W9-DEA-500

THE IRWIN SERIES IN ECONOMICS

CONSULTING EDITOR

LLOYD G. REYNOLDS

YALE UNIVERSITY

BOOKS IN THE IRWIN SERIES IN ECONOMICS

ANDERSON, GITLOW, & DIAMOND (Editors) *General Economics: A Book of Readings* Revised Edition
BALASSA *The Theory of Economic Integration*
BEAL & WICKERSHAM *The Practice of Collective Bargaining*
BLAUG *Economic Theory in Retrospect*
BORNSTEIN & FUSFELD *The Soviet Economy: A Book of Readings*
BRANDIS *Economics: Principles and Policy*
BUCHANAN *The Public Finances*
BUSHAW & CLOWER *Introduction to Mathematical Economics*
CARTTER *Theory of Wages and Employment*
DAVIDSON, SMITH, & WILEY *Economics: An Analytical Approach* Revised Edition
DAVIS, HUGHES, & MCDOUGALL *American Economic History: The Development of a National Economy*
DUE *Government Finance: An Economic Analysis* Revised Edition
DUE & CLOWER *Intermediate Economic Analysis* Fourth Edition
DUNLOP & HEALY *Collective Bargaining: Principles and Cases* Revised Edition
GAMBS & WERTIMER *Economics and Man*
GORDON *The Investment Financing and Valuation of the Corporation*
GRAMPP & WEILER (Editors) *Economic Policy: Readings in Political Economy* Third Edition
GROSSMAN, HANSEN, HENDRIKSEN, MCALLISTER, OKUDA, & WOLMAN (Editors) *Readings in Current Economics* Revised Edition
GUTHRIE *Economics* Revised Edition
HALM *Economics of Money and Banking* Revised Edition
HARRISS *The American Economy: Principles, Practices, and Policies* Fourth Edition
HIGGINS *United Nations and U.S. Foreign Economic Policy*
JOME *Principles of Money and Banking*
KINDLEBERGER *International Economics* Revised Edition
KUHLMAN & SKINNER *The Economic System*
LEE *Economic Fluctuations: Growth and Stability* Revised Edition
LOCKLIN *Economics of Transportation* Fifth Edition
MEYERS *Economics of Labor Relations*
PEGRUM *Public Regulation of Business*
REDDAWAY *The Development of the Indian Economy*
SCITOVSKY *Welfare and Competition: The Economics of a Fully Employed Economy*
SHAW *Money, Income, and Monetary Policy*
SIEGEL *Aggregate Economics and Public Policy*
SIRKIN *Introduction to Macroeconomic Theory*
SNIDER *Introduction to International Economics* Revised Edition
SPENCER, CLARK, & HOGHET *Business and Economic Forecasting: An Econometric Approach*
SPENCER & SIEGELMAN *Managerial Economics: Decision Making and Forward Planning*
VANEK *International Trade: Theory and Economic Policy*
WILCOX *Public Policies Toward Business* Revised Edition

GENERAL ECONOMICS

GENERAL ECONOMICS

A BOOK OF READINGS

EDITED BY

THOMAS J. ANDERSON, JR.

PROFESSOR OF ECONOMICS AND CHAIRMAN OF DEPARTMENT

ABRAHAM L. GITLOW

PROFESSOR OF ECONOMICS

DANIEL E. DIAMOND

ASSISTANT PROFESSOR OF ECONOMICS

ALL OF
SCHOOL OF COMMERCE, ACCOUNTS, AND FINANCE
NEW YORK UNIVERSITY

REVISED EDITION

1963

RICHARD D. IRWIN, INC.

HOMEWOOD, ILLINOIS

REVISED EDITION
First Printing, January, 1963

Library of Congress Catalogue Card No. 63-8446

PRINTED IN THE UNITED STATES OF AMERICA

To

JO H. ANDERSON

BEATRICE A. GITLOW

ESTHER R. DIAMOND

PREFACE

The reception accorded the original edition of this book indicates the utility of a collection of readings. A revised edition was deemed desirable in order to up-date the materials and to improve further the selections.

Attainment of these objectives necessitated a reduction in the number of items included in the book from 64 to 57. Of the 57 items, 43 are new. In making these major changes, the editors continued, when possible, to use complete items. Other editorial criteria used in making selections have been: (1) relevancy, (2) quality, (3) readability, (4) capacity to stimulate student interest, (5) comprehensibility to elementary economics students, and (6) supplementation rather than duplication of materials already available in basic texts. Thought was devoted to the achievement of broad and balanced coverage of major topics normally included in general economics courses. An effort was made to present opposing viewpoints on controversial questions. Space limitations, however, made it impossible to present every point of view, while simultaneously including items of substantial length.

The organization of selections into nine major parts, as well as the sequence of appearance in each part, was designed to achieve coherence and a logical flow of ideas. At the same time, the editors believe that flexibility is preserved, so that any individual instructor may use the materials in the order of his own preference.

Practice differs with respect to introducing the individual selections in a book of readings. In this one, the editors decided there was merit in preparing a composite introduction to each major part. This seems to give students a better insight into the flow of ideas from one item to the next.

Some users of the first edition expressed the opinion that inclusion of review and essay-type questions would improve the usefulness of the book. We are pleased to follow this suggestion. These questions are located at the end of each major division of the book.

The editors express gratitude to the copyright holders and authors who granted permission for the inclusion of their materials in this volume. Their respective names will be found in the footnote reference to each selection. Acknowledgment is also made of the helpful suggestions of our colleagues at New York University and Professor Lloyd G. Reynolds, of Yale University and Consulting Editor of the Irwin Series in Economics. It is a pleasure to acknowledge the assistance of the secretarial staff, Economics Department, School of Commerce, Accounts and Finance, especially Mrs. Sharon Goldfarb. To their wives, the editors once again express thanks for aid, encouragement, and patience. Needless to say, none of the aforementioned persons share responsibility for any shortcomings of this book.

THOMAS J. ANDERSON, JR.
ABRAHAM L. GITLOW
DANIEL E. DIAMOND

New York University
October, 1962

TABLE OF CONTENTS

B. Communism in Practice

I FUNDAMENTAL CONCEPTS

Economics is the study of man's use of scarce resources in achieving the satisfaction of his wants, both individual and community. Alfred Marshall, famous English economist at the turn of the century, explored the nature and scope of the subject in his great work *Principles of Economics*, from which appropriate excerpts have been taken. Economists have become very active in applying economic analysis to problems of government, business, labor, and, indeed, society at large. Kenneth Boulding, Professor of Economics at the University of Michigan, reviews the skills which characterize economic analysis.

The huge diversity and limitlessness of human wants as well as the scarcity of both human and natural resources comprise the basic economic problem. To advance his well-being, man has developed two outstanding techniques for achieving greater output with any given use of resources. These techniques are: (1) specialization, and (2) the use of capital. Classical statements of the importance of these techniques are made by Adam Smith, father of modern Political Economy, in his famous *Wealth of Nations*, and by Eugen von Böhm-Bawerk, noted Austrian economist, in his esteemed work *Positive Theory of Capital.* Solomon Fabricant, Director of Research, the National Bureau of Economic Research, and Professor of Economics at New York University, presents a statistical review of the changes in the efficiency with which productive factors have been used in the American economy. Ewan Clague, U.S. Commissioner of Labor Statistics, looks to the future in his discussion of the "Social and Economic Aspects of Automation."

A. Economics and Economists

1. DEFINITION OF ECONOMICS*

Alfred Marshall

THE SUBSTANCE OF ECONOMICS

Economics is a study of men as they live and move and think in the ordinary business of life. But it concerns itself chiefly with those motives which affect, most powerfully and most steadily, man's conduct in the business part of his life. Everyone who is worth anything carries his higher nature with him into business; and, there as elsewhere, he is influenced by his personal affections, by his conceptions of duty and his reverence for high ideals. And it is true that the best energies of the ablest inventors and organizers of improved methods and appliances are stimulated by a noble emulation more than by any love of wealth for its own sake. But, for all that, the steadiest motive to ordinary business work is the desire for the pay which is the material reward of work. The pay may be on its way to be spent selfishly or unselfishly, for noble or base ends; and here the variety of human nature comes into play. But the motive is supplied by a definite amount of money: and it is this definite and exact money measurement of the steadiest motives in business life, which has enabled economics far to outrun every other branch of the study of man. Just as the chemist's fine balance has made chemistry more exact than most other physical sciences; so this economist's balance, rough and imperfect as it is, has made economics more exact than any other branch of social science. But of course economics cannot be compared with the exact physical sciences: for it deals with the ever changing and subtle forces of human nature.

The advantage which economics has over other branches of social science appears then to arise from the fact that its special field of work gives rather larger opportunities for exact methods than any other branch. It concerns itself chiefly with those desires, aspirations and other affections of human nature, the outward manifestations of which appear as incentives to action in such a form that the force or quantity of the incentives can be estimated and measured with some approach to accuracy; and which therefore are in some degree amenable to treatment by scientific machinery. An opening is made for the methods and the tests of

* Alfred Marshall, *Principles of Economics* (8th ed.; London: Macmillan and Co. Ltd., 1920), pp. 14–15, 25–26.

science as soon as the force of a person's motives—*not* the motives themselves—can be approximately measured by the sum of money which he will just give up in order to secure a desired satisfaction; or again by the sum which is just required to induce him to undergo a certain fatigue.

It is essential to note that the economist does not claim to measure any affection of the mind in itself, or directly; but only indirectly through its effect. No one can compare and measure accurately against one another even his own mental states at different times: and no one can measure the mental states of another at all except indirectly and conjecturally by their effects. Of course various affections belong to man's higher nature and others to his lower, and are thus different in kind. But, even if we confine our attention to mere physical pleasures and pains of the same kind, we find that they can only be compared indirectly by their effects. In fact, even this comparison is necessarily to some extent conjectural, unless they occur to the same person at the same time.

. . . . .

To conclude provisionally: economists study the actions of individuals, but study them in relation to social rather than individual life; and therefore concern themselves but little with personal peculiarities of temper and character. They watch carefully the conduct of a whole class of people, sometimes the whole of a nation, sometimes only those living in a certain district, more often those engaged in some particular trade at some time and place: and by the aid of statistics, or in other ways, they ascertain how much money on the average the members of the particular group they are watching are just willing to pay as the price of a certain thing which they desire, or how much must be offered to them to induce them to undergo a certain effort or abstinence that they dislike. The measurement of motive thus obtained is not indeed perfectly accurate; for if it were, economics would rank with the most advanced of the physical sciences; and not, as it actually does, with the least advanced.

2. THE SKILLS OF THE ECONOMIST*

Kenneth E. Boulding

My principal objective in this essay is to examine some of the contributions which economics, as a distinct discipline, makes to the culture of our day. It is appropriate to begin by asking what economics is—which is really to ask what economists are. One recalls the famous remark at-

* Kenneth E. Boulding, *The Skills of the Economist* (Cleveland: Howard Allen Inc., 1958), pp. 1, 3–4, 9–23, 27–31.

tributed to Professor Jacob Viner that economics *is* what economists *do.* I therefore approach the contribution of economics by way of the skill of the economist, for if economists have anything to contribute to the culture of our time, it is through the employment of those special skills which have been developed in the study of economics.

. . . .

Before we examine the skill of the economist we should ask, "Who *are* the economists?" This is an embarrassing question. There are no recognized tests by which economists can be distinguished from those who may claim but who do not deserve the name. We have no professional qualifying examination as do the lawyers, the doctors, the accountants, and in some places, I understand, the beauticians. I know of no one who has been prevented from joining the American Economic Association or any other economic association for reasons of professional incompetence. We have no priesthood guarding the sacred fire handed down from Adam Smith. We do not even follow the practice of so many professions in improving their economic status by raising barriers to entrance. We may understand monopoly but we certainly do not practice it. Indeed, we are one of the few professions which deliberately, it would seem, attempts to undermine its economic status by actually encouraging students to enter it and by refusing to impose any professional standards.

Some unkind souls may want to deny us the status of a profession altogether. Moreover, it is a common belief that where two or three economists are gathered together there are always three or four varieties of economics present. We are popularly supposed to be divided by schools and racked by dissent, speaking with no common voice and being therefore quite unworthy of the name of science.

If these things be true it is an act of daring to claim there is a skill of the economist. Nevertheless, in spite of the divisions among us, and in spite of many signs of scientific immaturity, my experience with non-economists convinces me there is something, however humble, which can properly be called skill among those who recognize themselves as economists.

. . . .

. . . the skill of the economist depends on his ability to abstract a system from the complex social and physical world around him. The basis of the economist's system is the notion of a commodity. The economist sees the world not as men and things, but as commodities, and it is precisely in this abstraction that his peculiar skill resides. A commodity is anything *scarce,* that is; in order to get more of it a quantity of some other commodity must be relinquished.

Scarcity is most obviously manifested in the institution of exchange where one commodity is given up and another acquired by one party and the first commodity is acquired and the second given up by the other party. Exchange, however, is not the only manifestation of scarcity.

There are economic systems, like that of Robinson Crusoe, in which there is no exchange in the literal sense of the word. Nevertheless, there is scarcity in the sense that Crusoe's resources of time and energy are limited and therefore the various commodities acquire a value in substitution—what economists generally call *alternative cost*. Thus, if Crusoe wishes to build a house he must do without the things he might have acquired, or might have enjoyed, with the time spent in building the house. In this sense his house might be *worth* so many fish, or so many coconuts, or so many hours of dreaming in the sun which he had to give up in order to build it. From his point of view this alternative cost is a form of exchange, almost as if he had bought the house from someone else with fish or coconuts.

Similarly it is not difficult to see that all production is essentially a form of transformation of commodities akin to exchange. The miller exchanges flour for wheat by grinding it. The milkman exchanges milk-in-the-dairy for another commodity, milk-in-the-house, by transporting it from the dairy to the doorstep. It is not too much to claim that the phenomenon of exchange is at the heart of the economist's abstraction and the ability to recognize and analyze exchange constitutes the core of his skill.

An economic system, then, is a system of commodities which are exchanged (i.e., re-shuffled by their owners), produced (transformed from other commodities) and consumed (destroyed). If this process is to be continuous there must be a constant stream of some original commodity or commodities (factors of production) which then undergo the processes of transformation, exchange, and eventual consumption. The system can be regarded from various points of view along the scale from static to dynamic. A purely static snapshot of such a system would reveal various commodities in the possession of various organizations and owners. For each owner or organization a physical balance sheet can be made up listing the various commodities (assets) which he (or it) possesses or controls. Even at this stage the existence of a financial system as well as a system of physical commodities is apparent—debts, money, and securities as well as iron, steel, wheat and houses. These financial assets have the interesting property that they generally appear in at least two balance sheets—in one as a positive item and in another as a negative item. Thus a debt is a positive item in the balance of the creditor and a negative item in the balance sheet of the debtor. Debts and other financial instruments are, however, commodities in the sense that they are exchangeable for other things.

Even in taking a static snapshot of the system it is possible to observe a phenomenon akin to *pricing*. The various heterogeneous physical balance sheets can be reduced to homogeneous financial balance sheets by the process of *valuation*—which in essence means expressing each asset (positive or negative) in terms of some common denominator or *nu-*

meraire by multiplying it by a *valuation coefficient.* Thus suppose, what is usual though not necessary, that the numeraire is money—let us say dollars. Suppose then that the valuation coefficient of wheat is $2.00 per bushel. Any quantity of wheat in bushels can then be expressed as a dollar value by multiplying it by the appropriate coefficient of valuation. Fifty bushels of wheat would thus appear as $100. When all the items of a physical balance sheet are similarly reduced to a single numeraire (dollars), the total can be summed (both positive and negative items) and the sum is the *net worth* of the individual or organization concerned.

We now let the system begin to move. A complex system of events is observed. Some assets are consumed, as food is eaten, clothes wear out, fuel is burned, houses decay. Some assets are being exchanged among various owners or organizations in the process of buying and selling. Some assets are being produced, partly by the consumption of other assets, partly by the use of labor, land, and equipment. The use of these things, incidentally, is not the same thing as their consumption. In a given time period we can observe a universe of dynamic economic quantities: we observe amounts of commodity consumed, produced, transformed, exchanged, and the ratios of transformation (prices and costs) at which exchange and production transformations take place.

In the very simple model known as the stationary state or stationary equilibrium (Schumpeter's "Circular Flow"), all the balance sheet quantities continually reproduce themselves, like the trees of the forest, so that, even though there is constant change the whole system remains unchanged. Every time a commodity is consumed an equivalent amount is produced; every time a loan is paid back a new one is incurred. Both the human population and the population of all commodities and assets are in stationary equilibrium, with constant age distributions, births equal to deaths, and so on. This state of affairs is never found in reality though it has been approximated in some stationary societies.

In our society especially, the economic scene is continually changing. Populations of men and of things are constantly changing—usually growing, but some may be declining even in a generally advancing society as they are displaced by superior forms. Old processes and old commodities are constantly being displaced by new processes and new commodities. These changes frequently come in waves—one growth curve flattening off and then another coming along to accelerate the pace of change once more. The succession of growth curves gives the impression of cycles around the statistical trend. In addition to these apparent cycles there may be true cycles superimposed on the growth curves by certain dynamic instabilities of the system resulting, for instance, in a downward dip of the growth curves at the end of a growth period instead of a mere flattening off.

Such a system is immensely complex, and, if it is to be analyzed, various analytical devices and tricks must be used to reduce the intolerably complex mass even of this abstract system to manageable dimensions. In spite of the dynamic nature of the general system the most powerful tool which has been employed to date is still the idea of an *equilibrium* position of the various variables. This is a notion which can be employed usefully in varying degrees of looseness. It is an absolutely indispensable part of the toolbag of the economist and one which he can often contribute usefully to other sciences which are occasionally apt to get lost in the trackless exfoliations of purely dynamic systems.

The familiar equilibrium of demand and supply is the classical example of this method and it should not be despised even in a day of difference equations and linear programming. The equilibrium value of any economic variable, say the price of wheat, is that point at which there are no net forces making for change. If we may go beyond the strictly abstract world of commodities and recognize that they are in fact created, consumed, and exchanged by human beings, we may then say that, when an economic quantity is in equilibrium, no one who has the power to change it has the will and no one who has the will has the power.

Thus, in the competitive equilibrium of supply and demand, the price is such that the "market is cleared"—that is, the quantity offered for sale and the quantity offered for purchase are equal. Sellers would like a higher price, but, if one seller raises his price above the others he will sell nothing; if all sellers raise their prices together there will be excess supply—that is, the quantity offered will exceed the quantity demanded and some sellers will be left unsatisfied and, in a competitive market, will respond by lowering their price. Similarly buyers would like a lower price but do not have the power to lower it for a like reason. Even if they all lower their price together there will be unsatisfied buyers who will have both the power and the will to raise it again.

The equilibrium of demand and supply for a particular commodity can easily be generalized mathematically to the whole universe of commodities and we get the *general equilibrium systems* of Walras and Pareto. The ability to work with systems of general equilibrium is perhaps one of the most important skills of the economist—a skill which he shares with many other scientists, but in which he has perhaps a certain comparative advantage.

A general equilibrium system is one in which relationships exist among the variables so that only one, or a limited number, of sets of values of the variables is possible which satisfy *all* the relationships. The relationships are so defined that a failure to satisfy any one of them is either impossible (where the relationship is a formal identity) or results in changes in one or more variables through the behavior of some person or other agency capable of affecting the variables. The latter type of relationship may be called a *behavior equation* because, if it is not satisfied, behavior ensues in the direction of an attempt to satisfy it. In a general system, with many equations and many unknowns, behavior which is directed towards satisfying one behavior equation is likely to result in upsetting certain other behavior relationships with secondary, tertiary, and even further levels of behavior resulting. Nevertheless, if the system is stable, a divergence from the position of general equilibrium (at which all the behavior equations are satisfied), must result in overall behavior which will eventually restore the equilibrium.

General equilibrium systems are of course met with in most, if not in all, sciences. The equations of motion of a solar system are one example; ecosystems in biology are another important example. The general principles of all such systems are essentially similar. A number of essential variables are selected. All possible identities relating these variables are formulated. Suppose there are m of these. Then n—m behavior equations relating the various identities are postulated. These behavior identities must be based on some empirically founded postulate regarding the behavior of the prime elements of the system. Such a system is called a *model*. It is clear that the building of models is not a purely mechanical process but requires skill of a high order—not merely mathematical skill but a sensitivity to the relative importance of different factors and a critical, almost an artistic, faculty in the selection of behavior equations which are reasonable, tentative hypotheses in explaining the behavior of actual economies.

It is not enough, however, merely to set up a model with n equations and n unknowns. It is necessary to explore the *properties*, especially the dynamic properties of the model if it is to have any validity as an instrument of analysis or of prediction. Unfortunately, the more complex the model the more difficult it is to study its properties.

Three rather separate skills have been developed by economists to deal with this problem. The most general of these skills might be described as the method of plausible topology. We generally do not know the exact form of the behavior functions of our models. Nevertheless, we do know something about the general topological characteristics of these functions—i.e., their general shapes—even without extensive empirical investigation. Many of these topological assumptions can be derived from purely logical, or *reductio ad absurdum*, arguments. The famous *law of diminishing returns* is a good example. This, in any of its various forms, is an expression of the general topology of production or transformation functions of all kinds. In the case of the application of variable to fixed factors, the law can be demonstrated from the *reductio ad absurdum* argument that, if it were not true, we could grow all the world's food in a single flowerpot. Even in the somewhat more controversial form of eventually diminishing returns to scale, with all factors variable, certain *apriori* reasonings (e.g., the impossibility of making scale models of any organizational structure) are the foundations of the principle.

In certain other cases the topological assumptions about the nature of behavior functions are based on very broad general knowledge of human nature derived from introspection and non-quantitative observation. This is not to be despised as a source of valid knowledge, even in this day of econometrics and survey research. It is, after all, the kind of practical knowledge on which we depend in the conduct of our daily lives and in the innumerable small predictions in regard to human behavior on which all human interaction is based. When I stretch out my hand to an acquaintance I am in effect predicting that he will do the same and I am usually justified! The assumptions about the shape of demand and supply curves are, in large part, of the above nature. They are assumptions which have been abundantly confirmed in more quantitative, empirical research and even the exceptions to the general rules, in the shape of positively sloped demand curves for inferior goods, or backward sloping supply curves for individual labor, are very well understood and can easily be derived from equally plausible assumptions about the nature of preference functions. The assumed topology of the consumption function (relating consumption to income) in the Keynesian system is likewise an example of the method of plausible topology. It is not necessary to conduct elaborate empirical research to establish its validity as a first approximation regardless of how important second approximations, involving other variables, may turn out to be in the matter of economic forecasting.

The usefulness of graphical methods in economics is closely related to this method of plausible topology. The analysis of two or three variables graphs can express general assumptions about the topology of functions more simply than algebraic expressions. When it comes to the generalization of the analysis to more than three dimensions, graphic analysis tends to break down, whereas algebraic analysis does not, even though the weaknesses of conventional algebra persist. It may well be that the generalized topological analysis which mathematicians are now developing may turn out to be an important analytical tool for the economist.

The more variables a model contains the more difficult the task of exploring its properties. One of the most important skills of the economist, therefore, is that of *simplification of the model.* Two important methods of simplification have been developed by economists. One is the method of partial equilibrium analysis, generally associated with the name of Alfred Marshall and the other is the method of aggregation, associated with the name of John Maynard Keynes.

The partial equilibrium method consists essentially in the exploration of cross-sections in two or three dimensions of the n-dimensional model. This is the real meaning of the *ceteris paribus* (other things being equal) assumption. We can illustrate again from the equilibrium of demand and supply. In the complete model we recognize that the quantity depends on many variables besides the price of the commodity concerned—for instance, on incomes and their distribution (which in turn depend on the quantities of other commodities and their prices), on prices of substitute or complementary commodities, on selling costs, or even on the weather or the political news. The quantity supplied similarly depends on a host of variables. Nevertheless, in order to explore the most significant properties of the general model, we assume all variables constant except the price and quantity of the particular commodity, and draw the familiar intersecting demand and supply curves to determine the equilibrium price. What we have done here is to cut the general n-dimensional figure with a plane in the price-quantity dimensions, going through the points in the other dimensions which correspond to the variables assumed constant. Having explored the properties of the model in this plane, we can now assume a change in one of the other variables, and in effect draw another plane across the model. Thus, by degrees, we explore its whole topology. We see therefore that the method of partial equilibrium is in no sense contradictory to the method of general equilibrium—it is, in fact, a method, and a highly successful method within limits, for exploring the properties of the general equilibrium models. Only if it is taken as an end in itself does it contradict the principles of general equilibrium.

Writers like Marshall and Wicksteed are skilled in the method of particular equilibrium but from them the student can often get a better notion of the properties of general equilibrium systems than he can by studying Walras' formal mathematical expositions of general equilibrium or even the empirical model-builders like Leontief or Lawrence Klein. By the time Wicksteed, for instance, has finished explaining how money contributed to a Chinese famine relief fund in England actually relieves famine in China, there is hardly a corner of the world that we have not explored. By then the student should have a fair idea of the immense ramifications of a general equilibrium model.

The second method for the simplification of general equilibrium models is the method of aggregation. This consists in adding and otherwise combining large masses of variables and treating the resultant aggregate as if it were a single homogeneous variable capable of entering into behavior equations which express in some measure the behavior of the whole aggregates in relation to one another. Thus if the particular equilibrium method consists essentially of *slicing* the n-dimensional model, the method of aggregation consists in *squashing* it—in compressing great complex chunks of n-space into a single line through the construction of indices of aggregates.

Instead of working with a thousand different quantities of output of a thousand different commodities, we make an index of output as a whole and use this as a single dimension in our model. This is the economics of the bludgeon rather than of the scalpel. Nevertheless it has an important place in the understanding of the gross dimensions and properties of the system. Furthermore it enables us to understand the mass phenomena of the system—such as mass unemployment, inflation or deflation—much better than the more refined methods of partial equilibrium analysis. It should be observed that the method of aggregation is not confined to economics. We resort to it constantly in other sciences and in daily life, whenever it is necessary to reduce a complex multidimensional mass of data to some unitary measure. When a professor grades a class, for instance, he is bludgeoning a complex mass of personality and achievement data into a simple (and misleading) linear scale of grades. Psychologists use the method constantly in the construction of tests, and even in the physical and biological sciences there is probably more aggregation of essentially heterogeneous data than is generally recognized. In economics however, the problems, the successes, and the failures of the method of aggregation show up with remarkable clarity. It is here perhaps the economist has a peculiar contribution to make.

The most striking example of both the success and the intrinsic difficulties of the method of aggregation is to be found in the simple Keynesian models. It is hardly too much to say that the understanding of the Keynesian model constitutes the difference between an almost total failure to comprehend the phenomena of mass unemployment and a reasonable understanding of its essential nature. It is a remarkable tribute to the power of the method that a model so crude and so full of faults should at the same time be so powerful in producing what might be called rough comprehension—and rough comprehension is infinitely better than no comprehension at all!

. . . . .

There are two areas I have not yet mentioned in which the economist can claim some special skill. . . . The first is the theory of maximization, or more generally, the theory of rational behavior. The second is the theory of difference equations, or of dynamic processes.

In the course of his pursuit of the laws which govern the universe of commodities, it has proved to be impossible for the economist to insulate himself altogether from the world of human and organizational behavior. Consequently the economist has developed an elaborate theory of *economic behavior*, based on the simple assumption that the individual maximizes something, something which is a function of the set of variables which are relevant to the individual's economic position and some of which are under his control. This theory is known as the *marginal analysis*. In the case of the firm the maximand is generally assumed to be some measure of financial profits. In the case of the household an abstract preference-quantity known as *utility* is supposed to be maximized, though, as I hope to show, the assumption of profit maximization in the case of the firm is a highly special case, valid only under certain conditions. Even in the case of the firm it must generally be assumed that "utility" is maximized.

This theory of behavior is far removed from those based on stimulus and response patterns in psychology or on crisis and adjustment patterns in sociology. The economist is not much of an economic man when it comes to borrowing from other sciences. Generally speaking, if, in the pursuit of the world of commodities he stumbles into the world of men, he prefers to make up his own psychology on the spot rather than borrow from the psychologists. The psychologists, not unnaturally, are somewhat critical of this insular behavior. Nevertheless, once it is understood that the economist's interest is not human behavior but the behavior of commodities then his development of something as psychologically peculiar as the marginal analysis takes on more meaning. The core of the economist's interest is not human behavior as such but the *behavior functions* which relate his economic quantities, his prices, and his quantities of commodity produced, consumed, or exchanged. The marginal analysis has retained the interest of the economist because it seems to yield as a *conclusion* the assumptions about behavior functions which are the *postulates* of economic analysis proper.

Any other behavior theory would be just as acceptable to the economist which yielded the same conclusions and helped answer the following type of question: "Do higher prices mean smaller purchases?", "Do higher wages mean smaller output?" The marginal analysis has provided what seemed to be a reasonable answer to these questions, or at least a rationale for obtaining those answers, and its long-continued popularity with the economists is undoubtedly related to the failure of substitute theories of behavior to provide any answers at all. It is possible, as I shall indicate later, that we are on the verge of developing better and more relevant theories of behavior. The economist will not give up the marginal analysis, however, until something emerges which is clearly of more use to him for his special purposes.

In spite of all the space given to it in the textbooks of economics the marginal analysis appears to be more of a front porch than an integral part of the edifice of economics. It is a large and imposing porch trimmed with fine arches and handsome diagrams but it could be torn down and a different structure erected without seriously affecting the main building.

If the marginal analysis is a front porch, process analysis is perhaps the back porch—something which has been developed by economists but which clearly leads into other fields and other uses. If we know exactly how tomorrow is related to today we can obviously proceed to an indefinite series of tomorrows. Tuesday can be derived from Monday, and now having got Tuesday we can derive Wednesday, and from Wednesday, Thursday, and so on to the Day of Judgment. The astronomers got there with this game long before the economist and one wonders how possible it will be to find stable relationships of this sort (i.e., difference equations) in the social sciences. It is certainly worth trying, and the predictive power of economics, like that of any other science, depends on its ability to find stable difference equations within its universe of variables. However, skill in the analysis of these dynamic processes is not peculiar to the economist. It is something he must share with many other sciences.

Perhaps the best way to test the skill of the economist is to put him in the position of Economic Adviser to the Philosopher King (or President!). If he has any skill at all it will soon be revealed. One needs, of course, a proper humility. There are a great many questions on which the economic adviser cannot presume to give advice, even fundamental questions regarding the most desirable structure of the economic system, or relatively trivial questions about a tariff on buttons. Also there are a great many economic questions which are bound up with matters of peace and war, with the retention of power and the satisfaction of political obligations, with social justice and the racial or cultural stratifications of society, in which the economist has no special competence.

When, however, it comes to the question of what to do about a depression or an inflation, whether price control can be applied without rationing, what sort of public finance leads to inflation, and even on some of the more obvious conditions of economic development, the economist has something to say by virtue of his peculiar skills even if only to give a sense of direction. And if one compares the kind of answers and understanding which the economist is able to give to the question, for instance, of how we avoid or get out of a depression, with the kind of professional answers that the political scientist might give when asked what policies decrease the possibility of war, or the answers a sociologist might give to the question of what policies promote happy families or good race relations, the economist may at least be pardoned a touch of the disagreeable pride that comes from odious comparison.

B. Production and Productivity

3. SPECIALIZATION*

Adam Smith

OF THE DIVISION OF LABOUR

The greatest improvement in the productive powers of labour, and the greater part of the skill, dexterity, and judgment with which it is any where directed, or applied, seem to have been the effects of the division of labour.

* Adam Smith, *The Wealth of Nations* (New York: Random House, Inc., 1937), pp. 3–5, 7–9.

The effects of the division of labour, in the general business of society, will be more easily understood, by considering in what manner it operates in some particular manufactures. It is commonly supposed to be carried furthest in some very trifling ones; not perhaps that it really is carried further in them than in others of more importance: but in those trifling manufactures which are destined to supply the small wants of but a small number of people, the whole number of workmen must necessarily be small; and those employed in every different branch of work can often be collected into the same workhouse, and placed at once under the view of the spectator. In those great manufactures, on the contrary, which are destined to supply the great wants of the great body of the people, every different branch of the work employs so great a number of workmen, that it is impossible to collect them all into the same workhouse. We can seldom see more, at one time, than those employed in one single branch. Though in such manufactures, therefore, the work may really be divided into a much greater number of parts, than in those of a more trifling nature, the division is not near so obvious, and has accordingly been much less observed.

To take an example, therefore, from a very trifling manufacture; but one in which the division of labour has been very often taken notice of, the trade of the pin-maker; a workman not educated to this business (which the division of labour has rendered a distinct trade), nor acquainted with the use of the machinery employed in it (to the invention of which the same division of labour has probably given occasion), could scarce perhaps, with his utmost industry, make one pin in a day, and certainly could not make twenty. But in the way in which this business is now carried on, not only the whole work is a peculiar trade, but it is divided into a number of branches, of which the greater part are likewise peculiar trades. One man draws out the wire, another straights it, a third cuts it, a fourth points it, a fifth grinds it at the top for receiving the head; to make the head requires two or three distinct operations; to put it on, is a peculiar business, to whiten the pins is another; it is even a trade by itself to put them into the paper; and the important business of making a pin is, in this manner, divided into about eighteen distinct operations, which, in some manufactories, are all performed by distinct hands, though in others the same man will sometimes perform two or three of them. I have seen a small manufactory of this kind where ten men only were employed, and where some of them consequently performed two or three distinct operations. But though they were very poor, and therefore but indifferently accommodated with the necessary machinery, they could, when they exerted themselves, make among them about twelve pounds of pins in a day. There are in a pound upwards of four thousand pins of a middling size. Those ten persons, therefore, could make among them upwards of forty-eight thousand pins in a day. Each person, therefore, making a tenth part of forty-eight thousand pins, might be considered as making four thousand eight hundred pins in a day. But if they had all wrought separately and independently, and without any of them having been educated to this peculiar business, they certainly could not each of them have made twenty, perhaps not one pin in a day; that is, certainly, not the two hundred and fortieth, perhaps not the four thousand eight hundredth part of what they are at present capable of performing, in consequence of a proper division and combination of their different operations.

In every other art and manufacture, the effects of the division of labour are similar to what they are in this very trifling one; though, in many of them, the labour can neither be so much subdivided, nor reduced to so great a simplicity of operation. The division of labour, however, so far as it can be introduced, occasions, in every art, a proportionable increase of the productive powers of labour.

. . . .

This great increase of the quantity of work, which, in consequence of the division of labour, the same number of people are capable of performing, is owing to three different circumstances; first, to the increase of dexterity in every particular workman; secondly, to the saving of the time which is commonly lost in passing from one species of work to another; and lastly, to the invention of a great number of machines which facilitate and abridge labour, and enable one man to do the work of many.

First, the improvement of the dexterity of the workman necessarily increases the quantity of the work he can perform; and the division of labour, by reducing every man's business to some one simple operation, and by making this operation the sole employment of his life, necessarily increases very much the dexterity of the workman. A common smith, who, though accustomed to handle the hammer, has never been used to make nails, if upon some particular occasion he is obliged to attempt it, will scarce, I am assured, be able to make above two or three hundred nails in a day, and those too very bad ones. A smith who has been accustomed to make nails, but whose sole or principal business has not been that of a nailer, can seldom with his utmost diligence make more than eight hundred or a thousand nails in a day. I have seen several boys under twenty years of age who had never exercised any other trade but that of making nails, and who, when they exerted themselves, could make, each of them, upwards of two thousand three hundred nails in a day. The making of a nail, however, is by no means one of the simplest operations. The same person blows the bellows, stirs or mends the fire as there is occasion, heats the iron, and forges every part of the nail: In forging the head too he is obliged to change his tools. The different operations into which the making of a pin, or of a metal button, is subdivided, are all of them much more simple, and the dexterity of the person, of whose life it has been the sole business to perform them, is usually much greater. The rapidity with which some of the operations of those manufactures are performed, exceeds what the human hand could, by those who had never seen them, be supposed capable of acquiring.

Secondly, the advantage which is gained by saving the time commonly lost in passing from one sort of work to another, is much greater than we should at first view be apt to imagine it. It is impossible to pass very quickly from one kind of work to another, that is carried on in a different place, and with quite different tools. A country weaver, who cultivates a small farm, must lose a good deal of time in passing from his loom to the field, and from the field to his loom. When the two trades can be carried on in the same workhouse, the loss of time is no doubt much less. It is even in this case, however, very considerable. A man commonly saunters a little in turning his hand from one sort of employment to another. When he first begins the new work he is seldom very keen and hearty; his mind, as they say, does not go to it, and for some time he rather trifles than applies to good purpose. The habit of sauntering and of indolent careless application, which is naturally, or rather necessarily acquired by every country workman who is obliged to change his work and his tools every half hour, and to apply his hand in twenty different ways almost every day of his life; renders him almost always slothful and lazy, and incapable of any vigorous application even on the most pressing occasions. Independent, therefore, of his deficiency in point of dexterity, this cause alone must always reduce considerably the quantity of work which he is capable of performing.

Thirdly, and lastly, every body must be sensible how much labour is facilitated and abridged by the application of proper machinery. It is unnecessary to give any example. I shall only observe, therefore, that the invention of all those machines by which labour is so much facilitated and abridged, seems to have been originally owing to the division of labour. Men are much more likely to discover easier and readier methods of attaining any object, when the whole attention of their minds is directed towards that single object, than when it is dissipated among a great variety of things. But in consequence of the division of labour, the whole of every man's attention comes naturally to be directed towards some one very simple object. It is naturally to be expected, therefore, that some one or other of those who are employed in each particular branch of labour should soon find out easier and readier methods of performing their own particular work, wherever the nature of it admits of such improvement.

4. INDIRECT PRODUCTION*

Eugen von Böhm-Bawerk

THE NATURE OF CAPITAL

The end and aim of all production is the making of things with which to satisfy our wants; that is to say, the making of goods for immediate consumption, or Consumption Goods. . . . We combine our own natural powers and natural powers of the external world in such a way that, under natural law, the desired material good must come into existence. But this is a very general description indeed of the matter, and looking at it closer there comes in sight an important distinction which we have not as yet considered. It has reference to the distance which lies between the expenditure of human labour in the combined production and the appearance of the desired good. We either put forth our labour just before the goal is reached, or we, intentionally, take a roundabout way. That is to say, we may put forth our labour in such a way that it at once completes the circle of conditions necessary for the emergence of the desired good, and thus the existence of the good *immediately* follows the expenditure of the labour; or we may associate our labour first with the more remote causes of the good, with the object of obtaining, not the desired good itself, but a proximate cause of the good; which cause, again, must be associated with other suitable materials and powers, till, finally,—perhaps through a considerable number of intermediate members,—the finished good, the instrument of human satisfaction, is obtained.

The nature and importance of this distinction will be best seen from a few examples; and, as these will, to a considerable extent, form a demonstration of what is really one of the most fundamental propositions in our theory, I must risk being tedious.

A peasant requires drinking water. The spring is some distance from his house. There are various ways in which he may supply his daily wants. First, he may go to the spring each time he is thirsty, and drink out of his hollowed hand. This is the most direct way; satisfaction follows immediately on exertion. But it is an inconvenient way, for our peasant has to take his way to the well as often as he is thirsty. And it is an insufficient way, for he can never collect and store any great quantity such as he requires for various other purposes. Second, he may take a log of

* Eugen von Böhm-Bawerk, *The Positive Theory of Capital* (London: Macmillan and Co. Ltd., 1891), pp. 17–22.

wood, hollow it out into a kind of pail, and carry his day's supply from the spring to his cottage. The advantage is obvious, but it necessitates a roundabout way of considerable length. The man must spend, perhaps, a day in cutting out the pail; before doing so he must have felled a tree in the forest; to do this, again, he must have made an axe, and so on. But there is still a third way; instead of felling one tree he fells a number of trees, splits and hollows them, lays them end for end, and so constructs a runnel or rhone which brings a full head of water to his cottage. Here, obviously, between the expenditure of the labour and the obtaining of the water we have a very roundabout way, but, then, the result is ever so much greater. Our peasant needs no longer take his weary way from house to well with the heavy pail on his shoulder, and yet he has a constant and full supply of the freshest water at his very door.

Another example. I require stone for building a house. There is a rich vein of excellent sandstone in a neighbouring hill. How is it to be got out? First, I may work the loose stones back and forward with my bare fingers, and break off what can be broken off. This is the most direct, but also the least productive way. Second, I may take a piece of iron, make a hammer and chisel out of it, and use them on the hard stone—a roundabout way, which, of course, leads to a very much better result than the former. Third method—Having a hammer and chisel I use them to drill a hole in the rock; next I turn my attention to procuring charcoal, sulphur, and nitre, and mixing them in a powder, then I pour the powder into the hole, and the explosion that follows splits the stone into convenient pieces—still more of a roundabout way, but one which, as experience shows, is as much superior to the second way in result as the second was to the first.

Yet another example. I am short-sighted, and wish to have a pair of spectacles. For this I require ground and polished glasses, and a steel framework. But all that nature offers towards that end is silicious earth and iron ore. How am I to transform these into spectacles? Work as I may, it is as impossible for me to make spectacles directly out of silicious earth as it would be to make the steel frames out of iron ore. Here there is no immediate or direct method of production. There is nothing for it but to take the roundabout way, and, indeed, a very roundabout way. I must take silicious earth and fuel, and build furnaces for smelting the glass from the silicious earth; the glass thus obtained has to be carefully purified, worked, and cooled by a series of processes; finally, the glass thus prepared—again by means of ingenious instruments carefully constructed beforehand—is ground and polished into the lens fit for short-sighted eyes. Similarly, I must smelt the ore in the blast furnace, change the raw iron into steel, and make the frame therefrom—processes which cannot be carried through without a long series of tools and buildings that, on their part again, require great amounts of previous labour. Thus, by an exceedingly roundabout way, the end is attained.

The lesson to be drawn from all these examples alike is obvious. It is—that a greater result is obtained by producing goods in roundabout ways than by producing them directly. Where a good can be produced in either way, we have the fact that, by the indirect way, a greater product can be got with equal labour, or the same product with less labour. But, beyond this, the superiority of the indirect way manifests itself in being the only way in which certain goods can be obtained; if I might say so, it is so much the better that it is often the only way!

That roundabout methods lead to greater results than direct methods is one of the most important and fundamental propositions in the whole theory of production. It must be emphatically stated that the only basis of this proposition is the experience of practical life. Economic theory does not and cannot show *a priori* that it must be so; but the unanimous experience of all the technique of production says that it is so. And this is sufficient; all the more that the facts of experience which tell us this are commonplace and familiar to everybody. But *why* is it so? The economist might quite well decline to answer this question. For the fact that a greater product is obtained by methods of production that begin far back is essentially a purely technical fact, and to explain questions of technique does not fall within the economist's sphere. For instance, that tropical lands are more fruitful than the polar zone; that the alloy of which coins are made stands more wear and tear than pure metal; that a railroad is better for transport than an ordinary turnpike road;—all these are matters of fact with which the economist reckons, but which his science does not call on him to explain. But this is exactly one of those cases where, in the economist's own interest—the interest he has in limiting and defining his own task—it is exceedingly desirable to go beyond the specific economic sphere. If the sober physical truth is once made clear, political economy cannot indulge in any fancies or fictions about it; and, in such questions, political economy has never been behind in the desire and the attempt to substitute its own imaginings! Although, then, this law is already sufficiently accredited by experience, I attach particular value to explaining its cause, and, after what has been said as to the nature of production, this should not be very difficult.

In the last resort all our productive efforts amount to shiftings and combinations of matter. We must know how to bring together the right forms of matter at the right moment, in order that from those associated forces the desired result, the product wanted, may follow. But, as we saw, the natural forms of matter are often so infinitely large, often so infinitely fine, that human hands are too weak or too coarse to control them. We are as powerless to overcome the cohesion of the wall of rock when we want building stone as we are, from carbon, nitrogen, hydrogen, oxygen, phosphor, potash, etc., to put together a single grain of wheat. But there are other powers which can easily do what is denied to us, and these are the powers of nature. There are natural powers which far exceed the possibilities of human power in greatness, and there are other natural powers in the microscopic world which can make combinations that put our clumsy fingers to shame. If we can succeed in making those forces our allies in the work of production, the limits of human possibility will be infinitely extended. And this we have done.

The condition of our success is, that we are able to control the materials on which the power that helps us depends, more easily than the materials which are to be transformed into the desired good. Happily this condition can be very often complied with. Our weak yielding hand cannot overcome the cohesion of the rock, but the hard wedge of iron can; the wedge and the hammer to drive it we can happily master with little trouble. We cannot gather the atoms of phosphorus and potash out of the ground, and the atoms of carbon and oxygen out of the atmospheric air, and put them together in the shape of the corn of wheat; but the organic chemical powers of the seed can put this magical process in motion, while we on our part can very easily bury the seed in the place of its secret working, the bosom of the earth. Often, of course, we are not able directly to master the form of matter on which the friendly power depends, but in the same way as we would like it to help us, do we help ourselves against it; we try to secure the alliance of a second natural power which brings the form of matter that bears the first power under our control. We wish to bring the well water into the house. Wooden rhones would force it to obey our will, and take the path we prescribe, but our hands have not the power to make the forest trees into rhones. We have not far to look, however, for an expedient. We ask the help of a second ally in the axe and the gouge; their assistance gives us the rhones; then the rhones bring us the water. And what in this illustration is done through the mediation of two or three members may be done, with equal or greater result, through five, ten, or twenty members. Just as we control and guide the immediate matter of which the good is composed by one friendly power, and that power by a second, so can we control and guide the second by a third, the third by a fourth, this, again, by a fifth, and so on,—always going back to more remote causes of the final result—till in the series we come at last to one cause which we can control conveniently by our own natural powers. This is the true importance which attaches to our entering on roundabout ways of production, and this is the reason of the result associated with them: every roundabout way means the enlisting in our service of a power which is stronger or more cunning than the human hand; every extension of the roundabout way means an addition to the powers which enter into the service of man, and the shifting of some portion of the burden of production from the scarce and costly labour of human beings to the prodigal powers of nature.

And now we may put into words an idea which has long waited for expression, and must certainly have occurred to the reader; the kind of production which works in these wise circuitous methods is nothing else than what economists call Capitalist Production, as opposed to that production which goes directly at its object, as the Germans say, "*mit det nackten Faust.*" And Capital is nothing but the complex of intermediate products which appear on the several stages of the roundabout journey.

5. PRODUCTIVITY CHANGE*

Solomon Fabricant

IMPORTANCE OF THE FACTS

Productivity has been much discussed in recent years, and too frequently misunderstood.

Productivity deserves the attention that it has received, for it is a measure of the efficiency with which resources are converted into the commodities and services that men want. Higher productivity is a means to better levels of economic well-being and greater national strength. Higher productivity is a major source of the increment in income over which men bargain and sometimes quarrel. And higher—or lower—productivity affects costs, prices, profits, output, employment and investment, and thus plays a part in business fluctuations, in inflation, and in the rise and decline of industries.

Indeed, in one way or another, productivity enters virtually every broad economic problem, whatever current form or new name the problem takes—industrialization, or research and development, or automation, or tax reform, or cost-price squeeze, or improvement factor, or wage inflation, or foreign dollar shortage.

Despite its importance and the wide attention paid it, productivity is a subject surrounded by considerable confusion. For this there are a number of reasons. First, people employ the same term but mean different things. As a consequence, various figures on productivity change come into use, and these often differ in significant degree. Further, the rate of productivity change is not a fixed quantity. Our figures will show that it varies from one period to another. What the past or current rate of productivity change is will depend on the particular period for which the calculation is made. If no reference is made to the period, and if the period varies considerably from one context to another, confusion re-

* Solomon Fabricant, *Basic Facts on Productivity Change* (New York: National Bureau of Economic Research, 1959, Occasional Paper 63), pp. 1–10, 29–37. A fuller statement is given in John W. Kendrick, *Productivity Trends in the United States.*

sults. In addition, the statistical information available for calculating productivity indexes is deficient in various respects. Better or worse—or merely different—methods of meeting these deficiencies, enumerated below, often yield results that differ appreciably. Failure to specify the methods and the assumptions involved in the process of estimation, or failure to understand them, adds to the confusion.

As I have said, the questions into which productivity enters are important. They are also difficult. We all have far to go before any of us can claim to understand fully the process of productivity change, its causes, or its consequences, or to see clearly the way to deal with the issues involved. But surely the way to more effective policy would be clearer if the basic facts of productivity change were established and widely known.

. . . . .

THE LONG-TERM RATE OF INCREASE IN NATIONAL PRODUCTIVITY

Over the sixty-four years between 1889 and 1953—the period which has been examined most closely and for which presently available statistics are most adequate—the rate of increase in productivity has been as follows:

Physical output per manhour in the private economy has grown at an average rate that appears to be about 2.3 per cent per annum.

Comparing output with a measure of labor input in which a highly paid manhour of work counts for proportionately more than a low-wage manhour yields a measure of productivity for the private economy that grew at a significantly smaller rate—about 2.0 per cent per annum.

A measure of productivity for the private economy that compares output not only with labor input (so determined) but also with tangible capital, each weighted by the market value of its services, grew still less rapidly—about 1.7 per cent per annum.

All these indexes of productivity in the private economy rose somewhat more rapidly than the corresponding indexes for the economy as a whole, including government, when the usual measurements of government output and input are utilized. For the total including government, productivity rose about 1.5 per cent per annum.

This list presents the main broad measures of long-term productivity increase that John Kendrick has calculated for the American economy. It is by no means complete. Kendrick goes to some trouble to provide still other measures that differ in definition of output or input, in the degree to which they cover the economy, or in details of estimation. However, as Table 1 indicates, these alternative calculations yield results similar to those just given and we may therefore concentrate on the above measures. They differ enough among themselves to raise a serious question about the meaning and measurement of productivity.

Productivity, I have mentioned, is a measure of the efficiency with which the nation's resources are transformed into the consumption, investment, and other goods that satisfy individual or collective wants. Now we can become more (or less) efficient in the use of a particular type of resource, say, plant and equipment, as well as of resources taken as a whole. A given volume of product might be obtained from a smaller amount of plant and equipment, used in conjunction with an unchanged amount of labor, land, inventory, and other resources. This would be a real gain. It would be proper to consider it the result of an increase in efficiency (if fluctuations due to weather and the like were not the cause); and we could measure the increase in efficiency by calculating the ratio of an index of physical output to an index of the volume of plant and equipment. We could also refer to this ratio as a productivity index, as is frequently done. It is necessary to note, however, that we would have to be sure that all resources other than plant and equipment had in fact remained constant (or equivalently, that we had been able to eliminate the effect of changes in them by appropriate statistical techniques), before we could interpret the index as reflecting change in efficiency.

We would also have to recognize that the importance of the change so calculated depended on the size of the particular input—in this case, the services of plant and equipment—relative to other inputs. If the services of plant and equipment constituted a small fraction of total input, doubling the ratio of product to plant and equipment would have much less significance than if these services constituted a large fraction. In other words, an adequate index of productivity for a single resource requires not only eliminating the effect of changes in other resources, but also somehow taking into account the relative importance of the resource.

When other resources are used in significant volume, and change occurs in the volume of such resources used (which is almost always the case), a measure of productivity based on a single resource might tell us little or nothing of change in the efficiency with which this resource was being utilized. It might not even point in the right direction. For example, output per unit of plant and equipment might have fallen because plant or equipment was being substituted for labor or other resources. Yet the efficiency with which plant and equipment was being used might have risen.

Nor would the index of output per unit of plant and equipment (or any other single resource) provide reliable information on the efficiency with which all resources were being used. Only if all other resources were of small importance, or moved in the same direction (indeed, in virtually identical proportion) as plant and equipment would an index of productivity based on plant and equipment alone provide a reasonably accurate answer to that question. Yet that is the question with which we are primarily concerned.

As a general rule, therefore, it is better not to limit productivity in-

TABLE 1

BROAD MEASURES OF THE LONG-TERM RATE OF INCREASE IN PRODUCTIVITY IN THE UNITED STATES

Average annual percentage rates of change, 1889–1953

	Aggregate of Industries for Which Individual Productivity Indexes Are Available	Entire Private Domestic Economy	Entire Economy, including Government		
			"National Security" Version of Output	"Peace-time" Version of Output	Dept. of Commerce Version of Output
Gross physical output per unweighted manhour	2.3	2.3	2.2	2.0	2.2
Net physical output per unweighted manhour		2.3	2.2	2.0	2.2
Gross physical output per weighted manhour	1.9	2.0	1.8	1.6	1.8
Net physical output per weighted manhour		2.0	1.8	1.6	1.8
Gross physical output per unweighted unit of tangible capital	1.0	1.2	1.0	0.9	1.0
Net physical output per unweighted unit of tangible capital		1.2	1.0	0.9	1.1
Gross physical output per weighted unit of tangible capital	1.0	1.0	0.8	0.7	0.8
Net physical output per weighted unit of tangible capital		1.1	0.9	0.7	0.9
Gross physical output per weighted unit of labor and tangible capital combined	1.7	1.7	1.5	1.4	1.5
Net physical output per weighted unit of labor and tangible capital combined		1.7	1.6	1.4	1.6

Source: John W. Kendrick, "Productivity Trends in the United States" (a forthcoming report of the National Bureau of Economic Research), especially Chapter 3 and Appendix A. The underlying indexes, reproduced in part in Tables A and B, below, are subject to some revision. Use was made by Kendrick of estimates developed in other National Bureau studies by Kuznets, Goldsmith, Blank, Tostlebe, Ulmer, Creamer, Borenstein, and Barger, among others, as well as of data published by the Departments of Commerce and of Labor.

Gross output differs from net output by the amount of depreciation and other items of capital consumption, in the case of the national indexes; and also by the amount of materials, fuel, and supplies consumed, in the case of the industries covered in the first column of figures (except agriculture). See Kendrick for a fuller explanation of those differences; and also for a detailed explanation of the difference between the weighted and unweighted indexes.

Industries for which individual productivity indexes are available for 1889–1953 include farming, mining, manufacturing, transportation, and communications and public utilities. The detailed list is given in Table B.

The three sets of indexes for the entire economy differ mainly in the treatment of defense outlays in the calculation of national product and of inputs. The "national security" and "peacetime" versions of national product are based largely on concepts developed by Kuznets; the Department of Commerce version is that currently published by its Office of Business Economics.

dexes that purport to measure change in efficiency to a comparison of output with a single resource. The broader the coverage of resources, generally, the better is the productivity measure. The best measure is one that compares output with the combined use of all resources.

Information on all resources is not available, however. Until rather recently, economists interested in measuring the rate of increase in national productivity had to make shift with labor input alone—first, in terms of number of workers, then in terms of manhours. This is still true for most individual industries, narrowly defined, even on a historical basis, and for both individual industries and the economy as a whole on a current basis.

For this reason, the most widely used index of productivity—the one I cited first—is simply physical output per manhour. It is a useful index, if its limitations are recognized. Because in the economy at large and, as we shall see, in most—not all—individual industries, labor input is by far the most important type of input (measured by the fraction of income accruing to it), the index based on manhours alone is not often in serious error. It is a fair approximation to a more comprehensive index of efficiency. But as such it is usually subject to an upward bias, as the figures cited indicate.

The bias in output per manhour results not only from the omission of capital input. The usual index of output per manhour fails also to take into account change in the composition or quality of labor. That is, manhours worked by persons of different skills, levels of education, and lengths of experience are treated as if equivalent, thus ignoring important forms of human capital that aid in production and contribute to wage and salary differentials. The index of output per weighted manhour—the second index cited—catches some of this intangible capital, for the labor in industries with high rates of pay is given a heavier weight than that in low-pay industries. However, the procedure of weighting is only a step in the right direction. All the labor within an industry is still assumed to be homogeneous. Perhaps more important, broad advances in education and the like, which improve the quality of labor in industries generally, are not taken into account. And differences in labor quality are imperfectly measured by pay differentials, since these are influenced by such other factors as the non-economic advantages and disadvantages of particular occupations, differences in the cost of living, and uncompleted adjustments to changes in demand and supply. The figures previously given—the difference between the rate of increase in output per manhour and in output per unit of labor (weighted manhours), which is 0.3 per cent per annum—therefore indicate the direction but not the degree of bias arising from the neglect of change in the quality of labor.

With respect to tangible capital, we are in a better position. In recent years the available information on tangible capital has been broadened, worked over, pieced out, and put into usable form, and this has helped greatly to expand the coverage of inputs for productivity indexes. The data on tangible capital are still far from perfect. In calculating them, difficulties of all sorts are involved—the treatment of depreciation, the problem of allowing for changes in prices, and the proper valuation of land, among others. These problems have not been entirely solved, but we appear to be sufficiently close to a solution to warrant use of the data. With them, output per unit of tangible capital may be computed (Table 1). This is informative; but, like output per unit of labor, it is an incomplete index of productivity. It tells only part of the story.

Indexes of productivity based on the comparison of output with the input of both labor and tangible capital are better measures of efficiency than those based on labor input or capital input alone.

Indeed, the best currently available approximation to a measure of efficiency is such an index. As we have seen (it is the third index cited initially in the text), it indicates a rate of growth of productivity that is significantly below the rate for output in relation to labor input alone. That it is lower will not be a surprise, since it is well known that tangible capital has increased substantially more than the labor force: tangible capital per weighted manhour has risen at the average annual rate of 0.9 per cent. Because the services of labor have become more and more expensive relative to those of tangible capital, there has been a strong incentive for business firms and other producers to substitute capital for labor. Yet—and this may be surprising—capital increased less rapidly than did output. On net balance, output per unit of tangible capital rose by about 1 per cent per annum. Technological advance and the other means to improved efficiency have led to savings of capital as well as of labor.

Surprising, also, may be the fact that the difference between productivity measured in terms of labor and tangible capital combined and productivity measured in terms of labor alone is no more than the three-tenths of one per cent per annum that we have found. The reason is the relatively high weight given labor in combining it with tangible capital. Obviously, manhours cannot be combined with dollars of tangible capital without translating each of them into comparable units. The appropriate unit is a dollar's worth of services in a reference base period. If a manhour of labor commands two dollars in the base period and a hundred dollars of capital equipment commands six dollars of net revenue per year (whether in rent, profits, or otherwise is immaterial), we count the hundred dollars of equipment as equivalent to three manhours. Because, in production, use is made of many more manhours than of even hundreds of dollars of capital, labor as a whole gets a much greater weight than does capital. The weights for the private economy are currently as 8 to 2. The index of output per unit of labor and capital combined—which rose at the rate of 1.7 per cent per annum in the private economy—is thus, in effect, a weighted average of the index of output per unit of labor—2.0 per cent per annum—and of the index of output per unit of capital—1.0 per cent.

I have called this weighted index the best available approximation to the measure of efficiency that we seek. It is approximate for more reasons than those already given. One is the problem of measuring output, which involves combining into a meaningful aggregate a changing variety of old and new goods. A special difficulty arises in putting a figure on the quantity of services produced by government to meet collective wants. This accounts for the greater confidence most statisticians have in the estimate of productivity for the private economy, exclusive of government, and explains the plurality of estimates given in Table 1 for the economy inclusive of government.

A general deficiency of all the measures of output—and thus of productivity—is their failure to take adequate account of change in the quality of output. This, it is likely, subjects them to a downward bias. And, to repeat, the indexes of output per unit of labor and tangible capital combined, though broader than any other indexes now available, fail to cover adequately the investment in education, science, technology, and social organization that serves to increase production—a point to which we shall have to return.

The technical questions raised above (which I have selected from a host) are, of course, matters primarily for the producer rather than the user of productivity statistics. But for the user it is important to be aware of the sharp differences made in the rate of growth of productivity by technical choices not always specified: whether output or input is defined in one way rather than another, or weights of components of output and input are determined by this rather than that method, or data are selected or estimated from one or another source.

Measured in any of the ways listed above, however, productivity in the United States has grown at a remarkable average rate over the past two-thirds of a century. The more comprehensive indexes, in which output is compared with both labor and capital input, indicate a doubling of efficiency every forty years. The index of output per (unweighted) manhour indicates a doubling even more frequently—every thirty years. Not many of the countries for which corresponding records might be constructed would show average rates as high or higher over so long a period. Over shorter periods, it is very likely, our long-term rate has been exceeded in various countries. This has happened here, as well as elsewhere, as we shall see in a moment. But it is safe to say that the United States' long-term rate is not low in relation to the experience of other countries over comparable periods. It may appear low only in comparison with aspirations—the long-term rates dreamt of by countries embarked on ambitious programs of economic development, or the rates some of our own citizens believe we need to reach and maintain if we are to meet some of the urgent problems that confront us.

. . . . .

PRODUCTIVITY AND THE RISE IN REAL HOURLY EARNINGS

Productivity increase means more goods and services—more real income—available for distribution per unit of resources. Has the rise in productivity been reflected in the hourly real earnings of workers, as would be expected?

Real earnings per hour of work in the private domestic economy rose over the period since 1889 at an average annual rate about equal to the rate of increase in product per manhour, and greater than the rate of increase in product per weighted unit of labor and capital combined.

During recent decades, real hourly earnings have increased more rapidly, on the average, than during earlier decades. The change in the trend of real earnings thus matches the change in the trend of productivity noticed earlier, though the data do not permit a confident conclusion on their relative timing.

Long-term trends in hourly earnings in individual industries roughly paralleled the trend in the general average of hourly earnings. There was little systematic difference in rate of increase in hourly earnings between industries in which productivity rose very rapidly and those in which productivity rose slowly; or between those industries with high or low, or relatively rising or falling, capital per manhour.

These facts support the conclusion of generations of economists that over the long run the dominant factor in the general rise of real hourly earnings has been the increase in national productivity, and that the more rapid rise in earnings generally than in output per unit of labor and tangible capital combined has resulted largely from greater scarcity of labor relative to capital and from improved quality of labor.

The facts on real earnings in the economy at large may be inferred from the information already presented, plus one other piece of evidence. This is an estimate of the percentage of national income received in the form of wages and salaries, including allowances for the labor of farmers and other proprietors. The percentage seems to have fallen somewhat between 1889 and 1899, moved along a horizontal trend over the period to 1929, and then returned to the 1889 level in recent decades. The index of real earnings per hour of work is obtained simply by multiplying an index of this percentage by the index of real national product per manhour. The derived index of real hourly earnings is shown in Chart 1, and its rate of growth, in Table 2.

The same facts lead also, it should be noted, to the conclusion that the rate of return on capital—total non-labor income per dollar of tangible capital, both in constant prices—has fallen considerably in relation to the real hourly earnings of labor, but not absolutely. This is consistent with such other information as is available on trends in interest rates and in rates of return on property. Productivity increase thus offset the effects of the rise in capital per worker, and prevented the appearance of the absolute long-term decline in the rate of return on capital that might otherwise have been expected.

CHART 1
REAL HOURLY EARNINGS COMPARED WITH PRODUCTIVITY AND TOTAL INPUT PER MANHOUR, 1889–1957
Estimates for the Private Domestic Economy

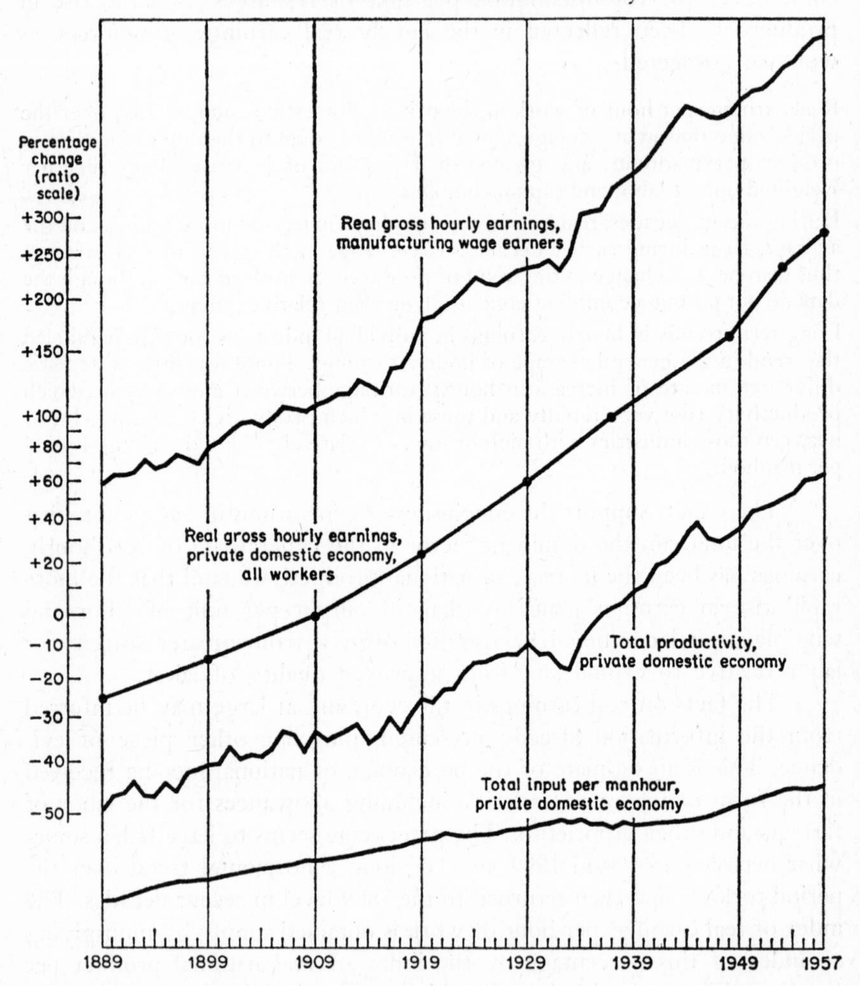

The upward drift of real earnings in relation to total productivity does not appear to be seriously in doubt, despite gaps in the underlying statistics, difficulties in distinguishing labor income from property income (as in agriculture), and differences of opinion on a variety of questions (such as whether income should be measured before or after income tax). But it is well to check the crudely derived data on earnings, available at best for occasional years only, with direct evidence on the annual movement of real hourly earnings.

For this purpose we make use of the index of real hourly earnings of manufacturing wage earners since 1889 shown in Chart 1 and sum-

TABLE 2

AVERAGE RATES OF INCREASE IN PRODUCTIVITY, TOTAL INPUT PER MANHOUR, AND REAL HOURLY EARNINGS, 1889–1957

	Average Annual Percentage Rate of Change		
	1889–1957	1889–1919	1919–1957
Output per unit of labor and capital combined, private domestic economy	1.7	1.3	2.1
Total input per manhour, private domestic economy	0.6	0.7	0.5
Real hourly earnings, private domestic economy, all workers (including proprietors and family workers)	2.4	1.7	3.0
Real hourly earnings, manufacturing, wage earners	2.3	1.9	2.6

Source: Tables A and C.

marized in terms of its average annual rate of increase in Table 2. The index, greatly improved over that previously available, we owe to Albert Rees and Clarence Long, who re-examined the available wage statistics for the period prior to World War I, reconsidered the methods and weights used in combining them into an index, and constructed a new cost of living index.

The agreement between the two indexes is surprisingly good. Of course, the index of real hourly earnings for the entire private economy covers also the real hourly earnings of manufacturing wage earners, and some degree of similarity must therefore be expected. However, wage earners in manufacturing have seldom numbered more than a fourth or fifth of all workers, and the parallelism is so close as to indicate virtual identity of the long-term percentage change in the real hourly earnings of manufacturing wage earners with the percentage change in the real hourly earnings of all other workers—that is, those in non-manufacturing and the salaried workers and proprietors of manufacturing—except possibly in the recent period.

The parallelism is all the more surprising because the economy-wide index reflects the increase in wages caused by the shift of workers from low-pay industries, such as agriculture, to high-pay industries, whereas the manufacturing index reflects such shifts only within the manufacturing sector. Further, the manufacturing index relates to wage earners alone, and thus cannot reflect adequately the rise in hourly earnings that might be expected to result from investment in education. However, the index of hourly earnings of factory wage earners has undoubtedly been affected by factors peculiar to manufacturing, and these might have worked to push up relative earnings in factories. It is tempting to speculate further about the complex of factors that lies behind the similarities between the two indexes of hourly earnings, but this is hardly worth while before more work has been done to improve the estimates;

and in any case speculation can only prompt—not take the place of—the hard labor of unraveling and weighing the factors involved.

This much seems clear and is important: Both the manufacturing index and the index for the entire private economy show that real hourly earnings rose substantially more rapidly than productivity over the period 1889–1957.

The new index of real hourly earnings in manufacturing, as well as the derived index of real hourly earnings for the entire private economy, leads to a substantial revision of prevailing impressions concerning the historical relation between productivity and real wages prior to World War I. It has long been thought, for example, that real hourly wages in manufacturing rose by only 8 per cent between 1890 and 1914, despite much greater concurrent increases in productivity. Rees's index for the twenty-four-year period shows a much larger gain in real wages, a rise that is much more in line with the productivity increase of the time. The present data indicate that real hourly earnings have normally, not always, moved up more rapidly than national productivity—output per unit of labor and tangible capital—and that, as in the case of national productivity, the rate of increase in real hourly earnings was greater in recent decades than in earlier decades.

To help explain the greater rise in real hourly earnings than in productivity two factors were singled out at the beginning of this section: increasing scarcity of labor relative to capital, and improved quality of labor. The trend in both combined is suggested by the rise of total input (weighted manhours and tangible capital) per manhour, in Chart 1. On each of the two factors a comment is necessary.

First, the decline in labor input relative to capital (or to total input) is not unambiguous evidence of increasing labor scarcity. The technological and other changes that have played a part in raising efficiency might also have altered the relative usefulness of labor and capital—an essential ingredient in their scarcity—in favor of the one or the other. If the technological and other changes back of productivity increase were not neutral in this respect, they would have tended to push the rate of return for labor relative to that for capital in one or the other direction.

Second, the shift of labor from lower- to higher-pay industries is at best a very rough measure of the improvement in the quality of the labor force. If more adequate allowance could be made for quality improvement, our measure of labor input would probably rise more than is now indicated; labor input relative to tangible capital would decline less; and productivity would rise less. Our inability—as yet—to measure quality of labor adequately thus probably leads us to overemphasize in some degree the contribution of productivity and labor scarcity to the rising trend of real hourly earnings, and correspondingly to underemphasize the contribution of investment in education and other forms of personal capital.

The information we have on the economy as a whole provides

CHART 2

RELATION BETWEEN CHANGE IN PRODUCTIVITY AND REAL HOURLY EARNINGS, AND PRODUCTIVITY AND PRICE OF PRODUCT, 33 INDUSTRY GROUPS

Indexes for 1953 Relative to 1899

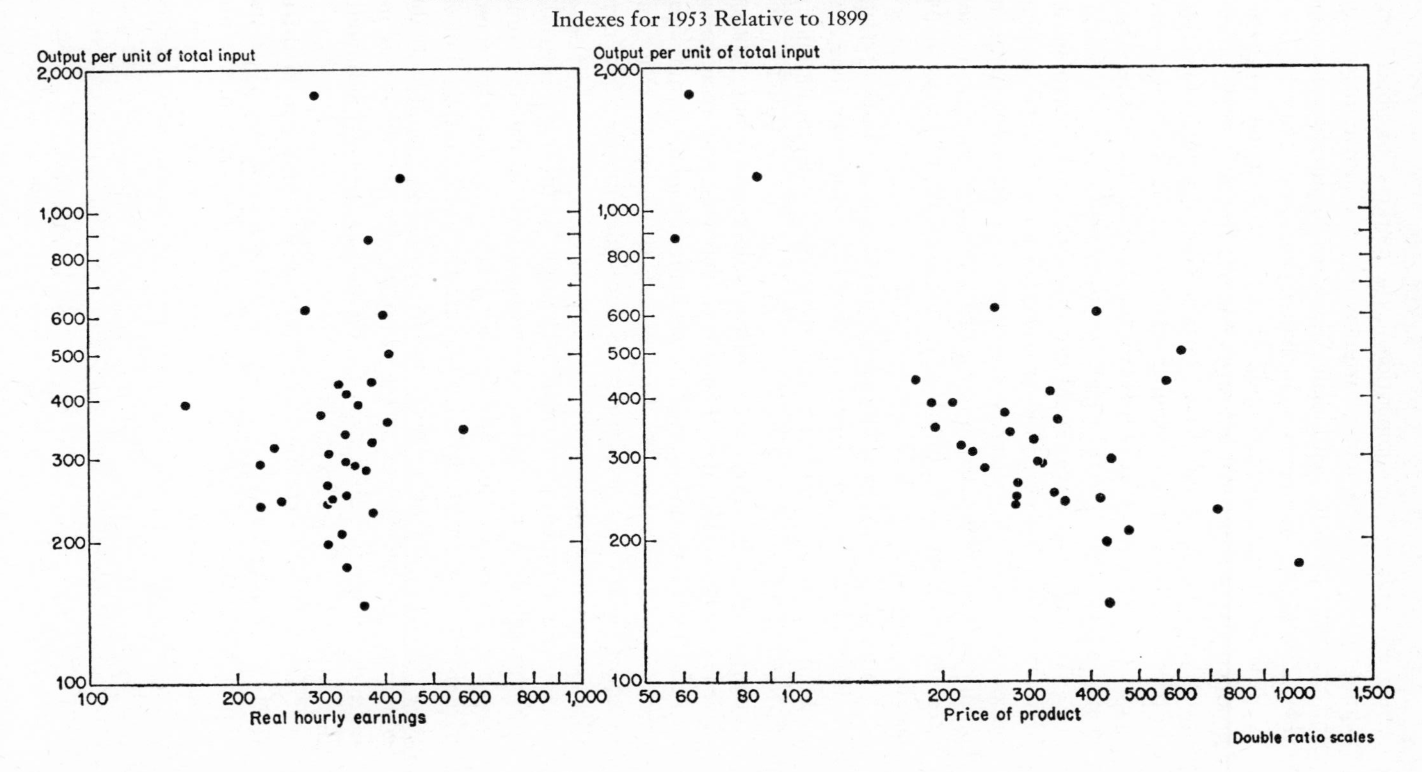

strong evidence of the competition in the markets for goods, labor, and capital that causes real hourly earnings to rise with national productivity and the other factors mentioned. Additional important evidence is provided by the developments in individual industries (Chart 2).

As we should expect to find in a competitive economy, the trends in productivity in individual industries and the trends in their hourly earnings are only weakly correlated. That is, hourly earnings in different industries moved up at fairly similar rates. The parallelism we noticed between the trend of real hourly earnings in manufacturing and in the economy at large is a fairly general phenomenon.

We find also, as we should expect, that there is a stronger relation between an industry's trend in productivity and the trend in its product prices. As a rule, in industries with high rates of productivity increase, product prices fell in relation to the prices of other goods, while in industries with low rates of productivity increase, relative prices of products usually increased.

To find *closely* parallel changes in the average rates of wages and salaries paid by different industries would be surprising. The American economy is one in which economic advance has brought not only greater efficiency but also other changes—in the type of labor used by different industries, in the relative scarcity of the skills they employ, in the values placed on the various noneconomic advantages and disadvantages of working in them, and in other determinants of demand and supply. So continuous has the flow of changes been that adjustment to them has never stopped. The exceptions to the rule are therefore many in Chart 2, and they invite study.

As for the general level of real wages, a fuller explanation of its historical changes must take account also of the behavior of money wages, retail prices, and productivity during the business cycles and periods of inflation and deflation that are found in the record of the past seven decades. And it is hardly necessary to add that it must take account of still other factors peculiar to particular periods, as well as of the more or less gradual changes in the markets for labor, goods, and capital that have taken place over the years.

But the chief determinants of the longer-run trends in the general level of real wages and in the level of real wages in individual industries appear to be those with which we began our discussion.

6. AUTOMATION: IMPLICATIONS*

Ewan Clague

MEASURES OF TECHNOLOGICAL CHANGE

The broadest effect of changing technology is on the economy as a whole, and it is measured by indexes of changing output per man-hour of labor. Attention is centered upon labor because, for the economy as a whole, it is by far the largest input—comprising as much as four-fifths of the total cost of production—and because the workers constitute the group who bear the brunt of the consequences of technological change.

Over the period 1909–59, the average annual change in real product per man-hour for the private economy as a whole was 2.3 percent. What the increase in output per man-hour will be for 1961 is not yet known, but some impression of the impact of productivity changes upon the Nation's labor force can be given. If it should amount to a modest 2.5 percent, the labor displacement would be 1.5 million workers; if the increase turns out to be 3 percent, the displacement would be nearly 2 million workers. In other words, technological change affects many workers every year.

Of course, displacement is not equivalent to unemployment. A worker whose job has disappeared may be transferred to another job in the same company and may never experience any unemployment at all. Others may experience varying periods of unemployment before finding other jobs. Still others may become occupationally obsolete and have to retire from the labor force. So productivity rates cannot be converted directly into unemployment figures.

The best way to interpret these figures is to point out that the Nation could produce in 1961 the same output as in 1960 with 1.5 million fewer workers (or 2 million). However, if the real product of the economy increases as much as productivity, then these workers (or an equivalent number of others) would be reabsorbed. Of course, such a slow rate of growth would not provide enough jobs to reduce the existing number of unemployed or to employ the additional new workers entering the labor market this year. It is the combined effect of all these factors which makes the unemployment problem what it is today.

Technological change has its strongest impact on individual firms or

* Ewan Clague, "Social and Economic Aspects of Automation," *Monthly Labor Review,* Vol. 84, No. 9 (September, 1961), pp. 957–60.

specific industries. The accompanying table shows how widely industries can differ in output per man-hour over the same period of time. At one extreme, in the cigarette industry, there was a net gain from 1919 to 1926 of more than 160 percent, while in the lumber industry there was an actual loss. The remaining industries ranged widely in between these extremes. So the effect of technological change can be much more pronounced in one industry than in another, even within one sector of the economy, such as manufacturing.

But even with respect to specific industries, productivity is not closely correlated with unemployment. Much depends upon how fast (if at all) the industry is growing. Note in the table that some industries with significant increases in output per man-hour nevertheless required more man-hours to turn out greatly increased output (motor vehicles, petroleum, cement). Another pattern was a large expansion in production, accompanied by an even greater increase in output per man-hour, thus causing some reduction in man-hours (cigarettes; chemicals; alloyers, rolling mills, and foundries; sugar refining; blast furnaces, steel works, and rolling mills). A third pattern was an actual decline in production, which nearly always resulted in a substantial decline in man-hours (agricultural machinery, beehive coke, flour, leather, cigars). In other words, the growth rate of the industry has a moderating influence upon the unemployment which could result from improved technology. In fact, a rapidly expanding industry can provide increasing employment along with the large-scale displacement of labor.

The man-hours shown in the table do not necessarily reflect the actual employment situation. There were substantial reductions in working hours between 1919 and 1926 (the shift from a 12-hour to an 8-hour day in the steel industry, for example). Some of the industries which reduced their man-hours of labor did not actually cut the number of workers employed by them.

Just as there are wide variations in productivity among industries, so there are marked (and sometimes surprising) variations among firms in the same industry. The chart (on page 39) shows the wide range of plant productivity performances in several industries, not necessarily for each plant as a whole but for its performance in the production of a particular product—a dozen work shirts, a dozen shoes, etc. Productivity is expressed as the man-hours of labor required per unit of output. The plants which were studied in this survey were classified into four groups, ranging from the lowest unit man-hours (the most efficient) to the highest (the least efficient). In foundries, the range from highest to lowest was about 4 to 1, in mixed fertilizers, nearly 3 to 1, in men's work shirts, nearly 2 to 1. Only in the shoe industry was there a moderately narrow range of labor utilization.

Even this chart does not disclose the maximum range of differences. Some firms in the most efficient group had performances lower than the

PERCENT CHANGE IN OUTPUT PER MAN-HOUR, PRODUCTION, AND MAN-HOURS, 34 MANUFACTURING INDUSTRIES, 1919–26

Industry	Output per man-hour: Change	Output per man-hour: Rank of Change—highest to lowest	Production: Change	Production: Rank of Change—highest to lowest	Man-hours: Change	Man-hours: Rank of Change—highest to lowest
Cigarettes	+161.5	1	+73.5	6	−33.6	32
Chemicals	+104.3	2	+48.5	14	−27.2	29
Alloyers, rolling mills, and and foundries[1]	+101.1	3	+69.5	7	−15.7	23
Motor vehicles	+83.8	4	+135.6	1	+28.0	5
Coke (byproducts)	+83.8	5	+77.8	4	−3.3	17
Petroleum	+80.4	6	+120.8	2	+22.4	7
Agricultural machinery[2]	+78.4	7	−20.1	33	−55.2	33
Newspapers	+77.0	8	+75.7	5	−.9	16
Cane sugar refining	+71.2	9	+29.8	21	−24.2	28
Glass group	+70.8	10	+58.7	12	−7.1	19
Blast furnaces, steel works, and rolling mills	+70.4	11	+36.7	19	−19.8	24
Primary smelting and refining of nonferrous metals	+67.3	12	+41.1	16	−15.7	22
Paper	+53.5	13	+53.8	13	+.1	15
Coke (beehive)	+49.7	14	−33.7	34	−55.7	34
Cement	+43.7	15	+101.3	3	+39.9	3
Slaughtering	+38.0	16	+6.1	24	−23.1	27
Silk and rayon goods	+36.6	17	+38.5	18	+1.4	13
Flour and other grain mill products	+35.8	18	−9.6	31	−33.4	31
Leather	+33.8	19	−5.2	30	−29.1	30
Canning and preserving	+32.4	20	+46.3	15	+10.5	9
Knit goods[1]	+29.6	21	+35.7	20	+4.7	12
Planing mills[1]	+27.4	22	+60.6	11	+26.1	6
Fertilizers	+27.3	23	+.3	27	−21.2	26
Furniture	+26.1	24	+67.3	8	+32.6	4
Pulp	+24.9	25	+26.5	22	+1.3	14
Clay products	+18.2	26	+65.7	9	+40.2	2
Ice cream	+18.2	27	+40.0	17	+18.4	8
Woolen and worsted goods	+17.4	28	+2.4	26	−12.9	21
Cigars	+11.8	29	−11.3	32	−20.7	25
Paints and varnishes	+11.4	30	+61.8	10	+45.4	1
Cotton goods	+8.1	31	+16.5	23	+7.9	11
Chewing and smoking tobacco and snuff	+7.6	32	−3.1	29	−9.9	20
Boots and shoes	+6.4	33	−.1	28	−6.1	18
Lumber	−3.2	34	+5.6	25	+9.2	10
Mean	+47.2	....	+38.6	....	−37.3	....
Median	+36.2	....	+39.3	....	−6.6	....

Source: Bureau of Labor Statistics.
[1] Covers 1919–25.
[2] Covers 1920–26.

group average, and some firms in the highest group had requirements still higher than that group average.

The import of these plant performances is that the high-labor plants are on the margin of survival. A technological improvement in the advanced plants would be likely to push these marginal plants out of business. A firm in difficulty will close its high-cost plants, or perhaps the whole firm will be forced into bankruptcy. Then all the workers are unemployed. In that small segment of our economy, the impact is 100 percent. In a small or medium-size community, this misfortune could generate a distressed area. Furthermore, the opportunities for the displaced workers to find other jobs there are likely to be extremely limited, and it is not easy to pick up the family and move elsewhere.

A few years ago, the Bureau of Labor Statistics, in cooperation with the Institute of Labor and Industrial Relations of the University of Illinois, conducted a survey of a shutdown of a steel car manufacturing plant in Mt. Vernon, Ill. Nearly 2,000 workers were laid off in the shutdown. Among the 1,500 workers who were covered by the study, 12 percent were still unemployed 2 years later, 11 percent were underemployed, and 9 percent had left the labor force.

EFFECTS OF TECHNOLOGICAL CHANGE

The benefits flowing from technical improvements in production are so well known and so generally recognized that there is no need to do more than record them. The overall rate of productivity gain is the most important factor in the Nation's rate of economic growth. The labor force is increasing at an estimated rate of about 1.5 percent a year. This could produce a 1.5-percent annual increase in total output. However, the increased output due to a larger supply of workers doesn't provide more goods and services for each worker and his family. A growth rate of 4 or 5 percent can only be achieved through higher productivity, which in turn will yield a higher level or standard of living. Shorter hours and leisure time are also fruits of technological efficiency.

We must bear in mind, however, that these changes have social and economic costs which must be met. Our problem as a Nation is how to distribute these costs equitably and how to share the benefits and the burdens of industrial change. Some industries and occupations are experiencing serious problems. In agriculture, for example, the employment of farmers and farm workers combined has declined from more than 11 million in 1919 to about 6 million in 1959. Particularly in the last 25 years, there has been a persistent shift of workers out of agriculture into industrial and commercial employment. In bituminous coal mining, a work force of about 550,000 production workers in 1919 had fallen to less than 150,000 in 1959. In railroad transportation, the number of workers employed declined nearly 40 percent from 1947 to 1959. In manufacturing, the peak employment of nearly 18 million workers (all employees) was reached in 1943 and has never been attained since; employment in manufacturing in 1959 was less than it was in 1953.

Substantial shifts in employment have also occurred within industry groups. White-collar employment has increased and blue-collar employment decreased, especially in the unskilled jobs. For example, within the manufacturing group itself, the number of workers (all employees) averaged about 15½ million in 1948 and the same number in early 1961.

AVERAGES OF MAN-HOURS PER UNIT OF OUTPUT, FOUR SELECTED INDUSTRIES, 1949

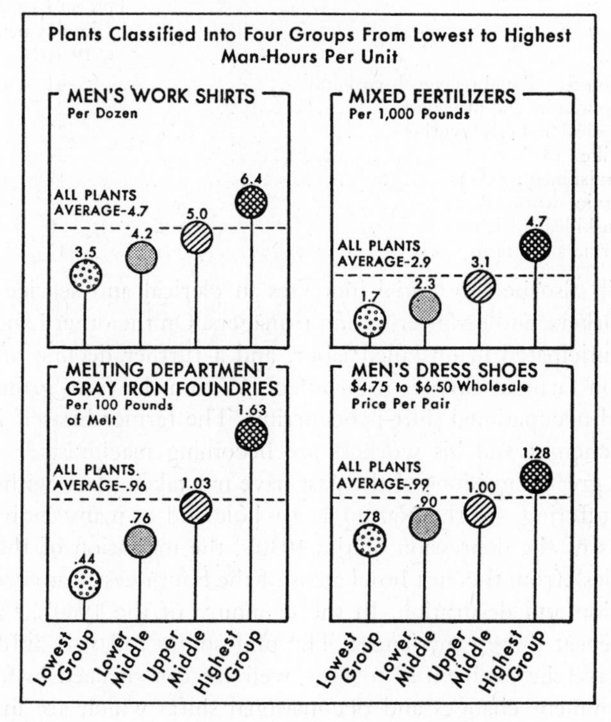

However, in the intervening period, production workers in plants declined by about 1½ million, while the supervisory and clerical workers in the offices increased by 1½ million. This shift has meant a significant change in jobs and occupations, even without a change in the total number of persons employed.

The workers who are unemployed today reflect in their characteristics the consequences of these past trends. In West Virginia, Pennsylvania, Kentucky, Ohio, and Illinois, there is widespread unemployment among coal miners (or ex-coal miners, as many of them now are). Cities dominated by heavy durable goods industries have high rates of unemployment; furthermore, the unemployed in those cities have a significant proportion of male heads of families, workers with 10 or more years of seniority. These are not occasional workers, lightly attached to the labor market; they are permanent, full-time workers. Some of them are experiencing serious unemployment for the first time in 20 years. Finally, many of them are unskilled or semiskilled—factory operatives who have limited capacities for other jobs.

The outlook for the future is for a continuation of most of these past trends. In the manpower projections which the Department of Labor has made up to 1970, the most rapidly growing occupational group will be the professional and technical workers:

	Percent Change in Employment, 1960–70
Professional and technical workers	41
Proprietors and managers	24
Clerical and sales workers	27
Skilled workers	24
Semiskilled workers	18
Service workers	25
Unskilled workers	0
Farmers and farm workers	−17

There will also be substantial increases in clerical and service workers, skilled workers, and proprietors and managers. On the other hand, no gain at all is anticipated in unskilled labor, and a further decline of as much as a million farm workers is in prospect. Within the farm group itself, a substantial occupational shift is occurring. The farmer himself is becoming a biochemist and his workers are becoming machinists.

The great transitions of the past have not taken place without much loss and suffering—to the Nation as a whole and to many individuals. In the depths of the depression of the 1930's, the migration of the "Okies" and "Arkies" from the dust bowl areas of the Southwest was accompanied by privation and destitution. In the economy of the 1960's, there is no need to repeat those experiences. The philosophy today is different. But we still have the problem as to how well we can succeed in facilitating the employment changes and occupational shifts which are in prospect and at the same time ease the burdens of those who must make the changes.

Part I: Questions for Analysis

1. *a*) How does Alfred Marshall define "economics"? Contrast this definition with the one in your textbook.
   b) Upon what does the special skill of the economist depend, according to the view of Kenneth Boulding?

2. *a*) To what development does Adam Smith attribute "the greatest improvement in the productive powers of labour"? Discuss its principal advantages.
   b) Illustrate this development with a modern example.
3. Discuss the nature of *roundabout production*, as discussed by Eugen von Böhm-Bawerk. Outline Böhm-Bawerk's account of how such a roundabout system might be used to improve the water supply of a peasant householder.
4. *a*) What methods of measuring productivity change are described by Solomon Fabricant?
   b) What happened to productivity in the American economy during the period from 1889 to 1953?
   c) Did the trend in productivity which you describe above affect the real hourly earnings of workers during this period? If so, in what way?
5. *a*) What benefits may one reasonably expect to follow from technical improvements in production, including the development of automation?
   b) Ewan Clague points out that such benefits from technical innovations in production "have social and economic costs which must be met." What are some important examples of such costs in this country since World War I?

II MONEY, BANKING, AND THE PRICE LEVEL

As men developed specialization in their productive activities, they found it necessary to trade their surpluses with one another. Early societies accomplished this by barter, a direct exchange of goods for goods. The cumbersome and inefficient nature of this trading technique led to one of mankinds greatest innovations, money. Adam Smith gives a vivid account of its origin. William Davenport gives a fascinating account of a contemporary primitive money and exchange system. The Board of Governors of the Federal Reserve System presents an overview of the modern monetary system of the United States.

One of the major problems involved in the use of money is the fluctuation which takes place in its value. It is important to measure the direction and degree of changes in the value of money. The principal measuring technique developed for this purpose is the index number. Wesley C. Mitchell, the moving spirit in the founding of the National Bureau of Economic Research and famous business cycle analyst, discusses the origin and use of index numbers. Arnold E. Chase, Chief of the Division of Prices and Cost of Living of the U.S. Bureau of Labor Statistics, presents a current discussion of index numbers. Perhaps the best known and most widely used index in the United States today is the Consumer Price Index, popularly called the "Cost of Living Index." The Bureau of Labor Statistics, which is the governmental agency responsible for the preparation and publication of this index, explains it. Ewan Clague describes the revision of the Consumer Price Index which is currently under way and which is scheduled for completion in 1964.

A. Money and the Banking System

7. ORIGIN OF MONEY*

Adam Smith

OF THE ORIGIN AND USE OF MONEY

When the division of labour has been once thoroughly established, it is but a very small part of a man's wants which the produce of his own labour can supply. He supplies the far greater part of them by exchanging that surplus part of the produce of his own labour, which is over and above his own consumption, for such parts of the produce of other men's labour as he has occasion for. Every man thus lives by exchanging, or becomes in some measure a merchant, and the society itself grows to be what is properly a commercial society.

But when the division of labour first began to take place, this power of exchanging must frequently have been very much clogged and embarrassed in its operations. One man, we shall suppose, has more of a certain commodity than he himself has occasion for, while another has less. The former consequently would be glad to dispose of, and the latter to purchase, a part of this superfluity. But if this latter should chance to have nothing that the former stands in need of, no exchange can be made between them. The butcher has more meat in his shop than he himself can consume, and the brewer and the baker would each of them be willing to purchase a part of it. But they have nothing to offer in exchange, except the different productions of their respective trades, and the butcher is already provided with all the bread and beer which he has immediate occasion for. No exchange can, in this case, be made between them. He cannot be their merchant, nor they his customers; and they are all of them thus mutually less serviceable to one another. In order to avoid the inconveniency of such situations, every prudent man in every period of society, after the first establishment of the division of labour, must naturally have endeavoured to manage his affairs in such a manner, as to have at all times by him, besides the peculiar produce of his own industry, a certain quantity of some one commodity or other, such as he imagined few people would be likely to refuse in exchange for the produce of their industry.

Many different commodities, it is probable, were successively both thought of and employed for this purpose. In the rude ages of society,

* Adam Smith, *The Wealth of Nations* (New York: Random House, Inc., 1937), pp. 22–28.

cattle are said to have been the common instrument of commerce; and, though they must have been a most inconvenient one, yet in old times we find things were frequently valued according to the number of cattle which had been given in exchange for them. The armour of Diomede, says Homer, cost only nine oxen; but that of Glaucus cost an hundred oxen. Salt is said to be the common instrument of commerce and exchanges in Abyssinia; a species of shells in some parts of the coast of India; dried cod at Newfoundland; tobacco in Virginia; sugar in some of our West India colonies; hides or dressed leather in some other countries; and there is at this day a village in Scotland where it is not uncommon, I am told, for a workman to carry nails instead of money to the baker's shop or the alehouse.

In all countries, however, men seem at last to have been determined by irresistible reasons to give the preference, for this employment, to metals above every other commodity. Metals cannot only be kept with as little loss as any other commodity, scarce any thing being less perishable than they are, but they can likewise, without any loss, be divided into any number of parts, as by fusion those parts can easily be reunited again; a quality which no other equally durable commodities possess, and which more than any other quality renders them fit to be the instruments of commerce and circulation. The man who wanted to buy salt, for example, and had nothing but cattle to give in exchange for it, must have been obliged to buy salt to the value of a whole ox, or a whole sheep, at a time. He could seldom buy less than this, because what he was to give for it could seldom be divided without loss; and if he had a mind to buy more, he must, for the same reasons, have been obliged to buy double or triple the quantity, the value, to wit, of two or three oxen, or of two or three sheep. If, on the contrary, instead of sheep or oxen, he had metals to give in exchange for it, he could easily proportion the quantity of the metal to the precise quantity of the commodity which he had immediate occasion for.

Different metals have been made use of by different nations for this purpose. Iron was the common instrument of commerce among the ancient Spartans; copper among the ancient Romans; and gold and silver among all rich and commercial nations.

Those metals seem originally to have been made use of for this purpose in rude bars, without any stamp or coinage. Thus we are told by Pliny, upon the authority of Timæus, an ancient historian, that, till the time of Servius Tullius, the Romans had no coined money, but made use of unstamped bars of copper, to purchase whatever they had occasion for. These rude bars, therefore, performed at this time the function of money.

The use of metals in this rude state was attended with two very considerable inconveniences; first with the trouble of weighing; and, secondly, with that of assaying them. In the precious metals, where a small difference in the quantity makes a great difference in the value, even the business of weighing, with proper exactness, requires at least very accurate weights and scales. The weighing of gold in particular is an operation of some nicety. In the coarser metals, indeed, where a small error would be of little consequence, less accuracy would, no doubt, be necessary. Yet we should find it excessively troublesome, if every time a poor man had occasion either to buy or sell a farthing's worth of goods, he was obliged to weigh the farthing. The operation of assaying is still more difficult, still more tedious, and, unless a part of the metal is fairly melted in the crucible, with proper dissolvents, any conclusion that can be drawn from it, is extremely uncertain. Before the institution of coined money, however, unless they went through this tedious and difficult operation, people must always have been liable to the grossest frauds and impositions, and instead of a pound weight of pure silver, or pure copper, might receive in exchange for their goods, an adulterated composition of the coarsest and cheapest materials, which had, however, in their outward appearance, been made to resemble those metals. To prevent such abuses, to facilitate exchanges, and thereby to encourage all sorts of industry and commerce, it had been found necessary, in all countries that have made any considerable advances towards improvement, to affix a public stamp upon certain quantities of such particular metals, as were in those countries commonly made use of to purchase goods. Hence the origin of coined money, and of those public offices called mints; institutions exactly of the same nature with those of the aulnagers and stampmasters of woollen and linen cloth. All of them are equally meant to ascertain, by means of a public stamp, the quantity and uniform goodness of those different commodities when brought to market.

The first public stamps of this kind that were affixed to the current metals, seem in many cases to have been intended to ascertain, what it was both most difficult and most important to ascertain, the goodness or fineness of the metal, and to have resembled the sterling mark which is at present affixed to plate and bars of silver, or the Spanish mark which is sometimes affixed to ingots of gold, and which being struck only upon one side of the piece, and not covering the whole surface, ascertains the fineness, but not the weight of the metal. Abraham weighs to Ephron the four hundred shekels of silver which he had agreed to pay for the field of Machpelah. They are said however to be the current money of the merchant, and yet are received by weight and not by tale, in the same manner as ingots of gold and bars of silver are at present. The revenues of the ancient Saxon kings of England are said to have been paid, not in money but in kind, that is, in victuals and provisions of all sorts. William the Conqueror introduced the custom of paying them in money. This money, however, was, for a long time, received at the exchequer, by weight and not by tale.

The inconveniency and difficulty of weighing those metals with exactness gave occasion to the institution of coins, of which the stamp, covering entirely both sides of the piece and sometimes the edges too, was supposed to ascertain not only the fineness, but the weight of the metal. Such coins, therefore, were received by tale as at present, without the trouble of weighing.

The denominations of those coins seem originally to have expressed the weight or quantity of metal contained in them. In the time of Servius Tullius, who first coined money at Rome, the Roman As or Pondo contained a Roman pound of good copper. It was divided in the same manner as our Troyes pound, into twelve ounces, each of which contained a real ounce of good copper. The English pound sterling in the time of Edward I., contained a pound, Tower weight, of silver of a known fineness. The Tower pound seems to have been something more than the Roman pound, and something less than the Troyes pound. This last was not introduced into the mint of England till the 18th of Henry VIII. The French livre contained in the time of Charlemagne a pound, Troyes weight, of silver of a known fineness. The fair of Troyes in Champaign was at that time frequented by all the nations of Europe, and the weights and measures of so famous a market were generally known and esteemed. The Scots money pound contained, from the time of Alexander the First to that of Robert Bruce, a pound of silver of the same weight and fineness with the English pound sterling. English, French, and Scots pennies too, contained all of them originally a real pennyweight of silver, the twentieth part of an ounce, and the two-hundred-and-fortieth part of a pound. The shilling too seems originally to have been the denomination of a weight. *When wheat is at twelve shillings the quarter,* says an ancient statute of Henry III. *then wastel bread of a farthing shall weigh eleven shillings and four pence.* The proportion, however, between the shilling and either the penny on the one hand, or the pound on the other, seems not to have been so constant and uniform as that between the penny and the pound. During the first race of the kings of France, the French sou or shilling appears upon different occasions to have contained five, twelve, twenty, and forty pennies. Among the ancient Saxons a shilling appears at one time to have contained only five pennies, and it is not improbable that it may have been as variable among them as among their neighbours, the ancient Franks. From the time of Charlemagne among the French, and from that of William the Conqueror among the English, the proportion between the pound, the shilling, and the penny, seems to have been uniformly the same as at present, though the value of each has been very different. For in every country of the world, I believe, the avarice and injustice of princes and sovereign states, abusing the confidence of their subjects, have by degrees diminished the real quantity of metal, which had been originally contained in their coins. The Roman As, in the latter ages of the Republic, was reduced to the twenty-fourth part of its original value, and, instead of weighing a pound, came to weigh only half an ounce. The English pound and penny contain at present about a third only; the Scots pound and penny about a thirty-sixth; and the French pound and penny about a sixty-sixth part of their original value. By means of those operations the princes and sovereign states which performed them were enabled, in appearance, to pay their debts and to fulfil their engagements with a smaller quantity of silver than would otherwise have been requisite. It was indeed in appearance only; for their creditors were really defrauded of a part of what was due to them. All other debtors in the state were allowed the same privilege, and might pay with the same nominal sum of the new and debased coin whatever they had borrowed in the old. Such operations, therefore, have always proved favourable to the debtor, and ruinous to the creditor, and have sometimes produced a greater and more universal revolution in the fortunes of private persons, than could have been occasioned by a very great public calamity.

It is in this manner that money has become in all civilized nations the universal instrument of commerce, by the intervention of which goods of all kinds are bought and sold, or exchanged for one another.

8. MONEY IN A CONTEMPORARY PRIMITIVE ECONOMY*

William Davenport

One of the most exotic kinds of money in the world today is a belt two inches wide and 30 feet long made of glue, fibers and feathers, particularly the downy red feathers plucked from the breast, head and back of a tropical forest bird. The red-feather currency of the Santa Cruz Islands of the southwest Pacific nonetheless fits the most rigorous definition of the term "money." It serves as a means of accumulating wealth and as a universal medium of exchange in the highly diversified commerce that flows among these islands. The currency itself is fully interchangeable, each belt having a precisely negotiable value in terms of other belts. Against the recent invasion of the Australian pound, moreover, the red-feather money has kept its integrity. It is still the only acceptable specie for the purchase of brides, fine pigs and certain forms of labor.

This improbable currency demonstrates that the use of money is not an economic sophistication limited to high civilizations. Many, but by no means all, primitive peoples have devised moneys of their own. Al-

* William Davenport, "Red-Feather Money." Reprinted with permission.

though the forms of the currencies are as diverse as any of man's inventions—running the gamut of animal, vegetable and mineral matter in the live, raw and processed states—the maintenance of these so-called primitive monetary systems requires the balancing of the same equation of supply and demand that confronts the U.S. Treasury and the Federal Reserve System.

If a currency is to serve as a common denominator of value, its value in turn must be carefully regulated. This is one of the most delicate operations in the management of a modern state. It involves adjustment of the demand for as well as supply of money, achieved by control over both the flow and the production of the currency. To a certain extent, especially for purposes of international exchange, the Western capitalist economies still refer their currencies to the value of gold on the world market. But in the main it is the scope of the modern state's authority and the extent of its jurisdiction that effectively fix the value of its currency.

Lacking the power to regulate demand (by such devices as manipulation of the interest rate), primitive societies must rely on measures that control the supply of currency against the demand in their completely free markets. Frequently the supply is limited by natural or social circumstances beyond the control of its users, much as the scarcity of gold or silver once set the value of the dollar or the pound. Often, however, the nature of the currency is such that the society could "mint" it without limit. Scarcity is then maintained by some convention that, through consumption, destruction or deterioration, renders the currency valueless and withdraws it from circulation.

The red-feather currency system shows both principles in operation. The supply of new money is regulated by the availability of the red feathers and by the output of the hunters and artisans who make the money; old currency goes out of circulation because it loses value as its color fades. Produced by the natives of Santa Cruz Island itself, the red-feather currency circulates throughout most of the islands in the group. In these islands, where the indigenous political organization has never extended beyond a single village, it functions as international currency, the common medium of exchange among peoples who speak different languages and live in contrasting ecological settings.

The Santa Cruz Islands, part of the British Solomon Islands Protectorate, are scattered over some 15,000 square miles of the Pacific Ocean just north of the New Hebrides Islands. Santa Cruz, a volcanic island, is the largest in the group as well as its financial center. About 25 miles to the north is a chain of small coral islets called the Reef Islands, and midway between these and Santa Cruz is Tinakula, a volcano too spectacularly active for human settlement. The Duff Islands, 60 miles northeast of the Reefs, are remnant peaks of a narrow volcanic ridge. The only other large islands of the group are Utupua and Vanikoro, respectively some 40 and 60 miles south of Santa Cruz.

Partly as the result of a long history of inhospitality to visiting mariners and missionaries, the islands were left pretty much to themselves even through the first two decades of this century, when colonial powers were asserting dominion over other islands in the Pacific. It was not until 1923 that the British assumed direct administration of the islands, which they had claimed since 1899, and only since World War II has the Santa Cruz group actually been drawn into the current of world affairs. Today some 7,000 people inhabit the islands, most of them concentrated along the north coast of Santa Cruz and in the eastern Reef Islands. The people of the Duffs and the western Reefs speak a Polynesian language and are racially similar to the Polynesians of the central Pacific islands. The darker Melanesians of the eastern Reefs and Santa Cruz itself speak four local languages that constitute an independent language family. Melanesians also live on Utupua and Vanikoro, but their three languages belong to the large Malayo-Polynesian family. The cultures of Santa Cruz and the islands north of it are similar in spite of language and racial differences, and it is through this area that the red-feather money circulates. Utupua and Vanikoro have different cultures and do not use feather currency, although their economy is closely linked to that of the red-feather islands.

Diversity and specialization, necessitated in part by differences in geology and geography, characterize the economies of the islands. Santa Cruz, where there is plenty of arable land, exports taro root and yams, the staple vegetables of these people, to the Reef Islands, where the sandy soil will not grow good root crops. The natives of certain islands and districts with particular types of reef offshore, with lagoons or with easy access to the deep sea are exporters of fish; pigs are bred in sandy areas where coconuts for feeding are plentiful, and several kinds of arboriculture are associated with the rainfall and forest cover peculiar to other areas. But specialization goes beyond ecology. Such arts as the raising and training of hunting dogs, canoe building, weaving, the manufacturing of bark cloth, tools and ornaments—and currency making—are indigenous to one or another small island or to one village on an island. Each of these specialized industries and crafts is regarded by its practitioners as a right inherited in the family line, and only individuals in the proper line of succession may manufacture currency, go shark fishing, build canoes or follow any other trade.

This primitive division of labor requires in many instances that raw or semiprocessed materials be brought from one district or island to another, where the goods are finished for local consumption or for export. In the busy commerce of the interisland economy goods are rarely bartered. They are sold for currency: feather money or, increasingly, Australian currency. For all who participate the motivation of this trade goes beyond the exchange of necessities and native luxuries; the islanders buy and sell for the express purpose of making money. The accumula-

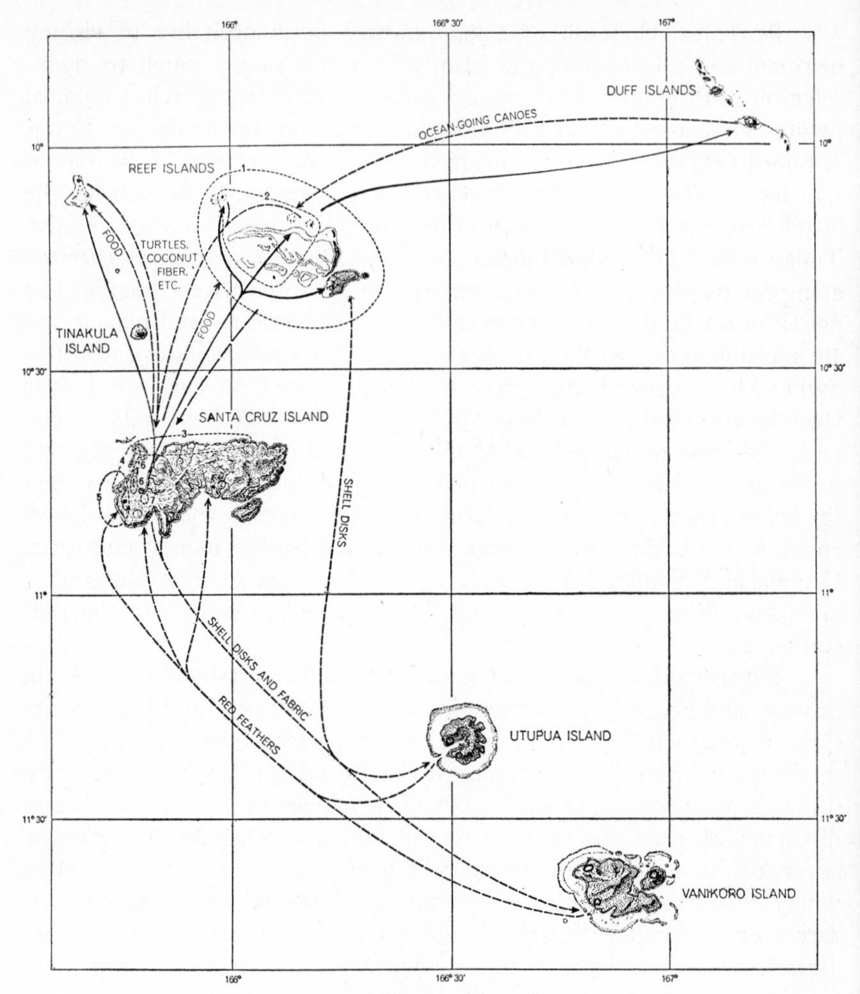

1 EXPORTERS OF WOMEN
2 NAVIGATORS AND TRADERS
3 ARBORICULTURE
4 PIG BREEDING
5 SHARK FISHING
6 SPECIALIZED CRAFTS
7 TARO GROWING

——— RED-FEATHER CURRENCY
— — WOMEN
- - - - GOODS AND PRODUCE
O FEATHERS AND SHINGLES
• CURRENCY BINDING

ECONOMIC MAP of the Santa Cruz group shows the specialized areas of origin of some of the major agricultural and manufactured products and the complex trade pattern made feasible by the red-feather monetary system. Feather money, which is made only in certain districts of Santa Cruz Island, circulates there and in the Reefs and Duffs.

tion of money is the way to prestige. But since the currency itself is perishable, prestige finds its tangible expression in spending as well as in accumulation, above all in helping to buy brides for members of one's family and friends and in giving feasts. Prestige won in these ways is the source of political power and authority.

The red-feather currency is made only on Santa Cruz Island. It is made on contract for a specific purchaser, who negotiates individually with the three different hereditary specialists whose combined skills are required for its manufacture. The first specialist snares the little jungle bird whose down supplies the red color of the money. The second makes individual platelets of pigeon feathers and decorates each with a band of the red down. The third assembles the platelets by binding them on two cords to form a belt.

The bird on which the entire system depends is a small scarlet-

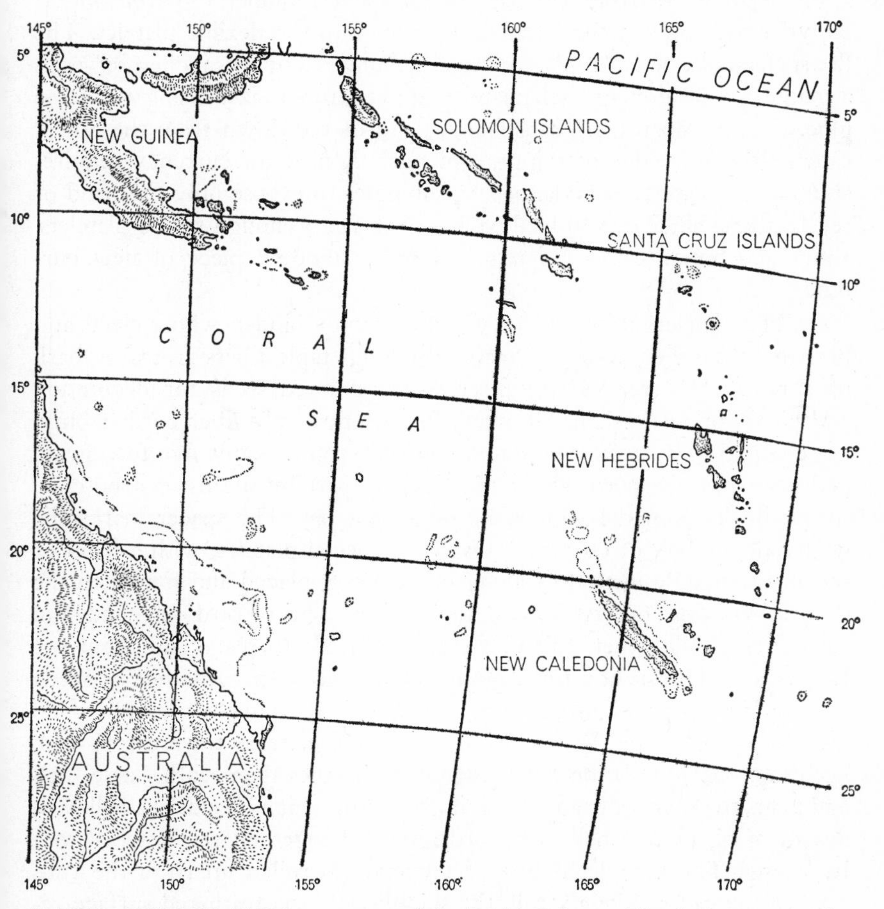

SANTA CRUZ ISLANDS are a part of the British Solomon Islands Protectorate in the southwest Pacific. They were largely untouched by outside influences until after World War II.

colored honey eater (*Myzomela cardinalis*) of the rain forest. The bird snarer makes portable perches covered with the sticky latex of a forest tree and fastens at the top of each either a live decoy of the species or a flower that the honey eater likes. Hanging a number of these perches in adjacent trees, he shields himself behind a blind of betel palm leaves and attracts birds into the area by chirping with a whistle made from a tree bud. Investigating the flower or the decoy, the honey eaters approach the sticky perch and are caught by their wings or feet. The bird snarer plucks the red down from the birds' breasts, heads and backs; he does not deliberately kill them in the process, but they usually die as a result. In the half-shell of a coconut he packs tightly the down of 10 birds, and this is the basic unit in which he deals.

The platelet maker usually secures his own pigeon feathers, shooting the gray Pacific pigeon (*Ducula pacifica*) with bow and arrow. With a mucilage made from the sap of the paper mulberry (*Broussonetia papyrifera*), he glues the feathers together into the flexible platelet. The flat surface of a wooden platen, usually about 2¼ by 1¼ inches, serves as a gauge for fashioning each platelet in the proper size. Using the same glue, the craftsman tacks a half-inch band of red down from the honey eaters along one edge of the gray platelet. A piece of currency requires about 1,500 platelets, overlapped like shingles to expose only the band of red feathers. Since one 10-bird packet of down is enough for 50 platelets, about 300 honey eaters are required for a standard piece of new currency.

The platelets are passed on to the currency binder, who collects and prepares the other necessary materials: long-staple fibers from the bark of a rain-forest tree (*Gnetum gnemon*), colored seeds for decoration and pieces of turtle shell. He stretches two three-ply fiber cords from a large stump to a springy sapling set in the ground about five feet away, and he spaces the cords about two inches apart by means of a notched spacer made from the wing bone of a fruit bat. The spacer marks the center of the belt of currency. Over it a special platelet, with a band of red in the middle instead of along one edge, is placed and bound to the cords. Working outward from the center, first toward one end and then toward the other, this craftsman proceeds to place and wrap the feather shingles one at a time. He maintains the proper distance between the cords with a sliding bat-bone spacer that he moves a quarter of an inch for each platelet. When he has bound 750 platelets toward each end, he brings the foundation cords together, sheathes them with turtle shell and plaits them into a triangular end piece into which he works a hallmark design of his own. Finally the cords, braided together, are fastened to a bark ring. The completed belt of currency is rolled up from the ends toward the center like a scroll, the shingling of the feathered surface resembling the scales of a snake when its spine is flexed.

All three of the skills involved in the manufacturing of feather money are believed to have been given to mortals by munificent spirits who still inhabit the island, keeping a watchful eye on the work of their protégés. None of the tasks requires exceptional skill or a lengthy apprenticeship, but the craftsman depends on secret incantations and talismans to keep in close communion with the spirits. The right to pursue a currency-making skill comes with the inheritance of these magic secrets; no unauthorized person will risk the anger of the spirits by making his own currency. Many of the islands' other specialties have their own supernatural trappings, which reinforce the restrictions imposed by heredity. No specialty is regarded as superior to any other and none, not even currency making, is likely to be more lucrative than another. The specialists plying each trade compete with one another, and the hereditary lines in each occupation are sufficiently numerous and dispersed so that no individual or small group can easily obtain a monopoly or control over the market.

Feather currency has absolutely no other use than as a medium of exchange, a standard of value and a store of wealth. It is not worn or displayed. In other words, it has no inherent usefulness; it is a true money. Yet it is produced and circulated in a free market, controlled only by supply and demand and by the principle of devaluation over time. Inflation is avoided, in spite of the constant issuance of new money, by the depreciation and withdrawal from circulation of old money.

The size and richness of color of a new piece of currency determine its original value. These two criteria are reducible to the number of birds and the amount of labor that go into its manufacture. In addition to the down of 300 birds, the average piece embodies 500 or 600 man-hours of work by the three specialists. But the width and sometimes the length of a belt can vary. And the red hue can be more or less saturated depending on how much down was used or the extent to which the less admired orange feathers were discarded.

Depreciation comes with time from damage by vermin and molds as well as from the wear and tear of handling. Great care is taken to protect the currency. The double coils are wrapped tightly, first in a dried fan-palm leaf and then in many layers of bark cloth. Looking more like a bundle of rags than something of value, the coils are stored on a shelf under which the household fire is kept smoldering. The heat inhibits molds, the smoke keeps insects and other vermin away and the wrappings protect the money from smoke damage. In spite of these precautions, each piece of currency eventually deteriorates. When the last bit of color disappears, the belt is discarded.

The value of most currencies is referred ultimately to some standard; in the Santa Cruz Islands the standard is the unseemly combination of pigs and marriage payments. The minimum payment made to the bride's family by the groom's kin at marriage—the bride price—always consists of 10 units of currency graduated in value from a new or nearly perfect

No. 1 ("bottom") piece to a No. 10 ("top") piece, which is just above the threshold of no value. The negotiation of a bride price calls for a session of formalized bargaining, involving the close examination of each coil of currency. Everyone concerned has a clear idea of the range of quality appropriate to each of the 10 units. Thus the bride price supplies not only a basic standard for the value of feather money but also a scale of ideal images in terms of which the "denomination" of any piece of currency can be expressed.

The progression is not arithmetic but geometric: each piece is worth twice as much as the one below it on the scale. If a "top" piece is given an arbitrary value of one, then a No. 6 piece is worth 16 and a "bottom" piece is worth 512. These values are not explicit. No one says that a piece is "worth 128" but all understand that an ideal No. 6 belt has a par value of two No. 7 belts. In the terminology of the pig standard, the pieces from No. 1 to No. 5 are called "porkers," because a pig suitable for a feast can be bought with currencies in this range; pieces from No. 6 to No. 10 are called "sucklings," because they will buy only pigs too small to be eaten. Except for the negotiation of bride prices, there is remarkably little haggling over the price of any purchase. The buyer of a pig or canoe or taro roots offers what he considers a fair amount of currency, and the seller accepts. If the seller feels he has been underpaid, he can seriously damage the buyer's reputation by gossiping about the transaction and refusing to deal with him again.

As in the purchase of a bride, certain other purchases must be made with specified pieces of high value. The seller has no obligation to "make change," so currency is exchanged ahead of time. This can be done by anyone, but some men who are particularly adept at money changing specialize in it and make a profit. These transactions take place before an informal gathering of witnesses in the men's clubhouse of a village, where the pieces of currency are draped over a horizontal bar for close comparison. Regardless of who has initiated the deal, the piece of greatest value (the "high piece") is hung over the center of the bar. Alongside it (and always in the direction of the Nembo River, a spring-fed stream symbolically associated with the currency spirits) is hung the "base piece," the most valuable of the belts to be exchanged for the high piece. On the other side is hung the "crown piece," the piece that makes up the difference in value between the base piece and the high piece. Values are matched in terms of the 10-point scale. For example, if the high piece is an average No. 6 and the base piece is a fine No. 7, a middling No. 7 may suffice as a crown.

In this manner the par value of the high piece is agreed on. But the price at which it now actually sells is something else again. Because high-value currency is scarcer than low-value currency, the owner of the high piece is a seller in a seller's market. The buyer (the owner of the base and crown pieces) must offer additional currency. It is not only that the high piece is newer; there are fewer new pieces in circulation. Hence market value is correlated to scarcity. The greater the par value of the high piece, the greater the spread between this value and the market price. (It is as though a $10 bill were worth a little more than two fives and a $20 bill worth more than two tens by a still larger margin.) It is the difficulty and expense of obtaining high-value pieces on the exchange market that ultimately leads a man to contract with the three currency specialists for a new piece.

Since all the feather currency originates on Santa Cruz Island, it must flow continually from its source to the Reef and Duff islands, where it is not manufactured. To maintain this one-way flow of currency the Reef Islanders have traditionally exported some of their women to Santa Cruz. Today the women go only as wives but once some went as concubines. Concubines were clearly distinguished from wives: they were shared by a group of men; they did no gardening or other domestic chores; having no dwelling of their own, they lived in the men's clubhouse. On the other hand, a concubine's possessors could purvey her services as a prostitute, sell her outright or even kill her without fear of retaliation. None of these things could be done with wives. But since the purchase price of a concubine was 10 times higher than a bride price, selling a girl into concubinage had its attractions for many Reef Island families. The British Government has forbidden the practice, but Reef Island women still go south as wives. Their bride prices are the main source of currency for their home islands. An imported wife brings extra prestige to a Santa Cruz man, and bride prices for Reef women run about twice as high as they do for domestic wives.

The Duff Islanders get their feather currency not by selling women but by building large sailing canoes that carry on interisland traffic in passengers and cargo. The men of the Duffs do not engage in that traffic themselves; they sell the canoes for feather currency to the people of a few of the western Reef Islands, who in turn specialize in voyaging and trading throughout the islands. These mariners sail even to the southern islands of Utupua and Vanikoro in search of trade. The two islands are outside the feather-currency area, but their people until recently depended on the canoes to bring them the shell disks and lengths of woven cloth they used as currency. For these precious items they traded, at fixed rates, packets of red honey eater feathers, and these were resold on Santa Cruz to the makers of feather currency. In this manner the two different money systems became interlocked and interdependent, and the economies of north and south remain so today, even though there is no longer any traffic in currency materials.

Since the end of World War II the Santa Cruz monetary system has come under pressure from the world outside. More and more Australian money has flowed into the islands; it circulates along with the feather currency and is completely interchangeable with it. Today the rate of exchange is roughly one shilling for a piece of feather money of minimum value. This makes the par value of a No. 1 piece 512 shillings, or about 25 Australian pounds. Figured in terms of labor (at the prevailing net wage rate for unskilled labor in the central Solomons, where most Santa Cruz men work at some point in their lives), the value of a new piece of currency is roughly comparable: about 20 to 24 pounds.

Plantation wages have nearly trebled since 1945. The great increase in the quantity of Australian money within the Santa Cruz group has caused a precipitate fall in its value in terms of local goods. Once a shilling bought 10 pounds of native tobacco; now it buys half a pound. During the same period, in an effort to increase copra production by channeling more islanders into plantation work, the colonial administration has taken steps that tend to depress interisland and intervillage trade in domestic products. Less feather currency is needed and less is being produced. At the moment there are only five men on Santa Cruz who bind currency, whereas a decade ago there were more than a dozen. Yet marriages go on as before, and men still refuse to marry off their daughters without receiving the traditional red-feather payment. Indeed, there is no area of the islands' economy in which confidence in the feather currency has been shaken. The craft and agricultural specialists still demand red-feather money for their best products.

With the value of feather currency rising as it becomes scarcer and that of Australian money dropping as it becomes more abundant, the market price of feather currency in Australian pounds has increased nearly 20 times in the past 15 years. Although it is recognized that 25 Australian pounds is the appropriate par value for a new piece of feather money, it takes considerably more than that to induce the currency specialists to turn one out. This is, to be sure, not true in the case of the bird snarers. As a result of the decreased production of feather money, the *Myzomela cardinalis* population has been increasing; the snarers can take birds more easily and in more accessible places and they would be willing to work for the old rates. But the labor involved in making platelets and binding new currency has not diminished. Like skilled artisans anywhere, the specialists in these processes prefer to charge more and work less. In pricing their labor they are mindful not only of today's high market but also of the fact that the value of their product in Australian money is likely to be even greater as time passes. As a result the production of feather currency has now fallen behind even the currently reduced demand. As the "bad" Australian money drives out the "good" red-feather currency in accordance with Gresham's law, a simple society in the South Seas is experiencing a monetary crisis familiar to many more sophisticated economies.

9. MONEY, CREDIT, AND THE FEDERAL RESERVE SYSTEM*

Board of Governors, The Federal Reserve System

The principal function of the Federal Reserve is to regulate the flow of bank credit and money. Essential to the performance of this main function is the supplemental one of collecting and interpreting information bearing on economic and credit conditions. A further function is to examine and supervise State member banks, obtain reports of condition from them, and cooperate with other supervisory authorities in the development of policies conducive to a system of strong individual banks.

Other important functions include the provision of cash-balance or payment services to the member banks of the Federal Reserve System, the U.S. Government, and the public. These services are chiefly the following: handling member bank reserve accounts; furnishing currency for circulation and making currency shipments; facilitating the clearance and collection of checks; effecting telegraphic transfers of funds; and acting as fiscal agents, custodians, and depositaries for the Treasury and other Government agencies.

Since the main concern of the Federal Reserve is the flow of credit and money, these words must be given meaning. . . . This can best be done by considering these four questions: (1) What is money and how is it used? (2) How is money related to bank deposits and to bank credit? (3) How do changes in credit and monetary conditions affect the lives of the people? (4) By what means does the Federal Reserve regulate credit and money?

Money and Its Uses

Money is most meaningfully defined in terms of how it is used. Money serves as: (1) a means of payment; (2) a standard of value; and (3) a store of purchasing power.

As a means of payment, money allows individuals to concentrate their productive efforts on those activities for which they are best equipped and in which they are trained to engage. Money is what people receive in return for their services and what they use to buy the goods and other things they need for themselves and their families.

As a standard of value, money provides the means by which a day's work can be equated with a family's food, housing, and other bills, in-

* Board of Governors, *The Federal Reserve System* (4th edition, Washington, D.C.: U.S. Government Printing Office, 1961), pp. 4–12.

cluding what is set aside for old age or for children's education. It is thus the measuring rod in terms of which producer and consumer choices can be assessed and decided.

As a store of purchasing power, money enables us to set aside some of our present income for future spending or investing. It is a way in which labor and work expended in the present can be saved for education, old age, and for the many contingencies that individuals and families are likely to meet.

Because money has all these uses, it is vital and necessary to the functioning of our economic system. If money were impaired as a means

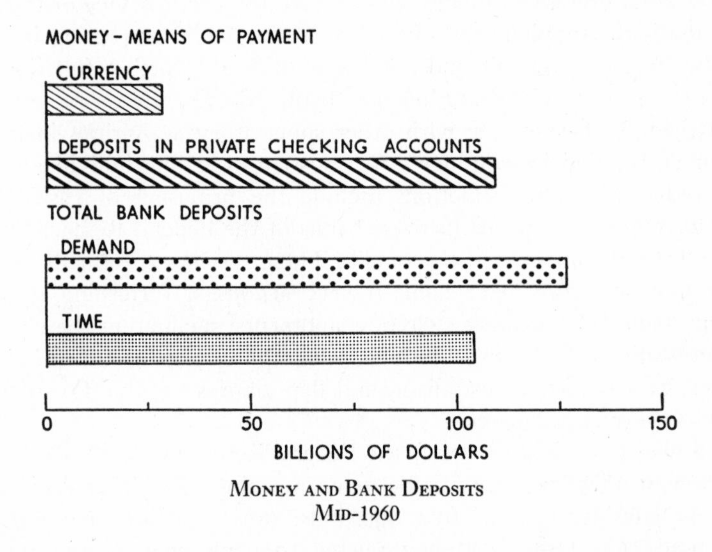

Money and Bank Deposits
Mid-1960

of payment, or a standard of value, or a store of purchasing power, the economy's ability to grow and to produce and distribute goods in accordance with the needs and wishes of the people would be jeopardized.

Currency, Bank Deposits, and Bank Credit

In the United States circulating paper money and coins of all kinds (currency) and the demand deposits held by banks perform all the functions of money. The reason that currency and demand deposits are both money is not far to seek. When a person has $10 of paper money and coin in his pocket and $100 in his checking account in the bank, he is in a position to spend $110 at any time. These two sums represent his active cash balance; they serve the same general purpose and each can be converted into the other at any time; that is, currency can be converted into a demand deposit by taking it to a bank, and a demand deposit can be converted into currency by taking it out of a bank.

The amounts of currency and of demand deposits at mid-1960 are shown in the chart on this page. It will be seen that the amount of demand deposits is far greater than the amount of currency. Banks also hold savings and other time deposits on which an interest return is paid. The amount of such deposits held at commercial and mutual savings banks at mid-1960 is also shown in the chart.

All bank deposits basically represent amounts owed by banks to depositors. They come into existence as banks extend credit to customers by exchanging bank deposits for the various assets that banks acquire—promissory notes of businesses and consumers, mortgages on real estate, and Government and other securities.

Demand deposits differ importantly from savings and other time deposits. Time deposits are not transferable by check. While convertible into demand deposits or currency, savings deposits of individuals are subject to prior notice of conversion, and other time deposits are not payable prior to maturity except in emergencies. Thus savings and time deposits, while serving a store-of-value function, are not in themselves means of payment; only currency and demand deposits serve in this active monetary role.

It has long been customary for people to keep most of their money in banks and to make most of their payments by drawing checks on their demand deposits with banks. Habits in this respect, however, change from time to time. Sometimes people keep more of their money in pocketbooks and sometimes less. Sometimes they hold more of their money in demand deposits and sometimes less. Such changes in money habits can have important consequences.

For a general idea of money, the two kinds—pocket money and deposits in checking accounts—should be considered together. For the most part both kinds originate in bank credit, that is, the loans and investments of commercial banks. The Federal Reserve influences the flow of bank credit by affecting its general availability and cost to borrowers. Changes in the loans and investments of banks are the major factor in bringing about changes in the nation's money supply.

How Credit and Monetary Changes Affect People

Superficially, it might seem that the more credit and money people have the better off they are. In fact, however, it is not the number of dollars that all the people have available that is important, but what those dollars will buy today as compared with earlier periods and as compared with the future.

People have different tests of whether they as individuals have enough money. To the manufacturer, the test is whether he has or can borrow at a reasonable cost enough dollars to buy his raw materials, pay the wages of his employees, and make other payments necessary to a profitable level of operation and to a sustained strong credit position. The farmer, the merchant, and the banker have similar tests. To the consumer, the test is whether he has or can borrow enough money, at a cost and on repayment terms that he can meet, to buy what he needs. Essentially, however, people are concerned mainly with what they can do with the dollars they earn, are indebted for, or need to borrow. The ultimate test, in other words, is the stability of the purchasing power of the dollar over time.

In a dynamic and growing economy, enough credit and money is that amount which will help to maintain high and steadily rising levels of production, employment, incomes, and consumption and to foster a stable value for the dollar. When credit, including bank credit, becomes unduly scarce or excessively hard to get and costs too much, factories and stores may curtail operations and lay off employees. Smaller payrolls mean hardship for workers, who curtail their purchases; merchants feel the decline in trade and reduce their orders for goods. Manufacturers in turn find it necessary to lay off more workers. A serious depression, unemployment, and distress may follow.

When credit is excessively abundant and cheap, the reverse of these developments—an inflationary boom—may develop. An increase in the volume and flow of money resulting from an increase in the supply and availability of credit, coupled with a lowering of its cost, cannot in itself add to the country's output. If consumers have or can borrow so much money that they try to buy more goods than can be produced by plants running at capacity, this spending only bids up prices and makes the same amount of goods cost more. If merchants and others try to increase their stocks so as to profit by the rise in prices, they bid up prices further. Manufacturers may try to expand their plants in order to produce more. In doing so, they will bid up interest rates, wages, and prices of materials. In the end they raise their own costs.

The nation as a whole does not profit from conditions of price inflation because production costs, prices of finished products, wages, and the cost of living will rise together or in closely linked sequence. At some point the upward spiral will break, perhaps because prices of finished goods get so high that ultimate consumers, even though many of them receive higher wages, can no longer buy the goods produced. Then a downward spiral will develop. The higher that values have risen, the more abruptly and lower they are likely to fall and the greater will be the associated unemployment and distress.

The above recital is oversimplified in that it does not include all the factors that affect the level of economic activity. Nevertheless, it shows how the lives of people are affected if, on the one hand, credit is too scarce or hard to get and too dear or if, on the other hand, it is too plentiful or easily obtainable and too cheap. By influencing the flow of bank credit, with resulting effects on the flow of money and the flow of credit generally, the Federal Reserve influences the economic decisions that people make.

How the Federal Reserve Influences Credit and Money

. . . Practically all of the money that people use reaches them, directly or indirectly, through banks. They may receive their pay in cash, but the employer who pays them will have cashed a check at a bank or may have borrowed from a bank before making up his payroll. Therefore, the flow of money in the country depends greatly on the activities of commercial banks in accommodating the credit and monetary requirements of industry, trade, agriculture, and all the other sectors of economic life.

The ability of commercial banks to extend credit and provide cash-balance and payment services to the people depends on the amount of reserve funds the banks have. This amount is directly affected by Federal Reserve operations. Banks can extend credit to customers or invest money in securities only in proportion to the reserves at their disposal. . . .

What needs to be understood first is that the Federal Reserve, through influencing the availability and cost of additional bank reserves, can influence the amount of credit the banks may extend to the public through loans and investments. The reserve position of banks affects directly the willingness of banks to extend credit and the cost, or rate of interest, that borrowers from banks will have to pay to obtain it. In this way the Federal Reserve has the power to influence the country's over-all credit situation and its money supply.

While the Federal Reserve directly influences the availability and cost of bank credit and thereby affects the total flow of credit, a great variety of other forces also affect the total flow of credit in the economy. These include, among others, governmental policies in regard to expenditures, taxes, and debt; the distribution of income among different groups of the population and the allocation of income between current consumption and saving; the bargaining strength and policies of management, labor, agriculture, and other sectors of the economy; the course of foreign trade and foreign investment; the prospects for peace or war; and the expectations of businesses and consumers as to future changes in economic activity, especially in prices.

Thus the Federal Reserve alone cannot assure favorable economic conditions nor can it direct whether bank or any other credit shall flow into particular channels. But it can affect the general flow of credit and money as economic conditions change and thus help to counteract instability resulting from other forces.

B. The Price Level and Its Measurement

10. THE HISTORY OF INDEX NUMBERS*

Wesley C. Mitchell

THE HISTORY OF INDEX NUMBERS

The honor of inventing the device now commonly used to measure changes in the level of prices probably belongs to an Italian, G. R. Carli. In an investigation into the effect of the discovery of America upon the purchasing power of money, he reduced the prices paid for grain, wine, and oil in 1750 to percentages of change from their prices in 1500, added the percentages together, and divided the sum by three, thus making an exceedingly simple index number. Since his book was first published in 1764, index numbers are over 150 years old.

It was in England, however, where practically the same device had been hit upon by Sir George Schuckburg-Evelyn in 1798, that the theory and practice of index numbers were chiefly developed. The generation that created the classical political economy was deeply interested in the violent price fluctuations that accompanied the Napoleonic wars and the use of an irredeemable paper currency from 1797 to 1821. Several attempts were made to measure these fluctuations, and in 1833 G. Poulett Scrope suggested the establishment of a "tabular standard of value."

Interest in the study of price fluctuations lagged somewhat in the forties; but the great rise of prices after the Californian and Australian gold discoveries started fresh investigations. W. S. Jevons in England and Adolf Soetbeer in Germany gave a powerful impetus to the theoretical discussion and the practical computation of index numbers. The problem changed somewhat in form but received even more attention after 1873, when a prolonged fall of prices began. In the sixties the chief aim of investigation had been to discover the relations between the rise of prices and the increased production of gold; in the seventies and eighties the chief aim was to find the relations between the fall of prices and the restrictions placed upon the free coinage of silver. The weightiest theoreti-

* Wesley C. Mitchell, "The Making and Using of Index Numbers," *Index Numbers of Wholesale Prices in the United States and Foreign Countries,* U.S. Bureau of Labor Statistics Bulletin No. 284 (Washington, D.C.: U.S. Government Printing Office, October, 1921), pp. 7–11.

cal contributions of this period were made by Prof. F. Y. Edgeworth, who served as secretary of a committee appointed by the British Association for the Advancement of Science "for the purpose of investigating the best methods of ascertaining and measuring variations in the value of the monetary standard."

The problem of price fluctuations entered upon another phase when the world-wide rise of prices which began in 1896–97 had been under way for several years. After 1900, and more insistently after 1910, complaints about the rising cost of living became common in all civilized countries. Efforts to measure this increase as well as efforts to explain it multiplied.

Index numbers are both troublesome and expensive to compile, yet now in the United States not less than seven wholesale-price series are currently maintained, four of them by financial papers. In England there are four important series; in France one; in Germany, before the beginning of the World War, there were three; while the Governments of Canada, Australia, South Africa, India, Netherlands, and New Zealand now publish official index numbers, and private investigators have made series for Italy, Japan, Belgium, Denmark, Norway, Austria, Spain, and Sweden, although not all of these were kept up during the war period. This list may well be incomplete at present, and is almost certain to require additions within a short time.

Most of the series just mentioned have been established but recently. The oldest—that of the *London Economist*—was begun in 1869. Sauerbeck's English series dates from 1886, Conrad's German series from 1887 (though in a sense it continues investigations made by Laspeyres in 1864), and Bradstreet's American series from 1897. Of the remaining index numbers regularly published at present, all date from years since 1899, and the majority from years since 1909.

With this increase in numbers there has come an improvement in quality. The early index numbers were made by private investigators, at irregular intervals, from such price quotations as chance had preserved. As public appreciation of the importance of measuring changes in price levels has developed, the work has more and more been assumed by financial journals and Government bureaus. This shift has produced a greater measure of continuity in the series, as well as greater frequency, regularity, and promptness in the publication of the results. Even more important is the improvement in the character and the scope of the price quotations from which the index numbers are made. Whereas the individual investigator had to take what he could get in the way of data, financial journals and Government bureaus can collect those current prices that are best adapted for statistical treatment, and can give better assurance of the representative value of their quotations and the uniform quality of the commodities included in successive years.

This improvement in the quantity and quality of index numbers is as marked in the United States as elsewhere. Price quotations had been published with more or less care and system by various newspapers and periodicals for many years before the first effort to compile an average of price variations was made. In 1881, Mr. H. C. Burchard, Director of the Mint, made an index number covering the years 1825 to 1880 from quotations that had been printed in certain reports of the Secretary of the Treasury, supplemented by quotations from a New York newspaper. But his data were of uncertain quality and his series was allowed to lapse after 1884. After an interval of eight years, the Senate Committee on Finance authorized a more ambitious effort. Under the direction of Dr. Roland P. Falkner, the statistician of this committee, the (then) Department of Labor made a huge collection of price quotations, running back as far as 1840, and compiled an index number including more than 200 commodities for the years 1860 to 1891, and 85 commodities for 1840 to 1891. But this also was a single investigation, and the United States did not have an index number regularly maintained year after year until the establishment of Bradstreet's series in 1897. A quasi continuation of the Senate Finance Committee's work, covering the years 1890–1899, was prepared by Dr. R. P. Falkner, and published by the Department of Labor in March, 1900. Another shortlived series was begun by Prof. John R. Commons and Dr. N. J. Stone in the *Quarterly Bulletin* of the Bureau of Economic Research later in the same year. In January, 1901, the second continuous American series was started by *Dun's Review* and gradually carried back to 1860; the third, covering the years 1890 to date, was added by the Federal Department of Labor in March, 1902. Other series of this type were begun by Thomas Gibson's weekly market letters in 1910, by the *New York Times* Annalist in 1913, and by the Federal Reserve Board in 1918.

This activity in the making of index numbers was accompanied by a rapid growth of the literature of the subject. Among the later contributions dealing with theoretical issues, the first place belongs to the work of an American scholar, Mr. C. M. Walsh. His great treatise upon the *Measurement of General Exchange-Value*, published in 1901, is still the most comprehensive book upon the subject. But the bibliographies that aim to cover the field now include hundreds of items, and to them must go the student who wishes a guide to further reading.

Some of the more important new series known to have been established since the war are the series compiled by the Price Section of the War Industries Board and published in its "History of Prices During the War," the series compiled by the Federal Reserve Board from data gathered by the United States Bureau of Labor Statistics, the series designed by the same board for making international comparisons, the series published by the United States Food Administration in 1918 in a pamphlet entitled "General Index Numbers of Food Prices on a Nutritive Value Base," the series established by the *London Times* for Great Britain and by the Handelstidning for Sweden, the series for Italy compiled by Prof.

Ricardo Bachi, the series compiled by the Bank of Japan, and those published by the Governments of South Africa and New Zealand.

THE DIFFICULTIES OF MEASURING CHANGES IN THE LEVEL OF PRICES

It is a curious fact that men did not attempt to measure changes in the level of prices until after they had learned to measure such subtle things as the weight of the atmosphere, the velocity of sound, fluctuations of temperature, and the precession of the equinoxes. Their tardiness in attacking that problem is the more strange because price changes had frequently been a subject of acrimonious debate among publicists and a cause of popular agitation. Long before the high development of the credit system and a class of permanent wage earners practical issues of grave importance were raised by the instability of prices, as the disturbances created in sixteenth-century Europe by the inflow of American silver and gold abundantly show. Perhaps disinclination on the part of "natural philosophers" to soil their hands with such vulgar subjects as the price of provisions was partly responsible for the delay; but after all a number of eminently "respectable" men wrote upon economic topics in every generation after the days of Columbus—to go no further back. Nor can the technical difficulties of the problem explain this tardiness; for the mathematical intricacy of index numbers, and even the necessity of allowing for changes in the pure silver content of coins, are obstacles far less formidable than those surmounted long before in other fields of research.

Probably the chief cause of delay was that averages of price fluctuations did not promise to command much confidence after they had been made. The quotations available for use by the early investigators were few in number and often of doubtful accuracy. Carli, for example, dealt with only three commodities; Shuckburg-Evelyn with 12. About the vastly greater number of unrecorded price fluctuations the one firmly established fact was that they exhibited bewildering diversity. Under these circumstances, could an average made from a few samples be accepted as a reliable measure of changes in the general level of prices? And if averages could not be trusted, why trouble to devise a plan of making them? So writers upon prices long contented themselves with statements about the fluctuations of particular commodities, and with indefinite assertions that the purchasing power of money had changed little or changed much. So, also, when certain bold investigators did finally venture to make index numbers, no one was particularly impressed by the significance of their achievement.

This lack of faith in the validity of averages of price variations was overcome rather slowly, partly in consequence of improvements in business organization. The multiplication of commercial newspapers and the more systematic keeping of private and public records provided a larger and more accurate body of quotations. Improved means of transportation made wholesale prices in the larger cities basic for many local markets. The grading and standardizing of commodities increased the number of articles which could be accepted as substantially uniform in quality from one year to the next. More important still was the discovery by statisticians that social phenomena of most kinds, though seeming to result from the uncontrolled choice of individuals, yet reveal a striking regularity when studied in large numbers. The demonstration that a formerly unsuspected regularity lay hidden in one set of numerical data after another encouraged economists to believe that the known price variations might after all be fair samples of the more numerous unknown variations. The general similarity of the results reached by different investigators using dissimilar data confirmed this faith. Thus emboldened, economic statisticians devoted much time to extending the scope, and improving the technique of index numbers. And their growing confidence in the trustworthiness of their series was gradually imparted to the public.

Today few, if any, competent judges doubt the validity of index numbers or the substantial accuracy of the results they show when properly constructed from carefully collected data. Indeed the danger at present is rather that the figures published will be taken too absolutely as a complete representation of the facts about price fluctuations. It is therefore well to begin a study of index numbers, not by analyzing the finished series, but by inspecting the actual changes in prices from which they are made, and which they purport to summarize. In no other way, indeed, can the value and the limitations of index numbers be learned.

11. CONCEPTS AND USES OF PRICE INDEXES*

Arnold E. Chase

It must be obvious to all statisticians and economists that there is relatively little that is new in index number theory. There has been significant growth during the past decade, however, in the understanding and use of index numbers by business and labor leaders, by the government, and by the general public. This is particularly true of the price indexes compiled by the Labor Department's Bureau of Labor Statistics. It is apparent to statisticians, both those who compile index numbers and those who attempt to use them, that the available indexes are not exactly

* Arnold E. Chase, *Concepts and Uses of Price Indexes* (Washington, D.C.: U.S. Bureau of Labor Statistics, 1960, mimeographed), pp. 1–16.

suited to all desired uses and that they are frequently misused by the public.

The purpose of this paper is to evaluate the price indexes and other price statistics compiled by the Bureau of Labor Statistics against uses of price data as we now understand them. For this purpose it is convenient to divide the major functions of price indexes into three principal categories:

(1) guide to maintenance of economic equities
(2) deflation of value aggregates to estimate physical quantities
(3) general economic intelligence.

These groupings of major functions will be described briefly, the general usefulness of the present indexes for these purposes will be evaluated and, finally, some needed changes and additions will be suggested.

MAINTENANCE OF ECONOMIC EQUITIES

Most uses of the Consumer Price Index by the public, and many uses of the Wholesale Price Index, can be classified as relating to the measurement of changes in economic equities. It should be pointed out that this term, as used here, relates to maintaining the economic stability of a bargain previously agreed to, and not to the initial equitableness of the bargain itself. Price trends, when compared with trends of wages, profits, and other incomes, depict economic distortions that take place from time to time as the economy moves through business cycles, or as different groups gain or lose bargaining power in markets. In fact, the C.P.I. was initiated during World War I primarily for use in adjusting wage scales to advancing living costs, especially in the shipbuilding industry. From that time on, the C.P.I. has been designed largely to serve as a yardstick for measuring changes in the purchasing power of workers and their families. In recent years especially, the efficacy of this role for the C.P.I. has been recognized in the escalator clauses that have been included in many labor-management contracts tying wage adjustments to changes in consumer prices.

Maintenance of economic equities, as a principle, also applies to the non-working members of our population, including dependents and retired persons. Family welfare allowances, alimony, survivor benefits, and other annuities are adjusted from time to time more or less in accord with changes in the C.P.I. It is well known, however, that these adjustments generally are not made as promptly, or as fully in accord with changes in consumer buying power, as are wage and salary adjustments for the working population.

The element of maintaining economic equities also enters into many contracts between business firms. This is especially true of long-term contracts which would not be feasible unless they included provisions for adjustments to the changing price level from time to time.

The Bureau of Labor Statistics Wholesale Price Index is used more commonly for this purpose than the C.P.I., though both are used to some extent.

The Federal Government and other governmental units also make use of the price indexes in escalating contracts as well as in preparing cost estimates for public works programs and other budget items for which contracts may run over a considerable period. The Federal Government, in particular, in some of its open-end supply contracts and its major long-range public works programs has need for price indexes.

DEFLATION OF VALUE AGGREGATES TO ESTIMATE PHYSICAL QUANTITIES

It is hardly necessary to enumerate the many reasons why means are needed to deflate value aggregates to estimate physical quantities. These uses are quite familiar to all statisticians, especially those uses relating to deflation of the National Product Accounts, the compilation of production indexes, and productivity studies. An excellent paper on this subject was presented by Mr. Sidney A. Jaffe at the meetings of the American Statistical Association in 1958. It should be noted, however, that these uses of price indexes are confined largely to professional statisticians and economists who, being more discriminating than the general public, have been more specific in their criticisms of the present indexes.

GENERAL ECONOMIC INTELLIGENCE

In addition to their uses of price indexes to measure changes in economic equities, consumers, businesses, and governments are making increasing use of the price indexes in their day-to-day decisions regarding buying, selling, production, and general economic policies. For example, at least a part of the tapering off in the upward trend of business activity during the past few months has been attributed to recent relative stability in prices which has encouraged consumers and business firms alike to be less concerned about advance buying or advance ordering than in the recent past.

The great amount of discussion that has taken place in recent years regarding inflation has awakened interest in the price indexes as measures of inflation. It probably is in this area more than any other that these indexes have been improperly used. During the first half of 1958, for example, the continued advance in the C.P.I. in the face of declining economic activity prompted some people to say, possibly somewhat facetiously, that we were experiencing both inflation and deflation at the same time. What was really happening, of course was that some prices were continuing to reflect past pressures, and that the level of farm and food prices was affected by certain cyclical and unusual weather influences. Some statisticians and economists have turned to use of the implicit GNP deflator because of the unsuitability of the C.P.I. and W.P.I. as measures of changes in prices of the whole range of national output. However, even the GNP deflator does not serve adequately as a measure of inflation.

There has been a great deal of interest recently in the position of the United States in world markets. Attempts have been made to compare wage, price, and productivity levels between the United States and other countries which are competing with us in world markets. These efforts have been largely ineffectual because of the lack of adequate price measures not only for foreign countries but for the United States as well.

A final major use of the price indexes is as an economic indicator. Unfortunately, changes in prices as measured by the present indexes become apparent rather late with respect to the timing of monetary and fiscal actions. However, the price indexes do provide a useful measure of the effectiveness of such actions some time after they have been taken.

EFFICIENCY OF PRESENT PRICE MEASURES

There probably is no index or other statistic in the world that has been subject to more intense professional and public scrutiny than the BLS Consumer Price Index. This is proper, since the index is of such great importance, and so directly affects the public interest. Within the resources that have been provided and the limitations of present index number techniques, the C.P.I. and the W.P.I. probably serve the purposes for which they are intended as well as can be expected. All of us are aware that there are certain limitations inherent in these two important price indexes as measured against present and anticipated needs for such indexes. These shortcomings can be examined only briefly in this paper.

LIMITATIONS IN SCOPE

The major limitations in scope need only to be enumerated and related to the uses made of the indexes. They can be corrected with proper planning and availability of resources. The C.P.I., for example, covers only urban wage-earner and clerical-worker families of two or more persons. To the extent that prices of goods and services purchased by other groups in the population move differently, economic adjustments based on the C.P.I. are likely to be inequitable.

Even within the group covered, losses or gains in real purchasing power by subgroups at different income levels resulting from divergent price movements for various goods and services are obscured in the C.P.I. For example, the climb in the index over the past few years has been caused to a large extent by advances in prices of essential services, including medical care. It is logical to expect that low income groups, and especially older persons, have suffered more from this development than higher income groups. It also is evident that any movement of food prices which diverges from the movement of prices for other items affects low-income or large families differently from high-income or small families.

Within its present framework, some limitations on the quality and usefulness of the C.P.I. are due to lack of adequate resources. As uses of the C.P.I. have multiplied, demands have arisen for more and more detail by groups, cities, subgroups, special combinations of various kinds, and even for individual items. While the present scope is generally satisfactory for an index of all items and cities combined, for the more specific, detailed uses, the number of items and qualities priced has been too limited; too few quotations per item have been obtained within restricted geographic areas; and only a minimum number of sampling points (cities) have been covered. With this limited coverage, estimating procedures that rely on similarity of price movements for priced and unpriced items, for different cities, and for a variety of stores have been adopted without sufficient examination of their effects on all parts of the index. While no evidence is available to indicate that these imputation procedures have caused the C.P.I. to be inaccurate for its major uses, it seems desirable to subject them to intense scrutiny and testing when the basic information required for this purpose can be assembled. Furthermore, the limited coverage does not yield sufficient information on a regular basis to produce what would seem to be a natural use of the prices for individual items, that is, place-to-place comparisons of living costs. From the standpoint of economic intelligence, there is legitimate need and great public demand for this type of information, as distinct from changes in prices over time.

In spite of the fact that more than 2,000 commodities representing about 55 percent of total industrial and agricultural shipments in primary markets are priced for the W.P.I., it too suffers from certain scope limitations which affect its usefulness with respect to each of the three major purposes for which it is employed. These limitations arise largely out of its lack of coverage of industrial and commercial services, costs of maintenance and replacement of existing facilities, and prices of special Government procurement items, as well as significant gaps in product groups now presumed to be covered. It should be noted that the character of the problem with respect to the scope of the W.P.I. differs somewhat from that of the C.P.I. in that most uses of primary market price data involve group, subgroup, or item indexes rather than the over-all index.

Somewhere within the framework of price information available; but presumably not within the scope of either the present C.P.I. or W.P.I., there also is need to include prices of equities, such as real estate and common stocks. It generally is agreed that this element is most important in any measure of inflation, but its exact significance and methods of handling it in evaluating inflationary or deflationary pressures obviously require further study.

LIMITATIONS IN CONCEPTS

The basic objective of the C.P.I. is to measure changes in the cost of a specific level of living over time. It is well known that, to this end, the index is compiled from prices for a fixed market basket using fixed weights so that, presumably, only price changes are reflected. To a considerable extent, the same general concept is followed in the W.P.I. though, of course, the basis for inclusion of items in the index and the sources of weight derivation are fundamentally different.

In spite of the difficult problems which this procedure presents from the standpoint of adjusting for changes in the quality of items actually offered in the market, the introduction of new items, and the disappearance of old items, this still appears to be the only sound method of measuring price changes in a way which is suitable for the primary uses made of these indexes. The market basket composition and the weights must be changed periodically, of course, when comprehensive revisions are undertaken.

At the same time, recognition should be given to persistent attempts by the public to use these indexes for purposes for which they are not suitable; notably the C.P.I., to measure changes in "the cost of living" as this term is generally understood by the public. There is some logic in this, of course, inasmuch as the C.P.I. measures the price change component of cost-of-living changes, which generally is the most significant element. However, the public usually fails to distinguish clearly between those changes in their expenditures resulting from price changes and those which reflect changes in the quality or quantity of various items bought. It seems logical to conclude that the public is reaching for a type of statistic which is not available and, therefore, that it is making use of the nearest available substitute.

The question arises as to exactly what many professional and nonprofessional users of price indexes really need and want that is not being supplied by the present indexes. Unfortunately, the answer to this question is not very clear, but this does not mean that the question should be ignored. On the other hand, it should be the subject of immediate intensive study.

For one thing, we know that the public very quickly becomes accustomed to any improvements in their standards of living which accrue from time to time. Does this mean that a price index should be devised which would more promptly incorporate a rise in the level of living and measure price changes for the new market basket rather than for the old one? The present C.P.I. measures changes in prices for a specified level of living which is held constant. Even when a comprehensive revision of items and weights is undertaken to reflect a significant change in the level of living, it is carried out in a manner that does not affect the level of the index. Would the general public be better satisfied if statistics were available which would show them how much of their increase in current expenditures and commitments represented a higher level of living and how much resulted from higher prices?

The latter distinction is exceedingly important from an economic standpoint. There may be one justification for adjustments in incomes to maintain the purchasing power of any particular economic group, thus maintaining its status quo, and quite another for adjustments which would alter the sharing of increased real national output through a redistribution of income shares. A very special indication of changes in levels of living, as distinct from adjustments for price changes, can be derived to some extent from the City Worker's Family Budget and the Elderly Couple's Budget compiled by the B.L.S., but these budgets are available only at infrequent intervals. The same is true of comparisons that may be made of consumer expenditure patterns, as revealed by the periodic surveys of consumer expenditures.

The concepts just discussed are distinct from, but related to the question which is being raised frequently of late regarding the effects of quality changes on the present C.P.I. and W.P.I. The importance of this problem tends to be exaggerated in some quarters, particularly as it affects month-to-month, or even year-to-year changes in the B.L.S. price indexes. Over the longer run, however, if real quality changes continue to be made in the same direction, their effects may tend to accumulate.

Where changes recognizable by commodity specialists take place in the quality of items priced, they are linked into the price series so that they do not affect the level of the indexes. It should be noted, however, that many such changes which commonly are characterized as quality improvements in accordance with merchandising practices, do not in fact represent any greater utility to the consumer. Furthermore, even if adjustments are impossible for some minor but nevertheless real quality changes that take place in items priced for the C.P.I., the effects of these changes on the index should be weighed against known biases in the opposite direction, in evaluating the over-all accuracy of the index.

With respect to the W.P.I., the problem of distinguishing between real price changes that are significant over the whole range of national output and price changes that reflect changes in the quality or utility of national output is even more difficult, because of changing technology, and greater possibilities for substitution of materials and processes which may or may not affect the economic utility of the items involved. Here again, it is easy to exaggerate the influence of unmeasurable quality changes on the validity of the W.P.I. for indicating actual short-run price changes. This statement is not meant to minimize the difficulty or significance of the problem of making proper adjustments in W.P.I. price series for quality changes, but to place it in its proper perspective from a practical standpoint. The B.L.S. employs groups of commodity specialists who spend a great deal of their time in contact with manufacturers and distributors attempting to determine the validity of claims of quality improvements and devising procedures for handling them in both the W.P.I. and the C.P.I.

While the present procedural concept of the W.P.I. is believed to be basically sound for most of its present uses, the organization of the index and its subindexes is now being opened up for complete reexamination. The objective is to devise an index structure that will conform better to needs of the users. More attention should be given to the needs of those who attempt to use primary market series to (1) measure price trends for commodities and services entering into specific types of further production, (2) compare price trends or price levels of finished products at different market levels, or (3) adjust or evaluate price trends of a product or group of products against production costs, profits, or some other related economic factor.

A large question still remains as to the types of price indexes which should be made available to meet needs that cannot be met appropriately by indexes using the procedural concepts of the present C.P.I. and W.P.I. These needs are primarily in the area of deflation of value aggregates, but some of them also are in the field of general economic intelligence, especially with respect to measurement of inflation.

To meet these needs, what may be required is a battery of price indexes, some of which might be Paasche-type (current-weighted) and others Laspeyre-type, i.e., corresponding to the present C.P.I. and W.P.I. General price indexes which would combine price movements of certain commodities and services at different market levels—consumer and other—might serve many useful purposes. In the opposite direction, indexes so constituted as to permit more direct studies of changes in price structures for major industries, or major products appear to represent an important need. A better index of sensitive commodity prices seems clearly desirable. There is a considerable demand for seasonally-adjusted indexes.

The above suggestions are illustrative, rather than exhaustive. It seems likely that some of these needs and many others will be discussed in the forthcoming report of the Price Statistics Review Committee, headed by Dr. George Stigler. In the meantime, the B.L.S. is carrying out some improvements in the price indexes on a limited scale, and studying other improvements. Major changes in or additions to the present series, however, must await further study and testing, and the provision of additional resources. Those who are interested in improvements in the price indexes should be advised that the collection of data and compilation of indexes are costly, and that each major improvement will require substantial additional funds.

IMPROVEMENTS NOW BEING MADE OR STUDIED BY B.L.S.

Highlights of improvement work now underway in the B.L.S. price indexes include: (1) re-weighting of the W.P.I. with data from the 1958 Census of Manufacturers, (2) filling some of the major gaps in pricing for the W.P.I., (3) study of the basic structure of the W.P.I., and (4) development of plans for experimental pricing to be done in connection with revision of the C.P.I., concurrently with the Consumer Expenditure Surveys now in progress.

Some of the major objectives of this experimental pricing are to provide the basis for selection of items to be priced for the revised C.P.I. in such a way that estimates of error may eventually be possible; to determine the validity of the "price families" concept and the imputations that have been made; and to examine differentials in price movements in different types of outlets located in various parts of metropolitan areas.

Plans also are being made for a maintenance program for the C.P.I. after the current comprehensive revision is completed. The purpose of these plans is to provide a sounder basis for making necessary adjustments in the price composition and weighting factors of the C.P.I. between comprehensive revisions, and a sounder basis for determining when the next comprehensive revision is needed.

12. THE CONSUMER PRICE INDEX*

U.S. Bureau of Labor Statistics

THE CONSUMER PRICE INDEX

Background and Uses

The Consumer Price Index prepared by the Bureau of Labor Statistics is a statistical measure of changes in prices of the goods and services bought by families of city wage earners and clerical workers. The index was initiated during World War I, when prices rose rapidly, for use in wage negotiations, particularly in shipbuilding centers. Coverage was gradually extended to include industrial cities throughout the country

* U.S. Bureau of Labor Statistics, *Techniques of Preparing Major B.L.S. Statistical Series*, Bulletin No. 1168 (Washington, D.C.: U.S. Government Printing Office, December, 1954), pp. 63–66, 69, 72–73.

and estimates of nationwide changes in consumer prices were published at intervals beginning in October 1919. Regular publication was begun in February 1921. Weights used in these early indexes were based on surveys of family expenditures conducted during the period from 1917 to 1919. In the fall of 1935 the Bureau introduced improved methods of calculating the index, and in 1940 completed revision of the weights to correspond with 1934–36 family expenditure patterns as determined by another extensive study of family consumption. During World War II, when many items were scarce and goods were rationed, the weights were adjusted to reflect these conditions; in 1950 the Bureau again adjusted weights to reflect the effect of postwar changes in spending patterns. The most recent comprehensive revision of the index, begun in November 1949, was completed in January 1953, and weights representing 1951–52 spending patterns were introduced.

Since price change is one of the most important factors affecting the cost of living over short periods of time, the Bureau's index provides a satisfactory approximation of changes in the cost of living of urban wage-earner and clerical-worker families. Widespread acceptance of this use is shown by the inclusion in labor-management agreements of automatic wage adjustment clauses based on the Index, particularly after 1950. It has been estimated that, in early 1951, wages of several million employees were adjusted according to changes in the Consumer Price Index. In addition, the index is used as a measure of changes in the purchasing power of the consumer's dollar, and as a guide in the formulation of broad economic and social policy.

. . . . .

Index Measurement

The complete title of this index, popularly referred to as "The Consumer Price Index," is "Index of Change in Prices of Goods and Services Purchased by City Wage-Earner and Clerical-Worker Families."

The index is concerned with price changes involving retail prices of foods, clothing, house-furnishings, fuel, and other goods; fees paid to doctors and dentists; prices in barbershops and other service establishments; rents; rates charged for transportation, electricity, gas, and other utilities; etc. Prices are those charged to consumers, including sales and excise taxes.

The different goods and services priced for the index are representative of the goods and services bought by city wage-earner and clerical-worker families to use, replace, and add to their possessions, as determined in a comprehensive survey of family incomes and expenditures. These families are defined as units of 2 or more persons who live in the 3,000 towns, cities and suburbs of the United States, ranging in size from small cities of 2,500 population to the largest cities. The heads of these families are wage earners or salaried clerical workers, including craftsmen, factory workers, laborers, clerks, sales and service workers (except domestic service workers). Many of the families have two or more wage or salary workers; as a result, average family incomes are higher than average individual earnings. (Families with incomes after taxes of $10,000 or more are excluded.) The average size of the families included in the index was estimated to be about 3.3 persons, and their 1952 average family income after taxes was estimated at about $4,160. These families represent about 64 percent of all persons living in urban places and about 40 percent of the total United States population.

Price changes from some past reference date, in percentage terms, are averaged for the various goods and services. The resulting index number is the measure of price change from that past period (expressed as 100) to any later date. Through December 1952, the index was calculated using the average of the 5 years 1935–39 as a base. It was then changed to the base of 1947–49 = 100 to correspond to other indexes published by Government agencies, as recommended by the Office of Statistical Standards, Bureau of the Budget. Index numbers as published from month to month compare prices at each date with the average level of prices in these 3 years.

Prices are obtained in 46 cities so selected that their populations are representative of the entire population of the 3,000 cities in the United States. Prices in all 46 cities are then combined into the National Index.

Separate indexes are calculated for the 20 largest of the 46 cities—monthly for the 5 largest, and quarterly for the 15 others.

The index measures the effect of price changes on the cost of the goods and services in the family "market basket." The contents of the "market basket"—that is, the quantities and qualities of goods and services that represent what families bought in 1951–52—is assumed to remain the same, so that the change in cost from month to month is the result of *changes in prices*. The index does not purport to measure the changes in spending of families that result from changes in their standards of living. It measures only the change in spending caused by changes in prices.

The "Index Market Basket"

The Bureau conducted a Nationwide Survey of Consumer Expenditures in 1950 to determine what goods and services urban wage-earner and clerical-worker families buy. The representative sample of cities in this survey included all of the 12 largest urban areas with populations of more than 1,000,000 people, and a sample covering 85 of the large, medium-size, and small cities. This sample was selected to account for the characteristics of different city types which affect the way families spend their money. The most important characteristics were size, climate, density of the population, and level of income in the community.

In each city the Bureau selected a representative sample of families from the entire population, including all family types and income classes.

Interviewers visited and interviewed each family and obtained a complete record of the kinds, qualities, and amounts of foods, clothing, furniture, and all other goods and services the family bought in 1950, together with the amount spent for each item. These records for all wage-earner and clerical-worker families of two or more persons were averaged together for each city, to form the basis for index weight determination.

The development of index weights from these survey results involved two major steps: (1) the averaging of variations in spending patterns reported by individual families, correcting the data for sampling and reporting errors and adjusting for unusually high purchases of automobiles, TV sets, and other consumer durable goods in 1950, and (2) the adjusting of survey data for price and income changes that had occurred after the survey year 1950.

The first step required the determination of stable relationships between average family income and average family expenditures on major categories of consumer goods and services, and also the development of relationships between expenditures on major commodity groups and expenditures for subgroups and items within these major groups. These relationships were discovered through a detailed analysis of the 1950 Consumer Expenditure Survey results which compared average expenditure patterns among the 91 cities included in the survey. This analysis defined the relationship between family average income and average expenditures for three major categories—food and alcoholic beverages, housing, and all other goods and services combined. Next, distributions of average expenditures on these major categories to successive groups and subgroups of items were determined; for example, the proportion of expenditures on all goods and services other than food and housing going to clothing, the proportion of clothing expenditures going to men's clothing, the proportion of men's clothing expenditures going to outerwear, and so on.

Finally, the distributions of expenditures to individual items included in the smallest subgroups of goods and services were based on average ratios of item to subgroup expenditures within groups of cities that showed approximately the same relationships. Adjustments for unusually high 1950 spending for automobiles and some other items were based on time series studies which estimated normal rates of growth in family expenditures on these items.

Thus, an average 1950 expenditure of wage-earner and clerical-worker families, adjusted for sampling and reporting errors, and the abnormal spending pattern following the Korean outbreak, was estimated for each item of expense; and these item expenditures were related to average 1950 family income.

The second step in creating weights for the revised index adjusted these average expenditures to the fiscal year 1951–52. This was accomplished by applying the stable income-expenditure relationships established for 1950 to estimated average family incomes for the 1951–52 period. This fiscal period was taken only because necessary information for the calendar year 1952 was not available at the time. Average 1951–52 incomes were estimated from regressions of 1950 average family income from the Consumer Expenditure Survey on average gross weekly earnings of production workers.

Since various local factors other than income affect the level of housing expenditures and relationships among component parts of total housing costs, no income-expenditure relationship could be established for this group. The ratio of homeowners to renters had not changed significantly between 1950 and the 1951–52 period. Therefore, the expenditure weights for housing required only the adjustment of the 1950 reported expenditures on rent, fuels, repair, and maintenance items, for price changes since 1950. For homeownership costs, estimation of expenditures for home purchase and interest payments and the rate of home purchase required to maintain the 1951–52 level of homeownership were developed from the 1950 survey and from census data.

The index "market basket" thus represents the customary buying pattern of city wage-earner and clerical-worker families in the period 1951–52. It includes television receivers and frozen foods that were not a part of family living patterns a few years ago, and it includes other important changes that have occurred in the amounts, kinds, and qualities of things people buy.

Prices Used in the Index Calculation

The sample of about 300 items, priced for the revised index, was selected to represent the average price movement of all goods and services bought by city wage-earner and clerical-worker families. It includes items that are relatively important in family spending, items that are representative of price change for large groups of related commodities, and items that have distinctive price movements of their own. In some cases, several qualities are priced to represent a single item.

During 1950 and 1951 the Bureau priced and studied the price changes of hundreds of items in order to expand and bring up to date the price information available in the Bureau's records. Items were then stratified within groups having similar characteristics with respect to physical description, use, and other price determining characteristics, into "price families" of items whose prices fluctuate similarly over reasonably long periods of time. Within each "price family" those items which were of outstanding importance in family spending were selected to represent price changes on all other items in the group. The number of items selected depended on the prevalence of items within a "price family" with high relative importance to total expenditures. Where only one item was selected, it was assigned the total expenditure weight of the group it represented; where two or more items were chosen, the total weight of unpriced items was assigned to them proportionate to their own importance in the group. Since price relationships change over time, the "price families" of items established for index item selection are reexamined periodically to determine whether price-change imputation patterns require adjustment.

Among the 300 items included in the sample are all the goods and services that are outstanding in family purchases, so that the priced items directly represent the greater part of total family expenditures. Intercity differences in the list of priced items were limited to commodity groups where differences in the kinds of goods purchased were highly significant, such as fuels and certain types of clothing, in order to standardize the pricing procedures as much as possible. Small differences in qualities of items offered for sale in the respective cities are reflected in city-to-city variations in the descriptive specifications used in obtaining current prices.

Prices of the 300 items are collected at regular intervals—some monthly, others less frequently—and the successive prices are compared to calculate price changes. It is important to be certain, however, that the calculation shows only price change and not changes which are due to other factors, such as quantity or quality differences. For example, the price of pork chops can vary considerably, depending upon how near the center of the loin they are cut. If center-cut pork chops are priced 1 month and end-cut the next, the price of pork chops might seem to have gone down. But in fact this would reflect a difference in quality, not a change in price. To prevent this, insofar as possible, the Bureau has prepared detailed specifications to describe the items that are priced for the index. These specifications are carefully written with the advice of manufacturers and retailers of the items. For example, the following is a specification for one of the men's shirts priced:

Style............. Business, fused or similarly constructed collar, attached; barrel cuffs.
Fabric............ Cotton broadcloth, white.
Yarn.............. Combed.
Thread count...... 136 × 60 or 128 × 68.
Finish............ Residual shrinkage 1 percent or less.
Construction....... Full cut; clean workmanship; 31 to 32 yards per dozen based on 36-inch fabric.
Size range......... 14 to 17 inch neckband.
Brand............. Manufacturer's nationally advertised.

When the Bureau's agents price these shirts, they examine the merchandise in the stores to make sure that the prices they record meet this specification.

· · · · ·

Limitations

(1) *Limitations of Measurement.* The Consumer Price Index is not an exact measurement. It is subject to the many kinds of limitations that

are always present in statistical calculations. The Bureau makes every effort, within the resources allotted to it, to keep the total effect of statistical errors to a minimum, and continually studies the nature of the errors, looking for ways to improve the index.

One kind of limitation arises from sampling procedures. Expenditures for items in the "market basket" are based on interviews with about 8,000 wage-earner and clerical-worker families; price changes are based on prices of about 300 items, collected in about 2,000 food stores and 4,000 other retail stores and establishments; rents are obtained from about 30,000 tenants. Prices are collected in 46 cities, some every month, some every 3 months, and some every 4 months. Thus, the index is based on samples of families, items, stores, and cities that are only a fraction of the total. There is even a "sample" of time, since information is collected only at certain periods.

The degree of error introduced into the index through sampling depends primarily on the amount of variation in price change that exists within groups of items and between stores and cities. To gain about the same degree of accuracy throughout the index, therefore, the number of price observations obtained for any item is conditioned by its price variability and its importance in the total index. For example, prices of fresh vegetables, which are important in the family food budget, change frequently and have different seasonal patterns in different cities; they differ considerably from item to item and from store to store. To measure the average change in prices of all vegetables satisfactorily, a large number of them must be priced in a fairly large number of stores each month in every city. On the other hand, prices of men's nationally advertised brand shirts do not change often, and the same kind of shirt sells for the same price in almost all stores. These can be priced less frequently and in fewer stores, and still measure the price change satisfactorily.

Another kind of error may occur in the index because people who give information cannot always report exactly. In making surveys of consumer expenditures to determine the basic "market basket," the Bureau has found that families can estimate very well what they spend in a year for rent, or electricity, or automobile, but not all can remember all their expenses for men's shirts, or women's hose or other things that are bought frequently. Some report less than they actually bought, some more, so that these errors of recall tend to cancel out. The Bureau uses the most modern survey methods and highly trained interviewers to keep these reporting errors in the "market basket" to a minimum, and the survey results are compared with information obtained by other organizations whenever possible so that the figures can be adjusted if necessary.

The Bureau takes precautions to guard against errors in pricing which might affect the index most seriously. Price agents are well trained to recognize qualities of goods on the store shelves, and they take the selling prices as marked or as reported by the merchant. Sales prices and discounts are recorded, as well as premium prices and special charges. However, sales prices are included in the index calculation only if the goods offered on sale are in good condition, meet the Bureau's specifications, and the sale is of sufficient duration to allow most consumers to take advantage of the price reductions. Discounted prices are used if they apply generally to all customers; they are not used if offered to special types of buyers only, or if affected by the bargaining skills of the buyer.

The index, therefore, does not reflect all sales and discounts offered in retail stores, or the effect of savings the housewife may make in "shopping around." Nor does it reflect all special charges, such as tips and "under-the-counter" premium payments, that are not reported to the Bureau's price agent.

One of the principal sources of potential error in the index is in the estimation of price change for items which are important in family spending, but not included in the list of items priced. Also, failure to observe price changes in localities in which price trends differ from those in which prices are collected, introduces errors of estimation in the measurement of the national trend. In the past, the Bureau omitted from its pricing list some items which were difficult to price satisfactorily, and limited its price collections to large cities only. However, within the limits of funds available for price collection work, efforts were made to check on price trends in noncovered areas and to keep error of estimation low.

The revision of the Consumer Price Index, completed in January 1953, was the most comprehensive undertaken since the mid-thirties, and was designed to reduce still further the effects of errors. In addition to developing a new "market basket" for the index, the Bureau introduced many important improvements in pricing and calculation methods. For example, changes in costs of shelter to homeowners, including repairs and maintenance of homes, are now priced directly where formerly they were measured by changes in rents; the Bureau now prices meals in restaurants instead of assuming that restaurant prices move like prices of foods purchased in stores. Changes in prices of used cars are measured directly where formerly they were imputed from price trends of new automobiles. Although the pricing procedures used for these items are still imperfect, they represent an improvement over past practices. Many items of food and other goods and services were added to the pricing list to improve the accuracy of the index measurement. Small cities have been added to the index coverage to make it more representative of price changes that are experienced by all urban wage-earner and clerical-worker families, since price trends in large and small cities may differ under certain circumstances.

(2) *Limitations in Use.* The Consumer Price Index is specifically designed to measure the average change in prices of goods and services bought by urban wage-earner and clerical-worker families. Conse-

quently, the index must be applied carefully when used for other purposes. The index represents all wage-earner and clerical-worker families, but not necessarily any one family or small groups of families. There are limitations on the application of the index to very low or very high income groups, to elderly couples, to single workers, or to other groups whose level or manner of living and spending are different from the average of all worker families. To the extent that these groups spend their income differently and are therefore differently affected by price changes, the index is not exactly applicable. On the other hand, when the index is applied to all city families or to the total urban population, the limitations are not considered to be serious, since the wage-earner and clerical-worker family group represents such a large proportion (nearly two-thirds) of these populations.

The index is not to be used to measure the changes in *total family spending*, since it measures only the effect of *price* change and does not take into account other factors, such as higher or lower incomes or income taxes. The index does not reflect the experience of the individual housewife, as she "shops around" to take advantage of the lowest prices, nor does it show the full effect of paying premium prices for scarce items. The index also does not reflect the change in costs experienced by families who move from one city to another or who change from renting to owning their own home.

Comparisons of city indexes show how much prices have changed in one city compared with another since the base period 1947–49. They do *not* show whether prices are higher or lower in one city than in another.

Because the index, like the other economic series prepared by the Bureau, serves the needs of all sections of the public, an effort is made to provide as much information about it as possible, and to consult the users on ways of making the index better and more useful. Committees of advisors drawn from business and labor organizations and from professional associations advise on problems that arise; they were active in the comprehensive program of index revision completed January 1953. Other outside technical experts are also consulted on occasion.

13. UPDATING THE CONSUMER PRICE INDEX*

Ewan Clague

PERIODIC REVISION OF INDEX

The Bureau of Labor Statistics is now in the third year of a five-year program of revising the Consumer Price Index. This is a step which has to be undertaken about once in a decade. The current index was last revised as of January 1953. The forthcoming revision will take effect as of January 1964.

Periodic revisions of the index are absolutely essential to keep it up to date. During the past ten years there has been a marked and widespread rise in the American standard of living. The real incomes of American families have risen, on the average, approximately one-third since the early 1950's. As people's income rises, their buying patterns change. This makes it necessary to re-study the expenditures of American families for the various goods and services in the family budgets. These expenditure surveys are now being made. They will cover all types of *families—urban, suburban, rural nonfarm* and *rural farm.* The Department of Agriculture is cooperating with us in these surveys. For the first time in more than 20 years we shall have a comparative picture of the spending habits of all classes of American families. This survey will provide information of great value on the consumption characteristics of our economy.

For the purpose of the index revision, we shall use the expenditure data for the index families (which include wage earners and clerical employees) to develop a revised and modernized "market basket" of goods and services, which we will then price each month for the Consumer Price Index.

OVERLAPPING OF OLD AND REVISED INDEXES

The last revision took effect just as the Eisenhower Administration took office. Labor and management had known for three years that the revision was under way. Both groups had been notified that the old index would be discontinued when the revised index was issued. However, at the last minute the President received petitions from both labor and man-

* Ewan Clague, *Escalation, Productivity, Wages and Costs—Do the Figures Tell the Story?* (Washington, D.C.: U.S. Bureau of Labor Statistics, Feb. 15, 1962, mimeographed), pp. 13–16.

agement groups, urging that the old index be continued for a period of six months in order to permit the parties to adjust to the change. Rather than run the risk of having some contracts opened up, the Administration (*not* the BLS) made the decision for a six months' extension through June 1953.

Mindful of this past experience, we plan to make a budget request in the 1964 fiscal year for funds sufficient to provide for a six months' *overlap* of the *old* and the *revised indexes* in *1964*. Even though we have already announced the revision date, and warned both parties to make preparation for the change, we feel sure that there will be last-minute appeals for continuation of the old index.

CHANGE OF BASE

For the past year, we have been notifying users of the index about this forthcoming change from the present base (1947–49 average equals 100) to the new base (1957–59 average equals 100). At our next release date in late February, when the shift to the new base will be made effective on the January index, we shall explain again just what we are doing and why.

Nevertheless, in spite of all we have done and will do to explain the situation, I am certain that we will have newspaper editorials in various sections of the country next month criticizing us for plotting to conceal inflation. For your information, here are the facts on this point.

First, the decision to change the base was made several years ago during the Eisenhower Administration. The change has been known to statisticians of the government for about three years, and it was announced to the general public over a year ago. Second, the decision was made by the Office of Statistical Standards of the Budget Bureau, not by the BLS. The decision was based (*a*) upon the need to update base periods from time to time in order to keep the statistics meaningful to the public, and (*b*) upon the desirability of having uniformity of base for all Federal statistical series. We in the BLS agreed with the decision of the Budget Bureau. Finally, we are going to *continue to publish the old indexes*, not only on the *1947–49 base*, but *also* on a *1939 base*. People who want to know the rise in the index from the pre-war period, or from 1947–49, will have the figures available every month. The change in base is not designed to, and will not in fact, conceal the behavior of the index.

THE INDEX IN THE BUSINESS CYCLE

When escalation adjustments are made quarterly, or even semi-annually, the Consumer Price Index creates some problems for both management and labor during business recessions. The index lags behind the turns in business, either up or down. *Labor* experienced the effect of this in the spring of 1950, when the auto workers took a wage loss of 2 cents per hour, due to a decline in the index at a time when business recovery had been under way about six months. *Business* firms suffered in the recession of 1958, when the index continued to climb upward for nearly a year after the business downturn began. It was the 1958 experience which disillusioned some management representatives with the escalation formula.

We in the Bureau have frequently pointed out this characteristic lag of the index. We published articles in the *Monthly Labor Review* in 1958 and 1959 sketching the behavior of the index during the major business recessions from 1921 to 1958. Our study showed that the index, even in the deepest depressions, is slow to respond to changing business conditions.

We have now been in a business recovery period for about a year, but the index is showing the lowest rate of annual increase of any year since 1955. It is only when business recovery blossoms into full prosperity and high employment that the index begins to rise more sharply.

Part II: Questions for Analysis

1. Explain why, according to Adam Smith, (*a*) money exchange has been superior to barter, (*b*) metals proved superior to other commodities as money materials, and (*c*) coined money proved superior to uncoined bars of metal.
2. Discuss the following aspects of the production and use of *red-feather money* in the Santa Cruz Islands:
   a) the operations involved in the manufacture of a red-feather money belt;
   b) the factors which tend to discourage overissue and depreciation of the red-feather money; and
   c) the operation of Gresham's Law in connection with the red-feather money and Australian currency.
3. *a*) Explain how the Federal Reserve System can influence the nation's money supply.
   b) What, in principle, is the appropriate quantity of money for a dynamic and growing economy to have? What happens if the money supply becomes inadequate? If it becomes excessive?
4. *a*) What economic condition stimulated the original study of index numbers? How long have such numbers been in use?
   b) What developments have encouraged an increasing use of index numbers and an improvement in their accuracy?
5. Arnold E. Chase of the Bureau of Labor Statistics mentions three major functions of price indexes: (*a*) to serve as a guide to the maintenance of

economic equities, (*b*) to serve as a deflator of value aggregates to estimate physical quantities, and (*c*) to promote general economic intelligence. Discuss and illustrate each of these functions.

6. Explain why it is essential that the Consumer Price Index be revised periodically. Summarize the principal changes being made in this index, which is expected to appear in revised form in January of 1964.

III AGGREGATE ECONOMIC ACTIVITY

Fluctuations in the value of money are the inverse of fluctuations in the price level. Both are associated with cyclical changes in the general level of economic activity, which have a profound impact on man's well-being. Recurrent waves of economic expansion and contraction, identified as the business cycle, have upset modern industrial societies. A classical description of the course of events in a hypothetical and representative business cycle is given by Wesley C. Mitchell. Geoffrey H. Moore, of the National Bureau of Economic Research, provides a set of measurements of past recessions with which any current recession can be compared. The depression phase of the business cycle was long regarded as a temporary aberration, from which the economy would return itself to full employment without government intervention. In sharp contrast, the problem of depression is presented by John Maynard Keynes as requiring large-scale government intervention. His essential thesis, which has been a source of great controversy, is presented in an excerpt from the notable work *The General Theory of Employment, Interest and Money*. Two different evaluations of the impact and survival value of Keynesian ideas are presented by Seymour E. Harris and Henry Hazlitt.

The idea of government action to maintain a high level of employment led in the United States to enactment of the Employment Act of 1946, which commits the Federal Government to the use of its powers for the purpose of preserving prosperity. The two excerpts which complete this part review the fiscal and monetary policies used to implement the Employment Act, and also make recommendations to strengthen these policies.

A. The Business Cycle

14. NATURE*

Wesley C. Mitchell

THE NATURE OF BUSINESS CYCLES

Fifteen times within the past one hundred and ten years, American business has passed through a "crisis." The list of crisis years (1812, 1818, 1825, 1837, 1847, 1857, 1873, 1884, 1890, 1893, 1903, 1907, 1910, 1913, 1920) shows that the periods between successive crises have varied considerably in length. Further, no two crises have been precisely alike and the differences between some crises have been more conspicuous than the similarities. It is not surprising, therefore, that business men long thought of crises as "abnormal" events brought on by some foolish blunder made by the public or the government. On this view each crisis has a special cause which is often summed up by the newspapers in a picturesque phrase "the Jay Cooke panic" of 1873, "the railroad panic" of 1884, "the Cleveland panic" of 1893, "the rich man's panic" of 1903, "the Roosevelt panic" of 1907.

Longer experience, wider knowledge of business in other countries, and better statistical data have gradually discredited the view that crises are "abnormal" events, each due to a special cause. The modern view is that crises are but one feature of recurrent "business cycles." Instead of a "normal" state of business interrupted by occasional crises, men look for a continually changing state of business—continually changing in a fairly regular way. A crisis is expected to be followed by a depression, the depression by a revival, the revival by prosperity, and prosperity by a new crisis. Cycles of this sort can be traced for at least one century in America, perhaps for two centuries in the Netherlands, England, and France, and for shorter periods in Austria, Germany, Italy, Spain, and the Scandinavian countries. Within a generation or two similar cycles have begun to run their courses in Canada and Australia, South America, Russia, British India, and Japan.

At present it is less likely that the existence of business cycles will be denied than that their regularity will be exaggerated. In fact, successive cycles differ not only in length, but also in violence, and in the relative prominence of their various manifestations. Sometimes the crisis

* Wesley C. Mitchell, *Business Cycles and Unemployment* (New York: McGraw Hill Book Co., 1923), pp. 5–18.

is a mild recession of business activity as in 1910 and 1913; sometimes it degenerates into a panic as in 1873, 1893, and 1907. Sometimes the depression is interrupted by an abortive revival as in 1895, sometimes it is intensified by financial pressure as in 1896 and 1914. Sometimes the depression is brief and severe as in 1908, sometimes it is brief and mild as in 1911, sometimes it is both long and severe as in 1874–1878. Revivals usually develop into full-fledged prosperity, but there are exceptions like that of 1895. Prosperity may reach a high pitch as in 1906–1907 and 1916–1917, or may remain moderate until overtaken by a mild crisis as in 1913, or by a severe panic as in 1893.

These differences among business cycles arise from the fact that the business situation at any given moment is the net resultant of a complex of forces among which the rhythm of business activity is only one. Harvest conditions, domestic politics, changes in monetary and banking systems, international relations, the making of war or of peace, the discovery of new industrial methods or resources, and a thousand other matters all affect the prospects of profits favorably or adversely and therefore tend to quicken or to slacken the pace of business. The fact that the rhythm of business activity can be traced in the net resultants produced by these many factors argues that it is one of the most constantly acting, and probably one of the most powerful, factors among them.

To give a sketch of the business cycle which will be applicable to future cases, it is necessary of course to put aside the complicating effects of the various special conditions which at any given time are influencing profits, and to concentrate attention upon the tendency of the modern business system to develop alternate periods of activity and sluggishness.

Even when the problem is simplified in this way, it remains exceedingly complex. To keep from getting lost in a maze of complications, it is necessary to follow constantly the chief clue to business transactions. Every business establishment is supposed to aim primarily at making money. When the prospects of profits improve, business becomes more active. When these prospects grow darker, business becomes dull. Everything from rainfall to politics which affects business exerts its influence by affecting this crucial factor—the prospects of profits. The profits clue will not only prevent one from going astray, but will also enable one to thread the business maze slowly, if he chooses, taking time to examine all details, or to traverse the maze rapidly with an eye only for the conspicuous features. Needless to say, in this chapter we shall have to move rapidly.

Plan of Discussion

Since business cycles run an unceasing round, each cycle growing out of its predecessor and merging into its successor, our analysis can start with any phase of the cycle we choose. With whatever phase of the cycle we start, we shall have to plunge into the middle of things, taking the business situation as it then stands for granted. But once this start has been made, the course of the subsequent discussion is fixed by the succession of phases through which the cycle passes. By following these phases around the full cycle we shall come back to the starting point and end the discussion by accounting for the situation of business which we took for granted at the beginning.

With full liberty of choice, it is well to start with the phase of the cycle through which American business is passing at present—the phase of revival after a depression. The first task will be to see how such a revival gathers momentum and produces prosperity. Then in order will come a discussion of how prosperity produces conditions which lead to crises, how crises run out into depressions, and finally how depressions after a time produce conditions which lead to new revivals.

This whole analysis will be a brief account of the cycle in general business. But it is important to note that different industries are affected by business cycles in different ways. Some industries, for example, are hit early and hit hard by a decline in business activity, while other industries are affected but slightly. This aspect of the subject has received scant attention from investigators so far, and it cannot be adequately treated until the various industries have collected far more systematic records of their changing fortunes than are now available outside a narrow field. But with the cooperation of trade associations and certain business men we have collected some data that show how important and how promising is further work along similar lines. This material concerning the effect of business cycles upon particular industries will be presented in the next chapter after the cycle in general business has been traced.

Revivals and the Cumulation of Prosperity

A period of depression produces after a time certain conditions which favor an increase of business activity. Among these conditions are a level of prices low in comparison with the prices of prosperous times, drastic reductions in the cost of doing business, narrow margins of profit, ample bank reserves, and a conservative policy in capitalizing business enterprises and in granting credits.

These conditions are accompanied sooner or later by an increase in the physical volume of purchases. When a depression begins, business enterprises of most sorts have in stock or on order liberal supplies of merchandise. During the earlier months of dullness they fill such orders as they can get mainly from these supplies already on hand, and in turn they buy or manufacture new supplies but sparingly. Similarly, families and business concerns at the end of a period of prosperity usually have a liberal stock of clothing, household furnishings, and equipment. For a while they buy little except the perishable goods which must be continuously consumed, like food and transportation. But after depression has lasted for months, the semi-durable goods wear out and must be replaced or repaired. As that time comes there is a gradual increase of buying, and as the seller's stocks are gradually reduced, there is also a slow increase of manufacturing.

Experience indicates that, once begun, a recovery of this sort tends to grow cumulatively. An increase in the amount of business that a merchant gets will make him a little readier to renew his shabby equipment and order merchandise in advance of immediate needs. An increase in the number of men employed by factories will lead to larger family purchases and so to more manufacturing. The improving state of trade will produce a more cheerful state of mind among business men, and the more cheerful state of mind will give fresh impetus to the improvement in trade. It is only a question of time when such an increase in the volume of business will turn dullness into activity. Sometimes the change is accelerated by some propitious event arising from other than business sources, for example, good harvests, or is retarded by some influence, such as political uncertainties. Left to itself, the transformation proceeds slowly but surely.

While the price level is often sagging slowly when a revival begins, the cumulative expansion in the physical volume of trade presently stops the fall and starts a rise. For, when enterprises have in sight as much business as they can handle with their existing facilities of standard efficiency, they stand out for higher prices on additional orders. This policy prevails even in the most keenly competitive trades, because additional orders can be executed only by breaking in new hands, starting old machinery, buying new equipment, or making some other change which involves increased expense. The expectation of its coming hastens the advance. Buyers are anxious to secure or to contract for large supplies while the low level of quotations continues, and the first definite signs of an upward trend of quotations brings out a sudden rush of orders.

Like the increase in the physical volume of business, the rise of prices spreads rapidly; for every advance of quotations puts pressure upon someone to recoup himself by making a compensatory advance in the prices of what he has to sell. The resulting changes in prices are far from even, not only as between different commodities, but also as between different parts of the system of prices. In most but not all cases, retail prices lag behind wholesale, the prices of staple consumers' behind the prices of staple producers' goods, and the prices of finished products behind the prices of raw materials. Among raw materials, the prices of mineral products reflect the changed business conditions more regularly than do the prices of raw animal, farm, or forest products. Wages rise sometimes more promptly, but nearly always in less degree than wholesale prices; discount rates rise sometimes more slowly than commodities and sometimes more rapidly; interest rates on long loans move sluggishly in the early stages of revival, while the prices of stocks—particularly of common stocks—generally precede and exceed commodity prices on the rise. The causes of these differences in the promptness and the energy with which various classes of prices respond to the stimulus of business activity are found partly in differences of organization among the markets for commodities, labor, loans, and securities; partly in the technical circumstances affecting the relative demand for and supply of these several classes of goods; and partly in the adjusting of selling prices to changes in the aggregate of buying prices which a business enterprise pays, rather than to changes in the prices of the particular goods bought for resale.

In the great majority of enterprises, larger profits result from these divergent price fluctuations coupled with the greater physical volume of sales. For, while the prices of raw materials and of wares bought for resale usually, and the prices of bank loans often, rise faster than selling prices, the prices of labor lag far behind, and the prices which make up overhead costs are mainly stereotyped for a time by old agreements regarding salaries, leases, and bonds.

This increase of profits, combined with the prevalence of business optimism, leads to a marked expansion of investments. Of course the heavy orders for machinery, the large contracts for new construction, etc., which result, swell still further the physical volume of business and render yet stronger the forces which are driving prices upward.

Indeed, the salient characteristic of this phase of the business cycle is the cumulative working of the various processes which are converting a revival of trade into intense prosperity. Not only does every increase in the physical volume of trade cause other increases, every convert to optimism make new converts, and every advance of prices furnish an incentive for fresh advances, but the growth of trade helps to spread optimism and to raise prices, while optimism and rising prices both support each other and stimulate the growth of trade. Finally, as has just been said, the changes going forward in these three factors swell profits and encourage investments, while high profits and heavy investments react by augmenting trade, justifying optimism, and raising prices.

How Prosperity Breeds a Crisis

While the processes just sketched work cumulatively for a time to enhance prosperity, they also cause a slow accumulation of stresses within the balanced system of business—stresses which ultimately undermine the conditions upon which prosperity rests.

Among these stresses is the gradual increase in the costs of doing business. The decline in overhead costs per unit of output ceases when enterprises have once secured all the business they can handle with their standard equipment, and a slow increase of these costs begins when the expiration of old contracts makes necessary renewals at the high rates of interest, rent, and salaries which prevail in prosperity. Meanwhile the operating costs rise at a relatively rapid rate. Equipment which is antiquated and plants which are ill located or otherwise work at some disadvantage are brought again into operation. The price of labor rises, not only because the standard rates of wages go up, but also because of the prevalence of higher pay for overtime. More serious still is the fact that the efficiency of labor declines, because overtime brings weariness, because of the employment of "undesirables," and because crews cannot be driven at top speed when jobs are more numerous than men to fill them. The prices of raw materials continue to rise faster on the average than the selling prices of products. Finally, the numerous small wastes, incident to the conduct of business enterprises, creep up when managers are hurried by a press of orders demanding prompt delivery.

A second stress is the accumulating tension of the investment and money markets. The supply of funds available at the old rates of interest for the purchase of bonds, for lending on mortgages, and the like, fails to keep pace with the rapidly swelling demand. It becomes difficult to negotiate new issues of securities except on onerous terms, and men of affairs complain of the "scarcity of capital." Nor does the supply of bank loans grow fast enough to keep up with the demand. For the supply is limited by the reserves which bankers hold against their expanding liabilities. Full employment and active retail trade cause such a large amount of money to remain suspended in active circulation that the cash left in the banks increases rather slowly, even when the gold supply is rising most rapidly. On the other hand, the demand for bank loans grows not only with the physical volume of trade, but also with the rise of prices, and with the desire of men of affairs to use their own funds for controlling as many business ventures as possible. Moreover, this demand is relatively inelastic, since many borrowers think they can pay high rates of discount for a few months and still make profits on their turnover, and since the corporations which are unwilling to sell long-time bonds at the hard terms which have come to prevail try to raise part of the funds they require by discounting notes running only a few years.

Tension in the bond and money markets is unfavorable to the continuance of prosperity, not only because high rates of interest reduce the prospective margins of profit, but also because they check the expansion in the volume of trade out of which prosperity developed. Many projected ventures are relinquished or postponed, either because borrowers conclude that the interest would absorb too much of their profits, or because lenders refuse to extend their commitments farther.

The credit expansion, which is one of the most regular concomitants of an intense boom, gives an appearance of enhanced prosperity to business. But this appearance is delusive. For when the industrial army is already working its equipment at full capacity, further borrowings by men who wish to increase their own businesses cannot increase appreciably the total output of goods. The borrowers bid up still higher the prices of commodities and services, and so cause a further expansion in the pecuniary volume of trade. But they produce no corresponding increase in the physical volume of things men can consume. On the contrary, their borrowings augment that mass of debts, many protected by insufficient margins, which at the first breath of suspicion leads to the demands for liquidation presently to be discussed.

The difficulty of financing new projects intensifies the check which one important group of industries has already begun to suffer from an earlier-acting cause. The industries in question are those which produce industrial equipment—tools, machines, plant—and the materials of which this equipment is made, from lumber and cement to copper and steel.

The demand for industrial equipment is partly a replacement demand and partly a demand for betterments and extensions. The replacement demand for equipment doubtless varies with the physical quantity of demand for products; since, as a rule, the more rapidly machines and rolling stock are run, the more rapidly they wear out. The demand for betterments and extensions, on the other hand, varies not with the physical quantity of the products demanded, but with the fluctuations in this quantity.

To illustrate the peculiar changes in demand for industrial equipment which follow from this situation, suppose that the physical quantity of a certain product varied in five successive years as follows:

First year	100,000 tons
Second year	95,000 tons
Third year	100,000 tons
Fourth year	110,000 tons
Fifth year	115,000 tons

This product is turned out by machines each of which will produce one hundred tons per year. Thus the number of machines in operation each year was:

First year	1,000 machines
Second year	950 machines
Third year	1,000 machines
Fourth year	1,100 machines
Fifth year	1,150 machines

Each year one-tenth of the machines in operation wears out. The replacement demand for machines was therefore:

First year	100 machines
Second year	95 machines
Third year	100 machines
Fourth year	110 machines
Fifth year	115 machines

The demand for additional machines was far more variable. Neglecting the first year, for which our illustration does not supply data, it is plain that no additions to equipment were required the second year when fifty of the machines in existence stood idle, and also none the third year. But after all the existing machines had been utilized new machines had to be bought at the rate of one machine for each one hundred tons added to the product. Hence the demand for additions to equipment shown by the number of machines in operation was:

First year	no data
Second year	none
Third year	none
Fourth year	100 machines
Fifth year	50 machines

Adding the replacement demand and the demand for additions to equipment, we find the total demand for industrial equipment of this type to be:

First year	no data
Second year	95 machines
Third year	100 machines
Fourth year	210 machines
Fifth year	165 machines

Of course the figures in this example are fanciful. But they illustrate genuine characteristics of the demand for industrial equipment. During depression and early revival the equipment-building trades get little business except what is provided by the replacement demand. When the demand for products has reached the stage where it promises soon to exceed the capacity of existing facilities, however, the equipment trades experience a sudden and intense boom. But their business falls off again before prosperity has reached its maximum, provided the *increase* in the physical quantity of products slackens before it stops. Hence the seeming anomalies pointed out by J. Maurice Clark:

> The demand for equipment may decrease . . . even though the demand for the finished product is still growing. The total demand for [equipment] tends to vary more sharply than the demand for finished products. . . . The maximum and minimum points in the demand for [equipment] tend to precede the maximum and minimum points in the demand for the finished products, the effect being that the change may appear to precede its own cause.

When we add to the check in the orders for new equipment arising from any slackening in the increase of demand for products, the further check which arises from stringency in the bond market and the high cost of construction, we have no difficulty in understanding why contracts for this kind of work become less numerous as the climax of prosperity approaches. Then the steel mills, foundries, machine factories, copper smelters, quarries, lumber mills, cement plants, construction companies, general contractors, and the like find their orders for future delivery falling off. While for the present they may be working at high pressure to complete old contracts within the stipulated time, they face a serious restriction of trade in the near future.

The imposing fabric of prosperity is built with a liberal factor of safety; but the larger grows the structure, the more severe become these internal stresses. The only effective means of preventing disaster while continuing to build is to raise selling prices time after time high enough to offset the encroachments of costs upon profits, to cancel the advancing rates of interest, and to keep producers willing to contract for fresh industrial equipment.

But it is impossible to keep selling prices rising for an indefinite time. In default of other checks, the inadequacy of cash reserves would ultimately compel the banks to refuse a further expansion of loans upon any terms. But before this stage has been reached, the rise of prices may be stopped by the consequences of its own inevitable inequalities. These inequalities become more glaring the higher the general level is forced; after a time they threaten serious reduction of profits to certain business enterprises, and the troubles of these victims dissolve that confidence in the security of credits with which the whole towering structure of prosperity has been cemented.

What, then, are the lines of business in which selling prices cannot be raised sufficiently to prevent a reduction of profits? There are certain lines in which selling prices are stereotyped by law, by public commissions, by contracts of long term, by custom, or by business policy, and in which no advance, or but meager advances can be made. There are other lines in which prices are always subject to the incalculable chances of the harvests, and in which the market value of all accumulated stocks of materials and finished goods wavers with the crop reports. There are always some lines in which the recent construction of new equipment has increased the capacity for production faster than the demand for their wares has expanded under the repressing influence of the high prices which must be charged to prevent a reduction of profits. The unwillingness of producers to let fresh contracts threatens loss not only to contracting firms of all sorts, but also to all the enterprises from whom they buy materials and supplies. The high rates of interest not only check the current demand for wares of various kinds, but also clog the effort to maintain prices by keeping large stocks of goods off the market until they can be sold to better advantage. Finally, the very success of other enterprises in raising selling prices fast enough to defend their profits aggravates the difficulties of the men who are in trouble; for to the latter every further rise of prices for products which they buy means a further strain upon their already stretched resources.

As prosperity approaches its height, then, a sharp contrast develops between the business prospects of different enterprises. Many, probably the majority, are making more money than at any previous stage of the business cycle. But an important minority, at least, face the prospects of declining profits. The more intense prosperity becomes, the larger grows this threatened group. It is only a question of time when these conditions, bred by prosperity, will force some radical readjustment.

Now such a decline of profits threatens worse consequences than the failure to realize expected dividends, for it arouses doubt concerning the security of outstanding credits. Business credit is based primarily upon the capitalized value of present and prospective profits, and the volume of credits outstanding at the zenith of prosperity is adjusted to the great expectations which prevail when the volume of trade is enormous, when prices are high, and when men of affairs are optimistic. The rise of interest rates has already narrowed the margins of security behind credits by reducing the capitalized value of given profits. When profits themselves begin to waver, the case becomes worse. Cautious creditors fear lest the shrinkage in the market rating of the business enterprises which owe them money will leave no adequate security for repayment; hence they begin to refuse renewals of old loans to the enterprises which cannot stave off a decline of profits, and to press for a settlement of outstanding accounts.

Thus prosperity ultimately brings on conditions which start a liquidation of the huge credits which it has piled up. And in the course of this liquidation, prosperity merges into crisis.

Crises

Once begun, the process of liquidation extends very rapidly, partly because most enterprises which are called upon to settle their maturing obligations in turn put similar pressure upon their own debtors, and partly because, despite all efforts to keep secret what is going forward, news presently leaks out and other creditors take alarm.

While this financial readjustment is under way, the problem of making profits on current transactions is subordinated to the more vital problem of maintaining solvency. Business managers concentrate their energies upon providing for their outstanding liabilities and upon nursing their financial resources, instead of upon pushing their sales. In consequence, the volume of new orders falls off rapidly; that is, the factors which were already dimming the prospects of profits in certain lines of business are reinforced and extended. Even when the overwhelming majority of enterprises meet the demand for payment with success, the tenor of business developments undergoes a change. Expansion gives place to contraction, though without a violent wrench. Discount rates rise higher than usual, securities and commodities fall in price, and as old orders are completed, working forces are reduced; but there is no epidemic of bankruptcies, no run upon banks, and no spasmodic interruption of the ordinary business processes.

At the opposite extreme from crises of this mild order stand the crises which degenerate into panics. When the process of liquidation reaches a weak link in the chain of interlocking credits and the bankruptcy of some conspicuous enterprise spreads unreasoning alarm among the business public, then the banks are suddenly forced to meet a double strain—a sharp increase in the demand for loans, and a sharp increase in the demand for repayment of deposits. If the banks prove able to honor both demands without flinching, the alarm quickly subsides. But if, as in 1873, 1893, and 1907, many solvent business men are refused accommodation at any price, and if depositors are refused payment in full, the alarm turns into panic. A restriction of payments by the banks gives rise to a premium upon currency, to the hoarding of cash, and to the use of various unlawful substitutes for money. A refusal by the banks to expand their loans, still more a policy of contraction, sends interest rates up to three or four times their usual figures, and causes forced suspensions and bankruptcies. Collections fall into arrears, domestic-exchange rates are dislocated, workmen are discharged because employers cannot get money for pay-rolls or fear lest they cannot collect pay for goods when delivered, stocks fall to extremely low levels, even the best bonds decline somewhat in price, commodity markets are disorganized by sacrifice sales, and the volume of business is violently contracted.

Depressions

The period of severe financial pressure is often followed by the reopening of numerous enterprises which had been shut for a time. But this prompt revival of activity is partial and short-lived. It is based chiefly upon the finishing of orders received but not completely executed in the preceding period of prosperity, or upon the effort to work up and market large stocks of materials already on hand or contracted for. It comes to an end as this work is gradually finished, because new orders are not forthcoming in sufficient volume to keep the mills and factories busy.

There follows a period during which depression spreads over the whole field of business and grows more severe. Consumers' demand declines in consequence of wholesale discharges of wage-earners, the gradual exhaustion of past savings, and the reduction of other classes of family incomes. With consumers' demand falls the business demand for raw materials, current supplies, and equipment used in making consumers' goods. Still more severe is the shrinkage of producers' demand for construction work of all kinds, since few individuals or enterprises care to sink money in new business ventures so long as trade remains depressed and the price level is declining. The contraction in the physical volume of business which results from these several shrinkages in demand is cumulative, since every reduction of employment causes a reduction of consumers' demand, and every decline in consumers' demand depresses current business demand and discourages investment, thereby causing further discharges of employees and reducing consumers' demand once more.

With the contraction in the physical volume of trade goes a fall of prices; for, when current orders are insufficient to employ the existing industrial equipment, competition for what business is to be had becomes keener. This decline spreads through the regular commercial channels which connect one enterprise with another, and is cumulative, since every reduction in price facilitates, if it does not force, reductions in other prices, and the latter reductions react in their turn to cause fresh reductions at the starting point.

As the rise of prices which accompanies revival, so the fall which accompanies depression is characterized by marked differences in degree. Wholesale prices usually fall faster than retail, the prices of producers' goods faster than those of consumers' goods, and the prices of raw materials faster than those of manufactured products. The prices of raw mineral products follow a more regular course than those of raw forest, farm, or animal products. As compared with the general index numbers of commodity prices at wholesale, index numbers of wages and interest on long-time loans decline in less degree, while index numbers of discount rates and of stocks decline in greater degree. The only important group of prices to rise in the face of depression is that of high-grade bonds.

Of course, the contraction in the physical volume of trade and the fall of prices reduce the margin of present and prospective profits, spread discouragement among business men, and check enterprise. But they also set in motion certain processes of readjustment by which depression is gradually overcome.

The operating costs of doing business are reduced by the rapid fall in the prices of raw materials and of bank loans, by the increase in the efficiency of labor which comes when employment is scarce and men are anxious to hold their jobs, by closer economy on the part of managers, and by the adoption of improved methods. Overhead costs, also, are reduced by reorganizing enterprises which have actually become or which threaten to become insolvent, by the sale of other enterprises at low figures, by reduction of rentals and refunding of loans, by charging off bad debts and writing down depreciated properties, and by admitting that a recapitalization of business enterprises—corresponding to the lower prices of stocks—has been effected on the basis of lower profits.

While these reductions in costs are still being made, the demand for goods ceases to shrink and begins slowly to expand—a change which usually comes after one or two years of depression. Accumulated stocks left over from prosperity are gradually exhausted, and current consumption requires current production. Clothing, furniture, machinery, and other moderately durable articles which have been used as long as possible are finally discarded and replaced. Population continues to increase at a fairly uniform rate; the new mouths must be fed and new backs clothed. New tastes appear among consumers and new methods among producers, giving rise to demand for novel products. Most important of all, the investment demand for industrial equipment revives; for, though saving slackens it does not cease, with the cessation of foreclosure sales and corporate reorganizations the opportunities to buy into old enterprises at bargain prices become fewer, capitalists become less timid as the crisis recedes into the past, the low rates of interest on long-term bonds encourage borrowing, the accumulated technical improvements of several years may be utilized, and contracts can be let on most favorable conditions as to cost and prompt execution.

Once these various forces have set the physical volume of trade to expanding again, the increase proves cumulative, though for a time the pace of growth is kept slow by the continued sagging of prices. But while the latter maintains the pressure upon business men and prevents the increased volume of orders from producing a rapid rise of profits, still business prospects become gradually brighter. Old debts have been paid, accumulated stocks of commodities have been absorbed, weak enterprises have been reorganized, the banks are strong—all the clouds upon the financial horizon have disappeared. Everything is ready for a revival of activity, which will begin whenever some fortunate circumstance gives a sudden fillip to demand, or, in the absence of such an event, when the slow growth of the volume of business has filled order books and paved the way for a new rise of prices.

Such is the stage of the business cycle with which the analysis began, and, having accounted for its own beginning, the analysis ends.

15. MEASURING RECESSIONS*

Geoffrey H. Moore

The purpose of this report is to provide a set of measurements of past business cycle recessions with which any current recession can be compared. The contractions in business activity that the American economy has experienced from time to time have, of course, varied widely in severity. Yet even severe depressions have often begun gradually. How soon can a severe decline be detected? How do the relative declines in the various available measures of economic activity compare with one another as a contraction develops? How can one determine whether a contraction that is currently under way is already or is going

* Geoffrey H. Moore, *Measuring Recessions* (New York: National Bureau of Economic Research, 1958, Occasional Paper 61), pp. 259–65. Reprinted in Geoffrey H. Moore (ed.), *Business Cycle Indicators* (Princeton, N.J.: Princeton University Press for National Bureau of Economic Research, 1961), pp. 120–27.

to be smaller or larger than those that have occurred in the past? How can one judge when it is about to end? The measurements presented here suggest possible ways of providing answers to questions such as these. Although the body of the report deals with measurements for recessions that have already run their full course, we shall, at the end, show how the method has worked out from month to month during the recession that began in 1957.

First, let us glance at the historical record of twenty-four business contractions given in Tables 1 and 2. The peak dates are the months when expansion of aggregate economic activity culminated and contraction began, as judged from a variety of statistical records; the trough dates specify when contraction culminated and expansion began. The meas-

TABLE 1

THE DURATION OF BUSINESS CYCLE EXPANSIONS AND CONTRACTIONS IN THE UNITED STATES, 1854–1957

Business Cycle			Duration of	
Trough	Peak	Trough	Expansion (months)	Contraction (months)
Dec. 1854	June 1857	Dec. 1858	30	18
Dec. 1858	Oct. 1860	June 1861	22	8
June 1861	Apr. 1865	Dec. 1867	46	32
Dec. 1867	June 1869	Dec. 1870	18	18
Dec. 1870	Oct. 1873	Mar. 1879	34	65
Mar. 1879	Mar. 1882	May 1885	36	38
May 1885	Mar. 1887	Apr. 1888	22	13
Apr. 1888	July 1890	May 1891	27	10
May 1891	Jan. 1893	June 1894	20	17
June 1894	Dec. 1895	June 1897	18	18
June 1897	June 1899	Dec. 1900	24	18
Dec. 1900	Sep. 1902	Aug. 1904	21	23
Aug. 1904	May 1907	June 1908	33	13
June 1908	Jan. 1910	Jan. 1912	19	24
Jan. 1912	Jan. 1913	Dec. 1914	12	23
Dec. 1914	Aug. 1918	Mar. 1919*	44	7
Mar. 1919*	Jan. 1920	July 1921*	10	18
July 1921*	May 1923	July 1924	22	14
July 1924	Oct. 1926	Nov. 1927*	27	13
Nov. 1927*	Aug. 1929*	Mar. 1933	21	43
Mar. 1933	May 1937	June 1938*	50	13
June 1938*	Feb. 1945	Oct. 1945	80	8
Oct. 1945	Nov. 1948	Oct. 1949	37	11
Oct. 1949	July 1953	Aug. 1954	45	13
Aug. 1954	July 1957		35	
Average, 24 cycles, 1854–1954			29.9	19.9

For an explanation of the method used to determine the business cycle peak and trough dates and some tests of their validity, see Arthur F. Burns and Wesley C. Mitchell, *Measuring Business Cycles* (National Bureau of Economic Research, 1946), Ch. 4. A few of these dates (designated by an asterisk) have been revised since the Burns-Mitchell report, and the list has been carried forward to date.

* Revised.

TABLE 2

Measures of the Duration and Amplitude of Business Cycle Contractions in the United States, 1920–1954

Business Cycle: Peak	Business Cycle: Trough	Mos. from Peak to Trough	Unemployment Rate, Annual: At Peak[a] (per cent)	Unemployment Rate, Annual: At Trough[a] (per cent)	Unemployment Rate, Annual: Change in Rate[a]	Unemployment Rate, Monthly: At Peak[b] (per cent)	Unemployment Rate, Monthly: At Trough[b] (per cent)	Unemployment Rate, Monthly: Change in Rate[b]	Nonagricultural Employment	Industrial Production	Gross National Product	Personal Income	Bank Debits Outside N.Y.C.	Retail Sales
									(percentage change from peak to trough[b])					
1. Contractions in Chronological Order														
Jan. 1920	July 1921	18	4.0	11.9	+7.9	—	—	—	—	−29.0	—	—	−22.5	−4.2
May 1923	July 1924	14	3.2	5.5	+2.3	—	—	—	—	−16.3	−2.3[c]	+0.1[c]	−3.1	−1.7
Oct. 1926	Nov. 1927	13	1.9	4.1	+2.2	—	—	—	—	−5.7	+0.3[c]	+0.8[c]	+8.7	0
Aug. 1929	Mar. 1933	43	3.2	23.6	+20.4	0.58	24.96	+24.4	−30.7	−50.1	−49.6[c]	−49.8	−61.9	−43.3
May 1937	June 1938	13	14.3	19.0	+4.7	11.53	19.77	+8.2	−10.0	−31.5	−11.9[c]	−11.2	−16.5	−14.1
Feb. 1945	Oct. 1945	8	1.2	3.9	+2.7	0.11	0.34	+0.2	−7.9	−29.4	−10.9[c]	−4.1	−1.0	+8.7
Nov. 1948	Oct. 1949	11	3.4	5.5	+2.1	3.96	6.99	+3.0	−4.1	−7.7	−3.2[c]	−3.7	−5.3	−0.3
July 1953	Aug. 1954	13	2.5	5.0	+2.5	2.63	5.93	+3.3	−3.4	−9.5	−2.0[c]	−0.2	+0.2	−0.8
July 1957						4.23								
2. Contractions in Order of Severity (excl. February–October 1945)														
Oct. 1926	Nov. 1927	13	1.9	4.1	+2.2	—	—	—	—	−5.7	+0.3	+0.8	+8.7	0
July 1953	Aug. 1954	13	2.5	5.0	+2.5	2.63	5.93	+3.3	−3.4	−9.5	−2.0	−0.2	+0.2	−0.8
Nov. 1948	Oct. 1949	11	3.4	5.5	+2.1	3.96	6.99	+3.0	−4.1	−7.7	−3.2	−3.7	−5.3	−0.3
May 1923	July 1924	14	3.2	5.5	+2.3	—	—	—	—	−16.3	−2.3	+0.1	−3.1	−1.7
Jan. 1920	July 1921	18	4.0	11.9	+7.9	—	—	—	—	−29.0	—	—	−22.5	−4.2
May 1937	June 1938	13	14.3	19.0	+4.7	11.53	19.77	+8.2	−10.0	−31.5	−11.9	−11.2	−16.5	−14.1
Aug. 1929	Mar. 1933	43	3.2	23.6	+20.4	0.58	24.96	+24.4	−30.7	−50.1	−49.6	−49.8	−61.9	−43.3

All data are adjusted for seasonal variations. For sources, see Appendixes A and B. For a ranking of amplitudes of business cycle expansions and contractions from 1879 to 1933 see Table 156 in Burns and Mitchell, *op. cit.*

[a] Based on annual averages for the following business cycle peak and trough years: P, 1920; T, 1921; P, 1923; T, 1924; P, 1926; T, 1927; P, 1929; T, 1932; P, 1937; T, 1938; P, 1944; T, 1946; P, 1948; T, 1949; P, 1953; T, 1954; P, 1957. The annual data are from Stanley Lebergott, "Annual Estimates of Unemployment in the United States, 1900–1954," in *The Measurement and Behavior of Unemployment* (National Bureau of Economic Research, Special Conference Series 8, 1957), pp. 215–16.

[b] Based on three-month averages centered on business cycle peak and trough months, except as noted. The peak standings from which the percentage changes are computed are given in Appendix A.

[c] Based on changes between the following business cycle peak and trough quarters; P, I 1920; T, III 1921; P, II 1923; T, III 1924; P, III 1926; T, IV 1927; P, III 1929; T, I 1933; P, II 1937; T, II 1938; P, I 1945; T, IV 1945; P, IV 1948; T, IV 1949; P, II 1953; T, III 1954; P, III 1957.

ures of duration show that five of the eight contractions since 1920 have lasted roughly a year (11 to 14 months). One was somewhat shorter (8 months), one somewhat longer (18 months), and one very much longer (43 months). Before 1920, contractions frequently lasted more than a year—indeed, ten out of sixteen between 1857 and 1919 lasted 18 months or more. The reasons for the apparent reduction in the typical length of contraction are not fully known, and we do not know whether it can be counted on as a permanent shift. The intervening intervals of expansion have typically been substantially longer than the contractions, many of them lasting two or three years. This has been just as true since 1920 as it was before.

The durations of the expansions and the contractions are not sufficiently uniform or regular to give one more than a very rough notion about how long an expansion or contraction might be expected to last when it has just begun. After a year or so has elapsed, however, it may be of some help to know how frequently or infrequently phases of given lengths occur. Thus at the end of 1956 one could say this about the expansion that had begun in August 1954:

"If the current expansion were to continue through all of 1957, it will have lasted forty months. In the National Bureau's business cycle chronology covering the past 100 years there are only five expansions (out of twenty-four) that lasted as long as forty months: June 1861–April 1865, forty-six months; December 1914–August 1918, forty-four; March 1933–May 1937, fifty; June 1938–February 1945, eighty; and October 1949–July 1953, forty-five. Four of these expansions encompassed major wars, and one was the recovery from the Great Depression. Clearly, if the present expansion extends through 1957 without a setback it will establish a new precedent." This bit of information in itself, of course, was not enough to forecast a recession, but it could usefully be considered together with other more direct and more important evidence. It now appears that the expansion came to an end in July 1957, that is, after 35 months (see below).

Table 2 shows the size of the declines between the business cycle peak and trough dates since 1920, as registered by several widely used measures of business activity. Clearly, a contraction that appears more severe than another by one measure may appear less severe by another measure. The 1953–54 contraction was somewhat greater than 1948–49 when measured in terms of the percentage decline in industrial production or the increase in the unemployment rate, but somewhat less than 1948–49 when measured by the percentage decline in gross national product or in nonagricultural employment. Nevertheless, one can construct at least a rough ranking of the contractions according to severity.

At the top of the list of recent contractions, obviously, is the contraction that began in 1929—the longest and deepest. The only other that comes close to it in the National Bureau's 100-year chronology is the contraction of 1873 to 1879. Next most severe among those since 1920 are the contractions of 1920–21 and 1937–38. Both were very sharp and fairly short, but that of 1937–38 began when unemployment was still at a very high level, much higher than in 1920. The contraction of 1923–24 was of moderate amplitude, not unlike that of 1948–49. The most recent contraction, 1953–54, was in most respects of slightly lesser magnitude than the contraction of 1948–49, yet greater than that of 1926–27, and certainly more widely recognized. There remains the brief contraction after World War II, February–October 1945, which marked the transition from a wartime to a peacetime economy, and which is the most difficult of all to characterize because different measures yield such different results. However, in terms of its impact upon the well-being of the population it must surely be classed among the more modest of those in our list.

In order to have a definite scale we shall use the following ranking of contractions according to severity, excluding the 1945 episode because of its special character. The ranking is based partly on the information in Table 2 (see second section of table) and partly on other information bearing on the depth of these contractions. . . .

Contraction	Rank
Oct. 1926 Nov. 1927	1 (mildest)
July 1953 Aug. 1954	2
Nov. 1948 Oct. 1949	3
May 1923 July 1924	4
Jan. 1920 July 1921	5
May 1937 June 1938	6
Aug. 1929 Mar. 1933	7 (most severe)

We can then construct, for each of these contractions, measures that show by how much business activity declined from the peak as the contraction continued, and compare such measures with the above ranking. Such measures should tell us at about what stage—that is, how many months after the contraction began—the relative severity of each recession became evident, and how it manifested itself in different aspects of economic activity, such as production, employment, incomes, prices. Similar measures constructed during the course of a current contraction can then be used to appraise its severity and its scope compared with earlier contractions.

One of the prerequisites for such an analysis is that the current contraction is known or is believed to have begun, so that the date from which it starts, i.e., the peak of the business cycle, can be fixed. Of course, such a date may be selected tentatively, when a contraction is only suspected. If the assumption turns out to be an error, the error need not long persist. Experience suggests that the date of the peak can be determined with reasonable accuracy fairly soon after it occurs.

Study of materials developed along these lines . . . suggests the following tentative conclusions:

1. When a business recession begins, most broad indicators of aggregate economic activity (production, employment, income, trade) show relatively slight declines, and during the first six months of the recession the magnitude of the declines bears little relation to the ultimate severity or depth of the recession.

2. About six months after a recession begins, the percentage declines from the peak month to the current month in most economic aggregates are smaller in mild recessions than in severe recessions, and this ranking is maintained in succeeding months with little change.

3. When such comparisons are made for types of economic data that typically begin declining before a recession starts (for example, new orders, construction contracts, the average workweek, stock prices) the distinction between mild and severe recessions begins to appear as early as three or four months after the recession begins, and is also substantially maintained in succeeding months.

4. Although frequently both mild and sharp business contractions have ended within about a year, the recovery to the previous peak level has been accomplished much more quickly after mild contractions. Hence the period of depressed activity has been much longer when the contraction proceeded at a rapid rate.

5. While the above conclusions suggest that a rough ordering of recessions according to severity can be made within four to six months after the onset, they do not imply that either the ultimate depth or the duration of recessions can be reliably forecast by this means. Many factors not taken into account by the method, such as governmental measures taken to combat depression, have an important bearing on the severity and duration of business contractions. The method appears useful primarily in providing a yardstick against which a current decline in various aspects of economic activity can be gauged, and thereby facilitating a more accurate and enlightened appraisal of what has already taken place. This in itself might facilitate the development of appropriate counter-cyclical programs.

6. Measures of the strength of various counter-cyclical factors (for example, unemployment compensation payments, increased governmental expenditures, easier credit terms, lower taxes) at similar stages of recession might be developed on the same plan as described here, although it is not attempted in this study. Such measures might be of assistance in judging the prospects for further business contraction or for a resumption of economic expansion.

7. Several months before a recession comes to an end and an upturn in aggregate activity occurs, a progressive narrowing of the scope of contraction ordinarily becomes visible. Fewer activities continue to decline, more begin to rise. It appears first in series of the "leading" type.

The more extensive and more sustained this reduction in the scope of the contraction is, the more likely that it marks the real end of recession rather than an abortive recovery. Information of this sort may help to identify an upturn in aggregate activity at about the time it occurs or shortly thereafter.

8. When the methods developed in this investigation are applied to the business contraction that began in July 1957, we find that:

a. After eight months of contraction, i.e., through March 1958, most indicators have declined more than in the corresponding periods of the four milder contractions since 1920 (1923–24, 1926–27, 1948–49, 1953–54) and less than in the three more severe contractions (1920–21, 1929–30, 1937–38).
b. The intermediate position of the 1957–58 contraction first became apparent in data for the leading indicators for November 1957, i.e., four months after the peak of July 1957. It was confirmed by most indicators of aggregate economic activity when data for February 1958 became available.
c. In contractions of the severity indicated for the 1957–58 contraction, it would be in line with previous experience if the level of economic activity generally remained below the previous peak level (July 1957) for a period ranging from a year and a half to two and a half years.
d. One of the outstanding features of the first eight months of the 1957–58 contraction has been the relatively modest decline in personal income. The rise in consumers' prices has been less unusual, since increases occurred during the first eight months of four of the seven business contractions since 1920.

9. The tentative findings reported above need to be tested further. The method could usefully be tested on declines that did not reach business cycle proportions. Comparisons based on a different method of dating downturns—e.g., dating the downturn from the peak in the specific series being compared—should be made, and other ways of measuring the severity of recessions should be explored. The empirical results should be examined in the light of the hypotheses that have been advanced to account for variations in the severity of business cycle contractions. Work along these lines will be facilitated now because electronic computer programs are available to handle the computations.

B. Theory of Aggregate Effective Demand

16. AS STATED BY KEYNES*

John Maynard Keynes

A brief summary of the theory of employment . . . may, perhaps, help the reader at this stage, even though it may not be fully intelligible. The terms involved will be more carefully defined in due course. In this summary we shall assume that the money-wage and other factor costs are constant per unit of labour employed. But this simplification, with which we shall dispense later, is introduced solely to facilitate the exposition. The essential character of the argument is precisely the same whether or not money-wages, etc., are liable to change.

The outline of our theory can be expressed as follows. When employment increases, aggregate real income is increased. The psychology of the community is such that when aggregate real income is increased aggregate consumption is increased, but not by so much as income. Hence employers would make a loss if the whole of the increased employment were to be devoted to satisfying the increased demand for immediate consumption. Thus, to justify any given amount of employment there must be an amount of current investment sufficient to absorb the excess of total output over what the community chooses to consume when employment is at the given level. For unless there is this amount of investment, the receipts of the entrepreneurs will be less than is required to induce them to offer the given amount of employment. It follows, therefore, that, given what we shall call the community's propensity to consume, the equilibrium level of employment, *i.e.* the level at which there is no inducement to employers as a whole either to expand or to contract employment, will depend on the amount of current investment. The amount of current investment will depend, in turn, on what we shall call the inducement to invest; and the inducement to invest will be found to depend on the relation between the schedule of the marginal efficiency of capital and the complex of rates of interest on loans of various maturities and risks.

* John Maynard Keynes, *The General Theory of Employment, Interest and Money* (London: Macmillan and Co., 1957 reprint), pp. 27–34; used by permission of the copyright holder, Harcourt, Brace and Co., Inc., New York.

Thus, given the propensity to consume and the rate of new investment, there will be only one level of employment consistent with equilibrium; since any other level will lead to inequality between the aggregate supply price of output as a whole and its aggregate demand price. This level cannot be *greater* than full employment, *i.e.* the real wage cannot be less than the marginal disutility of labour. But there is no reason in general for expecting it to be *equal* to full employment. The effective demand associated with full employment is a special case, only realised when the propensity to consume and the inducement to invest stand in a particular relationship to one another. This particular relationship, which corresponds to the assumptions of the classical theory, is in a sense an optimum relationship. But it can only exist when, by accident or design, current investment provides an amount of demand just equal to the excess of the aggregate supply price of the output resulting from full employment over what the community will choose to spend on consumption when it is fully employed.

This theory can be summed up in the following propositions:

(1) In a given situation of technique, resources and costs, income (both money-income and real income) depends on the volume of employment N.

(2) The relationship between the community's income and what it can be expected to spend on consumption, designated by D_1, will depend on the psychological characteristic of the community, which we shall call its *propensity to consume*. That is to say, consumption will depend on the level of aggregate income and, therefore, on the level of employment N, except when there is some change in the propensity to consume.

(3) The amount of labour N which the entrepreneurs decide to employ depends on the sum (D) of *two* quantities, namely D_1, the amount which the community is expected to spend on consumption, and D_2, the amount which it is expected to devote to new investment. D is what we have called above the *effective demand.*

(4) Since $D_1 + D_2 = D = \phi(N)$, where ϕ is the aggregate supply function, and since, as we have seen in (2) above, D_1 is a function of N, which we may write $\chi(N)$, depending on the propensity to consume, it follows that $\phi(N) - \chi(N) = D_2$.

(5) Hence the volume of employment in equilibrium depends on (i) the aggregate supply function, ϕ, (ii) the propensity to consume, χ, and (iii) the volume of investment, D_2. This is the essence of the General Theory of Employment.

(6) For every value of N there is a corresponding marginal productivity of labour in the wage-goods industries; and it is this which determines the real wage. (5) is, therefore, subject to the condition that N cannot *exceed* the value which reduces the real wage to equality with the marginal disutility of labour. This means that not all changes in D are compatible with our temporary assumption that money-wages are

constant. Thus it will be essential to a full statement of our theory to dispense with this assumption.

(7) On the classical theory, according to which $D = \phi(N)$ for *all* values of N, the volume of employment is in neutral equilibrium for all values of N less than its maximum value; so that the forces of competition between entrepreneurs may be expected to push it to this maximum value. Only at this point, on the classical theory, can there be stable equilibrium.

(8) *When employment increases,* D_1 *will increase, but not by so much as* D; since when our income increases our consumption increases also, but not by so much. The key to our practical problem is to be found in this psychological law. For it follows from this that the greater the volume of employment the greater will be the gap between the aggregate supply price (Z) of the corresponding output and the sum (D_1) which the entrepreneurs can expect to get back out of the expenditure of consumers. Hence, if there is no change in the propensity to consume, employment cannot increase, unless at the same time D_2 is increasing so as to fill the increasing gap between Z and D_1. Thus—except on the special assumptions of the classical theory according to which there is some force in operation which, when employment increases, always causes D_2 to increase sufficiently to fill the widening gap between Z and D_1—the economic system may find itself in stable equilibrium with N at a level below full employment, namely at the level given by the intersection of the aggregate demand function with the aggregate supply function.

Thus the volume of employment is not determined by the marginal disutility of labour measured in terms of real wages, except in so far as the supply of labour available at a given real wage sets a *maximum* level to employment. The propensity to consume and the rate of new investment determine between them the volume of employment, and the volume of employment is uniquely related to a given level of real wages—not the other way round. If the propensity to consume and the rate of new investment result in a deficient effective demand, the actual level of employment will fall short of the supply of labour potentially available at the existing real wage, and the equilibrium real wage will be *greater* than the marginal disutility of the equilibrium level of employment.

This analysis supplies us with an explanation of the paradox of poverty in the midst of plenty. For the mere existence of an insufficiency of effective demand may, and often will, bring the increase of employment to a standstill *before* a level of full employment has been reached. The insufficiency of effective demand will inhibit the process of production in spite of the fact that the marginal product of labour still exceeds in value the marginal disutility of employment.

Moreover the richer the community, the wider will tend to be the gap between its actual and its potential production; and therefore the more obvious and outrageous the defects of the economic system. For a poor community will be prone to consume by far the greater part of its output, so that a very modest measure of investment will be sufficient to provide full employment; whereas a wealthy community will have to discover much ampler opportunities for investment if the saving propensities of its wealthier members are to be compatible with the employment of its poorer members. If in a potentially wealthy community the inducement to invest is weak, then, in spite of its potential wealth, the working of the principle of effective demand will compel it to reduce its actual output, until, in spite of its potential wealth, it has become so poor that its surplus over its consumption is sufficiently diminished to correspond to the weakness of the inducement to invest.

But worse still. Not only is the marginal propensity to consume weaker in a wealthy community, but, owing to its accumulation of capital being already larger, the opportunities for further investment are less attractive unless the rate of interest falls at a sufficiently rapid rate; which brings us to the theory of the rate of interest and to the reasons why it does not automatically fall to the appropriate level, . . .

Thus the analysis of the Propensity to Consume, the definition of the Marginal Efficiency of Capital and the theory of the Rate of Interest are the three main gaps in our existing knowledge which it will be necessary to fill. When this has been accomplished, we shall find that the Theory of Prices falls into its proper place as a matter which is subsidiary to our general theory. We shall discover, however, that Money plays an essential part in our theory of the Rate of Interest; and we shall attempt to disentangle the peculiar characteristics of Money which distinguish it from other things.

The idea that we can safely neglect the aggregate demand function is fundamental to the Ricardian economics, which underlie what we have been taught for more than a century. Malthus, indeed, had vehemently opposed Ricardo's doctrine that it was impossible for effective demand to be deficient; but vainly. For, since Malthus was unable to explain clearly (apart from an appeal to the facts of common observation) how and why effective demand could be deficient or excessive, he failed to furnish an alternative construction; and Ricardo conquered England as completely as the Holy Inquisition conquered Spain. Not only was his theory accepted by the city, by statesmen and by the academic world. But controversy ceased; the other point of view completely disappeared; it ceased to be discussed. The great puzzle of Effective Demand with which Malthus had wrestled vanished from economic literature. You will not find it mentioned even once in the whole works of Marshall, Edgeworth and Professor Pigou, from whose hands the classical theory has received its most mature embodiment. It could only live on furtively, below the surface, in the underworlds of Karl Marx, Silvio Gesell or Major Douglas.

The completeness of the Ricardian victory is something of a curiosity and a mystery. It must have been due to a complex of suitabilities in the doctrine to the environment into which it was projected. That it reached conclusions quite different from what the ordinary uninstructed person would expect, added, I suppose, to its intellectual prestige. That its teaching, translated into practice, was austere and often unpalatable, lent it virtue. That it was adapted to carry a vast and consistent logical superstructure, gave it beauty. That it could explain much social injustice and apparent cruelty as an inevitable incident in the scheme of progress, and the attempt to change such things as likely on the whole to do more harm than good, commended it to authority. That it afforded a measure of justification to the free activities of the individual capitalist, attracted to it the support of the dominant social force behind authority.

But although the doctrine itself has remained unquestioned by orthodox economists up to a late date, its signal failure for purposes of scientific prediction has greatly impaired, in the course of time, the prestige of its practitioners. For professional economists, after Malthus, were apparently unmoved by the lack of correspondence between the results of their theory and the facts of observation;—a discrepancy which the ordinary man has not failed to observe, with the result of his growing unwillingness to accord to economists that measure of respect which he gives to other groups of scientists whose theoretical results are confirmed by observation when they are applied to the facts.

The celebrated *optimism* of traditional economic theory, which has led to economists being looked upon as Candides, who, having left this world for the cultivation of their gardens, teach that all is for the best in the best of all possible worlds provided we will let well alone, is also to be traced, I think, to their having neglected to take account of the drag on prosperity which can be exercised by an insufficiency of effective demand. For there would obviously be a natural tendency towards the optimum employment of resources in a Society which was functioning after the manner of the classical postulates. It may well be that the classical theory represents the way in which we should like our Economy to behave. But to assume that it actually does so is to assume our difficulties away.

17. KEYNESIAN ECONOMICS: AN EVALUATION*

Seymour E. Harris

Like other great economists, Keynes was affected by the events of the contemporary world. Twenty years, largely of depression in Great Britain, provided the background, though he did not by any means neglect the problems of inflation.

The sputtering of the capitalist machine made a lasting impression on him. In 1933 he had written "the decadent international but individualistic capitalism in the hands of which we find ourselves after the war is not a success. It is not intelligent, it is not beautiful, it is not just, it is not virtuous—and it doesn't deliver the goods. In short, we dislike it and we are beginning to despise it. But when we wonder what to put into its place, we are extremely perplexed."

Keynes devoted most of his life to assaults on laissez faire; these assaults culminated in the great book, *The General Theory of Employment, Interest and Money*, published in 1936.

What is this New Economics or *the* Keynesian Revolution?

1. *It is an emphasis on the objective of full employment.* Whereas the older economics had stressed the problems of most effective use of labor, resources and capital, and assumed full employment, Keynes concentrated his attention on employment. His major task was to solve the problem of unemployment.

2. *It is an attempt to find out why unemployment persists in nonwar periods.* Keynes insisted that the older economics assumed that what was produced was sold: there could not be general overproduction. But the new economics showed that all income is not spent; that some goods produced are not sold and hence losses are incurred and workers discharged. Investment may not equal the gap between the amount people wish to consume and the amount the economy is capable of producing. Hence expenditures on consumption and investment may fall short of total output and income earned. Hence thrift may well, under certain conditions, rise to be excessive.

Even Professor Pigou, Keynes's most formidable opponent, recently acknowledged the strength of Keynes's position here. ". . . there can be no doubt that in the period of the great slump many people did

* The selection from *John Maynard Keynes*, pp. 45–50, by Seymour E. Harris (Copyright 1955 Seymour Harris) is used by permission of Charles Scribner's Sons.

believe that thriftiness or economy would merely transfer employment from consumption to investment. . . . This was a great blunder. Nobody doubts any longer that Keynes's argument . . . is the only correct one . . . it is also applicable in a general way to the conditions of the actual world. . . ."

3. *Its major tasks are diagnosis and therapy.* Here Keynes is confronted with his greatest obstacles. His cures seem too easy to a world that had been taught the virtues of thrift, of free markets, of hard work, of monetary restraints, of the gold standard, of budgetary balance, of structural changes and especially wage-cutting to meet the needs of a dynamic world.

Thrift: His attack on thrift, one of the previous unassailable fortresses of capitalism, especially shocked the world. His weapon was primarily progressive taxation which would tend toward less inequality in income distribution and so stimulate consumption and reduce the gap between consumption and income.

Free Markets: Though he supported free markets generally, control of the rate of interest was to be a powerful weapon in his program. In order to preserve freedom in most markets, the market for capital must be controlled: the rate of interest must be depressed. Why? So as to encourage investment, for the extension of investment depends on a comparison of the expected return on capital with the cost of money, that is the rate of interest: the higher the former and the lower the latter the more investment; and this would tend to fill the gap between consumption and income.

Monetary Manipulation: To get the rate of interest down, it is necessary to raise the prices of securities and assets. When securities yielding 4 per cent rise from one hundred dollars to two hundred dollars in price, the rate of interest falls from 4 to 2 per cent. The technique had to be monetary expansion. This approach suggests inflation, and in fact Keynes went out of his way to establish the respectability of mercantilists who had stressed the relation of increased money and prosperity, even to say a good word for the under-world economists who, crackpots though they might have been, at least saw the need of monetary stimulation.

Gold: Over a period of thirty years, Keynes more than anyone else contributed to the repudiation of the gold standard. His antagonism stemmed from the fact that under a gold standard the monetary authority's freedom to manufacture money (and hence deal with unemployment) is restricted.

The Balanced Budget: Before Keynes, an unbalanced government budget in peace times was considered reckless finance which would bring inflation and bankruptcy. Now the view is widely held that unbalanced budgets *in depression* are symptoms of sound anti-cyclical policy. His penchant for unbalanced budgets stemmed from his conviction that private spending, even when buttressed by appropriate interest rate and tax policies, would not be adequate to take all the goods produced off the market. It therefore becomes a responsibility of government in periods of deficiency of spending to supplement private spending by spending in excess of tax receipts. In this manner, wastage of unemployment would be reduced and the finances for these outlays would be provided largely out of increased tax revenues springing from the resulting higher national income. In short, the larger government expenditures could, in considerable part, be self-financed because they would restore prosperity and taxable capacity.

Wage-Cutting: Depressions are not likely to be treated in the future by general wage-cutting. Keynes had taught the world that wage-cutting could indeed mean lower costs; but equally reduced buying. In a famous banana parable, he showed how wage-cutting could destroy a paradise. But his works also showed that economic health would not be induced by wage spiralling.

Before Keynes, the emphasis in economics was on the effective allocation of labor, capital and management; that is, apply the factors of production where they would yield the largest returns; and on the distribution of rewards. Ricardo, whose influence was great, would restrict economics to the laws of distribution. He had written to Malthus:

> Political Economy you think is an enquiry into the nature and causes of wealth —I think it should be called an enquiry into the laws which determine the division of the produce of industry amongst the classes who concur in its formation. No law can be laid down respecting quantity, but a tolerably correct one can be laid down respecting proportions. Every day I am more satisfied that the former enquiry is vain and delusive, and the latter only the true objects of the science.

In their general analysis, economists neglected the problem of employment. Except in special studies of the trade cycle, the assumption in general treatises on economics was of full employment: the problem of unemployment was abstracted by assuming that there was no unemployment.

Keynes changed all of this. The concern of theoretical economics and of the economic engineer with high or full employment is largely Keynes's doing. This shift of emphasis from studies of costs, demand, value, and prices of the individual enterprise or industry, of the degree of monopoly, of productivity, of the optimum size of the business unit, of the division of the product—the shift from almost exclusive consideration of these problems to that of employment, and wastages associated with less than full employment, is the contribution, directly and indirectly through those he inspired, of J. M. Keynes.

Even in such fields as international trade, this shift of emphasis has been revolutionary. Ever since the days of Ricardo, the fundamentals of the classical theory of international trade had been unassailed. Its primary, if not exclusive, interest was in the best allocation of factors of production and output on the basis of availability (cheapness) of labor, capital, raw materials, etc. Here is the theoretical underpinning of free trade.

Now Keynes and his followers inserted a new note. They wanted to know what international trade does to employment. They concentrated their attention on the relation of exports and imports, the exportation of capital and accompanying pressures on foreign exchanges, on gold movements, on monetary supplies, and on the rate of interest. If Britishers export capital, they buy (say) American dollars and if this is not compensated by (say) a rise of exports or a decline of imports, gold is lost and the central bank contracts the monetary supplies and prices and output then fall. A rise of exports, vis-a-vis imports, for example, is significant because like a rise of investment (in turn frequently related to an increase in money), it causes an increase of income and employment, a multiple of the original increase of exports. Keynes turned attention to the significance of surpluses and deficits in international accounts for the problem of employment and unemployment.

Related to all of this was the concentration on income and demand, or what the economist calls macro-economic as against micro-economic concepts. Keynes, with a full-blown theory of income formation and of the ingredients of income, and particularly with his emphasis on effective demand (i.e., the point of intersection of the curve representing aggregate-supply price and aggregate-demand price), more than anyone else, directed attention to the problems that would interest the practitioner: total demand, income, employment, unemployment, economic therapy. The resulting stampede to the study of income formation and employment has been spectacular.

In the process of studying total demand and supply, Keynes unleashed his vigorous attack on Say's Law, that sacrosanct axiom of classical economics which assumed that supply creates its own demand: what is produced is purchased; goods without a buyer are excluded. As J. S. Mill put it:

> What constitutes the means of payment for commodities is simply commodities. Each person's means of paying for the productions of other people consist of those which he himself possesses. All sellers are inevitably, and by the meaning of the word, buyers. Could we suddenly double the productive powers of the country, we should double the supply of commodities in every market; but we should, by the same stroke, double the purchasing power. Everybody would bring a double demand as well as supply; everybody would be able to buy twice as much, because every one would have twice as much to offer in exchange.

Keynes often exaggerated to make a point; and he undoubtedly gave the impression that Say's Law was more widely held than it actually was. But this is not nearly so important as is the fact that, through a skillful attack on Say's Law, he exposed the danger for economics of a failure to concentrate on demand. He was inclined to take potential output for granted. Here he would trust the engineers and business men. But to him the number one economic problem was why we do not realize the potentialities of our resources and productive ingenuity. The answer was inadequate demand; and the cure lay in treatment of demand. Simply, we do not buy all that can be produced.

18. KEYNESIAN ECONOMICS: ANOTHER EVALUATION*

Henry Hazlitt

1. DO DEFICITS CURE UNEMPLOYMENT?

. . . . .

In Keynesian policy, unemployment is never to be corrected by any reduction of money-wage-rates. Keynes recommends two main remedies. One is deficit spending (sometimes euphemistically called government "investment"). How good is this remedy? It was tried in the United States (partly because of Keynes's recommendations) for a full decade. What were the results? Here are the deficit in the Federal budget, the number of unemployed, and the percentage of unemployed to the total labor force, year by year in that decade. All the figures are from official sources:

	Deficit (billions)	Unemployed (millions)	Percentage of Unemployment
1931	$ .5	8.0	15.9
1932	2.7	12.1	23.6
1933	2.6	12.8	24.9
1934	3.6	11.3	21.7
1935	2.8	10.6	20.1
1936	4.4	9.0	16.9
1937	2.8	7.7	14.3
1938	1.2	10.4	19.0
1939	3.9	9.5	17.2
1940	3.9	8.1	14.6

In the foregoing table the deficits are for fiscal years ending on June 30; the unemployment is an average for the full calendar year. (The deficit figures therefore lead the unemployment figures by six months.) Advocates of deficit spending, no doubt, will try to find a partial negative

* Henry Hazlitt, *The Failure of the "New Economics"* (Princeton, N.J.: D. Van Nostrand Co., 1959), pp. 421–26.

correlation between the size of the deficit and the subsequent number of unemployed. But the central and decisive fact is that heavy deficits were accompanied by mass unemployment. The average unemployment of the ten-year period was 9.9 millions, which was 18.6 per cent of the total working force.

The average deficit in this ten-year period was $2.8 billion, which was 3.6 per cent of the gross national product of the period. The same percentage of the gross national product of 1957 would mean an annual deficit of $15.6 billion.

2. DOES CHEAP MONEY CURE UNEMPLOYMENT?

The other main Keynesian remedy for unemployment is low interest rates, artificially produced by "the Monetary Authority." Keynes incidentally admits . . . that such artificially low interest rates can only be produced by printing more money, *i.e.*, by deliberate inflation. But we may let this pass for the moment. The question immediately before us is: Do low interest rates prevent mass unemployment?

The policy of cheap money has had an even longer trial than the policy of planned deficits. Let us look at the record of interest rates and unemployment for the same period that we have just reviewed, adding, however, 1929 and 1930. In the table below, the first column after that of the years represents the average rate in each year (the average of daily prevailing rates) of prime commercial paper with a maturity of four to six months. I have chosen this rate rather than that on three-month Treasury bills because it is the most available statistical series reflecting the short-term interest rates at which business actually borrows. (Actually, the greatest volume of business borrowing from banks in the U.S. consists of "line-of-credit" loans; but these vary with the more sensitive commercial-paper rate.) The final column once again gives the percentage of unemployed to the total labor force. Both sets of figures are from official sources:

Year	Commercial Paper Rate (%)	Percentage of Unemployment
1929	5.85	3.2
1930	3.59	8.7
1931	2.64	15.9
1932	2.73	23.6
1933	1.73	24.9
1934	1.02	21.7
1935	.75	20.1
1936	.75	16.9
1937	.94	14.3
1938	.81	19.0
1939	.59	17.2
1940	.56	14.6

In sum, over this period of a dozen years low interest rates did *not* eliminate unemployment. On the contrary, unemployment actually *increased* as interest rates went down. In the seven-year period from 1934 through 1940, when the cheap money policy was pushed to an average infra-low rate below 1 per cent (.77 of 1 per cent) an average of more than 17 in every 100 persons in the labor force were unemployed.

Let us skip over the war years when war demands, massive deficits, and massive inflation combined to bring over-employment, and take up the record again for the last ten years:

Year	Commercial Paper Rate (%)	Percentage of Unemployment
1949	1.49	5.5
1950	1.45	5.0
1951	2.16	3.0
1952	2.33	2.7
1953	2.52	2.5
1954	1.58	5.0
1955	2.18	4.0
1956	3.31	3.8
1957	3.81	4.3*
1958 (June)	1.54	6.8*

* (Unemployment percentages before 1957 are based on Department of Commerce "old definitions" of unemployment; for 1957 and 1958 they are based on the "new definitions," which make unemployment slightly higher—4.2 per cent of the labor force in 1956, for example, instead of the 3.8 per cent in the table.)

It will be noticed in this table that though the commercial-paper interest rate in this period averaged 2.24 per cent, or three times as high as that in the seven years from 1934 through 1940, the rate of unemployment was not higher, but much lower, averaging only 4.2 per cent compared with 17.7 per cent in the 1934–40 period.

And within this second period itself the relationship of unemployment to interest rates is almost the exact opposite of that suggested by Keynesian theory. In 1949, 1950, 1954, and June of 1958, when the commercial-paper interest rate averaged about 1.5 per cent, unemployment averaged 5 per cent and over. In 1956 and 1957, when commercial-paper rates were at their highest average level of the period at 3.56 per cent, unemployment averaged only 4 per cent of the working force.

It is very difficult, if not impossible, to prove a positive proposition in economic theory by the use of statistics; but it is not difficult to *disprove* such a proposition (unless it is elaborately qualified) by statistics. We must conclude at least that *neither deficit spending nor cheap money policies are enough by themselves to eliminate even prolonged mass unemployment, let alone to prevent unemployment altogether.*

3. RACE WITH THE PRINTING PRESS

But these are the chief Keynesian remedies for unemployment. In 1936, reviewing the *General Theory*, which had appeared in the same year, Professor Jacob Viner ventured a prediction:

> Keynes's reasoning points obviously to the superiority of inflationary remedies for unemployment over money-wage reductions. In a world organized in accordance with Keynes's specifications there would be a constant race between the printing press and the business agents of the trade unions, with the problem of unemployment largely solved if the printing press could maintain a constant lead and if only volume of employment, irrespective of quality, is considered important.

This characterization has proved, in part, remarkably prophetic. There may be some doubt whether the problem of unemployment has been "largely solved." But we have certainly been *trying* to solve it since 1936 in accordance with Keynes's specifications, and we have certainly embarked upon a race between the printing press and the trade unions.

And our failure to solve the problem of unemployment even by this method is partly the result of a development Professor Viner could hardly have been expected to foresee: the spread of "escalator" clauses in labor contracts which provide not only for automatic increases with every increase in the cost of living, but for so-called "productivity" increases which come into effect whether marginal labor productivity actually increases or not.

The truth is that the only real cure for unemployment is precisely the one that Keynes's whole "general theory" was designed to reject: the adjustment of wage-rates to the marginal labor productivity or "equilibrium" level. This does not mean a uniform *en bloc* adjustment of "the wage level" to "the price level." It means the mutual adjustment of specific wage-rates and of prices of the specific products various groups of workers help to produce. It means also the adjustment of various wage-rates to each other and of various prices to each other. It means the *coördination* of the complex wage-price structure. It means the maintenance of a free, fluid, dynamic equilibrium, or a constant tendency toward such an equilibrium, through the economic system.

In sum, neither government spending, nor low interest rates, nor an increase in the money supply is either a necessary or a sufficient condition for the existence of full employment. What is necessary for full employment (using the word in a working, practical sense) is a proper relation among the prices of different kinds of goods and a proper balance between costs and prices, particularly between wages and prices. This functional balance will tend to exist when wage-rates are free and fluid and competitive, and not dictated by arbitrary union coercion.

When this balance exists, full employment and maximized production and prosperity will tend to follow. When this balance does not exist, when wage-rates are pushed above the marginal product of labor, and profit margins are doubtful or disappear, there will be unemployment.

C. Economic Stabilization: Problems and Policies

19. THE FULL EMPLOYMENT OBJECTIVE*

Joint Economic Committee, U.S. Congress

Short Title

Section 1. This Act may be cited as the "Employment Act of 1946."

Declaration of Policy

Sec. 2. The Congress declares that it is the continuing policy and responsibility of the Federal Government to use all practicable means consistent with its needs and obligations and other essential considerations of national policy, with the assistance and cooperation of industry, agriculture, labor, and State and local governments, to coordinate and utilize all its plans, functions, and resources for the purpose of creating and maintaining, in a manner calculated to foster and promote free competitive enterprise and the general welfare, conditions under which there will be afforded useful employment opportunities, including self-employment, for those able, willing, and seeking to work, and to promote maximum employment, production, and purchasing power.

Economic Report of the President

Sec. 3. (a) The President shall transmit to the Congress not later than January 20 of each year an economic report (hereinafter called the "Economic Report") setting forth (1) the levels of employment, production, and purchasing power obtaining in the United States and such levels needed to carry out the policy declared in section 2; (2) current and fore-

* Joint Economic Committee, U.S. Congress, *Employment Act of 1946, As Amended* (85th Cong., 1st sess.) (Washington, D.C.: U.S. Government Printing Office, 1957), pp. 1–4.

seeable trends in the levels of employment, production, and purchasing power; (3) a review of the economic program of the Federal Government and a review of economic conditions affecting employment in the United States or any considerable portion thereof during the preceding year and of their effect upon employment, production, and purchasing power; and (4) a program for carrying out the policy declared in section 2, together with such recommendations for legislation as he may deem necessary or desirable.

(b) The President may transmit from time to time to the Congress reports supplementary to the Economic Report, each of which shall include such supplementary or revised recommendations as he may deem necessary or desirable to achieve the policy declared in section 2.

(c) The Economic Report, and all supplementary reports transmitted under subsection (b) of this section, shall, when transmitted to Congress, be referred to the joint committee created by section 5.

Council of Economic Advisers to the President

Sec. 4. (a) There is created in the Executive Office of the President a Council of Economic Advisers (hereinafter called the "Council"). The Council shall be composed of three members who shall be appointed by the President, by and with the advice and consent of the Senate, and each of whom shall be a person who, as a result of his training, experience, and attainments, is exceptionally qualified to analyze and interpret economic developments, to appraise programs and activities of the Government in the light of the policy declared in section 2, and to formulate and recommend national economic policy to promote employment, production, and purchasing power under free competitive enterprise. Each member of the Council shall receive basic compensation at the rate of $16,000 per annum. The President shall designate one of the members of the Council as Chairman.

(b) The Council is authorized to employ, and fix the compensation of, such specialists and other experts as may be necessary for the carrying out of its functions under this Act, without regard to the civil-service laws and the Classification Act of 1949, as amended, and is authorized, subject to the civil-service laws, to employ such other officers and employees as may be necessary for carrying out its functions under this Act, and fix their compensation in accordance with the Classification Act of 1949, as amended.

(c) It shall be the duty and function of the Council—

(1) to assist and advise the President in the preparation of the Economic Report;

(2) to gather timely and authoritative information concerning economic developments and economic trends, both current and prospec-

tive, to analyze and interpret such information in the light of the policy declared in section 2 for the purpose of determining whether such developments and trends are interfering, or are likely to interfere, with the achievement of such policy, and to compile and submit to the President studies relating to such developments and trends;

(3) to appraise the various programs and activities of the Federal Government in the light of the policy declared in section 2 of this title for the purpose of determining the extent to which such programs and activities are contributing, and the extent to which they are not contributing, to the achievement of such policy, and to make recommendations to the President with respect thereto;

(4) to develop and recommend to the President national economic policies to foster and promote free competitive enterprise, to avoid economic fluctuations or to diminish the effects thereof, and to maintain employment, production, and purchasing power;

(5) to make and furnish such studies, reports thereon, and recommendations with respect to matters of Federal economic policy and legislation as the President may request.

(d) The Council shall make an annual report to the President in December of each year.

(e) In exercising its powers, functions, and duties under this Act—

(1) the Council may constitute such advisory committees and may consult with such representatives of industry, agriculture, labor, consumers, State and local governments, and other groups, as it deems advisable;

(2) the Council shall, to the fullest extent possible, utilize the services, facilities, and information (including statistical information) of other Government agencies as well as of private research agencies, in order that duplication of effort and expense may be avoided.

(f) To enable the Council to exercise its powers, functions, and duties under this Act, there are authorized to be appropriated (except for the salaries of the members and the salaries of officers and employees of the Council) such sums as may be necessary. For the salaries of the members and the salaries of officers and employees of the Council, there is authorized to be appropriated not exceeding $345,000 in the aggregate for each fiscal year.

Joint Economic Committee

Sec. 5. (a) There is established a Joint Economic Committee, to be composed of seven Members of the Senate, to be appointed by the President of the Senate, and seven Members of the House of Representatives, to be appointed by the Speaker of the House of Representatives. The party representation on the joint committee shall as nearly as may be feasible reflect the relative membership of the majority and minority parties in the Senate and House of Representatives.

(b) It shall be the function of the joint committee—

(1) to make a continuing study of matters relating to the Economic Report;

(2) to study means of coordinating programs in order to further the policy of this Act; and

(3) as a guide to the several committees of the Congress dealing with legislation relating to the Economic Report, not later than March 1 of each year (beginning with the year 1947) to file a report with the Senate and the House of Representatives containing its findings and recommendations with respect to each of the main recommendations made by the President in the Economic Report, and from time to time to make other reports and recommendations to the Senate and House of Representatives as it deems advisable.

(c) Vacancies in the membership of the joint committee shall not affect the power of the remaining members to execute the functions of the joint committee, and shall be filled in the same manner as in the case of the original selection. The joint committee shall select a chairman and a vice chairman from among its members.

(d) The joint committee, or any duly authorized subcommittee thereof, is authorized to hold such hearings as it deems advisable, and, within the limitations of its appropriations, the joint committee is empowered to appoint and fix the compensation of such experts, consultants, technicians, and clerical and stenographic assistants, to procure such printing and binding, and to make such expenditures, as it deems necessary and advisable. The cost of stenographic services to report hearings of the joint committee, or any subcommittee thereof, shall not exceed 25 cents per hundred words. The joint committee is authorized to utilize the services, information, and facilities of the departments and establishments of the Government, and also of private research agencies.

(e) There is authorized to be appropriated for each fiscal year, the sum of $125,000, or so much thereof as may be necessary, to carry out the provisions of this Act, to be disbursed by the Secretary of the Senate on vouchers signed by the chairman or vice chairman.

(f) Service of one individual, until the completion of the investigation authorized by Senate Concurrent Resolution 26, 81st Congress, as an attorney or expert for the joint committee, in any business or professional field, on a part-time basis, with or without compensation, shall not be considered as service or employment bringing such individual within the provisions of sections 281, 283, or 284 of title 18 of the United States Code, or of any other Federal law imposing restrictions, requirements, or penalties in relation to the employment of persons, the performance of services, or the payment or receipt of compensation in connection with any claim, proceeding, or matter involving the United States.

20. FISCAL POLICY*

Joint Economic Committee, U.S. Congress

I. FISCAL POLICY AND THE EMPLOYMENT ACT'S OBJECTIVES

The Employment Act of 1946 added to the practice of Government a new responsibility and function, that of contributing to achieving and maintaining a high and steady rate of employment, stability in the general level of prices, and a high rate of economic growth. The language of the Employment Act does not explicitly set forth the second and third of these objectives. In practice, it has been widely construed to include these objectives. In fact, of course, the Employment Act did not change the existing relationships between Government and the economy; the actions of Government have always been consequential in these respects. The Employment Act's principal significance is its express recognition of this fact and its statement of intention that such considerations be made explicitly the objective of Government action and that such actions be specifically adjusted to contribute to achieving these broad economic objectives.

The act calls upon the Federal Government to—

> . . . use all practicable means consistent with its needs and obligations and other essential considerations of national policy, . . . to coordinate and utilize all its plans, functions, and resources for the purpose of creating and maintaining, in a manner calculated to foster and promote free competitive enterprise and the general welfare, conditions under which there will be afforded useful employment opportunities, including self-employment, for those able, willing, and seeking to work, and to promote maximum employment, production, and purchasing power.

This directive clearly embraces the policies guiding the Federal Government's revenues and expenditures, i.e., Federal fiscal policy.

To the extent that the rate of employment and the level of prices are sensitive to changes in total demand, the implications of fiscal policy for achieving and maintaining economic stability are, in general, quite clear. Fiscal policy should seek to offset fluctuations in total demand which, on the one hand, would threaten an undesirably high level of unemployment, and on the other, would result in aggravating upward pressures on prices by creating conditions of excess demand.

* Joint Economic Committee, *Staff Report on Employment, Growth, and Price Levels* (Washington, D.C.: U.S. Government Printing Office, 1959), pp. 205–17.

Early postwar period experience appeared to emphasize the concurrence of trends in the price level and in the rate of employment. Increasing unemployment and falling prices were regarded as the pattern of recession, i.e., inadequate aggregate demand, while rising prices were associated with a tight labor market, i.e., excess demand. More recently, however, the divergence of trends in employment conditions and in price movements has led to separate identification of stability in the employment sense and in the price level sense as objectives of public policy. Downward rigidities and upward flexibility in wage rates and in many prices pose the problem of directing fiscal policy toward maintaining a level of total demand adequate to serve the employment stabilization objective without inflation, or alternatively, toward restricting total demand adequately to achieve stability in the price level without at the same time producing serious unemployment.

A distinction has also been made in recent years between the policy objective of stable high employment and economic growth. With a growing labor force, achieving stability in the rate of employment obviously means an expansion of total production. Moreover, stability in this sense is an important requirement for a high rate of capital formation in the private sectors of the economy; recession is a major deterrent to economic growth. The policy question today, however, is not merely whether growth in total output can be assured but how high a rate of growth is desirable.

Stabilizing employment at a higher rate than has prevailed on the average during the postwar period would in itself represent a major contribution to economic expansion. Moreover, minimizing lapses from high employment means not only more production available to meet all the demands of the economy but also, in the aggregate, less risk attendant upon private investment. But an additional element of the problem today is to use the Nation's productive capacity, at whatever rate is deemed appropriate, to a greater extent for the purpose of making possible a still larger volume of output in the future.

Fiscal policy aimed at a higher rate of growth, therefore, must be concerned not merely with adjusting total demand to the requirements of high employment and a stable price level, but also explicitly with channeling a larger proportion of total demand into growth-generating activities. In the last analysis, this requires devoting a larger proportion of total available resources to private capital accumulation, public investment, research, education, and similar intangible activities aimed at increasing productivity. Whether principal emphasis should be given to increasing tangible assets or an increase in technical skills and knowledge, whether the most productive growth-generating activities are plant and equipment outlays or more basic research, whether private capital additions should result in a more intensive or a more diversified capital structure, and whether a relatively large or small proportion of the increased efforts to expand productive capacity and productivity should be in the private or public sectors are assuredly important policy problems. Whatever the answer to these questions, however, the aggregate result is likely to be a relative increase in components of gross national product other than private consumption and a consequent increase in saving, both private and public, relative to the total national income. Fiscal policy, if it is to contribute to a higher rate of growth, must be concerned with the composition as well as the total volume of economic activity.

Other broad social, political, and economic objectives are also the concern of fiscal policy. The impact of Government fiscal activities on the distribution of income, both by income level and by type of income share, has long been a major issue of public policy. So indeed has been the influence of fiscal policy on competitive conditions and the opportunities for new enterprise. . . .

A. Dimensions of Fiscal Policy

The Federal fiscal structure is an elaborate system of specific expenditures and revenue devices. The *immediate* objectives of most expenditure programs are the satisfaction of social wants, not necessarily the Employment Act objectives. By the same token, the specific elements of the Federal revenue system were not originally nor are they now determined primarily on the basis of these objectives. The basic function of fiscal *policy* is to arrange these myriad elements of the fiscal system in such a way that while serving their individual purposes they will as well serve the broader objectives of the Employment Act. Fiscal policy, therefore, has a dual aspect.

1. *Short-run Economic Stabilization.* The Employment Act objectives of fiscal policy, in turn, have a twofold focus. The language of the act appears to emphasize the orientation of public policy toward maintaining economic stability, in the sense both of a high rate of employment and stability in the general price level. Considering the background of this legislation and the widely prevalent fears of postwar depression at the time it was conceived, this emphasis on the short-run problem of stability is easily understood. And although postwar experience appears to have demonstrated substantial inherent resistance in the U.S. economy against prolonged and deep underemployment and deflation, it has not shown the same resistance to more moderate economic reversals, still less to inflation. The short-run stabilization focus of the Employment Act and of fiscal policy, therefore, is certainly warranted, even if the magnitude of the problem appears to be different from that originally conceived.

In the context of fiscal policy, the economic stability problem is a twofold one. In the first place, there is the problem of minimizing the undesirable shocks which changes in Government activity may impose on the economy as a whole or on some important section thereof. A national defense emergency is certainly the most dramatic example of this problem. The attendant increases in Government demands upon the resources of the economy can hardly be constrained by considerations of economic stabilization. Any change in the composition or volume of Government demand, moreover, may involve the same sort of economic shocks. Since the immediate objective of most Government programs is not economic stability but to achieve some more specific goal, and since, in a dynamic society, these other objectives are hardly likely to remain constant for very long, Government is likely to be a source of economic instability, of changing pressures on resources, the rate of their employment, their prices, and the prices of the goods and services they produce.

The corollary of the destabilizing impact of changing Government demands is the capacity of fiscal policy to offset economic instability. Changes in taxes, or in expenditures, or in both may be used to compensate for changes in private demands or in demands by Government which would otherwise give rise to recessionary or inflationary trends.

2. *Secular Focus on Economic Growth.* While the background of the Employment Act explains its emphasis on economic stabilization, emphasis in public policy has turned increasingly to economic growth over the long run. The objective of achieving and maintaining a high rate of growth has assumed a status of equal importance with the stabilization goals explicitly stated in the act. . . . This emphasis introduced additional problems for fiscal policy, since it focuses concern on the impact of fiscal developments on the composition as well as on the aggregate level of economic activity. It therefore raises thorny issues about the character of Government activity and the distribution of fiscal burdens, traditionally the most politically sensitive aspects of public finance.

In summary, fiscal policy cannot seek to pursue a "neutral" course with respect to the Employment Act's objectives. The expenditure and revenue-raising activities of Government will affect the level and the composition of economic activity, will impinge on the conditions determining the rate of employment, the level of prices, and the rate of economic expansion whether or not expressly and deliberately formulated with these objectives in mind. In a free, representative, self-governing society, the obligation of Government to serve the people is matched by the obligation of the people to make sure that Government serves them well. This obligation cannot be discharged if fiscal policy is divorced from the Employment Act.

B. Constraints Against the Use of Fiscal Policy to Achieve the Employment Act's Objectives

The practice of fiscal policy aimed at maintaining a high rate of employment, stability in the general level of prices, and a high rate of economic growth is not easy. Indeed, the constraints on the vigorous, prompt use of fiscal policy for these purposes are numerous and varied.

In the first place, the fact that the fiscal structure consists of numerous and diverse expenditure and tax elements imposes limitations on the use of fiscal policy to achieve broad economic objectives. Those responsible for formulating fiscal policy may be in substantial agreement with respect to broad objectives. This global decision must then come to grips with the problem of determining the specific changes in expenditures or taxes necessary to achieve the objective. These decisions may well be made on the basis of considerations which are remotely, if at all, related to the global economic policy objectives. Ineffectual or undesirable changes, or more likely, fiscal inertia, may often result from the interaction of political considerations.

There are other serious obstacles to the use of fiscal policy for the achievement of broad economic policy goals. The most significant is the fact that, except in times of national emergency, there is little likelihood of a consensus, among those responsible for formulating public policies, with respect to the relative priorities of policy objectives. Changes in these priorities will involve changes in fiscal impact. The quick association of change in fiscal burden, in other words, with change in policy objectives in itself acts as a deterrent to easy agreement about what fiscal policy should seek to do.

Arraying the priority of policy objectives also involves the difficulty of clear delineation of objectives. How much and what kind of economic growth is sought? What is "reasonable" stability in the price level and what measure of "the price level" should be used? At what rate is employment "full"? The determination of policy priorities involves trading off gains with respect to the various objectives. The representative political process does not lend itself to making such marginal determinations quickly and smoothly. In a dynamic setting, they will often be reached only after the conditions which impelled the determination in the first place have changed. Fiscal policy, therefore, is likely to be sluggish, and often, at least from the vantage point of hindsight, out of tune with the times.

An offsetting factor is the fortunate fact of automatic responsiveness or "built-in" flexibility of both revenue and expenditure structures. The tendency of Federal expenditures, particularly transfer payments to persons, to rise and for receipts to fall during periods of recession, and for the reverse to occur during periods of economic expansion, without explicit, discretionary action reduces—but does not eliminate—the inherent sluggishness of fiscal policy with respect to the stabilization objective.

A further difficulty is that the stabilization problem may not be one of aggregate excess or deficient demand, so that fiscal measures of general impact may not be effective. Fiscal policy aimed at achieving the broad economic policy objectives of employment and price level stability and a high rate of growth is conventionally discussed in aggregative terms, despite the fact that it consists of a large number of specific fiscal components. Analytically, this conception involves no serious difficulty so long as the actual economic developments with which the policy is to cope are, similarly, broad, aggregate movements. But the important economic developments to which public policy may have to be addressed may be sectoral changes involving no excess demand but which lead to a rise in the price level because of downward rigidities in prices and wages. The customary prescription for an increase in the budget surplus under these circumstances is likely to take the form of efforts to achieve price level stability by way of depressing the level of total demand below that at which full employment can be maintained.

An additional difficulty is that arising from lack of knowledge and agreement about policy mechanics. Even assuming consensus about policy objectives and willingness to use any policy means to achieve them, the problem remains of determining which means are in fact optimum. The assumption is that different combinations of policy techniques and fiscal devices will have significantly different effects on the economy. The "mix" of policy techniques, therefore, should be adjusted in the light of the mix of policy objectives. This presupposes, however, a substantial amount of knowledge about the specific effects of alternative mixes of policy devices. But this is the very substantive area in which so much of the debate about public economic policy has centered, particularly in the years since 1954. It is, indeed, one of the major issues which has occasioned this inquiry by the Joint Economic Committee. Without substantial agreement among policymakers with respect to at least proximate conclusions on this question, fiscal action is likely to coincide with "good" policy, given policy objectives, only haphazardly.

Acknowledging these limitations on the use of fiscal policy to achieve broad economic objectives certainly does not imply that they should be complacently accepted. On the contrary, concern with the institutional constraints on a purposive fiscal policy is directed at pointing up the importance of finding the means to eliminate or mitigate them. Economic theory posits, and the historical record confirms, that fiscal actions may have a powerful impact on the level and character of economic activity. That such effects may occur, willy-nilly, without efforts on the part of a self-governing society to control them can imply only indifference on the part of that society to its economic fate. Such indifference is belied by this study undertaken by the Joint Economic Committee and the numerous similar inquiries in the past.

C. The Mechanics of Fiscal Policy

Fiscal policy aims at achieving the stabilization and growth objectives set forth above primarily through its influence on the level and composition of total money demand for goods and services. In the aggregate, this influence is the difference between Government expenditures (or in a number of very important instances, orders) which add to the volume of current demand, and taxes which reduce non-Government expenditures by reducing the disposable income of taxpayers. The extent of the increase or decrease in total non-Government expenditures resulting from these Government expenditures and taxes depends on the spending patterns of affected taxpayers and of the recipients of the payments by the Government. The composition of total demand is affected by fiscal actions both by virtue of the specific Government expenditures and by the differential impact of the various revenue sources.

1. *Basic Budget-Income Relationships.* In a simple aggregative analysis, fiscal policy will increase the level of total economic activity if the Government's contribution to total demand through its expenditures is not fully offset by the contraction of private demand resulting from the taxes imposed by the Government. If all resources are substantially fully employed, this expansion of total demand will be reflected in an increase in prices. If there is idle capacity and unemployment, expansionary fiscal policy will result in increases in output or in prices, depending on the initial impact of the increase in demand in terms of the rate of capacity utilization and the fullness of employment in the immediately affected lines of activity and the mobility of resources.

In general, if the fiscal impact is to be neither expansionary nor contractionary, an increase in the budget surplus (or decrease in deficit) is called for when Government purchases of goods and services are increasing and the reverse is required when purchases are declining, i.e., the change in receipts should exceed the change in purchases. This is because Government purchases add dollar for dollar directly to total demand but an equal amount of taxes will not reduce taxpayers' expenditures dollar for dollar unless changes in their income are entirely reflected in changes in their expenditures. Accordingly, equal increases in Government purchases and taxes will increase total demand; equal decreases will contract total demand.

Without reference to explicit non-Government spending functions, however, it is impossible to determine whether any given surplus or deficit budget is expansionary or contractionary in any absolute sense. Changes in non-Government spending functions, by the same token, may alter the expansionary or contractionary impact of any given amount of budget surplus or deficit. One cannot safely generalize that budget surpluses are contractionary and deficits are expansionary, although one can say that compared to no budgetary change, an increase in surplus or reduction in deficit is contractionary while a reduction in surplus or increase in deficit is expansionary.

2. *Differences in Effects on Income of Different Types of Expenditures and Revenue Sources.* Differences in the composition of fiscal changes have different implications for the impact of overall fiscal policy on the level of total economic activity. Government expenditures for the purchase of goods and services have a larger impact on total demand than

do transfer payments, which are not made for current production. (Transfer payments are frequently treated as negative taxes, implying that their impact on total demand will be of the same magnitude, but opposite sign as an equal amount of income taxes.) Moreover, the immediate demand and price effects of various types of Government purchases may very well differ, depending on the immediate availability and the degree of specialization of the productive services and capacity required to produce the goods and services, the volume of inventories of raw materials and final products involved, and similar conditions.

Similarly, the immediate demand effects of equal changes in various taxes may differ. Musgrave has calculated, for example, that consumption expenditures would change by $700 million in response to a $1 billion change in individual income taxes effected by a flat percentage cut in all bracket rates, $825 million in response to a $1 billion change in excises (assuming consumers adjust their outlays in response to real rather than current money income changes), and $500 million in response to a $1 billion change in the corporation income tax.

Equal changes in surplus or deficit, therefore, may have different consequences for the level and composition of total demand, depending on the specific fiscal ingredients of these surpluses or deficits and non-Government spending functions.

3. *Built-in Fiscal Stabilizers.* The change in income related to the change in surplus or deficit described above assumes a once and for all change in either expenditures or receipts (or both). The fiscal structure, however, contains features which result automatically in changes in receipts and in expenditures in response to changes in income. For example, a reduction in income reflected in a fall in employment will lead, under present statutory arrangements, to an increase in transfer payments in the form of unemployment compensation. The same reduction in income will result in a decline in various tax receipts at any given level of tax rates, the extent of the decline depending on the income elasticity of the various taxes. By the same token, an increase in income will result automatically in a decline in transfer payments and a rise in tax receipts.

Discretionary fiscal actions to expand or contract the level of total demand, therefore, will result in automatic changes in some fiscal components in an opposite direction. The net change in surplus or deficit, therefore, will be less than that of the discretionary fiscal action itself.

The greater the degree of "built-in flexibility" in the fiscal structure, the less, other things being equal, need be the discretionary fiscal action taken to moderate any destabilizing development. In view of the "stickiness" of discretionary fiscal action, increasing the automatic responsiveness of the fiscal structure to changes in income is, in itself, widely regarded as an important objective of fiscal policy. These automatic fiscal responses, however, cannot fully replace discretionary action for stabilization purposes, except insofar as the effects of automatic changes on income result in changes in private spending patterns.

An offsetting consideration is the fact that taxes respond not merely to changes in real activity but to changes in the price level as well. To the extent that price level fluctuations and changes in the rate of employment are in the same direction, automatic fiscal responses will tend to moderate instability in both. But when increases in the price level coincide with steady or declining employment rates, built-in flexibility may result in undue restraint on the level of total demand from the point of view of maintaining a high rate of employment.

4. *Repercussions of Fiscal Developments on Monetary Conditions.* Fiscal policy developments also affect the level and composition of total economic activity through their impact on monetary conditions. An increase in the deficit (or reduction in surplus) generally means that the Government will add directly to the total demand for loanable funds, while the opposite fiscal change generally reduces total demand for loanable funds. In addition, monetary conditions will also be affected by the expansionary or contractionary influence of fiscal policy on aggregate demand. With a given supply of money and credit, an expansionary fiscal policy "tightens" monetary conditions and a restrictive fiscal policy eases them. The actual change in monetary conditions, of course, depends on actions affecting the supply as well as the demand for loanable funds. Fiscal policy influences on monetary conditions, therefore, may at times be offset or reinforced by monetary policy changes.

Differences in specific fiscal ingredients of the surplus or deficit, as indicated, may have differential consequences for both the level and composition of total demand which in turn may also affect the composition and level of demand for loanable funds. These changes in monetary conditions will affect the level and composition of total demand. Indirect or "feedback" effects on Government revenues and expenditures, therefore, result not merely as the direct product of automatic stabilizers times initial demand response to discretionary fiscal actions, but also from the secondary consequences stemming from changes in monetary conditions.

5. *The Impact of Government Orders of Economic Activity.* In a number of important instances, changes in Government orders—or obligations—more accurately measure the impact of Government demand on the economy than changes in expenditures. The principal reason for this is that budget expenditures are recorded as such at the time disbursements are made, but a disbursement is sometimes made considerably after the time that a Government order for goods and services has been placed. It is the order which in fact gives rise to the production activity in the private sector of the economy, while the expenditure may reflect the conclusion of this Government-generated activity.

Hard-goods procurement actions of the Department of Defense frequently demonstrate this timelag between the initial impact of Government activity and expenditures. Assume, for example, an 18-month production leadtime for a given category of military hard goods. Activity in the private sector of the economy will be generated by placing an order in this category. The private contractor undertaking to fill the order will, at the time the order is placed (or perhaps even before, if intent to place the order has been expressed to him), begin to acquire the resources required for its completion. It is, therefore, at the order stage that the procurement action will have its initial and often major impact on the markets for labor, raw materials, and financial resources, in this instance, as much as 18 months before the procurement transaction is recorded in budget terms. Indeed, the budget expenditure may coincide in time with a reduction in Government impact on total demand.

The impact of Government orders on economic activity cannot be directly traced in changes in gross national product. Until the actual disbursement of funds, no change will be shown in Government purchases. Gross private domestic investment, however, will expand, other things being equal, by virtue of the increase in aggregate inventories, reflecting the addition to stocks at various stages in the production process of filling the Government order. As deliveries are made with the completion of the order, the national income account measure of gross private domestic investment will be reduced, other things being equal, while the Government purchases account will rise. At this point there is no further direct expansionary effect attributable to the Government purchase. The Government disbursement, however, does result in a transfer of liquidity from the Government to the private sector, which may be of consequence for the level of private activity.

Apart from these direct effects on the private sector, the Government order may result in a substantial induced income effect. The increase in gross private domestic investment, for example, may significantly exceed the inventory change, both because of new capital outlays required to fill the order and because of expansionary effects on investment in other lines of activity. If the Government order represents an initial phase of a new procurement program, anticipations in a wide area of business activity, as well as in that immediately involved, may be favorably influenced. By the same token, cancellation of any specific order may have adverse effects on anticipations of a magnitude substantially in excess of those directly attributable to the immediately affected line of business. Similarly, completion of an order may signal the "phasing out" of a procurement program, with the same sort of widespread impact on anticipations. Interruptions of a procurement program by holding back of orders previously expected, by delaying deliveries of completed orders, or by stretching out progress payments may also have adverse effects on anticipations and on investment in general.

The difference in timing between order and expenditure has its counterpart in revenue changes and, quite possibly, in other Government expenditures. The expansionary impact of the Government order will expand tax revenues and reduce the level of transfer payments, other things being equal. (Depending on monetary policy actions, there may also be an overall reduction in liquidity, reflected in higher interest payments by the Government.) An increase in budget surplus (or reduction in deficit), therefore, may emerge soon after the order is placed and before Government disbursements are made. Other things being equal, this rise in receipts will taper off as the order moves toward completion, so that a reduction in surplus or increase in deficit may develop when the Government disbursement is actually made (to the extent that the order results in expansion of investment and income lasting beyond the actual direct production on the order, the rise in revenues may continue beyond the increase in Government outlays, moderating this budget change). From the point of view of stabilization policy, of course, this succession of budget shifts toward surpluses and deficits is likely to be more appropriate than a closer coincidence in time of the increase in revenues with the increase in Government outlays.

In general, if the composition of Government demand does not materially change, period-to-period changes in expenditures provide an adequate approximation of the impact of Government demands on the economy. For appraisal of multiperiod trends in which the composition of Government expenditures is relatively stable, the differences in time between orders and expenditures may be of little consequence. In other circumstances—for example, analysis of short periods of time in which significant changes in the composition of Federal outlays occur—reference to expenditure data rather than the flow of Government orders may be quite misleading.

II. THE RECORD OF POSTWAR FISCAL POLICY

The record of postwar Federal fiscal policy offers highly instructive insights concerning the impact of Federal fiscal developments on the stability and growth of the American economy. In a dynamic environment, history may be a poor instructor. Nevertheless, the postwar record affords a wide variety of examples of the types of problems with which fiscal policy has been, and is likely to continue to be, faced. . . .

. . . .

In reviewing the impact of postwar fiscal policy on economic stability, the following major conclusions emerge:

(1) *Changes in the volume and character of Federal Government demands, particularly for defense purposes, have been an important source of economic instability.* The postwar period has seen several rising and falling waves of defense procurement activity, in connection with the Marshall Plan, the Korean war, the post-Korean defense program, and most recently the post-sputnik defense program. Because of the relatively high rate of change in military technology, these changes in defense programs are likely to involve requirements for new specialized production facilities. They therefore have had a sizable impact on business spending for new plant and equipment in addition to their more immediate impact on the volume of activity in the durable goods industries in general. Each of the several sharp cutbacks in defense orders dur-

ing the postwar period has been associated with a decline in durable goods activity, in plant and equipment outlays, in inventories, and in economic activity throughout the economy. Each of the rising waves of defense demands, similarly, has coincided with rising activity in durables, expanding plant and equipment outlays, inventory accumulation, and strong expansionary trends throughout the economy. The available data do not support a firm assertion that changes in defense demands were the sole source of these fluctuations in durables and plant and equipment, but the coincidence of movement is so close as to support the conclusion that defense programs exert an extremely significant influence, both directly and indirectly, in this regard.

With the single exception of the Korean war, however, changes in defense demands have not been accompanied on a timely basis by discretionary fiscal action to compensate for their disturbing impact. Such compensatory action as has been taken has been delayed until inflationary or recessionary pressures have had an opportunity to make themselves widely felt.

It may well be that failure to moderate the destabilizing effects of changing defense activities is a result of inadequate emphasis in policy formulation, in both the administration and the Congress, on Defense Department obligations and too much emphasis on near-term changes in expenditures. Because of the lag between defense orders for hard goods and budget disbursements, undertaking compensatory adjustments for changes in expenditures rather than orders defers such action until the destabilizing influence has taken effect.

(2) *Except during the Korean war period, Federal postwar fiscal policy has relied almost exclusively on discretionary changes in expenditures and on built-in stabilizers for purposes of achieving economic stability. Discretionary tax changes have not been employed even in the face of strong recessionary and inflationary developments throughout the economy.* Reductions in tax rates in 1948 and in 1954 certainly contributed to moderating the recessions of 1949 and 1953–54, respectively. In the former case, however, the reductions were enacted despite the general assumption that inflationary, rather than recessionary, influences dominated the economy. In the latter case, the reductions were automatic, pursuant to the Revenue Act of 1951; their effective date was 6 months after the recession had begun. Earlier enactment had been proposed by the Committee on Ways and Means in the House, but was opposed by the administration on budgetary grounds.

(3) *While the automatic stabilizers served to moderate both economic declines and booms once underway, they have not been adequate to prevent major fluctuations in rates of employment and output.* Within the Federal revenue system, the corporation income tax has been highly responsive to broad cyclical movements in the economy. This sensitivity has had little apparent significance with respect to capital outlays. Individual income tax liabilities, on the other hand, have responded,

in general, to a lesser degree to abrupt changes in economic conditions. In particular, they have been relatively insensitive, particularly in the post-Korean period, to sharp drops in employment. During the 1957–58 recession, for example, changes in the volume of transfer payments made more than twice as great a contribution to stabilizing disposable personal income as did changes in personal tax payments. The principal stabilizing influence, however, appeared to be outside the immediate framework of the fiscal system altogether.

(4) *The effectiveness of stabilizing fiscal action, either discretionary or automatic, is significantly affected by monetary conditions.* Under conditions of extremely high liquidity in the private sectors of the economy, even very large budget surpluses may prove inadequate to restrain inflationary expansion of total demand. This appears to have been the situation in 1946 and 1947. In the post-Korean period of increasing illiquidity, on the other hand, the responsiveness of the economy as a whole to quite modest changes in fiscal conditions appears to be relatively substantial.

(5) *So-called "traditional" fiscal policy, relying on broad changes in the relative levels of receipts and expenditures, is poorly suited to deal with inflationary pressures originating in strong shifts in demand among sectors of the economy rather than in excessive total demand.* More important than the magnitude of the change in budget surplus under conditions of dynamic demand changes is the source of the surplus. Presumably, if the objective sought is to curb inflationary price pressures at their source, selective tax increases and/or expenditure cuts should be aimed specifically at the sectors in which demand increases are likely to give rise to upward price movements. To do so, however, would limit the process of dynamic adjustment through relative price changes.

On the whole, the record of Federal fiscal policy aimed at economic stabilization throughout the postwar period is not very heartening. . . .

21. STRENGTHENING MONETARY POLICY*

The Commission on Money and Credit

MEASURES FOR STRENGTHENING MONETARY POLICY

INSTRUMENTS OF GENERAL MONETARY CONTROL

The major instruments of general monetary policy are the power to buy and sell securities in the open market, the power to fix discount rates

* The Report of the Commission on Money and Credit, *Money and Credit: Their Influence on Jobs, Prices and Growth* (c) 1961. Prentice-Hall, Inc., Englewood Cliffs, N.J. Reprinted by permission, pp. 62–76.

and regulate other conditions of member bank borrowing, and the power to alter the reserve requirements of member banks within limits specified by the Congress.

Open Market Operations

Open market operations constitute the primary instrument of monetary control. These operations are flexible with respect to timing and magnitude, and the initiative for their use lies with the Federal Reserve. The major issue on the conduct of open market operations is the policy followed by the Federal Reserve from 1953 until early in 1961 to confine such operations to short-term government securities, generally to Treasury bills.

Between 1951 and 1953 the directive to the manager of the open market account included the instruction to "maintain orderly conditions" in the government securities market. In 1953, the Federal Reserve made explicit its philosophy of favoring free and unpegged markets. It directed that henceforth open market operations would be confined to affecting bank reserves as economic conditions warranted; that this was to be accomplished by operations in short-term securities, except to correct already disorderly markets; and that support of the market by buying new or maturing issues during periods of Treasury financings would be discontinued. This policy has become known as the "bills-only" or more recently the "bills-preferably" policy.

The argument advanced in support of the bills-only policy is that it minimizes the *direct* influence of open market operations on the structure or pattern of interest rates without sacrificing any of the total impact on these variables, because such impacts flow principally from the effect on reserves. Investors and dealers in Treasury securities are thus assured that "free market forces" will determine the structure of security prices, and this, in turn, will improve the "breadth, depth, and resiliency" of the market. The influence of Federal Reserve policy actions on intermediate-term and long-term yields takes place indirectly—as the forces of arbitrage and substitution transmit the effect of changes in bank reserves and bill yields to all maturities.

The bills-only policy has been a subject of controversy ever since it was adopted. Many critics have argued that the potency of Federal Reserve is reduced. They believe it is preferable to operate on occasion in the long-term market to correct incipient disorderly market conditions rather than to wait until they become worse. The assumption that rate changes in the short end of the market are transmitted rapidly and completely to intermediate and longer maturities has been questioned.

. . . . .

The crucial question is the actual difference in the effect on long-term rates from open market sales or purchases of bills versus bonds. The evidence shows that there is a difference, but that the difference is small.

Open market operations achieve their principal effect on yields by altering bank liquidity. The impact on the short-term yields is far greater than that on long-term yields regardless of the maturity of the instrument used. Nevertheless, the differential effects and their timing are important, and the bills-only policy reduces the effectiveness of open market operations to alter the structure of interest rates. Much larger changes in Federal Reserve holdings of bills and thus in bank reserves may be necessary to effect desired changes in long-term rates indirectly than would be necessary to obtain the same changes by direct operations in longer-term securities.

The Commission recommends the continued use of open market operations as the normal or usual instrument of general monetary policy. Instead of relying on a "bills-only" policy, the Federal Reserve should be willing, when domestic or international conditions warrant, to influence directly the structure as well as the level of interest rates in pursuit of countercyclical monetary policies and should deal in securities of varied maturities. This recommendation does not mean a return to a pegged structure of prices and yields for government securities. And the normal use of open market operations in bills to carry out technical and seasonal changes in bank reserves is appropriate.

Discount Policy

Under present arrangements, member banks may obtain bank reserves by borrowing from Federal Reserve banks. This privilege permits an individual bank to correct a temporary deficiency in its reserve position arising from unexpected withdrawals of currency or deposits. The discount rate is the charge on such borrowings, and this rate is altered from time to time as an instrument of monetary policy.

It is frequently argued that the discount privilege is no longer necessary and that during periods of restraint it provides a loophole through which the banking system is able to offset the effect of open market operations. The argument for retaining the privilege is that it provides a smoother means of adjustment to temporary and local situations than would be available otherwise, and that any slippage in the process of general monetary restraint can be easily offset by open market operations.

The Commission concludes that the discount facility should be retained as a source of temporary credit. The Federal Reserve should provide liquidity directly to the commercial banks in times of general or regional economic distress. The Commission urges that the banking system be assured this will be done.

Changes in the discount rate are generally used to support and strengthen the effectiveness of open market operations. Under this general policy, changes in the discount rate tend to follow movements in market rates. However, because market rates move continuously whereas changes in the discount rate are made infrequently, the relationship between the discount rate and market rates varies. Changes in this differential often have effects that tend to counter those pursued by open market operations. During a period of restraint, the relative advantage of borrowing reserves increases as market rates of interest increase faster than the discount rate. Banks in tight reserve positions increasingly tend to borrow rather than to sell short-term securities, and this reduces the restraint until such time as discount rates are increased relative to market rates. When market rates fall relative to the discount rate, the advantage of using idle funds to repay indebtedness to the Federal Reserve increases over using them to buy securities. This lessens the easing of credit conditions being pursued by open market policy.

Numerous proposals have been put forward to eliminate the effect caused by a changing relationship between the discount rate and market rates. One proposal is for the Federal Reserve to change the discount rate much more frequently than it does now. Another is that discretionary changes in the discount rate should be abolished altogether and the discount rate should be determined automatically each week by the current rate on short-term Treasury bills. A third proposal is a compromise between the present discretionary procedure and the fully automatic rule. Changes in the discount rate would be tied to changes in the Treasury bill rate but the *spread* between the two rates would be changed periodically on a discretionary basis.

An objection to the proposal of frequent changes is that changes in the discount rate currently serve as a signal of a major shift in monetary policy, and this advantage would be lost if the changes occurred too often. Tying the discount rate to a single market rate holds the danger that that particular rate might move out of line with other short-term market rates and would pull the discount rate also out of line. The third proposal would provide nothing which is not equally possible under the present fully discretionary system. If the Federal Reserve chooses to do so, it can now change the rates weekly, and it can inform the public directly whenever a given change represents a basic shift in policy rather than a technical readjustment. The Commission favors the fully discretionary system and urges that it be administered to avoid effects counter to those sought by open market operations.

Discount rates are now set for each Federal Reserve bank by vote of its board of directors subject to the review and approval of the Federal Reserve Board. However, credit markets have become essentially national in character, and the possibility of utilizing differential regional discount rate policies is negligible. Regional differences in discount rates would be ineffective in view of the active market for federal funds and Treasury bills. Under these circumstances a national discount rate policy is appropriate to correspond with a national open market policy.

The Commission recommends that a fully discretionary, uniform rediscount rate be established for all Federal Reserve banks.

The twelve Federal Reserve banks administer the function of lending to member banks in their respective districts. The principles used by each bank in judging an application for a loan are based on uniform regulations issued by the Board governing the discount privilege, and discount administration of the banks is examined periodically by the Board. Nevertheless, there are claims that administrative criteria differ somewhat among districts.

Clearly the intent of the Federal Reserve Board is to have discount administration relatively homogeneous among the twelve Federal Reserve banks, and the Commission urges continued efforts to assure uniform standards of discounting practice. Uniform standards, of course, mean that like circumstances result in like treatment, at the same time permitting differences in practice where regional differences in economic conditions or needs require.

Reserve Requirements

The reserve position of the banking system depends on the relationship between the volume of reserves held and the volume of reserves required. Both factors can be controlled by the Federal Reserve, and countercyclical adjustments in the reserve position of member banks can be achieved either by changes in reserve requirements or through open market operations. Since 1951 the Federal Reserve had made countercyclical use of changes in member bank reserve requirements only during recessions. Requirements have been reduced to ease monetary conditions, but they have not been increased as a restrictive monetary measure.

While changes in reserve requirements are a powerful instrument of credit control, they are awkward and cumbersome in comparison with open market operations and present difficult problems of adjustment for many medium-sized and small banks. Even the customary changes in required reserve ratios of ½ of 1 percent supply or absorb a very large quantity of reserves. While smaller changes could be made, it appears that under normal circumstances changes in reserve requirements are less finely adjustable than open market operations.

It is argued that changes in reserve requirements have an advantage over open market operations because they affect all member banks directly and immediately, whereas the initial effects of open market operations are commonly concentrated in the major national money markets. There is little clear evidence to indicate that the effects of open market operations are slower than those following reserve requirement changes. Nor is it clear, in view of the other lags involved in monetary policy, that any difference in timing is large enough to be important.

The Commission believes that the power to change reserve requirements should be used only sparingly and favors major reliance on the use of open market operations for countercyclical adjustments.

. . . . . .

Since 1913, member banks have been divided into three groups with respect to reserve requirements on demand deposits—central reserve city banks, reserve city banks, and country banks. According to legislation enacted in 1959, the first class of banks is to be abolished by mid-1962. Reserve requirements for central reserve city and reserve city banks were made identical on December 1, 1960. The act of 1959 also provided that the Federal Reserve may permit all or part of vault cash to be counted as reserves, instead of only deposit balances at Federal Reserve banks.

The geographical distinction was based on conditions prevailing almost a century ago when the National Banking Act was passed. The elimination of the reserve differentials would provide more precise control over the money supply than is now possible. Shifts of funds between country banks and reserve city banks change the total amount of required reserves and thus change the amount of excess reserves within the banking system. With identical requirements, such shifts of funds would be of much less significance in managing the money supply. Now that vault cash is included in reserves, equalization is more feasible than formerly, because banks in different locations or with different categories of depositors have to carry differing amounts of vault cash.

The Commission recommends that the demand deposit reserve requirements for all member banks be made identical and that the classification of banks into country banks and reserve city banks be eliminated.

Reserve requirements on time and savings deposits are already uniform for all member banks. The level of these requirements and the form in which they must be held, however, is significantly different from those required of competing thrift institutions. The Commission believes it unnecessary to require statutory reserves against savings and time deposits in banks and competing institutions. Management and supervisory authorities are able to see to it that such liquidity as may be necessary with respect to such deposits is maintained.

The Commission recommends that existing statutory reserve requirements against savings and time deposits be repealed, and that pending repeal of such requirements, those banks and competing thrift institutions subject to them be permitted to hold reserves in the form of either cash or Treasury securities with maturities up to five years.

The reserve base required to support a long-run expansion in the stock of money can be supplied either through open market operations or through a reduction in required reserve ratios. Which method is used will affect the leverage with which monetary control operates, that is, the multiple by which demand deposits can be increased or decreased for any change in required reserves; net Treasury interest costs; and the level of bank earnings.

Reducing required reserve ratios increases the leverage of monetary control. Increased leverage has some advantages for economic stabilization. A given change in available reserves will induce a greater change in total bank loans and investments and in the money supply, the lower is the required reserve ratio. However, a lower reserve ratio may increase the difficulty of dealing with short-run variations in factors affecting bank reserves such as changes in float, currency in circulation, or the gold stock. These effects can be offset with a smaller amount of open market operations, but to the extent that they are not, their net disruptive effect will be larger when required reserve ratios are low and leverage is high.

A second consideration bearing on the level of reserve requirements is the interest cost on the Treasury debt. The same volume of demand deposits can be supported either by a relatively small volume of reserves and a low level of reserve requirements or a larger volume of reserves and higher reserve requirements. In the second situation the Federal Reserve banks would have a larger amount of earning assets, and because these assets consist largely of Treasury securities, more of the Treasury debt would be held by the Federal Reserve and less would be in the hands of the public. And because the Federal Reserve pays over 90 percent of its net earnings to the Treasury, the net interest cost to the Treasury would be less. Treasury interest costs would also be lower because less of the debt would have to be publicly held and lower interest rates on all new Treasury issues would be likely.

Another consideration affecting the growth of the money supply is the level of bank earnings, because if demand deposits are to grow, then commercial banks must also grow. A bank's ability to expand its loans and investments and its deposits is limited not only by the volume of its reserves and its required reserve ratio but also by the volume of its capital and its required capital–asset ratio.

Whether a bank will be able to expand to take advantage of an improved reserve position will depend on its capital position. If individual banks insist on maintaining or are required by supervisory authorities to maintain a specified capital–asset ratio as a prudent protection against losses, then a bank can expand its earning assets only if it can enlarge its capital at a corresponding pace. Increased capital depends on adequate earnings. If capital is built up from retained earnings, then total earnings must be large enough to permit this; or if capital is to be obtained from new stock issues, the earnings rate must be high enough to make this course attractive both to the banks and to investors.

The level of reserve requirements affect the level of bank earnings, because the required reserves of member banks are nonearning assets. The higher the required reserve ratio, the smaller the proportion of bank assets in the form of earning assets and the lower the level of earnings. Conversely, lower reserve requirements make possible higher bank earnings. If the current level of reserve requirements permits an adequate level of earnings to attract the necessary capital at current levels of interest rates and other bank charges, then the reserve base for an expanding money supply can be met through open market operations. On the other hand, if the required reserve ratio does not permit an adequate level of earnings at the existing levels of interest rates and bank charges, then either the level of interest rates and bank charges must rise or the reserve ratio must be reduced to permit the increased earnings necessary for the growth of commercial banks and the money supply.

The Commission recommends that Congress continue to grant to the Federal Reserve Board a range within which reserve requirements can be set for demand deposits, perhaps from 8 to 18 percent, so that the Board can adjust the specific level to meet the needs of growth or to meet emergency needs.

SELECTIVE CONTROLS

One suggestion frequently made for strengthening the effectiveness of monetary policy is that more use should be made of selective monetary measures. The traditional and continuing focus of Federal Reserve policy on general monetary control exercised through changes in the over-all reserve positions of commercial banks does not attempt to direct the allocation of credit among competing uses. If selective controls were used, the authorities could alter the terms and conditions on which credit is made available for particular purposes regardless of the reserve position imposed by general controls. Today the only selective control available to the Federal Reserve authorities is the power to alter margin requirements on credit granted by any lender—banks and others—for the purpose of purchasing or carrying listed securities.

Proposals for selective controls over other specific uses of credit are usually directed toward controlling volatile sectors of spending, such as spending on consumer durable goods, housing, inventory accumulation, and industrial plant and equipment. Expenditures for these depend heavily on the use of credit, but they do not respond rapidly to changes in general credit conditions. Thus they can be reached quickly through general monetary policies only by imposing credit conditions on the economy as a whole that might not be appropriate. Influencing these expenditures directly, through selective controls, would make monetary policy more effective. At least three related issues are involved in the question of selective credit controls: the degree to which government should intervene in the allocation of resources; the type of intervention; and the specific means available for intervention in particular types of expenditure.

The Degree and Type of Intervention

The debate on the appropriate degree of government intervention is frequently conducted entirely on grounds of doctrine. Some hold that intervention in resource allocation is undesirable in itself, except in time of war. Others believe that intervention to achieve accepted goals that cannot otherwise be attained is legitimate and desirable. The important issue is not the choice between intervention and nonintervention but between one type of intervention and another.

Existing credit controls are already selective, partly by conscious policy and partly because of the differential effects flowing from general credit controls. In addition to the margin regulations designed to curb stock market speculation, general monetary measures affect short-term interest rates more than long-term rates, housing expenditures more than business expenditures for plant and equipment and inventories, and expenditures for consumer durable goods more than for nondurable goods. There are also other deliberate selective controls in force elsewhere in the government for altering resource allocation. Federal credit agencies redirect credit flows in favor of such sectors as residential housing, slum clearance, agriculture, transportation, small business, and exports. General and specific tax and expenditure policies affect the distribution of resources between public goods and private goods, between aggregate saving and spending, between investment in tangible goods and intangibles such as research and education, and among particular kinds of consumer goods and services.

Selective credit controls attempt to influence the level and composition of output by regulating the volume and terms of lending for specific purposes. The effectiveness of such selective credit controls depends primarily on whether the purpose of the loan can be identified accurately by the collateral offered as security or by other means. Mortgage and consumer credit for the purchase of houses or automobiles and credit granted to purchase securities generally meet the test of loan identification by purpose through the collateral offered. It is not possible to identify the purpose of business borrowing by the collateral offered. To control such lending another type of identification device than any thus far used would be required. Unless private lenders can identify the purpose of the loan readily, evasion of control may be so easy as to make the control ineffective.

Whether the Federal Reserve should be granted additional powers to alter the pattern of credit and resource allocation through the exercise of new selective controls is a practical matter. It hinges largely on whether particular types of changes in the composition of spending among broad classes of output not readily affected by general controls can be identified *at the time* as being so destabilizing as to threaten the achievement of major economic objectives, and on whether there are efficient means to affect these types of spending and output in the desired directions.

Consumer Credit

One opinion that has been expressed on the long-run impact of consumer credit on the economy is that the demand for installment borrowing has been so strong that it has diverted loan funds to consumption from business investment possibly to the detriment of economic growth. Another opinion has been that consumer credit has grown so fast and on such easy terms that overburdened consumers are dangerously vulnerable to any decline in income receipts.

In spite of the large increase in outstanding consumer credit in the postwar period, the evidence does not suggest that consumers, in the aggregate, are now overburdened with debt, although specific families may be. Many low income families are devoting a fifth or more of their income to installment payments. If these families should suffer a modest decline in income, the burden of existing debt could become too heavy. However, this problem of individual overindebtedness is likely to continue even with selective controls over credit terms.

A more frequently expressed concern about consumer credit and particularly installment credit is that it is a source of cyclical instability. The demand for consumer durable goods has been cyclically volatile, and the use of credit to finance purchases has aggravated an already unstable situation. Net extensions of credit, the excess of new extensions over repayment, has added significantly to durable goods purchases in cyclical upswings. The need to continue payments on the downswing has deprived consumers of purchasing power when incomes were falling and has intensified the fall-off in durable goods sales. And changes in general credit conditions have not had any prompt or discernibly significant effect on cycles in consumer credit.

The difficulty of efficient administration of selective controls over consumer credit is a major argument against them. Past experience shows that evasion is a constant problem. A minimum ratio of down payments on some durable goods, such as automobiles, have been bypassed by changing ostensible trade-in allowances. The growth of leasing could permit consumers to acquire cars on terms which might differ significantly from those being imposed by the credit authorities.

Regulation of consumer credit terms might contribute to cyclical stability, but it would require a large and complex administration to be fully effective. The benefits to stability promised by such a system must be weighed against the cost and inconvenience of installing and managing it.

During wartime emergencies, direct controls over the output and sale of consumer durables probably would be imposed, and if so, consumer credit control would be redundant.

During more normal periods, it might be useful to discourage undue loosening of credit terms when the demand for durables is an important source of inflationary pressure. But as a regular countercyclical tool of stabilization its practical possibilities are limited.

The Commission is almost evenly divided as to the desirability of granting standby authority to the Federal Reserve Board for consumer credit controls. In the absence of a consensus, no recommendation is made except to urge an investigation of better forms of such controls which could be administered more effectively if they should be needed.

Residential Housing Credit

The arguments for variable controls over the terms of housing mortgages are similar to those for consumer installment credit controls. But because the exchange of existing houses for new houses is not common, many of the administrative difficulties of evasion do not arise.

However, setting appropriate goals for the desired volume of residential construction presents a difficult and serious problem. The elimination of the interest rate ceilings imposed on Veterans Administration and Federal Housing Administration mortgages, . . . would remove one cause of the present countercyclical variation of housing construction. The imposition of selective controls, however, would permit a restoration of all or part of such countercyclical variation that might be lost through the removal of interest rate ceilings.

. . . the Commission recommends that the terms of housing loans insured or guaranteed under VA and FHA programs be varied in support of the countercyclical and price stabilization policies of the government. These changes would be administered by the VA and FHA. No further power to change credit terms on residential mortgages by the Federal Reserve Board is believed necessary.

Business Credit

The instability of business spending for inventory accumulations and for plant and equipment purchases has contributed significantly to cyclical fluctuations. General monetary controls do not appear to have rapid effects on either, and it is argued that selective controls might have.

Setting and altering the terms of lending for specific uses of credit might have little effect. Businesses could employ internal funds for the uses carrying the most onerous terms and borrow for those uses which the control authorities were attempting to encourage the most or discourage the least. Thus, differential selective credit controls over business uses of funds would be difficult to enforce. And if the concept of different terms for different uses is sacrificed to close loopholes in enforcement, selective credit controls become virtually identical to general credit controls. A blanket classification for all loans to business would also virtually amount to general credit control, although it could vary the cost of business borrowing relative to other categories of borrowing.

Even noncredit controls pose serious administrative problems. Expenditures for business plant, equipment, and inventory are not homogeneous categories. There are important differences of behavior within a category among industries in the economy and among different companies in the same industry. These differences would inevitably call for an intricate network of administrative adjustments to make a selective control effective.

No seemingly effective selective credit control device has yet been devised for regulating these volatile business expenditures. It may well be that more effective controls of such expenditures than general credit measures will be necessary to achieve our major economic objectives, and the Commission suggests that possible methods of influencing inventory and business investment expenditures on a selective basis be investigated by the government.

Part III: Questions for Analysis

1. Would it be possible, according to the analysis of business cycles by Wesley C. Mitchell, for a decline in the total demand for industrial equipment to result from a slowing down in the rate of expansion of industrial production? Use hypothetical data to support your conclusion.
2. *a*) List the measures of the duration and amplitude of business cycle contractions employed by Geoffrey H. Moore.
   b) Indicate the severity of the contraction, as recorded by each of these measures, for the period from August, 1929 to March, 1933; also, for the period from July, 1953 to August, 1954.
3. *a*) Summarize the theory of aggregate effective demand as stated by John Maynard Keynes.
   b) What change in emphasis in economics, according to Seymour E. Harris, resulted from the *Keynesian Revolution?*
   c) What is the conclusion of Henry Hazlitt with respect to the effectiveness of Keynesian methods in reducing unemployment? How does he test the effectiveness of such methods?
4. Discuss the objectives of the Employment Act of 1946, and the methods by which these objectives are to be attained.
5. *a*) The Joint Economic Committee Staff has stated that fiscal policy, if it is to contribute to a higher rate of economic growth (as well as to economic stability) "must be concerned with the composition as well as the total volume of economic activity." Why is this the case?
   b) Present a summary of the principal conclusions of the Joint Economic Committee Staff as to the impact of postwar fiscal policy on economic stability in this country.
6. Indicate the recommendations made by the Commission on Money and Credit to strengthen monetary policy with respect to a "bills only" policy in open-market operations, with respect to a uniform discount rate, and with respect to reserve requirements of member banks against demand deposits.

IV ECONOMIC GROWTH

The impact of long-run economic growth on human welfare is perhaps more keenly recognized in the mid-twentieth century than ever before. The explosion of population growth and of aspirations for higher standards of living, particularly in the underdeveloped countries of the world, emphasize this observation. What economic system is most conducive to economic growth? The Russians preach the alleged merits of communism. We advance the benefits of a free economy. The course of events in the neutral underdeveloped countries in achieving economic growth will influence the outcome of the contest between the superpowers of the contemporary world.

The issue of growth in a context of ideological rivalry is explored in some detail in the items included in this part of the book. In almost all of the underdeveloped nations of the world, population pressure is a problem. An historic statement of the problem is made by Thomas Robert Malthus, English minister whose ideas contributed to the early nineteenth century designation of economics as the "dismal" science. Kingsley Davis, a contemporary population expert, analyzes the current population problem of underdeveloped countries.

Economic growth is as difficult to achieve as it is important. W. W. Rostow reviews the stages of growth through which an economy evolves on the way to high mass consumption. Frederick Harbison, Director of the Industrial Relations Section of Princeton University and Benjamin Higgins, Professor of Economics at the University of Texas, discuss economic and noneconomic factors important to the achievement of this objective. B. K. Nehru, Indian Ambassador to the United States, highlights the point that, in the absence of substantial aid from Western countries, underdeveloped countries will follow the pattern of dictatorship in their efforts to achieve rapid economic growth. Recognizing this threat, the Western nations have contributed to the establishment of an impressive roster of development-lending institutions.

A. Population Growth and Poverty

22. THE CLASSICAL VIEW*

Thomas Robert Malthus

STATEMENT OF THE SUBJECT. RATIOS OF THE INCREASE OF POPULATION AND FOOD

In an inquiry concerning the improvement of society, the mode of conducting the subject which naturally presents itself, is,

1. To investigate the causes that have hitherto impeded the progress of mankind towards happiness; and,

2. To examine the probability of the total or partial removal of these causes in future.

To enter fully into this question, and to enumerate all the causes that have hitherto influenced human improvement, would be much beyond the power of an individual. The principal object of the present essay is to examine the effects of one great cause intimately united with the very nature of man; which, though it has been constantly and powerfully operating since the commencement of society, has been little noticed by the writers who have treated this subject. The facts which establish the existence of this cause have, indeed, been repeatedly stated and acknowledged; but its natural and necessary effects have been almost totally overlooked; though probably among these effects may be reckoned a very considerable portion of that vice and misery, and of that unequal distribution of the bounties of nature, which it has been the unceasing object of the enlightened philanthropist in all ages to correct.

The cause to which I allude, is the constant tendency in all animated life to increase beyond the nourishment prepared for it.

It is observed by Dr. Franklin, that there is no bound to the prolific nature of plants or animals, but what is made by their crowding and interfering with each other's means of subsistence. Were the face of the earth, he says, vacant of other plants, it might be gradually sowed and overspread with one kind only, as for instance with fennel: and were it empty of other inhabitants, it might in a few ages be replenished from one nation only, as for instance with Englishmen.

This is incontrovertibly true. Through the animal and vegetable

* Thomas Robert Malthus, *An Essay on the Principle of Population* (London: Ward, Lock, and Co., 1890), excerpts from pp. 1–11.

kingdoms Nature has scattered the seeds of life abroad with the most profuse and liberal hand; but has been comparatively sparing in the room and the nourishment necessary to rear them. The germs of existence contained in this earth, if they could freely develop themselves, would fill millions of worlds in the course of a few thousand years. Necessity, that imperious, all-pervading law of nature, restrains them within the prescribed bounds. The race of plants and the race of animals shrink under this great restrictive law; and man cannot by any efforts of reason escape from it.

In plants and irrational animals, the view of the subject is simple. They are all impelled by a powerful instinct to the increase of their species; and this instinct is interrupted by no doubts about providing for their offspring. Wherever therefore there is liberty, the power of increase is exerted; and the superabundant effects are repressed afterwards by want of room and nourishment.

The effects of this check on man are more complicated. Impelled to the increase of his species by an equally powerful instinct, reason interrupts his career, and asks him whether he may not bring beings into the world, for whom he cannot provide the means of support. If he attend to this natural suggestion, the restriction too frequently produces vice. If he hear it not, the human race will be constantly endeavouring to increase beyond the means of subsistence. But as, by that law of our nature which makes food necessary to the life of man, population can never actually increase beyond the lowest nourishment capable of supporting it, a strong check on population, from the difficulty of acquiring food, must be constantly in operation. This difficulty must fall somewhere, and must necessarily be severely felt in some or other of the various forms of misery, or the fear of misery, by a large portion of mankind.

That population has this constant tendency to increase beyond the means of subsistence, and that it is kept to its necessary level by these causes, will sufficiently appear from a review of the different states of society in which man has existed. But, before we proceed to this review, the subject will, perhaps, be seen in a clearer light, if we endeavour to ascertain what would be the natural increase of population, if left to exert itself with perfect freedom; and what might be expected to be the rate of increase in the productions of the earth, under the most favourable circumstances of human industry.

It will be allowed that no country has hitherto been known, where the manners were so pure and simple, and the means of subsistence so abundant, that no check whatever has existed to early marriages from the difficulty of providing for a family, and that no waste of the human species has been occasioned by vicious customs, by towns, by unhealthy occupations, or too severe labour. Consequently in no state that we have yet known, has the power of population been left to exert itself with perfect freedom.

Whether the law of marriage be instituted, or not, the dictate of nature and virtue seems to be an early attachment to one woman; and where there were no impediments of any kind in the way of an union to which such an attachment would lead, and no causes of depopulation afterwards, the increase of the human species would be evidently much greater than any increase which has been hitherto known.

. . . . .

It may safely be pronounced, therefore, that population, when unchecked, goes on doubling itself every twenty-five years, or increases in a geometrical ratio.

The rate according to which the productions of the earth may be supposed to increase, it will not be so easy to determine. Of this, however, we may be perfectly certain, that the ratio of their increase in a limited territory must be of a totally different nature from the ratio of the increase of population. A thousand millions are just as easily doubled every twenty-five years by the power of population as a thousand. But the food to support the increase from the greater number will by no means be obtained with the same facility. Man is necessarily confined in room. When acre has been added to acre till all the fertile land is occupied, the yearly increase of food must depend upon the melioration of the land already in possession. This is a fund, which, from the nature of all soils, instead of increasing, must be gradually diminishing. But population, could it be supplied with food, would go on with unexhausted vigour; and the increase of one period would furnish the power of a greater increase the next, and this without any limit.

. . . . .

Europe is by no means so fully peopled as it might be. In Europe there is the fairest chance that human industry may receive its best direction. The science of agriculture has been much studied in England and Scotland; and there is still a great portion of uncultivated land in these countries. Let us consider at what rate the produce of this island might be supposed to increase under circumstances the most favourable to improvement.

If it be allowed that by the best possible policy, and great encouragements to agriculture, the average produce of the island could be doubled in the first twenty-five years, it will be allowing, probably, a greater increase than could with reason be expected.

In the next twenty-five years, it is impossible to suppose that the produce could be quadrupled. It would be contrary to all our knowledge of the properties of land. The improvement of the barren parts would be a work of time and labour; and it must be evident to those who have the slightest acquaintance with agricultural subjects, that in proportion as cultivation extended, the additions that could yearly be made to the former average produce must be gradually and regularly diminishing. That we may be the better able to compare the increase of population and food, let us make a supposition, which, without pretending to accuracy, is clearly more favourable to the power of production in the earth, than any experience we have had of its qualities will warrant.

Let us suppose that the yearly additions which might be made to the former average produce, instead of decreasing, which they certainly would do, were to remain the same; and that the produce of this island might be increased every twenty-five years, by a quantity equal to what it at present produces. The most enthusiastic speculator cannot suppose a greater increase than this. In a few centuries it would make every acre of land in the island like a garden.

If this supposition be applied to the whole earth, and if it be allowed that the subsistence for man which the earth affords might be increased every twenty-five years by a quantity equal to what it at present produces, this will be supposing a rate of increase much greater than we can imagine that any possible exertions of mankind could make it.

It may be fairly pronounced, therefore, that, considering the present average state of the earth, the means of subsistence, under circumstances the most favourable to human industry, could not possibly be made to increase faster than in an arithmetical ratio.

The necessary effects of these two different rates of increase, when brought together, will be very striking. Let us call the population of this island eleven millions; and suppose the present produce equal to the easy support of such a number. In the first twenty-five years the population would be twenty-two millions, and the food being also doubled, the means of subsistence would be equal to this increase. In the next twenty-five years, the population would be forty-four millions, and the means of subsistence only equal to the support of thirty-three millions. In the next period the population would be eighty-eight millions, and the means of subsistence just equal to the support of half that number. And, at the conclusion of the first century, the population would be a hundred and seventy-six millions, and the means of subsistence only equal to the support of fifty-five millions, leaving a population of a hundred and twenty-one millions totally unprovided for.

Taking the whole earth, instead of this island, emigration would of course be excluded; and, supposing the present population equal to a thousand millions, the human species would increase as the numbers, 1, 2, 4, 8, 16, 32, 64, 128, 256, and subsistence as 1, 2, 3, 4, 5, 6, 7, 8, 9. In two centuries the population would be to the means of subsistence as 256 to 9; in three centuries as 4096 to 13, and in two thousand years the difference would be almost incalculable.

In this supposition no limits whatever are placed to the produce of the earth. It may increase for ever and be greater than any assignable quantity; yet still the power of population being in every period so much superior, the increase of the human species can only be kept down to the level of the means of subsistence by the constant operation of the strong law of necessity, acting as a check upon the greater power.

OF THE GENERAL CHECKS TO POPULATION, AND THE MODE OF THEIR OPERATION

The ultimate check to population appears then to be a want of food, arising necessarily from the different ratios according to which population and food increase. But this ultimate check is never the immediate check, except in cases of actual famine.

The immediate check may be stated to consist in all those customs, and all those diseases, which seem to be generated by a scarcity of the means of subsistence; and all those causes, independent of this scarcity, whether of a moral or physical nature, which tend prematurely to weaken and destroy the human frame.

These checks to population, which are constantly operating with more or less force in every society, and keep down the number to the level of the means of subsistence, may be classed under two general heads—the preventive, and the positive checks.

The preventive check, as far as it is voluntary, is peculiar to man, and arises from that distinctive superiority in his reasoning faculties, which enables him to calculate distant consequences. The checks to the indefinite increase of plants and irrational animals are all either positive, or, if preventive, involuntary. But man cannot look around him, and see the distress which frequently presses upon those who have large families; he cannot contemplate his present possessions or earnings, which he now nearly consumes himself, and calculate the amount of each share, when with very little addition they must be divided, perhaps, among seven or eight, without feeling a doubt whether, if he follow the bent of his inclinations, he may be able to support the offspring which he will probably bring into the world. In a state of equality, if such can exist, this would be the simple question. In the present state of society other considerations occur. Will he not lower his rank in life, and be obliged to give up in great measure his former habits? Does any mode of employment present itself by which he may reasonably hope to maintain a family? Will he not at any rate subject himself to greater difficulties, and more severe labour, than in his single state? Will he not be unable to transmit to his children the same advantages of education and improvement that he had himself possessed? Does he even feel secure that, should he have a large family, his utmost exertions can save them from rags and squalid poverty, and their consequent degradation in the community? And may he not be reduced to the grating necessity of forfeiting his independence, and of being obliged to the sparing hand of Charity for support?

These considerations are calculated to prevent, and certainly do prevent, a great number of persons in all civilised nations from pursuing the dictate of nature in an early attachment to one woman.

If this restraint does not produce vice, it is undoubtedly the least evil that can arise from the principle of population. Considered as a restraint on a strong natural inclination, it must be allowed to produce a certain degree of temporary unhappiness; but evidently slight, compared with the evils which result from any of the other checks to population; and merely of the same nature as many other sacrifices of temporary to permanent gratification, which it is the business of a moral agent continually to make.

When this restraint produces vice, the evils which follow are but too conspicuous. A promiscuous intercourse to such a degree as to prevent the birth of children, seems to lower, in the most marked manner, the dignity of human nature. It cannot be without its effect on men, and nothing can be more obvious than its tendency to degrade the female character, and to destroy all its most amiable and distinguishing characteristics. Add to which, that among those unfortunate females, with which all great towns abound, more real distress and aggravated misery are, perhaps, to be found, than in any other department of human life.

When a general corruption of morals, with regard to the sex, pervades all the classes of society, its effects must necessarily be, to poison the springs of domestic happiness, to weaken conjugal and parental affection, and to lessen the united exertions and ardour of parents in the care and education of their children:—effects which cannot take place without a decided diminution of the general happiness and virtue of the society; particularly as the necessity of art in the accomplishment and conduct of intrigues, and in the concealment of their consequences necessarily leads to many other vices.

The positive checks to population are extremely various, and include every cause, whether arising from vice or misery, which in any degree contributes to shorten the natural duration of human life. Under this head, therefore, may be enumerated all unwholesome occupations, severe labour and exposure to the seasons, extreme poverty, bad nursing of children, great towns, excesses of all kinds, the whole train of common diseases and epidemics, wars, plague, and famine.

On examining these obstacles to the increase of population which I have classed under the heads of preventive and positive checks, it will appear that they are all resolvable into moral restraint, vice, and misery.

Of the preventive checks, the restraint from marriage which is not followed by irregular gratifications may properly be termed moral restraint.

Promiscuous intercourse, unnatural passions, violations of the marriage bed, and improper arts to conceal the consequences of irregular connexions, are preventive checks that clearly come under the head of vice.

Of the positive checks, those which appear to arise unavoidably from the laws of nature, may be called exclusively misery; and those which we obviously bring upon ourselves, such as wars, excesses, and many others which it would be in our power to avoid, are of a mixed nature. They are brought upon us by vice, and their consequences are misery.

The sum of all these preventive and positive checks, taken together, forms the immediate check to population; and it is evident that, in every country where the whole of the procreative power cannot be called into action, the preventive and the positive checks must vary inversely as each other; that is, in countries either naturally unhealthy, or subject to a great mortality, from whatever cause it may arise, the preventive check will prevail very little. In those countries, on the contrary, which are naturally healthy, and where the preventive check is found to prevail with considerable force, the positive check will prevail very little, or the mortality be very small.

In every country some of these checks are, with more or less force, in constant operation; yet, notwithstanding their general prevalence, there are few states in which there is not a constant effort in the population to increase beyond the means of subsistence. This constant effort as constantly tends to subject the lower classes of society to distress, and to prevent any great permanent melioration of their condition.

These effects, in the present state of society, seem to be produced in the following manner. We will suppose the means of subsistence in any country just equal to the easy support of its inhabitants. The constant effort towards population, which is found to act even in the most vicious societies, increases the number of people before the means of subsistence are increased. The food, therefore, which before supported eleven millions, must now be divided among eleven millions and a half. The poor consequently must live much worse, and many of them be reduced to severe distress. The number of labourers also being above the proportion of work in the market, the price of labour must tend to fall, while the price of provisions would at the same time tend to rise. The labourer therefore must do more work, to earn the same as he did before. During this season of distress, the discouragements to marriage and the difficulty of rearing a family are so great, that the progress of population is retarded. In the meantime, the cheapness of labour, the plenty of labourers, and the necessity of an increased industry among them, encourage cultivators to employ more labour upon their land, to turn up fresh soil, and to manure and improve more completely what is already in tillage, till ultimately the means of subsistence may become in the same proportion to the population, as at the period from which we set out. The situation of the labourer being then again tolerably comfortable, the restraints to population are in some degree loosened; and, after a short period, the same retrograde and progressive movements, with respect to happiness, are repeated.

23. THE CONTEMPORARY SITUATION*

Kingsley Davis

The amazing increase in the earth's population in recent years, justly described as an "explosion," is shown by the United Nations latest projections to be merely a forerunner of a still greater burst of human multiplication to come. Only sixteen years from now, according to the U.N.'s *medium* estimates, the earth will contain a billion more people than now, and in forty-one years nearly four billion more. The rate of increase during the second half of the present century will be *twice* as fast as it has been during the first half.

Here are the U.N.'s figures:

PAST

	1900	1925	1950
World population (in millions)	1,550	1,907	2,497
Percentage increase in 25 years		23%	31%
Years to double population at this rate		84	64

FUTURE

	1975	2000
Population (in millions)	3,830	6,280
Percentage increase in 25 years	53%	64%
Years to double population at this rate	41	35

Are these estimates accurate, or do they merely serve to scare us into "doing something about population"? The answer is that these are not "scare-projections." They are the most systematic and responsible population forecasts on a global basis we have.

Admittedly, nobody can predict future populations with certainty. The world's inhabitants in the year 2000 may exceed six billion or may number only a few thousand sufferers from nuclear radiation. Since future populations depend on what people do and decide, there is nothing automatic about them. The U.N. projections are based on statistical models that show what will happen if each nation's population follows the course implicit in its present stage of development. Only some world catastrophe or revolutionary innovation would cause the estimated world total by the close of the century to be far wrong.

If anything, the U.N. estimates are conservative. Not only do the

* Kingsley Davis, "The Other Scare: Too Many People," *New York Times Magazine*, March 15, 1959, pp. 13, 108, 110, 112, 114.

experts who prepared them regard them as so, but it is a curious fact that nearly all modern forecasts of population have proved too low. In 1924, for example, two reputable experts, Pearl and Reed, forecast a world population of 1.8 billion in 1950, but the correct figure turned out to be 2.5 billion. Each new set of forecasts exceeds the old set. This being true, the picture the U.N. figures give is ominous. By 1975 the number of people being added to the human race *each year* will be 77 million, and by 2000, 126 million!

Why is this speed-up taking place? Reduced to the simplest terms, the reason for the coming rise in the already unprecedented rate of increase is this: Two-thirds of the world's peoples still live in under-developed countries where spectacular declines in death rates are occurring with little change in traditionally high birth rates. At the same time, the industrial countries have had a post-war recovery in births which, along with a continued steady drop in mortality, has brought their population growth back to pre-Depression rates. Since the under-developed countries can lower their death rates still further, and since the other nations seem disinclined to return to the low fertility level of the Depression, the net result is an anticipated scale of human growth scarcely dreamed of a few years ago.

It follows that the countries expected to have the greatest ballooning of population—the poorer ones—are precisely the wrong ones to have it. If the medium U.N. projections hold true, the currently under-developed areas will grow twice as fast as the industrial countries. Their share of the earth's people will rise from 65.5 per cent in 1950 to 76.3 per cent in 2000. This means that the poorer regions, to make any headway against the more advanced nations, must buck a very strong current. So far they are losing the fight, because the gap in wealth between them and the developed nations is widening.

One mitigating circumstance is that among both the industrial and the nonindustrial countries it is the "new" ones that are showing the fastest population growth. In the industrial group, for example, those in the New World are expected to increase nearly three times as fast as the older industrial countries of central and northern Europe; and in the non-industrial group tropical Latin America is scheduled to multiply roughly twice as rapidly as nonindustrial Asia. This tendency will prevent the world's most densely settled areas as a whole from showing the highest rates of population growth.

It is not true, as some fear, that the Communist countries will necessarily outmultiply the free world. According to the U.N. projections, these nations will have roughly the same proportion of the world's people in 1975 and in 2000 as they have now—about 35 per cent.

The reason for this is that both the Communist and the free blocs include industrial and non-industrial peoples in nearly the same proportion. The Communist bloc contains neither the world's fastest growing region (tropical Latin America) nor the slowest growing region (northwestern Europe). If, therefore, communism does not spread by conquest, the world will probably remain two-thirds non-Communist. The "if," however, is a big one.

From a numerical standpoint, Red China is the world's most important nation. With 650 million people, she now encompasses nearly one-fourth of the human race, and her population is apparently increasing above the average world rate, with an absolute increment each year of approximately 15 million (almost equal to the entire population of Canada). By 1975, according to U.N. medium estimates, her population will reach 894 million, more than four times ours at that time. By the end of the century China may well have more than 1.5 billion.

Although Russia is expected to expand its population more slowly than China, it still will gain slightly over the United States. The figures for the world's four most populous nations, today and in 1975, are:

Today	Population (millions)	Ratio (U.S.-1)
U.S.A.	175	1.0
U.S.S.R.	208	1.2
India	406	2.3
China	650	3.7
1975		
U.S.A.	217	1.0
U.S.S.R.	275	1.3
India	563	2.6
China	894	4.1

Although we think our population is growing rapidly—and so it is, at just about the current world average—the gains south of our border make ours seem small. Mexico's birth rate, for instance, is 47 per 1,000 as against 25 for us, and her death rate 12.9 as against our 9.6.

The resulting rate of natural increase (the difference between the birth and death rates) is more than twice ours. Indeed, the population growth in Mexico, as in some other parts of Latin America, is close to 3.5 per cent a year—a rate which, if continued, will double the population in twenty years and increase it tenfold in sixty-seven years!

What are likely to be the chief consequences of this immense increase in world population? Some of the dangers may be clearly foreseen.

The central fact is that population growth will tend to be greatest where people are poorest. In this desperate situation the less developed nations will hardly be squeamish about the means they adopt to further their national goals. Caught in the predicament of having an ever larger share of the world's people and an ever smaller share of the world's resources, they will be driven to adopt revolutionary policies.

Obvious possibilities along this line are the reduction of population growth by speeding birth control and/or the transformation of the economy by totalitarian methods.

Not only is the glut of people in the poorer areas itself conducive to communism, but in the past communism has made its gains by conquest rather than by population growth. In 1920 it held less than one-tenth of the world's people under its fist; today it holds more than one-third. The lack of unity in the rest of the world against communism suggests that Red expansion may continue. If this happens, and if the conquests are made in the poorer countries, superior population growth will join territorial expansion in increasing communism's share of the world.

One of the questions of the future centers on China, whose sheer size poses a major political problem for the world—including Russia. The Communist bloc has achieved greater cohesion among its member nations than has the free world, but, as Yugoslavia and Hungary have shown, nationalism can plague the Communist group too. This may be a negligible factor so long as it concerns only the lesser satellites, but it can become acute when the "satellite" has three times the population of Russia.

At the moment China is not quite in a position to challenge Russia or America. She has more manpower than anything else; indeed, she has too many people and too fast a rate of increase to realize her economic or military potential. But she is apparently bent on converting her weakness into strength by radical economic methods. To the surprise of the Russians, China is outcommunizing Russia. By the tightest of controls she is directing her masses into the most productive channels and trying to avoid the dissipation of scarce capital that would result if these masses were allowed more than a subsistence consumption.

In addition, the Chinese state is directly transforming excess people into capital by using underpaid surplus labor on vast schemes of public construction. At the same time, appalled by the annual population increase, the Government has fostered a program of diffusing birth-control methods, and it has made a huge effort to settle sparsely inhabited areas in the north and west.

These measures cannot all be laid to communism. The policies, and to some extent Chinese communism itself, are the result of the desperate situation in which China finds herself in view of her low economic development and her runaway population growth. In any case the picture of a Communist élite organizing and driving an ocean of humanity evidently frightens the Russians themselves.

If the venture succeeds, China, with a projected 1975 population almost double the expected figures for the United States and Russia combined, would be the strongest contender for world leadership. Such a mass, equipped with modern arms and disciplined by a dictatorship, if bent on conquest, could be stopped only by a united world outside.

In the Western Hemisphere our own superiority of numbers, which has long bolstered our leadership of the area, is destined to diminish quickly. Whereas in 1920 we had more inhabitants than the rest of the hemisphere put together, in 1975 we will probably have only two-thirds as many as the other nations, and in the year 2000 less than half. Brazil, the hemisphere's second most populous nation, in 1920 had only a fourth as many people as we did; it will probably have half as many in 1975.

One question raised in connection with population trends is that of color. If color prejudice were the strongest force in the world, and if all so-called "non-whites" were united, they would certainly dominate the whites. The areas controlled or soon to be controlled by non-whites embrace about 64 per cent of the human population; and this preponderance is likely to increase to about 72 per cent by the year 2000.

But race has never been the main basis of conflict, and if it were it would not crudely pit all "whites" against all "non-whites." Far more important are differences of religion, culture and nationality. The conflict of Moslems and Hindus in the Indian subcontinent has nothing to do with race, nor does the antagonism between Arabs and Jews in the Middle East, between Chinese and Malays in Malaya, or between South and North Koreans.

One potent source of conflict, however, is international migration, which creates alien minorities or majorities within nations. Future growth will probably increase migratory pressures and, as a result, bring stiffened barriers to such movement. Human migration, when unrestricted, generally flows from areas of low income to areas of high income. Since the fastest future population growth will be in under-developed areas, and since their relative poverty is growing greater rather than less, the demand there for admission to industrial lands will become enormous.

In 1950 almost 56 per cent of the world's people lived in the already crowded and impoverished agrarian regions of Asia, North Africa, Middle America and the Caribbean. According to the U.N. projections, the same regions will contain 59 per cent by 1975 and 65 per cent in 2000.

To keep their *proportion* simply at the 1950 level, they would have to send out, by 1975, 140 million emigrants and, from 1975 to 2000, about 571 million. In view of the troubles attending a few thousands of Caribbean and West African immigrants in Britain, the slaughter accompanying the movement of only twelve million migrants between India and Pakistan, the present plight of Arab refugees, and the history of alien fifth columns in many lands, human movement on such a fantastic scale seems inconceivable except by conquest.

The dangers implicit in the present and future uncontrolled population trends raise the question, what can we do about it?

The late Pope Pius thought, hopefully, that interplanetary travel might alleviate the earth's population pressures. But merely moving people on the earth itself is costly. For example, adding 1,000 migrants to Canada's population is estimated to entail capital outlays of $12 to $13 million. Assuming that an individual could be moved to another planet at the ridiculously low cost of $1 million, it would take $45,000 billion to get rid of the earth's current increase for one year—a sum exceeding the earth's total income.

The curious thing about such drastic suggestions is that they assume man to be permanently and blindly driven by his own reproduction. They say, in effect, that the only way for human beings to avoid starvation is to emigrate into space, produce food out of algae and wood, or give up every enjoyment for sheer, grinding subsistence. If the assumption were true that the limit to population is a shortage of food, man's numbers would be increasing fastest in areas where food is most abundant, but this is not the case. No human population lives merely to eat.

Actually, the main cause of death rates in the past has been not scarcity of food but the prevalence of disease. The unprecedented population growth of recent decades has been due chiefly to the control of infectious diseases. It is unrealistic to calculate the "carrying capacity" of the earth as a way of finding an "ultimate limit" to population growth.

All such ideas focus too exclusively on the death rate. They assume that growth will be limited, if it is limited at all, by some death-dealing agency such as starvation, disease or war. But human beings, unlike other animals, can voluntarily control their population growth by limiting their reproduction. They have already demonstrated this capacity in industrial societies.

We are thus living in the key period of a new demographic revolution. The first step in this change was the drastic decline of death rates all over the world, especially in nonindustrial areas, brought on by twentieth-century science. The decline, still going on, has not come automatically, but has been achieved by a vast and costly international effort. As a consequence of the decline, the high birth rates once needed to offset the death rates are no longer necessary. Yet in nonindustrial and some industrial areas high birth rates continue.

They continue in part because it takes time for parents to realize the new hardships resulting from excessive family size, but in the main because no effort remotely comparable to the public health effort has been made to help parents reduce their reproduction. Our tax dollars go generously to help control malaria, bilharzia, yaws, dietary deficiency and a hundred other ills throughout the world, but virtually none go to protect the people of under-developed areas from the appalling effect of this beneficient work—overpopulation.

A vital issue of our time is the next step in the new demographic revolution. Will world leadership make an attempt to control births as well as deaths? Will the frantic multiplication of people be reduced by planned effort rather than by possible catastrophe?

So far, official thinking in the West about this matter has been dominated by obscurantist attitudes dating from the Middle Ages, when death rates were high. Most of the so-called "theories of population" unconsciously distract attention from the main problem because they assume that reproduction must go blindly on.

We therefore find some of the advanced nations, where birth control is practiced—for instance, Belgium, the United States and the Soviet Union—officially uncooperative on this subject in their dealings with the under-developed nations. The latter, however, are beginning to show themselves to be less superstitious. Some of them (Japan, China, India, Mauritius, Puerto Rico) are going ahead on their own with birth-limitation programs.

With the U.N. projections showing starkly what lies ahead unless action is taken, a policy of intransigence in this matter seems hard to justify. It is inhumane to have impoverished populations growing so fast that their economic development is hindered. It is shortsighted, in a world increasingly dependent on science, to have the bulk of the next generation reared in regions that cannot afford even an elementary education. It encourages parasitism to give economic aid and migratory opportunities to peoples who are irresponsible about such an important matter as reproduction.

It remains to be said that excessive population growth seems to intensify the struggle for scarce raw materials, to build up explosive migration pressures and to encourage *lebensraum* wars, and that communism is making its greatest conquests precisely in the impoverished and crowded countries. Thus the leading nations of the West might well consider giving every encouragement, including money, to foreign countries in their efforts to control fertility, simultaneously setting an example by officially encouraging birth control at home.

B. Processes and Ingredients of Growth

24. STAGES OF GROWTH*

W. W. Rostow

It is possible to identify all societies, in their economic dimensions, as lying within one of five categories: the traditional society, the preconditions for take-off, the take-off, the drive to maturity, and the age of high mass-consumption.

* W. W. Rostow, *The Stages of Economic Growth* (Cambridge: Cambridge University Press, 1960), pp. 4–12.

THE TRADITIONAL SOCIETY

First, the traditional society. A traditional society is one whose structure is developed within limited production functions, based on pre-Newtonian science and technology, and on pre-Newtonian attitudes towards the physical world. Newton is here used as a symbol for that watershed in history when men came widely to believe that the external world was subject to a few knowable laws, and was systematically capable of productive manipulation.

The conception of the traditional society is, however, in no sense static; and it would not exclude increases in output. Acreage could be expanded; some *ad hoc* technical innovations, often highly productive innovations, could be introduced in trade, industry and agriculture; productivity could rise with, for example, the improvement of irrigation works or the discovery and diffusion of a new crop. But the central fact about the traditional society was that a ceiling existed on the level of attainable output per head. This ceiling resulted from the fact that the potentialities which flow from modern science and technology were either not available or not regularly and systematically applied.

Both in the longer past and in recent times the story of traditional societies was thus a story of endless change. The area and volume of trade within them and between them fluctuated, for example, with the degree of political and social turbulence, the efficiency of central rule, the upkeep of the roads. Population—and, within limits, the level of life—rose and fell not only with the sequence of the harvests, but with the incidence of war and of plague. Varying degrees of manufacture developed; but, as in agriculture, the level of productivity was limited by the inaccessibility of modern science, its applications, and its frame of mind.

Generally speaking, these societies, because of the limitation on productivity, had to devote a very high proportion of their resources to agriculture; and flowing from the agricultural system there was an hierarchical social structure, with relatively narrow scope—but some scope—for vertical mobility. Family and clan connexions played a large role in social organization. The value system of these societies was generally geared to what might be called a long-run fatalism; that is, the assumption that the range of possibilities open to one's grandchildren would be just about what it had been for one's grandparents. But this long-run fatalism by no means excluded the short-run option that, within a considerable range, it was possible and legitimate for the individual to strive to improve his lot, within his lifetime. In Chinese villages, for example, there was an endless struggle to acquire or to avoid losing land, yielding a situation where land rarely remained within the same family for a century.

Although central political rule—in one form or another—often existed in traditional societies, transcending the relatively self-sufficient regions, the centre of gravity of political power generally lay in the regions, in the hands of those who owned or controlled the land. The landowner maintained fluctuating but usually profound influence over such central political power as existed, backed by its entourage of civil servants and soldiers, imbued with attitudes and controlled by interests transcending the regions.

In terms of history then, with the phrase 'traditional society' we are grouping the whole pre-Newtonian world: the dynasties in China; the civilization of the Middle East and the Mediterranean; the world of medieval Europe. And to them we add the post-Newtonian societies which, for a time, remained untouched or unmoved by man's new capability for regularly manipulating his environment to his economic advantage.

To place these infinitely various, changing societies in a single category, on the ground that they all shared a ceiling on the productivity of their economic techniques, is to say very little indeed. But we are, after all, merely clearing the way in order to get at the subject of this book; that is, the post-traditional societies, in which each of the major characteristics of the traditional society was altered in such ways as to permit regular growth: its politics, social structure, and (to a degree) its values, as well as its economy.

THE PRECONDITIONS FOR TAKE-OFF

The second stage of growth embraces societies in the process of transition; that is, the period when the preconditions for take-off are developed; for it takes time to transform a traditional society in the ways necessary for it to exploit the fruits of modern science, to fend off diminishing returns, and thus to enjoy the blessings and choices opened up by the march of compound interest.

The preconditions for take-off were initially developed, in a clearly marked way, in Western Europe of the late seventeenth and early eighteenth centuries as the insights of modern science began to be translated into new production functions in both agriculture and industry, in a setting given dynamism by the lateral expansion of world markets and the international competition for them. But all that lies behind the break-up of the Middle Ages is relevant to the creation of the preconditions for take-off in Western Europe. Among the Western European states, Britain, favoured by geography, natural resources, trading possibilities, social and political structure, was the first to develop fully the preconditions for take-off.

The more general case in modern history, however, saw the stage of preconditions arise not endogenously but from some external intrusion by more advanced societies. These invasions—literal or figurative—shocked the traditional society and began or hastened its undoing; but they also set in motion ideas and sentiments which initiated the process by which a modern alternative to the traditional society was constructed out of the old culture.

The idea spreads not merely that economic progress is possible, but that economic progress is a necessary condition for some other purpose, judged to be good: be it national dignity, private profit, the general welfare, or a better life for the children. Education, for some at least, broadens and changes to suit the needs of modern economic activity. New types of enterprising men come forward—in the private economy, in government, or both—willing to mobilize savings and to take risks in pursuit of profit or modernization. Banks and other institutions for mobilizing capital appear. Investment increases, notably in transport, communications, and in raw materials in which other nations may have an economic interest. The scope of commerce, internal and external, widens. And, here and there, modern manufacturing enterprise appears, using the new methods. But all this activity proceeds at a limited pace within an economy and a society still mainly characterized by traditional low-productivity methods, by the old social structure and values, and by the regionally based political institutions that developed in conjunction with them.

In many recent cases, for example, the traditional society persisted side by side with modern economic activities, conducted for limited economic purposes by a colonial or quasi-colonial power.

Although the period of transition—between the traditional society and the take-off—saw major changes in both the economy itself and in the balance of social values, a decisive feature was often political. Politically, the building of an effective centralized national state—on the basis of coalitions touched with a new nationalism, in opposition to the traditional landed regional interests, the colonial power, or both, was a decisive aspect of the preconditions period; and it was, almost universally, a necessary condition for take-off.

. . . . .

THE TAKE-OFF

We come now to the great watershed in the life of modern societies: the third stage in this sequence, the take-off. The take-off is the interval when the old blocks and resistances to steady growth are finally overcome. The forces making for economic progress, which yielded limited bursts and enclaves of modern activity, expand and come to dominate the society. Growth becomes its normal condition. Compound interest becomes built, as it were, into its habits and institutional structure.

In Britain and the well-endowed parts of the world populated substantially from Britain (the United States, Canada etc.) the proximate stimulus for take-off was mainly (but not wholly) technological. In the more general case, the take-off awaited not only the build-up of social overhead capital and a surge of technological development in industry and agriculture, but also the emergence to political power of a group prepared to regard the modernization of the economy as serious, high-order political business.

During the take-off, the rate of effective investment and savings may rise from, say, 5% of the national income to 10% or more; although where heavy social overhead capital investment was required to create the technical preconditions for take-off the investment rate in the preconditions period could be higher than 5%, as, for example, in Canada before the 1890's and Argentina before 1914. In such cases capital imports usually formed a high proportion of total investment in the preconditions period and sometimes even during the take-off itself, as in Russia and Canada during their pre-1914 railway booms.

During the take-off new industries expand rapidly, yielding profits a large proportion of which are reinvested in new plant; and these new industries, in turn, stimulate, through their rapidly expanding requirement for factory workers, the services to support them, and for other manufactured goods, a further expansion in urban areas and in other modern industrial plants. The whole process of expansion in the modern sector yields an increase of income in the hands of those who not only save at high rates but place their savings at the disposal of those engaged in modern sector activities. The new class of entrepreneurs expands; and it directs the enlarging flows of investment in the private sector. The economy exploits hitherto unused natural resources and methods of production.

New techniques spread in agriculture as well as industry, as agriculture is commercialized, and increasing numbers of farmers are prepared to accept the new methods and the deep changes they bring to ways of life. The revolutionary changes in agricultural productivity are an essential condition for successful take-off; for modernization of a society increases radically its bill for agricultural products. In a decade or two both the basic structure of the economy and the social and political structure of the society are transformed in such a way that a steady rate of growth can be, thereafter, regularly sustained.

. . . , one can approximately allocate the take-off of Britain to the two decades after 1783; France and the United States to the several decades preceding 1860; Germany, the third quarter of the nineteenth century; Japan, the fourth quarter of the nineteenth century; Russia and Canada the quarter-century or so preceding 1914; while during the 1950's India and China have, in quite different ways, launched their respective take-offs.

THE DRIVE TO MATURITY

After take-off there follows a long interval of sustained if fluctuating progress, as the now regularly growing economy drives to extend modern technology over the whole front of its economic activity. Some 10–20% of the national income is steadily invested, permitting output regularly to outstrip the increase in population. The make-up of the economy changes unceasingly as technique improves, new industries accelerate, older industries level off. The economy finds its place in the international economy: goods formerly imported are produced at home; new import requirements develop, and new export commodities to match them. The society makes such terms as it will with the requirements of modern efficient production, balancing off the new against the older values and institutions, or revising the latter in such ways as to support rather than to retard the growth process.

Some sixty years after take-off begins (say, forty years after the end of take-off) what may be called maturity is generally attained. The economy, focused during the take-off around a relatively narrow complex of industry and technology, has extended its range into more refined and technologically often more complex processes; for example, there may be a shift in focus from the coal, iron, and heavy engineering industries of the railway phase to machine-tools, chemicals, and electrical equipment. This, for example, was the transition through which Germany, Britain, France, and the United States had passed by the end of the nineteenth century or shortly thereafter. . . .

Formally, we can define maturity as the stage in which an economy demonstrates the capacity to move beyond the original industries which powered its take-off and to absorb and to apply efficiently over a very wide range of its resources—if not the whole range—the most advanced fruits of (then) modern technology. This is the stage in which an economy demonstrates that it has the technological and entrepreneurial skills to produce not everything, but anything that it chooses to produce. It may lack (like contemporary Sweden and Switzerland, for example) the raw materials or other supply conditions required to produce a given type of output economically; but its dependence is a matter of economic choice or political priority rather than a technological or institutional necessity.

Historically, it would appear that something like sixty years was required to move a society from the beginning of take-off to maturity. Analytically the explanation for some such interval may lie in the powerful arithmetic of compound interest applied to the capital stock, combined with the broader consequences for a society's ability to absorb modern technology of three successive generations living under a regime where growth is the normal condition. But, clearly, no dogmatism is justified about the exact length of the interval from take-off to maturity.

THE AGE OF HIGH MASS-CONSUMPTION

We come now to the age of high mass-consumption, where, in time, the leading sectors shift towards durable consumers' goods and services: a phase from which Americans are beginning to emerge; whose not unequivocal joys Western Europe and Japan are beginning energetically to probe; and with which Soviet society is engaged in an uneasy flirtation.

As societies achieved maturity in the twentieth century two things happened: real income per head rose to a point where a large number of persons gained a command over consumption which transcended basic food, shelter, and clothing; and the structure of the working force changed in ways which increased not only the proportion of urban to total population, but also the proportion of the population working in offices or in skilled factory jobs—aware of and anxious to acquire the consumption fruits of a mature economy.

In addition to these economic changes, the society ceased to accept the further extension of modern technology as an overriding objective. It is in this post-maturity stage, for example, that, through the political process, Western societies have chosen to allocate increased resources to social welfare and security. The emergence of the welfare state is one manifestation of a society's moving beyond technical maturity; but it is also at this stage that resources tend increasingly to be directed to the production of consumers' durables and to the diffusion of services on a mass basis, if consumers' sovereignty reigns. The sewing-machine, the bicycle, and then the various electric-powered household gadgets were gradually diffused. Historically, however, the decisive element has been the cheap mass automobile with its quite revolutionary effects—social as well as economic—on the life and expectations of society.

For the United States, the turning point was, perhaps, Henry Ford's moving assembly line of 1913–14; but it was in the 1920's, and again in the post-war decade, 1946–56, that this stage of growth was pressed to, virtually, its logical conclusion. In the 1950's Western Europe and Japan appear to have fully entered this phase, accounting substantially for a momentum in their economies quite unexpected in the immediate post-war years. The Soviet Union is technically ready for this stage, and, by every sign, its citizens hunger for it; but Communist leaders face difficult political and social problems of adjustment if this stage is launched.

BEYOND CONSUMPTION

Beyond, it is impossible to predict, except perhaps to observe that Americans, at least, have behaved in the past decade as if diminishing relative marginal utility sets in, after a point, for durable consumers' goods; and they have chosen, at the margin, larger families—behaviour in the pattern of Buddenbrooks dynamics. Americans have behaved as if, having been born into a system that provided economic security and high mass-consumption, they placed a lower valuation on acquiring additional increments of real income in the conventional form as opposed to the advantages and values of an enlarged family. But even in this adventure in generalization it is a shade too soon to create—on the basis of one case—a new stage-of-growth, based on babies, in succession to the age of consumers' durables: as economists might say, the income-elasticity of demand for babies may well vary from society to society. But it is true that the implications of the baby boom along with the not wholly unrelated deficit in social overhead capital are likely to dominate the American economy over the next decade rather than the further diffusion of consumers' durables.

25. CAPITAL AND HUMAN RESOURCES*

Frederick Harbison

THE ASPIRATION TO INDUSTRIALIZE

If in history the twentieth century may be recognized as the Century of Science, it may also be characterized as an era of high expectations. Peoples and their leaders in all parts of the world are rejecting the notion that disease, squalor and poverty are predestined conditions of earthy existence. In the age of the radio and the airplane, communication is rapid and easy. Even in the most remote lands, people have heard of the great industrial progress of America and the more recent rapid development of Russia. They have seen what modern medicine and science can do to alleviate human misery in their native villages. They feel that a better life is possible, and, more important, they are beginning to expect that it may be achieved. Indeed, there is in progress a world-wide revolution which is more basic and universal than the French, the American, or the Russian revolutions. This new global upheaval is the revolution of rising aspirations.

A major manifestation of this global revolution is the quest for rapid industrialization. Because machine production is so superior to handicraft output, people think that industrialization holds the magic key to rising living standards and the better way of life. It is thought to be the means for rapid transformation of primitive agricultural and commercial societies into highly developed economies. The industrialized society is fast becoming a world-wide cultural norm.

The pressures to industrialize are both economic and political. In many countries, such as for example India and Egypt, population is increasing with alarming speed because death rates have been falling

* J. Douglas Brown and Frederick Harbison, *High-Talent Manpower for Science and Industry* (Princeton, N.J.: Industrial Relations Section, Princeton University, 1957), pp. 63–77.

while birth rates have remained constant. In such countries, substantial economic growth is critically needed even to keep living standards from falling, and rapid development with extensive industrialization is required if there is to be any long-run improvement in the economic welfare of the people. Industrialization, moreover, has become a universal index of national prestige and political independence. In the twentieth century, steel mills, dams and modern factories have replaced temples and pyramids as the outward symbols of national grandeur.

Thus, underdeveloped countries such as Egypt, India, Iraq, Turkey, and many other nations in Africa, Asia, and South America are committing themselves to very ambitious programs of industrial development. As peoples' aspirations outstrip the means of production and as new nationalist leaders hold out the prospect of a better life to the masses, these countries hope and expect to achieve a rate of economic growth which far exceeds that of the western capitalist countries in the past hundred years. In their rush to industrialize, the underdeveloped countries appear determined to run before they learn to walk.

In many respects the late-comers to industrialization are fortunate. If they are able to find the capital, they have access to advanced technology and machinery which the more advanced countries have taken decades or even centuries to develop. For example, it is possible for the latecomer to purchase a completely modern steel mill, a spanking new textile factory or an artificial fertilizer plant from countries such as England, Germany, Russia, Japan, or the United States. Or the late-comer may simply invite foreign interests to explore, exploit, and market its natural resources as in the case of petroleum development in the South American and Middle Eastern countries. The fruits of years of scientific progress are available to all who develop the capacity to consume them, and thus the initial industrialization of the underdeveloped countries need not wait upon new discoveries nor the development of an indigenous technology. For this reason, industrialization appears on the surface to offer not only a desirable but also an easy road to economic progress.

But, industrialization by forced marches is a painful process. Except in rare cases, consumption must be restricted in order to satisfy the insatiable appetite of economic progress for capital. The shift from agricultural and tribal ways of living to industrial employment is, in itself, a disrupting process, and the more rapid the transition, the more painful that process is likely to be.

The underdeveloped countries are thus faced with a dilemma. If they industrialize very rapidly, they must make painful sacrifices in the short run; if they industrialize too slowly, the living standards of their people will be depressed in the long run. If they are bent on rapid industrialization, they may be tempted to adopt the method of totalitarian regimentation, following the example of Russia or more recently of Communist China. If they stress welfare and human values, their rate of growth may not keep pace with increasing population. Here lies a great challenge to the free world: Can the means be found to enable the underdeveloped countries to industrialize with adequate speed without sacrificing human values and political democracy on the altar of economic progress?

There are many factors which bear upon a country's potential for industrial development. The availability of natural resources, the ability to attract and to accumulate capital, the creation of a stable government, and the availability of labor are all important. Yet in many respects the really critical factor is that of attracting, accumulating, and developing the high-level human resources which modern industrialization unconditionally demands.

The objective of this essay is to analyze the problems which the newly industrializing countries face in developing high-level manpower and to suggest policies which may be effective in solving them. In so doing, the assumption is made that these countries are committed to rapid industrialization as a means of economic development, and thus the question of the economic or social desirability of this course of development lies beyond the scope of this inquiry.

SOME UNDERLYING PROPOSITIONS

The analysis and conclusions which follow rest upon a series of propositions, or first approximate generalizations, which have been formulated on the basis of preliminary research on the scope and nature of manpower problems connected with the industrialization of underdeveloped countries. These propositions cannot be advanced at this time as definitive conclusions resulting from exhaustive inquiry; they are in some degree based upon impressions rather than systematic research; yet they provide a reasonably plausible framework for analyzing the human problems in economic development on the basis of the best information which is currently available.

The first proposition is that most underdeveloped countries, for both economic and political reasons, will attempt to base their industrialization on modern plants and advanced processes and machinery. This proposition may be supported on both logical and empirical grounds.

As already indicated, the most modern technology and machinery which the advanced countries have taken decades to develop is available to the late-comers to industrialization. The underdeveloped countries can purchase equipment and even entire plants from the already industrialized countries. For example, India is getting new steel plants from the United States and also from the Soviet Union. The machinery for most of the textile mills in Peru came from England. Egypt has imported an entire synthetic fertilizer plant from the United States, and she has purchased a basic steel works from Germany.

A typical example of the use of modern technology in an industrializing country is provided by the Misr textile enterprises in Egypt. The large Egyptian mills are among the most up-to-date if not the most modern in the world. Furthermore, they are equipped with the most advanced labor-saving machinery that money can buy. On the surface, this kind of development is hard to explain in a country where capital is so scarce and where labor is so cheap and plentiful. Outsiders, moreover, are amazed to learn that the Egyptian textile companies were able to get a law passed which prohibits the importation of used machinery, and they would also find it hard to believe that the Misr companies always scrap and never sell their obsolete machines. But Misr Group executives are of one mind on the importance of investing in modern machinery; their reasoning runs as follows:

First, the most modern machinery is necessary for the production of cotton goods of very fine quality. In foreign markets, Egypt's comparative advantage lies in the manufacture of fine yarns and fine woven cotton goods because her cotton is of the long and extra-long staple variety. In order to earn more foreign exchange for the country, the Misr cotton textile plants have been shifting their production from coarse to fine counts. The argument is that fine yarn and cloth are not so much the result of expert labor as of modern machinery. As a managing director explained, "It is hands that spoil the product; if we can eliminate the handling of goods by workers, we can increase our production and improve our quality."

Second, if Egypt is to meet foreign competition, costs must be kept down. To bolster this argument Misr executives point out that labor costs constitute only 20 per cent of total production costs, whereas raw materials amount to over 60 per cent. A main advantage of modern machinery is that it substantially reduces waste of raw materials. These savings are said to be greater than the savings on labor. In the long run, so the argument goes, the competitive struggle for markets will be influenced more by the ability of manufacturers to install modern machinery than by their ability to substitute cheap labor for capital investments.

There are other explanations for the emphasis in Egypt on modern machinery which, though not openly stated, can be easily implied. The engineers and managers have received at home and abroad primarily technical education. Very few have studied the economics of production and even fewer have studied administration. As technicians they naturally want to buy the latest and best machinery which can be procured in any country. Another more fundamental explanation is connected with the desire of management and the government for international prestige. Modern plants run by Egyptians are a symbol of the country's capacity to industrialize. As the founder of the Misr industries, Talaat Harb Pasha, had preached many years before, industrialization is a necessary prerequisite of economic and political independence. The heads of the Misr companies are concerned with more than profits. They are as much if not more interested in acquiring status and commanding prestige for their contributions to the country's economic development.

The second proposition is that industries requiring large capital investments appear to require a correspondingly large investment in managerial and supervisory resources. Or, put in a different way, the greater the expenditures for modern equipment and machinery, the greater is the proportionate need for highly trained people in the labor force.

This proposition is quite easy to support on logical grounds. Large investments in machinery and processes are usually associated with relatively large enterprises. A large enterprise, being more complex than a small one, naturally requires more and better trained managerial resources. Also, if the machinery and processes themselves are complicated, engineers, chemists, or other technical staff specialists are required. To the extent that machinery may displace unskilled or skilled labor, it usually requires greater investment in personnel who specialize in planning, production scheduling, engineering, and "control" of all kinds. Thus an additional cost involved in investment in modern processes or labor-saving machinery is that of procuring and developing the managerial resources necessary to utilize and to control it. If a business organization must employ a battery of technicians to supervise and control more complicated processes, there is also need for more experienced and expensive top management to coordinate their activities and to plan for future development.

On empirical grounds, this relationship can be illustrated by a rough comparison which we have made of steel mills in Germany, the United Kingdom, and the United States. The first comparison was made between a German and an American company, each producing a roughly comparable range of productions and employing approximately the same total personnel (between 17,000 and 18,000 men). In comparison with the American company, the German enterprise had quite old machinery and processes which were in most respects inferior to that in the American company. Largely for this reason, the total annual production of the German company was only half that of its American counterpart.

The contrast in investment in managerial resources between the two companies was quite evident. In comparable steel making and rolling departments, the American company used three foremen to every one in the German mill, and the educational level of the American foremen was in practically all cases much superior to that of the German foremen. In the German plant a greater burden of supervision was placed upon the group leader, an experienced skilled workman, whereas in the American company the supervisory functions were performed by fulltime salaried foremen who were members of management. Some of the American foremen had master's degrees and 15 per cent had college degrees, but none of the German foremen had any equivalent higher education. In the States, moreover, foremen quite frequently advanced into the upper ranks of management; in Germany, the position of foreman is generally the highest step in the ladder of promotion for workers; only on rare occasions do the German foremen become members of middle or upper management. An even more striking contrast existed with respect to senior technical staff which comprises persons such as process engineers, chemists, specialists in industrial engineering, personnel, production control, and quality control. Here the American company employed 430 persons as compared with only 43 in the German enterprise. It was obvious that the top managers and the superintendent in the States had a great many highly trained assistants to perform technical work. In Germany, the members of top and middle management did most of the technical work themselves. For this reason, a much higher proportion of the managers and superintendents in the German company were themselves highly trained engineers, whereas many of their counterparts in the American company had either no formal technical training or perhaps merely a liberal arts college education.

The management spokesmen of the German company, who had visited the American mill and thus were familiar with its equipment and processes, pointed out that the "greater depth" in managerial organization in America was largely attributable to the greater investment in machinery and processes, and that as the German company embarked upon its program of modernization of equipment, it would be necessary to recruit and develop many more foremen and senior technical staff specialists. The German company also pointed out that its current investment in foremen and staff specialists was almost twice as large as twenty years ago when even older processes and more primitive machinery were used.

This steel mill comparison, though it is admittedly suggestive rather than conclusive, indicates that there may be a direct and positive relationship between investment in technology and investment in organization. We have noticed the same general relationships in the other companies with which we are acquainted. A thin managerial organization is usually associated with relatively extensive utilization of non-managerial labor forces and relatively primitive production methods, whereas a relatively deep managerial organization is almost always found in enterprises which have the largest investment in technology, particularly in labor-saving machinery.

A third proposition is that managerial resources are probably the principal element determining the productivity of labor, assuming that capital and natural resources are constant. A labor force is recruited, trained, developed, and managed by the managerial organization, and the skills and qualities of manpower probably depend more on what the management does than on any natural or innate characteristics of labor itself. This proposition, like the previous ones, seems to be plausible on both logical and empirical grounds.

An essential management function is the selection, training, and development of the persons comprising the labor force. Most, though not all, skills of manual labor and even clerical employees are acquired on the job. Another management function is to provide the incentive for work. To these functions we can add many more which directly affect the productivity of labor; proper lay-out of machinery and processes, work study, breakdown of jobs in order to economize on use of critical skills, safety programs, systems for appraising performance and discovering talent, and many other related techniques. Such techniques of "scientific management," however, are expensive. They require the employment of specialized personnel and investment of time on the part of members of the line organization. Even more important, they require relatively high levels of education, experience, and training among the members of the managerial organization.

In some respects, of course, the efficiency of labor resources may be independent of the organization which employs them. The more important factors here may be levels of education, conditions of health, nutrition, and general experience with and attitudes toward work. The organization, however, is able to influence these factors, at least in part. Attitudes toward work can be molded by management; companies can provide medical services and adequate diets for employees; and some firms in underdeveloped countries even provide facilities for general education of members of the labor force. In the industrially advanced countries, of course, the laboring population may be generally more efficient because of long tradition and previous experience with industrial enterprises, and the development of high labor productivity in a primitive society may thus require a much higher investment in managerial resources than in countries with a long industrial tradition. In short, one cannot deny that some innate factors have influence on the quality of labor resources; the main contention is simply that *the management which employs labor* is probably the principal factor—the dominant force—in determining labor productivity with constant technology.

This contention has been fortified by observations of the utilization of labor resources in different enterprises. For example, in Egypt, the productivity of labor is very low, even in factories which technologically may be among the most modern in the world. In the best Egyptian factories four to six workers may be employed for every one in comparable establishments in the United States. But, managerial resources are scarce and managerial methods are quite primitive. Although there is an impressive awakening to the need for improvement of management on the part of progressive Egyptian enterprises, systematic procedures of selection and training operatives are not yet used. Programs for training and development of supervisors or middle management in the skills of handling people are almost non-existent. Time and motion study, job evaluation, and other techniques for the systematic combination of labor with processes are still quite rare. The explanation for this "thinness of management" is obvious. First, labor is plentiful and cheap, so that there is no pressure to make a large investment in organization in order to economize in the utilization of labor; second, specialists in techniques of scientific management are scarce, if they exist at all; and finally, the general level of existing managerial resources is not yet sufficiently high to utilize effectively modern techniques of manpower utilization.

Another convincing bit of evidence showing the relationship of labor productivity to organization is the "spotty" work performance which is evident in most factories, and particularly in those in the less developed countries. One frequently observes a very slow pace of work in most departments of a factory, whereas in one or two departments the work pace may be very high. In observing some teams of Egyptian workers on packaging operations, one may find instances where rhythm and speed of work is equal to that in the best American factories, this being all the more remarkable because they are employed in factories with unusually poor labor productivity as a whole. The explanation for these spotty examples of labor efficiency lies in the peculiar or rare skills of the individuals planning or supervising these particular departments. The same spottiness also is apparent when one compares different factories in the same labor market. This evidence, of course, is suggestive rather than conclusive. Nevertheless, it leads to a strong presumption that the productivity of labor may be primarily a function of the effectiveness of the managerial organization.

The fourth proposition is that rapid industrialization and rising living standards are more likely to contribute to social and political instability than to happiness and harmony in the developing country. Industrialization raises the aspirations of workers, and at the same time it gives them greater reason to speak out against things which annoy them. Because industrialization requires in most cases the disintegration of traditional social systems and the imposition of new structures of working relationships, it is likely to lead to instability and widespread discontent, particularly in the early stages of development.

As people get more, they want more. According to an old saying, "an adequate standard of living for any person is usually thought by him to be about 25 per cent more than he has." As the standard of living of industrial workers is raised, their needs and aspirations also rise. The following experience of a Middle East oil company may be typical of almost any industrial enterprise which does a good job of developing its labor force.

This company has had notable success in selecting, training and committing an indigenous labor force for its far-flung installations. By any previous standards, the workers have enjoyed pay, housing, food, and medical care which are excellent. Their standard of living as compared with that of their fellow-countrymen is extremely high, as is their level of training and education. There is no evidence, however, that these workers are happier than their half-starved fellow Arabs who have not become industrial workers. The problems of the oil workers are reflected in the kinds of grievances they present to management. Here are some of their demands.

1. Wage increases and housing conditions more nearly equal to those of the expatriate personnel (with air-conditioning and other improvements).
2. Two days off before annual vacations to prepare for vacation and two additional days at the end of vacation to prepare to return to work.
3. Training on company time for everyone requesting such training. (The company had, of course, always contended that training was a prerequisite to advancement on the job. The demand for free training as a *right* for all workers, however, was somewhat embarrassing!)
4. Promotion of more Arabs to higher positions in the company.
5. Recognition of employee representatives for purposes of negotiation of terms of employment.

Obviously, such demands are not those of poverty-stricken and destitute labor. They reflect the aspirations of workmen who are becoming accustomed to high living standards.

An even more striking example of the effect of progress on aspirations is the case of Kuwait. Because of oil, Kuwait is now probably the richest country in the world, in terms of income per head of native population. The Sheiks of Kuwait, moreover, have invested the greater part of their revenues from oil in the country. In this tiny hot desert Sheikdom of less than 200,000 people, there are over fifty magnificent new schools, ranging from kindergartens to a technical institute. There are modern hospitals and health centers which provide complete medical care for everyone free of charge. Around the town of Kuwait are dual highways and new apartment buildings. This phenomenal and almost unique economic progress has taken place entirely within two decades, most of it in fact within the past six or seven years. From all outward appearances, Kuwait is an economic Utopia. Nevertheless, the Kuwaiti, now that they are getting education, are beginning to press for constitutional government despite the most benevolent policies of the Sheiks. They want more and better housing as a matter of right. They want more automobiles delivered more quickly and more cheaply. They want better air-conditioning equipment, a better water supply, and more dual highways. With all this, they are beginning to question the extent to which the Ruler should exercise unilateral authority over their lives.

It is clear that the more rapidly a country progresses, the greater are the aspirations of its people. Industrial development requires educational development; both demand changes in pre-existing attitudes, customs and folkways. Neither are opiates for the people; on the contrary, they are strong stimulants of men's desire for more.

At the same time, industrialization creates hardships, grievances, and widespread discontent. It requires a new structuring of the labor force. Factory organization establishes new physical surroundings, new methods and codes of discipline, new working arrangements and social groups. The manager replaces the head of the family or the leader of the tribe as the source of authority. The transition from agricultural work to industrial employment is difficult, and it is all the more painful if it is rapid. Thus, industrial workers everywhere have grievances. In particular, they chafe at the exercise of managerial authority over their day-to-day lives. In some cases they harbor deep resentment and experience extreme frustration. In short, among industrial workers there is always open or latent protest. The feeling of protest is partly negative, stemming from resentment of authority or dissatisfaction with conditions, and partly positive, stemming from aspirations. But irrespective of its causes, it is present among factory workers in all countries whether developed or underdeveloped.

The clear inference to be drawn here is that successful industrialization of presently underdeveloped countries will depend not alone on technological skill but also upon managerial ability to deal effectively with the problems of workers. Indeed, the development of administrative and organizational skills is in many respects the most baffling problem facing these countries today. The really important question is whether industrialization is spearheaded by authoritarian measures which subjugate workers to new and more harsh systems of subordination or whether it is achieved in a manner that will enhance the dignity, worth and freedom of human beings.

THE DEVELOPMENT OF STRATEGIC HUMAN RESOURCES

On the basis of the propositions set forth above, the problems which the underdeveloped countries face as they industrialize are quite apparent. They will be impelled for political as well as economic reasons to utilize modern machinery and techniques in their factories. They will need to build roads, railways, airports, power plants, dams, and irrigation systems. This kind of development requires the accumulation of large amounts of capital. It likewise necessitates intensive generation and accumulation of highly trained human resources, for in the underdeveloped countries the shortage of ability is usually just as acute if not more critical than the shortage of capital. Unless a country can develop the high-level human resources which modern industrialization unconditionally demands, it simply will not be able to utilize the funds which may be forthcoming for its development. In all of the presently underdeveloped countries, therefore, the scarcity of strategic human resources is likely to be at one time or another the limiting factor in economic growth.

The strategic human resources for industrial development include entrepreneurs, administrators, managers, scientists, engineers, and other technical personnel. Depending upon the political and economic systems of particular countries, such persons may be employed by the state, by private enterprise, or by quasi-governmental enterprise. In all societies they constitute only a small minority of the population, but they are the agents and the prime movers of industrialization. They are the pregnant minority which bears the seeds of industrial society. . . . They are the "seed-corn" of economic progress.

Thus, the core of the manpower problem in the industrializing countries is the development of these strategic, "seed-corn" resources. As pointed out earlier, the upgrading of the masses into a skilled and productive labor force is dependent in large measure upon the effectiveness of managerial and professional personnel. If the "seed-corn" is of high quality, then the means will be found readily to build the proper kind of industrial labor force. But the generation of "seed-corn" talent, like the building of dams, electric power plants, roads, and modern factories, is a time-consuming process. It calls for long-range forward planning, and in countries with limited resources, it may require that priority be given to intensive training of a strategic minority even at the expense of partial or temporary postponement of general education of the masses. . . .

26. NONECONOMIC FACTORS*

Benjamin Higgins

POLITICAL FACTORS

Political as well as economic factors combined to create an atmosphere conducive to economic development of the Western world in the eighteenth and nineteenth centuries. These favorable factors may be divided into two main categories: the politics of the technically superior country during the period and the politics of the relatively underdeveloped areas at the same time.

Politics of Technically Superior Countries

During the eighteenth century, economic development was largely a matter of developing new industries and areas within the geographic area subject to control by the government concerned. The political ad-

* Reprinted from *Economic Development* by Benjamin Higgins. By permission of W. W. Norton & Company, Inc., New York, 1959, pp. 249–62.

vantages of this sort of development are too obvious to need stressing here. It will be more fruitful to compare the politics of the technically superior countries during the nineteenth century, when the United States, Canada, Australia, and the New World generally enjoyed rapid growth, with the politics of the technically superior countries today. During the eighteenth and nineteenth centuries, the technically superior countries were the United Kingdom, France, Holland, and Germany. For our purposes, however, we can concentrate our attention on the United Kingdom, as the dominant power in that period. Similarly, the technically superior countries today are the United States and Canada, and possibly Australia, Switzerland, Sweden, Germany, France, and Russia; but we can usefully concentrate on the policies of the United States because of its overwhelming importance in the world economy.

Let us first consider foreign trade policy. During most of the period under consideration, the United Kingdom followed a policy of free trade. There were, of course, good reasons for this policy line. The United Kingdom enjoyed virtually a monopoly position with respect to the sale of its manufactured goods, and a monopsony position in the purchase abroad of agricultural raw materials and foodstuffs. Perhaps because its monopoly-and-monopsony position is somewhat less secure, the United States has followed a high tariff policy rather than a free trade policy. Difficulties in marketing their output of raw materials and foodstuffs, because of the high tariff policy pursued by the United States, operate as a retarding influence on the economic development of the now underdeveloped areas.

The United Kingdom was also a heavy importer. After 1825, its balance of trade in commodities became unfavorable. From 1873 on, its balance of trade in goods and services combined was unfavorable: Great Britain financed its trade deficit from the large amounts of interest and profits earned on its heavy investment abroad. Not only was its balance of trade unfavorable, but the volume of British imports was high relative to national income, probably averaging some 25 per cent. The United States, by contrast, not only has a high tariff but has consistently maintained favorable balances of trade in recent years. Moreover, its imports are a very small fraction of gross national income, averaging less than 5 per cent. Relative to the scale of its own economy and of the present-day world economy, the United States is providing a much less advantageous market for the products of underdeveloped areas, with respect both to the balance and to the volume of trade, and perhaps with respect to the terms of trade as well.

A similar contrast appears with respect to foreign investment. Professor Cairncross has recently estimated that if the United States were to lend abroad on a scale equivalent in terms of *per capita* real income to that of the United Kingdom during the nineteenth century, the United

States would have had in 1952 600 billion dollars of foreign investments, on which it would have earned 30 billion dollars a year. In other terms, to match the flow of capital from the United Kingdom in the nineteenth century, relative to its *per capita* real income, the United States would have to carry out the entire Marshall Plan twice every year! The scale of foreign aid and investment would need to be increased tenfold. There was no "chronic shortage of sterling" during the period of rapid growth of the United States, Canada, and Australia, but there is a "chronic shortage of dollars" today.

It has been suggested that the large scale of British foreign investment in the nineteenth century, although dictated largely by private economic interests, was consistent with domestic government policy. The French Revolution instilled a deep-seated fear in Britian's elite, and a feeling that the masses deserved—or might insist upon—more consideration than they had received in the past. There was, therefore, a wish in high places to obtain cheap food. Frontier developments using British capital made cheaper food possible. Thus apart from the immediate economic interest in developing underdeveloped countries through large-scale foreign investment, there was a more subtle political purpose.

Finally, the technically superior countries were able to enforce stability in underdeveloped areas. Originally the "underdeveloped areas" were within their own borders. Later, colonies assumed paramount importance. Later still, the United States and the Dominions became major recipients of foreign investment. Perhaps it was less easy for the United Kingdom to police investments in the Dominions than in its colonies, and less easy in colonies than within its own borders; but the superior military force of the United Kingdom was one factor in promoting confidence among investors. In the underdeveloped countries today, even slight suggestion that Western powers are trying to exercise physical control may cause serious trouble for foreign investors. In Indonesia in 1952, the technically superior country (the United States) found itself unable even to obtain a Mutual Security Administration agreement which included military aid—a single example of the difficulty the technically superior country faces in dealing with the underdeveloped areas today.

During the nineteenth century the technically superior countries confronted no major political challenge in underdeveloped areas. The United Kingdom, France, Holland, and Germany, might be rivals but they had a common interest in maintaining political stability in underdeveloped areas. Today, one set of powers has a distinct interest in fomenting unrest in those areas. Efforts of the technically superior country to enforce stability may drive underdeveloped countries into the enemy camp. This fact naturally affects the attitudes of potential investors in the technically superior countries, whether private or governmental, toward investment in the now less developed areas.

Politics of Underdeveloped Areas

In sharp contrast to the current situation in underdeveloped areas, in the New World during the eighteenth and nineteenth centuries nationalism seldom took a form antipathetic to foreign capital. Even in the United States, which won its independence from the British Empire through a revolution, nationalist feeling imposed no serious obstacles to a large and continuous flow of British capital into the country. In colonies, and even in areas which were not legally colonies at all, forced labor and expropriation of property played their roles in economic development, as Bronfenbrenner has pointed out.

How different is the current situation in the underdeveloped countries, most of which are now sovereign nations. Far from being able to force labor or expropriate property, the foreign investor is more apt to find himself at the mercy of powerful trade unions backed by government arbitration boards, and threatened with outright expropriation of his property, or import and immigration restrictions, and foreign exchange controls which are tantamount to expropriation. In many underdeveloped countries today, risks of unpredictable and injurious government action, often based on nationalist sentiment, are added to the normal risks attendant upon investment abroad.

Moreover, in the New World of the eighteenth and nineteenth centuries development was undertaken mainly by and with people from the investing countries themselves. As Cairncross has demonstrated, capital and labor flowed together from the Old World to the New. The emigrants who provided the management and the labor force for foreign undertakings spoke the same language and represented the same culture as those providing the capital. This situation naturally led to a higher degree of confidence in foreign investment than can be expected where governments insist on use of nationals of a culture alien to the investor, as they do in many of the present underdeveloped areas. For similar reasons, search for new natural resources by foreign capitalists was more attractive in the New World in the eighteenth and nineteenth centuries than it is in most underdeveloped areas today. Then there were no problems with regard to transfers of profits when earned, or with regard to personal and corporation income taxes, visas for managerial and technical personnel, land leases, and the like. These same conditions facilitated a higher rate of technological progress, since the movement of capital was usually accompanied by a transfer of skills and of technical knowledge.

Another aspect of the internal policies of the underdeveloped areas which is inimical to rapid development is insistence on early introduction of a full-fledged welfare state. In the now advanced countries, the welfare state appeared only after generations of industrialization. In the present underdeveloped areas, the usual policy seems to reverse this process. Most of these countries want the blessings of the welfare state today, complete with old age pensions, unemployment insurance, family allowances, health insurance, forty-hour week, and all the trimmings. Similarly, trade unions became powerful in the now advanced countries only after considerable industrial development had taken place. The statistics are none too good, but it seems likely that the material standard of living of European wage earners *declined* in the first stages of the Industrial Revolution. In terms of actual welfare, industrial slum dwellers in eighteenth-century England were almost certainly worse off than the peasants who were their forebears—and perhaps worse off than the Indonesian *tani* today. Many of the now underdeveloped areas, on the other hand, are encouraging the development of trade unionism in advance of industrialization. In some countries the trade unions, backed by governmental arbitration boards, are demanding higher wages, shorter hours, and "fringe benefits" which do not reflect any commensurate rise in man-hour productivity. Especially where the employer is a foreigner, trade-union members are nationals, and nationalist sentiments run high because of recent release from colonialism, governments are hard put to it to support employers against trade unions, even where economic development is adversely affected by crippling demands. Too few of the trade-union leaders of underdeveloped countries have learned the hard lesson that a higher standard of living for labor as a group requires higher productivity of labor as a group.

Finally, as Hansen has suggested, the fiscal systems of most Western countries in the early stages of industrial development were such as to redistribute income from poor to rich. Taxes consisted almost entirely of customs and excise duties, which fell relatively heavily on the poor, who spent most of their incomes for consumers' goods. Income and inheritance taxes were unknown. Government expenditures, on the other hand, were of a type benefiting mainly the upper-income groups: interest on government bonds, subsidies to private enterprise, transport facilities, and the like. However reprehensible these fiscal systems may have been from the social viewpoint, they added to the flow of savings and investment, and thus accelerated economic development. Most underdeveloped countries today want exactly the opposite kind of fiscal system, with progressive income and inheritance taxes and social security expenditures, designed to improve the distribution of income and wealth. Laudable as these policies are on social grounds, they tend in themselves to reduce the flow of savings and investment and so to retard economic growth.

SOCIOLOGICAL FACTORS

Sociological, as well as economic and political, factors coincided to favor rapid economic growth of the Western world in the eighteenth and nineteenth centuries. There is a whole literature purporting to show how the Reformation raised the propensity to save. The byword of Puritanism was "make what you can, but save what you can." This attitude helped produce a flow of savings sufficient to finance the introduction of new commodities and new techniques brought by the Industrial Revolution. This attitude is lacking in most of the underdeveloped countries today. Not only are these countries poor, so that large volumes of savings entail real sacrifices, but even among the higher-income groups, both the propensity to consume and the propensity to import are high. Especially in urban centers, one sees desire to emulate the Western nations with regard to consumption; hence, unless policy is specifically designed to prevent it, a large share of increases in income tends to be spent on imports. An initial increase in income fails to produce significant increases in savings, and it leads to a deterioration of the balance of payments unless prevented from doing so by policy. Thus, initial increases in income generated by development are likely to be dissipated in higher levels of consumer spending. The people of underdeveloped areas are more eager to consume the goods of the Western world, than they are to duplicate the saving and the quantity and quality of work which have produced the higher standard of living in the West.

A second contrast, which need not be labored for economic historians, is that between present efforts in underdeveloped areas to achieve geographic and occupational shifts on a voluntary basis with the drastic effects of the enclosures in Europe. However painful may have been the social impact of the enclosures, they were a very effective device for moving people out of agriculture into urban industry. The attachment to the village way of life in many of the underdeveloped areas makes it more difficult to achieve the industrialization which is necessary for high standards of living.

Another sociological factor is the difference between incentives in a society organized around the undivided family and those in a society based on the immediate-family unit. The rapid expansion of the European economies in the eighteenth century and of some New World economies in the nineteenth was based on a social system organized around immediate-family units. Whatever the merits or demerits of this system from other points of view, it offered effective economic incentives. The social unit concerned in a choice between income and leisure, between consumption and saving, between more children and a higher living standard, was the social unit that derived the immediate benefit from it. If a man worked overtime for extra pay, his own immediate family benefited from his decision. If he decided to limit his family, he could be reasonably sure that he could provide a better life for the children he did have. If he saved money, it was his own children who benefited from his sacrifice.

In the extended family system prevalent among underdeveloped countries, this consistency between the decision-making social unit and the benefiting social unit does not exist. The man who works harder than others may merely find himself taking care of a larger number of distant relatives, while his own children benefit little from his extra effort. If he limits the number of his own children, he may only be obliged to take care of a larger number of nephews and cousins. His savings may be regarded as at the disposal of the extended family unit as a whole, rather than for his own wife and children alone. Under these conditions, the incentive to work harder or longer, to save, and to practice birth control are obviously much diluted. Either the social organization must change, or the basic choices must be presented in a different fashion, so that the social unit that makes the decision will itself derive any benefit that accrues from it.

A final sociological factor is the "backward-sloping supply curves" of effort and risk-taking in underdeveloped countries. Nearly all observers of individual behavior in these countries point to the difficulty of encouraging additional effort, or additional risk-taking, by the promise of higher money income. One need not agree with Boeke that the people of underdeveloped areas are fundamentally different in their motivation from those of advanced countries to believe that stagnation is self-reinforcing. At whatever level stagnation sets in, it has the effect of converting upward-sloping supply curves of effort and risk-taking into backward-sloping curves. To have an incentive to work harder or better, or to take additional risks with one's capital, one must have a clear picture of the use to which additional income is to be put. A strong "spirit of emulation," or a high "demonstration effect," occurs only where some people actually show that additional effort or risk-taking pays off. "Keeping up with the Joneses" is a dynamic force only when one sees the Joneses move to a higher standard of living. If life in the village has been much the same for generations, and if no one in the village has before him the picture of people moving to ever higher standards of living through their own efforts or their own willingness to risk capital, expending additional effort, or accepting additional risk, will seem rather absurd. Here is still another of the vicious circles so common in the field of development in underdeveloped areas: a progressive society inculcates attitudes and provides incentives favorable to economic growth; a stagnant one does not.

This analysis only appears inconsistent with the foregoing argument concerning the high marginal propensity to import. If national income rises for some extraneous reason, such as increasing export prices, people will wish to spend a large share of the increased income on imported semiluxuries. But the villagers see no easy way of raising their incomes through their own efforts or initiative, because they do not have before their eyes enough examples of people succeeding in doing so. Thus their wish for imported semiluxuries provides no effective incentive for additional effort or risk-taking. Still another vicious circle:

the "spirit of emulation" is necessary to provide incentives to harder and better work and increased enterprise, but if that spirit takes the form of a wish for imported semiluxuries, it aggravates balance of payments problems.

TECHNOLOGICAL FACTORS

Finally, technological factors were more favorable to development in the Western world during the eighteenth and nineteenth centuries than they are in the underdeveloped countries today. The simplest of these technological factors is the extent of the resource endowment. If one compares the United States or Canada with Libya or East Pakistan in terms of per capita resource endowment the contrast is apparent. In countries like Indonesia, where there is great diversity of resources, the contrast is less clear; some observers have spoken of Indonesia as a country "rich in natural resources." Closer examination of the Indonesian position in terms of the extent and quality of resources in relation to its population of 85 million people suggests that, although Indonesia is certainly better off than many of the underdeveloped areas, it is far indeed from being as well endowed with natural resources as most of the now advanced countries.

Moreover, in the underdeveloped countries the present factor endowment, in terms of proportions in which land, labor, and capital are available, is a drag on development. The very essence of economic development is a fall in the ratio of agricultural employment to total employment. But the proportions in which factors of production are available in underdeveloped areas favor agriculture against industry: labor is abundant, even redundant, land is relatively limited; capital is very scarce. In agriculture, relatively good results can be obtained by labor-intensive techniques, with much labor and little capital applied to available land. Industrialization with known techniques requires a much higher capital-labor ratio.

Some recent analysis suggests that the techniques which would maximize total value output in underdeveloped countries, even assuming that enough capital was available to introduce them, would not provide full employment. Here is a dilemma: unemployment is a serious social phenomenon; yet maximum value product is needed, not only to raise standards of living at the moment, but in order to permit a ratio of savings and investment to income which would generate continued economic growth.

Unfortunately, technological research has been carried on mainly in countries where labor is a relatively scarce factor. Technological progress is regarded as a synonym for labor-saving devices. Little scientific endeavor has been directed toward raising production in countries where capital is scarce and labor abundant, and where consequently, labor-saving devices make little sense. No advanced technology has yet been discovered which is suited to the factor-proportions of underdeveloped countries. Perhaps such a technology does not exist; but it is important to find out. Meanwhile, the lack of technological advance adapted to their factor-proportions is a serious obstacle to development of underdeveloped areas—an obstacle that scarcely existed in the Western world during its Industrial Revolution.

A related technical problem is the apparent discontinuity in the production function with respect to capital supply. Certain types of production process are inefficient unless carried on at a minimum scale which is itself large in terms of capital requirements. For example, one of the most hopeful projects on the horizon in Indonesia is the complex of power, aluminum, fertilizer, and related industries constituting the Asahan program. A project of this kind runs into hundreds of millions of dollars, yet it is not worth undertaking on a small scale.

Moreover, evidence is accumulating to suggest that raising *per capita* income by a given percentage amount requires a larger percentage addition to the stock of capital in underdeveloped countries than it does in advanced countries. This difference reflects partly the extremely high capital cost involved in providing social capital, such as housing, community facilities, public utilities, and transport, as industrialization takes place. Even in agriculture, however, the incremental capital-output ratio may be very high where land reform is necessary, involving shifts to new types of agriculture, or where expansion requires land reclamation, jungle clearance, and the like. Here is still another vicious circle. Advanced countries can add to their *per capita* income with a smaller (percentage) sacrifice of current income than can underdeveloped countries.

Capital-saving inventions have been suggested as a solution to this problem. However, it is essential to distinguish between capital-saving inventions and capital-saving innovations. Probably most inventions are capital saving, in the sense that they reduce the capital required per unit of output, once the new plant is in place. In this sense, it seems likely that even the steam railroad was a capital-saving invention; capital required per ton-mile of freight carried is probably less on a modern railway than it was with horses and wagons. However, capital-saving inventions of this type do not help very much, if the capital requirements for *introducing* them are beyond the means of underdeveloped countries. In other words, the *installation* of a new technique that may ultimately be capital saving may require very large amounts of capital indeed. Even capital-saving inventions are easier for advanced countries to introduce than for underdeveloped ones. Where a great deal of capital has already been accumulated, capital-saving inventions can be introduced by using existing replacement funds. Where the capital stock is low, however, replacement funds will be insufficient for major innovations, even if they consist in introduction of capital-saving inventions. What underdeveloped countries need is not merely capital-saving inventions in this sense but means of raising productivity without increasing the current rate of total investment, *even temporarily*. Clearly, the technical requirements of this sort of innovation are much more severe than for capital-saving inventions of the usual sort.

There is also a problem of scale, or a discontinuity, on the side of demand. As Rosenstein-Rodan has pointed out, the establishment of a shoe factory may prove unprofitable in an underdeveloped country, since so small a share of the income created by investment in a shoe factory will return to the producer of shoes. Only large-scale expansion, consisting of development of a few industries of very large scale or of a great many small-scale industries, will raise income sufficiently to generate significant increases in demand for all commodities.

Moreover, there is reason to suspect that a collection of small industries has lower "leverage effects" than a single large one involving the same initial amount of total investment. The construction of a railway, opening up new territory, facilitating population movements, and making necessary the development of new communities, is likely to have a greater aggregate effect on investment than a collection of shoe factories, textile plants, and the like, even if the initial investment is equally large in both cases. Again we are confronted with a vicious circle. It is difficult to industrialize without the increases in income which would provide the demand for increased output of industrial goods, but such increases in income are difficult to achieve without industrialization.

In those underdeveloped countries which rely heavily on exports of the traditional plantation staples, still another technological problem arises. Most of these industries involve a combination of highly mechanized processing operations with labor-intensive agricultural operations, a combination which puts the plantation industries in an extremely awkward position. The large amount of capital required in the processing plants means that these plants must operate close to capacity if they are to be profitable. But operating *plants* to capacity requires the operation of *plantations* to capacity. Full use of the productive capacity of the plantations would require cultivation of all the land previously conceded to these estates, and the employment of a full labor force working effectively for a full week of at least forty hours. With losses of productive land through destruction, squatters, expropriation, blights, disease, and inadequate maintenance . . . the output of many plantations is no longer sufficient to keep the plants operating at capacity. In addition, the effective working week on many plantations is considerably less than what is required. Finally, in direct contrast to the process that took place in other countries during their period of rapid economic advance, growing strength of labor organization and consequent increases in wage rates are preceding, instead of following, increases in labor productivity.

The question is, therefore, whether the productivity of labor can be raised as fast as wage rates, so as to prevent labor costs from rising to a point where the whole operation becomes unprofitable. Certainly, much can be done to improve labor skills, and much more to increase the quantity and quality of effort expended. However, increases in labor productivity from this side will require a long and difficult process of training, not only to improve skills but to increase the sense of social obligation on the part of workers, and to bring an understanding of the relationship of their own efforts to their standard of living. As replanting takes place, higher-yield and disease-resistant strains can be introduced; but this, too, is a slow process, and one that will raise output per hectare considerably more than output per man-hour. The scope for technological progress in the sense of mechanization, or introduction of labor-saving devices, appears to be limited in most plantation industries, although the problem merits further study. The necessity of careful selection in picking and cutting, the importance of skilled tapping, the need to utilize land to the full, and the like, restrict the degree to which labor can be replaced by equipment on the plantations themselves. Meanwhile, no such limitations to technological progress and cost reduction occur in the production of substitute materials through synthetic processes, such as the manufacture of synthetic rubber, nylon fibers, mineral oils, and the like.

AN IMPOSSIBLE TASK?

In our whole review of strategic factors in economic growth, we have discovered only one with respect to which the now underdeveloped areas have a comparative advantage over the Western world of the eighteenth and nineteenth centuries. All underdeveloped countries have a large sector of their economies, in which the majority of their people are occupied, with levels of technique and skill far below that of the advanced countries or of the more advanced sector of their own economies. There is accordingly an opportunity for a high rate of technological progress, through the application of the most advanced technical knowledge available to the underdeveloped sector.

Even this advantage, however, is doubtful; the equipment and technical skills that have been so effective in raising levels of productivity in the West are largely inappropriate to the factor-proportions of underdeveloped countries. Almost without exception, the technical advances of the Western world have been designed to replace labor with machinery. In countries where capital is scarce and labor redundant, such labor-saving devices cannot add so much to the productivity of the economy as a whole. Even if labor-saving devices can raise the total value of output in underdeveloped countries, they may do so at the cost of adding to the pool of disguised unemployment. In every other respect, the now underdeveloped countries seem to be at a disadvantage as compared to Europe and the New World at the beginning of their periods of rapid economic development.

Must our conclusion be that the task of developing the now underdeveloped areas is an impossible one? My own answer to this question is no: if both the underdeveloped countries and the advanced countries agree on the necessity of economic development of underdeveloped areas; if they understand what is required to obtain this development and recognize the magnitude of the task; and if they accept it nevertheless.

27. ACCUMULATING THE INGREDIENTS: FREEDOM OR DICTATORSHIP?*

B. K. Nehru

One of the most disquieting features of international society today is the continuous state of unrest that prevails over large parts of Asia, Africa and Latin America. We seem to move from crisis to crisis, with the Security Council of the United Nations in almost permanent session. As soon as a measure of stability is achieved in one part of the world, a new conflict erupts somewhere else; and about the only thing one can predict with some certainty is that there are many more crises brewing which have not yet got to the stage of catching the headlines.

Complex and bewildering as the crises of our times appear to us, however, they are not without a parallel in human history—and comparatively recent history, at that. And the gratifying part about the historical experience I have in mind is that it points to the only permanent remedy for our present-day ferment of discontent.

I venture to suggest that the violent upheavals in many parts of the world today are but an international version of the conflicts that raged within the nation-states of Europe in the eighteenth and nineteenth centuries. If the nation-states of Europe have not collapsed under the pressure of internal conflicts among different classes, but have emerged instead as dynamic and harmonious societies, it is as a result of certain definite policies adopted to bridge the difference between group and group. It is precisely the kind of measures which saved the nations of Europe from erosion from within that are required today, on an international level, for the preservation and strengthening of international society.

* B. K. Nehru, "$2,700 a Year or $70 a Year," *New York Times Magazine*, April 16, 1961, pp. 22, 116, 117.

The American people have long considered, and rightly, that their own revolution found a natural echo in many lands for many years to come. "The shot heard round the world" was followed a few years later by the storming of the Bastille. For a hundred years thereafter and more the states of Europe, when they were not at war with each other, were engaged in dealing with revolution at home, opposing to it sometimes the organized force of the state, and attempting at other times to deal in a more sophisticated manner with the causes of the revolutionary outbreaks from which they suffered.

Why was it that the people of France revolted in 1789? Why were there revolutions, uprisings, and widespread national unrest in 1830 and in 1848 in France, Germany, Italy, Austria, Hungary and Poland? Why was even the mature and stable society of Great Britain rocked to its foundations by popular agitation? What was the genesis of Nihilism in Russia, the St. Petersburg uprising in 1905, the bread riots which followed, and, finally, the holocaust of the October Revolution?

The human race is not prone to indulge in disorder for its own sake; if there is a history of continuous disorder, it is obvious that the people occupied with it lack something which they regard as more valuable than the maintenance of the regime, of the law under which they live. All the European revolutions, and the disorders which did not reach the stage of revolutionary violence, can be traced to the frustration of two of the most fundamental desires of man: the desire for liberty and the desire for bread.

The European system of the time concentrated political power in the hands of a hereditary monarchy tempered sometimes by a hereditary nobility. As almost invariably happens, this political power was exercised for the benefit of those who wielded it, while those outside the pale suffered the consequences. One of the consequences was an extreme inequality in the distribution of wealth; so much so that in countries not lacking in production there were large segments in society which could not earn enough to live a life that could by any standards be regarded as human.

The system was unjust; but it had prevailed with little change for centuries. Why was it that at this particular period of history large masses of people in Europe became so dissatisfied with it that they were willing to shatter to bits old institutions hallowed by tradition at great material cost to themselves?

There was, of course, the force of ideas, for it is ideas that guide the action of those who wield the arms. The philosophers and the men of the Age of Reason had preached the virtues of liberty and equality. And it was these ideas, born of the meditations of secluded philosophers, that filtered down ultimately to the illiterate and "swinish multitude," "the great unwashed," and made them resolve to rebuild the system under which they lived.

But the intellectual acceptance of ideas does not provide a sufficient motive force for those great earthquakes of humanity which are known as revolutions. Nor does emptiness of the human stomach—a very powerful force indeed—explain why revolutionary forces erupted at the time they did in Europe. The poor had, of course, always been poor since the dawn of history. But the poor had been in good company for, apart from a very small handful of those who lived somewhat better, the entire mass of humanity had been poor.

It was during the late eighteenth and nineteenth centuries, when the winds of technical change began to sweep across Europe, that this began to be no longer true. The wealth created by trade and commerce, and later by the Industrial Revolution, had been substantial. The rich had become very much richer and were using their wealth for luxury and ostentation and display. The poor had had no benefit at all from this accumulation of wealth to the nation; they were as poor as they ever had been before, if not, on occasion, poorer. And it was this new spectacle of poverty in the midst of plenty and the growing realization that poverty was no longer inevitable that essentially sparked the revolutions of the time.

The remarkable thing about the nation-states of Western Europe, however, is that despite the trials and tribulations to which they were subject throughout the nineteenth century, and contrary to the dire prophesies of Karl Marx, they have managed to survive. And they have survived not as weak and feeble organisms, but as vital, dynamic, growing societies, integrated within themselves. What was it that effected this change?

What effected this change was that the nation-state took steps to see throughout the nineteenth century that the causes of discontent were removed. Political power was gradually transferred from those who held a monopoly of it to the entire mass of the adult population. Economic inequality was reduced so that the benefits of the new productive powers which humanity had discovered were not restricted to any one group but were shared by the community as a whole. Combinations of working men were permitted in order that the bargaining power of the poor should be increased.

Laws regulating factories insured that those working in them were not reduced to the level of animals. Acts governing education insured that the children of the poor, not only those of the rich, were given access to knowledge. Medical care was continuously made cheaper and more easily accessible.

In essence, all these reforms meant a reduction in the inequality of real incomes. And the great over-all instrument which enabled all these reforms to be financed was the progressive income tax.

It is the policy of all nation-states today, whether they are governed by parties of the Right or by those of the Left, to insure that there are transferences of wealth from the rich to the poor; not only from rich individuals to poor individuals, but also from the richer areas within the community to the poorer areas within that same community. With growing evidence of sufficiency for all and the development of a sense of responsibility on the part of those who have more, the discontents of yesterday and the scars of hurt pride they produced have all but disappeared.

Few people in the nineteenth century could have analyzed clearly the basic causes of the discontents of their times. To them the times were merely out of joint. It is only the hindsight of history that enables us to get a glimpse of what really was then happening.

Equally understandably, the basic causes responsible for the turmoil in the international world today are not always apparent to those who are living through them. But if we look around today at conditions in the world, can we really escape the conclusion that much of the contemporary stresses and strains in international society are the exact counterparts of the stresses and strains with which the nation-states of the nineteenth century were faced?

At the same time, are not the methods of restoring stability to, and of strengthening, international society today exactly those which were applied during the nineteenth century within the nation-state? The difference, of course, is that whereas the discontent within the nation-state was that of individuals, the discontents within international society are those of nations.

I said earlier that the two fundamental causes of the revolutions and disorders of the nineteenth century were the desire for liberty and the desire for bread. Internationally, the twentieth century started off with an equilibrium which though manifestly unjust, seemed so stable as to be able to endure for eternity.

The colonial system which had deprived the majority of the human race of political liberty caused, by the very act of that deprivation, a great intensification of the desire for liberty. One consequence of that deprivation of liberty was the growth of nationalism, for nationalism never develops so fast nor grows so strongly as in opposition to an alien power.

The nationalist movements of Asia and Africa were a constant threat to the maintenance of the status quo in the earlier half of this century. The demand for freedom could, at last, no longer be resisted and the internal strength which the colonies developed, together with changes in the ideas of the majority of the colonial powers themselves, has led to the rapid liquidation of colonial empires since the end of the last world war.

While the desire for liberty is thus in the process of being satisfied, the desire for bread is not. There are, internationally speaking, the same inequalities of wealth between nations that were prevalent between individuals within the nation-states of the nineteenth century. Also, as happened in those states before they took themselves in hand, these inequalities are growing.

The average per capita income of the developed parts of the world (Europe, North America, Australia and Japan) is $1,200 per annum. The same figure for the underdeveloped world is $125 per annum. These averages conceal the true contrast, which is better illustrated by comparing the two ends of the scale.

At one end is the United States, with a per capita income of $2,700 per annum; near the other end of the scale is India, with one-third of the population of the non-Communist under-developed world, with a per capita income of $70 per annum. The existing discrepancies are so great that even if the under-developed societies develop at a much faster rate than the developed ones the difference between them would still continue to grow.

A 3 per cent rate of growth in the American economy would increase per capita incomes by $81 per annum—the increase being more than the total income of the Indian. An increase at the presently unimaginable rate of 10 per cent would increase the Indian income by only $7 per annum, so that at the end of twelve months the difference between the American's income and the Indian's income would be even greater than it is today.

The people in the underdeveloped world are not content with this situation any more than the under-privileged European in the nineteenth century was with his. Once again, poverty is nothing new and its continuance would not have aroused discontent had it continued to be regarded as inevitable. But, like the have-not rioters of Paris or the have-not Chartists of England, the have-not nations of the world see today that poverty is not the will of God and that there are nations in which it has been removed by the hand of man.

Unfortunately, the analogy between the nation-state of the nineteenth century and international society today breaks down in one vital respect. In the case of the nation-state, the gradual spread of political power among the masses of the people, combined with the growing accumulation of capital and technical know-how within the nation-state itself, provided the natural means for eradicating the contrast between the "haves" and the "have-nots."

In the case of the international society of today, however, the achievement of political independence among the "have-nots" provides no automatic means of harnessing the growing wealth of the "haves" for the betterment of the "have-nots."

The great reforms within the nation-state of the nineteenth century consisted in essence in raising the standard of living of the mass of the citizenry by taking a part of the annual growth in the already large incomes of the rich and devoting it, through public expenditures, to ends which helped the under-privileged to increase their incomes.

In international society today there is no such mechanism. The United Nations is very far from a world government. The means through which it operates are not the organized force of the state, but moral persuasion. It cannot abolish colonialism by force, as slavery was abolished by force. It cannot tax rich nations for the benefit of poor nations, as the nation-state taxed the rich for the benefit of the poor.

And yet it would appear to me that what is required today is precisely to fashion ways and means which would enable the have-not nations to share in the prosperity that is technically available to the whole human race.

It is true that, left wholly to themselves, the poorer nations will, in due course of time, be able to banish poverty from their midst. But they will have to pay a price in social organization which must necessarily result in the destruction of the liberty of the individual—for a totalitarian form of government is demonstrably better suited for the initial economic development of poor societies than the slow-moving and complicated processes of democracy.

It would, therefore, appear essential for organized international society, if it wishes to insure the continuance of the values of justice and freedom on which it claims to be founded, to respond to the needs of its weakest members and help them to overcome the difficulties with which they are faced. These needs are multifarious, but they can be comprehensively described as the need for economic growth.

The factors restricting the growth of the economies of the under-developed countries—or in other words, the factors which keep them poor—are many and they vary from country to country. For the removal of some, no help can come from the outside. People must by themselves develop the strength to face the sacrifices necessary for economic development and must by themselves learn how to organize so that they can work together for the attainment of their national aspirations. What can be supplied from the outside is technical assistance—in its widest sense—and developmental capital.

There are societies which require teachers, doctors, administrators, lawyers and the like. The outside world can surely provide the means by which personnel of this kind can be trained in large numbers. There are others which are short of technicians in certain branches of industrial or agricultural practice; these can be supplied from abroad. But what all under-developed countries are short of is developmental capital—a poor society, like a poor man, cannot save enough and, therefore, invest enough, to enable its income to grow at a rapid enough rate.

Many of the under-developed countries are at a stage of development where large amounts of capital cannot be usefully absorbed; in those countries conditions have first to be created which will enable investment to be usefully carried out. There are, however, some countries which have reached a stage where the only shortage is that of capital; and the absolute amounts required are so large and in such fields that they are wholly beyond the capabilities of the private investor to supply.

It is for this reason that government-to-government and international programs of foreign aid have come into being. No firm estimates have ever been really made as to what it would cost either the developed or the under-developed world to pursue a program of rapid economic development in the under-developed countries. But the general consensus seems to be that the figure involved for external aid is somewhere around $7 billion a year, matched by several times this amount from the under-developed world itself.

This figure may seem high in absolute terms, but when it is remembered that the income of the developed parts of the world is somewhere around $1,000 billion a year, that this income is increasing between $30 to $40 billion a year, and that the expenditure on armaments alone is around $100 billion a year, the figure seems to fall into its correct perspective.

A certain amount of capital does flow at present from the industrially advanced countries to the less developed lands either by way of private investment or by way of loans and grants from governmental agencies and international organizations. The precise measurement of the net developmental capital that is presently available, however, is not as simple a matter as one might suppose. A number of adjustments have often to be made to what commonly passes as aid in order to arrive at figures which represent truly the net addition to the amount of capital available for the development of the less developed countries.

According to one estimate, the net capital outflow to the non-Communist developing countries amounted to some $4.5 billion a year in 1959 and 1960. Of this, $2.6 billion was from the U.S.—$1.75 billion by way of economic assistance, $0.2 billion as technical assistance and $0.65 billion as net private foreign investment.

Other countries in the West supplied a total of about $0.9 billion, and the U.S.S.R. another $0.5 billion. The remainder came in the form of economic assistance from the International Bank ($0.35 billion) and in technical assistance from non-U.S. sources ($0.15 billion).

If the critical minimum level of net capital outflow to the developing countries is accepted as of the order of $7 billion per annum, what we need is an increase of 50 per cent over the level already attained. Whether this increase should come mainly through international agencies or through bilateral channels, and how it should be distributed among the contributing countries, are questions that need not detain us here.

It is, I think, fairly clear that for some years to come, at any rate, the bulk of the increase that is required will have to come from bilateral channels of government-to-government assistance as distinguished from private funds or international agencies.

At the same time, there is no reason why even essentially bilateral effort cannot admit of a measure of coordination and common determination among a group of countries. But whatever the method employed for increasing the flow of developmental capital to the newly emerging nations, there is, I think, no doubt that unless this flow is increased without delay to the critical minimum level I have mentioned above, there is every danger that the significant effort already being made will itself be frustrated.

The U.N. General Assembly at its last session adopted a resolution recommending that there should be a transfer of capital from the developed countries to the under-developed equal to 1 per cent of the national income of the former. It would appear that the Kennedy Administration is in sympathy with this proposal, for there are welcome indications that it wishes to urge that the burden of financing the external needs of the under-developed world should be shared by the richer countries on some such basis.

The essence of the argument that I have endeavored to develop is that the roots of the threat with which national societies were faced in the nineteenth century lay in the maldistribution of political power and economic well-being; that the roots of the present international discontents are exactly the same, except that the maldistribution is between nations and not individuals; that the nation-states stabilized themselves by correcting this maldistribution, first through broadening the base of political power, and next through using the authority of government to reduce inequalities of income; that international society should endeavor to achieve the same ends by ending colonialism as soon as practicable and transferring wealth to the poorer nations; that the sacrifices involved in the task are by no means great; but that, whereas in the case of national governments this was done compulsorily, in the case of international society this will have to be done on a voluntary basis, since we do not as yet have a government of the world.

28. INTERNATIONAL DEVELOPMENT LENDING INSTITUTIONS*

The Federal Reserve Bank of New York

In recent years the efforts of major industrial nations to provide more economic assistance to the less developed countries have pro-

* The Federal Reserve Bank of New York, "International Development Lending Institutions," *Monthly Review*, Vol. 43, No. 9 (September, 1961), pp. 156–61.

ceeded along two separate but related lines. Not only have they enlarged their bilateral aid programs, but they have also taken steps to increase both the number and the activities of international institutions designed to finance economic development.

The first, and for some years after World War II the only, international long-term lending institution was the International Bank for Reconstruction and Development (IBRD), whose fifteenth anniversary will be observed this month in Vienna where the annual meetings of the bank and the International Monetary Fund are being held. The IBRD was organized to supply capital-hungry parts of the world with the long-term funds needed for economic reconstruction or development at a time when there was little hope that private capital, unaided, would risk international investment outside the Western Hemisphere. Although the IBRD's original capital was doubled in 1959, thus adding substantially to its capacity to mobilize capital resources for the developing countries, it had become clear even earlier that its lending facilities needed to be supplemented by other forms of development finance. Accordingly, two supplementary institutions were set up as IBRD affiliates—the International Finance Corporation in 1956 and the International Development Association in 1960. In addition, another major institution, the Inter-American Development Bank, was established in 1960 to promote development on a regional basis.

THE INTERNATIONAL BANK FOR RECONSTRUCTION AND DEVELOPMENT

Among international institutions, the IBRD has not only the longest experience in the field of development financing, but also by far the largest resources. On June 30, 1961, its subscribed capital amounted to $20 billion, and the aggregate of the loans it had extended totaled more than $5½ billion. The bank, which now has seventy member countries, is governed by a board of directors chosen by its members, with the voting power of each director determined by the size of the capital subscription of the country or countries he represents. The United States subscription of $6.4 billion is slightly less than a third of the total.

The IBRD was designed to stimulate the flow of long-term investment capital across national frontiers and thereby to contribute to the development of economic resources and growth of production and income, particularly in the nonindustrial areas of the world. According to its charter, its purpose is to "promote private foreign investment by means of guarantees or participations in loans and other investments made by private investors; and when private capital is not available on reasonable terms, to supplement private investment by providing, on suitable conditions, finance for productive purposes out of its own capital, funds raised by it, and its other resources." As matters turned out, the IBRD found it neither practical nor prudent to give its guarantee to loans raised in private capital markets by borrowers with widely varying credit ratings. Consequently, from the beginning it concentrated on making, from its own resources, direct long-term loans for productive projects.

The IBRD's funds have been derived from three major sources which have varied in relative importance over the past fifteen years (see Chart I). Initially, the IBRD relied heavily on its own subscribed capital,

CHART 1

IBRD: Sources of Funds

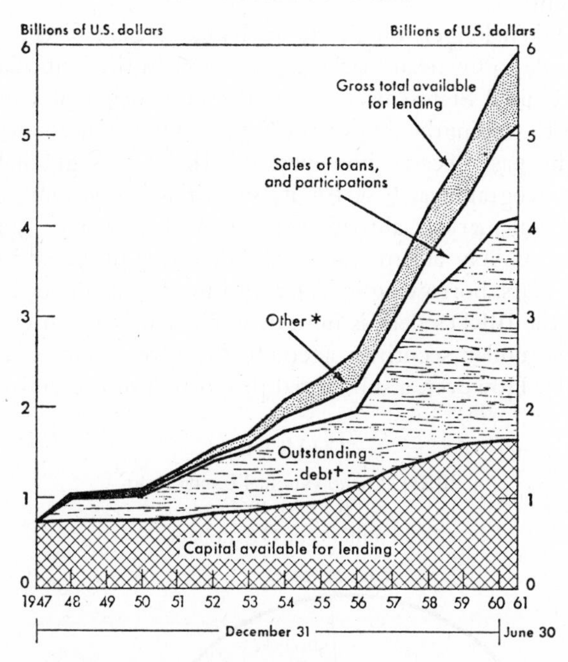

* Consists of repayments of principal and income from operations and exchange adjustments.
† Including commitments to borrow $207 million.
Source: International Bank for Reconstruction and Development.

of which $2 billion has been paid in. Second, the IBRD has raised funds by issuing its own bonds and notes, which are of course backed by the capital subscriptions of its members. A third source, which has lately become quite important, has been the sale of participations in IBRD loans to private investors. In addition, in more recent years the IBRD's available funds have been swelled by its sizable earnings and, at the same time, loan repayments have freed resources for new loans. All in all, from the start of its operations through mid-1961 the IBRD had available for lending a gross total of almost $6 billion.

IBRD Bond Issues

The most important single source of IBRD's funds today is the sale of its obligations on the world's capital markets. Some $2.2 billion of its bonds and notes were outstanding at the end of June 1961.

Once the bank had overcome the initial investor resistance to a new type of security as well as legal barriers to the purchase of its bonds by various institutional investors, it became extremely successful in floating large and frequent issues in the United States. Moreover, a rising amount of dollar bonds and notes, originally sold in the United States, soon found their way into the portfolios of individual and institutional investors outside this country.

It has taken longer, on the other hand, to gain direct access on a substantial scale to financial markets elsewhere. In the immediate postwar period, the United States market was the only one that could provide funds. With the strengthening of the foreign industrial countries' economies over the past decade, however, the IBRD was gradually able to broaden the geographical base for its securities issues. During the early 1950's, as capital markets abroad were opened up, small issues began to be sold both publicly and privately in Western Europe and Canada. In more recent years, borrowing in Western Europe was stepped up sharply.

While the IBRD's debt is now denominated in seven currencies, its United States dollar securities account for three fourths of the total (see Chart II). However, a substantial proportion of the dollar debt—up-

CHART II

IBRD: OUTSTANDING FUNDED DEBT
JUNE 30, 1961
In millions of U.S. dollars

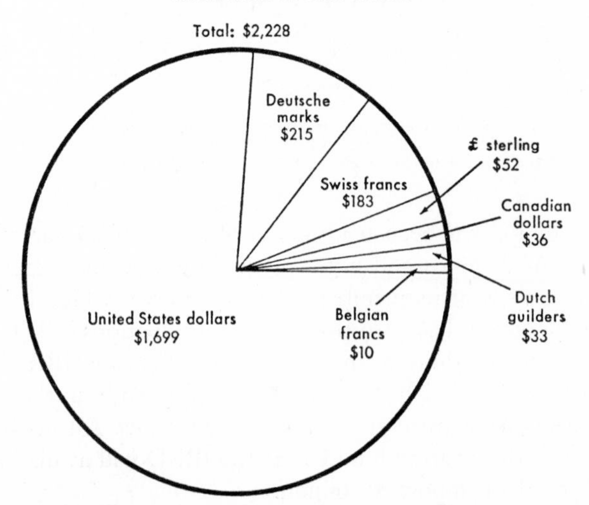

Source: International Bank for Reconstruction and Development.

ward of 40 per cent—is estimated to be held outside the United States, so that the institution now owes more than half of its total funded debt to investors abroad.

IBRD Loan Operations

Although access to capital markets abroad has not always been easy, the IBRD has not been hampered in its lending activities by lack of funds. Any limitation on its loan operations has come rather from a dearth of loan projects that are suitable under the IBRD's standards. These standards are, in certain respects, similar to those of the private investor, except that on loans to private entities the IBRD charter requires a government guarantee. The productive character of the projects submitted by would-be borrowers is appraised, and repayment prospects are assessed according to exacting criteria. The IBRD does not normally lend for projects involving social overhead cost, such as schools, housing, or hospitals, which do not produce revenue and cannot be expected to lead to direct and prompt increases in the borrowing country's productive potential and foreign-exchange earning capacity. It may also find it impossible to finance worthy and productive projects in cases where the borrowing country's over-all ability to service the loan is in doubt because of an already-heavy foreign debt burden or poor balance-of-payments prospects. It is indicative of the rigorousness of the IBRD's standards that there has never been a default among the approximately 300 loans made since 1946.

Except for some $500 million of war reconstruction loans to Western Europe in 1947 and 1948, IBRD lending has been devoted to stimulating economic development. Until the early 1950's its loan operations remained fairly modest, but the pace has since then quickened considerably and new loan commitments have for several years averaged about $700 million annually (see Chart III). A certain slackening has become noticeable of late, however, in part because some of the IBRD's borrowers have by now established a sufficient credit standing with private investors so as to be less dependent on its loans. At the same time, other borrowers have accumulated heavy foreign debt burdens which are likely to make difficult the servicing of additional loans.

IBRD loans have been heavily concentrated in public utilities, particularly in two major categories that are usually the prerequisites of industrial expansion—power and transportation facilities (see Chart IV). Next in importance in the IBRD portfolio are loans for the construction or development of basic industrial facilities, followed in turn by loans for agricultural improvement, irrigation, and the like. The projects assisted by the IBRD have touched every corner of the globe and have included construction of some of the world's largest dams, whole networks of roads to open up isolated regions to industrialization and agricultural development, huge port installation projects, and the rehabilitation of entire national railway systems. IBRD funds have also helped finance the establishment and expansion of steel, cement, fertilizer, and numerous other heavy and light manufacturing industries, as well as the development of mineral and other natural resources.

IBRD loans are medium or long term, mostly in the 15- to 25-year range, depending on the nature of the project financed. They are repayable in semiannual instalments, normally beginning after a grace period of

CHART III

IBRD: Loans by Geographical Areas

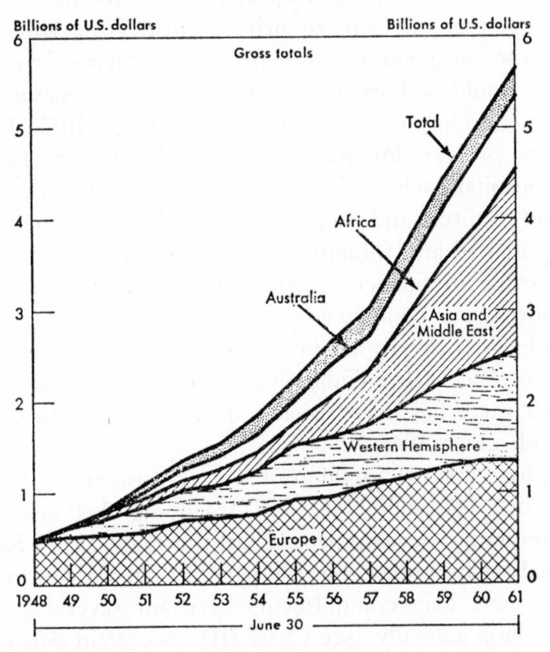

Source: International Bank for Reconstruction and Development.

two to five years. The interest rate they carry (currently 5¾ per cent) is based upon the rate at which the IBRD raises funds in the market, to which is added a 1¼ per cent service charge. Because of the nature of the projects financed, most IBRD development loans are quite large, ranging in size from several million up to as much as $100 million. For the same reason, many are extended to government-owned or government-controlled sectors of the economy. When making industrial loans, however, the IBRD prefers to finance privately owned concerns, in the belief that manufacturing is usually best left to private enterprise. While the government-guarantee requirement and the relatively modest scale of private industrial undertakings in underdeveloped countries make it difficult to administer such assistance directly, the IBRD has found ways to channel funds to private industry through local development banks, many of which have been created at IBRD initiative.

The IBRD generally limits its financial assistance on an investment project to the foreign exchange portion of the cost of the project. This limitation cannot, of course, be applied rigidly in the case of countries, such as Japan, that are already producers of capital equipment and where the direct import costs of a development project may therefore be small in relation to the total cost. The main objective of the policy has been to ensure that the borrowing country, through taxation or by other means, mobilizes local resources to make a significant contribution of its own to the investment effort. Until now, however, progress toward this objective has been rather modest and some borrowers have conse-

CHART IV

IBRD: Loans by Purpose
June 30, 1961

Gross totals in millions of U.S. dollars

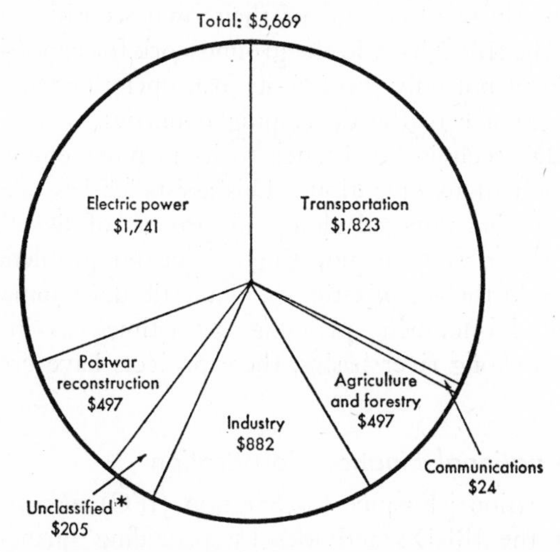

* These represent loans made to local development institutions and reloaned by the latter.
Source: International Bank for Reconstruction and Development.

quently failed to secure maximum possible results from the use of IBRD resources. Also, in order to ensure maximum benefits from the aid granted, the use of the proceeds from an IBRD loan is not tied. Procurement can be effected in any IBRD member country or in Switzerland which, without being a member, has cooperated closely with the IBRD. In general, on any sizable project, the IBRD requires competitive bidding on contracts under its credits.

The IBRD, Private Capital, and Economic Development

The IBRD remains faithful to its mission of not competing with, but on the contrary encouraging, private foreign investment. In the first place, it has made relatively few loans to the more industrialized countries of the world, where funds can usually be secured on private capital markets. Until recently, to be sure, it has been lending heavily to two industrial countries that are considered rather special cases—Italy, whose southern half remains underdeveloped, and Japan, where industrialization is still proceeding at an extremely rapid pace. However, the IBRD is now encouraging these two countries to raise elsewhere the funds needed to continue their development programs.

At the same time, to help broaden the market for its borrowers' obligations, the IBRD has frequently arranged to sell to private investors portions of the loans held in its portfolio or to have private lenders participate in some of its new loans. In most cases, the IBRD has kept the longer maturities, while private institutions have bought or participated in the shorter ones, without requiring a formal guarantee from the IBRD. As the credit standing of IBRD borrowers has improved, some of them have supplemented IBRD loans with funds raised simultaneously by the public issue or private placement of their own securities in the United States. Finally, the IBRD has laid the groundwork for expansion of private foreign investment not only through its loan operations but also through its technical assistance to the developing countries.

The IBRD's technical assistance to its member countries has been an invaluable part of its operations. This assistance has taken many different forms and has covered almost all aspects of development planning and execution, from engineering advice on problems of specific projects to help in the organization of domestic development banks and in broad-range development planning. Sometimes, as in the case of the Indus and Mekong river basins, these projects have crossed national borders.

The International Finance Corporation

The International Finance Corporation (IFC) was created in 1956 to supplement the IBRD's activities by providing finance for private undertakings under riskier circumstances than the IBRD and without the latter's government-guarantee requirement. It acts as a catalytic agent in the process of development, securing as much private participation in its investments as possible and eventually revolving its own funds by turning its successful investments over to private investors.

The IFC's financial resources are limited and its operations have been modest in scope. Although it is allowed by its charter to raise funds in the market, until now it has relied solely on its $97 million of capital funds. So far, the IFC has committed $45 million to forty industrial ventures in eighteen countries. The IFC confines its investment activities to privately owned and managed enterprises engaged in productive industrial activities—manufacturing, processing, or mining. The enterprises financed are usually of medium scale, the IFC's investments ranging in size from $100,000 up to as much as $4 million. Generally, the IFC provides no more than half of the finance required for a project, expecting the remainder of the required capital to come from private sources, domestic or foreign. Private interests have, in fact, supplied about three fourths of the total capital used in the various IFC development projects.

Although the IFC, like the IBRD, is prohibited from investing in equities, it has developed ways of providing venture-type capital. The IFC is instructed by its charter to obtain a return on its investment commensurate with the risks undertaken and comparable with the returns obtained by private investors. This has led it to negotiate with its borrowers complex investment formulas that add some equity features—such as stock options and participations in profits—to what are formally fixed-interest loans. On the whole, the use of these devices has vastly complicated the IFC's operations and has constituted a serious obstacle to its expansion. Moreover, equity capital is often badly needed in new and expanding enterprises, which may already be overburdened with debt in their initial years of operation. To meet this need, a charter amendment has been proposed that would allow the IFC to make nonvoting equity investments. If the amendment is ratified by the member governments, the IFC hopes to be better able to promote the expansion of private enterprise and to induce more local and foreign private investors to join in such activities.

THE INTERNATIONAL DEVELOPMENT ASSOCIATION

The International Development Association (IDA) was established in the fall of 1960 to fill a gap of a different nature in IBRD's operations: to make long-term development loans on more flexible terms than are possible for the IBRD. In the words of Eugene Black, who is president both of the IBRD and of the new institution, the IDA, is to assist "countries whose foreign exchange situation is such that they cannot borrow abroad at all on conventional terms" and "those whose foreign debt service burden over the short and medium term is already so high that they cannot prudently borrow, on conventional terms, all of the external capital which they require to carry out their priority programs." IDA credits, like those of the IBRD, are to be repaid in the currency borrowed, in order to avoid the accumulation of large quantities of local currencies with little or no international usefulness. However, the debt servicing burden is to be minimized by very lenient repayment terms. The IDA is empowered to finance projects of high developmental priority, whether or not they are directly productive. Its activity may therefore be spread over a broader range of investments than the IBRD's, including those of a primarily social character, such as housing or sanitation works.

The IDA, whose membership consists of about three quarters of

IBRD member countries, is to receive subscriptions in instalments over the next four years of over $900 million. However, only the industrialized countries—including, besides Western Europe and the United States, Canada, Australia, Japan, and the Union of South Africa—are being required to make their subscriptions available in gold or freely convertible currencies. Hence IDA's effective resources will amount to only about 80 per cent of its total subscriptions.

The IDA's charter provides that the adequacy of the institution's resources will be reviewed periodically with a view to increasing the members' subscriptions. Initially, the IDA's convertible-currency resources are expected to support a lending rate of about $150 million a year. Subsequently, the institution's ability to help meet the developing countries' financing needs will largely depend upon the willingness of the developed member countries to provide additional funds—upon their willingness, in effect, to internationalize a greater part of their development aid. Discussing the IDA's prospects at the United Nations Economic and Social Council recently, Mr. Black said:

> It is to be hoped that in due course the obvious need, and IDA's record of performance, will together justify a substantial increase in IDA's financing capacities, and also that countries contemplating an expansion of their aid programs may see fit to channel a part of the additional funds through the IDA. Such a pooling of resources is by far the most effective and satisfactory means of coordinating development aid.

THE INTER-AMERICAN DEVELOPMENT BANK

The Inter-American Development Bank (IDB) differs from the IBRD and its two affiliates in that it is a regional, rather than world-wide, institution. It was organized early in 1960 by the members of the Organization of American States and aims to promote the general economic development and economic integration of Latin America. Its membership includes the United States and nineteen Latin American republics.

The IDB is divided into two financially distinct entities: an Ordinary Banking Operations component that makes loans on approximately commercial terms to finance immediately remunerative projects in countries capable of bearing the debt-servicing burden; and a Fund for Special Operations which provides credit to countries in special need and which also finances undertakings that will increase the recipient's productive capacity only indirectly and slowly (including, in particular, investments in health, housing, and the like). Loans from the latter fund are repayable in part or entirely in the borrower's own currency and are made at relatively low rates of interest and for long periods, with amortization beginning only after a generous grace period.

By using its ordinary capital only for commercial-type loans, the IDB should be able to supplement its members' subscriptions by mobilizing private capital in much the same way as has the IBRD. The ordinary capital, like that of the IBRD, includes a paid-in portion of about $400 million and a callable portion of $450 million to serve as backing for bond issues. The groundwork for such issues is already being laid in both the United States and Western Europe. In addition, the IDB has already obtained participations by United States banks in a substantial number of the regular loans it has extended so far.

The Fund for Special Operations, on the other hand, is to obtain its resources solely from the $150 million subscribed by member countries. As the fund's convertible-currency holdings may be quickly depleted, owing to the local-currency repayment feature to be used in most of its loans, provision has been made for eventual increases in the members' contributions.

Because the IDB aims to supplement rather than replace existing sources of development finance in Latin America, it is expected to make special efforts to coordinate its activities with those of other lending institutions. A beginning has already been made in this direction with a highway loan to Honduras in cooperation with the IDA, and a housing credit to Colombia in collaboration with the United States Development Loan Fund. The regional character of the IDB offers good opportunities for working out a coordinated approach to development lending on both the hemisphere and the country level. Of the more than $115 million of loans authorized to date, approximately $79 million have been extended to banks and local development institutions, which will relend the funds generally for small-scale projects in agriculture, industry, and mining, in accordance with over-all plans worked out with the IDB's assistance.

The IDB is also administering, at the request of the United States, the larger part of the $500 million appropriated by the Congress last May for social development projects in Latin America. Loans under this program are to be on flexible terms, to finance important social projects, such as land improvement, water supply, and low-cost housing, and to foster the adoption by the recipient countries of the basic tax, land, and other reforms that will make rapid economic development possible.

CONCLUSIONS

While the supply of development capital available from international development lending institutions will undoubtedly remain only a small fraction of total requirements, the contribution of these institutions has already been significant. Through its loans, the IBRD has helped greatly in laying the foundations for economic growth in many countries. Moreover, the economic and technical advice offered by the IBRD, as an international institution, has sometimes been accepted more readily than if the advice had come from any national source.

Beyond this, it has become clear that international lending institutions can effectively enlist the help of private capital to assist in the task of development financing. The experience of the IBRD, in particular, has shown that such institutions can very usefully play, in the international sphere, a role similar to that of financial intermediaries in national capital markets.

Finally, it is now widely recognized that the current multiplication of lending agencies at both the government and the intergovernmental levels calls for ever-closer coordination of aid-giving activities. The specific type of financing offered by some of the agencies, or the nature of their approach, may in themselves define broad areas of specialization. There may nevertheless be instances when the various lenders find themselves in competition with one another, or even working at cross purposes, if they do not reach agreement on common principles, consistent with the over-all development objectives of those receiving assistance. The feasibility of effective interagency cooperation has been demonstrated many times in the past in the joint ventures of the IBRD with lending agencies of the United States and other governments, including the consortium of nations providing assistance to India and Pakistan, as well as in some of the first undertakings by newcomers like the IDA and the IDB.

Part IV: Questions for Analysis

1. Over-population is one of the formidable problems that many underdeveloped nations face in their quest for material well being.
   a) Present this problem as it was formulated by Malthus around the turn of the 19th century.
   b) As presented by Kingsley Davis, what is the current nature of the problem?
2. *a*) Discuss the several stages of economic growth as viewed by W. W. Rostow.
   b) Discuss the nature and importance of capital and human resources in achieving meaningful economic growth.
3. According to Benjamin Higgins, what role do non-economic factors play in influencing economic growth? Identify and describe the nature of these non-economic considerations.
4. Although the ingredients of economic growth are the same for all nations the method of accumulation may vary widely.
   a) In the opinion of the Indian Ambassador to the United States, B. K. Nehru, how does the simultaneous existence of very rich and very poor countries contribute to international instability?

b) In Ambassador Nehru's view, what will be the consequences of this situation if the richer western nations do not materially assist poorer nations? Do you agree? Explain.

5. *a*) Identify and explain the special features of each of the major international development lending institutions.

   b) What role do these institutions play in providing capital funds to the underdeveloped nations? In your opinion, is this method superior to aid from individual nations? Explain why or why not.

V COMPETITION, MONOPOLY, AND PUBLIC POLICY

Our nation's economic system relies principally on the market mechanism as the instrument through which resource allocation and distribution decisions are made. Traditional economic thought assumed that markets were fundamentally competitive in nature. Accordingly, it gave relatively little attention to departures from the competitive ideal. Reality, coupled with refinement of analytical techniques and language, has led modern economists to distinguish a variety of market structures.

John Maurice Clark, Professor Emeritus of Economics at Columbia University, defines competition. Substantial departures from the competitive ideal resulted in various reactions in public policy. One of the earliest and most significant was the attempt to preserve competitive markets by making unreasonable restraints of trade and monopoly illegal. The antitrust laws, which embody this policy, are discussed and evaluated by Theodore J. Kreps of Stanford University. However, significant departures have been made from the antitrust laws. Our farm program, in its price support and output restriction aspects, represents a basic departure from the attempt to preserve competition. This deviation, which affects what is otherwise the most perfectly competitive sector of the American economy, is a source of considerable controversy. Karl Brandt, Director of the Food Research Institute at Stanford University, provides guidelines for a constructive revision of present agricultural policy.

The existence of certain industries, characterized by conditions which make insistence on competitive markets inefficient and impractical, has led to government adoption of the public utility approach. This approach recognizes natural monopolies, gives them legal status, and regulates them. It is evaluated by James C. Bonbright, Professor Emeritus of Economics at Columbia University.

Our economy is characterized by widespread use of administered prices, both product and factor prices. Three excerpts which conclude this part analyze and evaluate the relationships between administered prices and the price level. Gardiner C. Means, coiner of the expression "administered prices," argues that inflation in the period 1955–57 was significantly influenced by such prices. Jules Backman, Research Professor of Economics at New York University, denies that inflation is caused by price administration; he attributes price-level changes to other factors, such as changing demand-and-cost conditions. Charles L. Schultze, Professor of Economics at Indiana University, offers another explanation, emphasizing changes in the composition of demand.

A. Competition and Public Policy

29. DEFINING COMPETITION*

John Maurice Clark

WHAT IS COMPETITION?

Competition is an indispensable mainstay of a system in which the character of products and their development, the amount and evolving efficiency of production, and the prices and profit margins charged are left to the operation of private enterprise. In our conception of a tenable system of private enterprise, it is a crucial feature that the customer should be in a position (as Adam Smith put it) to exert effective discipline over the producer in these respects. Otherwise, government would feel constrained to undertake discipline over these matters—as it does in the field of public-service industries. It is competition that puts the customer in this strategic position, hence its crucial character. It is the form of discipline that business units exercise over one another, under pressure of the discipline customers can exercise over the business units by virtue of their power of choosing between the offerings of rival suppliers. Competition presupposes that businesses pursue their own self-interest, and it harnesses this force by their need of securing the customer's favor. By reason of this discipline, business, which is profit minded, has to become production minded as a means of earning profits dependably.

This has its seamy side, as when the pressures of competition toward reducing money costs of production lead to substandard wages and working conditions, which increase the human costs of industry or lead to deterioration of the quality of products. These defects arise from a variety of causes: handicapped or relatively inefficient employers may be forced to make up for their disadvantages by lower money wages and may be able to do so because the competition they face as hirers of labor is less compelling than their competition as sellers of products; or customers may be poor judges of products, or certain qualities of products may be inscrutable. These are defects of a serviceable institution. In an impossibly perfect, omnipresent, and equal competition, they would presumably not arise; but that is an unattainable ideal. In the actual market place they have to be dealt with, and mitigated, by a variety of public and private measures adapted to the causes at work, including the "coun-

* John Maurice Clark, *Competition as a Dynamic Process* (Washington, D.C.: The Brookings Institution, 1961), pp. 9–18.

tervailing power" of organized labor, which uses anticompetitive pressures and has its own seamy side. Many of the remedies are themselves subject to abuse.

These defects are responsible for the view held in some quarters that it is the inherent tendency of competition to sacrifice serviceability to "vendibility" and to debase or impair the human values it touches. These things can happen; but if they were the whole story, the system of private business would not exhibit the strength it does today. Remedies that sustain the "level" of competition are in the interest of the business community, as well as the broader community of citizens. This is a more generally applicable course of action than the one envisioned a half-century ago by Gerald Stanley Lee, in a small volume entitled *Inspired Millionaires*, based on the idea that there existed men of wealth whose dominant motive was to use it to benefit humanity. To such a person, his first prescription was: "get a monopoly." Free yourself from the competitive compulsions that force you to squeeze down costs and prevent you from putting human values first.

The attraction of this procedure might have been somewhat dimmed by a hard-headed contemplation of the methods by which monopolies are established and defended. The element of truth in the prescription might better have been expressed in terms of organizing one's processes of production efficiently enough to give a margin of superiority affording leeway for experiments in promoting human values, not all of which need justify themselves by increasing profits. This, being consistent with competitive checks, would have been more clearly defensible.

A secure monopoly—if such a thing exists or can exist in industry or trade—might be able to save some of the wastes of competitive marketing. After spending part of the savings on public-relations advertising, it might choose to give the public some share of the resulting net economy. Indeed, there are quite cogent reasons why it might do this, or at least might refrain from exploiting to the utmost its immediate power over profits. Nevertheless, we would oppose such a monopoly, regardless of its good performance, because this performance would rest on its arbitrary choice. It would have power, if it chose, to make larger profits by giving the customer less for his money rather than more. The choice to give him more would depend too much on its enlightenment and good will.

While the good performance of our economy is more dependent on such qualities than many of us realize, our resources in this direction are limited. They are already heavily taxed or overtaxed by the requirements of good faith and responsibility in many relationships essential to the economic process and concerned with maintaining the level of competition. They would surely be overtaxed by laying upon them the whole burden of making economically correct decisions in the central matter of amounts produced and prices charged. In such decisions the opposition between private and community interest, is direct and powerful. Hence we do well to seek to keep these decisions subject to forces that are visibly and tangibly cogent, after the fashion of impersonal and competitive "economic law." So we are unwilling to leave in uncontrolled private hands the kind of power that goes with monopoly.

The patent system, with its grant of temporary legal monopoly, is less of an exception than might seem on the surface, as will appear later when we discuss innovation. Innovations are first selected and their value tested by their success in competition with existing practice. If innovation is to be stimulated by public policy, it is hard to devise a totally different system that would not depend more on arbitrary or bureaucratic judgment. Imperfections in the operation of the system present difficult problems, as we shall see, but do not destroy this general principle.

When an industry is recognized as a "natural monopoly," controls of the public utility kind are resorted to, imposing an enforceable obligation to render adequate service at reasonable charges. But we would quite rightly shrink from extending this system to the whole of industry and trade. And where effective competition exists, the customer does not need this sort of protection. Given a chance to choose between the offers of rival producers, his protection rests with his own ability to make an intelligent choice, plus his willingness to take the trouble involved. As to his ability, when he is faced with the inscrutable qualities of many products of modern applied science, there are difficulties, as we shall see, and there are various things that can be done about them, starting with various ways of giving the customer the most appropriate kinds of information. Minimum standards of quality may be set, publicly or privately, and some harmful products may be prohibited. But public control of output and price is not called for to meet this kind of need.

The customer can put pressure on the producer to create a supply corresponding to demand, produced at economical cost and sold at a price reasonably related to cost. "Consumer sovereignty" may be effective in this primarily quantitative sense; but it should be noted with some emphasis that this is not all there is to serviceability. Serviceability depends on how well the customer's patronage reflects those needs and interests that are properly identified with his welfare—using the term in its generally accepted meaning. This is more than an economic problem—a fact which is often used as a pretext for ignoring its economic aspects. The forces shaping our wants include the arts of salesmanship, at a time when our increased consuming power makes it disturbingly easy to become so preoccupied with the *mélange* of trifles or worse that salesmanship offers that we lose something really indispensable—a sense of worthwhile purpose in life. At the utilitarian level, we shall accept consumer sovereignty as an agency that is demonstrably limited and fallible, in need of practical aids to getting what is wanted—aids that can be furnished. Yet with all its defects this agency is indispensable in a society in which the task of shaping worthwhile lives is basically voluntary, rather than dictated by central authority.

So far we have been speaking of the effect of competition, from the standpoint of the alternative choices it offers to the customer, but without trying to define competition as an activity of the producers. For the present purpose, the most useful kind of definition is one that is full enough to suggest some of the important differences in degree and kind of situation, objective, and activity that the realistic student should be prepared to encounter. This kind of definition might also help to explain why competition is so many things to so many different people. They may take hold of it at different points and encounter different aspects, like the blind men and the elephant. Our elephant should have legs, tail, trunk, tusks, and ears. The following definition is framed with this in mind.

Competition between business units in the production and sale of goods is the effort of such units, acting independently of one another (without concerted action), each trying to make a profitable volume of sales in the face of the offers of other sellers of identical or closely similar products. The pursuit of profits includes attempting to minimize losses if that is the best the situation permits. The process normally involves rivalry, though this may or may not be direct and conscious. In perhaps the chief example, the case of staple farm products sold on organized exchanges, the rivalry of the growers is indirect and for the most part unconscious. In contrast, business units consciously attempt to get customers away from their rivals by the relative attractiveness of their offers. To the extent that the customer does his choosing effectively, the way to secure his business is to offer him good value for his money, backed by dependable information about the product. To the extent that he is incompetent or otherwise unable to choose effectively, specious selling appeals and scamped products have their opportunity. Business firms as buyers are better equipped and more competent than most consumers, and the methods of selling to them reflect this. But even with business buyers, the seller must bring his product to their attention. There may be rivalry between products not closely similar—this is ordinarily called "substitution" rather than "competition." We shall later examine the problem of defining the distinction between them.

Rivalry may be active or latent. In the latter case it has its most visible effect when it becomes active; but if this possibility influences the conduct of active competitors without waiting for the latent rivalry to become active, then latent competition as such has some effectiveness. It may come from the potential entry of new firms, but it is nowadays often a matter of an existing producer branching out into a new type of product or a new market. Much of the most formidable competition takes this form.

Where profits are attainable, competitors may aim at the largest feasible short-run profit, or at a profit thought of as reasonable and probably the best attainable in the long run. The point in either case is that the feasible profit and the methods of pursuing it are limited by the return for which other competitors are willing and able to produce goods and offer them to buyers. The aim may be to excel the attractiveness of their offerings, or to equal it, or to come as near equaling it as possible, in cases in which the rival has something that is, at least for the time being, inescapably superior as a sales appeal. In the latter case, the first firm is under pressure to find ways of improving the appeal of its offerings. Or the aim may be merely to secure enough business to survive.

The attempt to excel may be called aggressive competition, in effect if not in intent; it may or may not be aimed at a particular rival's business. The attempt to equal a competitor's offer or minimize a rival's advantage is clearly defensive. Under competition the one implies the other, and it takes both kinds to make an effectively competitive situation —certainly in industry and trade and probably in agriculture. A proper understanding of the processes of competition in industry and trade requires a recognition of the different and complementary roles of aggressive and defensive actions. This distinction has been recognized, but its basic importance does not appear to have been developed.

Overlapping this, but not coextensive with it, is the distinction between moves of an initiatory character, including moves responding merely to the general situation in which a competitor finds himself, and responses precipitated by specific moves of a rival or rivals—responses of the nature of parries or ripostes. They may imitate the rivals' moves, or may be countermoves of a different sort. Initiatory moves may be aggressive, as defined above; or they may be made by a competitor who is in a defensive situation, in an attempt to improve his position by trying something fresh. This distinction between initiation and response has been more fully recognized than the distinction between aggression and defense. In fact, it is the basis of that theory which claims that effective competition occurs only when firms making initiatory moves disregard the responses their rivals will make. Where competitors are few and a competitive action by one has a substantial impact on his rivals, they are virtually certain to make some kind of response. If the initiator of the move does not have foresight enough to anticipate this, experience will soon drive it home to him. To assume that he ignores it requires him to be far more stupid than businessmen are. If competition really depends on this kind of stupidity on the part of businessmen, its prospects are not good.

Fortunately, this pessimistic view contains only part of the truth, and a part that is seldom fully controlling. Businessmen are not only able to anticipate that rivals will respond, but to devise moves of sorts that cannot be easily and quickly neutralized by rivals' responses. And it is not necessary that all should initiate such moves; if some do, resulting competitive pressures will spread, not instantly or in precisely predictable forms, but, in general, effectively. For this purpose, it is important that firms differ in situations and perspectives. Fewness does not eliminate the incentive to improve productive efficiency or to increase the attractiveness of the product; and the resulting differences tend to spill over into price competition, often of irregular sorts. Anticipation that rivals will respond does not carry certainty as to how prompt or effective the responses will be. This uncertainty allows some firms to hope that, as the outcome of initiating a competitive move, they may end with an improved relative market position, which will mean increased profits for them, after profits in the industry as a whole have reached a normal competitive state. There are a variety of conditions that may lead some firms to this kind of an expectation, including the hope of avoiding a worsening of the firm's market position if it fails to make competitive moves when other firms are doing so. At the best, gains may be progressive over time. This, in nonmathematical language, is a rudimentary explanation of the paradox of competition, whereby single firms see an advantage in actions that tend to eventuate in reduced profits for the entire industry. This explanation supplies some essential elements that are left out of the simplified theoretical model that runs in terms of an "individual demand function" substantially more elastic than the industry function.

The forms which this condition may take hinge on the different means competitors may use in making their offerings attractive to customers. These include the selection and design of a product, selling effort to bring it to the favorable notice of potential customers, and price. The appeal of a seller's offer is a joint resultant of all three. Nevertheless, it has meaning to distinguish "competition in price" from competition in selling effort or product design. Any one of the three may change while the others do not. Indeed, estimates of the probable effects of such single variations are implied in the attempt to devise the most effective joint combination. But all three are tied together by the fact that they all need to be appropriate to one another and to the type and level of market demand the seller is aiming to reach.

The attempt to attract the customer's trade, in this three-sided appeal, costs money, whether it takes the shape of a high-quality product, an expensive selling campaign, or a low price. To make a profit on this money outlay or sacrifice, efficient and economical production is needed; and the more economical the production, the more effective the selling inducements can be made, consistently with profits. Therefore, though low-cost production is not a direct act of rivalry (a producer *may* reduce his costs and pass none of the benefit on to his customers), it is an essential enabling factor and as such is part of the whole process. A struggling competitor may have to reduce his costs if he is to stay in business at all. So it may be added as a fourth means of competitive appeal.

Most of these responses take time and involve uncertainty, starting with the responses of the customers that determine how effective the initial move is, after which rivals' responses take further time. The outstanding exception is an openly quoted reduction in the price of a standardized product. Here response can be prompt and precise; and the expectation of such responses can interfere with the competitive incentive to reduce prices and tends to shift price action to the more irregular forms, which create problems of their own, or to increase competitive emphasis on moves in the field of product and selling effort, which present a different array of problems as to the conditions of effective and serviceable competition. Competition over distance also presents its special problems in identifying serviceable forms of competitive price behavior. All in all, the conditions of serviceable competitive behavior in price, product, or selling effort leave much to be defined.

For example, does competition improve or deteriorate quality? Actually, it can do either or both. How can we judge the conditions determining whether the range of quality offered corresponds to the range desired or misrepresents it? By what criteria can we appraise the productiveness or wastefulness of the indispensable function of advertising or balance its informative and perverting effects on the guidance of demand? Would genuine competition drive prices down to marginal cost? Whose marginal cost, and short-run or long-run? The simplified formulas of abstract theory have too-often bypassed such questions. Or would genuine competition cause prices to fluctuate continually with every change in the relation of "demand and supply" (or rather, of demand and productive capacity)? If a given price remains unchanged for weeks or months, is price competition nonexistent during those intervals?

To answer the last question first, the decisive fact seems to be that the purpose of a firm in setting a price on its goods is to sell the goods at the price that has been set. If a price is set competitively, it would be absurd to claim that the price competition ended with the setting of the price and before any goods had been sold. The selling of the goods is part of the price competition. What remains is an arguable question how often prices should change, and such questions do not belong in a definition. The same applies to the other controversial questions about how competitive prices should behave. A definition should facilitate the study of such questions, not foreclose it by purporting to give a final answer.

Perhaps some of the difficulties can be reduced by accepting the consequences of the proposition that effective competition requires both aggressive and defensive actions. A second saving consideration is that price competition must, in reason, include some way in which prices can rise, on occasion, without concerted action. Some conceptions appear to leave room only for price reductions except when demand exceeds capacity. As to specific behavior, it is clear that price competition is something different for a wheat grower, a cement manufacturer, an automobile producer, or Macy's department store.

For the competition to be effective, the crucial thing seems to be that prices be independently made under conditions that give some competitors an incentive to aggressive action that others will have to meet, whenever prices are materially above the minimum necessary supply prices at which the industry would supply the amounts demanded of the various grades and types of products it produces. What profit or loss a given competitor will individually make will depend on whether he is a high-cost or a low-cost producer, and on whether the industry is shrinking or expanding.

It may be worth while calling attention to certain things that this definition does *not* set up as essential characteristics of competition. It does not limit it to cases in which the seller merely accepts a going price, which he has no power to influence. It does not define competition as a struggle to excel, after the simile of a race, in which there can be only one winner. It does not incorporate the effort to maximize profits—still less their actual maximization—as part of the definition of competition. The definition needs to leave room for competing firms that may conceive their aims in ways not necessarily inconsistent with the attempt to maximize profits, but including elements that are formulated in different terms. Perhaps the chief trouble with the conception of maximization is its implication of a precision which is unattainable and can be misleading. Secondarily, the meaning of profit maximization is ambiguous unless the time perspective that controls the firm's policy is carefully specified. Incidentally, and paradoxically, the producer who is likely to be trying hardest to maximize his profits is the one who is not making any—he is struggling for survival.

Finally, the definition does not require that each form of competition should be active at every moment, in the sense of new technical methods, new products, new selling tactics, or changed prices. All these may remain unchanged between active moves and may still embody the resultant of active and effective competitive forces. If so, this implies that preparedness is under way for further moves as occasion may present the need or the opportunity. Of course, this preparedness may lapse into ineffectiveness; but the producer who allows this to happen in his own establishment is likely to find himself fatally outclassed. And if preparedness is active, it is likely to eventuate in action.

30. THE ANTITRUST LAWS*

Theodore J. Kreps

WHAT IS THE MEANING OF ANTITRUST POLICY?

Historically antitrust policy, like a gnarled oak subjected to unsystematic pruning by weather, animals, and man, has grown irregularly, inconsistently, from various origins in several directions.

While under English common law there were remedies against "forestalling, regrating, and engrossing," antitrust policy debates in the United States started with Granger agitation in the 1870's against high and discriminatory freight rates. The term "antitrust" was the public battlecry against the Standard Oil trust of 1879 and against other industrial concerns which used the trust method of combination. First fruits of the agitation against monopoly evils were the so-called Granger laws, by which several Western States subjected railroads to varying degrees of public regulation, followed by antitrust legislation in some of the Southern States. After the famous decision in *Munn* v. *Illinois*, the regulatory authority of the Federal Government was invoked. Congress passed the Interstate Commerce Act in 1887 and the Sherman Act in 1890. The latter outlawed "combinations in restraint of trade" and monopoly or attempts to monopolize.

According to a recent decision of the Supreme Court: The Sherman Act was designed to be a comprehensive charter of economic liberty aimed at preserving free and unfettered competition as the rule of trade. It rests on the premise that the unrestrained interaction of competitive forces will yield the best allocation of our economic resources, and the greatest material progress, while at the same time providing an environment conducive to the preservation of our democratic political and social institutions.

Only a few antitrust cases were instituted during the first decade of the Sherman Act. Government efforts to use the new statute to break up industrial monopolies met a serious reverse in 1895. In a suit brought to prevent acquisition of additional refineries by the Sugar Trust, the Supreme Court ruled that Congress had no power to legislate concerning manufacture, which was held to be an inherently local pursuit, and fur-

* Theodore J. Kreps, *An Evaluation of Antitrust Policy: Its Relation to Economic Growth, Full Employment, and Prices*, Joint Economic Committee, Study Paper No. 22, Study of Employment, Growth, and Price Levels (86th Cong., 2d. sess.) (Washington, D.C.: U.S. Government Printing Office, January, 1960), pp. 2–5.

ther that a combination of manufacturers did not violate the Sherman Act since it affected interstate commerce only indirectly.

Respect for the antitrust law was restored by Theodore Roosevelt's "trust-busting" campaign and by Supreme Court decisions during his administration. In the *Northern Securities* case the Court ordered dissolution of a company which had been formed to hold the stock of competing railroads in the Northwest. And in the "beef-trust" case the Court ordered dissolution of a packing combine alleged to be restricting competition in the meat industry. The latter decision brought manufacturing within the scope of the Sherman Act, thus removing the handicap to antitrust enforcement seemingly imposed by the 1895 decision in the sugar case.

A new guide to antitrust enforcement was established in 1911 when the Supreme Court, in decisions ordering dissolution of the Standard Oil Co. and the American Tobacco Co., promulgated the "rule of reason."

A decade of increasing popular debate and agitation over trusts led all groups in 1912 to pledge "an increasing warfare in Nation, State, and city against private monopoly in every form." A plan of action had been outlined as early as 1900 which sounds strangely modern:

> Existing laws against trusts must be enforced and more stringent ones must be enacted, providing for publicity as to the affairs of corporations engaged in interstate commerce, requiring all corporations to show, before doing business outside the State of their origin, that they have no water in their stock, and that they have not attempted, and are not attempting, to monopolize any branch of business or the production of any article of merchandise; and the whole constitutional power of Congress over interstate communication shall be exercised by the enactment of comprehensive laws upon the subject of trusts.

In 1912 it was furthermore advocated that there be enacted a declaration by law of the conditions upon which corporations should be permitted to engage in interstate trade. Specifically included among such conditions were—

> the prevention of holding companies, of interlocking directors, of stock watering, of discrimination in price, and the control by any one corporation of so large a portion of any industry as to make it a menace to competitive conditions.

On October 15, 1914, the Clayton Act was passed which forbade a corporation to acquire any stock of a competing corporation in the same industry or line of commerce and prohibited a holding company from acquiring the stock of two or more competing corporations, where such acquisition would substantially lessen competition or restrain commerce or tend to create a monopoly. The act prohibited certain trade practices where the effect would be substantially to lessen competition or promote monopoly. And it forbade interlocking directorates among large corporations that were competitors. The new law, however, did nothing to change the "rule of reason."

A companion act of September 26, 1914, set up the Federal Trade Commission and gave it power to investigate activities of corporations engaged in interstate commerce, to report violations of the antitrust laws to the Attorney General, and to enter cease and desist orders against corporations which it found were engaging in "unfair methods of competition in commerce" or violating provisions of the Clayton Act.

In 1926 the Federal Trade Commission created a special division to supervise trade-practice conferences, in which it cooperated with businessmen in defining practices to be regarded as "unfair methods of competition" banned by the Trade Commission Act. Numerous trade-practice conference agreements were negotiated and promulgated, preventing so-called guerrilla competition and promoting "smoothness and stability of business operations." After 1930 this activity died down as did that of the Antitrust Division. The latter instituted but five cases in 1931 and only three in 1932.

The first attack of the Roosevelt administration on the problem of destructive competition was a scheme of industrial control that required partial suspension of the antitrust laws. When the national industrial recovery bill was before the Senate, June 7, 1933, Senator Wagner, Democrat of New York, asserted that the Sherman Act was based on an outworn economic philosophy and had failed to prevent excessive concentration of wealth or to protect the economic opportunities of small business and consumers. He held that NRA codes would fulfill the objectives of the antitrust laws by making "competition constructive rather than ruinous" and by permitting "cooperation whenever a wise policy so dictates."

The Supreme Court in the famous *Schechter* decision put an end to the National Recovery Administration.

In the meantime, concentrated economic power was being restricted or subjected to Government control by laws to separate investment banking from commercial banking, to regulate issuance of securities, to limit operations of public utility holding companies and to strengthen Clayton Act prohibitions against price discrimination, among other reforms. In 1938, Congress authorized the formation of the Temporary National Economic Committee which recommended a large number of changes in our patent laws and in antitrust legislation generally. But few thus far have won enough support to be embodied into law.

There did take place, however, a considerable increase in antitrust activity. Before 1935 appropriations to the Department of Justice for antitrust enforcement had ranged from $100,000 to $300,000 a year. Before the end of World War II they began to exceed $2 million and more a year.

Law is often obliquely made by changing the enforcement machinery; thus the fivefold increase in the Antitrust Division's appropriation between 1938 and 1942 was a more important contribution to an effective antitrust policy than all of the amendments to the Sherman Act ever passed.

Antitrust policy thus, is a summation of legislation (1) prohibiting combinations in restraint of trade, judicially amended by the "rule of reason"; (2) of legislation prohibiting monopoly, attempts to monopolize, or mergers lessening competition; (3) of legislation prohibiting some restrictive business practices per se such as price fixing and interlocking directorates; and (4) of legislation limiting to actual differences in cost such discriminatory practices as might tend to "lessen competition." But it is more than legislation. It covers also deliberate suspension during both World War periods and the Korean war, also de facto nonenforcement except during the Theodore Roosevelt-Taft administrations and the years 1938 to 1941, 1946–50, and recently. Not to be forgotten is the vast area of statutory exemption from Federal antitrust policy: all intrastate commerce, public utilities, agriculture, most activities of organized labor, transportation including shipping, airlines and railroads, oil imports and production, retail prices, and certain exports.

31. AGRICULTURE: THE COMING DECADE*

Karl Brandt

I believe it to be one of the legitimate functions of economists that they make their contribution to the development and performance of our political economy by putting before the American people, their legislators and administrators alternative courses of policies and by evaluating comparative costs, major results and expectable side effects. It is for the body politic to choose and decide. It is the economists' duty to keep the body politic well informed, first of all on the range of alternative means to arrive at certain ends. In this sense I put an additional alternative set of guidelines on the docket of our profession for preliminary discussion and for later testing and weighing against a number of other alternative packages of farm policy measures. . . .

Studies of agricultural policy issues on both sides of the Atlantic stretching over 35 years have taught me that the "agricultural problem" is in all countries a perennial part and parcel of the dynamic process of economic development and of the dislocations and adjustments which are integral elements in it. Under any democratic form of government, farm

* Karl Brandt, "Guidelines for a Constructive Revision of Agricultural Policy in the Coming Decade," *Journal of Farm Economics*, Vol. XLIII, No. 1 (February, 1961), pp. 1–12.

policy tends to become an increasingly hot political and social issue as the accelerated rise in productivity of manpower in agriculture requires people to shift from rural to urban employment. The ever-changing symptoms of the farm problem can be tackled by an unlimited variety of public policy programs. But the hard core of the farm problem, namely, the structural change involved in a nation's economic growth can never be "solved" in the same sense as one can solve problems of a temporary emergency nature. Being concerned chiefly with the social impact and pains of economic growth, the legislative treatment of the farm problem can diminish the political friction and heat it causes. However, it is well to realize that farm legislation reaches in all countries to the very life of liberty and the core of the values that orient an economic system, the more so the smaller the farm population gets. Farm legislation calls for warm hearts and cool heads.

I

In the coming decade foreign affairs will outweigh domestic issues far more than in the past because our military security will depend heavily on closest cooperation with our allies. This in turn presupposes more and more economic cooperation within the Atlantic Community including Latin America, and with the free parts of Asia. These vital relations reduce the leeway for potential domestic adjustments by any measures of restriction of imports and of foreign exchange controls.

Compelling evidence makes it abundantly clear that in this turbulent and deeply divided world our country will face in the years ahead a most crucial test of its leadership among the free nations. To meet the challenge in all its interlocked diplomatic, military, political, and economic aspects requires that we develop, expand, and utilize our productive resources with drive, imagination, and wisdom. With an assured vigorous growth of our population, appropriate efforts at further improving health, education, and research, and continued thrift, formation and wise investment of capital of our citizens, the foundations for greater national security and welfare appear excellent. Provided the nation and its statesmen are alert and act with prudence, that is: given appropriate public policy, prospects are good that with growing productivity and a rising real output of goods and services per capita, the economy will offer ample opportunities to our people for a sustainable high rate of employment and for the improvement of income while we simultaneously discharge our heavy responsibilities in mutual security, foreign trade and investment, particularly in less developed countries.

However, it must be realized that such growth and performance of the national economy is bound to face a much harder competition in coming years than in the period since the end of World War II.

To assure a continued stable and prosperous development of the

Western countries requires that the stability of convertible currencies, recently achieved, be extended, and that foreign trade be liberalized further. This puts a high priority on the maintenance of the integrity of the U.S. dollar as the world's foremost reserve currency. Only if we succeed in containing inflation in the domestic economy will it be possible to hold the balance of trade and the balance of payments in such conditions that the dollar remains a hard, freely convertible currency, and that a liberal foreign trade policy prevails.

Due to the strong revival and vigorous expansion of the industrial exports of Western Europe and Japan, there will be less latitude for price increases of U.S. products than during the postwar years in which U.S. industries had a practical monopoly of supply. Increasing competition from Soviet Bloc countries in world trade and in financing of underdeveloped countries will make domestic price stability even more mandatory lest unemployment hit industries that have priced themselves out of their foreign markets.

If these assumptions about the changed impact of the international situation on our national economic policy should be basically correct, it would demand even more than in the past that productive resources be allocated to the uses where they contribute the optimal yield to the social product. In a dynamic economy this calls for a high mobility of resources. Most of all, it calls for the geographic and vocational mobility of the greatest of all resources: manpower.

Within the American economy a universally unique feature of our dynamic progress is the structural improvement and the unprecedented rise in productivity in agriculture. These have yielded a steady flow of labor to the urban economy, and assured for it an abundant and dependable supply of food and fibers at reasonable prices. In its utilization of land and capital resources and its output agriculture is today an extremely well-integrated part of the national economy, which performs in accord with economic principles as any other part of it. Originally, nearly all other economic activities were integrated into agriculture, as is best illustrated by the fact that in Jefferson's time 90 percent, sixty years ago 50 percent, of the American population were gainfully employed in agriculture. Today less than 10 percent are still in agriculture.

The farm problem is commonly considered as the result of a sudden revolution or explosion of technology. There is, indeed, a great deal of improvement in machines, tools, plants, animals, feed, and fertilizer. But the essence of the change lies in improved input-output ratios and cost-revenue ratios. The persistence of very powerful price relations between factors and products has forced cumulative shifts in the operations of the firm in agriculture. The much steeper rise of farm wages than of total operating costs of labor-saving machinery has induced the continued substitution of capital for labor. The heavy capital investment in farm machinery and the economies of scale possible in its full utilization have led to acreage enlargement of operational units. The high excess of marginal revenues over marginal costs, still attainable anywhere in the U.S. in the application of more fertilizer and water to crops and pastures, has led to the boosting of yields per acre, or the substitution of purchased inputs for land. In fact the main increase in the output of crops during the last two decades can be explained by increased input in seed, pesticides, fertilizer (chiefly nitrogen), and water. This increase has contributed a considerable share to the increase of output per man-hour which was otherwise due to a reduction in input of labor. The institutional circumstance that for some major crops the supported market price is obtainable only for the output of a specified acreage allotment adds a further powerful economic incentive to increased use of yield boosting kinds of input. Allotments are, indeed, a powerful output accelerator.

As a result of these cost-price relations, which promote intensification and which governmental price supports have accentuated, the aggregate output has exceeded total utilization. This is the part of the farm problem that concerns the 2 million commercial farms and even more the U.S. Treasury.

Despite a large transfer of manpower out of agriculture, there is still a considerable excess of manpower left in agriculture. This is chiefly the problem of low-incomes of many of the people on the other 2 million farms, although by no means of all of them.

II

Major economic defects of the methods chosen in agricultural legislation are the following:

A price guarantee for a few commodities interferes with the relations between prices of all farm products and all factors, and thereby interferes unintentionally with all supply responses of our agricultural economy.

Price support as the chief method of farm income support sets each support level above equilibrium and gives powerful incentive to excess production.

The raising of a commodity price above a competitive market level subsidizes non-agricultural producers of substitute products, such as man-made fibers, and competing farmers abroad, e.g., producers of cotton. Both effects shrink the potential demand in domestic and foreign markets.

Insofar as agricultural exports must be subsidized, this is an additional drain of Treasury funds.

Due to excess production, support prices are actually fixed prices.

The guarantee against price changes for a select few commodities puts a premium on the risk-free expansion of their output.

Fixed grain prices vis-a-vis free livestock prices induce farmers to feed less and to sell more to the CCC as livestock prices fall.

Restrictive acreage allotments establish a premium on intensification and therefore are ineffective as output controls, while they tend to freeze the location of production.

Marketing quotas are more effective in controlling market supply of a commodity, but they shift the use of resources and thereby the surplus to other commodities. They are applicable and enforceable only for the part of the commodity stocks which are exchanged in the market.

The price-fixing legislation has resulted in truly gigantic stockpiles of unwanted grain and other farm commodities held by the Government, at enormous costs in interest, storage, losses, and transportation. This in itself is a perpetual serious misallocation and waste of scarce resources. It is a waste of a part of the taxpayers' income and has entrenched vested interests of third parties that benefit from surplus holding and handling.

Despite being sealed off from the current market, the excess stocks exert a depressive influence on the markets in the U.S. and the world, particularly in view of the prospect of continued excess production.

So long as this stockpile exists there is no possibility of restoring a free market for the commodities concerned.

The price supports, acreage allotments, and marketing quotas have raised land values and land rents and thereby created rigidities in land utilization and vested interests in the perpetuation of such policies. While increased equities benefit operating and retiring farmers, the higher land values increase costs for future farmers.

The capitalization of revenues flowing from price support via acreage allotments increases the marginal physical and value productivity of land assets at the expense of returns to labor and capital assets.

The vast expenditures for price stabilization do not correct the regional maladjustment, such as the overproduction of wheat in the Great Plains, or the underemployment of manpower on the low-income farms of the Appalachian, the Piedmont, and the Ozark areas.

As a device for redistributing income to agriculture from within the economy, price supports are an inappropriate and wasteful means.

As a device to redistribute income within agriculture, price supports are even much less effective, because they prorate the increase in income according to the scale of operation.

Beyond outright donation, the disposal of surplus stocks can be achieved only by heavily subsidized exports, a policy which is counter to the national interest in a maximum liberalization of international trade.

The use of the surpluses under Public Law 480 as aid to underdeveloped countries is a costly *ex-post* method of assistance in which the recipient countries receive less than one-half of the costs to the U.S. Government, and in which it may perhaps recover no more than 10–15 percent of the costs after 10 to 20 years.

Price support by the CCC by means of non-recourse loans and purchases amounts to an open-end commitment of the Treasury, which renders control over the government expenditures ineffective.

III

In order to have some foundations on which to erect guideposts for a change, I offer a few observations on the essential features of the dynamics of agriculture.

There is no more than a minute grain of truth, if any, in such fundamentalistic assertions by some members of the profession as that due to physical, biological, and organizational circumstances, agriculture is unable to adjust supply to demand, and that it reacts perversely to prices.

The assertion that agriculture is denied a "just income" by being forced to operate in atomistic competition against monopolistic market power of industry, commerce, and labor is not supported by any conclusive evidence. To prove such causational relation calls for far more than demonstration of rigidities in "administered" prices or in certain wage rates of 17 million labor union members among a labor force of over 70 million people.

It must not be overlooked that corporate income is an extremely unstable item in our economy and that unions have no control over the volume of employment or the payroll of industries and hence no control over the income of even a fully unionized vocational group. That unions have considerable power in collective bargaining over working conditions for their members is another matter.

The income and financial situation of the commercial farm operators, particularly when due consideration is given to the continual increase in their equity, give no cause for national alarm about an emergency or the urgency of sharply expanding public income support, but a great deal of cause for pondering a review of the means of policy.

Our agriculture is far from being left to hopeless isolation of millions of atomistically competing farmers who increase production when prices make production unprofitable. On the contrary, it is excellently organized with a farmer-owned and operated up-to-date long-, medium-, and short-term farm credit system, a tax-privileged, well-organized, vast cooperative system of nearly 10,000 marketing, farm-supply, and service enterprises with over 20 million members, $13.5 billion annual turnover, vast capital assets, and extraordinary bargaining power. About 100 of the largest farmer coops do annually over $20 million business each. Our agriculture is serviced by a government-supported land grant college system with agricultural research stations in every State of the Union and by a Federal-State financed up-to-date farm advisory system available free of charge to every farmer in every county of the U.S. All farm people, though most are self-employed, have the same benefits as urban employees under social security legislation.

Agriculture is a system of private, overwhelmingly family-operated enterprises, which in its 2 million commercial units behaves so remarkably businesslike that it gears production in accordance with the effective demand—a demand which for price-supported commodities includes the U.S. Government's unlimited commitment to buy any amount offered. The trouble is chiefly one of a lag in effective mobility of resources, particularly manpower, and of adjustments in land values.

Government price-income support policies have reduced the mobility of resources. Allotments and quotas have enhanced the land value. Rational economic adjustment may require use of some land at lower intensity (i.e., less manpower and purchased inputs per acre) in larger operational units. But this involves a certain relative reduction in land value and land taxes. The greatest rigidities that interfere with the mobility of resources are the result of price fixing in combination with allotments.

Arguments on behalf of the gradual restoration of a market economy for agriculture and a less costly, more effective system of farm policy are usually countered with the accusation that this implies laissez-faire and an unfair denial of equal political subsidy treatment of agriculture, and with the absurd assertion that subsidies "built" the railroads, the airlines, and the maritime merchant fleets. Therefore, I want to stress that I do not believe in laissez-faire but in a strong government enforcing the rules of competition in a market economy and effectively promoting conditions favorable to economic growth and stability. The question cannot be whether the government should or should not use subsidies in dealing with the farm problem. The question is whether subsidies are being misused to make an economically untenable *status quo* socially bearable, or whether subsidies and intervention are self-liquidating and serve the purpose of keeping the farm economy basically free, self-adjusting, and capable of operating eventually without such aid. Subsidies are justifiable if they assist people in making adjustments and mitigate the hardships involved. The fast tax write-offs on farm equipment and storage facilities, freedom of all farmers from Federal tax on farm-used gasoline, and initially subsidized credit for rural electrification are also non-objectionable forms of subsidies.

However, to have the gross returns from all major farm products fixed and rationed among all farmers in a manner that is just or "fair to both consumers and producers" by the Congress, as some economists propose, appears to me neither compatible with the institutional and legal frame of our economic system, nor feasible.

While it is theoretically not impossible to control the output of 4 million farms by comprehensive control of land and capital inputs, I hold it politically inconceivable that the American people, particularly the farmers, would ever accept the degree of regimentation and law enforcement that would be necessary to execute such control. It is moreover questionable whether the total costs involved for the nation would not by far exceed the exhorbitant ones of the present price stabilization. Compulsory supply controls immediately create by definition illegal units of supply, i.e., a black market. To make it effective such control would have to ration all purchased inputs, such as fuel, fertilizer, machinery. It makes no difference whether the "comprehensive supply control" would be exercised by the Government, or by compulsory farmer-operated commodity cartels, or whether quotas would be made negotiable. The assignment to all farmer cartels would be to restrain competition, administer shares in the market, and reduce the mobility of resources. This would lay waste in the realm of food, feed, and fiber production the main source of wealth in the American economy.

If supply control should approach effectiveness, it would require extension to the industries which compete with farm production. Beyond that it seems fantastic to believe that in an integrated dynamic economy the conversion of a primary industry like agriculture into a politically directed state monopoly could stop there. Total cartelization of agriculture is only the beginning of total cartelization of the industries and trade. The historical precedent of this inescapable sequence under the Weimar Republic in Germany from 1928 to 1933 and its ominous finale under the Nazi regime, 1933–1945, should be sufficient deterrent to any repetition by contemporary eclecticists.

Insofar as the results of a decade of extensive research by many of our most competent analysts on the supply function in agriculture are concerned, they have not gone beyond preliminary exploration and in my judgment do not provide any reliable quantitative knowledge with which a supply control system could be operated with any accuracy.

The assumptions by some economists about the possibility of reducing aggregate output to market equilibrium by withdrawing enough crop acreage by expansion of the conservation reserve up to 60 or 80 million acres impress me as unwarranted and extremely expensive illusions. At best the conservation reserve provides additional opportunities for the retirement of elderly farm people chiefly on marginal units. There is no evidence in support of the idea that idling of acreage at public expense could become an effective decelerator of growth of aggregate output of agriculture.

The unsatisfactory results of the present farm policy are almost exclusively the result of maladjusted legislation, not of administrative failure in its execution.

The overruling economic argument against a policy change toward effective lifting of farm income beyond the present level by supply restriction lies in the implied substantial jacking up of food and fiber prices to the consumer and the inevitable escalator effect on wages and prices. The cost-push inflation involved in it would tend to cause serious unemployment in export industries and deterioration of the balance of trade. Hence such policy would tend to imperil the exchange rate of the U.S. dollar. The savings in the Federal Budget by reduced CCC stocks would largely be lost in higher export subsidies.

IV

The foregoing assumptions about the needs of economic policy in general and of agricultural legislation in particular lead me to suggest, for discussion and getting them tested within the economic profession for their economic validity as well as their practicability, guidelines for a possible alternative course in legislation for agricultural adjustment aid, that go in a different direction from those of fascism or the corporate state. There are quite a few proposals. Professor Hendrik S. Houthakker's "Transitional Acreage Payments" plan, which he abbreviates as TAP, would bridge the gap between "artificially high" support prices and presumably lower prices riding in a free market over a transition period of five years. Payment per acre would be the same for all farmers, giving low-yield farmers proportionately more than under the present system. Professor Houthakker calls it a subsidy for past, but not for future inefficiency. He anticipates that acreage controls, government purchases, and export subsidies will become unnecessary and that the danger of increasing surpluses will disappear.

Professor Houthakker assumes that the "farm bloc's power" may vanish overnight. I do not believe that the assumed power of the farm bloc is what has kept legislation in the same tracks for 27 years. I believe the causes lie much deeper, namely, in what has so aptly been analyzed by J. S. Davis as agricultural fundamentalism. I would add to it that as an indestructible strand of a society's timeless memory all urban people have a fond affection for the farm, from which they or their forebears all came. It is the *Paradise Lost Complex* of modern metropolitan electorates that creates the phenomenon of increasing will to grant farm aid as the proportion of farm votes diminishes, a phenomenon typical of all industrial societies under representative forms of government.

Professor Boris C. Swerling has for several years worked out in great detail a Contributory Income-Insurance Plan for agriculture with initial Government contributions to the insurance fund. The insurance would be tied to the individual, not to the farm. It would be social insurance with an upper limit of something like $5,000 per individual, based on income tax records. The plan disassociates farm legislation from commodity stabilization altogether, is compulsory, lets prices settle at a free market level.

As a substitute for the price support policy the plan would, in my judgment, be unacceptable to the commercial farmers and their organizations and does not touch the question of what happens to the business of commercial agriculture and its gigantic investment within 4, 5, or 6 years.

I have already mentioned still another plan which envisages the correction of excess aggregate output by laying still 60 to 80 million acres of cropland by an increase of the conservation reserve. I consider this approach as a dead alley, unless productive acres, not whole farms, were fallowed under tight annual leases.

In view of the crucial need of a constructive alternative I put on the docket of our profession a course of legislation along the following lines:

A. Since the greatest maladjustment lies in the chronic underemployment of manpower in low-income farms, maximum assistance would be given by all competent Federal and State Government service agencies with particular emphasis on expansion of nonfarm employment.

B. The excess stocks of grain would be effectively eliminated from the U.S. and world grain markets by transferring title to a *Grain Conversion Board* under the statutory requirement that it cannot dispose of any of its stocks as grain but must convert all of them over a period of 6 to 8 years to staple livestock products and sell them exclusively in newly to be developed foreign markets and exclusively on the basis of long-term delivery contracts with food dispensing agencies abroad, particularly in new industrial areas of less developed countries where protein supplements to the diet are needed. These war-surplus disposal and market development transactions would be carried out by existing private enterprises and business firms. The Board would also be entitled to donate certain quantities to foreign charity. The high but limited cost of such disinvestment should be no deterrent vis-a-vis the absence of any constructive alternative and the extraordinary benefit of regaining a market free from the duress of the surpluses.

C. The Government would gradually (over a period of say four years) and progressively disengage itself from intervention in the commodity markets, thereby assist in the recuperation of their natural buoyancy in the absence of depressive surpluses, and it would simultaneously reprivatize the carrying of all visible stocks in first and second hand.

D. During this transitional period of disengagement the Government would financially assist producers of chronic surplus commodities in specified regions by buying from farmers, under specified contractual conditions, their allotments and marketing quotas, tapering the installment payments over the four years. One of the conditions would involve the farmer's commitments to fallow a specified percentage of his allotment acreage, with a tapering scale during the four years. Such massive financial aid would amount to indemnification for the abolition of unworkable means of farm policy adopted basically for war purposes and an institutional modification of the economy.

E. In order to get the Federal Budget expenditure for the farm program under control, the Congress would make a total appropriation for each fiscal year covering the expenditures involved in the indemnification, i.e., the purchase of the allotments.

F. The Government would give maximum support to agricultural exports by diplomatic efforts at removing discriminatory import restrictions abroad and by keeping U.S. markets open to foreign industrial products.

G. The Food-for-Peace Program would be continued.

This is a set of guidelines for a revision of agricultural legislation which I consider as one of several possible alternatives and which appears to me as an economically, socially, and politically constructive and feasible one. Legislation following these guidelines, properly administered, would adjust aggregate output via the market mechanism, without the fettering of farm enterprises or cartelization of industries, while protecting the economy against more inflation, and would shield the farmers against decline in their income and equity. Chiefly, such a program would create within a period of four years a situation in which the U.S. Treasury would no longer be mortgaged by, and the U.S. Government no longer be tied to, a continuation of anachronistic methods of farm policy. The precarious balance of payments situation makes a review of the Federal Budget item for agricultural price stabilization mandatory.

32. THE PUBLIC UTILITY APPROACH*

James C. Bonbright

This is a study of the standards of reasonable or optimum prices applied, or proposed for application, to that limited but vitally important class of business enterprises called "public utilities." Since the relevant standards must depend in part on the special character of the enterprises under review, a foreword on this character is in order. But the foreword will be brief, since it is designed merely to supplement the more extensive discussions in the general treatises on public utility law and economics.

The term "public utility" is one of popular usage rather than of precise definition, and writers are not uniform in extending its scope to newer types of regulated enterprise, such as radio and television broadcasting. For present purposes, however, the extension of the public utility concept need not concern us, since the basic principles of reasonable rates can best be developed by reference to the traditional public utilities

* James C. Bonbright, *Principles of Public Utility Rates* (New York: Columbia University Press, 1961), pp. 3–25.

—to those enterprises that have long been subject either to outright public ownership or else to government regulation of prices and of services. In the United States the control has usually taken the form of regulated private ownership, and this is the form that will be assumed throughout most of our discussion of price policy. It should not be inferred, however, that an economic theory of public utility rates which is valid under private ownership becomes invalid under public ownership, and vice versa. On the contrary, the essential principles, . . . apply with modification under both forms of organization.

For the purpose of this study an enterprise is not regarded as a public utility unless the regulation to which it is subject includes direct control of its rates of charge for services. But governmental price control alone is not enough to confer public utility status upon an enterprise or an industry. By a generally, though not universally, accepted linguistic convention, there is the further requirement that the primary purpose of the regulation must be, ostensibly at least, the protection of the public in the role of consumers rather than in the role either of producers or of taxpayers. For this reason if for no other, milk production was not converted into a public utility industry by the passage of state and Federal milk-price control laws; and the same statement applies to coal production under the former Guffey Act or to agriculture under the Federal farm-product price supports. To be sure, defenders of these price-support laws have often contended that they are really in the long-run interests of the consumers. But the defense comes from spokesmen for the producers.

Most public utilities can be divided conveniently into two major classes: (1) those enterprises which supply, directly or indirectly, continuous or repeated services through more or less permanent physical connections between the plant of the supplier and the premises of the consumer; and (2) the public transportation agencies. The most important members of the first class are the enterprises supplying electricity, gas, water, and telephone communication. The transportation agencies are sometimes divided into (1) the "steam" railroads along with competing forms of intercity public transportation, and (2) the local transit systems. Transportation, however, presents problems of unusual complexity and is therefore often reserved for special treatises that pay detailed attention, among other things, to the highly competitive nature of modern transport. This book will cite illustrations of rate-making problems in the railroad or local transit fields. But the systematic development of principles will have primary reference to the nontransport utilities, and especially to the electric companies. The reason for this narrowed emphasis lies in the closer approach to monopoly enjoyed by these latter companies along with the telephone systems.

Despite the distinction just drawn between the transportation agencies and the nontransport utilities, even most of the latter utilities do a transportation business if we use "transportation" in a broad sense to include what are more frequently called "transmission" and (in gas and electricity parlance) "distribution." True, a local utility company may have a production or manufacturing department, as does an electric company which generates its own power or a gas company which manufactures its own gas. But the transmission-distribution phase of the business is a vital part of most public utility systems and may constitute the major component of the total cost of service. Moreover, even though the entire utility system is usually subject to regulation, it is likely to have derived its recognized utility status from the department of the operations concerned with the transfer of the gas, or the electricity, or the telephone messages from one location to another. The economic significance of this fact will be noted in a later paragraph in this chapter.

"PRIVATE" BUSINESS VERSUS BUSINESS "AFFECTED WITH A PUBLIC INTEREST"

We have already in effect defined a public utility as any enterprise subject to regulation, including price regulation, of a type designed primarily to protect consumers. And in order to come still closer to traditional usage, we may amend the definition so as to make it apply only to those enterprises subject to regulation as a matter of long-run policy rather than as a temporary expedient in wartime or in some other emergency. But what are the special attributes of an enterprise, or of an industry of which the enterprise is a member, that give it "utility status" even in a country that has gone as far as has the United States in its reliance on the "automatic forces" of market competition for protection of consumer interests?

Down to the decade of the 1930s, the question just raised was often discussed as a legal problem—specifically, as a problem in constitutional law. Except in times of emergency, state and Federal legislatures were held by the Supreme Court of the United States to have no power to impose price restrictions on ordinary business enterprises. Statutes imposing such restrictions were held void as violations of constitutional guaranties of property rights, including the guaranties of the Fifth and Fourteenth Amendments. But exception was made of certain types of business said to have been "dedicated to a public use" or "affected with a public interest," and these types included the railroads and the familiar municipal utility companies. A layman might suppose that a list of all businesses affected with a public interest would be very long and that it would exclude only the producers of frivolous or luxury goods, which the community could very well do without. In fact, however, the early Supreme Court rulings were much more restrictive and did not go very far beyond the traditional public utility field in recognizing legislative power to fix prices or to impose upon private businesses restrictions not merely designed to protect "health, safety, and morals."

Perhaps the most plausible way to rationalize these early legal cases, which seem to deny any public interest in the production of vitally important goods and services, is to infer that what the courts were denying was the public importance of any single producing firm or enterprise rather than the public importance of an entire industry. But this rationalization would not fit *all* the cases; and it would be cogent only under the assumption of competition among many producers, no one of which has a sufficiently large share of the market to make its output or price-fixing policies a matter of general concern.

Today, however, any attempt to explain the early judicial distinctions between a public and private business has little more than historical interest, since the Supreme Court has now changed its own position, as indicated by the famous *Nebbia* case of 1934. Legislative proposals to place a given industry under price regulation may now be considered on their merits from the standpoint of economic and social policy, and without serious danger of upset by reason of conflict with the older, traditional legal doctrines. But this does not solve the problem; it merely shifts the emphasis from considerations that have seemed of special importance to lawyers and judges to considerations that seem valid to persons unindoctrinated in legal lore.

ESSENTIAL NATURE OF THE SERVICE AND PUBLIC UTILITY STATUS

The preceding paragraphs have followed custom in defining a public utility as any enterprise actually subject to regulation as a public utility. But this definition begs a question that must now receive attention: why certain types of enterprise are, or should be, singled out for this treatment whereas others are free from direct price control and from related types of regulation except, perhaps, in a period of emergency such as a war. Modern writers generally agree that no simple or single answer will suffice. The economic and social forces that have imposed regulation, say, on the electric power companies are multiple and complex. Moreover, they are not precisely the same as the forces that have imposed somewhat similar regulation, say, upon the interstate railroads.

Nevertheless, two attributes of a public utility business have received emphasis in the textbooks, and they will be discussed in turn. The first is the special public importance or necessity of the types of service supplied by utility enterprises; the second is the possession by utility plants of technical characteristics leading almost inevitably to monopoly or at least to ineffective forms of competition. As Clemens neatly puts it: "Necessity and monopoly are almost prerequisites of public utility status."

As to the character of public utility services considered as a group, few persons would deny that they are essentials of modern living rather than mere luxuries or conveniences. A well-functioning transportation system, for example, is a matter of life-and-death importance to the nation. Especially in a large city, even a temporary stoppage of electric power service is serious, and a prolonged cessation would be disastrous. This recognized public importance of adequate utility service, available without delay at reasonable rates and without unjust discrimination, certainly helped to account for the public demand for regulation even in a period of American history which was notably unfriendly toward "government interference with business."

But what the recognized importance of public utility service fails to account for is the restriction of regulation to services which, however essential they may be to the life of a community or the whole nation, are no more so than are the supplies of many commodities and services produced and distributed by unregulated business. Granted that electric power and telephone service are necessities of modern living rather than mere luxuries, so also are food, clothing, and housing. Yet the prices of these essential products are not subject to peacetime control of a public utility nature, with the partial exception of housing rentals in limited areas and under assumed conditions of abnormal scarcity. Indeed, if the supply of electric power is a necessity, so also must be the supply of the turbines, the generators, and the boilers needed for the production of this power. Yet the electric equipment companies are not treated as public utilities and are left as free to determine their own price policies as are other "private" industrial companies.

What must justify public utility regulation, then, is the necessity of the regulation and not merely the necessity of the product. Indeed, one may go further and note that modern public policy is far from satisfied with regulation limited to the protection of consumers in securing *essential* types and amounts of service at fair prices. Instead, it extends to the encouragement of abundant use of service, especially of electric service, stimulated by promotional rates that are nevertheless high enough to discourage wasteful consumption. The theory of public utility rate making would be a very limited and rather dull subject if it were merely a theory of the proper pricing of economic *necessities.*

What has just been said may seem so obvious as to be hardly worth mentioning. Indeed, I would not have stressed the point but for its bearing on the criteria of "reasonable" utility rates. One sometimes reads the contention that charges for public utility services should not be based on the ordinarily accepted standards of cost pricing, since these services are essentials of living and hence should be made freely available even to persons who cannot afford to pay the costs of production. What this contention ignores is the very weak correlation between necessities versus luxuries on the one hand and utility services versus non-utility products on the other. If the prices chargeable for all necessities were to be based on standards of ability to pay rather than on standards of cost pricing, then a reorganization of the country's entire price system would be in order.

The above-noted reference to essentiality of service as an earmark of a public utility should be distinguished from a related point of a more subtle character to be found in some of the literature, namely, the assertion that public utility services have a peculiarly *social* or *community* value, not reflected by the prices that individual consumers are willing to pay for them. This "social-value" theory will be discussed briefly at the end of this chapter. . . . But whatever its merits, I feel sure that it has been of only secondary influence in the American and British development of public utility regulation.

NATURAL MONOPOLY AND PUBLIC UTILITY STATUS

It is the general consensus of economists that the primary, even though not the sole, distinguishing feature of a public utility enterprise is to be found in a technology of production and transmission which almost inevitably leads to a complete or partial monopoly of the market for the service. Public utility regulation, if chosen in preference to outright public ownership, is therefore said to be a substitute for competition. . . .

This "natural-monopoly" theory of public utility regulation reflects an old and orthodox point of view. Properly qualified, I believe it to be sound. But it must be expressed today with more caution than would have been deemed necessary in earlier years. For, as modern economists have shown, the differences between a competitive industry in a realistic sense of competition and a monopoly, natural or unnatural, are far less sharp and less simple than was once assumed. Close approximations to "pure" or "perfect" competition are thought to be rarely if ever found in manufacturing or trading industries. On the other hand, even public utilities may face severe competition, typically of a substitute-product type, with respect to a large fraction of their services—sometimes with respect to the major fraction.

It follows that the traditional distinction between monopolistic public utilities and competitive private enterprises is an over-simplification, since the true distinctions are those of degree rather than of kind. In attempting to draw such a distinction, moreover, one should not overlook the possibility that some important industrial companies have avoided regulation, not because they have been more competitive than most utilities but rather because of the recognized difficulties of an extension of effective regulation to the manufacture of commodities. Efficient regulation of the American steel industry, or even of the aluminum industry, would present far more serious problems than has regulation of the electric power utilities or of the telephone companies. Reliance on a certain degree of competition, fortified by antitrust laws, may therefore be deemed the lesser evil.

ECONOMIES OF LARGE-SCALE PRODUCTION AND NATURAL MONOPOLY

The familiar statement that a public utility is a "natural monopoly" is meant to indicate that this type of business, by virtue of its inherent technical characteristics rather than by virtue of any legal restrictions or financial power, cannot be operated with efficiency and economy unless it enjoys a monopoly of its market. So great are the diseconomies of direct competition that, even if it gets an effective start, the competition will probably not long persist if only because it will lead to the bankruptcy of the rivals. But even if the competition is long lived, as has occasionally happened when the rivalry has taken a restrained form, it is wasteful of resources because it involves unnecessary duplication of tracks, of cables, of substations, etc.

What then are the special characteristics of a public utility enterprise or plant which give it a natural monopoly character not conceded to other industries? An answer frequently given is that public utilities operate under conditions, or "under the law," of decreasing costs, whereas competitive enterprises operate under conditions either of constant cost or else of increasing cost. This means that the larger the output of a utility plant per day or per month or per year, the lower will be the cost of production and distribution per kilowatt hour, or per thousand cubic feet of gas, or per passenger mile, etc. Consequently, only a company enjoying a monopoly of the supply of service in a given area can operate at maximum economy.

This rationale of the natural monopoly status of the public utility industries was given currency, years ago, by the late Professor Henry C. Adams, and has been repeated, with many variations, down to this day. Properly qualified, it remains valid. But a restatement is required. For, taken alone, the well-known economies of large-scale enterprise are by no means peculiar to the utility business. Instead, they are enjoyed by utilities in common with many unregulated types of enterprise, including steel companies, automobile companies, and chemical companies. Compared to some of the giant manufacturing companies and manufacturing plants, most utility systems are of a small-scale nature if measured by any of the conventional units of size.

What favors a monopoly status for a public utility is not the mere fact that, up to a certain point of size, it operates under conditions of decreasing unit cost—an attribute of every business, including a farm or a hand laundry. Nor is it even due to any indefinite extension of the declining-cost portion of a curve relating unit costs of production to scale of output. It is due, rather, to the severely localized and hence restricted markets for utility services—markets limited because of the necessarily close connection between the utility plant on the one hand and the consumers' premises on the other. As a deterrent to successful competition, this market restriction is far more serious than is the case with manufacturing companies which can ship their products throughout a wide region or even throughout the nation. An automobile plant may be large enough to enjoy the full economies of large scale without requiring more than a fraction of the American car market to sustain full-capacity output. But a gas distribution system in Yonkers, N.Y., or an electric distribution system in Evanston, Ill., has a market limited to the load of one city. Even if permitted to supply the entire load, the local distribution system will still be engaged in fairly small-scale business. Were it compelled to share its limited market with two or more rival plants owning duplicate distribution networks, the total cost of serving the city would be materially higher.

The reader may note that Yonkers is served by the gigantic Consolidated Edison Company, which also supplies gas and electricity to much of the area of New York City, and that Evanston is one of many cities served by the Commonwealth Edison Company, which also carries the entire Chicago electrical load. But growth in size through an extension of territory, while it may result in substantial economies of scale, is no adequate substitute for the opportunity of a utility to cultivate intensively whatever area it does serve.

What has just been said about the interplay of the factors of economies of scale and of localized markets points to the significance of the fact, already noted earlier in this chapter, that public utility companies are essentially transportation or transmission agencies. The technology of electric, gas, or telephonic transmission is such as to require a close connection between the plant on the one hand and the consumers' homes or factories on the other. This is even true, though less rigidly so, for a railroad plant. Not all forms of transportation are so strictly localized—not ocean shipping, for example, nor truck transport. But for this very reason, these two forms of transportation have a less well established utility status.

ARE PUBLIC UTILITY SERVICES NECESSARILY PRODUCED AT DECREASING UNIT COSTS?

One further point about the monopoly attributes of a public utility should be emphasized in this chapter because of its important bearing on measures of desirable or "optimum" rates of charge. The point concerns the assumption, sometimes accepted by American writers as if it were axiomatic, that a public utility, by virtue of the very characteristics which put it into this category of enterprise, supplies service under conditions of decreasing unit cost with increasing rates of output. For example, a 50 per cent increase in the annual output of electric power (other things equal, including price levels, load factors, and number of customers) may result in an increase in total cost of only, say, 25 per cent. In consequence, the incremental cost of the service—the unit cost of supplying more of it—will be lower than the average cost. And this excess of average over incremental or marginal cost is thought to prevail, not merely as a short-run phenomenon when existing plant capacity is temporarily redundant, but even as a long-run or chronic phenomenon exemplifying the economies of large-scale output. The implications of this supposed cost differential for policies of rate making . . . will be apparent to anyone familiar with modern price theory.

Stated as a general tendency or typical situation applicable to most types of utilities in the United States in the present stage of their expansion, this assumption that a utility operates on the declining-cost portion of a long-run unit-cost curve may be valid, although the available data in support of any such generalization are rather sketchy because of the currently inadequate state of public utility cost analysis. But the point to be stressed here does not concern the question of general tendency or typical situation. It concerns rather what seems to be a widespread assumption that a public utility *must* be producing on the declining-cost segment of a unit-cost curve in order to justify its claim to acceptance as a natural monopoly. This assumption is quite unwarranted. It ignores the point that, even if the unit cost of supplying a given area with a given type of public utility service must increase with an enhanced rate of output, *any specified* required rate of output can be supplied most economically by a single plant or single system.

By way of illustration, let us assume a region served by one electric utility which generates its own power in local plants. Three fourths of the generation is from economical hydroelectric plants at production costs (including capital charges on investment) of, say, ¼¢ per kilowatt hour. But since no additional water power is available within economical transmission distance, the remaining one fourth of the generation is by steam plants at a cost of, say, ¾¢ per kilowatt hour in an area of high fuel prices. Under these assumptions, the marginal or incremental cost of power generation will be ¾¢ per kilowatt hour, whereas the average cost is only 3¾ mills. In short, power is being produced under conditions of increasing unit cost. The increasing-cost behavior will be further emphasized if we also assume that, as more steam power is produced to meet the growing requirements of the area, even this power becomes more and more expensive to generate and transmit because of the absence of adequate condensing water or of good sites near the distribution network. To be sure, the increasing-cost tendency of the company's production department *may* be offset, or more than offset, by the declining-cost behavior of its distribution system. But there is no a priori ground for the assumption that the offset will be complete. Conceivably, the total kilowatt-hour costs of electric power in the area under review may rise as the rate of output increases, even assuming, as we do, no change in general price levels.

This hypothetical example of an electric utility company supplying power under conditions of increasing unit cost, irrespective of any change in price levels, may seem farfetched as an example applicable to this country today, although it may now apply to the Tennessee Valley Authority with its increasing reliance on steam power. But even when applicable, it does not belie the assumption that any given area can be supplied more economically by a public utility monopoly than by two or more companies operating in direct competition. For, on the one hand, the single company can secure the maximum advantages of economies of scale and of density, while on the other hand it is no more subject to the diseconomies of enhanced output resulting from scarcity of water power and of other natural resources than would two or more companies if called upon to supply the region with the same total output.

The current literature on electric power rates in Great Britain and France reveals no such general tendency as one finds in the American literature to take for granted long-run trends of decreasing costs with increasing rates of output. In France available water-power resources have been pretty well exploited, and additional output must come largely from thermal plants. In England, where water power has always been of minor importance, emphasis has been placed on the increasing-cost character of coal supply and also on the difficulties of securing desirable sites and good condensing water for new power plants. (Hence the vigor with which the British government is now pushing the development of atomic-power plants.)

What the parallel situation may be in the future with electric power in this country is a question on which I venture no opinion, although the limited opportunities for further water-power development and even the scarcity of good condensing water (in some areas) are well recognized. It may be that, with expected further increases in demand for power, economies of scale can still more than offset limitations of sites and of raw materials. Moreover, the coming of atomic power may change the situation. But with natural gas, the increasing-cost tendencies of the production end of this wasting-asset industry threaten to outpace the economies of large-scale transmission and distribution. Whether or not the American railways, as a whole, reflect a type of industry still subject to long-run decreasing costs is a controversial question, to which a confident answer is precluded by lack of adequate data. The telephone utilities, at least by their own contention and under the usual assumptions of the textbooks, are subject to increasing unit costs if the telephone subscriber or station rather than the telephone call is taken as the unit of measurement. But, so far as I am aware, the telephone industry, despite its vast facilities for statistical and economic research, has never seen fit to publish elaborate studies of its cost functions; and until these studies have been made, a degree of skepticism is justified. In any event, a telephone company does not present a standard example either of a firm or of an industry subject to "the law of increasing costs," since the character of the service rendered to any one subscriber changes significantly with a change in the number of other subscribers.

COMPETITION OF SUBSTITUTE SERVICES AS AN ALTERNATIVE TO RATE REGULATION

This brief discussion of the reasons that account for rate regulation of public utility companies in nearly all countries which have adhered to private ownership should not ignore a minority position expressed in this country, some years ago, by a group of economists with a strong antipathy toward "government interference with business." While their views have won but little favor either among other economists or with the general public, they are nevertheless entitled to careful attention as pointing to serious limitations of orthodox rate regulation.

The contention of these economists has been that the assumed monopoly status of a public utility is an illusion, or at least a gross exaggeration. True, there seldom exists that primary form of competition illustrated by two electric companies vying with each other for the patronage of the same customers. But what does exist is the competition of substitute services or products. For many purposes, the use of electricity is alternative to the use of gas, oil, or coal. Moreover, the large industrial and commercial customer has a feasible option to produce his own electricity if the power company will not quote him a favorable rate. Similarly, communication by telephone must compete with possible communication by telegram, by post, or by direct contact.

Those writers who have stressed this point of view would concede that there are limited uses and amounts of a utility service for which the consumer may have no feasible substitute. This is notably true, for example, of electricity for lighting, where gas, even if available and even if provided by a rival utility company, must be dismissed as obsolete. But the contention is that the high potential profits from a modern utility business do not lie in a policy of high prices designed to exploit the most urgent uses of service. On the contrary, they lie in a policy of low "promotional" prices, of the type that will maximize profits by a heavy volume of sales. Thus, even the small user of electricity for lighting and for minor appliances will be protected, without government regulation, by the self-interest of a company in setting rates low enough to encourage bountiful consumption for uses less urgent or subject to feasible substitutes.

The writers who thus insist upon the competitive character of a modern utility business do not limit their objection to regulation to the claim that it is unnecessary. Instead, they have urged that it is positively harmful since it must result, at least in the long run, in utility rates higher than would prevail with unregulated private ownership. Regulation of the traditional type purports to restrict companies to a standard "fair rate of return" on invested capital or on property "values." Hence, it is believed to stifle the initiative and the risk taking inherent in an effort by management to maximize profits through cost reductions and through the promotion of heavy volumes of sales. If free to set its own rates, an intelligently managed, profit-seeking company will be led to make experimental rate reductions in the hope that, perhaps after a delay of one or more years, the resulting increase in the demand for the service may yield higher profits than ever. But if subject to regulation, the same company will hesitate to make a rate cut, since the anticipated increase in demand is far from a certainty, and since the company will not long be permitted to enjoy the benefit of the increase even if it should be realized. Moreover, under regulation in actual practice, a voluntary decrease in rates is not easily and quickly reversed even if the resulting rate of return should prove disappointing.

These are forcible arguments, if not against all feasible forms of regulation then against the more orthodox forms. . . . But the question now to be raised is why these arguments have failed to carry widespread conviction. A really adequate answer will not be attempted here, since it would involve a detailed review of the actual history of corporate rate-making policy in this country under the influence of different forms and degrees of regulation including, in some areas, the almost complete absence of regulation. But two partial answers will be suggested.

The first answer is that, in actual experience, even those public utility managements that have been completely or relatively free from rate regulation of the "fair profit" type have not generally espoused a philosophy of low pricing designed to maximize long-run profits by the encouragement of widespread use of their services. Instead, they have acted in much the same way as have the managements of the more rigidly regulated companies, by revealing a marked degree of skepticism as to the alleged price elasticity of the demand for their products. On occasion, to be sure, laxly regulated private companies have made drastic rate reductions on their own initiative rather than on order from a public service commission. But these reductions may be attributed to the example of adjacent publicly owned plants or to the fear of public-plant competition. The famous and oft-cited example of the late Henry Ford's dramatic cut in automobile prices, followed, rather than preceded, by a cut in production costs, has not found many imitators in the public utility field. One may perhaps add that it has not been widely imitated in other fields nor even often repeated in automobile production.

Of more interest for the theory of public utility rate making is a second reason why any proposal to rely on competition has failed to win more converts. The point is that public utility companies, if free from rate regulation, would seldom be under competitive necessity to make *general* rate reductions in harmony with opportunities of cost reduction. Instead, they would be more likely to follow the policy of rate discrimination, otherwise known as "charging what the traffic will bear," thus enjoying at one and the same time the commercial advantages of a high price policy with respect to services for which the demand is inelastic, and of a low price policy with respect to services for which the availability of substitutes makes the demand highly elastic.

For this practice of price discrimination the mechanism of modern utility rate structures is admirably adapted. Through block rates, sometimes applied both to the "demand" charges and to the "energy" or "commodity" charges, favorable terms can be offered to large consumers who have a feasible option to generate their own electric power, while stiffer terms can be offered to small consumers. Still other devices of differentiation are available, such as special, low rates for services designed for special use. Not all of these differentials, to be sure, need be discriminatory in character. Indeed, all of them can be so administered as to conform to cost-of-service standards rather than to value-of-service standards. But an unregulated public utility is under no such limitation in the use of these instruments of monopoly power.

Let it not be supposed from the foregoing remarks that all forms and practices of rate discrimination are to be condemned as against the public interest. On the contrary, wise resort to discrimination of a value-of-the-service character is an essential tool of rate-making policy with respect to unsubsidized utilities that supply services at incremental costs lower than total average costs. But this very fact enhances the need for regulation. For it precludes the adoption of the proposal, sometimes made by persons who have not considered its logical consequences, to leave public utility companies the complete freedom to set their own rates subject only to a statutory mandate to avoid discrimination. Literally construed, the imposition of such a mandate would be fatal to private ownership. To be sure, even the traditional public utility laws are sometimes carelessly said to forbid discrimination. In fact, however, what they forbid is merely "undue" or "unjust" discrimination, thus placing upon commissions the major burden of interpreting and policing these ambiguous terms.

As already noted, the arguments against rate regulation have never won widespread support in their application to the so-called "municipal utilities" such as the electric power companies and the telephone companies. But arguments for much less restrictive standards of regulation have been receiving increasing attention and support with respect to the railroads. Largely because of the competition from the newer rival forms of transport, the railroads as a whole have been unable to earn rates of return that are adequate when measured by any of the conventional tests of adequacy. Even if completely free from rate control, only a few of them could expect to enjoy excessive rates of profit. Under these circumstances, and for the purpose of enabling them to compete more effectively with road, water, and air carriers, it has been proposed to amend the Interstate Commerce Act so as to permit them to set their own rates within a presumably wide band of minimum and maximum tolerable rates set by the Interstate Commerce Commission. Even within these limits, however, the Commission would still have the duty to enforce the rule against "unjust discrimination."

The merits of this proposal will not be discussed in this monograph on public utility rates, since only a transportation specialist, with an intimate knowledge of the technicalities of the different forms of transport, including a knowledge of their cost functions, is competent to have an expert opinion on its merits. In its favor is the argument that substitute-service competition is more nearly all-pervasive for intercity transportation than it is for the local utilities. But if the proposal should be adopted by an act of Congress, one may guess that part of the trouble associated with the enforcement of reasonable rates under the current standards of the Interstate Commerce Commission would be transferred to the problem of redefining and reapplying the rules against "unjust discrimination." In any event, the need for some form of government regulation will remain.

PUBLIC UTILITY SERVICES VERSUS "SOCIALIZED" SERVICES

The emphasis placed by the legal and economic literature on the distinction between a public utility and an unregulated "private" business has unfortunately tended to obscure another aspect of "the public utility concept" that is quite as important from the standpoint of rate theory. The fact is that a public utility enterprise is nonetheless a "business" even though subject to regulation and even when directly owned and operated by the government. This statement, at least, is in accord with the spirit of the concept both in British and in American usage. Stated more concretely and without the many qualifications required for strict accuracy, public utility services are designed to be sold at cost, or at cost plus a fair profit.

The thrust of this statement will be apparent if we compare the services supplied, say, by a municipally owned electric plant with other services supplied by the same city—for example, the construction and maintenance of streets and sidewalks. In all probability, the electricity will be sold at rates yielding a total revenue at least equal to cost including debt-service charges. Moreover, while the specific rate structure will not bear any very *close* relationship to the relative costs of different classes and amounts of service, a cost relationship will be present to an important degree. In short, the rates will be designed in accord with the old legal maxim, "Let the beneficiary bear the burden."

Not so with the city streets, nor with its parks, its zoological garden, its public schools, its health services, or its police system. These services are also costly to render, but the costs will be met directly or indirectly by taxation; and even the taxes will not be designed with any serious attempt at apportionment in relation to benefits received. The public schools, for example, are not only tuition free but are subject to compulsory attendance, and the payment of school taxes is not lightened for persons without children or for parents who choose to send their children to private schools. In short, the schools are not operated as a business, not even as a public utility business. They are "socialized" in a sense quite different from that which we have in mind if we refer to the "socialization" of an electric utility plant through municipal or state ownership. Only if a city, having taken over a private electric plant, were to abandon the effort to make it financially self-supporting in favor of free service, or of service supplied on an ability-to-pay basis, would it have socialized the electric service as it has socialized schools and public hospitals. In that event the city's electric department would have ceased to be a public utility.

Having drawn this sharp distinction between a public utility service and a fully "socialized" service, we must of course hedge the distinction in a manner required of nearly all attempts to classify social institutions. On the one hand, even private utility companies and railroads are sometimes required or induced to violate "business" or "economic" principles by supplying free service to indigent people, or by operating trains that fail to cover even their out-of-pocket costs, or by adherence to rate schedules designed to deal gently with low-income consumers. On the other hand, services supplied directly by government run the whole gamut from those rendered completely without charge (public vaccination) to services rendered at high profits (a European tobacco monopoly). Moreover, linguistic convention applies the term "public utility" to a type of enterprise *traditionally* supplying service at cost or at cost plus a profit, even though the cost principle is violated in a given instance; for example, the New York City subway system, which has not even been covering its operating expenses to say nothing of interest costs on the invested capital.

Despite these qualifications, the distinction just drawn between a public utility service and a completely socialized service is basic to the prevailing theories of reasonable public utility rates. For, with important reservations, these theories are variations of the major theme that the consumers of public utility services (1) should be free to take whatever types and amounts of service they are ready to pay for but (2) in return therefor should be required to pay rates not seriously out of line with costs of rendition.

This book would be a very different work both in its development of rate theory and in its conclusions on wise public policy if the author did not accept, in the main and with important qualifications, the orthodox view that those services presently known as public utility services should be sold on a cost principle. But the reader should be warned that this view is not universally accepted. Among those who have apparently rejected it is Professor Horace M. Gray, whose article on "The Passing of the Public Utility Concept" should be familiar to every student of public utilities. Gray believed that the concept had become outmoded partly because of the failure of regulation to accomplish the very objectives which it purported to accomplish, namely, to serve as an effective substitute for competition. But he also insisted that a cost-price standard of rate making is inappropriate for application to electric power supply or to the other vital services now largely supplied by private enterprise on "business principles." Social and national objectives, he believed, should supersede the limited objectives of a fair-profit or of a cost-price philosophy of rate making. At least, so I interpret his readiness to move away not only from private corporate ownership in its present form but also from the public utility concept as applied to a plant owned and operated directly by an agency of the government. . . .

B. Administered Prices and the Price Level

33. ADMINISTERED PRICES: AN EVALUATION*

Gardiner C. Means

Mr. Means. You see, the classical economists assumed that there was no zone of relative indifference, and it is the difference between the classical and what we actually have that is fundamental.

. . . Theoretical analysis indicates that, wherever a price can be administered, there is almost certain to be a zone of relative indifference

* Gardiner C. Means, "Statement," *Administered Prices*, Hearings, Part I, U.S. Senate Subcommittee on Antitrust and Monopoly (85th Cong., 1st. sess.) (Washington, D.C.: U.S. Government Printing Office, July 9–16, 1957), pp. 82–90.

within which various prices would produce practically the same profit, and observation supports this conclusion.

Also, it is important to notice that this zone of relative indifference and price administration itself does not depend on bigness or on having a monopoly. . . .

The necessity of adjusting to price changes made by competitors can narrow the breadth of the zone or can make it a zone for an industry and not for just a single firm, but I believe that such a zone of indifference is a pervasive fact in industries which operate on the basis of administered prices.

Once we accept this idea of a zone of relative indifference, it must be clear that the individual producer who is in a position to adopt a policy of administered prices does have an area of discretion within which he can choose to set one price rather than another and within which the price he actually sets is not determined by market forces even though market forces set limits on the area of his choice.

But the zone of relative indifference is not the only factor creating an area of price discretion for the price administrator. A second influence is the opportunity to choose between maximizing profits in the short run or in the longer run. Once a company is in a position to administer prices, if it aims to maximize its profits, it may have to choose between higher immediate profits and higher profits over a longer period. And often it will forego immediate profits for future profits. This may well be what happened immediately after the recent war when the established automobile companies were faced with a demand for cars far in excess of what they could supply. Instead of raising their prices to the level that would have maximized their current profits, they kept prices well below what the traffic would bear. Clearly these companies were not required by market force to keep their prices so low. It may have been that long-run profit considerations overweighed the advantages of greater immediate profits.

But whatever the reasons, in this case, the opportunity to choose a longer or shorter period to aim at profit maximization adds a second dimension to the area of discretion.

And this dimension, like the first, is not a product of bigness or of being a monopoly.

A third dimension to the area of discretion does arise from bigness and also from monopoly. Whenever a company is large enough in relation to its market to be vulnerable to governmental action under our antitrust laws, it may well choose to set prices lower than the most profitable for fear of stimulating Government intervention. This can further widen the discrepancy between the classical price and the actual price set, representing a further widening of the area of discretion in pricing.

There are other factors which can contribute to the area of discretion, but I have already given enough to show that administered prices involve an area of pricing discretion which lies entirely outside of classical theory.

Within this area, prices are not dictated by market forces. Within this area Adam Smith's unseen hand fails to operate. I have mentioned here examples in which price discretion has or may be used in favor of lower prices. But it can also be used to raise prices. I have been unable to discover purely economic forces which will ensure that this discretion will be used in a manner that would serve the public interest. Within this area, the decision is as open as the difference between the American and French traditions of pricing.

This clearly makes the administered price—its existence, the extent to which it is used, the ways in which it is used, and the economic areas in which it is most actively used—a subject of urgent concern to all who would understand the workings of our modern economy.

This is a matter for economic investigation and such investigation is badly needed. But, in the area of public policy, we can and should turn immediately to the effects of administered prices.

I have said I consider this price discretion to have an important bearing on our central economic problems and that it is therefore a matter of concern to public policy in regard to these problems. I would like now to develop this thought.

First, the problem of inflation. Some people have argued that inflation is solely a matter of the money supply and fiscal policy—that if the public's buying power in the form of liquid assets is increased, prices will rise; if buying power is reduced, prices will fall; and if the right amount of liquid assets is maintained prices will be stable.

This is good classical doctrine and if prices were actually controlled by market forces—if there were not a significant area of pricing discretion—I would be inclined to accept it.

But with the discretion implicit in administered prices, it would be possible to have a rise of prices without a prior increase in the public demand for goods. We have already seen that, by keeping their prices on the low side of the area of discretion, business can retard an inflation arising from too much buying power, as happened in the case of administered prices immediately after the war.

Conversely, if there were no excess in buying power, business enterprises could decide to raise their prices within the area of discretion so as to increase their unit profit margins.

This could lead to a considerable rise in price level without an initial increase in buying power simply as a result of decisions by price makers to move their prices to the upper margin of their respective areas of discretion.

If the higher prices had the effect of reducing sales, they could lead to reduced employment. And if fiscal and monetary expansion were used to support employment, the area of discretion within which prices could be set would be moved up the price scale and the process could be repeated.

In this manner, the area of discretion implicit in administered prices could lead to creeping inflation without an initial impetus from fiscal and monetary expansion while fiscal and monetary expansion might serve to maintain employment only at successively higher price levels. I suggest that we could properly call this type of inflation administrative inflation, in contrast to the traditional monetary inflation which arises from too much money chasing too few goods.

I should like to add that I do not believe administrative inflation is likely to lead to runaway inflation unless a reckless monetary and fiscal policy is pursued. The revision of administered prices tends to be fairly infrequent, with important lapses of time between, so that any large rise is likely to be spread over a considerable period of time. However, this is certainly something to be investigated.

The same upward spiraling of prices could be initiated through the area of price discretion in wage rates. Wage rates are themselves a form of administered price and, like other administered prices, administered wage rates are not closely controlled by market forces. If they are pushed up further than productivity can increase, the rise in costs is likely to be reflected in higher prices.

Whether in a particular case initiative for a rising price level comes from labor or business seems to be secondary to the fact that because of the area of discretion associated with administered prices and wage rates, a rise of prices can occur without the classic cause: excessive demand.

This presents us with a real problem of public policy and I don't begin to know how to handle it because, while we can see how administered prices can exist and what may cause them to be changed, we do not know enough about how administered prices are actually made and how, in fact, they are changed.

Certainly, we don't want government regulation of prices or government regimentation of the economy. Also we don't want creeping inflation. In these circumstances the recently employed technique of urging business and labor to help maintain stability is a logical first step—though how far it can take us is not clear.

If we knew more about the actual setting of administered prices and knew what we wanted to accomplish we might find measures to prevent or limit creeping inflation and do this in ways that are consistent with free enterprise and democratic procedures.

I would like to interject here that my reason for feeling that this is possible parallels my reason for feeling many years ago that we could maintain full employment.

In both cases it was strongly in the interests of labor, it was strongly in the interests of business, and it was strongly in the interests of the public that in one case we should maintain full employment, in the other case that we should not have creeping inflation.

We have developed procedures for dealing with the problem of maintaining employment and those procedures are consistent with our democratic system.

I believe we can do the same with respect to inflation arising not from too much buying power and fiscal and monetary policy, but arising from the area of discretion within which prices and wage rates are made.

I wish to give an example of the sort of thing that can be done and that is consistent with our system.

In the early days of the great depression, the President held a conference with business leaders who agreed to maintain wage rates as a contribution to recovery. The wage rate statistics show a very considerable adherence to this agreement well into 1931 and if a coordinate fiscal and monetary policy had been maintained—if we had known as much then as we know now about fiscal and monetary policy, this could have served to reduce the depression. Under what conditions would such a method help to hold against the inflationary use of the price-making discretion?

This would mean both discretion with respect to prices and discretion with respect to wage rates.

This whole field of price discretion and its relation to inflation needs intensive and, I believe, immediate study. It is not a matter which fits effectively into a study of inflation in the fiscal and monetary aspects. It is particularly appropriate to the background of this committee and the resources available to it. Such an investigation should not be concerned with derogation and should not be an attack on business or on labor, and should not be concerned only with monopoly in the legal sense. If all monopoly in this sense were eliminated the problem of administered prices, administrative discretion, and administrative inflation would still remain, but it is intensified by monopoly.

The problem is inherent in the character of modern business; it finds no answer in traditional economic theory because it involves behavior entirely outside that theory. It deserves to be investigated with a real effort to determine the area of discretion and the conditions under which discretion is exercised.

I want now to discuss administered prices in relation to employment, but the discussion will lead us back again to inflation. Administered prices are just as important to the problem of full employment as to that of inflation but the problem of employment is less immediately pressing because we have some understanding of it and have adopted a high employment policy to deal with its more important effects.

It was this problem which originally led me into the study of administered prices and their relative inflexibility. But that study was made more than 20 years ago and I believe there is a great need to reinvestigate the problem in the light of subsequent events.

In the case of employment as in that of inflation, it is the area of discretion which makes the operation of the economy different from that described in classical theory.

Classical theorists believed that market forces operated in such a way as to make the economic system self-correcting. If unemployment were excessive, reduced demand would lead to a general fall in prices and wage rates. This, in turn, would increase the real buying power of the money supply and stimulate real demand for goods and production at the lower level of prices.

Thus, excessive unemployment was regarded as only a temporary and self-correcting matter. So far as I can see, this view would be correct if prices were continuously determined by market forces as the classical theorists assumed. Some economists do not accept even this part of classical theory but the matter is largely academic.

What is more important is that there is fairly general agreement that if prices or wage rates or both are inflexible and do not respond fairly quickly to changes in demand or costs, there is no reason to expect an automatic tendency toward full employment.

This does not mean that there is general agreement on why particular shifts in demand and employment have occurred but only that inflexibility in prices or wage rates can prevent any classical tendency to automatic correction.

It is this agreement, I believe, more than any other one thing which has led to such widespread acceptance among economists of the idea of national responsibility for maintaining high employment through fiscal and monetary measures. The Government is relied on to maintain buying power so that we do not have to depend on a general decline in prices and wage rates to generate buying power when depression threatens.

The way in which administered prices operate to prevent an automatic correction of unemployment can be clearly seen in the behavior of wholesale prices during the depression of the 1930's. Chart I represents the general behavior of market and administered prices as groups. The solid line is a price index for those items in the BLS wholesale price index which changed less than 8 times in a period of 8 years and represents roughly a fifth of all the items in that index.

The dashed line is an index for those items in the BLS price index which changed practically every month in the same 8-year period and also represents about a fifth of all items. The chart only represents the major fluctuations in prices and leaves out the minor fluctuations in between.

I have simply taken the turning points or significant points and drawn straight lines connecting them.

From 1926 to 1929 the indexes for both administered and market prices reflect stability. Then from 1929 to 1932 market prices dropped precipitately while administered prices dropped only a little. Perhaps the BLS data somewhat understate the decline in the administered price index but various studies confirm the idea that the administered prices did not drop anything like the drop in market prices.

Then with economic recovery to 1937, market prices rose rapidly while the administered price index moved slowly so that the two indexes returned almost to the relation they held from 1926 to 1929.

I think it is also significant that we almost returned to full employment. You will see why that is significant in a moment.

With the recession of 1938, the two indexes separated again, and again came together with recovery.

This pattern of behavior is quite outside that which classical analysis would lead one to expect. Instead of a general decline in prices which would increase the real buying power of liquid assets, there was a distortion of the price structure with high prices and unemployment in one part of the economy and low prices and full employment in the other part.

That is particularly seen in agriculture as against industry but it is also true in some nonagricultural areas.

Indeed one might say that in the period of high employment and price stability from 1926 to 1929, market and administered prices were in relative balance with each other, that with depression they got out of balance, came back toward balance in 1937, were out of balance in 1938 and returned to balance along with full employment under the impact of war demand.

I emphasize this matter of balance because it seems to me more than fortuitous. The two indexes were in nearly the same relation in the high employment and stable price period 1913–14 as after the First World War in 1926 to 1929 in spite of the great price changes which occurred between these periods.

And again after the Second World War and the Korean war the two indexes assumed nearly the same relation in the high employment relatively stable-price period of 1953 to 1955.

This question of price balance seems to me to need investigation both from the point of view of employment and from that of inflation.

At the present time the latter aspect is the more important.

Let us examine the inflation after the Second World War in terms of balance. If we accept the relation of market and administered prices in 1926 to 1929 as representing approximate balance, and that is what theoretically you would expect in a period of full employment and relatively stable prices when the whole price structure would have an opportunity to get into approximate adjustment, we find that the price freeze in 1942 was made when the price structure was again in approximate balance.

Prices were then fairly stable through the rest of the war period though market prices were less effectively controlled than administered prices.

Then, price controls were removed and we had a big rise of prices, led by market prices. In this rise of prices and the later rise associated with the Korean war, the evidence seems to me clear that it was the great buying power in the form of liquid assets created by the war which forced inflation. This monetary inflation went on until the higher prices offset the urge to spend created by the large volume of liquid assets in the hands of the public and established a balance between prices, incomes, and the money supply.

The successive rounds of price and wage increase were a means to this adjustment but the area of discretion both in the case of prices and wage rates was, in my opinion, quite incidental to the inflation; in fact it probably acted as a very considerable brake.

By 1952 the full price impact of the increase in liquid assets appears to have spent itself and the readjustment to the higher price level was almost complete. Market prices which had overshot the new conditions fell back while administered prices came into adjustment so that, by 1953, the price structure in general was very close to being in the same balance as existed when prices were frozen in the war and as existed in the full employment stable price periods of 1926–29 and 1913–14.

This new price balance was roughly maintained for nearly 3 years though with some sagging in agricultural prices. Then in the middle of 1955, a new price advance began. I do not have reliable statistics to show the relative movement of administered and market prices in these latest years but I have indicated on Chart I my best estimates on the basis of the available material.

As far as I can discover this recent price rise has not been the result of excessive buying power or demand but, at least to a very considerable extent, has been a result of action within the area of discretion in which prices and wage rates are made. This is suggested by the rise of administered prices while market prices were stable or falling.

This is a new phenomenon. I do not find it anywhere in our history of prices.

. . . . .

In conclusion I wish to say that I believe administered prices lie quite outside the realm of traditional economic thinking and present serious problems which cannot find solution within the realm of traditional theory. There is need to find out more about this type of behavior. Why are administered prices changed when they are changed? Why not sooner? Why not later? And by what amounts are they changed and why not more or why not less? What are the factors which enter into these decisions and what is the latitute of discretion on the part of the price administrator?

CHART I

WHOLESALE PRICE BEHAVIOR

(Indexes: 1928–1929 = 100)

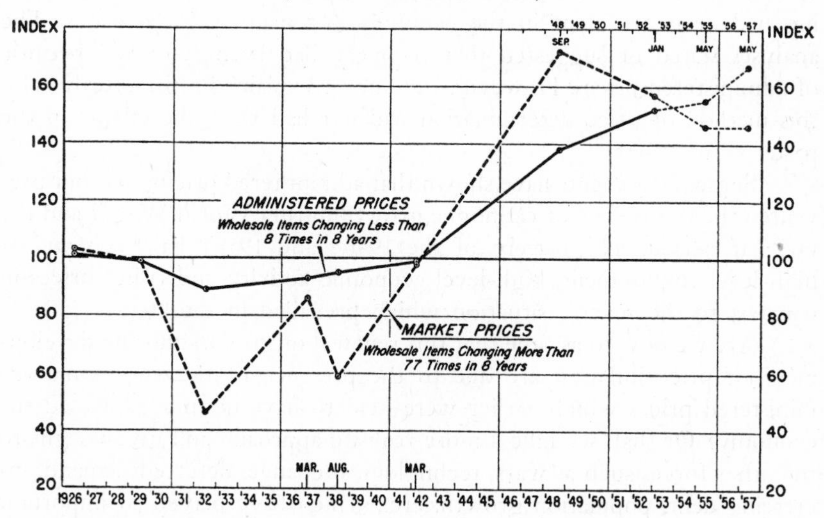

Price making in modern big business is often, perhaps usually, a complex and intricate matter. And it is likely to vary from one situation and industry to another. It will not be easy to disentangle what is relevant and what is not. But until we understand the actual pricing processes involved in price administration, we are quite as likely to make bad, as good, national policy decisions in these fields.

34. ADMINISTERED PRICES: ANOTHER EVALUATION*

Jules Backman

Congressional interest in administered prices is not new. A little less than a quarter of a century ago, Gardiner C. Means and others were blaming the post-1929 depression upon administered prices. Just prior to World War II, the Temporary National Economic Committee also devoted considerable time and effort to administered prices.

When the earlier efforts were made to determine the economic effects of administered pricing, the resulting analyses were colored by the

* Jules Backman, "Statement," *Administered Prices,* Hearings, Part III, U.S. Senate Subcommittee on Antitrust and Monopoly (85th Cong., 1st. sess.) (Washington, D.C.: U.S. Government Printing Office, 1957), pp. 1062–63, 1077–89.

depressed environment in which they were formulated. It is also not surprising to find that many of the ills that beset the economy at that time were attributed to administered prices even though this method of pricing had been prevalent in the economy for many prior decades. The analyses stated or suggested that recovery had been restricted because of administered prices. However, they never explained satisfactorily why this method of price determination had not had the same effects in the past.

Subsequent events have shown that administered pricing has not prevented the resurgence of economic growth during World War II and the postwar period. The pattern of the 1940's and 1950's has been one of high-level employment, high-level economic activity and rising prices in contrast to the reverse situation which prevailed in the 1930's.

Are we now to assume that this renewal of growth and the development of price inflation are due to the presence of the very same administered prices which earlier were held to have unduly depressed the economy? Or shall we take a more realistic approach and give weight to the other forces such as wars, technological change, deferred demand, increasing debt, population growth, etc., which have played so important a role in the dynamic expansion of the past decade? In both periods, administered prices were passive rather than initiating forces. In both periods, the causes of the changes are found in other dynamic factors in our economy.

. . . . .

Senator Estes Kefauver has stated that the Subcommittee on Antitrust and Monopoly " . . . is trying to come to grips with what is probably the nation's current Number One domestic economic problem—the problem of inflation. We are concerned particularly with the extent to which administered prices in concentrated industries may contribute to this problem." Gardiner Means and J. K. Galbraith agreed with Mr. Kefauver that administered prices did contribute to the most recent price rise. However, Means stated that he did "not believe that the area of discretion accompanying administered prices is likely to lead to runaway inflation unless a reckless monetary and fiscal policy is pursued."

Is inflation the result of rises in so-called administered prices? At the outset, it should be noted that this is a brand new theory. So far as I know, no similar allegation was made in earlier periods of inflation, although administered prices also were of considerable significance during those periods. In fact, in the early postwar years the failure to raise these so-called administered prices as much as may have been warranted by the shortages then prevailing was a stabilizing influence which held down the magnitude of the postwar price rise. Before we can determine what contribution, if any, is made by administered prices to inflationary pressures, we must understand the nature of inflation.

NATURE OF INFLATION

Historically, the major price inflations in this country and in the rest of the world have been associated either with an excessive expansion of money and credit or with large budgetary deficits for national governments or with some combination of both. The wartime and postwar inflations clearly were attributable to these forces. During the war and postwar years, our federal government accumulated budgetary deficits in excess of $200 billion; and the money supply (demand deposits plus

CHART 1

INDEXES OF WHOLESALE PRICES, CONSUMER PRICES AND THE VOLUME OF MONEY (DEMAND DEPOSITS AND CURRENCY) 1939–1957

(1939 = 100)

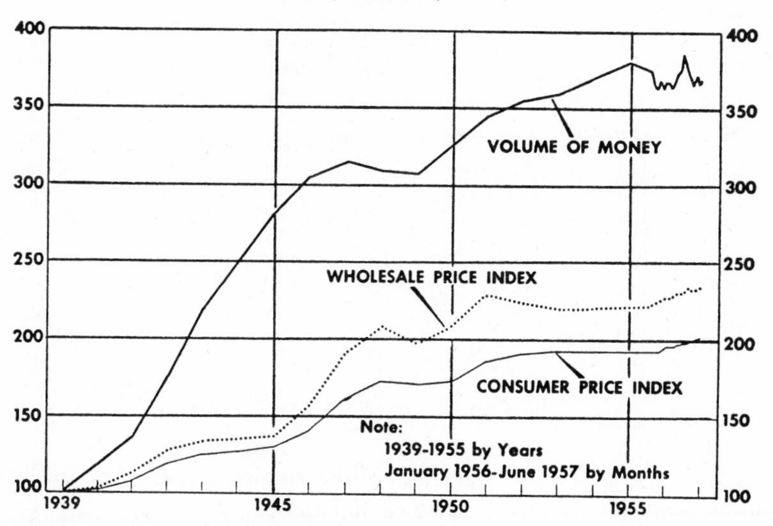

Source: Prices—U.S. Department of Labor, Bureau of Labor Statistics; Volume of Money—Federal Reserve Board.

currency) of the country increased from $36.2 billion in 1939 to $134.7 billion in April 1957—a rise of 272 per cent. With this explosive expansion of money and credit accompanying huge federal budgetary deficits, it is not surprising to find that the consumer price index has about doubled and that wholesale prices have increased about 134 per cent. Approximately nine-tenths of this price rise had taken place prior to 1953 and was the result of the monetary and fiscal inflation. Chart 1 shows the changes in prices and money supply since 1939.

During the past two years these fundamental forces of monetary and fiscal inflation have not been developing in our economy. In the fiscal year 1955–56, the federal government had a surplus of $1.6 billion in the executive budget and $4.5 billion in the cash budget. In the fiscal year which ended June 30, 1957, the federal budget was in the black by $1.6 billion, while the cash budget had a surplus of $2.8 billion. Clearly, the most recent rise in prices cannot be attributed to an unbalanced federal budget. Some persons insist that the high level of government spending is a primary factor in the rise in prices. That it plays a role is probable. However, we cannot ignore the fact that when the government on balance is taking more money from the private economy than it spends, which is the nature of a budgetary surplus, the government is acting as a deflationary, rather than an inflationary, influence on the economy.

TABLE 1

CHANGES IN CURRENCY, DEMAND DEPOSITS AND TOTAL BANK LOANS, ALL COMMERCIAL BANKS, SELECTED DATES, 1939-1957

	Demand Deposits Adjusted	Currency Outside the Banks	Total Loans
	(billions of dollars)		
Dec. 1939	29.8	6.4	17.2
Dec. 1945	75.9	26.5	26.1
Dec. 1949	85.8	25.4	43.0
Dec. 1954	106.6	27.9	70.6
Apr. 1955	104.5	26.7	72.9
Dec. 1955	109.9	28.3	82.6
Apr. 1956	106.1	27.0	85.3
Dec. 1956	111.4	28.3	90.3
Apr. 1957	107.3	27.4	91.0

Source: Board of Governors of the Federal Reserve System.

An examination of the changes in the volume of currency and bank deposits also fails to reveal renewed inflationary pressures.

Between April, 1956 and April, 1957, currency outside the banks increased from $27.0 billion to $27.4 billion, an increase of about 1½ per cent, and demand deposits adjusted increased from $106.1 billion to $107.3 billion, or a rise of only 1 per cent. In the preceding year (April, 1955 to April, 1956), currency outside the banks had increased by 1.1 per cent and demand deposits by 1.5 per cent. (See Table 1.) An expansion of one per cent a year in money supply is about one-third the normal rate of increase. Hence, there has been no increase in inflationary pressures because of increases in the money supply.

However, the dynamic nature of that money supply has changed. During the same two year period, commercial bank loans increased from $72.9 billion to $91.0 billion. The increase in loans has resulted in a more active use of demand deposits. This is shown by the increase in bank debits which indicate the velocity of demand deposits.

TABLE 2

BANK DEBITS, ALL REPORTING CENTERS, BY MONTHS, 1955–1957

	1955	1956	1957
	(billions of dollars)		
Jan.	163.4	187.4	204.4
Feb.	149.7	162.1	177.5
March	178.9	189.8	197.2
April	158.3	176.8	192.6
May	167.7	185.6	197.2
June	177.9	186.5	
July	161.7	181.3	
Aug.	167.3	183.8	
Sept.	169.0	167.2	
Oct.	175.8	193.1	
Nov.	173.2	185.2	
Dec.	200.5	201.9	

Source: Board of Governors of the Federal Reserve System.

Bank debits increased from $158.3 billion in April, 1955 to $176.8 billion in April, 1956 and $192.6 billion in April, 1957, or an increase of 21.7 per cent for the two year period and 8.9 per cent for the year ending April, 1957. This greater turnover of deposit money undoubtedly has contributed to the pressure for a price rise despite the relative stability of our total money supply. However, turnover of bank deposits is a *result* of business activity, not a cause of price rise. It is the boom which stimulates the velocity *and* the price rise. On balance it seems clear that there has been no significant impetus to inflationary trends as a result of the changes in the federal budget or in the supply of money and credit.

FACTORS LEADING TO HIGHER PRICES

The failure of the traditional inflationary forces to develop has led to a feverish search for the reasons for the price rise during the past two years. Examination of the wholesale price index shows that the major areas of price rise have been in those industries which have been most affected by the boom and/or those industries which have the highest proportion of labor costs to total cost.

When wage and other labor cost increases are greater than productivity gains, the resulting higher unit labor costs create pressure for higher prices. Chart 2 shows the war and postwar trends in wages and productivity. The steadily widening spread as money wages have increased far more than productivity is readily evident. This situation has prevailed throughout the war and post-war period. It was also true in 1956. The actual rise in labor costs has been greater than shown in Chart 2 because average hourly earnings do not include important fringe benefits.

CHART 2

INDEXES OF
REAL PRIVATE NON-FARM PRODUCT PER MANHOUR, ALL MANUFACTURING OUTPUT PER MANHOUR, AND ALL MANUFACTURING AVERAGE HOURLY WAGES,
1939–1956
(1940 = 100)

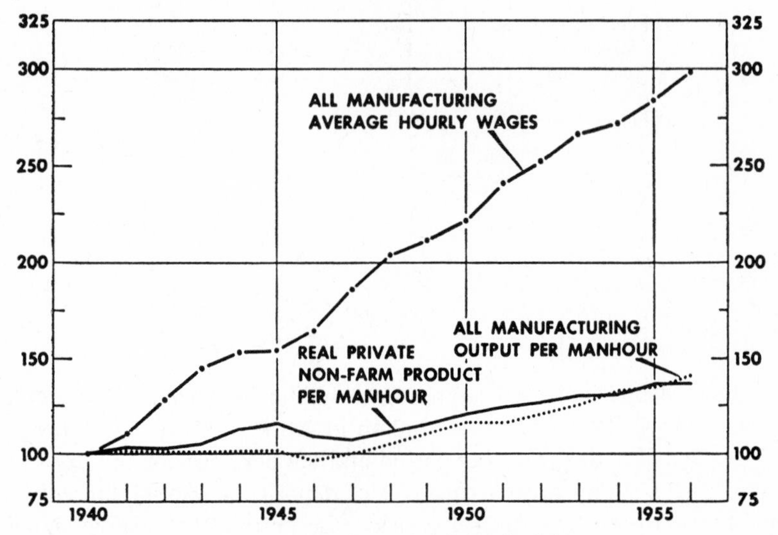

Source: U.S. Department of Labor, Bureau of Labor Statistics.

According to the data now available productivity gains in 1956 were relatively small.

Output per manhour for the nonfarm private economy showed no change in 1956.

Output per manhour for all manufacturing industries increased 2.7 per cent.

While productivity gains were lagging, wages and various fringe benefits rose substantially. Thus, average hourly earnings were $1.88 in 1955 and $1.98 in 1956, an increase of 5.3 per cent. In addition, pension and welfare programs were liberalized and other fringe benefits such as supplementary unemployment benefits (SUB) were paid. Total labor costs, therefore, rose by more than 5.3 per cent for all manufacturing industries in 1956. Clearly, labor costs rose more than productivity, thus leading to higher unit labor costs. According to estimates prepared by the U.S. Bureau of Labor Statistics, unit labor costs for the entire economy rose by 4.5 per cent in 1956. In the first five months of 1957, average hourly earnings in all manufacturing industries increased to $2.05, or a further rise of 3½ per cent above the 1956 average level—and further increases in wages and fringe benefits became effective after May. These rising labor costs have played a significant role in the pressure for higher prices.

PRICE TRENDS, 1955–1957

During the past two years (May, 1955 to June, 1957), the consumer price index has risen 5.3 per cent and the wholesale price index has risen 6.8 per cent. Most of this rise in wholesale prices occurred by the end of 1956 as Table 3 shows.

TABLE 3
WHOLESALE PRICE INDEX, 1955–1957
(1947–49 = 100)

	Total Index	Non Farm Non Food	Farm Products
May 1955	109.9	115.5	91.2
Dec. 1955	111.3	119.8	82.9
May 1956	114.4	121.7	90.9
Dec. 1956	116.3	124.7	88.9
Jan. 1957	116.9	125.2	89.3
Feb. 1957	117.0	125.5	88.8
Mar. 1957	116.9	125.4	88.8
Apr. 1957	117.2	125.4	90.6
May 1957	117.1	125.2	89.5
June 1957	117.4	125.2	90.9
July 30, 1957	117.9	125.5	92.8

Source: U.S. Department of Labor, Bureau of Labor Statistics.

During the first seven months of 1957, the non farm, non food index (industrial prices) was relatively stable within the narrow range of 125.2 to 125.5. The nominal rise in the total index in 1957 reflected the moderately higher prices for farm products and processed foods due in part to seasonal forces. Clearly, there has been no significant inflation in wholesale prices since the end of 1956.

In contrast, the consumer price index has continued to move forward. The CPI rose from 114.6 in February, 1956, the month from which the current rise started, to 118.0 in December. By June, 1957, the index had advanced to 120.2. The changes in the main components of the index are shown in Table 4:

From December, 1956 to June, 1957, the consumer price index rose 2.2 points. The major part of this increase was accounted for by the rise in food prices and housing (food, 1.0 point and housing 0.6 point). Transportation, medical and personal care, and reading and recreation accounted for the other 0.6 point increase reported during this period.

The continuing rise in the consumer price index in 1957 has reflected a combination of two forces: the delayed effects of earlier rises in wholesale prices and, secondly, the rise in prices of services, some of which are primarily labor costs (e.g. medical care) and of others, which

TABLE 4

CONSUMER PRICE INDEX, 1956–1957
(1947–49 = 100)

	Feb. 1956	Dec. 1956	June 1957	Per Cent Increase Feb. 1956 to June 1957	Per Cent Increase Dec. 1956 to June 1957
All items	114.6	118.0	120.2	4.9	1.9
Food	108.8	112.9	116.2	6.8	2.9
Housing—total	120.7	123.5	125.5	4.0	1.6
Housing—rent	131.5	134.2	135.0	2.7	0.6
Apparel	104.6	107.0	106.6	1.9	−0.4
Transportation	126.9	133.1	135.3	6.6	1.7
Medical care	130.9	134.7	137.9	5.3	2.4
Personal care	118.9	121.8	124.2	4.5	2.0
Reading & recreation	107.5	109.3	111.8	4.0	2.3
Other goods & services	120.9	123.8	124.6	3.1	0.6
Gas and electricity	111.7	112.0	112.3	0.5	0.3

Source: U.S. Department of Labor, Bureau of Labor Statistics.

have been lagging behind the war and postwar inflation (e.g. public utility rates and rents). It does not appear to represent the emergence of new inflationary forces. Chart 3 shows separately the changes in the prices of goods and of services included in the consumer price index. The

CHART 3

PRINCIPAL COMPONENTS OF THE CONSUMER PRICE INDEX,
ALL COMMODITIES VS. ALL SERVICES (Excl. Rent)
1939–1957
(1947–49 = 100)

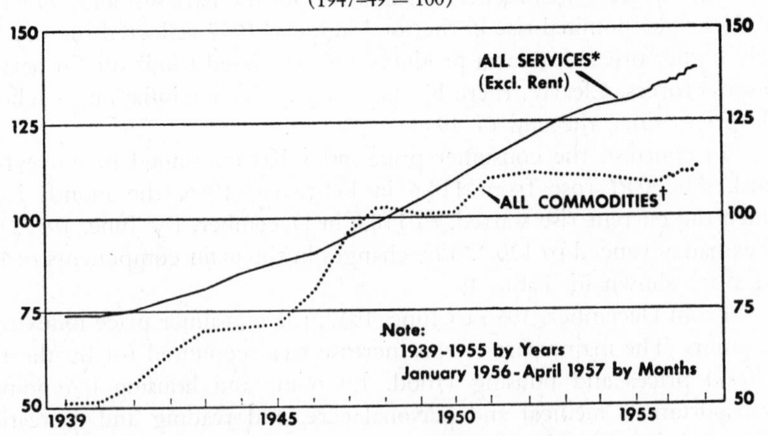

Source: U.S. Department of Labor, Bureau of Labor Statistics.

* All services includes such items as gas and electricity, dry cleaning and laundry, shoe repairs, telephone, public transportation, medical services, beauty and barber shop services, domestic service, auto repairs, auto insurance and registration, water rates, postage, and movie admission. It does not include residential rent.

† All commodities includes such items as food, apparel, solid fuel and fuel oil, house furnishings, radio and TV, prescriptions and drugs, toilet goods, automobiles, tires, gasoline and motor oil, tobacco products, alcoholic beverages, laundry soap and detergents, and newspapers.

steady climb in the prices of services is readily apparent. It has been particularly important since 1951.

ANATOMY OF PRICE CHANGES, 1955–1957

Table 5 shows the changes in the *major components* of the wholesale price index between May, 1955 and May, 1957. The over-all price rise has been 6.6 per cent. But an examination of the anatomy of the price rise shows it has been very uneven. Three major groups of prices have risen more than 10 per cent (machinery and motive products, metals and metal products, and fuel, power and lighting materials), while three major groups have actually declined (lumber and wood products, miscellaneous, and farm products). The industries with the largest price increases have been those most stimulated by the boom, particularly that in plant and equipment, and, in some instances, those industries with a relatively high labor content.

TABLE 5

CHANGES IN WHOLESALE PRICES, MAJOR GROUPS, MAY, 1955 TO MAY, 1957

(1947–49 = 100)

Major Groups	Index		Per Cent Increase or Decrease
	May, 1955	May, 1957	
Machinery and motive products	126.7	145.1	14.5
Metals and metal products	132.5	150.0	13.2
Fuel, power and lighting materials	107.0	118.5	10.7
Nonmetallic minerals, structural	123.2	135.0	9.6
Pulp, paper and allied products	117.7	128.9	9.5
Commodities other than farm products and foods	115.5	125.2	8.4
Hides, skins and leather products	92.9	99.0	6.6
All commodities	109.9	117.1	6.6
Furniture, other household durables	115.1	121.6	5.6
Rubber and rubber products	138.0	144.7	4.9
Foods, processed	102.1	104.9	2.7
Tobacco manufactures and bottled beverages	121.6	124.5	2.4
Chemicals and allied products	106.8	109.1	2.2
Textile products and apparel	95.0	95.4	0.4
Farm products	91.3	89.5	−1.9
Miscellaneous	91.4	89.4	−2.1
Lumber and wood products	123.5	119.7	−3.1

Source: U.S. Department of Labor, Bureau of Labor Statistics.

The lagging tendencies of farm prices reflect the huge surpluses accumulated in recent years while the decline in residential building was a primary factor in the price decline for lumber and wood products. Similarly, the relatively unchanged price level for textile products and apparel reflects the depressed conditions in those industries. Among the other industries with modest price rises, rubber and rubber products reflected the decline in automobile output; tobacco manufactures and bottled beverages are industries with a very small labor content; chemicals and allied products also have less than average labor costs as a per cent of the sales dollar. Thus, *it appears that the level of prosperity in an industry and/or the relative importance of its labor costs provide the primary explanations for the price behavior of the past two years.*

Table 6 shows the changes for the same price groups for the year from May, 1956 to May, 1957. The picture is essentially the same.

TABLE 6

CHANGES IN WHOLESALE PRICES, MAJOR GROUPS, MAY, 1956 TO MAY, 1957 (1947–49 = 100)

Major Groups	May 1956	May 1957	Per Cent Increase or Decrease
Fuel, power and lighting materials	110.8	118.5	6.9
Machinery and motive products	136.5	145.1	6.3
Nonmetallic minerals, structural	128.6	135.0	5.0
Furniture, other household durables	118.0	121.6	3.1
Commodities other than farm products and foods	121.7	125.2	2.9
Foods, processed	102.4	104.9	2.4
Tobacco manufactures and bottled beverages	121.6	124.5	2.4
All Commodities	114.4	117.1	2.4
Metals and metal products	146.8	150.0	2.2
Chemicals and allied products	106.9	109.1	2.1
Pulp, paper and allied products	127.3	128.9	1.3
Rubber and rubber products	143.5	144.7	0.8
Textile products and apparel	94.9	95.4	0.5
Hides, skins, and leather products	100.0	99.0	−1.0
Farm products	90.9	89.5	−1.5
Lumber and wood products	128.0	119.7	−6.5
Miscellaneous	96.1	89.4	−7.0

Source: U.S. Department of Labor, Bureau of Labor Statistics.

Table 7 shows the changes for 44 subgroups of products for the period from May, 1955 to May, 1957. This tabulation is particularly instructive concerning the behavior of administered prices during the period covered—and also the behavior of prices in concentrated industries as compared with others. As the table shows some administered prices have risen sharply, while others have declined.

An analysis of the May, 1955—May, 1957 price changes also shows that for several finished goods, the administered prices rose more or declined less than the market prices of their important raw materials.

Price administered meats, poultry and fish prices rose 6.8 per cent as compared with the rise of only 0.4 per cent for market price determined livestock and live poultry.

While market price determined grains declined 7.6 per cent, the price administered cereal and baking goods group fell only 1.5 per cent.

Market price determined fresh and dried fruits and vegetables recorded a

TABLE 7

CHANGES IN WHOLESALE PRICES, SUBGROUPS,
MAY, 1955 TO MAY, 1957
(1947–49 = 100)

Sub-Groups	Index May, 1955	Index May, 1957	Per Cent Increase or Decrease
Coal	100.4	123.3	22.8
Iron and steel	135.6	162.9	20.1
Construction machinery and equipment	134.3	157.6	17.3
Electrical machinery and equipment	126.5	148.2	17.2
Petroleum and products	111.5	129.8	16.4
Clay products	137.0	155.0	13.1
Fats and oils, inedible	53.2	59.2	11.3
Paper	128.9	142.4	10.5
Motor vehicles	122.0	134.7	10.4
Agricultural machinery and equipment	121.5	132.3	8.9
Footwear	111.4	121.1	8.7
Prepared paint	114.8	124.7	8.6
Furniture, household	113.1	122.4	8.2
Concrete products	118.2	126.7	7.2
Heating equipment	113.5	121.4	7.0
Meats, poultry, and fish	85.7	91.5	6.8
Dairy products and ice cream	104.0	110.7	6.4
Chemicals, industrial	117.6	123.6	5.1
Gas	111.0	116.5	5.0
Hides and skins	53.3	55.8	4.7
Tires and tubes	142.3	149.0	4.7
Leather	85.0	88.8	4.5
Wool products	106.1	110.9	4.5
Beverages, alcoholic	114.7	119.6	4.3
Gypsum products	122.1	127.1	4.1
Toys, sporting goods	113.2	117.5	3.8
Apparel	98.0	99.5	1.5
Nonferrous metals	137.8	139.9	1.5
Silk products	123.2	124.7	1.2
Television receivers	69.0	69.5	0.7
Cotton products	90.3	90.7	0.4
Livestock and live poultry	78.4	78.7	0.4
Drugs and pharmaceuticals	93.2	93.3	0.1
Cigarettes	124.0	124.0	0
Fruits and vegetables, canned and frozen	104.1	103.5	−0.6
Appliances, household	106.5	105.1	−1.3
Cereal and baking goods	118.3	116.5	−1.5
Lumber	124.2	120.6	−2.9
Electricity	97.8	94.9	−3.0
Radio receivers and phonographs	94.7	91.1	−3.8
Fertilizer materials	113.1	107.2	−5.2
Man-made fiber textile products	86.9	81.8	−5.9
Grains	92.4	85.4	−7.6
Fruits and vegetables, fresh and dried	118.7	109.0	−8.2

Source: U.S. Department of Labor, Bureau of Labor Statistics.

price decline of 8.2 per cent, while price administered canned and frozen vegetables showed a small decline of 0.6 per cent.

Nevertheless, there are also a number of interesting contrasts in price behavior during that two-year period.

Coal which has low concentration, high labor costs, and administered price had the largest rise, 22.8 per cent. Petroleum and products, a competitive product, with a higher concentration ratio rose 16.4 per cent. On the other hand, highly concentrated, low labor content, price administered cigarettes showed no change in price; and lumber, an industry with many producers and administered prices, had a price decline of 2.9 per cent.

Hides and skins' prices, which are market determined, rose 4.7 per cent, while price administered leather prices increased 4.5 per cent.

Man-made fiber textile products' prices declined 5.9 per cent, while the wool products' prices advanced 4.5 per cent and cotton products rose 0.4 per cent. These products are all price administered and have similar degrees of concentration although man-made fibers are highly concentrated.

Electrical machinery and equipment prices increased 17.2 per cent while prices of television receivers increased 0.7 per cent, prices of household appliances fell 1.3 per cent and prices of radio receivers and phonographs declined 3.8 per cent. In many instances these products are produced by the same companies.

Iron and steel products rose 20.1 per cent as compared with a rise of only 1.5 per cent for nonferrous metals although both are price administered.

Clay products' prices rose 13.1 per cent as compared with a rise of 4.1 per cent for gypsum products which are more highly concentrated.

Of the eleven groups of products for which prices did not increase between May, 1955 and May, 1957, nine are price administered in industries with varying degrees of concentration.

Industry	Per Cent Change in Prices
Cigarettes	0
Canned and frozen fruits and vegetables	−0.6
Appliances, household	−1.3
Cereal and baking goods	−1.5
Lumber	−2.9
Electricity	−3.0
Radio receivers and phonographs	−3.8
Fertilizer materials	−5.2
Man-made fiber textile products	−5.9

Only two groups of products for which prices declined are market determined:

Industry	Per Cent Change in Prices
Grains	−7.6
Fresh and dried fruits and vegetables	−8.2

While price administered products recorded varying increases in this two-year period, it is significant that for nine industries, prices failed to rise despite the fact that they were administered.

Moreover, for four additional industries, prices rose less than one per cent. Only one of these industries had market determined prices (livestock and live poultry) while the following three industries were price administered:

	Per Cent Increase
Drugs and pharmaceuticals	0.1
Cotton products	0.4
Television receivers	0.7

In general, these fifteen industries, with price rises of less than one per cent or price declines, did not participate fully in the 1955–57 boom. This fact, rather than price administration, explains price behavior in this area.

On the other hand, the eight industries with price increases of 10.5 per cent or more generally participated in the boom and were significantly affected by it.

If the analysis is confined to the experience in the year May, 1956 to May, 1957, the wide diversity of behavior for administered prices is again evident. The data are shown in Table 8. Some of the interesting exceptions to the administered price-inflation theme include the following:

The largest price rise was for meats, poultry, and fish (11.4 per cent) and the largest decline was for nonferrous metals (−12.6 per cent). Both groups of products have administered prices. Nonferrous metals are highly concentrated. Market determined grain prices also recorded one of the largest declines.

Fresh and dried fruits and vegetables, whose prices are largely market determined, declined 2.5 per cent while the more concentrated price administered canned and frozen fruits and vegetables declined 5.3 per cent.

Coal recorded a price rise of 10.2 per cent while cigarettes were unchanged in price. Petroleum and products had a price rise of 9.7 per cent.

Motor vehicles had a price rise of 4.3 per cent while prices declined 1.8 per cent for tires and tubes. Both industries are highly concentrated and have administered prices. Prices of tires and tubes were adversely affected by the decline in automobile output.

Hides and skins' prices, which are market determined, fell 5.4 per cent while closely related administered price of leather declined 4.4 per cent. However, administered price footwear rose 0.9 per cent. It should be noted that the latter is an industry with low concentration.

Cotton products prices declined 2.6 per cent, prices of man-made textile fibres rose 1.9 per cent and prices in the wool products group increased 7.8 per cent.

Electrical machinery and equipment prices rose 8.2 per cent, while the similarly administered prices of radio receivers and phonographs rose 1.7 per cent, television receivers rose only 0.3 per cent, and household appliances a nominal 0.1 per cent. The difference in the demand for the two groups of products provided a more significant explanation of this diverse behavior than did the fact the prices are administered.

Of the 44 subgroups included in the BLS wholesale price index, prices declined for twelve groups, were unchanged for two groups, and

TABLE 8

CHANGES IN WHOLESALE PRICES, SUBGROUPS, MAY, 1956 TO MAY, 1957
1947–49 = 100

Subgroups	May 1956	May 1957	Per Cent Change
Meats, poultry, fish	82.1	91.5	11.4
Coal	111.9	123.3	10.2
Petroleum and products	118.3	129.8	9.7
Electrical machinery and equipment	137.0	148.2	8.2
Iron and steel	150.8	162.9	8.0
Wool products	102.9	110.9	7.8
Construction machinery and equipment	146.6	157.6	7.5
Clay products, structural	146.1	155.0	6.1
Livestock and live poultry	74.4	78.7	5.8
Prepared paint	119.1	124.7	4.7
Agricultural machinery and equipment	126.5	132.3	4.6
Paper	136.2	142.4	4.6
Beverages, alcoholic	114.6	119.6	4.4
Motor vehicles	129.1	134.7	4.3
Concrete products	121.7	126.7	4.1
Furniture, household	118.0	122.4	3.7
Heating equipment	117.3	121.4	3.5
Dairy products and ice cream	107.9	110.7	2.6
Chemicals, industrial	120.8	123.6	2.3
Man-made fiber textile products	80.3	81.8	1.9
Electricity	93.2	94.9	1.8
Radio receivers and phonographs	89.6	91.1	1.7
Toys, sporting goods	115.8	117.5	1.5
Drugs and pharmaceuticals	92.1	93.3	1.3
Gas	115.4	116.5	1.0
Footwear	120.0	121.1	0.9
Cereal and bakery products	115.5	116.5	0.9
Television receivers	69.3	69.5	0.3
Appliances, household	105.0	105.1	0.1
Apparel	99.4	99.5	0.1
Cigarettes	124.0	124.0	0
Gypsum products	127.1	127.1	0
Silk products	125.0	124.7	−0.2
Fertilizer materials	109.1	107.2	−1.7
Fats and oils, inedible	60.3	59.2	−1.8
Tires and tubes	151.8	149.0	−1.8
Fruits and vegetables, fresh and dried	111.8	109.0	−2.5
Cotton products	93.1	90.7	−2.6
Leather	92.9	88.8	−4.4
Fruits and vegetables, canned and frozen	109.3	103.5	−5.3
Hides and skins	59.0	55.8	−5.4
Grains	90.5	85.4	−5.6
Lumber	130.4	120.6	−7.5
Nonferrous metals	160.0	139.9	−12.6

Source: U.S. Department of Labor, Bureau of Labor Statistics.

rose one per cent or less for six groups. Thus, in the year from May, 1956 to 1957, 20 out of the 44 subgroups had a price rise of one per cent or less or declined in price. 17 of these 20 industry groups had administered prices.

The various comparisons cited above have been stressed because they provide important exceptions to the role assigned to price administration. They show that there is no simple or certain relationship between concentration and price administration, on the one hand, and the direction or magnitude of price change on the other. *The depressed condition of demand (e.g. tires and tubes, lumber, nonferrous metals), stimulation of demand (e.g. the influence of Suez on petroleum products), relatively large raw materials costs (e.g. meats, poultry and fish, leather), high relative importance of labor costs (e.g. coal, iron and steel), relatively low labor costs (e.g. cigarettes, chemicals), the plant and equipment boom (e.g. machinery and equipment), and other factors provide more significant explanations for the recent behavior of prices than does the fact that most prices are administered.*

Of course, there are products which are concentrated, have administered prices, and also have had larger than average price rises. The point that is underlined by these many illustrations, however, is that there are also many concentrated industries in which administered prices have shown only small changes. Industries with low concentration and administered prices have recorded similar differences in price behavior.

In the light of the differences in behavior among "various concentrated industries with administered prices," it is difficult to understand how price administration *per se* can be responsible for the general price rise of the past year or two. Where other conditions have either favored or compelled the price rise, administered prices have risen. And where these other conditions have not favored a price rise, administered prices have failed to rise. Market determined prices have shown a similar responsiveness. *The primary pressures and responsibilities for price behavior, therefore, are found in these other factors, not in the fact of price administration.*

35. INFLATION: ALTERNATIVE EXPLANATIONS*

Charles L. Schultze

This study is concerned with the nature of inflation, and in particular with the rise in the general level of prices between 1955 and 1957. While there is little controversy over the nature and causes of inflation during periods of war or postwar reconversion, there is substantial dis-

* Charles L. Schultze, *Recent Inflation in the United States*, Study Paper No. 1, *Study of Employment, Growth and Price Levels*, Joint Economic Committee (86th Cong. 1st. sess.) (Washington, D.C.: U.S. Government Printing Office, 1959), pp. 1–3.

agreement over the causes of the relatively mild inflation of recent years. Those who believe that inflation stems, now as always, from "too much money chasing too few goods" are ranged against those who attribute postwar inflation to the upward pressure of wage costs on prices. This study concludes that creeping inflation can be explained by neither of these two lines of analysis. In particular its conclusions are:

1. The basic point at issue between the "demand-pull" and "cost-push" theorists relates to the sensitivity of prices and wages to changes in the demand for goods and services. If prices and wages are very sensitive, general monetary and fiscal policy can be designed to achieve full employment and price stability. The elimination of aggregate excess demand will choke off inflation without necessarily involving substantial unemployment. If prices and wages are relatively insensitive to moderate changes in demand, the converse holds true.

2. In the modern American economy prices and wages are much more sensitive to increases in demand than to decreases. As a consequence, a rapid shift in the composition of demand will lead to a general rise in prices, even without an excessive growth in the overall level of demand or an autonomous upward push of wages. Prices rise in those sectors of the economy where demands are growing rapidly, and decline by smaller amounts, or not at all, in sectors where demands are falling.

3. When the composition of demand changes rapidly, prices of semi-fabricated materials and components tend to rise, on the average, since price advances among materials in heavy demand are not balanced by price decreases for materials in excess supply. Wage rate gains in most industries tend to equal or almost equal those granted in the rapidly expanding industries. As a consequence, even those industries faced by sagging demand for their products experience a rise in costs. This intensifies the general price rise, since at least some of the higher costs are passed on in prices.

4. The resulting inflation can be explained neither in terms of an overall excess of money demand nor an autonomous upward push of wages. Rather it originates in excess demands in particular sectors and is spread to the rest of the economy by the cost mechanism. It is a characteristic of the resource allocation process in an economy with rigidities in its price structure. It is impossible to analyze such an inflation by looking only at aggregate data.

5. During the 1955–57 period the overall growth of monetary demand was not excessive. But there was a strong investment boom, offset by declining sales of automobiles and houses. This rapid shift in the composition of demand led to a general price rise, in which the capital goods industries played the major role.

6. If the rise in prices was not a result of an overall excess of monetary demand, neither was it primarily caused by an autonomous upward push of wage rates. There are many indications of this. For example, the

capital goods and associated industries accounted for two-thirds of the rise in industrial prices during the period, but in these same industries prices rose substantially more than wage costs. Profits per unit of output rose in the capital goods industries, although for the economy as a whole they declined.

7. The largest part of the rise in total costs between 1955 and 1957 was accounted for not by the increase in wage costs but by the increase in salary and other overhead costs. This increase in turn was associated with the investment boom. Business firms purchased large amounts of new equipment, hired extensive professional, technical, sales, and clerical staffs, and speeded up research and development projects. When output did not rise producers attempted to recapture at least some of these increased costs in higher prices. This "premature" recapture of fixed costs further accentuated the magnitude of the general price rise.

8. Overhead costs have been increasing as a proportion of total costs throughout the postwar period. This has intensified the downward rigidities in the cost structure of most industries.

9. These downward rigidities in prices and costs put a new floor under each successively higher price level and thus help create a long-term upward bias in prices.

10. While there is a secular upward drift to the price level, its magnitude is not to be judged by the size of the price increases during the 1955–57 period. These years were characterized by an abnormally large shift in the composition of demand and a particular combination of events which led to an abrupt rise in overhead costs.

11. Since it does not stem primarily from aggregate excess demand, but largely from excess demand in particular sectors of the economy, a slow increase in prices cannot be controlled by general monetary and fiscal policy if full employment is to be maintained. When, as in recent years, prices are rising during a period of growing excess capacity, a further restriction of aggregate demand is more likely to raise costs by reducing productivity than it is to lower costs by reducing wages and profit margins.

12. Monetary and fiscal policies which are directed specifically toward the sectors where demand is excessive, may, however, limit the inflationary effect of a rapid shift in the composition of demand. Between 1955 and 1957 a slower growth in investment demand, coupled with a more even rise in purchases of autos and housing would have resulted in a smaller price increase and a larger output gain.

13. The whole subject of selective tax and credit controls is beyond the scope of this study. Their application involves economic and social problems of substantial magnitude. This study does indicate that counter inflationary policy must be designed to take into account the composition as well as the magnitude of excess demand. By using monetary and fiscal policy to prevent excess *aggregate* demand from emerging, one type of

inflation—and that, the most harmful type—can be controlled. Even should aggregate demand rise no more rapidly than the supply potential of the economy, however, inflation can still take place if the composition of demand changes sharply. Faced with this situation we can attempt to alter the composition of demand by using selective controls or we can accept the moderate price increases which will otherwise occur. In either event, the problem cannot be solved by a further repression of demand through general monetary and fiscal policy.

Public policy statements in recent years have emphasized that wage-rate gains must stay within the bounds of productivity advances if inflation is to be avoided. This study on the other hand stresses the importance for price stability of the responsiveness of wages and prices to changes in demand. There is no single formula which can specify the appropriate relationship between changes in productivity, prices, and costs in particular industries. In a flexible economy individual wage-price-productivity relationships should reflect the strength of demands in each industry. If businessmen and labor leaders would become more demand conscious and less cost conscious, the overall wage-productivity relationship would take care of itself, so long as intelligent monetary and fiscal policies were pursued. Hence, if one must preach to business and labor about their obligations to the "public interest," the emphasis should lie on the need to orient price and wage decisions more closely to market conditions. The continual invocation of the phrase "wage rate gains on the average should not exceed productivity gains on the average" is not sufficient to enable management and labor in an individual business to determine the kind of price and wage behaviour on their part needed to achieve a greater stability of the price level in a full employment economy.

Part V: Questions for Analysis

1. The maturation of our economic system has resulted in substantial deviations from the precepts of traditional economic thought. This is particularly so in the areas of competition and monopoly. In the view of John Maurice Clark, what is the present status of competition in our economy today?
2. Attempts to retain a measure of competition have led to the adoption of antitrust laws.
   a) Trace the development of federal antitrust laws.
   b) As expressed by Theodore J. Kreps, what is our current antitrust policy?
3. Because of its special market situation, agriculture is exempted from antitrust jurisdiction. In the opinion of Karl Brandt, what are some guidelines

for a constructive revision of agricultural policy in the 1960's? Do you agree? Explain.

4. Public utilities also are exempted from antitrust jurisdiction.
   a) Discuss the principal characteristics of a public utility.
   b) As expressed by James C. Bonbright, what is the case for public utility exemption from antitrust jurisdiction?
   c) In Bonbright's opinion, what alternative approaches exist for dealing with the public utility problem? In your opinion, which method is preferable? Support your answer.
5. Our present market system is characterized by the wide-spread use of administered prices.
   a) What are administered prices?
   b) In the opinion of Gardiner C. Means, what role did administered prices play in the inflation of the 1955–57 period?
   c) Present the position of Jules Backman in this matter.
   d) In the view of Charles L. Schultze, what is the "real" explanation for this period of inflation?
   e) Present your viewpoint in this matter. Support it with appropriate evidence.

VI INCOME DISTRIBUTION AND PUBLIC POLICY

The distribution of a nation's output among its people is certainly one matter which arouses intense interest. This is true whether the question is examined from the standpoint of functional or of personal distribution. In the first instance, we deal with division of output among the productive factors (labor, capital, land, and enterprise). In the second instance, we are concerned with the sharing of the nation's goods and services among its consumer spending units. In both instances group interests create intense public pressures. A public policy which caters to a particular group interest may help that group in the short run, but harm the entire society, including that group, in the long run. John Stuart Mill, famous mid-nineteenth century economist and philosopher, discusses group interest and social welfare.

Concern over the historical pattern of functional distribution leads to various efforts at modification. In particular, we may note various efforts to modify market wages. Lloyd G. Reynolds, Sterling Professor of Economics at Yale University and Cynthia H. Taft, formerly Research Associate in Economics at Yale, discuss the efforts of unions to modify the wage structure. Professor Donald E. Cullen, of the New York State School of Industrial and Labor Relations, presents an analysis of governmental efforts to modify wages by means of minimum-wage legislation.

One of the significant efforts to modify personal distribution is through alterations in the tax structure. The principle of tax progression is a leading technique for accomplishing this goal. This principle of taxation affects incentives. Dan Throop Smith, of Harvard University, proposes reforms in our federal tax laws to minimize their adverse effects on incentives.

A. Distribution and Group Interest

36. GROUP INTEREST AND SOCIAL WELFARE*

John Stuart Mill

We next proceed to the evils arising from the prevalence of modes of action in the representative body, dictated by sinister interests (to employ the useful phrase introduced by Bentham), that is, interests conflicting more or less with the general good of the community.

It is universally admitted that, of the evils incident to monarchical and aristocratic governments, a large proportion arise from this cause. The interest of the monarch, or the interest of the aristocracy, either collective or that of its individual members, is promoted, or they themselves think that it will be promoted, by conduct opposed to that which the general interest of the community requires. The interest, for example, of the government is to tax heavily: that of the community is to be as little taxed as the necessary expenses of good government permit. The interest of the king, and of the governing aristocracy, is to be as little taxed as the necessary expenses of good government permit. The interest of the king, and of the governing aristocracy, is to possess, and exercise, unlimited power over the people; to enforce, on their part, complete conformity to the will and preferences of the rulers. The interest of the people is to have as little control exercised over them in any respect as is consistent with attaining the legitimate ends of government. The interest, or apparent and supposed interest, of the king or aristocracy is to permit no censure of themselves, at least in any form which they may consider either to threaten their power, or seriously to interfere with their free agency. The interest of the people is that there should be full liberty of censure on every public officer, and on every public act or measure. The interest of a ruling class, whether in an aristocracy or an aristocratic monarchy, is to assume to themselves an endless variety of unjust privileges, sometimes benefiting their pockets at the expense of the people, sometimes merely tending to exalt them above others, or, what is the same thing in different words, to degrade others below themselves. If the people are disaffected, which under such a government they are very likely to be, it is the interest of the king or aristocracy to keep them at a low level of intelligence and education, foment dissensions among them,

* John Stuart Mill, *Representative Government*, in *Great Books of the Western World* (Chicago: Encyclopaedia Britannica, 1952) Vol. 43, pp. 366–70.

and even prevent them from being too well off, lest they should "wax fat, and kick"; agreeably to the maxim of Cardinal Richelieu in his celebrated *Testament Politique*. All these things are for the interest of a king or aristocracy, in a purely selfish point of view, unless a sufficiently strong counterinterest is created by the fear of provoking resistance. All these evils have been, and many of them still are, produced by the sinister interests of kings and aristocracies, where their power is sufficient to raise them above the opinion of the rest of the community; nor is it rational to expect, as a consequence of such a position, any other conduct.

These things are superabundantly evident in the case of a monarchy or an aristocracy; but it is sometimes rather gratuitously assumed that the same kind of injurious influences do not operate in a democracy. Looking at democracy in the way in which it is commonly conceived, as the rule of the numerical majority, it is surely possible that the ruling power may be under the dominion of sectional or class interests, pointing to conduct different from that which would be dictated by impartial regard for the interest of all. Suppose the majority to be whites, the minority Negroes, or vice versa: is it likely that the majority would allow equal justice to the minority? Suppose the majority Catholics, the minority Protestants, or the reverse; will there not be the same danger? Or let the majority be English, the minority Irish, or the contrary: is there not a great probability of similar evil? In all countries there is a majority of poor, a minority who, in contradistinction, may be called rich. Between these two classes, on many questions, there is complete opposition of apparent interest. We will suppose the majority sufficiently intelligent to be aware that it is not for their advantage to weaken the security of property, and that it would be weakened by any act of arbitrary spoliation. But is there not a considerable danger lest they would throw upon the possessors of what is called realized property, and upon the larger incomes, an unfair share, or even the whole, of the burden of taxation; and having done so, add to the amount without scruple, expanding the proceeds in modes supposed to conduce to the profit and advantage of the labouring class? Suppose, again, a minority of skilled labourers, a majority of unskilled: the experience of many trade unions, unless they are greatly calumniated, justifies the apprehension that equality of earnings might be imposed as an obligation, and that piecework, payment by the hour, and all practices which enable superior industry or abilities to gain a superior reward might be put down. Legislative attempts to raise wages, limitation of competition in the labour market, taxes or restrictions on machinery, and on improvements of all kinds tending to dispense with any of the existing labour—even, perhaps, protection of the home producer against foreign industry—are very natural (I do not venture to say whether probable) results of a feeling of class interest in a governing majority of manual labourers.

It will be said that none of these things are for the real interest of the most numerous class: to which I answer, that if the conduct of human beings was determined by no other interested considerations than those which constitute their "real" interest, neither monarchy nor oligarchy would be such bad governments as they are; for assuredly very strong arguments may be, and often have been, adduced to show that either a king or a governing senate are in much the most enviable position, when ruling justly and vigilantly over an active, wealthy, enlightened, and high-minded people. But a king only now and then, and an oligarchy in no known instance, have taken this exalted view of their self-interest: and why should we expect a loftier mode of thinking from the labouring classes? It is not what their interest is, but what they suppose it to be, that is the important consideration with respect to their conduct: and it is quite conclusive against any theory of government that it assumes the numerical majority to do habitually what is never done, nor expected to be done, save in very exceptional cases, by any other depositaries of power—namely, to direct their conduct by their real ultimate interest, in opposition to their immediate and apparent interest. No one, surely, can doubt that many of the pernicious measures above enumerated, and many others as bad, would be for the immediate interest of the general body of unskilled labourers. It is quite possible that they would be for the selfish interest of the whole existing generation of the class. The relaxation of industry and activity, and diminished encouragement to saving which would be their ultimate consequence, might perhaps be little felt by the class of unskilled labourers in the space of a single lifetime.

Some of the most fatal changes in human affairs have been, as to their more manifest immediate effects, beneficial. The establishment of the despotism of the Caesars was a great benefit to the entire generation in which it took place. It put a stop to civil war, abated a vast amount of malversation and tyranny by praetors and proconsuls; it fostered many of the graces of life, and intellectual cultivation in all departments not political; it produced monuments of literary genius dazzling to the imaginations of shallow readers of history, who do not reflect that the men to whom the despotism of Augustus (as well as of Lorenzo de Medici and of Louis XIV) owes his brilliancy, were all formed in the generation preceding. The accumulated riches, and the mental energy and activity, produced by centuries of freedom, remained for the benefit of the first generation of slaves. Yet this was the commencement of a regime by whose gradual operation all the civilisation which had been gained insensibly faded away, until the Empire, which had conquered and embraced the world in its grasp, so completely lost even its military efficiency, that invaders whom three or four legions had always sufficed to coerce were able to overrun and occupy nearly the whole of its vast territory. The fresh impulse given by Christianity came but just in time to save arts and letters from perishing, and the human race from sinking back into perhaps endless night.

When we talk of the interest of a body of men, or even of an individual man, as a principle determining their actions, the question what would be considered their interest by an unprejudiced observer is one of the least important parts of the whole matter. As Coleridge observes, the man makes the motive, not the motive the man. What it is the man's interest to do or refrain from depends less on any outward circumstances than upon what sort of man he is. If you wish to know what is practically a man's interest, you must know the cast of his habitual feelings and thoughts. Everybody has two kinds of interests, interests which he cares for and interests which he does not care for. Everybody has selfish and unselfish interests, and a selfish man has cultivated the habit of caring for the former, and not caring for the latter. Every one has present and distant interests, and the improvident man is he who cares for the present interests and does not care for the distant. It matters little that on any correct calculation the latter may be the more considerable, if the habits of his mind lead him to fix his thoughts and wishes solely on the former. It would be vain to attempt to persuade a man who beats his wife and ill treats his children that he would be happier if he lived in love and kindness with them. He would be happier if he were the kind of person who could so live; but he is not and it is probably too late for him to become, that kind of person. Being what he is, the gratification of his love of domineering, and the indulgence of his ferocious temper, are to his perceptions a greater good to himself than he would be capable of deriving from the pleasure and affection of those dependent on him. He has no pleasure in their pleasure, and does not care for their affection. His neighbor, who does, is probably a happier man than he; but could he be persuaded of this, the persuasion would, most likely, only still further exasperate his malignity or his irritability. On the average, a person who cares for other people, for his country, or for mankind, is a happier man than one who does not; but of what use is it to preach this doctrine to a man who cares for nothing but his own ease, or his own pocket? He cannot care for other people if he would. It is like preaching to the worm who crawls on the ground how much better it would be for him if he were an eagle.

Now it is a universally observed fact that the two evil dispositions in question, the disposition to prefer a man's selfish interests to those which he shares with other people, and his immediate and direct interests to those which are indirect and remote, are characteristics most especially called forth and fostered by the possession of power. The moment a man, or a class of men find themselves with power in their hands, the man's individual interest, or the class's separate interest, acquires an entirely new degree of importance in their eyes. Finding themselves worshipped by others, they become worshippers of themselves, and think themselves entitled to be counted at a hundred times the value of other people; while the facility they acquire of doing as they like without regard to consequences insensibly weakens the habits which make men look forward even to such consequences as affect themselves. This is the meaning of the universal tradition, grounded on universal experience, of men's being corrupted by power. Every one knows how absurd it would be to infer from what a man is or does when in a private station, that he will be and do exactly the like when a despot on a throne; where the bad parts of his human nature, instead of being restrained and kept in subordination by every circumstance of his life and by every person surrounding him, are courted by all persons, and ministered to by all circumstances. It would be quite as absurd to entertain a similar expectation in regard to a class of men; the Demos, or any other. Let them be ever so modest and amenable to reason while there is a power over them stronger than they, we ought to expect a total change in this respect when they themselves become the strongest powers.

Governments must be made for human beings as they are, or as they are capable of speedily becoming; and in any state of cultivation which mankind, or any class among them, have yet attained, or are likely soon to attain, the interests by which they will be led, when they are thinking only of self-interest, will be almost exclusively those which are obvious at first sight, and which operate on their present condition. It is only a disinterested regard for others, and especially for what comes after them, for the idea of posterity of their country, or of mankind, whether grounded on sympathy or on a conscientious feeling, which ever directs the minds and purposes of classes or bodies of men towards distant or unobvious interests. And it cannot be maintained that any form of government would be rational which required as a condition that these exalted principles of action should be the guiding and master motives in the conduct of average human beings. A certain amount of conscience, and of disinterested public spirit, may fairly be calculated on in the citizen of any community ripe for representative government. But it would be ridiculous to expect such a degree of it, combined with such intellectual discernment, as would be proof against any plausible fallacy tending to make that which was for their class interest appear the dictate of justice and of the general good.

We all know what specious fallacies may be urged in defence of every act of injustice yet proposed for the imaginary benefit of the mass. We know how many, not otherwise fools or bad men, have thought it justifiable to repudiate the national debt. We know how many, not destitute of ability, and of considerable popular influence, think it fair to throw the whole burthen of taxation upon savings, under the name of realised property, allowing those whose progenitors and themselves have always spent all they received to remain, as a reward for such exemplary conduct, wholly untaxed. We know what powerful arguments, the more dangerous because there is a portion of truth in them, may be brought against all inheritance, against the power of bequest, against every advantage which one person seems to have over another. We know how easily the uselessness of almost every branch of knowledge may be proved, to the complete satisfaction of those who do not possess it. How many, not altogether stupid men, think the scientific study of languages useless, think ancient literature useless, all erudition useless, logic and metaphysics useless, poetry and the fine arts idle and frivolous, political economy purely mischievous? Even history has been pronounced useless and mischievous by able men. Nothing but that acquaintance with external nature, empirically acquired, which serves directly for the production of objects necessary to existence or agreeable to the senses, would get its utility recognised if people had the least encouragement to disbelieve it. Is it reasonable to think that even much more cultivated minds than those of the numerical majority can be expected to be will have so delicate a conscience, and so just an appreciation of what is against their own apparent interest, that they will reject these and the innumerable other fallacies which will press in upon them from all quarters as soon as they come into power, to induce them to follow their own selfish inclinations and short-sighted notions of their own good, in opposition to justice, at the expense of all other classes and of posterity?

One of the greatest dangers, therefore, of democracy, as of all other forms of government, lies in the sinister interest of the holders of power: it is the danger of class legislation; of government intended for (whether really effecting it or not) the immediate benefit of the dominant class, to the lasting detriment of the whole. And one of the most important questions demanding consideration, in determining the best constitution of a representative government, is how to provide efficacious securities against this evil.

If we consider as a class, politically speaking, any number of persons who have the same sinister interest—that is, whose direct and apparent interest points to the same description of bad measures; the desirable object would be that no class, and no combination of classes likely to combine, should be able to exercise a preponderant influence in the government. A modern community, not divided within itself by strong antipathies of race, language, or nationality, may be considered as in the main divisible into two sections, which, in spite of partial variations, correspond on the whole with two divergent directions of apparent interest. Let us call them (in brief general terms) labourers on the one hand, employers of labour on the other: including however along with employers of labour, not only retired capitalists, and the possessors of inherited wealth, but all that highly paid description of labourers (such as professions) whose education and way of life assimilate them with the rich, and whose prospect and ambition it is to raise themselves into that class. With the labourers, on the other hand, may be ranked those smaller employers of labour, who by interests, habits, and educational impressions are assimilated in wishes, tastes, and objects to the labouring classes; comprehending a large proportion of petty tradesmen. In a state of society thus composed, if the representative system could be made ideally perfect, and if it were possible to maintain it in that state, its organisation must be such that these two classes, manual labourers and their affinities on one side, employers of labour and their affinities on the other, should be, in the arrangement of the representative system, equally balanced, each influencing about an equal number of votes in Parliament: since, assuming that the majority of each class, in any difference between them, would be mainly governed by their class interests, there would be a minority of each in whom that consideration would be subordinate to reason, justice, and the good of the whole; and this minority of either, joining with the whole of the other, would turn the scale against any demands of their own majority which were not such as ought to prevail.

The reason why, in any tolerable constituted society, justice and the general interest mostly in the end carry their point, is that the separate and selfish interests of mankind are almost always divided; some are interested in what is wrong, but some, also, have their private interest on the side of what is right: and those who are governed by higher considerations, though too few and weak to prevail against the whole of the others, usually after sufficient discussion and agitation become strong enough to turn the balance in favour of the body of private interests which is on the same side with them. The representative system ought to be so constituted as to maintain this state of things: it ought not to allow any of the various sectional interests to be so powerful as to be capable of prevailing against truth and justice and the other sectional interests combined. There ought always to be such a balance preserved among personal interests as may render any one of them dependent for its successes on carrying with it at least a large proportion of those who act on higher motives and more comprehensive and distant views.

B. Efforts to Modify Market Wages

37. UNIONS AND THE WAGE STRUCTURE*

Lloyd G. Reynolds and Cynthia H. Taft

Economists have frequently viewed with alarm the rise of powerful labor syndicates able to influence the pricing and allocation of labor serv-

* Lloyd G. Reynolds and Cynthia H. Taft, *The Evolution of Wage Structure* (New Haven, Conn.: Yale University Press, 1956), pp. 167–69, 171–72, 175–79, 182–83, 185–86, 188–91.

ices. The apparent parallel with industrial monopoly, the interference with market pricing, and the possible limitation of free occupational choices provide a basis for legitimate apprehension. The great expansion of union strength in the United States during the thirties and forties has brought a new wave of critical comment and of proposals for curtailing union power.

Recent discussion of the impact of unionism has focused on two principal issues. One controversy has to do with the effect of unionism on the general level of money wage rates. Does strong unionism increase the likelihood of a rapid advance of wages and prices during periods of high employment? Does it contribute to secular inflation? A much older controversy, . . . has to do with the impact of unionism on relative wage rates. Does unionism distort the wage structure away from its "normal" pattern, with disruptive effects on relative prices, outputs, and resource allocation?

In addition to its direct impact on the wage structure, unionism has at least two possible indirect effects which can only be noted in passing. First, union rules undoubtedly alter workers' reaction patterns, employers' hiring and promotion practices, the channels through which labor moves into employment, and other features of the labor market. Seniority systems, for example, may reduce both the willingness and ability of workers to change employers, and may mean that interfirm competition for labor occurs principally at the bottom of the occupational structure. Discussion of these side effects is omitted here, partly for reasons of space, partly because research in this area is only in its infancy.

Second, unions might influence wages by controlling the number of workers admitted to particular occupations and industries. Indeed, it has sometimes been argued (or assumed) that this is the principal way in which unions influence the wage structure. Manipulation of wages via labor supply, however, implies a closed shop plus a policy of admitting to the union fewer workers than employers would be willing to hire at competitive wage rates. The closed shop has been used by only a minority of craft unions, while deliberate restriction of members is found in a still smaller number. Opinion is now shifting increasingly to the view that unions influence wage rates not by control of labor supply but by direct control of the employer. The sequence of events is not that supply is first reduced and then wages rise. Rather, wages are raised through direct negotiation with the employer under threat of strike action, and this limits the number of workers who can find employment at the bargained wage.

. . . Before embarking on the main discussion, several methodological comments are in order.

First, it is necessary to take account of all the dimensions of wage structure. Theoretical discussion has tended to focus on interindustry differentials and on the problem of whether unionism alters these in an anti-competitive way. Equally important, however, are personal differentials among workers in the same type of work, occupational differentials, interfirm differentials within an industry, and geographical differentials. The effect of unionism on each of these things must be appraised before its total impact can be judged.

Second, there is no warrant for the assumption that unionism is the only thing preventing attainment of a perfectly competitive wage structure. There is a growing body of evidence that the labor market is by nature an imperfect instrument and that all kinds of wage distortions exist even under nonunion conditions. To compare the wage structure which develops under collective bargaining with a hypothetical wage structure which might exist under perfect competition is an arbitrary and unreal procedure. The significant comparison is between the bargained wage structure and that which actually exists in imperfect nonunion labor markets. It may turn out that the bargained wage structure lies closer to the hypothetical competitive pattern than does the nonunion structure. In any event, the inquiry should not be biased by taking a position on this point before the evidence has been examined.

Third, the consequences of unionism cannot be discovered simply by deduction. General reasoning must be checked by systematic observation of bargained wage structures in different industries, different countries, and different time periods. We know relatively little about the mainsprings of union wage policy, and students of the subject are at odds on many points. There would be widespread agreement among informed observers, however, that the analogy with business monopoly is seriously misleading. It is reasonable to take profit maximization as a first approximation to business behavior, because a concern for profit is a condition of survival and growth for the firm. The trade union, however, is not engaged in buying and selling. It does not make a profit if wages are set high, nor does it become bankrupt if wages are set low. It is a regulatory agency engaged in determining the minimum standards under which production may continue, and is more nearly comparable to a local government than to a business organization.

· · · · · ·

PERSONAL DIFFERENTIALS

· · · · ·

The union frequently has some effect on the choice between time payment and incentive payment. While some unions have a distinct preference for incentive payment, the general tendency of unionism has probably been to retard the spread of incentive wage systems. Unions have frequently blocked the installation of incentive payment, and in some cases, such as the automobile industry, have caused its abandonment where it had long been established. Substitution of time payment for incentive payment makes it somewhat harder to relate individual earnings to output, but does not prevent this from being accomplished in a rough way through "measured day work" and other devices.

Where unions have accepted incentive payment, they have normally insisted on a voice in the structure and administration of the system. Unions have preferred systems under which earnings increase proportionately with output to decreasing piece-rate systems of the Bedaux or Gantt type. They have insisted that piece-rate earnings bear a consistent relation to a basic schedule of occupational hourly rates, usually termed "minimum," "guaranteed," or "fall-back" rates. By protecting workers against arbitrary cuts in piece rates, unionism may have encouraged them to work somewhat closer to their individual capacities than they feel safe in doing under nonunion conditions. Each of these effects appears desirable. The main thing to be set on the other side of the ledger is that some unions, where their strength is sufficient, have presented intransigent resistance to any adjustment of piece rates as production methods change. This tends over time to distort the earnings structure away from the structure of hourly base rates.

In the more common case of time payment, the union typically insists on a standard wage schedule which "rates the job, not the man." While for most large companies this is nothing new, in many smaller establishments union organization has forced the abandonment of personal rates and the development of a systematic wage structure. This is probably a net gain. . . .

Unions do not necessarily insist that every member of an occupational group receive the *same* wage. On the contrary, many unions prefer a system of rate ranges rather than single job rates. This is more flexible, provides greater opportunity for personal advancement over the course of time, and provides greater opportunity for the union to demonstrate that it is giving service to its members by pressing for individual adjustments within the established range. Certain craft groups . . . , have deliberately created a rate structure under which some members of the craft are able to earn much more than others. It seems unlikely that the dispersion of earnings among locomotive engineers, or among papermachine tenders, would be as great under nonunion conditions as it has become under collective bargaining. Unionism may thus make for less equality, rather than greater equality, among members of the same occupational group.

As regards criteria for advancement of individual workers within an established rate range, or from one level to another of a craft hierarchy, unions attach major importance to length of service while employers typically prefer freedom to reward superior efficiency. If the dispersion of efficiency levels within the group is wide, and if one assumes no correlation between efficiency and seniority, a strict seniority system may have undesirable results. In many situations, however, one or both of these conditions is absent, and a seniority system will not produce very different results from a merit system. It is also an open question how far nonunion employers, uncontrolled by contract rules, do actually make wage increases and promotions on an efficiency basis rather than on other grounds. While the net effect of union seniority rules is probably to worsen the earnings structure, the strength of this effect should not be exaggerated.

. . . . .

INTERPLANT DIFFERENTIALS

. . . . .

Collective bargaining clearly makes for reduction of wage differentials among firms competing in the same product market. Several factors work in this direction. The maxims of "equal pay for equal work" and "the standard rate" are deeply embedded in union thinking. Departure from the principle of equality requires justification, while conformity to it does not. There is likely to be pressure from union members in low-wage companies to be brought up to the wage level which other members are receiving for the same work. High-wage companies are also likely to favor industry-wide standardization on competitive grounds. The decisive factor making for wage uniformity is the pressure of competition in the product market. A firm which is allowed to pay less than the prevailing rates may, by undercutting prices, become a threat to the entire wage and price structure of the industry. A standard wage scale thus comes to be viewed by union and employers alike as a method of "stabilizing the industry," of "putting a floor under competition."

It follows that the area over which a union attempts to impose a standard rate will be related to the area of competition in the product market. In retail trade, service industries, building construction, and other local industries, the union may be expected to establish a standard scale in each locality; but it will not be considered essential to bring different localities to a common level. In industries where competition is regional or national in scope, on the other hand, the union will be under pressure to develop a standard scale for all employers regardless of location. The struggle of unions to establish greater wage uniformity can be traced in the history of many American industries. The list includes railroading, coal mining, basic steel, most branches of the textile industry, men's clothing, pulp and paper on the Pacific Coast, hosiery, pottery, flat glass, pressed and blown glassware. In some industries, wage equalization has been pursued via centralized negotiation with employers' associations. This does not appear to be essential, for in other industries the union has continued to bargain separately with each employer and has tried in the course of successive annual negotiations to herd them in the direction of a common wage level.

Analysis of experience in these industries suggests that the concept of wage equalization or wage uniformity is more complicated than may appear at first glance. Precisely what is to be equalized? The possibilities include:

1. Hourly rates for workers actually paid on a time basis. Equalization in this sense will equalize workers' hourly earnings, except for possible payment above the scale during periods of labor shortage. It will not equalize average direct labor cost per unit of output (referred to hereafter as unit labor cost), because of nonuniformity in both plant efficiency and in quality of labor.

2. Hourly minimum rates for workers paid on a piece-rate or other incentive basis. This will not equalize the average hourly earnings of workers on the same job in different companies, unless the companies follow identical standards of piece-rate determination. It is compatible with equalization of unit labor cost but will not by itself produce this result.

3. Piece rates per unit of output. This will not equalize workers' earnings, because of variations in both plant and worker efficiency. It will equalize unit labor cost but is compatible with wide variations in average total unit cost.

4. Earnings per unit of skill and effort required (Marshall's "efficiency earnings"). On this basis, piece rates in different plants would be so adjusted as precisely to offset variations in the quality of tools, materials, supervision, and other factors outside the worker's control. A worker putting forth a given amount of skill and effort would then earn the same amount regardless of the plant in which he was employed. Earnings of workers on the same job would not necessarily be equalized, but differences would reflect only differences in skill and effort among the workers themselves. Unit labor cost would of course not be equalized. Unit *total* costs would be more unequal than under method 3, because the least efficient firms in an industry would be obliged to pay the highest piece rates. Marginal firms would receive an added penalty and efficient firms a bonus under this arrangement.

From the worker's standpoint, only method 4 will equalize earnings for workers of equal efficiency. From the employer's standpoint, only method 3 provides assurance of equal unit labor costs throughout the industry. In general, the methods which will ensure uniformity of earnings will destroy uniformity of labor costs, and vice versa. It is possible to work out hypothetical conditions under which the two objectives could be achieved simultaneously, but there is little likelihood of these conditions actually being realized. Faced with this dilemma, both employers and unions seem to give greatest weight to uniformity of labor cost. An effort is sometimes made to protect workers against abnormally poor plant conditions by prescribing higher piece rates, extra payments, and so on; but beyond this earnings are left to fall where they may.

The consequences of a union's wage-leveling activities depend on what it is that the union undertakes to equalize, and on what the reasons were for inequality of wages in preunion days. It was suggested in the previous section that two main elements can be distinguished; differences in the quality of the labor employed, normally a minor factor; and difference in firms' wage-paying ability, normally the major factor. It is necessary to separate these for analysis and to ask concerning each: if interfirm differentials in an industry were due entirely to this element, what would be the effect of eliminating them?

Suppose, first, that interfirm variation in workers' hourly earnings is due entirely to differences in ability and effort; and consider for simplicity only the case of time rates. Differences in labor efficiency, then, are precisely reflected in different levels of hourly rates in the various firms. If an effort is now made to raise the wage levels of the lowest firms and impose a standard scale on the industry, this clearly will have a disturbing effect. It will impose higher unit labor costs on the firms with an inferior labor force. These firms will begin to suffer losses and will face elimination unless they can raise the quality of their labor force *pari passu* with the rise in their wage level. If the process of wage leveling is sufficiently gradual, if employers are reasonably free to alter their labor force by discharges and new hirings, and if the industry in question is a small factor in the total labor market, it may be quite possible for firms to make the necessary adjustments. The outcome may be a new equilibrium with a uniform quality of labor in all firms corresponding to the uniform level of hourly wage rates. This implies that many workers will have been forced out of this industry into others whose wage structure is either not standardized at all or is standardized at a lower level. There is no insuperable difficulty in imposing uniform quality requirements *within* a single (relatively small) industry, provided there remains sufficient room for quality variation *among* industries.

The effect of imposing a uniform scale of minimum hourly rates, while earnings are computed on a piece-rate basis, will be more moderate. It will impose considerable pressure on the firms with the poorest labor force. The pressure will not be so serious as that of uniform time rates, however, because there remains an escape valve in the gap between the hourly minimum and actual hourly earnings. The firms with an inferior labor force may survive partly by holding this gap considerably below that which exists in the superior firms. If the union will not permit this and insists on a uniform gap throughout, the effect becomes identical with that of uniform time rates.

Suppose, second, that the quality of labor is uniform throughout the industry, and that interfirm variation is due solely to differences in ability to pay. What happens when a union enters the industry and tries to enforce a uniform level of wages? The severity of the impact will depend on the kind of wage standardization which is attempted. A uniform scale of time rates will put heaviest pressure on the low-wage firms. Uniform minimum hourly rates for pieceworkers will exert somewhat less pressure. Uniform piece rates will exert even less pressure, but will still exert some. In order fully to offset their higher unit overhead costs, it will have been necessary for the less efficient firms to pay their workers, not merely less per hour, but also less per piece. Establishment of uniform piece rates will thus work some hardship upon them. An attempt to equalize *efficiency earnings* of pieceworkers, by setting higher piece rates where production conditions are unfavorable, will of course bear still harder on the marginal firms.

Any type of wage standardization will thus worsen the position of the marginal firms and threaten their survival. Their first reaction will doubtless be to reexamine their costs and endeavor to reduce them. This is the "shock effect," which has frequently been observed as an aftermath of minimum wage legislation. Some of the inefficiency of the high-cost firms may turn out to be removable, and wage increases may force management to take remedial action. After everything possible has been done in this direction, continued pressure for wage equalization can result only in eventual elimination of the highest-cost firms.

Cases in which union wage pressure actually produces a plant shutdown are rare in practice. Where a marginal firm would be put out of operation by enforcement of the standard wage scale, local union leaders and members will usually be willing to make concessions in order to protect their jobs. National leaders are more reluctant to permit payment under the standard scale and more insistent that inability to pay be fully demonstrated; but if the facts are clear, even national headquarters will usually approve a lower wage scale. Numerous instances of this sort have been pointed out in cotton textiles, pulp and paper, basic steel, and steel fabricating, and many additional illustrations could be given from other industries. Exceptions to the standard scale are usually regarded as temporary, and are frequently accompanied by a requirement that the employer take steps to improve plant efficiency. In some industries the union itself maintains an engineering department which provides free assistance to marginal employers who must improve their efficiency in order to survive.

. . . . .

GEOGRAPHICAL DIFFERENTIALS

. . . . .

Unionism appears thus far to have had only a slight effect on geographical differentials; and this effect has not always been in the same direction. In manufacturing and other industries characterized by interregional competition, union efforts to place different firms on an equal competitive basis have often involved a reduction of geographical differentials. There are exceptions, however, such as the pulp and paper industry, where the unions have followed a pragmatic policy of exploiting the wage-paying ability of each region as fully as possible, leaving differentials to fall where they may. In other cases the organizing ability of the union has varied considerably from region to region. In textiles, hosiery, clothing, and light industry generally, union progress in the South has been slow, and this has limited what could be done in narrowing regional differentials. In some of these cases the union may have widened geographical differentials for the time being, because it could exploit fully the wage-paying ability of firms in the North but was unable to do so in the South.

In other manufacturing industries, geographical differentials have been reduced and in a few cases eliminated entirely. Where differentials have been eliminated, as in flat glass and basic steel, there has typically been a combination of favorable circumstances: a high degree of unionization, a high degree of industrial concentration, and a situation in which the southern plants were subsidiaries of northern companies. It is easier in such a situation for the union to force acceptance of wage equalization, and for the industry to adjust to it, than in an industry which has hundreds of small, independent producers and is only partially unionized.

There is a regrettable lack of evidence concerning the impact of unionism on geographical differentials in local industries. It may well be that unionism, by entrenching itself first in the high-wage regions and communities, has for the time being widened differentials in such industries. This may be one reason why building construction wages in the South today are further below the northern level than they were forty years ago. If and when unionism spreads evenly throughout the industry, geographical differentials may tend to narrow once more.

. . . . .

OCCUPATIONAL DIFFERENTIALS

. . . . .

The effect of unionism on occupational differentials appears to have been slight, and rather different from what might have been expected from speculative reasoning. It seems logical that an industrial union, having a large percentage of low-skilled members, will favor a narrowing of occupational differentials, and that where the skilled men are organized separately in craft unions they will be able to widen their advantage over the unskilled. This hypothesis, however, does not stand up against the evidence. In the printing industry, differentials have been well maintained, the premium of compositors over binderywomen having fallen by only about one-fifth between 1938 and 1952. Other cases can be found, however, in which differentials have been drastically reduced despite the prevalence of craft organization. The building construction and railroad industries are two leading examples.

Turning to the industrial unions, one finds a similar diversity of experience. In several major industries, including the automobile industry, occupational differentials have been sharply compressed. In basic steel, however, there has been little reduction. In the woolen and worsted textile industry, the percentage differential of loom fixers over laborers has actually increased since the mid-thirties.

It does not appear, then, that there is any marked correlation between type of union organization and rate of decline in occupational differentials. A more detailed analysis would be necessary to confirm this observation. If correct, it raises interesting questions. Are the skilled members of an industrial union much more influential than one might suppose from their numbers alone? Are the skilled craft unions less aggressive and self-interested than one might expect on economic grounds? Are they restrained by regard for public opinion or by other considerations from advancing their already high wage scales at a disproportionate rate? Are they interested in raising the rates of the unskilled, possibly as an underpinning to their own position and a platform for future wage demands?

To the extent that unionism has had any net effect on occupational differentials, this has almost certainly been in the direction of narrowing them. One can find numerous instances during the thirties and forties in which a union sought and won an equal cents-per-hour increase for all employees, whereas the employer would have preferred a uniform percentage increase. The pulp and paper industry appears to be a leading example. It is difficult to find cases of the opposite sort. The cost-of-living escalator systems which were installed in many companies at union insistence during the forties and early fifties were invariably constructed to yield uniform cents-per-hour increases to all employees. One can conclude, then, that there has been some tendency for unionism to increase the use of uniform cents-per-hour wage adjustments, which necessarily reduce occupational differentials on a percentage basis.

. . . . .

INTERINDUSTRY DIFFERENTIALS

. . . . .

Much of the theoretical criticism of trade unionism has rested on a presumed distorting effect on interindustry differentials. Assuming that all industries are unionized and that the union in each industry follows a "monopolistic" wage policy, one might expect wages to be set highest in industries where the demand for labor is rising most rapidly, whether because of rising demand for the product or a rapid increase in labor productivity. There is some tendency in this direction even in the absence of union organization. Expanding industries tend to bid up wages somewhat to attract an adequate labor force, while stationary or declining industries take advantage of the imperfection of the labor market to lag behind the general pace of wage advance. Trade unionism, however, might be expected to accentuate this tendency for the expanding industries to outpace the others. A larger part of any increase in labor demand will be translated into wage increases and a smaller part into employment increases than would be the case without collective bargaining.

What evidence is there that these disruptive potentialities of collective bargaining are actually realized? The statistical evidence is by no means conclusive but suggests that the actual impact of unionism is much less than might have been expected on theoretical grounds.

A serious difficulty in interpreting the evidence is that there is a marked intercorrelation among the variables of rate of increase in man-hour output, degree of concentration, and extent of unionization, and particularly between the last two. Garbarino found a "Z" of 0.89 for the relation between unionization and concentration, which is above the 1 per cent level of significance. This is not surprising, for once the core of employer resistance has been penetrated, full unionization of a highly concentrated industry is simpler than unionization of an industry containing scores or hundreds of small concerns. The association of unionization with concentration seems mainly responsible for the fact that a simple correlation between rate of increase of earnings and degree of unionization yields a high positive coefficient. High concentration, in other words, tends to accompany *both* high unionization and a rapid rate of increase in earnings.

This still leaves the question of causation unsettled. It may be that highly concentrated industries show a rapid rate of wage increase *because* they are also highly unionized. It should be emphasized, however, that large, oligopolistic, and progressive firms seem in any event to follow a high-wage policy. This tendency can be traced back to the early decades of this century when union organization was very weak.

Garbarino, working with manufacturing data for 1923–40, concluded that "the relationship between unionism and earnings for this period seems to be rather vague. This result may well be due to the fact that the influence of unionism entered the picture so late in the time period." Ross and Goldner, after an examination of data for 1933–46, concluded that "New unionism (that is, unionization) has been a source of relative wage advantage during the 1933–46 period, whereas continuing unionism has not." Lester and Robie, after a study of seven industries characterized by strong unionization and regional or national collective bargaining, reported: "Generally speaking, wage and earning levels do not appear to have risen more rapidly under national and regional bargaining than for manufacturing as a whole." Dunlop found that economic variables have dominated the changes in interindustry differentials and that unionism has played a minor role. Rees, in a study of the fully unionized basic steel and bituminous coal industries during the inflationary period 1946–50, concluded that their wage levels probably rose somewhat less rapidly than they would have risen under nonunion conditions.

The only recent study which finds strong indications of union influence is that of Levinson, who concludes:

> For the period 1920 to 1933, there was a consistent positive correlation between the strength of unionism and the trend of money wages. Those groups of workers who were strongly unionized obtained much greater wage concessions than those who were not; furthermore, the wages of those groups of workers who became unionized during these years rose from the lower non-union level to the higher union level, while the wages of workers whose unionism was greatly weakened followed almost exactly the opposite pattern. For the remaining years, however—1914 to 1920, and 1933 to 1947—there was no significant correlation between the strength of unionism and the trend of money wages in the manufacturing, extractive, construction, and public utility industries.

Almost all studies except Levinson's have focused on manufacturing industries, and it is possible that one might find clearer indications of union influence by widening the focus to include construction, transportation, trade and service, and a variety of other industries. It would also be a rewarding task to try to reconcile the divergent methods and findings of the authors cited above. About all one can say at present is that the evidence is inconclusive. A few scholars believe that unionism has shown some tendency to widen interindustry differentials. The preponderant opinion is that union influence has been slight or even nonexistent.

If the preponderant view is correct, how can this result be explained? Why does unionism not wrench the interindustry wage structure apart as Simons and others anticipated? The answer appears to lie partly in the realities of union behavior and partly in the structure of labor markets. Wage bargaining is only one aspect of union activity, and in the case of old and secure unions it is by no means the most important aspect. As regards wage bargaining, there are indications that most union leaders function as "lazy monopolists." They are conservative institutional leaders who try to keep out of trouble both with employers and with their members, and to whom aggressive wage maximization would appear as a dangerous and quite unnecessary course.

Suppose, however, that this hypothesis about union behavior is wrong, and that one or more unions do endeavor to raise the wage levels of their industries at an abnormally rapid rate. The usual conclusion is that this will reduce employment in those industries, and that this will force the displaced workers to seek employment in other industries, whose wage level will then necessarily fall. This process can continue so long as the aggressiveness and power of the unions continues, and so long as there is any employment at all left for their members. The consequence must be an ever increasing gap between the bottom and top of the wage structure.

It is perhaps unfair to compare this essentially static argument with the dynamic movement of wages in actual labor markets. In actuality, however, it does not seem that the process just described could continue indefinitely. There appears to be at any given time a maximum feasible gap between the highest and lowest wages offered for comparable labor in the same labor market. To the extent that unions do work actively to force up the top strata of the wage structure, there are other forces working to push up the lower layers. These forces include the advance of legal minimum wage levels and of benefit rates under social insurance programs. They include employer fears of incipient or potential unionism in the unorganized industries. They include also employer and worker reactions expressed directly in the labor market.

Wage increases in some industries tend to influence the supply price of labor to other industries. The higher wages generate expectations among workers in the market and influence their conception of what is a reasonable or fair wage for a certain type of work. As the top of the wage structure rises, this minimum expectation also rises, and the lowest wage employers are under pressure to raise wages in order to recruit labor and to maintain the morale of their present work force. Nor do employers necessarily wait to be forced by supply pressures. They take it for granted that their wage levels should keep pace in a rough way with the movement of wages elsewhere in the market. They do not sit passively until an avalanche of displaced workers descends on them from the high-wage industries. The low-wage firms take positive action to keep within sight of the wage leaders; and the consequent increase in their wage (and price) levels may largely or even entirely prevent any displacement from occurring.

Beyond a certain point, then, an effort by the more highly organized and strategically situated workers to increase their advantage over the low-paid workers must become a futile attempt to rise by pulling at their own bootstraps. The market reactions just described operate most strongly, to be sure, during periods of high employment and may be largely suspended during severe underemployment. What may happen, therefore, is a cyclical alternation of low employment periods during which the well-organized workers widen their advantage over the ill-organized ones, and of high employment periods during which the latter narrow the gap.

38. MINIMUM WAGE LEGISLATION: EXPERIENCE*

Donald E. Cullen

THE CONFLICTING VIEWS

Several detailed studies have been made of the impact of minimum wage laws, but different analysts view these studies from quite different perspectives. For instance, those who doubt the value of wage regulation expect the evidence to show that higher wages for some have been offset by unemployment, lower wages, or higher prices for others. This expectation springs not from malice but from a widely accepted belief as to how our economic system works. Assume, these critics suggest, that you are an employer now paying half your workers less than $1.00 an hour. What would you do if tomorrow you were ordered to pay everyone at least $1.00? You might absorb the resultant cost increase by reducing your profits, but your profits may be too small to permit this and, even if they are large, why shouldn't you try to retain them for yourself, your stockholders, or to reinvest in the business? To do this, or perhaps just to break even if you are particularly hard hit, you might raise your prices, although you know this will reduce your sales volume (and hence employment) or you would have raised them before this.

If competition is so stiff that you cannot raise prices, then you will probably seek to cut your unit costs back to their former level by increasing the output you obtain for every dollar of your wage bill. This might be done by using more labor-saving machinery, or raising work standards, or hiring better workers to replace the least efficient among your present force—all of which means unemployment for somebody, since today's level of output will thus be met tomorrow by fewer workers. Finally, if the workers you lay off were not "worth" $1.00 to you, they probably will not be worth that to other employers and will consequently have to seek work in low-wage industries not yet covered by a wage law—which will depress wages even further in those industries.

To all this, proponents of wage regulation say that it is small wonder that economics long ago earned the title of "the dismal science." They point out that nearly every type of welfare legislation has been opposed initially with the same predictions of disaster, predictions which they feel are based on the homely philosophy that the poor are always with

* Donald E. Cullen, *Minimum Wage Laws*, Bulletin 43, N.Y. State School of Industrial and Labor Relations, Ithaca, N.Y., February, 1961, pp. 6–15.

us and for their own good it is best not to meddle with fate and free enterprise. Analysts of this persuasion turn to the impact studies in the knowledge that the country has not been ruined yet and therefore with the expectation of discovering that past minima have been absorbed quite easily. Their reasoning, which has achieved wide currency among economists specializing in labor problems, proceeds from three propositions.

First, as businessmen never tire of reminding economists, the real world is seldom as neatly ordered as theory implies. It is true that a competitive economy works quite well on the whole, but there is inevitably considerable slippage in a system as complex as our own. Workers cannot shift about as easily as capital; unorganized workers are frequently at a disadvantage in bargaining with their employers; businessmen would be less than human if they always strained every fiber to operate at peak efficiency, even when under no pressure to do so.

For these and other reasons, it is argued that one cannot comfortably assume that in a free market all workers tend to be paid as much as the market can bear for their services. Many employers know they have some discretion in setting the wages they pay, for there would be no point to their many wage surveys and elaborate job-evaluation programs if market forces alone determined wage rates. Thus, there are great variations in the wages paid for the same type of labor in the same industry or the same city, and who is to say that the janitor paid $.70 an hour on one side of town is not worth the $1.00 being paid the janitor on the other side of town? More to the point, who can safely predict that the first janitor will be laid off if he must be paid $1.00 an hour? Everyone has heard nonunion employers predict complete bankruptcy if forced to accept a union, and yet most survive when organized and devise ways of living with the union scale short of wholesale layoffs. They may intensify their selling efforts, improve their plant layout, increase the training of their present workers and selection standards for new ones, strengthen the quality of supervision, and in these and other ways absorb most of the shock of a wage increase which first appeared ruinous.

Second, organized labor has long urged that wage increases be recognized as not only a cost increase for employers but also an increase in the purchasing power of consumers. Particularly in the case of low-wage workers, it is argued, increases are spent immediately—long before employers can undertake, for example, any large-scale substitution of machinery for labor—and they are usually spent in a way which directly benefits certain low-wage industries: through retail stores and for such products as food and clothing.

Third, the few employers truly unable to pay a decent wage should not be in business in the first place. To those who hold this view, it is both cruel and senseless to assert that the richest country on earth should do nothing about employers who today are unable to pay their workers $40 a week. If society really needs some of these employers in business, then let them be subsidized, not by their few workers in the form of low wages, but by society as a whole through any of the several forms of government aid already being given, for other reasons, to employers in many industries. If these employers are not essential, let their share of sales and their workers go to those who can pay a living wage. This is a harsh remedy for those affected and they should be given every aid possible in adjusting, but their numbers, it is said, will be small compared to those who directly benefit from a legal minimum.

THE HAZARDS OF MEASUREMENT

And so the controversy between these opposing camps rages on, with many of the arguments used today being identical with those advanced fifty years ago. Why hasn't this dispute been settled long ago by an appeal to the facts of experience? Since 1912 there have always been minimum wage laws in effect somewhere in the nation, for some states continued to enforce such laws even during the 1923–1937 period when they could not have withstood a court challenge. Yet, during the first forty years of this long experience, only twenty scattered studies were made which attempted to gather statistics on the actual effect of one or another of these laws, and many of these studies were not of high quality. It was not until 1955, seventeen years after the FLSA was enacted, that Congress specifically directed the Secretary of Labor to supply it annully with data on the effects and adequacy of the act. Thus, until very recently the debate on this question has not been overburdened with facts.

The basic difficulty lies deeper than this, however, as evidenced by the widely differing interpretations placed upon the seven hundred pages of data which the Department of Labor has recently published on the impact of the $1.00 minimum. As indicated previously, this massive study was cited as supporting all three positions taken in the recent congressional debate: against any increase in the $1.00 rate, in favor of no more than $1.15, and in favor of $1.25. It would be easy but inaccurate to attribute these varying appraisals to nothing more than political expediency, for the fact remains that independent experts are similarly divided.

The essential reason why "the facts" on this question have proved inconclusive is that it is extremely difficult to separate out the effects of a legal minimum from the effects of dozens of other forces acting simultaneously in the economy. Changes in prices, wages, employment, and output are the result not only of changes in wage laws, but also of the interaction of shifting consumer tastes, management's investment decisions, the pattern of government taxing and spending, union activity, the discovery of new inventions, revolution in Cuba and recovery in Japan—the list is endless and, unfortunately for the analyst, none of these forces obligingly suspends operation when a new minimum wage is enacted.

No one seriously argues, for example, that the sole reason wages today are higher than in 1938 is the lifting of the FLSA rate over this period from $.25 to $1.00. Even if the period of comparison is narrowed to one or two years, however, there remain serious hazards in interpreting the law's effect. The $.25 minimum of 1938 and the $.30–$.40 range of 1939 were followed by the beginning of the defense and war boom in 1940; the $.75 minimum took effect just six months before the Korean invasion and the subsequent inflation of 1950–1952; and the $1.00 minimum became effective as the economy was expanding in 1956 prior to its relapse into the recession beginning in 1957.

In an effort to minimize the effects of these economy-wide changes, several studies have made before-and-after comparisons limited to a few weeks or months bridging the introduction of a new minimum, but these studies may be unintentionally biased in either direction. On the one hand, they may underestimate the negative effects of a minimum by not including long-range adjustments such as the introduction of labor-saving machinery (which can rarely be done overnight), the raising of hiring standards in filling future vacancies left by normal turnover, or even the complete shutdown of some plants which managed to survive the first few months of a new minimum but could not last indefinitely. On the other hand, "quickie" studies may magnify negative effects, since some managements, fearing the worst, produce furiously for inventory in the weeks just before a new minimum takes effect and then sharply reduce their level of operations in the period immediately following; or some employers may not discover for some time all of the ways in which they can absorb a wage increase without adverse employment or price effects; or if the plants least affected ultimately capture the sales volume lost by those hardest hit, an initial contraction or shutdown by low-wage plants may later be tempered or offset by employment expansion in high-wage plants.

This, then, is the central dilemma in attempting to measure the actual effects of minimum wage laws: the shorter the period examined, the greater is the danger of ignoring important long-run effects, but the longer the period, the greater is the difficulty of correcting for the effects of all the other economic forces constantly at work. This poses formidable problems of interpretation for even the most dispassionate observer. For instance, many studies have attempted to hold "all other things equal" by including in their sample only plants which were continuously in existence both before and after a legal minimum was applied. This approach obviously excludes plants wiped out by such a law and has been justifiably criticized as based on a logic which, by examining the health of identical soldiers before and after a war, could show that no soldier had been fatally wounded. On the other hand, this approach also excludes new plants which may have come into an affected industry, and even a complete count of the plants both begun and shut down during the relevant period would have to be carefully compared to the high rate of plant turnover which often characterizes low-wage industries at all times. The same type of problem is involved in attempting to assess post-minimum wage changes in prices, employment, mechanization, working hours (as opposed to numbers of workers), work procedures, and product lines.

Finally, the difficulty of assessing the impact of a national minimum wage "is aggravated by the relatively low minimums that have been set under the FLSA. In even the most affected low-wage industries, to have raised all workers to the minimum would have required only a 5–15 per cent increase in payrolls and a 1–3 per cent increase in total cost." Of course, the cost impact was far higher for some individual firms, but it was even lower for the average industry covered by the law and so low for the entire economy that the law's effect on such things as inflation and mass purchasing power probably cannot be measured at all.

To sum up, the question of how workers and employers fare under a minimum wage law is still unresolved, because (1) different people look at the evidence of past experience from quite different viewpoints, based on conflicting notions of how our economy operates, and (2) the evidence itself is so difficult to interpret that nearly everyone can point to some facts that appear to support his prior convictions.

THE EFFECTS ON WORKERS

When a new minimum wage goes into effect, a fairly predictable chain of events is touched off in those firms covered by the law which had been paying many of their workers less than the new standard. First, the occupational wage structure within these firms is sharply compressed, as wage increases granted to those formerly below the new minimum are seldom matched by similar increases to those already above the legal floor. Also, differentials among those previously below the minimum are often obliterated, since nearly all of this group—those who had been $.10 below, plus those who had been $.20 below, etc.—will usually be bunched together at or just above the new minimum. Second, most employers will sooner or later attempt to restore, at least partially, the pre-minimum occupational differentials; this might be done by subsequently increasing only the rates of the high-wage occupations or by distributing future general wage increases in such a fashion that rates for this group increase more rapidly than rates for those at the bottom of the structure. Third, many workers will feel certain non-wage effects of the new minimum in such forms as shorter working hours, increased production standards, or complete unemployment.

There is no argument over whether all of these effects occur, but only over their relative magnitudes. No one knows, for example, how many workers have benefited from these laws by either direct or indirect wage increases, although some crude estimates can be made. For the 1938–1945 period, when the national minimum was first established at $.25 and ultimately raised to $.40, the data on this point are particularly poor, but it is known that the final industry wage orders establishing the $.40 rate over the 1940–1944 period covered a total of 1.6 million workers who were receiving less than $.40 at the time the various orders were issued. When the minimum was raised to $.75 in 1950, there were approximately 1.3 million covered workers who had been receiving less than that, and the 1956 increase to $1.00 applied to about 2.1 million workers receiving less than $1.00 an hour.

These figures, however, tell only one part of the story. In some ways they overstate the beneficial effect of the law, and in some ways they understate it. For instance, it is regrettably true that many employers violate the law, either wittingly or unwittingly, and therefore many workers who are entitled to the minimum do not receive it. The extent of this problem is indicated in the following excerpts from an article analyzing Department of Labor data on the effects of the $1.00 minimum effective March 1, 1956:

> Minimum wage violations were found in 21% of investigations made for enforcement purposes between July and December 1956.
>
> Discovered underpayments of the minimum wage more than tripled between fiscal year 1956 and fiscal year 1957.
>
> If for every discovered violation of the minimum, three went undiscovered [this being the ratio of discovered to undiscovered underpayment estimated by the Department of Labor for fiscal year 1958], then about 310,000 covered employees were paid less than the minimum in fiscal year 1957. . . .
>
> The Department estimated that total underpayments both discovered and undiscovered totalled $80 million.

Also, in the underpayment cases which the Department does discover, it is able to obtain for the workers involved only about one half of the amount due them, for reasons to be explored later.

Some workers will suffer a partial or complete offset of their rate increase when their employers reduce the length of their work week. This course often is taken by hard-hit employers who previously have been operating on a work week of more than forty hours, since the requirement of the FLSA (and several state laws) that time and a half be paid for all weekly hours over forty is, and was meant to be, a powerful deterrent to longer hours. The importance of this factor was recognized in the recent Kennedy bill, originally designed to extend FLSA coverage to five million additional workers as well as to increase the minimum, which provided that the act's overtime requirements would not apply to newly covered employees during their first year of coverage and would then be introduced only in gradual steps, not reaching the normal forty-hour level until the fourth year of coverage. The extent to which rate increases have been offset by reduced hours is not known, but it should be recognized that, even if the offset were 100 per cent and no worker's take-home pay increased, labor would still consider it a very real net gain that those affected could henceforth earn the same weekly pay in fewer hours of work.

However, the hottest battles have been fought over the extent to which the wage increases granted to some workers by a legal minimum have been offset by the complete unemployment of others. It can safely be said that as a result of minimum wage laws some employers have been put completely out of business; some have been forced to cut back the size of their work force; some have laid off their least efficient workers and hired replacements considered to be more efficient; and all of these disemployment effects are more likely to occur in the businesses in which the cost impact of a legal minimum is great than in businesses in which it is negligible. This cautious summary is obviously not very helpful to anyone wishing to know how a particular legal minimum will affect *him* as a worker or employer, but there is little more that can be said with certainty because of the difficulties in interpreting the evidence which were discussed earlier in this chapter.

Consider certain facts gathered by the Department of Labor on the employment impact of the $1.00 minimum. Clearly no large proportion of the 2.1 million workers directly affected by the new minimum were laid off in 1956, as total employment in the country actually increased following the effective date of the amendment. In the first few months of this period, the Department made a special effort to seek out and follow up on all reports of situations in which the new rate was said to have adverse employment effects, including plant shutdowns; it could find by this method only 150 plants in which employment had suffered, and the total number of workers discharged in these plants because of the $1.00 rate was no more than 1,800. Further, in 15 low-wage industries surveyed, total employment fell, from any and all causes, only 3 per cent from 1955 to 1957, and it actually increased in 7 of these industries over this period bridging the introduction of the new rate.

Critics remain unimpressed by this selection of facts and instead point to others: since the economy was in a period of expansion which lasted up to the last half of 1957, the figures above underestimate what the minimum's effect would have been under conditions of stability or decline; the fact remains that total employment (and hours) in the fifteen low-wage industries *did* drop at a time when total employment in the economy was rising; and the most precise measure of the employment effects of the $1.00 minimum—a special survey of twelve industry segments in which individual plants were classified by the average wage increase necessary to meet the new minimum—clearly showed that the average high-impact (low-wage) plant lost more workers in the post-minimum period than did the average low-impact (high-wage) plant. All of this, it is said, confirms the prediction that the higher the legal minimum, the greater the offsetting toll exacted by market forces.

In brief, with the data now available, neither side of this dispute can prove its case to the satisfaction of the other. The most extensive minimum wage study ever made was that of the $1.00 rate; and yet no one really knows how many of the 2.1 million workers who had been receiving less than $1.00 benefited (or lost) solely from the new minimum, or by how much they benefited (or lost); and given the difficulties of measurement, it is doubtful that this issue will be resolved for some time.

Turning from the direct to the indirect effects of these laws, there are several ways in which their benefits to workers may be underestimated by data on the numbers previously receiving less than a newly applied minimum. There is first the effect on the wages of covered workers already at or above the new minimum but working in the same establishments as those whose wages are directly affected. Opinion on this matter has undergone an ironic reversal over the years. It has been mentioned that organized labor long opposed these laws for male workers out of fear that employers would pay no more than forced to by law, and that a legal minimum for some would thus tend to become a wage ceiling for all. Today, employers opposing these laws often assert that any wage increases they are forced to give their low-wage workers will have to be matched by equal increases to all their other workers in order to preserve morale and incentive, thereby increasing greatly a minimum's cost impact, and labor spokesmen strongly deny that this will or need occur.

The evidence suggests that some wage increases are given to high-wage workers at the same time a law forces direct increases for low-wage workers, but that these "indirect" increases are seldom as large as the direct. In certain low-wage industries surveyed in 1956, for instance, the average indirect increase given on the effective date of the $1.00 minimum amounted to 40 per cent of the direct increase. In succeeding years, these compressed occupational differentials do tend slowly to widen in affected establishments, but whether in most cases they eventually regain their previous levels is not known. In any event, any assessment of the benefits these laws confer on workers must include these indirect wage increases enjoyed by workers above the legal minimum.

The same holds true for two other types of indirect wage effects. Increases have been known to be granted to those not covered by the law but working closely with those who are covered and do receive increases. It is a moot point, however, whether this "ripple effect" goes so far as to increase wages in other industries by increasing the purchasing power of workers in low-wage industries; no adequate data are available on this point. It may be needless to add that critics view all these indirect wage effects as imposing the same cost burden as direct effects and therefore expect that they provoke offsetting reactions of some kind, including the possible "indirect effect" of lowering employment in uncovered industries.

Finally, mention should be made of certain worker benefits which resist measurement by the statistician's computer or the calculus of the economist. For any worker aided by a minimum wage law to escape at least the worst horrors of poverty, the increase this may afford in his self-respect and the total well-being of his family cannot be summed up in the dollars added to his paycheck, nor can it easily be counterbalanced by an arithmetically equivalent offset in the income received or the prices paid by the prosperous majority of citizens. By the same token, for the worker who is left without a job by such a law, the loss he may suffer cannot be easily absorbed by the wage increase granted the skilled worker "to preserve morale," nor by the expansion of distant high-wage plants now freed of his "unfair competition." Beneath the barrage of ambiguous statistics and partisan oratory concerning the effects of minimum wage regulation on workers, these are the values ultimately at stake.

C. Taxation and Incentives

39. REFORMING THE TAX SYSTEM*

Dan Throop Smith

Federal tax reform is urgently needed. It is recommended by taxpayers' groups and by economists. It is high on the list of proposed action by political leaders.

The peculiar and perverse character of our tax system is dramatized by the fact that it was cited by Khrushchev as evidence that we fail to use incentives to increase production to the extent that they are used in Communist Russia. It is indeed ironic that the Soviet leader in speaking of incentive should note to President Eisenhower that "in many ways you stifle it."

A few major areas stand out for reform in virtually all proposals. Reduction in the rates of the individual income tax together with broadening of the base and closing of loopholes to remove inequitable and uneconomic tax privileges stands at the top of most lists. Liberalization of

* Dan Throop Smith, "A Program for Federal Tax Reform," *American Economic Review, Papers and Proceedings*, Vol. L (May, 1960), pp. 470–86.

depreciation allowances on machinery and equipment together with a tightening to deny capital gains treatment to profits from any too-rapid depreciation comes second. A reform of the entire capital gains area is a third major subject. In addition to those three broad areas, a thorough reform should include: effective taxation of co-operatives and mutual financing companies to give substantial equality with ordinary taxable enterprise, a rationalization of the present haphazard excise tax system, a tightening of estate taxation to remove the present inducement to leave property in trusts extending over many years together with a reduction in rates, and a review of depletion allowances.

The structure of a tax system may be almost as important as the total level of taxation. With sufficient reform, we could probably support appreciably higher tax burdens than we now have, if that is desirable or inevitable. Without it, we shall reap accelerating social and economic damage from our systems. In various ways our present structure violates the three requisites of an acceptable tax system: fairness, minimum restraint on economic growth, and simplicity.

We shall not argue here the relative merits of private and government spending. Though taxation by itself is repressive, wise government expenditures may be highly productive; in fact, some government expenditure provides the essential base for the very existence of our society and economy. But increased government expenditures are not necessarily good, nor will they necessarily be any wiser than private spending. The defects of education, for example, seem mainly to arise from what are at last coming to be recognized as wrong emphasis on "life adjustment" courses and egalitarian standards of performance rather than from inadequate appropriations. Too liberal government assistance may undermine personal responsibility and initiative and even draw to a community recipients who are at best parasitic. Even if one deplores the frivolity of much private consumption and favors the expansion of some government programs—and there are probably few who do not—one may still regret the general scale of public spending and oppose increases in the aggregate level. The harmful effects of taxation as such must be matched against the presumably good effects of the expenditures which they finance.

A self-balancing tax reform could be developed, but any major tax reform program which is politically realistic probably would involve some immediate loss of revenue, though it would so improve the climate for economic growth that it would doubtless produce higher revenues within a short time.

Viewed abstractly, a surplus or deficit of 1 or 2 billions of dollars is relatively small in an economy of almost 500 billion dollars and a federal budget of 80 billion; it is no more than the margin of error in the best of estimates. Logically it should be regarded as a minor factor in comparison with other forces involving much larger expansions and contractions of credit, shifts in private spending, or cost increases. Still the immediate revenue effects may govern the time at which major tax reform may be prudently undertaken.

The budget has a symbolic importance which transcends abstraction and logic. It is a symbol of fiscal responsibility both domestically and internationally. For too long, there was a presumption that a balanced budget would prevent inflation. We now realize that it will not. But the inadequacy of a balanced budget, or of fiscal policy generally, to prevent inflation does not mean that the budget position is unimportant. Though a small deficit arising from changing conditions or errors in estimates is no basis for alarm, conscious action to throw a budget out of balance is likely to be taken as a symbol of irresponsibility which cannot be justified even for so good a purpose as tax reform. This is especially true when other forces are unfavorable, as they now are.

The failure to remove the ceiling on the interest rate for the public debt forces a reliance on short-term financing which in its actual impact may be quantitatively as important as a deficit of several billion dollars. Present restrictions on the interest rate make it almost inevitable that debt management will be inflationary. Until freedom is given for sound management, it is doubly important to keep the budget—the other area of Treasury impact—on a completely solid basis.

Attitudes towards inflation are also important. The country is now confronted with the realization that our creeping inflation has priced many American goods out of the world markets. Business, labor, and the public should expect to have some of the benefits of increasing productivity passed on to the consumer. Wage increases in excess of productivity increases are recognized as inflationary and unjustified. But national wage standards based on increased productivity in the most rapidly improving industries must lead either to inflationary cost increases in other industries or to widening disparities in incomes. It is not practicable or reasonable to have permanently wide wage differentials based on differences in the rate of technological improvement, increased mechanization, and capital investment in various industries. One can only hope that the benefits of the labor movement in furthering mass consumption, in opposing government ownership, and generally encouraging increased productivity will be matched by sound wage policy in the critical years ahead. The initiative for price reductions reflecting unusually high increases in productivity must come from business, but they should be expected by the public, with recognition that larger capital investments, which often are necessary for higher productivity, require sufficient profits to justify the investment.

The foregoing digressions suggest that tax reform, important though it is, should not be undertaken at the expense of even a briefly unbalanced budget, unless all other factors are favorable. One can only hope that room can be made soon for tax reform within a balanced budget or that inflationary forces will be so well under control that tax reform even at the cost of a temporarily unbalanced budget will be a sound and responsible act. Above all else, one must be reasonably sure that a budgeted amount for tax reform will not be diverted to other changes in the tax law which may have greater political appeal. With this background, we turn to the substance of reform.

INDIVIDUAL INCOME TAX RATES

The most important single reform is to reduce the excessive rates of the individual income tax and tighten the definition of taxable income to cut down on present abuses, legal and illegal, and assure more equal treatment of taxpayers.

Our present very high rates of tax were developed during the thirties and the World War II and Korean war periods. The circumstances involved a period of extreme economic egalitarianism in our dominant political attitudes (though the public opinion polls have indicated the belief that fair taxes on larger incomes should be much lower than they were in fact), a mistaken belief that Western civilizations had excessive savings (this gave an economic rationalization for confiscatory taxation), and the war periods when controls were widespread and limitations on individual income were but token sacrifices compared to those serving in the unpleasant parts of military life.

But the period of personal sacrifices has at least been suspended, and one hopes ended, some years ago. The controls have been dismantled in the interests of a free and dynamic economy. The fallacy of excessive savings and the mature economy has been exposed in both the more developed and the less-developed countries and recognized by both the public and economists, albeit grudgingly by a few of the latter. And with the general improvement in incomes through greater production, the egalitarian excesses of a quarter century ago are seen as more vindictive than rational. Most of those who still favor very high income tax rates as a matter of social philosophy have recognized that on balance they are bad because they distort personal and business decisions and lead to action and attitudes which may jeopardize the income tax itself.

It is manifestly not true, as is sometimes alleged, that high income taxation completely destroys incentive and brings economic growth to a halt. The nonpecuniary incentives for economic activity are numerous and powerful. The satisfaction of creative activity, power, status, leadership—all these can be realized in business. The pressures and disciplines within a large organization require continued effort and application, though the independent owner-manager of a company may slacken after he has realized his other goals. But pecuniary incentives are of some importance in all cases and repression of them cannot do other than repress economic growth. Moreover, damage from high taxes comes in more subtle ways than a simple lack of activity.

With high taxes, it becomes much more important to save a dollar of taxes than to earn another dollar of income. At a 90 per cent tax rate, it is ten times as important to save a dollar of taxes as to earn a dollar of income. This fact cannot do other than divert attention from production to tax minimization—an activity which involves perhaps the most flagrant sort of conflict between private and social net products.

The effects of high taxes in freezing people into their existing employment because of the impossibility of making up invested pensions foregone are familiar.

High taxes seem also to make the public more tolerant of fraud and loopholes and the Congress more susceptible to pleas for new special relief provisions. We still have among most social groups in this country a feeling that tax fraud is morally reprehensible. This is a tradition as precious as it is rare in the world. Very high rates strain the integrity of individuals. The rates put a premium on subterfuge, on expense account living, and on all devices which may come within the letter though they violate the spirit of the law.

As has been said many times before, our income tax has become a mass tax, not a class tax. Out of over 40 billion dollars estimated revenue for the current fiscal year, probably not over 800 million, or less than 2 per cent, comes from the rates above 50 per cent. In fact, only about 6 billion dollars, or one-seventh, comes from the entire range of progression above the basic rate of 20 per cent. By contrast, each percentage point on the basic rate involves 1.7 billion of revenue. Thus a reduction to 50 per cent at the top would cost not more than a reduction of one-half of one percentage point in the full scale of rates; a reduction of three percentage points in the full scale would cost almost as much revenue as the complete removal of all progression!

Problems of equity, economic policy, and politics intermingle in any consideration of rate reduction as part of tax reform. From the standpoint of equity, comparisons can be made in terms of changes in the amount of tax, in the rate of tax, and in net income after tax. The great misfortune and inequity in the period of increasing taxes occurred in 1932 when the normal tax was raised from 1½ to 4 per cent and the top bracket, presumably on the notion that rates should be changed proportionately, from 25 to 63 per cent. In terms of net income, this meant a reduction at the bottom from 98½ to 96 cents, or about 2½ per cent, while at the top the reduction was from 75 to 37 cents, or by more than 50 per cent. Since that date, subsequent increases have been tapered off at the top to avoid bumping into complete confiscation at 100 per cent. It was not adequately realized that, given a progressive structure, even a uniform increase in rates—that is, by the same number of percentage points—is progressive in terms of effects on net income; a proportional increase in rates is highly progressive; while a progressive increase in rates is likely to be confiscatory in its effects on net income. When rates are reduced, the converse is true and any appreciable reduction in the highest rates will have an effect on net income which could not be matched by the full removal of tax on the small incomes. The political arithmetic of taxation is built on different presentations of the effects of tax changes.

Since rate increases did not proceed on any logical pattern, real reform cannot be secured by reversing the historical increases. The best procedure is to set a goal of the most reasonable rate structure to meet revenue requirements, with minimum economic repression and distortions and maximum equity, and then proceed to it promptly or over a period of years as expanding revenues permit. There is no absolute standard for measuring total or marginal sacrifices from tax payments. Scientific analysis can give little help in reaching a consensus of popular opinion, which may intuitively take account of something like the economists' conflicting abstract concepts of equal sacrifice, minimum sacrifice, and proportional sacrifice.

The perverse effects of income taxation obviously increase as rates become higher. A 10 or 20 or 25 per cent marginal tax rate is not likely to decrease incentives or divert action into tax-saving maneuvers. Any rate above 50 per cent is likely to have a pronounced effect; the transition from keeping more than half to paying more than half can have a strong psychological impact. From the standpoint of fairness, high-bracket taxpayers have not only been denied the chance to share in increases in national income; their real net incomes have been irretrievably reduced over what they were in earlier years of lower taxes and lower income. By contrast, tax increases in the lower brackets fortunately have not prevented substantial general increases in real net income. Equity and economic policy thus both require disproportionate relief in the higher brackets.

BROADENING THE TAX BASE

The reduction in individual tax rates should be accompanied by a tighter definition of taxable income to increase the fairness of the tax law and to provide revenue to offset partially the immediate losses from lower rates. The theoretical concept that income should be measured by changes in net worth plus consumption, though intriguing to some, is neither practical nor sensible for taxation. The net of the tax gatherer should not be cast so wide that it includes items which it is not feasible to tax nor within the popular concept of income. This limitation rules out such favorite proposals as taxation of the rental value of an owner-occupied house as imputed income.

Tighter Standards on Expense Accounts and Other Fringe Benefits

Taxable income should include the value of new perquisites established primarily for tax avoidance but exclude conditions of employment and fringe benefits which existed before taxation was important or which have compelling nontax reasons. Thus the cost of payments of country club dues by an employer, travel expenses of family members except on long-term transfers, personal use of company transportation facilities and resorts, and personal entertainment under the guise of business activity should all be taxed to the individual beneficiary. By contrast, the value of meals in executive lunch rooms, the use of a company car for company business, not to mention well-furnished offices and secretarial assistance, should not be included in individual income. Expense account living may need additional controls, perhaps first by requiring segregation on a company's records of all expenses by and on behalf of individual employees. The variety of charges permitted under credit cards is an invitation to tax evasion; but the use of cards should facilitate audits. Taxation of the value of benefits to individuals is much more significant than denial of a deduction to employers; in fact, the denial of a deduction may not be appropriate if compensation, direct and indirect, is not unreasonable.

The travel expenses of professional people also require more intensive limitations. Travel to a resort or vacation area should not necessarily be made deductible merely by attendance at a convention or visits to hospitals, libraries, or short summer school courses. Travel expenses should be prorated if personal activities take any appreciable part of the time on a trip or disallowed completely if they take the majority of the time. Hotels which provide special rate cards to show that single occupancy of a room costs as much as double occupancy for the duration of a convention, thus making a wife's hotel bill deductible, should be held up to public ridicule.

Ultimate Denial of Deduction for State and Local Taxes

If the tax law were being developed anew, it would be preferable not to allow deductions for any taxes paid, federal, state, or local, except in computing net incomes on business activities. This would be a real simplification. It would help remove the present discrimination in favor of homeowners who can deduct their property taxes while renters have no deduction for any part of their rent. Unless very large reductions were made in the top brackets, however, total taxes might exceed or approach total income if the state and local taxes were not deductible. The disallowance of present deductions may be regarded as an ultimate goal in a reform but equitable only in conjunction with a substantial reduction in high-bracket rates.

Removal of the "Sick Pay" Exclusion

The present sick pay exclusion should be repealed in the interests of simplicity and equity. The law was tightened in 1954 by the insertion of a $100 weekly ceiling to prevent gross abuse of the existing provision for complete exemption of insured sick pay. It was also liberalized to remove discrimination against self-insured employers. It should now be repealed to remove the remaining petty abuses. The medical expense deduction gives what relief is necessary to extra costs of sickness; exemption of income is an inducement to malingering and not justified on grounds of fairness.

Maintenance of Split-Income Provision unless Community Property Concepts Can Be Ignored

The present split-income provision is justified only as a means to secure equality of treatment with the community property states. It would have been preferable to ignore that concept for purposes of the federal income tax, and it is hard to see what inequity there would be in achieving national uniformity in that way. The present split-income provision is capricious in giving relief to married couples in the middle-income brackets, with no relief at the bottom or top brackets. But it is vastly better than the alternative proposal for compulsory joint returns for all married couples. This would impose an annual progressive tax on marriages where both spouses have income. It is hard to think of a tax provision which would be more inequitable, immoral, and antisocial.

Denial of Interest Deduction

Deductions for interest are a source of continuing abuse. A few insurance companies show great ingenuity in creating special policies which are self-financing through deductions of interest on peculiar "loans" on the policy itself. The interest deduction gives a further benefit to homeowners with mortgages over renters. Enforcement of the disallowance on loans to carry tax-exempt bonds is difficult. Logically, an interest deduction is not necessary in computing personal income, as distinct from business income. The deduction might well be removed, as part of a general reform. This would substantially simplify the law.

Strict Examination of Charitable Contributions in Kind

The United States is conspicuous among nations for the extent of philanthropy. It is proper that our tax laws should be among the most generous in the world on charitable deductions. Abuse does exist, however, in excessive claims of value for gifts in kind, whether of art objects, business properties, or discarded furniture or clothing. A restriction of a deductible contribution to the cost to the contributor is appealing on grounds of equity, though it would not cover abuses in gifts of discarded property. On balance, however, the importance of philanthropy is so great that the present law, one may say regretfully, should be continued to allow deductions for fair market value but with strict standards of enforcement. There is too much room for collusion between donor and donees.

Removal of Tax Exemption for Future Issues of State and Local Bonds

Tax exemption of interest on municipal bonds has no more justification than the former tax exemption of salaries of municipal employees. Its inequity and its distortion of investment decisions have been thoroughly discussed. It should be discontinued on future bond issues. If necessary as a matter of intergovernmental relations, the federal government might make an annual payment equivalent to some stated fraction of interest paid, or some specified percentage of the loan, on future issues of taxable bonds. This could more than offset any increase in interest costs to the states and municipalities and still give a net gain to the federal government.

Maintain the Dividend-Received Exclusion and Credit

In spite of uncertainty about the incidence of the corporation income tax, some part of its aggregate burden rests on the corporation, thus making dividend income uniquely subject to some degree of double taxation. It is unsound economic policy, as well as unfair, to impose a tax penalty on the income from that form of capital which is most important for economic growth. The present relief, though small, is an important symbol of a reversal of the punitive attitude towards enterprise prevailing twenty-five years ago. The repeal of the relief would indicate a return to punitive and destructive taxation. Withholding of tax on both dividends and interest is desirable for the sake of equity and additional revenue, and the administrative problems probably are not insuperable.

Retirement Income Taxation

Though the present treatment of retirement income is not altogether logical or equitable, major proposed changes do not seem desirable on balance.

If a completely fresh start were possible, a better system could be devised. Social security benefits should be taxable. They became nontaxable only through an early ruling of doubtful soundness. Perhaps this could sometimes be reversed by statute if rates were reduced substantially. This would permit repeal of the cumbersome retirement income credit, now necessary to give substantially equal treatment to those who receive little or no social security benefits.

Employee pensions based on employers' contributions receive preferential tax treatment, but this is due to the difficulties and inequities in trying to impute to individual employees their appropriate shares of an employer's contribution to a pension plan with nonvested rights. Proposed deductions for contributions by self-employed people for their own retirement funds would present new complications and new discriminations against employees who do not in fact benefit from employee pension plans. There is no really good solution to this problem. It has been magnified by high tax rates. Hopefully, a reduction in taxes will minimize the sense of discrimination and forestall new complexities and discriminations.

The tax status of deferred compensation received under contracts is not clear, but deferral is increasingly common and apparently regarded as safe by many legal advisers so long as it is provided for in an original agreement and perhaps supplemented with some sort of continued potential services. The distinction between contracts originally providing for deferral and those where a previously agreed amount is later deferred seems unduly legalistic to many laymen, especially when the only conceivable reason for deferral is a large tax advantage. But the law should be made clear on this subject so that, if there is a benefit, it will be available to all. General availability of deferral, however, would give a distinct advantage to large well-established employers, publishers, and clients where the risks of loss under deferred payment are small. On grounds of equity and economic policy, an attempt should be made to restrict the use of deferred payment contracts, but the administrative problems are so formidable that action may be postponed with the hope that reduced tax rates, by reducing the advantages of deferral, will minimize the problem.

DEPRECIATION

Our tax allowances for depreciation are among the most restrictive in the world. With the great need for increased efficiency and production, we can no longer afford to maintain our present restrictions. But liberalization to permit faster write-off should be balanced by tightening to make profits on the sale of depreciated property taxable as ordinary income, instead of capital gains, to the extent of any excess depreciation. The authorization of declining balance depreciation in 1954 and changes in regulations to reduce controversy and give greater emphasis to expectations instead of historical experience were important changes, but they were not sufficient to meet the new problems and challenges.

Many other countries permit deductions in excess of actual cost of some categories of depreciable property or large initial deductions in the year of acquisition. Such large allowances do not seem necessary in this country under present circumstances, nor does an adjustment to reflect an excess of replacement cost over original cost, important though the problem of high replacement cost is in some industries. A faster recovery of original cost will help meet the problem of higher replacement cost as well as encourage and facilitate investment generally.

We cannot afford the immediate budget impact of complete freedom of choice on depreciation rates. The Canadian approach seems preferable. Broad categories of depreciable property should be established with statutory rates or lives somewhat shorter, perhaps two-thirds or three-quarters of the probable actual economic life in use. Taxpayers should be permitted to use even shorter lives if they can justify them on the basis of distinctive features in their own operations or expectations or, if they choose, to use longer lives. Since machinery and equipment are the most important forms of capital to increase productivity, the new approach might be confined to such investment at least at the start. Real-estate investments already have numerous tax advantages and are a source of a good deal of tax abuse, most of which would be removed by the repeal of the section permitting capital gains treatment of profits arising from over-depreciation and by other necessary changes to prevent avoidance of the ordinary tax as through corporate liquidations.

Faster depreciation will permit the generation of more internal funds for expansion and will permit outside financing or shorter terms, thus making funds more generally available. By permitting the recovery of capital more quickly when risks and prospects can be foreseen more clearly, it will also encourage the investment of such funds as are available.

A surprising controversy has developed among accountants over the proper way to present financial statements of companies using different methods of accounting for tax and book purposes. To avoid financial statements which contain accounts that are puzzling and in some respects misleading, it would seem desirable to permit new methods and rates of depreciation, including the declining balance method itself, only when it is used on a company's own books in ways that do not call for qualified certificates or special adjustments or accounts.

CAPITAL GAINS AND LOSSES

The tax treatment of capital gains and losses involves matters of definition, holding periods, and rates. The definition should be drastically tightened, the holding period lengthened (if any change is made in it), and the rate reduced on bona fide capital gains on property held over five or perhaps ten years.

Though the concept that accretions to wealth represent income appeals to some theorists, it does not correspond to ordinary ideas of income. An increase in value developing over many years is ordinarily regarded as being embodied in the capital of which it is a part. A tax on the gain, whether imposed during appreciation or on realization, is regarded as a capital levy by those subject to it and by many dispassionate observers.

Realized capital gains are regarded as a special form of taxable capacity in this country. We might be better off from the standpoint of economic development if we had no tax on capital gains, and certainly a country primarily concerned with economic growth should be extremely cautious about imposing one. The full taxation of gains, even with the most generous and elaborate form of income averaging, would probably do more damage to economic development here and elsewhere than any other single provision of a tax law. A reduction by half, to a 12½ per cent maximum, would do a great deal to thaw frozen investments and increase mobility of capital.

An extension of the existing provision for tax-free exchanges of residences and property used in trade or business to sales and reinvestments of securities deserves serious consideration. This rollover approach would significantly encourage investment and increase the fluidity of capital funds. If adopted, realized gains withdrawn from a capital fund and spent on consumption probably could and should be taxed at rates approximating ordinary income, subject to reasonable averaging.

But the definition of capital gains should be drastically tightened. Many things have been included in it which now bring the whole concept into understandable disrepute. Coal royalties, lump-sum withdrawals from pension plans, the gains from sales of life insurance policies (special institutions have been established to buy and redeem them), profits on quick sales of stock purchased under stock options, as well as the profits arising from excessive depreciation already discussed, should be excluded to increase the fairness of the law and to protect the integrity of the basically sound concept of capital gains.

There is little justification for a holding period as short as six months. Gains which develop and are realized in so short a period partake of trading profits which should be taxed as ordinary income. The short holding period does help to increase liquidity in the security markets, and that is desirable, but the disadvantages of lengthening of the holding period would be more than offset by the advantages of reduced rates on true long-term gains, and a combination of rate reduction and lengthened holding period would be both equitable and economically sound.

It would be a great simplification in the law if all corporate income and gains were taxed at the same rate. The special rate for capital gains of corporations is a relatively new addition to the tax law and does not arise from a need to recognize the difference in personal attitudes between income flows and capital accretions. The revenue gained from a repeal of the capital gains provisions for corporations could be matched by a reduction in the general rate of the corporate income tax. The idea is at least worth thorough consideration.

CO-OPERATIVES AND MUTUAL FINANCIAL ORGANIZATIONS

The present tax treatment of co-operatives gives them an altogether unjustified advantage over their fully taxable competitors. Co-operatives are no longer small organizations for joint action by a group of neighbors. They are large business concerns forcing taxpaying companies out of business in many lines of industry because of their ability to retain all earnings tax free indefinitely. Under a series of court decisions, both the co-operatives and their members can be exempt from tax indefinitely if the right sort of certificates of beneficial interest are issued to members.

The appropriate change in the law would be to tax co-operatives at corporate rates on all net retained earnings. This would still give them a great tax advantage over other business in permitting deductions for cash distributions of profits to members in computing the co-operatives' taxable income. But it would give equal treatment on retained earnings for expansion, thereby removing the most unfair part of the tax discrimination against ordinary business.

Co-operatives argue that they should be permitted to retain earnings tax free for ten or fifteen years, treating them as revolving funds. This would continue the gross discrimination against regular business, which would also like to have tax-free retention of earnings for ten or fifteen years.

Savings and loan associations and mutual savings banks also have an unfair advantage over taxpaying commercial banks in that they can retain earnings, in the form of a "bad debt reserve," up to 12 per cent of deposits, thus permitting indefinite tax-free expansion. These mutual organizations also have grown into big businesses, as evidenced by their solicitation of deposits from large corporations on a national basis. They long ago ceased to be neighborly self-help associations. Their taxation should be brought more nearly into line with that of their taxpaying competitors.

ESTATE TAXATION AND THE TAXATION OF TRUSTS

The present estate tax law almost forces people to leave estates in trusts for as many generations as is possible. Only one estate tax is paid, on the death of the creator of the trusts; the transfers to each succeeding life beneficiary and to the ultimate recipient of the body of the trust is not subject to additional gift or estate taxes. The effect of this strong tax inducement for trusteed property means that capital is likely to become passive instead of active, and the intermediate beneficiaries are forced into the position of rentiers, even though they desire to be active businessmen. It is hard to imagine a more perverse feature of a tax law in a country which aspires to personal activity and dynamic capitalism.

It would be much better to include the capital value of each trust in the estate of each life beneficiary on his death, and reduce the rates of tax to bring in the same amount of revenue. This would restore activity to both capital and individuals. It will be opposed strongly by those who regard trusts as separate legal entities, which they doubtless are for various legal purposes, but which they do not need to be and should not be for taxation.

The tax law should be further amended regarding trusts to prevent the use of separate trusts for income taxation. Multiple trusts permit incomes to be broken into innumerable fragments, and if they run for more than ten years to be taxed as separate entities and then revert to the original grantors. The law is exceedingly complex in this area, and most proposals to reduce the abuses of multiple trusts and multiple-generation trusts would make it even more complex. The following drastic change is suggested for consideration.

To the extent practicable, trusts created in the future should not be recognized as separate taxable entities. Trust income should always be taxed either to the grantor or to individual beneficiaries, and income taxability should go with estate tax responsibility. Thus, so long as property had not been transferred completely to another, it would remain subject to the estate tax of its grantor with its income taxable to him. The liability for income tax would be shifted to another at the same time as the responsibility for estate taxation. This change would make obsolete a vast amount of present estate planning and would doubtless create many problems of its own. Trusts have their place in estate planning apart from taxation and could be used. But their tax advantages have become so great and the reality of trusts as a taxable entity seems so remote to laymen, that a drastic approach to their tax treatment seems justified.

A final point on death taxes—and this, too, is a major one—would be to consider a change from an estate tax to an inheritance tax. Since the principal purpose of the tax seems to be to break up large aggregations of wealth, this purpose would be served more effectively, and certainly more fairly, if the tax were related to the amount received rather than the aggregate amount left. There would seem to be less taxpaying capacity, and obviously less concentration of wealth, if ten heirs divided 10 million dollars than if it all went to one. The states, to be sure, have found inheritance taxes very complicated because of the valuation of future interests when property is left in trust, but this problem would be reduced by the proposed change in the taxation of trusts themselves.

EXCISE TAXATION

The present selection of commodities and services for excise taxation makes no sense whatsoever, except for the traditional ones on liquor, tobacco, and gasoline, the latter now happily tied in with highway financing. But our reliance on excise taxation is the lowest in the world and we cannot afford to lose any of the revenue now derived from it. A broad-based tax at the manufacturers' or wholesalers' level to bring in the same amount of revenue is an obvious and much-needed reform. This basic reform can be stated thus simply; it is not developed at length, but it is of great importance.

Consumption taxation is less repressive of initiative and activity than income taxation and cannot lead to elaborate subterfuges for avoidance.

Consumption taxation, by exempting savings, is especially appropriate in less-developed countries which greatly need more savings; perhaps we could benefit from this approach also. When economic expansion is especially desired, a moderately progressive consumption tax instead of, not in addition to, progressive income taxation has much to recommend it, but its administrative complexities seem to make it unsuitable for the countries which could best use it on economic grounds.

Supplemental excises at very substantial rates on items of luxury consumption would be preferable to very high income tax rates and might be adopted to offset revenue losses from high-bracket rate reductions. However, there seem to be enough ways to tighten the income tax law to assuage any qualms about an outright reduction in the higher bracket rates without establishing special high-bracket excises.

Immediate action is necessary to prevent the reduction in the telephone tax, enacted earlier this year, from going into effect next year. There is no justification for singling out the service of this healthy growing industry for special relief. Each additional reduction in excises throws more of the tax burden on income taxation, the most repressive form of all. It is discouraging that those who retain lobbyists to secure excise tax relief do not realize this simple fact.

DEPLETION

Most of the familiar arguments for percentage depletion seem specious. Depletion allowances do not have to be reinvested in new properties, as is often presumed. Many other assets are economically exhaustible and many other types of activity are risky. A recovery of the actual cost, and no more than the actual cost, of a property is basic in our tax law. The fortunate circumstance that gives a value above cost is no reason for a tax-free recovery of that value, and perhaps even more than that value, by a depletion allowance quite unrelated to cost.

Some proponents of percentage depletion refer to an increase in the price of gasoline as a dire ultimate result of reduced depletion. Surely this puts their case in the weakest possible way. It suggests that percentage depletion subsidizes rapid consumption of exhaustible resources, hardly a sound policy from any standpoint.

The possible consequences of a reduction in depletion, however, require thorough analysis. With oil and minerals subject to international prices, changes in depletion would affect domestic production which is significant for security; the extent and nature of appropriate special tax treatment is by no means clear, however. Also, a reduction in depletion allowances would probably encourage further integration in the oil industry, since present values could be realized as capital gains and new purchasers of properties would establish high bases for cost depletion. There may be overriding considerations in these two areas justifying some sort of special taxation in the extractive industries, but they are not to be found in the common rationalizations advanced thus far.

In the meantime, a glaring loophole should be closed promptly. Recent court decisions permit percentage depletion on the value of some finished products rather than the value of the raw ingredients, on cement instead of rock, on bricks instead of clay. By analogy perhaps it can be taken on the value of coke instead of coal or on pig iron instead of iron ore. These decisions have permitted a several-fold increase in depletion allowances. The result is completely indefensible and should be promptly denied by legislation, unless the Supreme Court overturns the prevailing opinions of the lower courts.

CORPORATION INCOME TAX RATE

A reduction in the corporation income tax rate is desirable, but less important and more costly in revenue than the reduction in individual rates, more liberal depreciation, and lower rates on long-term genuine capital gains. The fact that business has adjusted as well as it has to a very high rate of corporate tax indicates that the tax is to a considerable extent shifted. This does not mean, however, that it is a "painless excise" and to be cherished as such. The fact of the tax has an adverse effect on decisions concerning capital outlays; the break-even point on new investments is increased in proportion to the tax. This point needs more recognition and consideration. It means that the corporation income tax impedes investment regardless of its incidence.

The new provision postponing part of the tax on life insurance companies until income is distributed may be a useful precedent for reform in the general corporation tax. A lower tax on retained earnings would encourage savings and facilitate expansion by this most available sort of equity capital. It would lower the break-even point on new commitments of funds. If a separate tax on distributions were adopted, then, and only then, a revision of the dividend-received credit might be in order to treat that part of the corporate tax as a withholding on stockholders with a grossing-up and credit by taxable stockholders. The lower tax on retained earnings is especially suited to underdeveloped countries, but we might benefit from the same policy as we seek to step up our own rate of expansion.

Part VI: Questions for Analysis

1. Commonly, the controlling groups in an economy seek to redistribute income in their favor.
   a) According to John Stuart Mill is such a course of action always in the best interests of the controlling group? Explain.
   b) Is this problem less likely to exist in a democracy than in a totalitarian society? Explain.
2. In our economy, labor unions have been engaged for some time in attempting to modify the wage structure.
   a) As presented by Reynolds and Taft, assess the impact of unionism on the choice between time payment and incentive payment.
   b) Do the same for wage differentials among firms competing in the same product markets; geographical wage differentials; occupational wage differentials; and interindustry wage differentials.
3. Minimum wage laws represent another attempt to modify the wage structure.
   a) Explain the essential features of minimum wage laws.
   b) What does Donald E. Cullen's review of several empirical studies of the effects of minimum wage laws reveal?
   c) Present your opinion of minimum wage laws.
4. An important vehicle for modifying personal income distribution is the tax structure. Discuss the possible injurious effects of progressive taxes on incentives. According to Dan Throop Smith, what revisions could be made in our tax structure to minimize these harmful effects? Do you agree with these recommendations? Explain.

VII INTERNATIONAL ECONOMIC RELATIONS

An essential characteristic of modern economic life is its interdependence, both domestic and international. Just as the specialized citizens of a nation depend economically upon one another for their mutual survival and welfare, so do modern industrial nations depend upon other countries for raw materials and markets. International trade, however, has not proceeded in the unfettered manner one might suppose from the preceding observations. Considerable numbers of people, exerting important political pressure, have pressed for protectionist policies. The free trade-protectionist controversy is represented here by two classical statements. On the protectionist side is an excerpt from Friedrich List's famous *National System of Political Economy*. Subtly and ironically arguing for free trade is Frederick Bastiat, from whose *Economic Sophisms* an extract was taken.

Controversy over the protectionist issue has long marked the foreign trade policy of the United States. In recent years, attention has centered on the U.S. balance-of-payments problem, the European Common Market, and the Reciprocal Trade Agreements Program. The economic revival of Western Europe and Japan, concurrent with continuing extensive foreign aid and military efforts by our country, have contributed to the creation of a serious U.S. balance-of-payments problem. The Federal Reserve Bank of San Francisco reviews the historical development of this problem. Robert R. Bowie, Dillion Professor of International Relations at Harvard, and Theodore Geiger, of the National Planning Association, discuss the enormous significance of the success of the European Common Market, and its importance to the United States and the world. President John F. Kennedy, in recognition of these fundamental changes, has recommended replacement of the Reciprocal Trade Program with a more liberal foreign trade policy. In any event, the American economy is faced with increased foreign competition. Otto R. Reischer, consulting economist, discusses the problems and processes of adjustment to such increased competition.

A. Protectionism in Classical Thought

40. A PROTECTIONIST VIEWPOINT*

Friedrich List

The practical importance of the great question of free trade between nations is generally felt in our day, as also the necessity of investigating, with impartiality, once for all, how far theory and practice have erred on this subject, and how far any reconciliation between them is possible. It is at least needful to discuss seriously the problem of such a reconciliation.

It is not indeed with any assumed modesty, it is with the feeling of a profound mistrust of his power, that the author ventures upon this attempt; it is after resisting many years his inclination, after having hundreds of times questioned the correctness of opinions and again and again verifying them; after having frequently examined opposing opinions, and ascertained, beyond a doubt, their inaccuracy, that he determined to enter upon the solution of this problem. He believes himself free from the empty ambition of contradicting old authorities and propounding new theories. If the author had been an Englishman, he would probably never have entertained doubts of the fundamental principle of Adam Smith's theory. It was the condition of his own country which begot in him, more than twenty years since, the first doubts of the infallibility of that theory; it was the condition of his country which, since that time, determined him to develop, first in anonymous articles, then in more elaborate treatises, not anonymous, contrary opinions. At this moment, the interests of Germany alone give him the courage to publish the present work; he will however not dissemble, that a personal motive is connected with those interests; that is, the necessity in which he is placed of showing by a treatise of some extent, that he is not quite incompetent to treat of political economy.

The author will begin, as theory does not begin, by interrogating History, and deducing from it his fundamental principles; this being done, an examination of former systems will follow, and his tendency being especially practical, he will, in conclusion, furnish a sketch of the later phases of commercial policy.

* Friedrich List, *National System of Political Economy* (Philadelphia: J. B. Lippincott and Co., 1856), pp. 69–82.

For greater clearness, we give here a cursory view of the principal results of his researches and meditations:

The association of individuals for the prosecution of a common end, is the most efficacious mode towards ensuring the happiness of individuals. Alone, and separated from his fellow-creatures, man is feeble and destitute. The greater the number of those who are united, the more perfect is the association, and the greater and the more perfect is the result, which is the moral and material welfare of individuals.

The highest association of individuals now realized, is that of the state, the nation; and the highest imaginable, is that of the whole human race. Just as the individual is happier in the bosom of the state than in solitude, all nations would be more prosperous if they were united together, by law, by perpetual peace, and by free interchange.

Nature leads nations gradually to the highest degree of association; inviting them to commerce by variety of climate, soil, and productions; and by overflowing population, by superabundance of capital and talents, it leads them to emigration and the founding of distant colonies. International trade, by rousing activity and energy, by the new wants it creates, by the propagation among nations of new ideas and discoveries, and by the diffusion of power, is one of the mightiest instruments of civilization, and one of the most powerful agencies in promoting national prosperity.

The association of nations, by means of trade, is even yet very imperfect, for it is interrupted, or at least weakened by war or selfish measures on the part sometimes of one and sometimes of another nation.

A nation may by war be deprived of its independence, its wealth, its liberty, its constitution, its laws, of its own special features, of that degree of culture and national well-being to which it may have attained; it may be wholly enslaved. Nations are thus the victims of each other, and selfish policy is continually disturbing and delaying the economical development of nations.

To preserve, to develop, and to improve itself as a nation is consequently, at present, and ever must be, the principal object of a nation's efforts. There is in that nothing false or selfish; it is a reasonable tendency, agreeing perfectly with the real interests of humanity; for it leads naturally to universal association, which is an advantage to men, so far as nations have reached the same degree of culture and power, and, consequently, so far as it may be realized, by way of association or confederation.

A universal association, proceeding from the overbearing influence and wealth of a single nation, based, consequently upon the subjection and dependence of all others, would result in the annihilation of separate nationalities, and national emulation; it would hurt the interests and wound the feelings of nations which deem themselves on the way to independence and the attainment of great wealth, as well as of high political importance; such an association would be only a repetition of what has already occurred in the attempt to subjugate the world, made by the Romans; an attempt that would be more successful in our days, by means of manufactures and commerce, instead of, as formerly, by the sword; though either mode would restore the world to barbarism.

The civilization, political education and power of nations, depend chiefly on their economical condition and reciprocally; the more advanced their economy, the more civilized and powerful will be the nation, the more rapidly will its civilization and power increase, and the more will its economical culture be developed.

In the economical development of nations, it is necessary to distinguish the following principal stages: the savage state, the pastoral state, the agricultural state, the agricultural and manufacturing state, and finally, the agricultural, manufacturing, and commercial state.

It is obvious that a nation possessing an extensive territory, enriched with varied resources and a numerous population, uniting agriculture and manufactures with an external and internal trade, is beyond comparison more civilized, politically more developed and more powerful than any merely agricultural country. But manufactures constitute the basis of external and internal trade, of navigation, of an improved agriculture, consequently of civilization and political power; and should any nation succeed in monopolizing all the manufacturing activity of the world, and in checking all other nations in their economical development by reducing them to the mere production of agricultural commodities and raw materials, and other indispensable local productions, it would undoubtedly attain to very wide, if not to universal dominion.

A nation that greatly values its independence and its safety, must make a vigorous effort to elevate itself as fast as possible, from an inferior to a higher state of civilization, uniting and perfecting as quickly as possible, its own agriculture, manufactures, navigation, and commerce.

The transition from the savage to the pastoral, and from the pastoral to the agricultural state, as well as the first progress in agriculture, is very efficiently promoted by free intercourse among manufacturing and commercial nations.

The elevation of an agricultural people to the condition of countries at once agricultural, manufacturing, and commercial, can only be accomplished under the law of free trade, when the various nations engaged at the time in manufacturing industry shall be in the same degree of progress and civilization; when they shall place no obstacle in the way of the economical development of each other, and not impede their respective progress by war or adverse commercial legislation.

But some of them, favored by circumstances, having distanced others in manufactures, commerce, and navigation, and having early perceived that this advanced state was the surest mode of acquiring and keeping political supremacy, have adopted and still persevere in a policy so well adapted to give them the monopoly of manufactures, of industry and of commerce, and to impede the progress of less advanced nations or those in a lower degree of culture. The measures enforced by such nations, taken as a whole, the prohibitions, the duties on imports, the maritime restrictions, premiums upon exports, &c., are called the protective system.

The anterior progress of certain nations, foreign commercial legislation and war have compelled inferior countries to look for special means of effecting their transition from the agricultural to the manufacturing stage of industry, and as far as practicable, by a system of duties, to restrain their trade with more advanced nations aiming at manufacturing monopoly.

The system of import duties is consequently not, as has been said, an invention of speculative minds; it is a natural consequence of the tendency of nations to seek for guarantees of their existence and prosperity, and to establish and increase their weight in the scale of national influence.

Such a tendency is legitimate and reasonable only so far as it renders easy, instead of retarding, the economical development of a nation; and it is not in opposition to the higher objects of society, the universal confederation of the future.

As human association ought to be considered under two points of view, that is to say, the cosmopolitan, embracing all the human race, and the political or merely national, every economy, private or public, ought to be considered under two different aspects, the individual, social and material power, by means of which riches are produced, and the interchangeable value of the products of industry.

There is, consequently, a cosmopolitan economy and a political economy, a theory of interchangeable value, and a theory of productive power. These doctrines are distinct in their essence, and require to be developed separately.

The productive power of nations is not solely dependent on the labor, the saving, the morality, and the intelligence of individuals, or on the possession of natural advantage and material capital; it is dependent also upon institutions and laws, social, political, and civil, but, above all, on the securities of their duration, their independence, and their power as nations. Individuals would be in vain laborious, economical, ingenious, enterprising, intelligent, and moral, without a national unity, without a division of labor and a co-operation of productive power. A nation cannot otherwise attain to a high degree of prosperity and power, nor maintain itself in the permanent possession of its intellectual, social, and material riches.

The principle of the division of labor has been hitherto but imperfectly understood. Industrial production depends much less on the apportioning of the various operations of a manufacture among several individuals, than on the moral and material association of those individuals for a common end.

This principle applies not only to a manufacture or to a rural industry; it extends also to every kind of national industry, agricultural, manufacturing, and commercial.

The division of labor and the combination of productive power take place in a nation when the intellectual power is applied so as to cooperate freely and efficiently with national production, when manufacturing industry and trade are equally and harmoniously developed.

A merely agricultural people in free intercourse with manufacturing and trading nations, will lose a considerable part of their productive power and natural resources, which must remain idle and unemployed. Its intellectual and political culture, and its means of defence, will thus be limited. It can possess neither an important navigation, nor an extensive trade; its prosperity, as far as it results from external commerce, may be interrupted, disturbed, or annihilated by foreign legislation or by war.

On the other hand, manufacturing industry is favorable to science, art, and political progress; it promotes the general welfare, increases population, public revenue, and the power of the country; it enables the latter to extend its influence to all parts of the world, and to found colonies; it sustains fisheries and navies, mercantile and national. By it only, can agriculture rise to any high degree of efficiency and perfection.

Agriculture and manufacturing industry united in the same nation, under the same political power, live in perpetual peace; they are disturbed in their reciprocal action, neither by war, nor by foreign legislation; they ensure to a nation the continued development of its prosperity, civilization, and power.

Agriculture and manufacturing industry are subjected by nature to special conditions.

The countries of the temperate zone are especially fit for the development of manufacturing industry; for the temperate zone is the region of intellectual and physical effort.

If the countries of the torrid zone are little favored in reference to manufactures, they possess, on the other hand, the natural monopoly of many precious commodities which the inhabitants of the temperate climates greatly prize. The exchange of the manufactured products of the one for the commodities of the other, constitutes a division of labor and a co-operation of productive power throughout the chief commercial nations, and mainly constitutes the great international trade of the world.

A country of the torrid zone would make a very fatal mistake, should it try to become a manufacturing country. Having received no invitation to that vocation from nature, it will progress more rapidly in riches and civilization if it continues to exchange its agricultural productions for the manufactured products of the temperate zone.

It is true that tropical countries sink thus into dependence upon those of the temperate zone, but that dependence will not be without compensation, if competition arises among the nations of temperate climes in their manufacturing industry in their trade with the former, and in their exercise of political power. This competition will not only ensure a full supply of manufactures at low prices, but will prevent any one nation from taking advantage by its superiority over the weaker nations of the torrid zone. There would be danger and damage in this dependence only so far as manufactures, important branches of trade, foreign commerce, and maritime power should become the monopoly of a single nation.

Nations of the temperate zone possessing extensive territory enriched with varied resources, have lost one of the richest sources of prosperity, civilization and power, if they do not succeed in realizing a national division of labor and a co-operation of national productive power, as soon as they possess the necessary conditions, economical, intellectual, and social, for accomplishing it.

By economical conditions, we understand an advanced stage of agriculture, which cannot be sensibly stimulated by the export of its products; by moral conditions, a high moral culture among individuals; by social conditions, we mean legal security to citizens for their persons and properties, and the free exercise of their moral and physical faculties; institutions regulating and facilitating trade, and suppressing all restraints upon industry, liberty, intelligence, and morality, as for instance, feudal institutions.

It is of the utmost concern for a nation uniting such advantages, first fully to supply its own wants, its own consumption, with the products of its own manufactures, then to form direct connections progressively with the countries of the torrid zone, transmitting to them, upon its own vessels, its manufactured products, receiving in exchange their commodities.

In comparison with this exchange of the manufactured products of the temperate, for the agricultural productions of the torrid zone, other international trade is of a secondary importance, if we but except the trade in a few special articles; wine, for instance.

The production of raw materials and commodities among the great nations of temperate climes, has no real importance but in regard to internal trade. An uncultivated nation may at the beginning advance its agriculture by the exportation of wheat, wine, flax, hemp, and wool; but no great nation ever arrived at wealth, civilization, and power, by such policy.

It may be stated as a principle, that a nation is richer and more powerful, in proportion as it exports more manufactured products, imports more raw materials, and consumes more tropical commodities.

Productions of the tropics serve to manufacturing countries of temperate climes, not only as raw materials and alimentary commodities, but also, and especially, as stimulants for agricultural and industrial labor.

The nation which consumes the greatest quantity of tropical commodities, will always be that of which the agricultural and manufacturing production is relatively the most considerable, and that which consumes the greatest quantity of its own products.

In the economical development of nations by means of external trade, four periods must be distinguished. In the first, agriculture is encouraged by the importation of manufactured articles, and by the exportation of its own products; in the second, manufactures begin to increase at home, whilst the importation of foreign manufactures to some extent continues; in the third, home manufactures mainly supply domestic consumption and the internal markets; finally, in the fourth, we see the exportation upon a large scale of manufactured products, and the importation of raw materials and agricultural products.

The system of import duties being considered as a mode of assisting the economical development of a nation, by regulating its external trade, must constantly take as a rule the principle of the industrial education of the country.

To encourage agriculture by the aid of protective duties is vicious policy; for agriculture can be encouraged only by promoting manufacturing industry; and the exclusion of raw materials and agricultural products from abroad, has no other result than to impede the rise of national manufactures.

The economical education of a country of inferior intelligence and culture, or one thinly populated, relatively to the extent and the fertility of its territory, is effected most certainly by free trade, with more advanced, richer, and more industrious nations. Every commercial restriction in such a country aiming at the increase of manufactures, is premature, and will prove detrimental, not only to civilization in general, but the progress of the nation in particular. If its intellectual, political, and economical education, under the operation of free trade, has advanced so far, that the importation of foreign manufactures, and the want of markets for its own products has become an obstacle to its ulterior development, then only can protective measures be justified.

A nation without extensive territory and of otherwise limited resources, which does not control the mouths of its rivers, or which has not suitable boundaries, cannot resort to the protective system, or at least cannot employ it with full success. It must be first enlarged by way of conquest or negotiation.

Manufacturing industry is concerned with so many branches of science and art, it implies so much experience, practice, and adaptation, that the industrial training and education of a country can proceed but slowly. All excessive or premature protection is expiated by a diminution of national prosperity.

No commercial policy is more dangerous and reprehensible than a sudden resort to absolute prohibition of foreign products. It may, however, be justified, when a country, separated from others by a long war, finds itself almost in a compulsory state of prohibitions in regard to foreign products, and under the absolute necessity of offering a high premium to the industry which will enable it to supply its own wants.

The return from such a condition must be by gradual transition from the prohibitive to the protective system, and should be effected by means of duties fixed by anticipation, and decreasing gradually. On the other hand, a nation which is to pass from free trade to the protective system should commence with low duties to be afterwards raised by degrees according to a suitable scale.

Duties thus fixed by anticipation must be strictly maintained by the government; it must be careful not to diminish them before the appointed time, and equally careful to raise them if they should prove insufficient.

Duties upon imports so high as absolutely to exclude foreign competition are prejudicial to the country which adopts them; for they suppress all rivalry between domestic and foreign manufacturers, and encourage indolence among the former.

When, under the rule of suitable and progressive duties, the manufactures of a country do not thrive, it is an evidence that the country does not yet possess the conditions requisite to a manufacturing people.

Duties designed to favor an industry should never be put so low as to endanger the existence of the latter from foreign competition. It should be a rule to preserve what exists—to protect national industry in its trunk and in its roots.

Foreign competition should not have more than its share in the annual increase of consumption. Duties should be raised when foreign commodities supply the greatest part or the whole of the increased annual consumption.

A country like England, which is far in advance of all its competitors, cannot better maintain and extend its manufacturing and commercial industry than by a trade as free as possible from all restraints. For such a country, the cosmopolitan and the national principle are one and the same thing.

This explains the favor with which the most enlightened economists of England regard free trade, and the reluctance of the wise and prudent of other countries to adopt this principle in the actual state of the world.

A quarter of a century since, the prohibitive and protective system of England operated to her detriment and to the advantage of her rivals.

Nothing could be more prejudicial to England than her restrictions upon the importation of raw material and food.

Union of customs and commercial treaties are the most efficient means of facilitating national exchanges.

But treaties of commerce are legitimate and durable only when the advantages are reciprocal. They are fatal and illegitimate when they sacrifice one country to another; when one country, to purchase advantage for its agriculture, sacrifices a manufacturing industry already well advanced; such a treaty was that of Methuen, a compact in which one party took the lion's share.

The treaty concluded between England and France in 1786 was one of those leonine treaties. And all the propositions made since by England and France to other countries are of the same nature.

If protective duties enhance for a time the price of domestic manufactures, they secure afterwards lower prices by means of internal competition; for an industry that has reached its full development can safely reduce its prices far below those which were necessary to ensure its growth, and thus save to its consumers the whole expense of transportation and the whole profits of trade, which are consequent upon imports of the same articles from other countries.

The loss occasioned by protective duties consists, after all, only in values; whilst the country thus acquires a power, by which it is enabled to produce a great mass of values. This loss in values must be considered as the price of the industrial training of the country.

Protective duties upon manufactured products do not press heavily upon the agriculture of a country. By the development of manufacturing industry, the wealth, population, consumption of agricultural products, rent, and exchangeable value of real estate are vastly increased, whilst the manufactured products consumed by farmers gradually fall in price. The gain, thus realized, exceeds, in the proportion of ten to one, the loss which agriculturalists incur by the transient rise of manufactured products.

Internal and external trade flourish alike under the protective system; these have no importance but among nations supplying their own wants by their own manufacturing industry, consuming their own agricultural products, and purchasing foreign raw materials and commodities with the surplus of their manufactured articles. Home and foreign trade are both insignificant in the merely agricultural countries of temperate climes, and their external commerce is usually in the hands of the manufacturing and trading nations in communication with them.

A good system of protection does not imply any monopoly in the manufacturers of a country; it only furnishes a guarantee against losses to those who devote their capital, their talents, and their exertions to new branches of industry.

There is no monopoly, because internal competition comes in the place of foreign competition, and every individual has the privilege of taking his share in the advantages offered by the country to its citizens; it is only an advantage to citizens as against foreigners, who enjoy in their own country a similar advantage.

But this protection is useful not only because it awakens the sleeping energies of a country and puts in motion its productive power, but because it attracts the productive power of foreign countries, including capital, both material and moral, and skilful masters as well as skilful men.

On the other hand, the absence of manufacturing industry in a nation long civilized, the productive powers of which cannot be sensibly excited by the export of raw materials and agricultural products, and, by the importation of foreign manufactures, exposes it to numerous and serious inconveniences.

The agriculture of such a country must necessarily suffer; for the surplus population, which, in a great manufacturing development, finds means of living in factories and creates a large demand for agricultural products, thus affording substantial profits to agriculture, will be reduced to the labor of the fields, and thence will follow a subdivision of farms and a small culture, both as prejudicial to the power and the civilization of a country as to its wealth.

An agricultural people consisting chiefly of proprietors of small estates, can neither fill the channels of internal trade with large quantities of commodities, nor furnish a large consumption for manufactured goods; in such a country, every one is limited almost to his own production and his own consumption. In circumstances like these, no complete system of communications can be established, and the immense advantages which they afford are lost to the country.

Hence ensues necessarily, moral and material, individual and political weakness. The danger is aggravated when neighboring nations pursue a different policy: some making progress in every respect, others retrograding; some hoping for a brighter future, the courage and enterprise of their people being aroused; the absence of hope extinguishing by degrees in others all courage, intelligence, and enterprise.

History is not without examples of entire nations having perished, because they knew not and seized not the critical moment for the solution of the great problem of securing their moral, economical, and political independence, by the establishment of manufacturing industry, and the formation of a powerful class of manufacturers and tradesmen.

41. A SATIRICAL VIEW OF PROTECTIONISM*

Frederick Bastiat

To Messieurs the Members of the Chamber of Deputies:

GENTLEMEN,—You are on the right road. You reject abstract theories, and have little consideration for cheapness and plenty. Your chief care is the interest of the producer. You desire to protect him from

* Frederick Bastiat, *Economic Sophisms* (New York: G. P. Putnam's Sons, 1922), pp. 60–65; used by permission of Ernest Benn Ltd., London, the copyright holder.

foreign competition, and reserve the *national market* for *national industry*.

We are about to offer you an admirable opportunity of applying your—what shall we call it?—your theory? No; nothing is more deceptive than theory—your doctrine? your system? your principle? But you dislike doctrines, you abhor systems, and as for principles you deny that there are any in social economy. We shall say, then, your practice—your practice without theory and without principle.

We are suffering from the intolerable competition of a foreign rival, placed, it would seem, in a condition so far superior to ours for the production of light that he absolutely *inundates* our *national market* with it at a price fabulously reduced. The moment he shows himself our trade leaves us—all consumers apply to him; and a branch of native industry, having countless ramifications, is all at once rendered completely stagnant. This rival, who is no other than the sun, wages war to the knife against us, and we suspect that he has been raised up by *perfidious Albion* (good policy as times go); inasmuch as he displays towards that haughty island a circumspection with which he dispenses in our case.

What we pray for is, that it may please you to pass a law ordering the shutting up of all windows, skylights, dormer-windows, outside and inside shutters, curtains, blinds, bull's-eyes; in a word, of all openings, holes, chinks, clefts, and fissures, by or through which the light of the sun has been in use to enter houses, to the prejudice of the meritorious manufactures with which we flatter ourselves we have accommodated our country—a country which, in gratitude, ought not to abandon us now to a strife so unequal.

We trust, Gentlemen, that you will not regard this our request as a satire, or refuse it without at least previously hearing the reasons which we have to urge in its support.

And, first, if you shut up as much as possible all access to natural light, and create a demand for artificial light, which of our French manufactures will not be encouraged by it?

If more tallow is consumed, then there must be more oxen and sheep; and, consequently, we shall behold the multiplication of meadows, meat, wool, hides, and, above all, manure, which is the basis and foundation of all agricultural wealth.

If more oil is consumed, then we shall have an extended cultivation of the poppy, of the olive, and of grape. These rich and exhausting plants will come at the right time to enable us to avail ourselves of the increased fertility which the rearing of additional cattle will impart to our lands.

Our heaths will be covered with resinous trees. Numerous swarms of bees will, on the mountains, gather perfumed treasures, now wasting their fragrance on the desert air, like the flowers from which they emanate. No branch of agriculture but will then exhibit a cheering development.

The same remark applies to navigation. Thousands of vessels will proceed to the whale fishery; and, in a short time, we shall possess a navy capable of maintaining the honour of France, and gratifying the patriotic aspirations of your petitioners, the undersigned candlemakers and others.

But what shall we say of the manufacture of *articles de Paris?* Henceforth you will behold gildings, bronzes, crystals, in candlesticks, in lamps, in lusters, in candelabra, shining forth, in spacious warerooms, compared with which those of the present day can be regarded but as mere shops.

No poor *resinier* from his heights on the seacoast, no coalminer from the depth of his sable gallery, but will rejoice in higher wages and increased prosperity.

Only have the goodness to reflect, Gentlemen, and you will be convinced that there is, perhaps, no Frenchman, from the wealthy coalmaster to the humblest vendor of lucifer matches, whose lot will not be ameliorated by the success of this our petition.

We foresee your objections, Gentlemen, but we know that you can oppose to us none but such as you have picked up from the effete works of the partisans of Free Trade. We defy you to utter a single word against us which will not instantly rebound against yourselves and your entire policy.

You will tell us that, if we gain by the protection which we seek, the country will lose by it, because the consumer must bear the loss.

We answer:

You have ceased to have any right to invoke the interest of the consumer; for, whenever his interest is found opposed to that of the producer, you sacrifice the former. You have done so for the purpose of *encouraging labour and increasing employment.* For the same reason you should do so again.

You have yourselves obviated this objection. When you are told that the consumer is interested in the free importation of iron, coal, corn, textile fabrics—yes, you reply, but the producer is interested in their exclusion. Well, be it so; if consumers are interested in the free admission of natural light, the producers of artificial light are equally interested in its prohibition.

But, again, you may say that the producer and consumer are identical. If the manufacturer gain by protection, he will make the agriculturist also a gainer; and if agriculture prosper, it will open a vent to manufactures. Very well; if you confer upon us the monopoly of furnishing light during the day, first of all we shall purchase quantities of tallow, coals, oils, resinous substances, wax, alcohol—besides silver, iron, bronze, crystal —to carry on our manufactures; and then we, and those who furnish us with such commodities, having become rich will consume a great deal, and impart prosperity to all the other branches of our national industry.

If you urge that the light of the sun is a gratuitous gift of nature, and that to reject such gifts is to reject wealth itself under pretence of encouraging the means of acquiring it, we would caution you against giving a death-blow to your own policy. Remember that hitherto you have always repelled foreign products, *because* they approximate more nearly than home products to the character of gratuitous gifts. To comply with the exactions of other monopolists, you have only *half a motive;* and to repulse us simply because we stand on a stronger vantage-ground than others would be to adopt the equation $+ \times + = -$; in other words, it would be to heap *absurdity* upon *absurdity*.

Nature and human labour co-operate in various proportions (depending on countries and climates) in the production of commodities. The part which nature executes is always gratuitous; it is the part executed by human labour which constitutes value, and is paid for.

If a Lisbon orange sells for half the price of a Paris orange, it is because natural, and consequently gratuitous, heat does for the one what artificial, and therefore expensive, heat must do for the other.

When an orange comes to us from Portugal, we may conclude that it is furnished in part gratuitously, in part for an onerous consideration; in other words, it comes to us at *half-price* as compared with those of Paris.

Now, it is precisely the *gratuitous half* (pardon the word) which we contend should be excluded. You say, How can national labour sustain competition with foreign labour, when the former has all the work to do, and the latter only does one-half, the sun supplying the remainder? But if this *half*, being *gratuitous*, determines you to exclude competition, how should the *whole*, being *gratuitous*, induce you to admit competition? If you were consistent, you would, while excluding as hurtful to native industry what is half gratuitous, exclude *a fortiori* and with double zeal, that which is altogether gratuitous.

Once more, when products such as coal, iron, corn, or textile fabrics are sent us from abroad, and we can acquire them with less labour than if we made them ourselves, the difference is a free gift conferred upon us. The gift is more or less considerable in proportion as the difference is more or less great. It amounts to a quarter, a half, or three-quarters of the value of the product, when the foreigner only asks us for three-fourths, a half, or a quarter of the price we should otherwise pay. It is as perfect and complete as it can be, when the donor (like the sun in furnishing us with light) asks us for nothing. The question, and we ask it formally, is this: Do you desire for our country the benefit of gratuitous consumption, or the pretended advantages of onerous production? Make your choice, but be logical; for as long as you exclude, as you do, coal, iron, corn, foreign fabrics, *in proportion* as their price approximates to *zero*, what inconsistency it would be to admit the light of the sun, the price of which is already at *zero* during the entire day!

B. Trade and the Free World in the Sixties

42. THE BALANCE-OF-PAYMENTS PROBLEM*

Federal Reserve Bank of San Francisco

THE DOLLAR STANDARD

Because of its large area, diversity of natural resources, and developed economic activity, the United States of 1914 was the closest counterpart of the London-centered British complex of trade and payments. Long before World War I, New York had become the clearing center for transactions between different parts of the country. This was the center for arranging for the exchange of manufactured goods for agricultural products and the distribution of imported goods, as well as the entrepot center for exports. Loans, deposits, and financial transactions were concentrated in New York, and the correspondent banking system permitted settlement of interior transactions through the New York clearing house.

Before World War I, the facilities required of an international money market were not provided by New York alone, but in cooperation with London; for example, the credit facilities required by the cotton trade of the South utilized both the New York and London facilities. The New York–London connection was the channel through which long-term capital was attracted to the United States and through which American funds found profitable employment. The London market enjoyed the advantage of traditional usage and of an efficient complex of financial facilities. World War I provided the opportunity for New York to emerge as a powerful international money market. The war caused the United States to become a creditor in the long-term area and also contributed to the provision by New York of the short-term financing required by American trade and to the establishment of an American foreign banking system.

The New York acceptance market grew rapidly during the war, and by 1917 the volume of acceptances outstanding amounted to $1 bil-

* Federal Reserve Bank of San Francisco, "The Search for Certainty in an Uncertain World," *Monthly Review*, July 1961, pp. 150–54; October 1961, pp. 201–5, 214–18.

lion, of which two-thirds was drawn to finance foreign trade. International bank balances in New York rose, influenced by the key role played by advances from the United States Treasury in financing the war after American entry and by capital flight from Europe. New sources of financing acceptance credit and a new distribution of international bank deposits had come into being. During the war, the New York Stock Exchange also gained importance in the distribution of international securities.

The wartime transformation of New York into an international money market occurred because the United States was the only major country on the gold standard, had impressive credit reserves, and represented immense real wealth. However, New York yet lacked the international confidence which London had earned over its long period of operation, and New York lacked certain facilities related to commodities, shipping, and foreign exchange which were available in London.

Private capital exports from the United States became prominent in the 1920's; however, they had an unsatisfactory character because insufficient attention was given to the repayment prospects of the borrower (particularly in the case of bond flotations) and because they were irregular in volume, as shown in the table below, thus exerting an unstabilizing effect upon the world economy.

The 1930's proved a difficult period; following the collapse of the New York stock market in 1929, the United States experienced a severe depression and a banking panic. The depression became world-wide, and international trade greatly contracted. In April 1933, the American dollar was allowed to depreciate in terms of gold, and the United States has been on a limited gold bullion standard since passage of the Gold Reserve Act of 1934. Within the next several years there occurred a very large inflow of gold to the United States due to unsettled exchange conditions and political conditions abroad.

The Dollar Shortage after World War II

Throughout the postwar period and right up to the present time, attention has been focused on the dollar. There have been two distinct phases to this problem. In the early postwar period, nations which had been devastated by war wanted to purchase goods from the United States but did not have either the exports or accumulated gold and dollar holdings to cover the needed imports. More recently, the major trading nations have been building up their gold and dollar balances (especially gold), as shown by the large payments deficits recorded by the United States in 1958–60, in preference to spending them on United States goods and services.

The United States was a major supplier of finance and material for the conduct of World War II, and American productive capacity and the dollar emerged from the war in very strong positions. The United States

NET PRIVATE AMERICAN CAPITAL EXPORTS,
LONG-TERM AND SHORT-TERM
(millions of dollars)

Year		Year	
1923	−33	1927	695
1924	517	1928	944
1925	621	1929	306
1926	181	1930	739

Source: Department of Commerce.

was almost the only major industrial nation among the belligerents which did not suffer severe damage to its industrial plant. Consequently, the Western European countries, which had been ravaged by the war, turned to the United States for the goods and services necessary to rebuild their industrial plant. Table 1 illustrates the gap between United States exports of goods and services and imports in the years immediately following the war. United States imports from the rest of the world provided only part of the dollars to pay for exports from this country. As the European economies recovered and their currencies were brought into closer alignment with prevailing cost and price structures through the devaluations of September 1949 and as the Korean war stimulated United States imports, the surplus of United States exports over imports began to decline in 1950.

TABLE 1

SELECTED ITEMS FROM THE UNITED STATES
BALANCE OF PAYMENTS, 1946–1960
(billions of dollars)

	Exports of goods and services	Imports of goods and services	Surplus on goods and services	Net U.S. capital exports	U.S. gold sales or purchases (−)	Increase in foreign holdings of dollars
1946	14.7	7.0	7.7	6.7	−0.6	−0.6
1947	19.7	8.2	11.5	7.9	−2.9	−1.7
1948	16.8	10.3	6.4	6.6	−1.5	0.5
1949	15.9	9.7	6.1	6.7	−0.2	*
1950	13.9	12.1	1.8	5.4	1.7	1.9
1951	18.9	15.1	3.7	4.5	*	0.4
1952	18.1	15.8	2.3	3.9	−0.4	1.5
1953	17.1	16.6	0.4	2.8	1.2	0.9
1954	17.9	16.1	1.9	3.5	0.3	1.2
1955	20.0	17.9	2.1	3.7	*	1.1
1956	23.7	19.8	3.9	5.5	−0.3	1.3
1957	26.7	20.9	5.8	6.1	−0.8	0.3
1958	23.3	21.1	2.3	6.1	2.3	1.2
1959	23.7	23.5	0.2	4.3	0.7	2.9
1960	27.3	23.3	4.0	7.3	1.7	2.2

* Less than $100 million.
Source: Department of Commerce.

The trade balance, however, was only part of the picture. In the early postwar period, the dollar deficit was met by grants or loans from the United States Government or by a decline in the international assets of other countries, primarily gold. From 1946 through 1949, $5.2 billion in gold flowed into the United States. But a substantial part of the deficit was met by the extension of economic aid and loans by the United States Government. In this way the United States provided the dollar exchange that was needed to finance its export balance. This means of settlement was not unique since Britain had followed a similar policy in earlier years of financing its exports by lending abroad to the importer nations. The only difference is that in the 1946–50 case grants were used to a greater extent than loans. The requirements of postwar reconstruction and the fact that the United States emerged intact and even stronger economically than before the war were thus instrumental in elevating the United States dollar to its position of prominence as a key currency.

The Supply of Dollars Increases in 1958–60

After the critical phase of the dollar shortage had passed by 1950 or thereabouts, the dollar continued to be highly regarded as a means of payment and international reserve currency, as evidenced by the steady build-up in foreign dollar balances in the United States. From $6 billion in 1946 foreign short-term dollar holdings in the United States rose to $21 billion by the end of 1960. Beginning in 1958, however, the United States started to incur large deficits in its balance of payments, and foreigners took a large part of their dollar gains in the form of gold. Nevertheless, claims of foreigners against dollars increased by $6.4 billion during the three years 1958–60 (excluding the United States subscription to the International Monetary Fund). The experience of 1958–60 seemed to indicate that not only had the dollar shortage ended but that there might be a surplus of dollars available for international payments and external reserves. Part of the lessening in the demand for dollars was due to the economic recovery of Western Europe and Japan and greater freedom in international payments consequent upon the introduction of nonresident convertibility at the end of 1958—goals which the United States supported. Part of the enlarged deficits was due to special, nonrecurrent circumstances.

The sharp rise in the United States payments deficit and its maintenance at high levels, together with an accelerated rate of gold losses, led to speculation against the dollar in the latter part of 1960. It was rumored that the United States would be forced to devalue the dollar because of the pressures against it. The lower level of interest rates in the United States relative to other nations also encouraged the movement of funds abroad. Steps taken by the United States to bring its payments into closer balance and the cooperation of other countries helped to weather the crisis of confidence since the underlying position of the United States was still strong. The dollar thus continues to be widely accepted as the leading international currency.

International Cooperation after World War II

After World War II, the dollar increased in importance relative to gold and sterling as an international currency. Since the end of the war, the functions performed by the dollar, the pound sterling, and gold have been supplemented by the creation of two international agencies which were conceived in the course of wartime discussions concerned with exchange stability and future balance of payments problems. These agencies—the International Monetary Fund (IMF) and the International Bank for Reconstruction and Development (often referred to as the World Bank)—were set up at the Bretton Woods Conference in 1944. These international agencies, mentioned briefly here, will be discussed in somewhat greater detail in a subsequent article in this series.

The International Monetary Fund was designed to promote and maintain a pattern of exchange rates sufficiently stable to encourage world trade and investment and at the same time sufficiently flexible to permit the orderly adjustment of exchange rates in order to deal with a fundamental balance of payments imbalance. To ensure stability of exchange rates, signatory nations are required to maintain their currencies within 1 percent of a given parity. To tide them over temporary payments difficulties, the IMF makes available to member nations short-term assistance from its pool of gold and currencies subscribed by members. On the other hand, the Fund Articles permit changes in exchange rate parities to correct a fundamental payments imbalance. This flexibility was built into the Agreement to avoid the competitive devaluations that had plagued world trade and payments in the 1930's. The Fund also provides a forum for international consultation on balance of payments problems.

The International Bank for Reconstruction and Development in turn was established to help meet the need for long-term investment capital in the war-devastated countries and in the less economically advanced areas of the world. The primary lending role of the Bank is supplementary to private international investment and to domestic investment, while its principal function is to increase the productive capacity of borrowing nations over the long haul and thus enable them to expand exports and earn foreign exchange. Two auxiliary agencies of the World Bank have been created recently: In 1956, the International Finance Corporation specializing in equity-type investments and in 1960 the International Development Association for long-term lending on easier terms. Both the Fund and the Bank carry out some of the functions borne primarily by the pound sterling and the dollar before World War II.

In addition to these world-wide international financial agencies, smaller regional arrangements appeared after the war. The European Payments Union (EPU), for example, was formed in September 1950 by the

Marshall Plan countries and operated as a mechanism for the regional, multilateral settlement of current accounts among its members, with facilities for extending credit. The EPU was an essential element in the restoration of multilateral trade in Europe until nonresident currency convertibility was achieved in December 1958. The European Economic Community (the Common Market) and similar regional groupings have also set up, or plan to set up, institutions on a smaller scale to provide long-term financing and facilities for consultation among members.

. . . . .

An Altered Trading Environment Confronted the United States in 1958–60

The experience of the United States with sizable balance of payments deficits in the three years 1958–60, sharply emphasized by the increase in the London gold price to $40 per ounce in October 1960 and speculative outflows of privately-held funds from the United States, and the recent problems encountered by the United Kingdom following the March 1961 revaluation of the German mark and the Netherlands guilder have stimulated discussion concerning the weaknesses and strengths of the current payments system. Initially, much of the discussion centered on the United States balance of payments position alone; but because short-term capital movements affected other countries such as the United Kingdom and Germany, as well, the discussion expanded into the more general topic of international liquidity. The problems arising out of the recent pressures on the United States dollar (and also the pound sterling) can be separated into three fairly distinct categories: (1) the restoration of balance between the external receipts and payments of a country in deficit, such as the United States or the United Kingdom, or of a country in surplus, such as Germany; (2) the ability to control or offset disruptive effects of sudden and large flows of "hot money" between countries, particularly from "key currency" countries; (3) the adequacy of international liquidity in the future.

The $11 billion in United States balance of payments deficits in 1958–60 aroused doubts in some quarters about the strength of the dollar. Up until 1950 United States Government and private capital exports, and from 1950 onwards the over-all balance of payments deficits, contributed to the reconstruction and recovery of the war-torn countries overseas and to the better distribution of gold and foreign exchange reserves among the various trading nations. But from 1958 through 1960, United States deficits jumped sharply to $3.5 billion or more each year, a level that obviously could not be sustained for any extended period of time. European countries, which were the principal gainers, moreover, no longer needed financial assistance for reconstruction or the build-up in reserves. Foreign-owned short-term dollar balances in this country had risen to $15 billion by the end of 1957 and totaled more than $21 billion by the end of

1960. The United States gold stock fell to $17.8 billion by December 1960, causing some to question the adequacy of United States gold reserves in relation to short-term liabilities to foreigners and in view of the requirement that 25 percent of Federal Reserve Bank note and deposit liabilities had to be backed by gold.

The reasons behind the striking increase in the excess of United States payments to foreigners over receipts, which resulted in the accumulation of these large foreign-owned dollar balances, were partly structural in nature and partly due to temporary developments. The Suez crisis and its aftereffects in 1956–57, crop shortages in Europe, and large cotton shipments abroad boosted exports to unusually high levels in 1957, followed by a sharp decline in 1958 as these special circumstances ceased to affect our trade. In addition, the lag in United States conversion to jet aircraft production and the 1959 steel and copper strikes were in part responsible for keeping our exports down, while the strikes and sizable imports of foreign passenger cars in 1958–59 operated to swell imports and reduce our surplus on merchandise trade. At the same time, the full impact of the recovery of Germany, Japan, and other industrial countries began to be felt in United States markets at home and abroad. These countries were now able to compete effectively with many United States products on the basis of price, style, quality, service, delivery time, and credit terms. The mobility of short-term funds, and their responsiveness to interest rate differentials or speculative prospects, was also enhanced by the adoption of nonresident currency convertibility by a number of leading countries at the end of 1958.

In addition to the part played by the altered trading environment and the greater sensitivity of short-term funds in increasing the deficit in 1958–60, United States policies had not adjusted fully to the changed circumstances. The emphasis of United States Government long-term

U.S. PAYMENTS DEFICITS IN 1958–60 DUE TO BOTH TEMPORARY AND STRUCTURAL DEVELOPMENTS

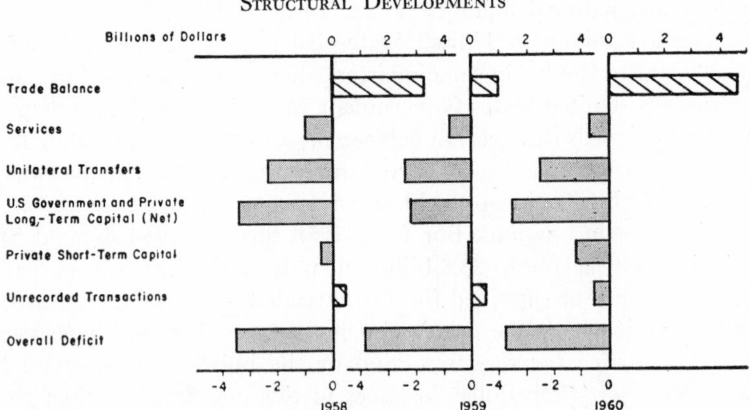

Source: United States Department of Commerce.

foreign aid programs had shifted largely from Western Europe to the countries of Asia, Africa, and the Near East. United States Government military expenditures abroad, on the other hand, still tended to be concentrated in countries with high and rising levels of gold and foreign exchange reserves; a large part of recent private direct investment has been in the industrial countries of Europe, encouraged partly by favorable tax treatment for earnings of foreign subsidiaries and partly by the establishment of the European Common Market; and foreign travel in the United States has not been actively promoted. Recently, the United States has stepped up its efforts to enlist the assistance of industrialized countries with improved reserve positions to help the United States achieve a better payments balance through continuing liberalization of international trade and capital movements, assumption of a large part of the burden of mutual defense, and increased aid to less developed areas of the world.

Large Short-term Capital Outflow after Mid-1960

From 1958 through mid-1960, the United States balance of payments deficit was caused primarily by weakness in the trade balance; the outflow of Government and private capital from the United States did not differ significantly from that of previous years. In the latter half of 1960, however, the widening of the deficit could be ascribed to sizable increases in the outward movement of both foreign and United States private short-term capital, which led to a gold outflow, rather than to the smallness of our merchandise trade surplus, which rose to an annual rate of $5 billion in the third quarter of the year and to $6 billion in the last quarter. Part of the short-term capital exports was due to divergent economic conditions in the United States and in Western Europe and Japan, which attracted funds to those countries where yields were higher and encouraged foreign short-term borrowing in the United States, where interest costs were lower and credit more readily available. Funds also moved out of the United States into foreign stocks and bonds because the prospects of capital appreciation under boom conditions were bright. Part of the outflow, however, was attributable to distrust of the dollar created by the continuing balance of payments deficits, the conversions of dollars into gold, and fear of inflation in the United States. Speculation against the dollar was also evident in the sharp rise in the London gold price in the fall of 1960, the influx of funds into Switzerland and the Netherlands where interest rates were no higher than in the United States, and in the unaccustomed outflow of funds from the United States through lags in payment for goods and services and possibly temporary investment of corporate cash in foreign money markets instead of repatriation to the United States as investment income. Speculation in favor of an upward revaluation of the German mark because of Germany's persistent balance of payments surplus was also instrumental in the movement of private liquid capital abroad.

Doubts about the competitiveness of United States products in domestic and foreign markets, which had been suggested by the decline in our surplus on goods and services in 1958 and 1959, were to some extent dispelled by the improvement in the trade balance throughout 1960. Various price indexes for the United States and other industrial countries provided little support for the view that United States prices as a whole had risen faster than those of her competitors, although it is true that productivity increases have been somewhat greater abroad. Special short-run factors that held down American exports and swelled imports in 1958 and 1959, such as the demand for the smaller foreign passenger cars and delays in jet aircraft deliveries, had disappeared by 1960. The satisfactory showing of other United States exports also did not indicate that United States products were over-priced. But the situation of the past three years has underlined the importance of keeping United States goods and services competitive with those of other industrial nations.

Some of the rise in the trade surplus in 1960, like that of short-term capital exports, was due to the strength of economic activity in Western Europe and Japan, which stimulated United States exports, and to the recession at home, which caused imports to drop off. Thus the conjuncture of a recession in the United States and boom conditions in Europe was responsible for both a larger trade surplus and the outward movement of short-term funds.

THE "BASIC" PAYMENTS DEFICIT

Measures to reduce or eliminate the "basic" balance of payments deficit should include the proper monetary and fiscal policies that will help to control inflationary pressures and still contribute most effectively

"Basic" U.S. Payments Deficits Sizable in 1958–60 but Small Surplus Recorded in First Half of 1961

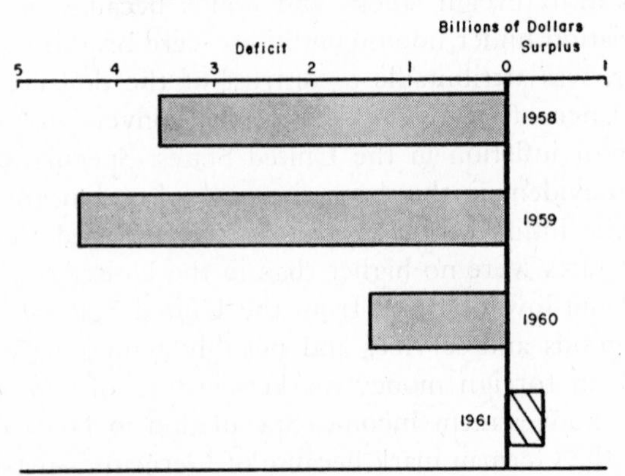

Note: Data for 1961 are figures for the first half of the year on the basis of seasonally adjusted annual rates.
Source: United States Department of Commerce.

to domestic stability and economic growth. Not only is it important that the United States remain competitive in order to export, but a substantial surplus on goods and services is essential if the United States wishes to achieve certain vital economic and political objectives. Continuing deficits of the size recorded in 1958–60, even after excluding the extraordinary short-term capital flows, suggest, moreover, an imbalance in our "basic" payments position which cannot be ignored in the interests of general economic stability and international monetary stability. Our "basic" balance of payments position should therefore be kept under constant surveillance and not lost among other more immediate problems such as "hot money" flows or longer run problems concerning the adequacy of international reserves.

Various Steps Have Been Taken to Reduce the Basic United States Deficit

Some steps have already been taken to increase our surplus on current transactions, such as export promotion programs, the required utilization of the proceeds of United States Government credits in this country, reductions in military expenditures overseas wherever possible, encouragement of foreign travel in this country, and the temporary lowering of the duty-free exemption for American tourists from $500 to $100. Foreign countries in turn have continued to remove quota restrictions on trade and have virtually eliminated discrimination against dollar goods. The member countries of the North Atlantic Treaty Organization have agreed to assume a larger share of the organization's expenses, while stepped-up programs of foreign aid announced by various countries should ease any additional financial load that the United States might assume in this direction. Advance repayments of postwar debt which have been made to the United States provide only temporary relief and do not reduce our "basic" deficit position.

Other measures, however, remain to be taken by both sides to restore a better international payments balance. When the boom in Europe tapers off and a vigorous recovery in the United States boosts imports, our surplus on goods and services will decline. From the first to the second quarter of 1961, the surplus had already fallen from $6.4 billion (at a seasonally adjusted annual rate) to $5.4 billion. Since every payments deficit is matched by a surplus elsewhere, action by the surplus countries to restore balance in their own international payments would ease the adjustment process for the deficit countries and minimize the need for deflationary measures by the latter countries. The continued accumulation of gold and foreign exchange reserves by the surplus country, moreover, constitutes consumption and investment foregone.

The actions taken so far to achieve a better balance in international payments have in general been those which have contributed to the further extension of multilateral trade, with its attendant benefits of optimum

U.S. TRADE SURPLUS MAY BE SMALLER AS ECONOMIC ACTIVITY RISES HERE AND TAPERS OFF ABROAD

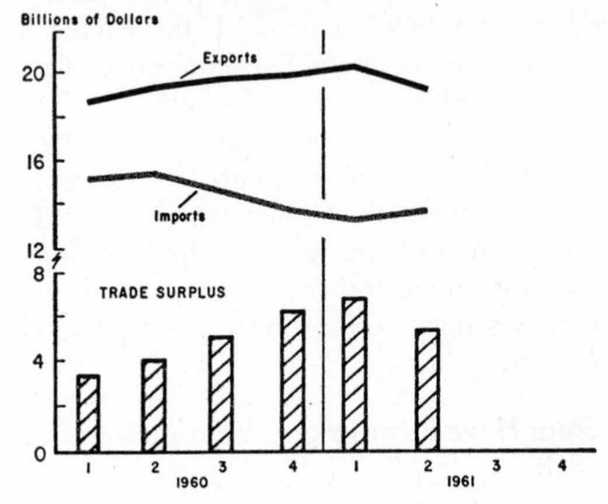

Note: Quarterly data at seasonally adjusted annual rates.
Source: United States Department of Commerce.

allocation of resources. The proposals that have been rejected, such as trade and exchange restrictions, deflation, and devaluation of the dollar, would, on the other hand, have been restrictive of trade and unsuited to the situation.

. . . . .

LONGER TERM LIQUIDITY

United States Payments Deficit Brings Longer Term Liquidity Requirements into Question

Not only did the United States balance of payments deficit pose problems concerning a "basic" imbalance in our payments situation and substantial shifts of private short-term money, but it brought to the fore the role of the United States dollar in supplying the longer term liquidity requirements of the international payments system. If the United States deficit were reduced, where would the rest of the world obtain liquid assets to add to their international reserves, outside of gold, without depriving some other country? At the present time, there is no over-all shortage of international liquidity despite the fact that a number of the underdeveloped countries have extremely small reserves. If these countries had larger reserves, they might be able to maintain imports at desired levels without trade and exchange restrictions. Some of the less developed countries, however, have made the deliberate choice to forego the "luxury" of larger "nonproductive" reserves in favor of what they feel is a more rapid rate of economic growth and development. The low level of their reserves reflects in usual cases, moreover, a lack of balance in their economy so that any volume of reserves would soon be exhausted. Other countries, on the other hand, continue to accumulate reserves in possible excess of needs. But this is essentially a problem either of maldistribution of external reserves among countries or the failure to reconcile the requirements of internal and external stability rather than a shortage of liquidity.

Freely fluctuating exchange rates or a widening of the margins for exchange rate movements have been frequently advanced as a means of reducing or even eliminating the need for reserves by placing the burden of adjustment to the balance of payments on exchange rates. Under a regime of freely fluctuating exchange rates, rates are theoretically left free to find their "equilibrium" level through the interplay of natural market forces of supply and demand. The advantages claimed for such a system are greater maneuverability for the monetary authorities in market operations, more realistic rates, and an effective and economical means of resisting and smoothing out temporary fluctuations in the balance of payments and combating the explosive effects of speculative capital movements. On the other hand, freely fluctuating exchange rates, with their element of risk, would tend to discourage international trade by increasing uncertainty and would impede adjustment to changes in the trade balance. The fluctuations might also tend to be cumulative and self-aggravating. When exchange rates are flexible and psychological factors dominate or when the underlying economic situation is suspect, disequilibrating rather than balancing capital movements may occur, as in the case of France in 1924–25 and 1937 and the United States in 1933. A system of fluctuating exchange rates works best when there is internal financial stability and external balance, in which case there is little need for flexibility and thus little difference from a fixed exchange rate policy.

OVERALL INTERNATIONAL LIQUIDITY ADEQUATE AT PRESENT ALTHOUGH SHARP VARIATIONS EXIST IN THE POSITIONS OF INDIVIDUAL COUNTRIES

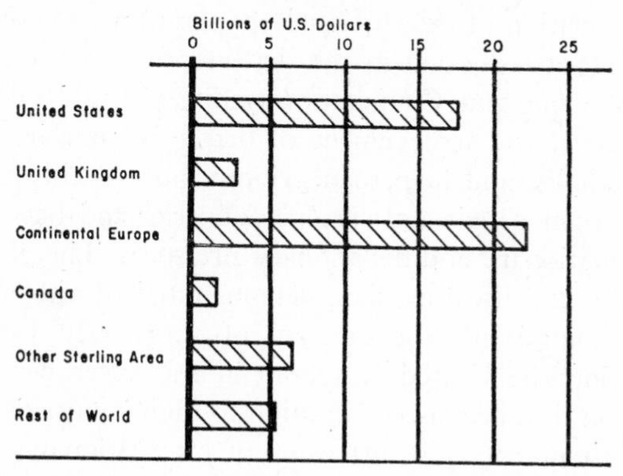

Note: Figures refer to June 30, 1961 except for "other sterling area" and "rest of world," which refer to March 31, 1961.
Source: International Monetary Fund.

Better Balance and International Cooperation Can Increase Liquidity

Over the longer run, a significant body of opinion has held that a larger supply of reserves will be necessary to take care of the anticipated expansion in world trade and production. But there is no fixed relation between the volume of transactions financed between countries and the volume of payments media. It is possible to reduce the need for reserves—and much can still be accomplished in this direction—as well as increase the supply to meet future needs. By working toward a better balance in international payments, for example, the demand for international liquidity can be reduced. If deficits and surpluses are minimized, the amount of reserves required by each country would be correspondingly smaller.

The continuation of international cooperation and consultation also can contribute to a reduction in the demand for reserves, both for the short run and the long run. Cooperation among central banks and governments can facilitate the achievement of better balance between internal and external stability and help to distribute more evenly the burden of adjustment between deficit and surplus countries and between countries experiencing inflationary and deflationary pressures. The closer coordination of monetary and fiscal policies, demonstrated by the actions of governments in dealing with the outflow of short-term funds from the United States and the United Kingdom in the latter part of 1960 and early in 1961, can thus be a useful addition to each country's range of economic policy instruments. The extension of International Monetary Fund consultations to countries that have adhered to Article VIII (the so-called "convertible" countries), in addition to the regular annual discussions with Article XIV members (those that still maintain restrictions on trade and payments for balance of payments reasons), is another constructive step by which the Fund can keep itself informed of developments in various countries and the policies being followed. The initiation of intergovernmental talks under the auspices of the Organization for European Economic Cooperation (OEEC) and its Economic Planning Committee during the period of "hot money" movements furnished an appropriate forum for discussions on mutual problems and possible solutions. The association of the United States and Canada as full members in the Organization for Economic Cooperation and Development, successor to the OEEC, should keep open this channel of communication between the leading industrial countries of the world. Intercentral bank cooperation under the aegis of the Bank for International Settlements has also proved workable, as illustrated by the Basle Agreement of March 1961. An observer from the United States has been attending meetings of the Bank for International Settlements, providing another point of contact between countries. The continued interchange of views through these vari-

INTERNATIONAL COOPERATION AND CONSULTATION BETWEEN GOVERNMENTS CAN BE FACILITATED THROUGH THE OECD

The members of the OECD are:

Austria	Germany	Luxembourg	Sweden
Belgium	Greece	Netherlands	Switzerland
Canada	Iceland	Norway	Turkey
Denmark	Ireland	Portugal	United Kingdom
France	Italy	Spain	United States

Source: Organization for Economic Cooperation and Development.

ous organizations should prove helpful in the formulation of future international economic policy and in efforts to improve international liquidity. Closer cooperation among countries in coordinating monetary and fiscal policies and regular consultation can assist nations to guard against the emergence of sharp divergencies in national policies which might exert strong pressures against particular countries or areas.

The Supply or Availability of International Reserves Could Be Increased

A number of suggestions have been put forward to enhance longer run international liquidity either by increasing the availability of present reserve holdings or by increasing the supply. At one end of the spectrum is the proposal for an increase in the price of gold, which has been advanced as a solution to all the problems arising from the balance of payments. The advocates of a rise in the world price of gold as a means of providing for additional liquidity in the long run base their support on the following points: (1) that the present international payments imbalance is due primarily to a shortage of gold, thus encouraging bilateralism and discrimination in trading arrangements; (2) that world trade has expanded much faster than the means of payment and that the gap will widen in the future; (3) that world gold production has lagged because of low gold prices; (4) that an increase in the price of gold is the necessary first step prior to the restoration of the gold standard system, which would eliminate most of the current payments problems. If the price of gold were doubled, for example, official gold reserves as of March 1961 would rise in value to $81.3 billion.

Objections, however, have been voiced to the view that a higher gold price is the best way to bolster international liquidity over the longer run. All the "profits" of the gold revaluation would theoretically be available to support higher levels of trade and economic activity. But such a step would tend to diminish confidence in the pound sterling and the dollar as international currencies if it were felt that greater liquidity could be met simply by periodic increases in the gold price. Countries might therefore reduce their foreign exchange reserves and hold more gold so that the increased liquidity arising from a higher gold price would be partly offset by the decline in their holdings of the two key currencies. A standard of value, such as gold and the dollar, the value of which was altered as commodity prices or the volume of transactions rose, would be a contradiction in terms. Moreover, a higher gold price would leave fundamentally unchanged the present distribution of gold reserves among foreign countries. Countries with large gold reserves—or with most of their international reserves in the form of gold—and gold-producing countries would benefit most, while those with small gold reserves or a high proportion of their reserves in foreign exchange would find that their relative position had deteriorated. In addition, countries with currently inadequate reserves would be liable to spend any increment to their holdings.

An increase in the gold price has also been opposed on other grounds. By expanding the monetary reserve base or through the income effects of larger domestic gold production or gold imports, a rise in the gold price would tend to be inflationary unless the monetary authorities neutralized its impact. From a political standpoint, a higher gold price would boost the value of both the current output and stock of gold in Russia and other Iron Curtain countries. As stated earlier, an increase in the price of gold would not affect the basic causes of imbalance and might only postpone needed corrective measures. There is also no consensus at the present time that present payments arrangements will be unable to supply the demand for increased liquidity in the future.

International liquidity could be augmented by expanding the functions of existing institutions or utilizing existing facilities more extensively. Fuller utilization of International Monetary Fund quotas, enlargement of the number of convertible currencies held by the Fund through adherence to Article VIII, or increase of Fund quotas would increase international liquidity without necessarily adding to the reserves of countries now holding adequate reserves. Greater use could also be made of Fund facilities in the ordinary course of meeting temporary balance of payments deficits, as has been proposed, instead of limiting their use to emergency situations, and drawings on the Fund could also be made more automatic and not contingent upon a particular course of action approved by the Fund. Two rather similar proposals to meet prospective increases in the need for reserves have been advanced, both of which can also be used to deal with the problems caused by the erratic movement of short-term funds. One of these proposals, outlined in principle by the Managing Director of the International Monetary Fund, Mr. Per Jacobsson, and presented to Fund members at their annual meeting in Vienna in September 1961, would set up a network of standby arrangements with the main industrial countries, under which the Fund would be able to borrow their currencies whenever the need for them arose in excess of current Fund holdings. The other proposal made by Mr. Edward M. Bernstein would establish a Reserve Settlement Account as a subsidiary institution to the Fund which would specialize in transactions connected with capital movements and conversion of reserve currencies. Fund members would purchase, up to stated amounts, interest-bearing notes of the Reserve Settlement Account, which could be used by the deficit countries in the exchange market or to meet conversions out of its currency. At the Fund meeting, the Jacobsson plan was accepted in principle, with the details to be worked out by the permanent directors representing the Fund membership.

New International Institutions Have Been Suggested to Meet Long-term Liquidity Needs

Some informed observers of the present scene feel, however, that existing institutions are not equipped to cope with the anticipated expansion in the demand for international liquidity and that new institutions must be formed. One of the more widely discussed proposals has been Professor Robert Triffin's proposal for a supranational institution in which gold and foreign exchange reserves would be concentrated. Under this proposal, the United States dollar and the pound sterling would eventually lose their status as reserve currencies. Triffin's plan resembles in some respects Lord Keynes' proposal for an International Clearing Union, which was submitted by the British during World War II in the course of discussions concerning the postwar international financial structure. This "international central bank" would be endowed with the authority to extend credits on a discretionary basis to members, and balances with the bank would be freely usable in settlement of all international transactions. Creation of liquid assets by the new institution would provide for the growing requirements of international trade, production and payments. International liquidity would be increased as needed, according to some predetermined formula. Under this plan, pressures on the dollar and sterling would supposedly be eliminated, and the flow of international capital facilitated.

Another blueprint for a new international financial institution has been drawn up by Mr. Maxwell Stamp of the United Kingdom. Briefly, the proposal calls for the issuance of gold certificates by the International Monetary Fund—or its successor—to countries in exchange for their own currency. These certificates would be given to an international economic development agency which would allocate these certificates to the less developed countries for import of capital equipment from the industrialized nations. The certificates could also be used to finance deficits and therefore would end up with the countries in over-all surplus in their balance of payments. Thus arrangements would be set up to link the surpluses of countries in a favorable payments position with aid to underdeveloped areas.

Critics discount some of the advantages claimed for the proposed credit-creating institutions and question whether they would be better able to withstand acute balance of payments pressures and general economic disturbances than the present mechanism. Some feel that confidence would be weakened and that the present discipline exercised by gold movements might be lost. Other criticisms are directed against the possibly illiquid nature of the new institution's proposed investments and other technical details of organization and operation. The price to the key currency countries under the Triffin plan has also been held to be excessive, entailing among other things intervention in their money markets through transfer of ownership of dollar and sterling balances to the international central bank.

43. THE EUROPEAN COMMON MARKET AND THE UNITED STATES*

Robert R. Bowie and Theodore Geiger

THE SIGNIFICANCE OF THE EUROPEAN COMMUNITY

The European Community could be a crucial turning point in the history of our century.

If it continues to develop, the Community can unify Europe's vast resources for common action at home and abroad, and can become a full partner of the United States in creating and defending a viable world order congenial to free societies.

* Robert R. Bowie and Theodore Geiger, *The European Economic Community and the United States*, Joint Economic Committee (87th Cong., 1st. sess.) (Washington, D.C.: U.S. Government Printing Office, 1961), pp. 3–14, 35–39.

The prospects for the European Community are encouraging. But whether they will be fully realized is not yet certain. The oldest of its three components—the European Coal and Steel Community—started operating as recently as 1952. With it, France, West Germany, Italy, the Netherlands, Belgium, and Luxembourg launched the process of continental integration. In the decade since, integration has had major setbacks and notable successes. The movement faltered in 1954 with the failure of the ambitious European Defense Community and the companion Political Community. Yet less than 2 years later it revived when the same countries—"the Six"—formed the other two undertakings now making up the European Community. One is Euratom, concerned with atomic energy. The other is the European Economic Community (EEC) also known as the Common Market. Having come into effect only about 4 years ago, January 1, 1958, the Economic Community still faces serious obstacles before it will be fully realized. And further steps will be needed to make the European Community an effective entity for wider purposes.

Yet the movement for European unity displays striking vitality and capacity to overcome obstacles and defeats. They may have delayed integration but they have not stopped it; and the Common Market in important respects is well ahead of schedule. The reason for this vitality and persistence is that European integration responds to deep-seated needs of our times.

A. The Impetus for Integration

Ours is a century of radical change in the world order. For four decades the order and structures inherited from the 19th century have been breaking up under the impact of nationalism, war, science and technology, and communism. The conflict with the Soviet bloc is a part of this process but only a part. That contest takes place in a world arena shaped by other basic forces. Indeed, its outcome may well turn mainly on the capacity to adapt to and cope with these forces.

In terms of industrial potential, trained people, and long tradition, Europe should be able to play a major part in meeting this challenge facing the West. The European Community is designed to enable Europe to play such a role.

The Schuman proposal in 1950 for the Coal and Steel Community must be seen in this perspective. At that time the central issues for the West were how to defend Europe from the Soviet military threat and how to revive its war-torn economy. By 1950, NATO had come into effect for defense and the Marshall plan was well underway for recovery. But these measures, vital as they were, could not, without more, assure a stable, prosperous, and secure Europe. European integration was proposed as the essential means to this end. These aims have inspired and determined the successive concrete measures along the route: The Coal and Steel Community, the Common Market, Euratom.

The driving forces behind European integration have been both political and economic:

(1) A key motive was to end the historic Franco-German enmity. The aim was to forge bonds firmly tying Germany to Western Europe by offering her a place as an equal member in a united Europe and a challenging outlet for the vital energies of her people.

This concept embodied a radical reversal of policy toward Germany. In 1948, the three Western Powers had agreed to formation of the Federal Republic of Germany and its Government had taken office in the fall of 1949. But policy toward Germany was still based on restraining her power and actions, through the occupation regime of the Allied High Commission, the Military Control Board, and the International Authority to control the Ruhr industries and enforce ceilings on their output. Had these policies and controls continued, they might have reproduced the friction and hostility that followed World War I. The Soviet threat made it all the more urgent to heal the wounds on the Western side. European integration of coal and steel was designed to enable Germany to join in the constructive task of "building Europe" on a basis which buried the past.

(2) By 1950 many in Europe had come to see that even countries as large as France and Germany were too small to assure a dynamic economy and the full benefits of technology, scientific advances, and research necessary for industrial efficiency and growth. Moreover, in France and Italy especially, it appeared that stagnation due to the lack of competition and enterprise could best be overcome within a larger framework. Competition from outside might strike a spark which could not be ignited from within.

The idea of a wider European market had great appeal. On the experience of the United States it appeared to offer the prospect of stimulating economic dynamism which would raise living standards and enable industries to compete better on the world markets.

(3) The European nations, once their shattered economies had begun to recover, naturally wished to have a greater part in shaping their own destiny. Yet the rise of the United States and of the Soviet Union as superpowers now dwarfed even the major nations of Europe. A larger European entity was needed to mobilize and use the potential of Europe.

These various objectives tended to reinforce each other. Only if France and Germany could pull together could Europe hope to shape its own political and economic future. Only dynamic industries could expect to flourish within any common market and compete in the outside world. Growing economies would enable Europe to develop and mobilize the resources for prosperity at home and a greater role in the world.

European integration was put forward by its proponents as the best route to these objectives. Cooperation among governments, as in the Organization for European Economic Cooperation (OEEC), was useful but not sufficient. The pursuit of these common purposes required some transfer of national authority to European agencies which were to exercise their powers in the interests of the whole community. A series of partial steps was to lead ultimately to a federal or confederal entity—a United States of Europe.

Undoubtedly, some who have supported the concrete steps have not necessarily shared this final goal. Even so, each of the practical measures has to some degree reflected the underlying conception of creating a European entity and not merely a form of cooperation among separate states. The High Authority of the Coal and Steel Community and the Commissions of Euratom and the Common Market share the duty to act for the Community as an entity in defining and pursuing common interests and common actions, just as in the still-born European Defense Community and the Political Community. This idea is central. It implies that there is a common European interest which should transcend the parochial interests of the members.

The other institutions of the European Community, based on a quasi-federal pattern, express the same conception. The Court, modeled on constitutional courts, is superior to the member states in applying the common rules; and the European Assembly is a symbol of European unity. The Council of Ministers is the one body where the members represent the governments. Its authority is substantial in all three treaties; it is greater in relation to the European Commission in the Common Market Treaty than in the earlier Coal and Steel Community. But even its decisions in various situations may be reached by less than unanimity—a sharp break with the intergovernmental tradition. Indeed, the European "federalists" saw the Council as the embryo of a future senate.

Its long-term political promise was certainly one of the major reasons for the persistence of the integration movement after the EDC defeat. But this political aspect was also a primary cause of the British refusal to take part. Britain had been among the leaders of European cooperation after the World War II. Indeed the main instruments for that purpose before 1950—the Brussels Treaty, the Council of Europe, the Organization for European Economic Cooperation (OEEC)—reflected the British concept of expanding cooperation among sovereign states, without definite political and institutional goals. The continental conception of a more organic kind of unification, whose ultimate goal is some form of supranational government, was uncongenial, even antipathetic, to most Britons.

This divergence between British and continental thinking about European unification had deep roots. Historically, as a seapower with farflung interests, the United Kingdom naturally has looked outward, away from Europe, and the pull of Commonwealth ties and remaining colonial commitments is strong. Unlike the continental peoples, the British did not suffer the humiliation of defeat and enemy occupation, and liberation by a non-European power—experiences which have done so much to bring into question among continental Europeans the validity of national sovereignty. The British, too, have sought to base their foreign policy on the premise of a special relationship with the United States. In all this there has been an echo of the traditional British policy of maintaining the European balance of power, which implied an aloofness from deep continental involvements.

Given such differences in experience and outlook, it was not surprising that British and continental strategies for unifying Europe should diverge, beginning with the proposal of the Schuman plan in 1950. During the following decade, the policies of Britain and the Six drew apart, as the European Community took shape in the Coal and Steel Community, Euratom, and the Common Market.

Even so, European integration contributed greatly to Western stability and strength in the 1950's. Most notably, it opened the door for Germany to return to Europe as a partner of France. The reconciling of France and Germany has been a major contribution of integration. It has succeeded so well that it is now taken for granted. While the effort in the European Defense Community to extend integration to defense proved premature, the new Franco-German relation which had developed by 1954 provided the essential basis for the alternative solution within Western European Union (WEU) and NATO. The phenomenal revival of Europe and the rapid rates of growth during the 1950's were due to many causes, but could hardly have occurred if the Western policies toward Germany had continued unchanged. And the idea of European integration gradually gained acceptance in wider circles both as a route to progress and an eventual goal. The speed with which the movement could be revived in 1956, after many had pronounced it dead, showed dramatically how deep were its roots.

B. Tasks Facing the Atlantic Nations

The radical changes in international conditions over the last decade have enhanced the significance of the European integration movement even further.

The 20th century revolution has moved into a new stage. The undermining of the old world order has about run its course. The old empires have been totally dismantled with a few residual exceptions. The Soviet bloc has vastly increased its power and influence. Nuclear weapons are now available to both sides on a scale adequate to destroy each other. The challenge of the coming decades is to fashion a new order to replace the old.

The Soviet Union is dedicated to molding this new order in its own image. The Communist leaders are confident that history is working their way, that their concept of world order will inevitably triumph.

Their confidence is not merely doctrinal. They see the strong forces of change as moving steadily in their favor. Conditions in the less developed nations offer them many tempting targets. The collapse of colonialism has launched scores of new nations—in Asia, Africa, and the Middle East—ill prepared for the staggering burdens of independence. Poor and illiterate, with too few trained people and weak institutions, with little capital and multiplying populations, they are impatient to build modern cohesive nations and to raise living standards. Communism will seek to exploit frustrations and disorder wherever they may occur.

The Western World cannot afford to underestimate the Communist threat, backed by growing overall strength. Today Soviet gross output is only about half our own but growing twice as fast; still it is likely to remain lower than our own for several decades despite the boasts of Soviet leaders. Even so, the Soviet Union is more and more able to concentrate resources on selected purposes—on investment, armaments, foreign aid, or outer space—in amounts rivaling or exceeding those of the West.

There has also been a notable change in the military balance. Throughout the last decade the United States had a nuclear superiority to compensate for its lesser strength in conventional forces. But Soviet nuclear-missile capabilities are now creating a nuclear stalemate. The full effects of this situation are still unclear. The Soviet leaders doubtless understand the dreadful import of all-out nuclear war. So long as our deterrant remains "credible," they appear to prefer other methods of expansion, although not forgoing "wars of liberation" or other forms of limited aggression. To them "peaceful coexistence" is a form of struggle utilizing all available means except all-out war. With new assurance and growing power, the Soviet Union is pursuing a more active policy, aimed at dividing the Western nations and at exploiting the revolution in the less developed countries.

If they are to meet this challenge, the Atlantic nations must clearly understand its double nature. It involves much more than merely defending against the growing Communist threat. It also requires a creative response to our epoch—a positive concept of where we want to go and how to adapt to and build on the forces of change which are now at work. These purposes are obviously long-term in character. They cannot be completed in one or two decades.

In these circumstances, the Atlantic nations, with their predominant power, must play a crucial role in carrying out both the defensive and creative purposes. In discharging that role, they face five basic tasks:

First, they must assure the security of the non-Communist world through military strength and deterrence.

Second, they must foster economic growth, independence, and viable societies in the less-developed regions.

Third, they must work out a common approach for their political and economic relations with the Communist bloc.

Fourth, they must enhance the vitality of their own societies and economies in order to provide the resources for carrying on these tasks.

Above all, in order to perform them, the Atlantic nations must develop political ties and institutions adequate to insure unity of purpose and effort.

C. Progress and Potential of European Community

The progress of the European Economic Community to date has shown its potential for increasing the capacity of the West to perform these urgent tasks.

The Economic Community established by the treaty goes far beyond a customs union. After the transition period of 12 to 15 years, the six separate economic units will have been welded into a new economic entity characterized not only by freedom from trade barriers among its members, but by free movement for capital and labor, common policies for agriculture and transport, common rules for the conduct of economic life within the area, and common policies for many aspects of its external economic relations.

The progress toward these several objectives has varied according to their nature. . . . In reducing tariffs and quotas on trade among the members and in developing a common external tariff, the Community has thus far done extremely well. Not only have the Six fulfilled the schedule fixed in the Treaty of Rome, but they decided in May 1960 to speed up, by a year, the tariff cuts among themselves and the application of external tariff. In general they have taken more "liberal" decisions toward lower external tariffs than many expected.

On agriculture, the headway has been much slower: this now poses the most serious problem for the Community. For farm products the treaty contemplates a uniform market, free of trade barriers, but managed by the Community and largely insulated from the world market. The differences among the members on farm programs and levels of support create serious problems of adjustment for the Community. The first segments of the Community program are now up for decision and will have to be followed by working out the detailed measures. Powerful sectional and national interests may impede agreement; but failure or serious delays could imperil the Common Market.

The Community has made only limited headway in developing common policies in other fields. On the provisions to control cartels and other private restrictions, the Commission has done preliminary work and submitted to the Council of Ministers the first regulations. Initial steps have also been taken to remove restrictions on capital movements, on the right of residents in one member to establish businesses or supply services in other parts of the Common Market, and on the mobility of labor in the Community. A start has likewise been made in concerting action among the monetary authorities of the Six and in developing a common commercial policy.

In general, the European Community has enjoyed high levels of economic activity, trade, and growth since its formation. Trade within the Common Market has been expanding dramatically, and trade with the United States and the rest of Europe has also grown. The Community has been growing much more rapidly than the United States or Britain, expanding its share of world trade, and steadily building up its monetary reserves. . . .

In part this prosperity reflects the continuation of economic stimuli which have been operating on the Continent for some years. But the Common Market has also clearly had its impact already. Since its formation trade between its members has increased even more rapidly than before. Businessmen of the Community and outside investors have been acting on the premise that a full customs union would exist within the Community by 1970 or earlier. They assume that the EEC will continue to expand at high rates. Their decisions on these premises will steadily reinforce integration.

The political development and consequences of the Economic Community are more difficult to appraise. The operations of the Community are doubtless less "supranational" than the European federalists would wish but the Commission plays a major role. While decisions rest more with the Council of Ministers than under the Coal and Steel Community and the Commission works closely with the member governments in developing its proposals, its treaty right to submit proposals and its relations with the European Assembly enable it to put pressure on the members of the Community. Moreover, the Commission's proposals aim not merely to reconcile national policies, but to lay the bases for common policies for the creation of a new economic entity. This concept of building a strong new entity is crucial and is not questioned within the Community.

At French initiative, the Six have been considering ways to coordinate political and related policies, though differing on methods and perhaps objectives. Recently they agreed on steps that appear to go well beyond a coalition of national states toward the creation of a coherent European power complex, carrying on from the activities of the existing Communities. Among the Six there are different views about the proper methods or institutions, with the French favoring a "union" led by closely cooperating states. The issue is still under debate, complicated now by the British request for adherence to the Community.

The British request to join is, in many respects, the strongest evidence of the growing political and economic significance of the European Community. The decision is a historic break with the long tradition of British policy toward the Continent.

In taking it, the British have decided to abandon the European Free Trade Area (EFTA) and to turn from the Commonwealth and from the hoped-for special realtionship with the United States. British attempts to find some way of linking the EFTA Seven with the ECE Six without full participation in EEC foundered on the fear that any such link would threaten, perhaps fatally, the Community's longer run political and institutional objectives. It thus became clear to the British that their full participation in the Community was the only course that would meet the political concern of the Six and of the United States; that the United States would be unlikely to oppose on commercial grounds; and that any French Government would find acceptable.

More basic reasons underlay the final decision. The success of the Common Market itself in helping to stimulate rapid growth rates in the Six was in striking contrast to the near stagnation of British productivity in the 1950's. To more and more people, entry into the Common Market seemed essential not simply to keep open this fast-growing market for British exports, but to obtain for the United Kingdom economy the stimulus of increased competition and of wider horizons. . . .

Political factors also had great—perhaps decisive—influence in inducing the move to join the Community. Foremost among them was the growing realization in Britain that, in a world where political and economic power were becoming so concentrated, a larger European unity was essential. Having suffered neither defeat nor occupation, Great Britain was inevitably slower than the Six in accepting the changed power situation in the postwar world. The relative decline of the United Kingdom in power terms has, however, been prominent in the recent public discussion about joining the Community. Its growing cohesion has underlined the prospect of a Britain overshadowed in the world's councils by this developing power complex. No doubt also the strong American backing for the Six forced many people to question whether any special relationship between the United Kingdom and the United States could survive under the new conditions.

But as in economic so in political terms: the British were motivated not simply by the disadvantages they saw for themselves in standing aloof but by the gains to be won by combining with the Six. Government statements and the recent debates in Parliament have shown that the vision of a strong, united Europe, of which the United Kingdom is a part, working in close and equal partnership with the United States, has begun to capture the British imagination.

Working out a mutually acceptable basis for British entry will not be easy. In applying to join, Great Britain has fully accepted the objectives of the Treaty of Rome and its institutions as they stand. Even so, solutions will have to be found for the difficult practical problems. . . . They include:

(*a*) the problem of trade in foodstuffs (especially wheat, meat, and dairy products) from Australia, New Zealand, and Canada, which now enjoy free entry into the British market;

(*b*) the problem of trade in tropical agricultural products and raw materials, especially from the newer Commonwealth members;

(*c*) the problem of low wage manufactures from developing Commonwealth members;

(*d*) the problem of adjusting British agriculture and support methods to the Common Market program;

(*e*) the arrangements to protect the legitimate interests of other EFTA members who are unable to join the European Community.

Each of these poses complex issues which affect influential poitical interests within the Community, the Commonwealth, and Great Britain. Skill, patience, and compromise will be needed to resolve them. The negotiations appear to have begun in a constructive spirit which augurs well for their success. And none of the governments will want to take the responsibility for the serious consequences of failure for the position of the West.

If, then, the negotiations succeed and Britain joins, what will be some of the consequences for the Community, assuming some of the other EFTA members also join?

Just how far and how fast the integration of the Six would proceed without the addition of the United Kingdom and other members is today extremely difficult to predict, and their addition makes prediction the more hazardous.

The British Government today appears as ready as the French and German Governments to accept the full economic implications of the Common Market, and key British civil servants and ministers are aware that the implications may, over time, prove to be very far-reaching. The British Government is probably no more ready than is the present French Government for a federal European state. Among the public at large, the goal of some form of politically united Europe would probably be more widely accepted on the Continent than in the United Kingdom. Nevertheless, the British decision to seek to join the European Community was, fundamentally, a political decision and public awareness and acceptance of the consequences are growing rapidly.

The accession of the United Kingdom (and other European countries) is likely to slow down somewhat the implementation of the Treaty of Rome, for the process of assimilating new members will consume the energies of Community officials that might otherwise be directed to pushing on with the development of the Community. And various questions, such as a further acceleration of the formation of a customs union and certain aspects of agricultural policy may well be postponed until the outcome of the negotiations with the United Kingdom is clear.

Of more importance, the addition of the United Kingdom and other European countries to the European Community will somewhat change the character of the Community. The change will be, in part, simply a function of increasing the size and decreasing the homogeneity of the group. In part it will be the result of some redistribution of the balance of interest within the Community. In part it will be the result of the fact that the United Kingdom brings with it complex worldwide economic and political commitments, a different legal system, and a host of other institutional and historical differences.

It is clear, then, that the new Community will be a different animal both in economic and in political terms from the existing Community and that this change in character will have important consequences. For example, in economic terms, the consequences for the international financial structure if the Six were to adopt a common currency would be of quite a different order than would be the consequences if the Community, including the United Kingdom, were to adopt a common currency. Similarly, the fact that virtually all intra-European trade will now become "internal trade" has many important implications in terms of international trade agreements, such as the GATT.

In institutional terms as well, the addition of the United Kingdom and other countries will inevitably mean more than simply adding a few more members to the Commission and readjusting the voting arrangements. With nine members, the Commission is already large. If, as should be done, the three Communities (EEC, Euratom, and the European Coal and Steel Community) are merged at the time of British accession, some radical reorganization of the composition of the executive will, in any case, be needed. Moreover, the enlarging of the Community could result in more, rather than less, influence and authority for the central institutions than exists today, since this may well prove to be the only way to avoid an excessively cumbersome institutional structure. Since the smaller European countries have traditionally resisted concentration of power in the hands of the larger members, some increase in power of an independent executive may prove the only way to make the new machine work.

It seems clear, then, that what is in prospect is a new European complex potentially capable of exercising great economic and political power. But it is impossible to predict how soon it will organize itself so that it can act as a unit in its external relations and thus use its great potential power effectively.

D. Partners for Common Tasks

An enlarged European Community creates both the need and the opportunity for common action and effective ties with the United States. As the new European entity emerges, the United States will have strong reasons of self-interest to coordinate its policies closely with the Community in trade, investment, international monetary arrangements, and other economic fields. Beyond this, the United States will have a major national interest in the new opportunities for common action to meet the external challenges to the West.

In the past, Atlantic cooperation has often been strained by the unequal size of the United States and its partners in NATO and in OECD. The disparity has produced friction, ill feeling, and frustration. The European nations tend to feel that their views are not given sufficient weight or influence on policy and that their role is not in keeping with their traditions and their resources. The United States has often felt that the Europeans do not carry their fair share of the burdens of defense, economic assistance, and political direction. Moreover, the large membership of NATO and OECD severely complicates the concerting of policy and often delays or waters down required action. There is no way to solve these tensions and difficulties on the basis of the present numbers and disparity of capacity and resources.

An enlarged European Community offers a constructive answer. If it develops fast enough and well enough, the key industrial nations of Europe will form a new entity able to take common decisions, to mobilize its resources for common purposes, and to participate more actively in its own defense. As the members merge their economies and develop their capacity for acting as a unit, they will for the first time be able to play the role of an equal partner with the United States, sharing equitably in the responsibilities and burdens which have hitherto rested mainly upon this country.

Thus the European Community should not endanger Atlantic cooperation but facilitate it. Only if the European nations are able to carry their share of the load, to adopt common policies to influence the world, will there be the foundation for the kind of Atlantic relations which is required to face the challenge of the coming decades.

The European Community therefore offers an effective means to enable the developed countries of the West to join together in discharging their common obligations and responsibilities. In tandem, the European Community and the United States can work for the creation of a more viable world order which can accommodate the needs and interests of the less developed countries as well. Together they can assure the growth of their own economies, provide their own people rising standards of life, and help the less developed nations in the gigantic effort to modernize. And finally they can concert more effectively for military defense against Communist aggression and for a common political approach designed to bring about ultimate changes in Soviet purposes and objectives.

Fulfilling this promise of the European Community depends on three conditions:

First, the members of the Community will have to develop their readiness and ability to act as a single entity. This is, of course, implicit in their ultimate goal of European federation or confederation. The Community seems likely to progress gradually to that goal. Meanwhile, the members of the Community will have to concert their policies so as to deal with the United States—and with other countries—as a unit. In the shorter term, this means that the central institutions of the European Community, particularly the Commission, must be given more power, and must develop the capacity to act on behalf of the members in their external relations. So far, the Six have made limited progress in this respect. More will have to be done once the United Kingdom and others have joined.

Second, the development of an effective and enduring bilateral partnership between the United States and the enlarged European Community is of fundamental importance. This partnership would cover the major economic, political, and military problems confronting the United States and the enlarged Community.

The two partners will have to work together much more intimately in these fields than in the past. NATO and OECD can serve as major instruments for such collaboration, if they are adapted to fit the new conditions. New agencies may ultimately be needed for coordination or joint action, but it would be unwise to try to blueprint them too early. For the first few years the two partners will have to learn better how to make the major adjustments required for working together more closely. Experience will help in defining the more formal ties or institutions necessary for the kind and degree of integration achieved and in prospect.

Third, the partnership must face outward toward the rest of the world. The building of their own resources and unity is valuable not merely for its own sake but to enable the Atlantic nations to discharge more effectively the crucial tasks facing them. On some matters mainly of interest to them, they will deal bilaterally with each other. But many problems also concern other nations and must be handled in ways enabling the others interested to participate. A close partnership of the two big Atlantic entities need not, and must not, prevent a broader community of nations willing to cooperate in the solution of common problems. Both are needed. The United States and the enlarged European Community must not be held back to what smaller or less industrialized countries are willing and able to do in the economic and political fields.

Aside from other factors, the disparities in economic, political, and defense capabilities would preclude the degree of economic integration, of coordinated defense policies, and of joint political actions which should characterize the direct partnership of the United States and the European Economic Community. Yet the two Atlantic entities cannot develop their own relations or realize the opportunities for constructive progress throughout the world without arrangements for participation of other nations concerned. While there will always be tension between these two requirements, neither can be satisfied without the other.

Thus, the opportunity offered by the European Community imposes heavy obligations on both the Europeans and the United States to see that it does come into being as rapidly as possible, that it grows in strength and influence, and that the United States and the European Community are able to work together effectively in pursuit of common purposes and in the discharge of common tasks.

To achieve this the Europeans have much to do. They must first make certain that the momentum of the Community is not lost in trying to solve the serious problems relating to agriculture and other common policies. They will have to resolve the issues involved in British accession to the European Community. And finally they will have to take rapidly the steps necessary to enable the enlarged Community to act as a unit, especially in its external relations.

For its part, the United States also has important obligations. If the partnership is to be effective, the United States will have to adopt a realistic and constructive policy on its own trade barriers. It will have to equip itself for serious negotiations with the enlarged Common Market for a general reduction of tariffs and other obstacles to trade. It will also have to be prepared to join in common measures relating to monetary, agricultural, and general economic policy. It will have to foster a partnership in extending of assistance to the less developed countries. And it will probably have to recognize the desire of the Europeans for more adequate means for their defense in order not to feel themselves hostages of Soviet atomic power.

Above all, success of the European Community and of an Atlantic partnership will depend heavily on how the United States conducts its general foreign policy and handles the inevitable crisis such as Berlin. Any actions in the cold war which impair the confidence of a major European ally would be likely to damage or undermine the European Community—or else to turn the Community away from the United States.

In both Europe and in the United States, many of the necessary actions will require major changes in traditional attitudes and approaches.

The experience of European integration indicates that hard decisions about trade and monetary policy are more likely to be politically acceptable if they are clearly seen to be part of a broader national purpose. The fact that the Six were engaged in creating a European Community, in order to restore Europe's status in the world and bring major economic and social benefits to its peoples, was one of the decisive factors in winning acceptance for sacrifices involved.

As the Marshall plan showed, Americans are prepared to pay the costs of national policies which can be understood as part of a larger creative purpose. The actions necessary to complete the European Community and create an Atlantic partnership fully meet this requirement. If the historic import of that Community and partnership is made clear, they should evoke the necessary support both in Europe and the United States.

. . . .

ECONOMIC IMPLICATIONS OF THE ENLARGED EUROPEAN COMMUNITY FOR THE UNITED STATES

Until the European Economic Community began to crystallize into reality, the United States might have been pictured as the leader of a score or more of advanced industrialized nations, devoted to the concepts of economic and political democracy, and allied by loose economic ties in the fields of trade, payments, and investment. In the decade or two to come, that image is likely to change dramatically. The Common Market, enlarged by the United Kingdom and others, will match the international economic role of the United States and in some respects exceed it. The structure of the industrialized world outside of the Communist bloc, therefore, will be dominated by two economic giants.

The possibilities and opportunities opened up by this change in the economic structure of the free world are far greater than is generally appreciated. Whether they are realized will depend upon the way in which the United States and the European Economic Community address themselves to their common economic problems of trade, payments, investment, monetary and fiscal policy, and the like.

A. Mutual Economic Dependence of the Enlarged Community and the United States

By way of introduction to that question, it will be useful to look at some of the general economic characteristics of the enlarged European Economic Community. At the present moment it is not certain how many nations besides the United Kingdom will join the original Six of the Common Market to form the enlarged Community; but Denmark, Norway, and Ireland are obvious candidates. While as yet unwilling to join as full members, Sweden, Switzerland, and Austria have indicated their intention of associating themselves in some way with the Community. Table V shows the main economic aggregates for the

TABLE V

ECONOMIC AGGREGATES FOR THE ENLARGED COMMON MARKET, CANADA AND THE UNITED STATES, 1960

Country	Estimated population midyear 1960 (millions)	Gross national product at current prices (billions)	National income: Total (billions)	National income: Per capita	Gold and foreign exchange reserves as of September 1961 (billions)
European Economic Community (Belgium, France, Germany, Italy, Luxembourg, Netherlands)	169.2	$179.1	$130.5	$ 771	$15.3
United Kingdom	52.5	65.1	56.7	1,080	3.6
Other prospective members or associates of EEC (Austria, Denmark, Ireland, Norway, Sweden, Switzerland)	30.9	38.0	30.9	1,000	4.9
Subtotal	252.6	282.2	218.1	863	23.8
Canada	18.0	37.1	28.3	1,572	1.9
United States	180.7	505.2	417.5	2,310	17.5
Grand total	451.3	824.5	663.9	1,471	43.2

Sources: OEEC, Statistical Bulletins, General Statistics, July and September, 1961; United Nations, Monthly Bulletin of Statistics, October 1961; IMF, International Financial Statistics, November 1961.

original Six, for the enlarged Common Market as it would be if it included all of these additional countries, for Canada, and for the United States.

The resulting percentages reveal the importance of the United States and the enlarged Common Market to each other and to the rest of the world. Under existing conditions, the enlarged Common Market would be sending a fifth of its total exports to the United States and would be obtaining a quarter of its total imports from the United States. In turn, over 30 percent of U.S. exports would go to the enlarged Common Market, and it would be the source of 27 percent of U.S. imports. As of the end of 1960, a fifth of U.S. private long-term investment abroad was in the enlarged Common Market, and over two-thirds of all private long-term foreign investment in the United States came from this source.

Of more immediate significance are the trade and investment relationship indicated in Table VI between the United States and the enlarged Common Market. In order to use available statistics, this table had to be constructed on the assumption that all members of the European Free Trade Area were full or associated members of the European Economic Community. Hence, the trade of all member coun-

TABLE VI

TRADE AND INVESTMENT RELATIONS BETWEEN THE UNITED STATES AND THE ENLARGED COMMON MARKET, 1960*

[Dollars in billions]

EEC exports to United States	$2.3
As percentage of EEC total exports	20
As percentage of U.S. total imports	16
EEC imports from United States	$3.8
As percentage of EEC total imports	27
As percentage of U.S. total exports	19
EFTA exports to United States	$1.6
As percentage of EFTA total exports	17
As percentage of U.S. total imports	11
EFTA imports from United States	$2.6
As percentage of EFTA total imports	22
As percentage of U.S. total exports	13
Combined EEC and EFTA exports to United States	$3.9
As percentage of EEC and EFTA total exports	19
As percentage of U.S. total imports	27
Combined EEC and EFTA imports from United States	$6.4
As percentage of EEC and EFTA total imports	25
As percentage of U.S. total exports	31
Total U.S. direct investments in EEC	$2.6
Total U.S. direct investments in EFTA	3.8
Total	6.4
As percentage of total U.S. direct investments abroad	20
Total EEC direct investments in United States	$1.4
Total EFTA direct investments in United States	3.2
Total	4.6
As percentage of total foreign direct investments in United States	67

* EEC and EFTA totals omit trade within each group and between groups.

Sources: OEEC Statistical Bulletins, General Statistics, July 1961; U.S. Department of Commerce: Statistical Reports, pt. 3, No. 61, 23 and 24; U.S. Department of Commerce, Survey of Current Business, August and October, 1961.

tries with one another could be considered part of the internal commerce of the enlarged Common Market and could be eliminated from the totals.

Together, these two giant economic units would be responsible for half of the world's total trade. With a combined population of 450 million, a consolidated gross national product of nearly $825 billion, and total monetary reserves of over $40 billion, the Atlantic partnership, if effectively organized, would be capable of carrying out all of the tasks . . . confronting the Western nations in the decades to come. To achieve such unified strength, however, the United States and the European Community will have to make major changes in their existing economic relations with each other.

These relationships will undoubtedly be modified by the specific conditions under which the United Kingdom and others join the Six, and thereafter by structural changes which will ensue within the Common Market. The individual members of the Common Market have, in varying degrees, been substantially dependent upon foreign trade, partly because of their meager endowments of natural resources in relation to their population. The removal of barriers to trade within the enlarged Community will in effect convert a substantial portion of their existing foreign trade into domestic trade and will further stimulate the growth of internal commerce. Nonetheless, the enlargement of the Common Market does nothing to improve the relation of population to natural resources and, as population and incomes grow, the need to import fuel, industrial raw materials, and certain kinds of food will increase.

It is axiomatic that trade increases among industrialized countries as they grow. Economic growth is essentially a process of increasing specialization and division of labor both within countries and among them. The more industrialized an economy and the higher its living standards, the more it will open up new fields of economic activity, institute new processes of production, and generate new products and services for consumption. Thus, as between the two most industrialized areas of the non-Communist world—the United States and the enlarged Common Market—there should continue to be over the long term greatly expanded opportunities for mutually advantageous trade both in production and in consumption goods.

The basic condition, therefore, for expanding economic relationships between the enlarged Community and the United States is that both have adequate rates of economic growth. In this respect, the performance of the Common Market has been much more satisfactory than that of the United States; indeed, its rate of economic growth has been double that of the American economy in recent years. Moreover, it seems reasonably certain that growth will continue at a high rate in the enlarged Common Market. Though the entry of the United Kingdom may initially lower the average—the United Kingdom's rate of growth has been even less satisfactory than that of the United States—the Community's growth rate will still be high, and membership in the Common Market should stimulate an improved British performance within a few years. The major uncertainty is not that the enlarged Common Market might fail to grow at an adequate rate, but that the United States would continue to be deficient in this basic respect. In this sense, realization of potential opportunities for increased trade and investment between the two large entities depends more upon the United States than on the European Community.

Thus, both for the United States and for other countries of the world, the prospect of an enlarged and dynamic Common Market opens up major new opportunities for expanding and mutually beneficial trade and other economic relations. However, whether and how soon these opportunities can be realized depends not only upon long-term growth factors but also upon the deliberate trade policies which the countries concerned will follow.

The fact that the enlarged Common Market will continue to be significantly dependent upon foreign trade should, even in the shorter run, help to predispose it toward a liberal foreign trade policy, though it is not sufficient by itself to guarantee such a policy. This factor will be reinforced by major economic, political and psychological considerations. The Community, too, recognizes the gains to be obtained from increased trade and investment. The Soviet menace and the habits of economic cooperation built up since World War II will continue to exert pressure toward the strengthening of the Common Market's ties with the other industrialized and many underdeveloped countries.

But the key question for the enlarged Common Market in deciding upon its orientation will be the outlook and policies of the United States. If the United States is eager for a strengthening of economic ties with the European Economic Community and for an outward-looking approach to economic relations with the other nations of the world, the chances that the Community will be disposed to a similar approach would be greatly increased. A contrary attitude on the part of the United States could turn the Common Market inward, increasing its potential protectionist features.

44. U.S. FOREIGN TRADE POLICY FOR THE SIXTIES*

President John F. Kennedy

To the Congress of the United States:

Twenty-eight years ago our nation embarked upon a new experiment in international relationships—the Reciprocal Trade Agreements Program. Faced with the chaos in world trade that had resulted from the Great Depression, disillusioned by the failure of the promises that high protective tariffs would generate recovery, and impelled by a desperate need to restore our economy, President Roosevelt asked for authority to negotiate reciprocal tariff reductions with other nations of the world in order to spur our exports and aid our economic recovery and growth.

That landmark measure, guided through Congress by Cordell Hull, has been extended 11 times. It has served our country and the free world

* President John F. Kennedy, *New Foreign Trade Program* (Washington, D.C.: U.S. Department of State, January, 1962), pp. 1–28.

well over two decades. The application of this program brought growth and order to the free-world trading system. Our total exports, averaging less than $2 billion a year in the 3 years preceding enactment of the law, have now increased to over $20 billion.

On June 30, 1962, the negotiating authority under the last extension of the Trade Agreements Act expires. It must be replaced by a wholly new instrument. A new American trade initiative is needed to meet the challenges and opportunities of a rapidly changing world economy.

In the brief period since this act was last extended, five fundamentally new and sweeping developments have made obsolete our traditional trade policy:

—*The growth of the European Common Market*—an economy which may soon nearly equal our own, protected by a single external tariff similar to our own—has progressed with such success and momentum that it has surpassed its original timetable, convinced those initially skeptical that there is now no turning back, and laid the groundwork for a radical alteration of the economics of the Atlantic alliance. Almost 90 percent of the free world's industrial production (if the United Kingdom and others successfully complete their negotiations for membership) may soon be concentrated in two great markets—the United States of America and the expanded European Economic Community. A trade policy adequate to negotiate item by item tariff reductions with a large number of small independent states will no longer be adequate to assure ready access for ourselves—and for our traditional trading partners in Canada, Japan, Latin America, and elsewhere—to a market nearly as large as our own, whose negotiators can speak with one voice but whose internal differences make it impossible for them to negotiate item by item.

—*The growing pressures on our balance-of-payments position* have, in the past few years, turned a new spotlight on the importance of increasing American exports to strengthen the international position of the dollar and prevent a steady drain of our gold reserves. To maintain our defense, assistance, and other commitments abroad, while expanding the free flow of goods and capital, we must achieve a reasonable equilibrium in our international accounts by offsetting these dollar outlays with dollar sales.

—*The need to accelerate our own economic growth*, following a lagging period of 7 years characterized by three recessions, is more urgent than it has been in years—underlined by the millions of new job opportunities which will have to be found in this decade to provide employment for those already unemployed as well as an increasing flood of younger workers, farm workers seeking new opportunities, and city workers displaced by technological change.

—*The Communist aid and trade offensive* has also become more apparent in recent years. Soviet bloc trade with 41 non-Communist countries in the less developed areas of the globe has more than tripled in recent years; and bloc trade missions are busy in nearly every continent attempting to penetrate, encircle, and divide the free world.

—*The need for new markets for Japan and the developing nations* has also been accentuated as never before—both by the prospective impact of the EEC's external tariff and by their own need to acquire new outlets for their raw materials and light manufactures.

To meet these new challenges and opportunities, I am today transmitting to the Congress a new and modern instrument of trade negotiation—the Trade Expansion Act of 1962. As I said in my state of the Union address, its enactment "could well affect the unity of the West, the course of the cold war, and the growth of our nation for a generation or more to come."

I. THE BENEFITS OF INCREASED TRADE

Specifically, enactment of this measure will benefit substantially every State of the Union, every segment of the American economy, and every basic objective of our domestic economy and foreign policy.

Our efforts to expand our economy will be importantly affected by our ability to expand our exports—and particularly upon the ability of our farmers and businessmen to sell to the Common Market. There is arising across the Atlantic a single economic community which may soon have a population half again as big as our own, working and competing together with no more barriers to commerce and investment than exist among our 50 States—in an economy which has been growing roughly twice as fast as ours—representing a purchasing power which will someday equal our own and a living standard growing faster than our own. As its consumer incomes grow, its consumer demands are also growing, particularly for the type of goods that we produce best, which are only now beginning to be widely sold or known in the markets of Europe or in the homes of its middle-income families.

Some 30 percent of our exports—more than $4 billion in industrial goods and materials and nearly $2 billion in agricultural products—already goes to the members and prospective members of the EEC. European manufacturers, however, have increased their share of this rapidly expanding market at a far greater rate than American manufacturers. Unless our industry can maintain and increase its share of this attractive market, there will be further temptation to locate additional American-financed plants in Europe in order to get behind the external tariff wall of the EEC. This would enable the American manufacturer to contend for that vast consumer potential on more competitive terms with his European counterparts; but it will also mean a failure on our part to take advantage of this growing market to increase jobs and investment in this country.

A more liberal trade policy will in general benefit our most efficient and expanding industries—industries which have demonstrated their advantage over other world producers by exporting on the average twice as much of their products as we import—industries which have done this while paying the highest wages in our country. Increasing investment and employment in these growth industries will make for a more healthy, efficient, and expanding economy and a still higher American standard of living. Indeed, freer movement of trade between America and the Common Market would bolster the economy of the entire free world, stimulating each nation to do most what it does best and helping to achieve the OECD target of a 50 percent combined Atlantic community increase in gross national product by 1970.

Our efforts to prevent inflation will be reinforced by expanded trade. Once given a fair and equal opportunity to compete in overseas markets, and once subject to healthy competition from overseas manufacturers for our own markets, American management and labor will have additional reason to maintain competitive costs and prices, modernize their plants, and increase their productivity. The discipline of the world marketplace is an excellent measure of efficiency and a force to stability. To try to shield American industry from the discipline of foreign competition would isolate our domestic price level from world prices, encourage domestic inflation, reduce our exports still further, and invite less desirable Governmental solutions.

Our efforts to correct our adverse balance of payments have in recent years roughly paralleled our ability to increase our export surplus. It is necessary if we are to maintain our security programs abroad—our own military forces overseas plus our contribution to the security and growth of other free countries—to make substantial dollar outlays abroad. These outlays are being held to the minimum necessary, and we are seeking increased sharing from our allies. But they will continue at substantial rates—and this requires us to enlarge the $5 billion export surplus which we presently enjoy from our favorable balance of trade. If that surplus can be enlarged, as exports under our new program rise faster than imports, we can achieve the equilibrium in our balance of payments which is essential to our economic stability and flexibility. If, on the other hand, our surplus should fail to grow, if our exports should be denied ready access to the EEC and other markets—our overseas position would be endangered. Moreover, if we can lower the external tariff wall of the Common Market through negotiation our manufacturers will be under less pressure to locate their plants behind that wall in order to sell in the European market, thus reducing the export of capital funds to Europe.

Our efforts to promote the strength and unity of the West are thus directly related to the strength and unity of Atlantic trade policies. An expanded export program is necessary to give this nation both the balance-of-payments equilibrium and the economic growth we need to sustain our share of Western military security and economic advance. Equally important, a freer flow of trade across the Atlantic will enable the two giant markets on either side of the ocean to impart strength and vigor to each other, and to combine their resources and momentum to undertake the many enterprises which the security of free peoples demands. For the first time, as the world's greatest trading nation, we can welcome a single partner whose trade is even larger than our own—a partner no longer divided and dependent, but strong enough to share with us the responsibilities and initiatives of the free world.

The Communist bloc, largely self-contained and isolated, represents an economic power already by some standards larger than that of Western Europe and hoping someday to overtake the United States. But the combined output and purchasing power of the United States and Western Europe—nearly a trillion dollars a year—is more than twice as great as that of the entire Sino-Soviet world. Though we have only half the population, and far less than half the territory, we can pool our resources and resourcefulness in an open trade partnership strong enough to outstrip any challenge, and strong enough to undertake all the many enterprises around the world which the maintenance and progress of freedom require. If we can take this step, Marxist predictions of "capitalist" empires warring over markets and stifling competition would be shattered for all time—Communist hopes for a trade war between these two great economic giants would be frustrated—and Communist efforts to split the West would be doomed to failure.

As members of the Atlantic community we have concerted our military objectives through the North Atlantic Treaty Organization. We are concerting our monetary and economic policies through the Organization for Economic Cooperation and Development. It is time now to write a new chapter in the evolution of the Atlantic community. The success of our foreign policy depends in large measure upon the success of our foreign trade, and our maintenance of Western political unity depends in equally large measure upon the degree of Western economic unity. An integrated Western Europe, joined in trading partnership with the United States, will further shift the world balance of power to the side of freedom.

Our efforts to prove the superiority of free choice will thus be advanced immeasurably. We will prove to the world that we believe in peacefully "tearing down walls" instead of arbitrarily building them. We will be opening new vistas of choice and opportunity to the producers and consumers of the free world. In answer to those who say to the world's poorer countries that economic progress and freedom are no longer compatible, we—who have long boasted about the virtues of the marketplace and of free competitive enterprise, about our ability to compete and sell in any market, and about our willingness to keep abreast of the times—will have our greatest opportunity since the Marshall plan to demonstrate the vitality of free choice.

Communist bloc nations have negotiated more than 200 trade agreements in recent years. Inevitably the recipient nation finds its economy increasingly dependent upon Soviet goods, services, and technicians. But many of these nations have also observed that the economics of free choice provide far greater benefits than the economics of coercion—and the wider we can make the area of economic freedom, the easier we make it for all free peoples to receive the benefits of our innovations and put them into practice.

Our efforts to aid the developing nations of the world and other friends, however, depend upon more than a demonstration of freedom's vitality and benefits. If their economies are to expand, if their new industries are to be successful, if they are to acquire the foreign exchange funds they will need to replace our aid efforts, these nations must find new outlets for their raw materials and new manufactures. We must make certain that any arrangements which we make with the European Economic Community are worked out in such a fashion as to insure nondiscriminatory application to all third countries. Even more important, however, the United States and Europe together have a joint responsibility to all of the less developed countries of the world—and in this sense we must work together to insure that their legitimate aspirations and requirements are fulfilled. The "open partnership" which this bill proposes will enable all free nations to share together the rewards of a wider economic choice for all.

Our efforts to maintain the leadership of the free world thus rest, in the final analysis, on our success in this undertaking. Economic isolation and political leadership are wholly incompatible. In the next few years, the nations of Western Europe will be fixing basic economic and trading patterns vitally affecting the future of our economy and the hopes of our less developed friends. Basic political and military decisions of vital interest to our security will be made. Unless we have this authority to negotiate and have it this year—if we are separated from the Common Market by high tariff barriers on either side of the Atlantic—then we cannot hope to play an effective part in those basic decisions.

If we are to retain our leadership, the initiative is up to us. The revolutionary changes which are occurring will not wait for us to make up our minds. The United States has encouraged sweeping changes in free-world economic patterns in order to strengthen the forces of freedom. But we cannot ourselves stand still. If we are to lead, we must act. We must adapt our own economy to the imperatives of a changing world, and once more assert our leadership.

The American businessman, once the authority granted by this bill is exercised, will have a unique opportunity to compete on a more equal basis in a rich and rapidly expanding market abroad which possesses potentially a purchasing power as large and as varied as our own. He knows that, once artificial restraints are removed, a vast array of American goods, produced by American know-how with American efficiency, can compete with any goods in any spot in the world. And almost all members of the business community, in every State, now participate or could participate in the production, processing, transporting, or distribution of either exports or imports.

Already we sell to Western Europe alone more machinery, transportation equipment, chemicals, and coal than our total imports of these commodities from all regions of the world combined. Western Europe is our best customer today—and should be an even better one tomorrow. But as the new external tariff surrounding the Common Market replaces the internal tariff structure, a German producer—who once competed in the markets of France on the same terms with our own producers—will achieve free access to French markets while our own producers face a tariff. In short, in the absence of authority to bargain down that external tariff, as the economy of the Common Market expands, our exports will not expand with it. They may even decline.

The American farmer has a tremendous stake in expanded trade. One out of every seven farm workers produces for export. The average farmer depends on foreign markets to sell the crops grown on one out of every six acres he plants. Sixty percent of our rice, 49 percent of our cotton, 45 percent of our wheat, and 42 percent of our soybean production are exported. Agriculture is one of our best sources of foreign exchange.

Our farmers are particularly dependent upon the markets of Western Europe. Our agricultural trade with that area is four-to-one in our favor. The agreements recently reached at Brussels both exhausted our existing authority to obtain further European concessions, and laid the groundwork for future negotiations on American farm exports to be conducted once new authority is granted. But new and flexible authority is required if we are to keep the door of the Common Market open to American agriculture, and open it wider still. If the output of our astounding productivity is not to pile up increasingly in our warehouses, our negotiators will need both the special EEC authority and the general 50 percent authority requested in the bill described later in this message.

The American worker will benefit from the expansion of our exports. One out of every three workers engaged in manufacturing is employed in establishments that export. Several hundred times as many workers owe their jobs directly or indirectly to exports as are in the small group—estimated to be less than one-half of 1 percent of all workers—who might be adversely affected by a sharp increase in imports. As the number of job seekers in our labor force expands in the years ahead, increasing our job opportunities will require expanding our markets and economy, and making certain that new United States plants built to serve Common Market consumers are built here, to employ American workers, and not there.

The American consumer benefits most of all from an increase in foreign trade. Imports give him a wider choice of products at competitive prices. They introduce new ideas and new tastes, which often lead to new demands for American production.

Increased imports stimulate our own efforts to increase efficiency, and supplement antitrust and other efforts to assure competition. Many industries of importance to the American consumer and economy are dependent upon imports for raw materials and other supplies. Thus American-made goods can also be made much less expensively for the American consumers if we lower the tariff on the materials that are necessary to their production.

American imports, in short, have generally strengthened rather than weakened our economy. Their competitive benefits have already been mentioned. But about 60 percent of the goods we import do not compete with the goods we produce—either because they are not produced in this country, or are not produced in any significant quantity. They provide us with products we need but cannot efficiently make or grow (such as bananas or coffee), supplement our own steadily depleting natural resources with items not available here in quantity (such as manganese or chrome ore, 90 percent or more of which must be imported if our steel mills are to operate), and contribute to our industrial efficiency, our economic growth, and our high level of consumption. Those imports that do compete are equal to only 1 or 1½ percent of our total national production; and even these imports create jobs directly for those engaged in their processing, distribution, or transportation, and indirectly for those employed in both export industries and in those industries dependent upon reasonably priced imported supplies for their own ability to compete.

Moreover, we must reduce our own tariffs if we hope to reduce tariffs abroad and thereby increase our exports and export surplus. There are many more American jobs dependent upon exports than could possibly be adversely affected by increased imports. And those export industries are our strongest, most efficient, highest paying growth industries.

It is obvious, therefore, that the warnings against increased imports based upon the lower level of wages paid in other countries are not telling the whole story. For this fear is refuted by the fact that American industry in general—and America's highest paid industries in particular—export more goods to other markets than any other nation; sell far more abroad to other countries than they sell to us; and command the vast preponderance of our own market here in the United States. There are three reasons for this:

(a) The skill and efficiency of American workers, with the help of our machinery and technology, can produce more units per man-hour than any other workers in the world—thus making the competitive cost of our labor for many products far less than it is in countries with lower wage rates. For example, while a United States coal miner is paid 8 times as much per hour as the Japanese miner, he produces 14 times as much coal—our real cost per ton of coal is thus far smaller—and we sell the Japanese tens of millions of dollars worth of coal each year.

(b) Our best industries also possess other advantages—the adequacy of low-cost raw materials or electrical power, for example. Neither wages nor total labor costs is an adequate standard of comparison if used alone.

(c) American products can frequently compete successfully even where foreign prices are somewhat lower—by virtue of their superior quality, style, packaging, servicing, or assurance of delivery.

Given this strength, accompanied by increasing productivity and wages in the rest of the world, there is less need to be concerned over the level of wages in the low-wage countries. These levels, moreover, are already on the rise, and, we would hope, will continue to narrow the current wage gap, encouraged by appropriate consultations on an international basis.

This philosophy of the free market—the wider economic choice for men and nations—is as old as freedom itself. It is not a partisan philosophy. For many years our trade legislation has enjoyed bipartisan backing from those members of both parties who recognized how essential trade is to our basic security abroad and our economic health at home. This is even more true today. The Trade Expansion Act of 1962 is designed as the expression of a nation, not of any single faction or section. It is in that spirit that I recommend it to the Congress for prompt and favorable action.

II. PROVISIONS OF THE BILL

New Negotiating Authority. To achieve all of the goals and gains set forth above—to empower our negotiators with sufficient authority to induce the EEC to grant wider access to our goods and crops and fair treatment to those of Latin America, Japan, and other countries—and to be ready to talk trade with the Common Market in practical terms—it is essential that our bargaining authority be increased in both flexibility and extent. I am therefore requesting two basic kinds of authority to be exercised over the next 5 years:

First, a general authority to reduce existing tariffs by 50 percent in reciprocal negotiations. It would be our intention to employ a variety of techniques in exercising this authority, including negotiations on broad categories or subcategories of products.

Secondly, a special authority, to be used in negotiating with the EEC, to reduce or eliminate all tariffs on those groups of products where the United States and the EEC together account for 80 percent or more of world trade in a representative period. The fact that these groups of products fall within this special or "dominant supplier" authority is proof that they can be produced here or in Europe more efficiently than anywhere else in the world. They include most of the products which the members of the Common Market are especially interested in trading with us, and most of the products for which we want freer access to the Common Market; and to a considerable extent they are items in which our own ability to compete is demonstrated by the fact that our exports of these items are substantially greater than our imports. They account for nearly $2 billion of our total industrial exports to present and prospective Common Market members in 1960, and for about $1.4 billion of our imports from these countries. In short, this special authority will enable us to negotiate for a dramatic agreement with the Common Market that will pool our economic strength for the advancement of freedom.

To be effective in achieving a breakthrough agreement with the EEC so that our farmers, manufacturers, and other free-world trading partners can participate, we will need to use both the dominant-supplier authority and the general authority in combination. Reductions would be put into effect gradually in stages over 5 years or more. But the traditional technique of trading one brick at a time off our respective tariff walls will not suffice to assure American farm and factory exports the kind of access to the European market which they must have if trade between the two Atlantic markets is to expand. We must talk instead in terms of trading whole layers at a time in exchange for other layers, as the Europeans have been doing in reducing their internal tariffs, permitting the forces of competition to set new trade patterns. Trading on such an enlarged basis is not possible, the EEC has found, if traditional item-by-item economic histories are to dominate. But let me emphasize that we mean to see to it that all reductions and concessions are reciprocal—and that the access we gain is not limited by the use of quotas or other restrictive devices.

Safeguarding Interests of Other Trading Partners. In our negotiations with the Common Market, we will preserve our traditional most-favored-nation principle under which any tariff concessions negotiated will be generalized to our other trading partners. Obviously, in special authority agreements where the United States and the EEC are the dominant suppliers, the participation of other nations often would not be significant. On other items, where justified, compensating concessions from other interested countries should be obtained as part of the negotiations. But in essence we must strive for a nondiscriminatory trade partnership with the EEC. If it succeeds only in splintering the free world, or increasing the disparity between rich and poor nations, it will have failed to achieve one of its major purposes. The negotiating authority under this bill will thus be used to strengthen the ties of both "Common Markets" with, and expand our own trade in, the Latin American Republics, Canada, Japan, and other non-European nations—as well as helping them maximize their opportunities to trade with the Common Market.

The bill also requests special authority to reduce or eliminate all duties and other restrictions on the importation of tropical agricultural and forestry products supplied by friendly less developed countries and not produced here in any significant quantity, if our action is taken in concert with similar action by the Common Market. These tropical products are the staple exports of many less developed countries. Their efforts for economic development and diversification must be advanced out of earnings from these products. By assuring them as large a market as possible, we are bringing closer the day when they will be able to finance their own development needs on a self-sustaining basis.

Safeguards to American Industry. If the authority requested in this act is used, imports as well as exports will increase; and this increase will, in the overwhelming number of cases, be beneficial for the reasons outlined above. Nevertheless ample safeguards against injury to American industry and agriculture will be retained. Escape-clause relief will continue to be available with more up-to-date definitions. Temporary tariff relief will be granted where essential. The power to impose duties or suspend concessions to protect the national security will be retained. Articles will be reserved from negotiations whenever such action is deemed to be in the best interest of the Nation and the economy. And the four basic stages of the traditional peril-point procedures and safeguards will be retained and improved.

—the President will refer to the Tariff Commission the list of proposed items for negotiations;

—the Tariff Commission will conduct hearings to determine the effect of concessions on these products;

—the Commission will make a report to the President, specifically based, as such reports are based now, upon its findings of how new imports might lead to the idling of productive facilities, the inability of domestic producers to operate at a profit, and the unemployment of workers as the result of anticipated reductions in duties; and

—the President will report to the Congress on his action after completion of the negotiations. The present arrangements will be substantially improved, however, since both the Tariff Commission recommendation and the President's report would be broader than a bare determination of specific peril points; and this should enable us to make much more informed use of these recommendations than has been true in the past.

Trade Adjustment Assistance. I am also recommending as an essential part of the new trade program that companies, farmers, and workers who suffer damage from increased foreign import competition be assisted in their efforts to adjust to that competition. When considerations of national policy make it desirable to avoid higher tariffs, those injured by that competition should not be required to bear the full brunt of the impact. Rather, the burden of economic adjustment should be borne in part by the Federal Government.

Under existing law, the only alternatives available to the President are the imposition or refusal of tariff relief. These alternatives should continue to be available.

The legislation I am proposing, however, provides an additional alternative called trade adjustment assistance. This alternative will permit the executive branch to make extensive use of its facilities, programs, and resources to provide special assistance to farmers, firms, and their employees in making the economic readjustments necessitated by the imports resulting from tariff concessions.

Any worker or group of workers unemployed or underemployed as a result of increased imports would, under this bill, be eligible for the following forms of assistance:

1. Readjustment allowances providing as much as 65 percent of the individual's average weekly wage for up to 52 weeks for all workers, and for as many as 13 additional weeks for workers over 60, with unemployment insurance benefits deducted from such allowances to the extent available;
2. Vocational education and training assistance to develop higher and different skills;
3. Financial assistance for those who cannot find work in their present community to relocate to a different place in the United States where suitable employment is available.

For a businessman or farmer adversely affected by imports, there should be available:

1. Technical information, advice, and consultation to help plan and implement an attack on the problem;
2. Tax benefits to encourage modernization and diversification;
3. Loan guarantees and loans otherwise not commercially available to aid modernization and diversification.

Just as the Federal Government has assisted in personal readjustments made necessary by military service, just as the Federal Government met its obligation to assist industry in adjusting to war production and again to return to peacetime production, so there is an obligation to render assistance to those who suffer as a result of national trade policy. Such a program will supplement and work in coordination with, not duplicate, what we are already doing or proposing to do for depressed areas, for small business, for investment incentives, and for the retraining and compensation of our unemployed workers.

This cannot be and will not be a subsidy program of Government paternalism. It is instead a program to afford time for American initiative, American adaptability, and American resiliency to assert themselves. It is consistent with that part of the proposed law which would stage tariff reductions over a 5-year period. Accordingly, trade adjustment assistance, like the other provisions of the Trade Expansion Act of 1962, is designed to strengthen the efficiency of our economy, not to protect inefficiencies.

Authority to grant temporary tariff relief will remain available to assist those industries injured by a sudden influx of goods under revised tariffs. But the accent is on "adjustment" more than "assistance." Through trade adjustment prompt and effective help can be given to those suffering genuine hardship in adjusting to import competition, moving men and resources out of uneconomic production into efficient production and competitive positions, and in the process preserving the employment relationships between firms and workers wherever possible. Unlike tariff relief, this assistance can be tailored to their individual needs without disrupting other policies. Experience with a similar kind of program in the Common Market, and in the face of more extensive tariff reductions than we propose here, testifies to the effective but relatively inexpensive nature of this approach. For most affected firms will find that the adjustment involved is no more than the adjustment they face every year or few years as the result of changes in the economy, consumer taste or domestic competition.

The purpose of this message has been to describe the challenge we face and the tools we need. The decision rests with the Congress. That decision will either mark the beginning of a new chapter in the alliance of free nations—or a threat to the growth of Western unity. The two great Atlantic markets will either grow together or they will grow apart. The meaning and range of free economic choice will either be widened for the benefit of free men everywhere—or confused and constricted by new barriers and delays.

Last year, in enacting a long-term foreign aid program, the Congress made possible a fundamental change in our relations with the developing nations. This bill will make possible a fundamental, far-reaching, and unique change in our relations with the other industrialized nations—particularly with the other members of the Atlantic community. As NATO was unprecedented in military history, this measure is unprecedented in economic history. But its passage will be long remembered and its benefits widely distributed among those who work for freedom.

At rare moments in the life of this nation an opportunity comes along to fashion out of the confusion of current events a clear and bold action to show the world what it is we stand for. Such an opportunity is before us now. This bill, by enabling us to strike a bargain with the Common Market, will "strike a blow" for freedom.

45. ADJUSTING TO INCREASED FOREIGN COMPETITION*

Otto R. Reischer

INTRODUCTION: THE SIGNIFICANCE OF READJUSTING TO INCREASED COMPETITIVE IMPORTS

This study examines various methods designed to minimize economic dislocations caused by increased competitive imports; the desirability of greater freedom of trade is taken for granted.

Withdrawal of tariff protection from an industry often entails severe losses to groups or individuals. Such losses are open to objection on social grounds, even though they result from a decision of the Government taken in the national interest. But these losses may also give rise to political opposition which can prevent or delay trade liberalization. Much could be gained, therefore, if it were possible to remove these objections to a policy shift from protection to adaptation by providing adjustment assistance to producers who, despite efficient operations, have suffered, or are being threatened with, serious injury from competitive imports.

Attrition of an industry due to general technological progress is not the same as damage inflicted on that industry by intensified import competition resulting from lowered trade barriers. In the latter case the damage results from a policy decision of the Government taken in the national interest—national in the sense that matters of trade and tariff policy are of a nationwide rather than regional, sectional, or local character. In following through this policy decision, the Federal Government may be expected to assume responsibility for mitigating some of these immediately adverse consequences of freer trade.

In the domestic economy of a free society like our own, where market forces are given reasonable play, technical progress tends to be equated with the "law of the market"—the operation of impersonal economic forces to which producers have to submit or perish. The Government is charged with keeping these forces operating at home and fosters them through antitrust and antimonopoly legislation and controls. The Government also is obliged to desist from directly influencing technical

* Otto R. Reischer, *Trade Adjustment in Theory and Practice*, Joint Economic Committee (87th Cong., 1st. sess.) (Washington, D.C.: U.S. Government Printing Office, 1961), pp. 1–11.

progress except in an upward direction. It assists such progress by issuing patents and undertaking research activities, public works and other forms of assistance.

In the area of foreign trade, however, the "law of the market" only rarely has been given free rein. Here market forces still are hemmed in by many restrictive devices dating back to a period when such restrictions were in fact beneficial on a nationwide basis, and when stable markets had to be secured for many of this country's infant industries. Behind the shield of tariffs, industries have grown up over the years, investments have been sunk in plant and equipment, and prosperous businesses have been built up.

Though firms within an industry differ in their ability to cope with new developments and new types of competition, domestic competition has had to be accepted as the law of the land, with a tradition going back many generations. But foreign competition has not had to be accepted, at least not until fairly recently. Foreign manufacturers are not covered by our legislation on labor standards and restraint of trade. Against their competition the tariff and other trade restrictions have been an effective shelter, not available against an industry's domestic competitors.

Economic progress in a free society cannot be dissociated from competition, and no cushioning is needed or desirable. In the foreign trade field, however, equity requires that the impact of a Government policy decision leading to increased import competition be accompanied by a policy to facilitate adjustments and minimize injury suffered by industries deprived of their accustomed shield against competitive imports.

The Government's objective in safeguarding competition on the domestic scene is to increase the general welfare; the same objective underlies the decision to increase competition in foreign trade. The objective would be realized in the long run (total adaptation) through the benefits from specialization according to the doctrine of comparative advantage. In the short run (partial adaptation) it would be achieved as a result of the stimulus of competition and of concessions obtained from our trading partners. In both instances, it may be noted, American exports are increased.

Withdrawal of protection from an industry accustomed to rely on it may contribute to the demise of a certain number of firms in that industry. Their number will vary in proportion to the measures they themselves take and the opportunity the Government gives them to make a satisfactory adjustment to the new competitive situation.

No firm or industry is entitled to a blanket dispensation from having to adjust its operations to changes in its economic environment. But the Government, by removing safeguards against injury from foreign competition which it had provided initially, incurs, as a matter of equity, an obligation to provide some form of assistance to these firms and industries now unable to make a satisfactory adaptation on their own. Increased competition from abroad is a relatively small matter compared with disturbances in the home market due to technological and other changes. The burden of that new obligation should therefore be rather small.

ECONOMIC AND PUBLIC POLICY ASPECTS OF TRADE ADJUSTMENT

Economic dislocations as a rule have more than one cause. If an industry is suffering in some degree from foreign competition, it is also suffering from a much larger array of ailments. Changed conditions of domestic demand or new sources of domestic supply often create the basic problem. But the processes of adjustment are similar, regardless of whether the dislocation stems from domestic or foreign causes.

Unassisted versus Assisted Readjustment

Two general types of readaptation can be distinguished: unassisted readaptation, and readaptation aided by government.

Unassisted readaptation may entail cost reduction, diversification of production, market research, and importing. In industries producing standardized commodities for a wide market, such as electrical manufacturing, chemicals, and iron and steel, opportunities for cost reduction are easily found. But even in small-scale manufacturing, cost reductions are found possible, through time and motion studies, for example. In general, however, import-sensitive industries may find more help in competing with foreign firms by analyzing consumer demand more carefully, and determining the changed characteristics of the market. Developing of new designs has been helpful, too.

Diversification has been another way firms have taken in adapting themselves to changed competitive situations. In the present context, this has meant branching out into lines not subject to import competition. But successful selection of new products requires detailed studies of market possibilities and production techniques, and not all firms suffering from import competition command the necessary financial resources and managerial skills to undertake the studies and apply the findings.

For producers of labor-intensive commodities unable to reduce costs to the level of competitors in low-wage countries making identical goods, the only solution has been in offering something distinctive, which usually has meant something more expensive.

There are many interesting examples of successful adaptation to rising foreign competition in the wake of tariff concessions. Manufacturers of bicycles turned to competitive models. They also use their facilities in the off-season for making other products—lawn-mowers, air-conditioning apparatus, equipment for gas stations and so on. Some woolen and worsted mills make automobile fabrics as well as apparel cloth; others are producing synthetic and blended fabrics. Manufacturers of hand-fashioned glass have begun to turn out Fiberglas. Manufacturers of fine household china also make hotel ware. And watch companies in addition to defense items are making watch cases and bracelets, men's jewelry, and electronic apparatus.

Producers of import-sensitive goods often have taken to selling imported goods to improve their position. Some watch manufacturers also are importers of Swiss watch movements, which they case and sell under their own or another trade name. Several bicycle manufacturers have made arrangements with foreign firms to market their products in the United States. American producers of dyestuffs also are engaged in importing. For, while the manufacturer is mainly interested in turning out the goods himself, importing as a sideline provides him with a more complete line of products, including items which can be procured more cheaply abroad than produced at home.

But unassisted readaptation may not always be enough for coping with a changed competitive situation. When, for example, an import-sensitive industry has been the sole or predominant source of employment in a community, a tariff reduction may push an already weak producer to the brink of disaster. This may not be a tariff problem pure and simple, for overspecialization too would have made the community vulnerable to any sudden change, whether of domestic or foreign origin. Whatever the cause, the remedy in these cases would be to broaden the industrial base and thereby create new opportunities for employment.

From the point of view of the workers, even a successful diversification program may involve considerable hardship. Labor is far from being perfectly mobile. Older workers in particular lack the inclination and the ability to find employment in other industries. Workers who do not move suffer losses in earnings because of downgrading in skill classification. And many a new job may be less satisfactory than the old.

To cope with such difficulties is in the first instance the responsibility of both management and labor in the affected industry, and of State and local authorities. But since such efforts often are inadequate, the Federal Government tends to assume responsibility for providing help, and has done so in the past. In fact, our Federal social security and unemployment assistance programs are reflections of that tendency, as is the recently adopted depressed area program. The thesis of this study is that more should be done.

Advocates of freer trade deny that the higher American wage scale makes this country more vulnerable to import competition originating in low-wage countries, since higher wages in our industries reflect higher productivity, and are therefore no indication of higher unit costs. However, this superiority holds true chiefly for standardized commodities which are turned out in quantity by mass production methods.

In producing such commodities, heavy investment of capital makes possible much larger output per worker per hour than in foreign plants not so well equipped. But relatively high wages in this country tend to be a serious handicap to low-capital producers in import-sensitive industries. The basic difficulty of these industries, however, is not the low wages paid abroad. Rather, it is the high competing wages paid by other American industries, based on the high level of productivity in American industry. The goods we export are produced by our most productive, highest wage industries.

No industry stands by itself in competition with foreign suppliers. Its changing cost structure vis-a-vis the cost structures of foreign competitors is to a major extent a reflection, indeed a function, of the changing cost patterns of the national economy in which it operates. Adaptation to increased imports is not an isolated phenomenon but a facet of the general process of economic adaptation and growth. One significant feature of this type of adjustment is that it represents a point of convergence of domestic and foreign economic policy. This brings us to the public policy aspects of assisted readjustment which will be discussed after a brief review of its economic aspects.

Economic Aspects of Trade Adjustment

The economic objective of assisted readjustment is to soften or spread out the impact on domestic producers of an increase in competitive imports resulting from freer trade. A major prerequisite of a workable adjustment program will be to convince these producers of the usefulness of making an adjustment. This prerequisite would be met by offering those American businessmen who bear the brunt of intensified import competition a program consistent with the free-enterprise system and which allows them to continue to exercise their managerial prerogatives. Such a program would include financial assistance and technical advice, but no detailed guidelines or prescriptions. Moreover, the program should be optional, and offered as an alternative to methods currently used for relieving injury resulting from freer trade, with appropriate administrative safeguards. Various types of assistance thus made available to businesses as and where needed would help them to carry the burden of the required adaptation.

Assistance in adjustment to economic change is intended to increase flexibility and mobility, not as compensation for injury. Greater flexibility and mobility are desirable in themselves, quite apart from any reductions in trade barriers with which adjustment assistance may be associated. Adjustment assistance also can be made preventive rather than remedial. It can be made available to those who merely expect to be (or face a threat of being) injured so that they may act before injury occurs.

From the viewpoint of the economy as a whole it seems best to focus such a program on the individual business firm immediately affected by increased imports. Workers and communities are affected by such imports less directly; their injury is a function of the extent to which the business firms employing the workers, or situated in the communities, fail to make the necessary adaptation.

Trade liberalization generally is more likely to take place when there is little resistance to moves of that sort, e.g., in times of comparative prosperity, when workers can shift without too much difficulty to jobs similar to those they had been doing before being dislocated. If necessary, workers can be given preference in existing public welfare and assistance facilities. Larger enterprises in general can be counted on to make necessary adjustments in operations without assistance. There would remain only the smaller business units to be looked after. A comprehensive adjustment program could then be devised for every type of industry.

The true test of a readjustment program would be the real economic gain it could produce through a shift of resources to more profitable employment. That gain is difficult to measure. Parts of it are quantifiable in money terms. Other parts defy that kind of measurement, being widely diffused through the economy.

The Public Policy Aspect of Trade Adjustment

Public policy enters into a program of assisted readjustment by virtue of the fact that through such a program the Government could insulate problems of *foreign* economic policy, of which tariff and trade policy is one variety, from *domestic* economic policy problems created by trade liberalization. Separating the effects of governmental action in the two areas would allow greater freedom of movement as well as greater precision in achieving the respective policy objectives.

At home, the major policy problem is to keep competition at least workable by preventing undue increases in concentration of economic power. Small units have to be kept from being pushed to the wall, and economic self-reliance among entrepreneurs is to be fostered.

In the domestic policy area also, the Government has to face a problem pertaining to the national security. It has to decide which industries and what portion of the labor force are important enough from a defense standpoint to be kept at their current tasks despite relatively and often uneconomically high costs.

The problem of national security also arises in the field of foreign economic policy, where we strive to maintain mutually beneficial economic relations with allied nations. To maintain these relations requires eventual achievement of relatively unrestricted trade. As a condition for fulfilling this requirement, this country will have to accept a sizable increase in the volume of imports. Since existing trade barriers in general are still too high to permit such an increase the Government is endeavoring to lower barriers accordingly. As a result, certain domestic industries are already suffering injury from increased import competition despite existing safeguards, and more industries are likely to do so before this particular policy objective is attained. The industries injured are mostly those who in some way had geared their operations to the existence of certain types of protection—to sustaining intervention by Government.

Continuance of such protection would mean, of course, that these industries would go on receiving indirect Government subsidies. The number of producers of those industries' products would be limited by virtue of a partial or total exclusion of foreign goods. And the price of the goods produced domestically would be kept substantially higher than if producers were subjected to competitive pressure from more freely admitted foreign goods.

The Government faces a dilemma in having to deal simultaneously with relatively inadequate competition at home (in the absence of advantageously priced imports), and excessive competition from abroad (from the viewpoint of national interest, that is). The dilemma cannot be resolved so long as the Government has to rely on trade restrictions, or sustaining intervention, as the only technique available for ordering these two conflicting tendencies. Whenever it now wishes to stop excessive foreign competition, the Government is forced, as it were, to pour out the baby with the bathwater: it can indeed curtail foreign competition, yet at the same time domestic competition is also weakened. If the Government adopted the technique of adaptive intervention, in conjunction with a tariff reduction, the baby would be lifted out of the bath before the tub is emptied, and the result would be greater precision in policy implementation: policy makers could then achieve the objectives of liberal trade policy without any paralyzing concern for protected home industries. Obliged for once to make adjustments to freer trade and increased competitive imports, these industries could then be granted assistance on a temporary basis during a transition period.

A trade adjustment program thus provides the Government with a tool for separating decisionmaking in the domestic economic sphere from decisionmaking in the foreign economic sphere. Once the concept of readjustment assistance is accepted, the Government can deal with requirements of protection for domestic industries in isolation from requirements of foreign economic policy. And consideration of the one need not be distorted by consideration of the other, and vice versa.

A Federal program of assisted adaptation would also have considerable political usefulness. If the appropriate legislation were passed, it would be easier for many Congressmen who, although convinced that freer trade is in the national interest, nevertheless have protected industries in their districts, to vote for tariff reduction. They would then better be able to face their protection-minded constituents by pointing to the existence of and the advantages offered by the trade adjustment programs.

The Gain from Trade Adjustment

Increased adaptability. Assisted readjustment to increased competitive imports basically aims at increasing the adaptability of this country's industrial structure to changed world trade conditions.

Implicit in greater adaptability is a better allocation of domestic resources. Spurred by a lowering of trade barriers, the domestic economy would gain in strength as marginal producers in import-sensitive industries are impelled to switch to other and more profitable pursuits. As imports rise, and assuming that other countries also lower trade restrictions, there would appear a tendency for exports to increase in payment for imports. This increase in exports would be a reflection of stronger foreign demand for specific American goods, such as products of the automotive and engineering industries, for example. This increased foreign demand will cause more resources to be attracted into existing and into new export industries, the latter springing up as new needs and opportunities are discovered in foreign markets. Foreign investment opportunities also would multiply, and domestic resources, especially capital goods, will be absorbed by such investments. With progressive easing of multilateral trading restrictions, the effect of freer trade will also be felt in the less specialized export industries, those which hitherto may have produced almost exclusively for the home market. With the increase in opportunities created by these developments, marginal producers initially displaced by greater import competition should find adaptation not beyond their reach, especially if appropriate assistance is made available.

With obstacles to freer trade being removed gradually and in conjunction with appropriate programs of assisted adaptation—other things remaining equal—a process of economic expansion will get underway at home and abroad. As expansion of production and trade continues over time, it may be possible for the Government to reduce its expenditures for various types of foreign economic assistance including military aid.

Foreign economic aid—in the absence of any significant freeing of trade that would allow an increase in the volume of goods exchanged between the United States and aid-recipient countries—may be considered as a concealed subsidy to certain groups of domestic producers. This subsidy serves to support those marginal elements of American industry that would stand to suffer from increased foreign competition. Such support is granted at the taxpayers' expense. If these marginal producers could adapt themselves to a new competitive situation involving the freer admittance of foreign goods, with or without assistance from the Government, certain industries in the aid-recipient countries could increase their exports to the United States. To the extent that these foreign producers would be able to take advantage of relaxed American protection, they could contribute to the prosperity of their own countries, with the result that the need for further substantial foreign aid may be lessened, with corresponding reductions in U.S. outlays.

A good deal of U.S. foreign aid has taken the form of orders placed with a foreign country's capital goods industries for production of weapons and materiel. Various national engineering and related industries have been strengthened in that way. When at some future point in time the present danger should subside, these national industries may be expected to continue producing durable goods, but of a nonmilitary character. If the respective internal market should prove too small for keeping these industries busy, they will seek outlets for their products in world markets. These efforts in the first instance will generate sustained pressure for freer trade on a global basis. With greater productive capacity all around, the need for greater international specialization and division of labor will increase in proportion. If by the time this need becomes urgent American trade policy should prove not flexible enough to cope with it (in part for the reason of not having adopted a policy of assisted adaptation of marginal segments of import-sensitive industries), another foreign-aid program, but of vastly greater dimensions, may have to be devised.

A seemingly unending vicious spiral threatens to emerge as seen from the simplified sequence of measures and conceivable countermeasures which follows: The military buildup in countries friendly to the United States continues for a time, with assistance from this country. A detente with the Soviet bloc is then assumed to set in. Armament industries in countries friendly to the United States then revamp operations and exert pressure for more exports. American trade policy, however, continues unchanged in a moderately restrictive vein (without a policy of assisted adaptation). The friendly countries thereupon retaliate by discriminating against American exports. At the same time they begin suffering from unemployment in their overgrown durable goods industries. One unfavorable development brings forth another. The economies of these countries become unstable, and one more economic aid from the United States becomes indispensable. The next move would be up to the Soviet bloc. With a renewed tightening of the international situation, the spiral goes into another turn, and U.S. economic aid once more is supplemented or transformed into military aid and "defense support." With successful and rapid adaptation to economic change this repetitive succession of events might be prevented.

The Probable Dimension of Trade Adjustment

Available evidence suggests that the extent of the readjustment problem will be much smaller than commonly expected. One reason for this is that the aggregate area of displacement of domestic produciton by imports is likely to be quite small in comparison with the national economy as a whole.

Shifts in production and marketing practices take time. Foreign products not only must compete pricewise with domestic products after paying freight and other charges, but must also conform to established tastes, and appropriate channels of distribution must be developed for them. Owing to these requirements, whatever readjustments by domestic producers must be executed can be made gradually, even if rates of duties were reduced more rapidly than, for example, at a rate of 5 percent per year.

Given unimpeded economic progress at home and abroad, there need be no fear lest resources freed by marginal enterprises not be taken up by others, such as business firms benefiting from an expansion in production for exports.

In a recent investigation concerning the qualitative effect of a conceivable tariff reduction in eight American industries, on the assumption that the reduction would be gradual and would not be undertaken in a period of general unemployment and falling national income, it was found that lower import duties would affect large-scale manufacturers only peripherally. Certain small-scale industries, though, with a high ratio of labor costs to total manufacturing costs, in some cases aggravated by declining markets, appear to be marginal from the standpoint of the American industry as a whole. Within these marginal industries, increased imports would hit marginal firms hardest. But tariff changes in general do not determine whether or not an entire industry will survive or disintegrate; they determine only the dimensions of the industry. And any lowering of tariff duties on commodities which are sensitive to import competition is a selective process in which only the fringes of an industry—the marginal firms—are cut off.

The small dimension of readaptation is matched by its probable low cost in real terms. The real cost of using resources in any given line of production is the return foregone by what these resources would yield in other lines. The real cost to the economy of not shifting resources from marginal firms in import-sensitive industries appears to be substantial. Conversely, the real cost of a readjustment program in terms of production sacrificed because of a reallocation of resources would be comparatively small. Besides, this small cost will be offset and exceeded, after a reasonable period of time, by the multiplier effect inherent in successful readaptation.

To sum up, the case for adjustment assistance in instances of dislocation by increased competitive imports may be restated briefly. Readjustment assistance can be advocated on two grounds: it benefits the economy through freer trade and better allocation of resources, and it solves the short-term problems that such shifts entail. The fact that freer trade benefits the economy is generally accepted. Since readjustment assistance would facilitate acceptance of imports, it would tend to promote removal of trade restrictions. And since assisted readaptation in the face of increased import competition may be expected to reduce opposition to a further lowering of trade barriers, a readjustment program becomes that much more desirable.

Past opposition to assisted readjustment has concentrated on two points: the administrative complications of the program, and its redundancy in the presence of a gradual lowering of tariff duties. It has been held that a readjustment assistance program could not possibly be instituted without very great difficulties of implementation. To this objection it may be replied that a simple program can be devised that would be no more cumbersome than current measures of protection, and possibly much less so.

It has also been asserted that with a gradual lowering of tariff rates there would be no need to bother with governmental aid in adaptation, since under such circumstances the necessary changes in the industrial structure would take place anyway. The answer to this objection is, that even in a situation like the present, when there exists legislation providing for a gradual decrease of tariff duties over a number of years, there is still a great deal of opposition to a freeing of trade, to judge from testimony before congressional committees studying our trade policy, and from the number of applications for relief from competitive imports processed by the Tariff Commission. Therefore, even with a gradual reduction of tariff duties, a comparatively simple trade adjustment program, that cuts down resistance to increased imports, would enhance the boon to economic progress.

Part VII: Questions for Analysis

1. American history, to the present day, reveals considerable controversy over the issue of freedom of trade.
   a) What position does Friedrich List take with respect to freedom of trade?
   b) Does Frederick Bastiat agree with List's position? If not, explain why Bastiat disagrees.
2. Friedrich List and Frederick Bastiat lived about a century ago. Do their writings on the question of freedom of trade have any relevance to the present day? If so, How?
3. *a*) The U.S. dollar is important in international trade. Trace the evolution of its position in world trade, as presented by the Federal Reserve Bank of San Francisco.
   b) In the years immediately following World War II there was a dollar shortage. More recently, the U.S. has faced a serious balance-of-payments deficit. Explain the profound changes which have taken place in the world which underlie this shift.

4. *a*) According to Robert R. Bowie and Theodore Geiger, what are the driving forces behind European integration? Why did England originally hold back from joining the European Economic Community? Why did England subsequently initiate action to join the EEC?
   b) Is the development of the EEC important to the United States? Support your answer.
5. *a*) Review the essential features of the proposed Trade Expansion Act of 1962, as transmitted by President John F. Kennedy to the Congress.
   b) What arguments did the President advance to support the proposed bill? Do you agree with them? Why?
6. Otto R. Reischer distinguishes between unassisted and assisted readjustment to increased foreign competition. What are the major points he makes in connection with the two types of readjustment? Do you think the federal government should aid industries hurt by foreign competition? Explain.

VIII THE PUBLIC ECONOMY

A major consequence of two world wars, continuing international tension, and a great depression is big government. However, there is considerable controversy as to the need for further growth. Barbara Ward, English economist, presents the affirmative argument, whereas Henry C. Wallich questions the desirability of such a development.

The budget is the instrument employed by government to record its expenditures and revenues. It is also employed for the purpose of planning the government's role in the economy.

Since the administrative budget, the one customarily referred to as "the budget," does not include certain important cash receipts and cash expenditures of the federal government, such as payments in and out of trust funds like Old Age and Survivors Insurance and Unemployment Insurance, it is vital that we note the origin and nature of both the cash budget and the national income accounts budget. In so doing we obtain a complete picture of the flow of funds to and from the federal government. The Council of Economic Advisers presents a discussion of the budget, showing the relationships of the administrative, cash, and national income accounts budgets. The extracts from *The Federal Budget in Brief*, fiscal year 1963, provide summary information on federal expenditures and revenues, as well as excerpts from President Kennedy's 1963 budget message to the Congress.

Government expansion has been financed by taxation and borrowing. The latter has resulted in the creation of a large public debt. Warren L. Smith, of the University of Michigan, discusses the size, burden, ownership, and structure of the national debt.

A. Growth

46. THE NEED FOR FURTHER GROWTH: A POSITIVE VIEWPOINT*

Barbara Ward

In the last year, an issue has come to the fore in America that could —particularly with an election ahead—provide the focus for a more precise and pointed debate than is usual amid the confused controversies of democratic politics.

The issue, at its simplest, is the question whether the United States is spending too much on its private necessities and enjoyments and, as a result, skimping the broad public needs and services that are vital to its very social and national existence.

Clearly, this is an urgent issue. In the public sector lie most of the critical necessities for survival. The arms race, the space race, the tough contest with the Soviets in the fields of economic assistance, basic research and education all depend, in very large measure, upon public expenditure. And, quite apart from these challenges of "competitive coexistence," some of the most urgent long-term needs of the community —in urban living, in provision for a bounding birthrate, in conservation, in water supplies—also depend heavily upon public spending. If its level is too low and the community is unwilling to raise it, safety abroad and amenity at home are alike endangered.

This, the critics maintain, has more than purely political and economic implications; it also raises moral questions of the first order. Wealth has always meant, above all else, elbowroom and choice, and history is strewn with the wreck of individuals and groups and classes who used this elbowroom to make frivolous and ridiculous choices—playing at shepherds and shepherdesses with Marie Antoinette, jumping horses over recumbent peasants with the Esterhazys, drinking champagne out of chorus girls' shoes with the rampant Edwardians, doing the year-long round of beaches, yachts and night spots with today's cafe society.

But if a whole nation acquires wealth beyond any earlier human dream, it, too, can opt for the trivial temptations of the rich. The modern moralists see in tail-fins and mink earmuffs more than the virtuosity of the ad men. They see a society corrupted, as so many rich groups have

* Barbara Ward, "The Great Silence in the Great Debate," *New York Times Magazine* (May 8, 1960), pp. 26, 89–90.

been corrupted in the past, by a scale of choice that exhilarates and bemuses and finally extinguishes all sense of the proper ends of man.

And, when all the political, social and moral implications of the issue are admitted, there remains one more over-riding reason for the central character of the debate. It points to the most sensitive area in the voter's make-up—his pocketbook. Whatever the long-term possibility that rapid economic growth could cover the rising need for both public and private expenditure, in the short run there is only one way to provide more funds for public needs—that is by lessening private spending. Higher taxes in one form or another—in other words, financial sacrifices—seem an inescapable consequence of any concrete policy of meeting public needs more fully.

There is thus no issue in current politics that could touch on so many fundamental points of national life—survival, amenity, economic sacrifice, the voters' choice. And all its themes could be further sharpened and defined by the coming electoral campaign, during which—if democracy is to work effectively—the issues should be set before the voters with all the thrust and clarity candidates can muster.

Given their urgency, one might even envisage these questions as the subject matter of debates as weighty and significant as the Lincoln-Douglas exchanges a century ago. Carried by television to the voters throughout the land, they might raise the campaign above trivialities and personalities and provide the world with a noble spectacle of free men determining their political destiny by the full exercise of reason and inquiry.

But the chances today seem not much to favor any such sharp focusing of the issues. In some fields the difficulty lies in the voter's sense that he does not command the facts. Ought he to side firmly with those who tell him America's defense posture is adequate when as many voices assure him that it is not? Can he determine whether Russia's rate of economic growth offers a threat to Western society when so many economists give not only a different estimate of the Russian threat but even disagree profoundly about America's growth rate? Should he be perturbed about the Soviet's apparent predominance in, for instance, the mobilization of engineers, linguists and scientists, or does it simply reflect different rates of expansion in the two populations?

Every now and then, he may feel he has a grip on some absolute comparison. A Soviet rocket has hit the moon. Russians, not Americans, photographed its dark face. But then the mists of controversy swirl back over the few peaks of hard fact and he is left with perhaps a sense of malaise but with little feeling of certainty or conviction.

Another obstacle to a clear definition of the issues is the apparent difficulty of assessing their scale and cost. There are a number of fairly general estimates. A survey made by the Twentieth Century Fund some years ago suggested that public expenditure fell short of requirements by some $9 to $10 billion annually. More recently, the Rockefeller Brothers Fund showed a level of non-defense public spending running at two-thirds the pre-war level. To return to the old proportion would also indicate a figure—like the Twentieth Century Fund's—of about $10 billion extra. If to this were added $4 to $5 billion for more defense spending and more economic assistance, it would take no time at all to reach a $95 billion budget.

This figure has to be set against a vast national income rising above $500 billion. Yet it presents so horrific an image to most voters that the tendency is to leave the price tag out of the argument. This can be done by talking of filling in tax loopholes and ending tax evasion, by pointing to future rates of growth which will take care of the extra expenditure and by leaving the actual degree of extra taxation somewhat shadowy. Yet these procedures, however understandable, serve only to confuse the debate and blur its sharp outline in a fog of generalities.

Another debate-stopper can be found in the reactions of those who say: "It may be that Russia is pulling ahead and that we are in danger of being outpaced by the totalitarians. But if we permit government at home to spend more, we shall so increase its encroachments on personal liberty that we will simply become totalitarians by another route. Why, therefore, fight the Russian dictatorship by means that create a dictatorship at home?"

This argument has in European ears an ominous resemblance to the debate in Britain over rearming against Hitler in the Thirties. The question was then asked why Britain should rearm to fight a dictatorial government when a large arms program inevitably meant total government intervention in Britain itself—an argument that played its part in insuring the country's awful nakedness before the German onslaught of 1940.

Today the fear of Big Government is so widespread and so well publicized in the United States that in many circles it is enough to state that a program, however essential, involves further government action and the discussion comes to an abrupt stop.

But the greatest obstacle to a great public dialogue is probably the little taste voters have for great issues in good times. "Peace and prosperity" gave Mr. Macmillan his victory last fall in a campaign as barren of urgent debate as any in Britain's history. It could have the same blanketing effect in the United States.

Peace may seem precarious under the shadow of the bomb and of Soviet pressure on Berlin. But in a sense Mr. Khrushchev has cried "wolf" so often that the risks seem too familiar to stir up immediate anxiety. Meanwhile, there is enough talk of disarmament in the headlines to mask the underlying threat.

As for prosperity, it is real enough, the pockets of unemployment are small, prices steady, growth rates have increased and many prophets are prepared to argue that with population increasing by 2 per cent a year and productivity by 3, such built-in accelerators will insure a 4 to 5 per cent rate of expansion throughout the Sixties and thus take care quite comfortably of both rising private and public needs.

The issues thus evaporate in a certain euphoria, and between the alternatives of strong action to re-equip American society for its domestic and international tasks and of allowing the "natural" trend of expansion to look after everything, there is no doubt that the second course has a very strong appeal. All this would change with any new, real and inescapable threat from the Communists. It could be undermined by a downturn in the economy. But the latter is not foreseen for 1960. As for the former, it is strictly unpredictable and so does not affect popular reactions.

There is therefore a risk that no large and sustained debate will be forthcoming on America's fate and future—and this could have far-reaching and tragic consequences both for the United States and for its allies. The issues in the debate will not become less urgent for being bypassed. The Communist challenge will not diminish by being overlaid, nor will the great forces of historical change wait until the community is ready to consider them. Democracies cannot survive on ignorance or indifference in an age of total communication and total engagement.

Yet what are the chances of anything like a serious dialogue breaking through the surface preoccupations and distractions of today's Western electorates? What hope is there, specifically, that 1960 could bring to the greatest of the democracies a shift of interest to deeper issues and more urgent needs?

Inevitably, the answer depends in some measure upon the leaders of opinion. The kind of campaign that the Presidential candidates decide to conduct will help to determine whether the public mind is jolted out of familiar ruts of self-interest and easy recrimination into wider awareness and engagement.

Responsible leaders in the whole communications industry—newspapers, magazines and television—will determine in some degree the breadth and pertinence of the public debate. Educators have a special opportunity since there is evidence from every side of less conformity and more adventurous interest among the young. All these are the men and women who can help set the *form* of the debate, and their responsibility is immense.

Nevertheless, they cannot carry the discussion forward if the electorate turns its back and walks away. The hope of democracy must be informed and widespread participation. What are its chances in the present crisis of our times?

There are perhaps some grounds for hope. If the present public mood is compared with that of the Twenties and Thirties, it is more informed and responsible. The context within which the public dialogue takes place has grown more ample. Parochialism has waned. The man in the street knows, even if only obscurely, that he is a man in the world as well.

Again, it is just possible that the present absorption of citizens in private needs and purchases represents no more than the first, astonished reaction of the *nouveaux riches*. The intoxication will not last and elbowroom, at some point, will bring not further dissipation but responsibility.

History provides some evidence of this. From group to group in the West, from Whig magnates to county burgesses, from landed gentry to rising businessmen, from inherited estates to earned property, some tradition of *noblesse oblige* has been handed on. The men who guided the reforms of Victorian England were, in the main, comfortable men who were moved, not by self-interest, but by public concern and Christian conscience.

Today, in relation to the world at large, Western electorates as a whole are comparable in wealth and elbowroom to the small middle class of a century ago. It is at least possible that they are susceptible to the same promptings of duty and compassion.

But these are only hopes, not certainties. The overriding impression is still one of puzzlement at best, of apathy at worst, and it would be a bold prophet who would say that either awareness or generosity is spreading at the same rate as the challenge and the need. And since there is no inevitable law by which free peoples, however inconsequential, always triumph over dictatorial systems, however dedicated, the lack of great and focused purposes in free society could still mean the end of free society itself.

47. THE NEED FOR FURTHER GROWTH: A QUESTIONING VIEWPOINT*

Henry C. Wallich

As President Kennedy's program unfolded after January 20, the financial storm flags that had gone up during and after the campaign came down abruptly. The outflow of gold, which had been nourished by campaign talk about easy money and big budgets, came to a halt. This was the financial world's way of saying that it regarded the program as moderate and not very different from what the Republican program would have been. It looked as if both parties had something to cheer about: the Democrats had their man, the Republicans had their program.

* Henry C. Wallich, "The Easy Chair: Private vs. Public, Could Kenneth Galbraith Be Wrong?" *Harper's Magazine*, Vol. 223, No. 1337 (October, 1961), pp. 12, 14, 16, 22, 25.

But it would scarcely be fair to the President's advisers, whose views are well known, to assume that a few months in office have fundamentally changed their minds. Their problem is that the gold flow is not just a barometer. It is a positive check. The United States cannot afford a program that would undermine confidence in the dollar. It puts the Administration's economists in the position of Oscar Wilde's French-speaking Englishman, who said not what he wanted to say, but what he could say. If and when the gold situation permits, their economic pronouncements will probably recover the familiar ring.

This ring has been made familiar by the writings of J. K. Galbraith, Seymour Harris, Arthur Schlesinger, Jr., Alvin Hansen, and others. It rejects our ancient American folklore that politicians spend too much. In its place it puts the intriguing notion that they spend too little. Public needs are underfinanced while private tastes are overindulged—that is the proposition.

The two parts of the proposition seem neatly to complement each other—too much of one, therefore too little of the other. In fact they don't. It is one thing to be irritated by certain manifestations of our contemporary civilization—the gadgets, the chrome, the tailfins, and the activities that go with them. It is quite another—and something of a *non sequitur*—to conclude from this that the only alternative to foolish private spending is public spending. Better private spending is just as much of a possibility. My contention here will be that to talk in terms of "public vs. private" is to confuse the issue. More than that, it is to confuse means and ends. The choice between public and private money is primarily a choice of means. The sensible approach for those who are dissatisfied with some of the ends to which private money is being spent, is to specify first what other ends are important and why. Having determined the ends, the next step is to look to the means. That is the order in which I propose to proceed here.

WHAT IS WRONG WITH PRIVATE SPENDING?

One may share the irritation of the new social critics as they look upon some of the fluff and the floss on our standard of living. My personal feelings can be characterized by noting that I have a 1951 car and no TV. The critics may want to bear in mind, however, that not all the money in this country is spent by people for whom life begins at $25,000. The median family income is $5,600. Would these critics of the affluent society want to try living on much less than that? When Galbraith inveighs eloquently against switchblades, narcotics, and other phases of juvenile delinquency, he deserves the support of all right-thinking representatives of what he calls the "conventional wisdom." But are the sources of these aberrations more intimately tied to affluence or to poverty? The exponents of the new social criticism may also want to remember the outcome of that "noble experiment," Prohibition. It should have taught us that it is futile to become our brother's dietitian. I hope that it has also imbued us with wholesome doubt about the moral right of some members of the community to regulate the lives of the rest.

Irritation with the poor judgment of other people who fail to appreciate one's own more advanced tastes is not new. It was a familiar situation during the 1920s. The critics then quoted T. S. Eliot's *The Waste Land*, and some went off to Paris in search of greener cultural pastures. The feeling behind the new social criticism is not dissimilar. Hence one might suppose that the reaction would likewise turn in a cultural direction. One might expect the critics of contemporary materialism to plead for more intensive preoccupation with things of the mind. Some fits and starts in that direction there have been, to be sure. But they have not been in the main stream of the movement. The principal alternative to private materialism that has been offered to us has been public materialism.

SIGNS OF QUALITY

Obviously, the quality of our culture could be greatly improved by public expenditures for education and support of the arts. The sales of good paperbacks and LPs are encouraging signs. But if contemporary materialism is to be leavened by such pursuits, it will be principally because large numbers of individuals make private decisions to that end. Social criticism is constructive if it helps precipitate these decisions. It obstructs a desirable evolution if it suggests that public creature comforts are the only alternative to private.

But while emphasis on nonmaterial ends seems sadly lacking in the new social criticism, the critics are right in pointing out that new material needs also have been carried to the fore by social and economic evolution—even though they mislabel them as public needs. In the good old days, when this was still a nation of farmers, most people had no serious retirement worries, there was no industrial unemployment problem, good jobs could be had without a college degree, most diseases were still incurable—in short, social security, education, and health care found primitive and natural solutions within the family and among the resources of the neighborhood. Today, these solutions are neither adequate nor usually even possible.

Meanwhile mounting wealth and advancing technology have brought within reach the means of meeting these needs. We can afford to live better in every way—more creature comforts, more leisure, more attention to matters of the mind and the spirit. At the same time we can take better care of retirement, of unemployment, of illness, of education, of the possibilities opened by research, than ever before.

There are indeed new needs. The citizen-taxpayer has his choice of meeting them, as well as all his other needs, in one of two ways. He can buy the goods or services he wants privately, for cash or credit. Or he can buy them from the government, for taxes.

The nation as a whole pays taxes to buy public services as it pays grocery bills to buy groceries. The tax burden may be heavier for some individuals than for others. But the nation as a whole has no more reason to complain about the "burden" of taxes than about the "burden" of grocery bills—and no more reason to hope for relief.

Of the two stores, the private store today still is much the bigger. The public store is smaller, but it is growing faster.

Each store has some exclusive items. The private store sells most of the necessities and all of the luxuries of life, and in most of these has no competition from the government side. The public store has some specialties of its own: defense, public order and justice, and numerous local services that the private organization has not found profitable. But there is a wide range of items featured by both stores: provision for old age, health services, education, housing, development of natural resources.

THE NEW NEEDS

The bulk of the new needs are in this competitive area. The fashionable notion is to claim them all for the public store and to label them public needs. The statistics say otherwise. They say in fact two things: First, the supply of this group of goods and services has expanded very rapidly in recent years; and second, they are being offered, in varying degrees, both by the private and the public suppliers. Let us run down the list.

Provision for Old Age Is Predominantly Private

The average American family, realizing that while old age may be a burden, it is the only known way to achieve a long life, takes care of the matter in three ways: (1) by private individual savings—home ownership, savings deposits, securities; (2) by private collective savings—life insurance, corporate pension funds; and (3) by public collective savings through social security. Statisticians report that the two collective forms are advancing faster than the individual. The increases far exceed the rise in the Gross National Product of almost 80 per cent (in current prices) over the past ten years; they do not indicate either that these needs are neglected or that they are necessarily public in character.

Education: the Bulk of It Is Public; but a Good Part, Particularly of Higher Education, Is Private

Total expenditures for all education have advanced in the last ten years from $9.3 billion to $24.6 billion ($19.3 billion of it public). Education's share in the national income has advanced from 3.8 per cent to 5.8 per cent. The silly story that we spend more on advertising than on education is a canard, though with its gross of over $10 billion, advertising does take a lot of money.

Health Expenditures Are Still Mainly Private

At considerable expense, it is now possible to live longer and be sick less frequently or at least less dangerously. In the past, most people paid their own doctors' bills, although health care for the indigent has always been provided by public action or private philanthropy. Since the war, the proliferation of health insurance has given some form of collective but private insurance to three-quarters of our 182 million people. This has greatly reduced pressure for a national health service along British lines. For the aging, whose health-care needs stand in inverse proportion to their capacity to pay or insure, public insurance has finally been initiated and needs to be expanded. The total annual expenditure on health is estimated at over $25 billion, a little more than on education. Of this, about $6 billion is public.

So much for the allegation that the "new needs" are all public needs. Now for some further statistics on the public store, which is said to have been neglected. Some of them could make an investor in private growth stocks envious. Research expenditures (mainly for defense and atomic energy) have gone from about $1 billion to over $8 billion in the last ten years. Federal grants to the states have advanced from $2.2 billion to $7 billion during the same period. Social-security benefits rose from $1 billion to over $10 billion. All in all, public cash outlays (federal and state) advanced from $61 billion to $134 billion over ten years, 57 per cent faster than the GNP.

For those who feel about public spending the way Mark Twain felt about whiskey, these figures may still look slim. (Mark Twain thought that while too much of anything was bad, too much whiskey was barely enough.) To others, the data may suggest that the advocates of more public spending have already had their way. Could their present discontent be the result of a not keeping their statistics up-to-date? In one of his recent pamphlets, Arthur M. Schlesinger, Jr. claims that the sum of the many neglects he observes (including defense) could be mended by raising public expenditures by $10 to $12 billion. That is well below the increase in public cash outlays that actually did take place in one single fiscal year, from $118.2 billion in 1958 to $132.7 billion in 1959. In the three fiscal years 1957–59, these outlays went up more than $31 billion, though the advance slowed down in 1960. More facts and less indignation might help to attain better perspective.

Some parts of federal, state, and local budgets have expanded less rapidly than those cited—in many cases fortunately. The massive build-up in defense expenditures from the late 'forties to the 'fifties has squeezed other programs. Unfortunately, on the other hand, some programs that both political parties have favored—including aid to education, to depressed areas, for urban renewal—have been delayed unduly by the vicissitudes of politics. But the figures as a whole lend little support to the thesis that politicians don't spend enough, and that the government store is not expanding fast enough.

THE CITIZEN IN THE STORES

The two stores—private and public—work very hard these days to capture the business of the citizen-taxpayer. Here is what he hears as he walks into the private store:

"The principal advantage of this store," the private businessman says, "is that you can shop around and buy exactly what you want. If I don't have it I'll order it. You, the consumer, are the boss here. To be sure, I'm not in business for charity but for profit. But my profit comes from giving you what you want. And with competition as fierce as it is, you can be sure the profit won't be excessive."

If the proprietor has been to Harvard Business School, he will perhaps remember to add something about the invisible hand which in a free economy causes the self-seeking of competitors to work for the common good. He will also, even without benefit of business school, remember to drop a word about the danger of letting the public store across the street get too big. It might endanger freedom.

As the citizen turns this sales talk over in his mind, several points occur to him. Without denying the broad validity of the argument, he will note that quite often he has been induced to buy things he did not really need, and possibly to neglect other, more serious needs. Snob appeal and built-in obsolescence promoted by expensive advertising don't seem to him to fit in with the notion that the consumer is king. Looking at the brand names and patents and trademarks, he wonders whether most products are produced and priced competitively instead of under monopoly conditions. The invisible hand at times seems to be invisible mainly because it is so deep in his pocket.

Bothered by these doubts, the citizen walks across the street and enters the public store.

"Let me explain to you," says the politician who runs it—with the aid of a horde of hard-working bureaucrats doing the chores. "The principles on which this store is run are known as the political process, and if you happen to be familiar with private merchandising they may seem unusual, but I assure you they work. First of all, almost everything in this store is free. We simply assess our customers a lump sum in the form of taxes. These, however, are based largely on each customer's ability to pay, rather than on what he gets from the store. We have a show of hands from the customers once a year, and the majority decides what merchandise the store is to have in stock. The majority, incidentally, also decides how much everybody, including particularly the minority, is to be assessed for taxes.

"You will observe," the politician continues, "that this store is not run for profit. It is like a co-operative, run for the welfare of the members. I myself, to be sure, am not in politics for charity, but for re-election. But that means that I must be interested in your needs, or you would not vote for me. Moreover, there are some useful things that only I can do, with the help of the political process, and in which you and every citizen have an interest. For instance, everybody ought to go to school. I can make them go. Everybody ought to have old-age insurance. I can make that compulsory too. And because I don't charge the full cost of the service, I can help even up a little the inequalities of life.

"By the way," the politician concludes, "if there is any special little thing you want, I may be able to get it for you, and of course it won't cost you a nickel."

The citizen has some fault to find with the political process too. He notes that there is not even a theoretical claim to the benefits of an invisible hand. Majority rule may produce benefits for the majority, but how about the other 49 per cent? Nor is there the discipline of competition, or the need for profits, to test economy of operation. There is no way, in the public store, of adjusting individual costs and benefits. And the promise to get him some small favor, while tempting, worries him, because he wonders what the politician may have promised to others. The political process, he is led to suspect, may be a little haphazard.

He asks himself how political decisions get to be made. Sometimes, obviously, it is not the majority that really makes a decision, but a small pressure group that is getting away with something. He will remember that—after payments for major national security and public debt interest—the largest single expenditure in the federal budget is for agriculture, and the next for veterans. He may also recall that one of the first budgetary actions of the new Administration was to increase funds for agriculture by $3 billion.

THE EXPANDING BELT

Next, the citizen might consider the paralyzing "balance-of-forces" effect that often blocks a desirable reshuffling of expenditures. The allocation of public funds reflects the bargaining power of their sponsors, inside or outside the government. A classical example was the division of funds that prevailed in the Defense Department during the late 'forties. Army, Navy, and Air Force were to share in total resources in a way that would maximize military potential. By some strange coincidence, maximum potential was always achieved by giving each service the same amount of money. It took the Korean War to break this stalemate.

What is the consequence of the balance-of-forces effect? If the proponents of one kind of expenditure want to get more money for their projects, they must concede an increase also to the advocates of others. More education means more highways, instead of less; more air power means more ground forces. To increase a budget in one direction only is as difficult as letting out one's belt only on one side. The expansion tends to go all around. What this comes down to is that politicians are not very good at setting priorities. Increases in good expenditures are burdened with a political surcharge of less good ones.

The last-ditch survival power of federal programs is a specially illuminating instance of the balance of forces. If a monument were built in Washington in memory of each major federal program that has been discontinued, the appearance of the city would not be greatly altered. In contrast, when the Edsel doesn't sell, production stops. But the government is still reclaiming land to raise more farm surpluses and training fishermen to enter an occupation that needs subsidies to keep alive. Old federal programs never die, they don't even fade away—they just go on.

The citizen will remember also the ancient and honorable practice of logrolling. The unhappy fate of the Area Development bill illustrates it admirably. As originally proposed, the bill sought to aid a limited number of industrial areas where new jobs were badly needed. It got nowhere in the Congress. Only when it was extended to a large number of areas with less urgent or quite different problems, were enough legislators brought aboard to pass it. Because of the heavy political surcharge with which it had become loaded, President Eisenhower vetoed the bill. A bill was finally enacted early this year, long after aid should have been brought to the areas that needed it.

Finally, the citizen might discover in some dark corner of his mind a nagging thought: Any particular government program may be a blessing, but could their cumulative effect be a threat to freedom? He has heard businessmen say this so often that he has almost ceased to pay attention to it. He rather resents businessmen acting the dog in the manger, trying to stop useful things from being done unless they can do them. He is irritated when he hears a man talk about freedom who obviously is thinking about profit. And yet—is there any conclusive rebuttal?

THE CITIZEN'S FAILURES

The citizen would be quite wrong, however, if he blamed the politician for the defects of the political process. The fault lies with the process, or better with the way in which the process, the politician, and the citizen interact. The citizen therefore would do well to examine some of his own reactions and attitudes.

First, when he thinks about taxes, he tends to think of them as a burden instead of as a price he pays for a service. As a body, the nation's taxpayers are like a group of neighbors who decide to establish a fire department. Because none is quite sure how much good it will do him, and because each hopes to benefit from the contribution of the rest, all are prudent in their contributions. In the end they are likely to wind up with a bucket brigade.

But when it comes to accepting benefits, the citizen-taxpayers act like a group of men who sit down at a restaurant table knowing that they will split the check evenly. In this situation everybody orders generously; it adds little to one's own share of the bill, and for the extravagance of his friends he will have to pay anyhow. What happens at the restaurant table explains—though it does not excuse—what happens at the public trough.

Finally, in his reaction to public or free services, the citizen takes a great deal for granted, and seldom thinks of the cost. Public beaches mistreated, unmetered parking space permanently occupied, veterans' adjustment benefits continued without need—as well as abuses of unemployment compensation and public assistance—are some examples. This applies also, of course, to privately offered benefits, under health insurance, for instance. The kindly nurse in the hospital—"Why don't you stay another day, dearie, it won't cost you anything, it's all paid for by Blue Cross"—makes the point.

By removing the link between costs and benefits, the political process also reduces the citizen's interest in earning money. The citizen works to live. If some of his living comes to him without working, he would be less than rational if he did not respond with a demand for shorter hours. If these public benefits increase his tax burden so that his over-all standard of living remains unchanged, the higher taxes will reduce his work incentive. Why work hard, if much of it is for the government?

THE POLITICAL DOLLAR AT A DISCOUNT

These various defects of the political process add up to an obvious conclusion: the dollar spent by even the most honest and scrupulous of politicians is not always a full-bodied dollar. It often is subject to a discount. It buys less than it should because of the attrition it suffers as it goes through the process, and so may be worth only 90 cents or 80 cents and sometimes perhaps less. The private dollar, in too many cases, may also be worth less than 100 per cent. But here each man can form his own judgment, can pick and choose or refuse altogether. In the political process, all he can do is say Yes or No once a year in November.

The discount on the public dollar may be compensated by the other advantages of government—its ability to compel, to subsidize, to do things on a big scale and at a low interest cost. Whether that is the case needs to be studied in each instance. Where these advantages do not apply, the private market will give better service than the political process. For many services, there is at least some leeway for choice between the private and public store—health and retirement, housing, research, higher education, natural-resource development. Defense, on the other hand, as well as public administration, public works of all kinds, and the great bulk of education—while perhaps made rather expensive by the political process—leave no realistic alternative to public action.

The argument I have offered is no plea to spend more or less on any particular function. It is a plea for doing whatever we do in the most effective way.

B. The Budget

48. THE NATIONAL INCOME ACCOUNTS BUDGET VIS-A-VIS OTHER BUDGETARY CONCEPTS*

The Council of Economic Advisers

The Federal budget has influenced economic activity in recent years in two ways: through the workings of the built-in stabilizers, and through discretionary changes in the budget program. It is not easy to separate these two influences. In order to do so, it is necessary, first, to view Federal fiscal transactions in the same accounting framework used to describe the whole economy. The *national income accounts budget* is a way of measuring and classifying Federal transactions which accords with the national income and product accounts for the economy. Second, it is convenient to have a numerical measure of the expansionary or restrictive impact of a budget program on the economy. The *full employment surplus* is such a measure. This section discusses these two somewhat unfamiliar but highly useful tools and then applies them in an analysis of recent and prospective budget policies.

THE NATIONAL INCOME ACCOUNTS BUDGET

The effects of Federal receipts and expenditures on the income stream are most accurately represented when the budget is viewed in the framework of the national income accounts. These accounts present a consistent record and classification of the major flows of output and income for the entire economy, including the transactions of the Federal

* *Economic Report of the President, January 1962* (Washington, D.C.: U.S. Government Printing Office, 1962), pp. 77–81.

Government. There are three major differences between the Federal budget as it is conventionally presented (the so-called "administrative budget") and the accounts of the Federal sector as they appear in the national income. The major differences between these two budgets, and between both of them and the consolidated cash budget, are schematically summarized in Table 7. There are other, less significant differences among the budgets, such as the treatment of intragovernmental transactions.

First, the national income accounts budget, like the consolidated cash budget, includes the transactions of the trust funds, which amount currently to about $25 billion per year and have a significant impact on

TABLE 7

MAJOR DIFFERENCES AMONG THREE CONCEPTS OF THE FEDERAL BUDGET

Item	Budget Concept		
	Administrative	Consolidated Cash	National Income Accounts
Timing of receipts	Collections	Collections	Accruals
Treatment of net loans and other credit transactions	Included	Included	Excluded
Treatment of trust fund transactions	Excluded	Included	Included

Source: Council of Economic Advisers.

the economy. Highway grants-in-aid, unemployment compensation payments, and social security benefits are examples of trust fund transactions. Because the traditional budget—or administrative budget—is primarily an instrument of management and control of those Federal activities which operate through regular congressional appropriations, it excludes the trust funds, which have their own legal sources of revenue.

Second, transactions between government and business are, so far as possible, recorded in the national income accounts budget when liabilities are incurred rather than when cash changes hands. This adjustment in timing affects both government purchases and taxes, shifting them to the point in time at which they are likely to have their principal impact on private spending decisions. The choice of an accrual, rather than a cash, basis for timing is particularly important for the highly volatile corporate income tax. Since these taxes are normally paid more than six months after the liabilities are incurred, payments of corporate income taxes, as recorded in the administrative budget, run substantially below accruals in a period of rising economic activity. For fiscal year 1962, this difference is estimated at about $3 billion.

Finally, unlike the administrative budget, the national income accounts budget omits government transactions in financial assets and already existing assets. The largest omission is the volume of loans extended by the Federal Government. This volume is estimated at $4 billion net of repayments in fiscal year 1962. While these loans have important effects on economic activity, they are properly viewed as an aspect, not of fiscal policy, but of monetary and credit policy. . . . Borrowers from the Federal Government, like borrowers from private financial institutions, acquire cash by incurring debts. They add thereby to their liquidity, but not directly to their incomes.

THE FULL EMPLOYMENT SURPLUS

As pointed out earlier in this chapter, the magnitude of the surplus or deficit in the budget depends both on the budget program and on the state of the economy. The budget program fixes both tax rates and expenditure programs. The revenues actually yielded by most taxes, and the actual expenditures under certain programs like unemployment compensation, vary automatically with economic activity. To interpret the economic significance of a given budget it is, therefore, essential to distinguish the *automatic* changes in revenues and expenditures from the *discretionary* changes which occur when the Government varies tax rates or changes expenditure programs. The discussion that follows runs in terms of the national income accounts budget.

In Chart 6 this twofold aspect of fiscal policy is portrayed for the fiscal years 1960 and 1962. Since tax revenues and some expenditures depend on the level of economic activity, there is a whole range of possible surpluses and deficits associated with a given budget program. The particular surplus or deficit in fact realized will depend on the level of economic activity. On the horizontal scale, Chart 6 shows the ratio of actual GNP to the economy's potential, labeled the "utilization rate." On the vertical scale, the chart shows the Federal budget surplus or deficit as a percentage of potential GNP.

The line labeled "fiscal 1960 program" represents a calculation of the budget surplus or deficit which would have occurred at various levels of economic activity, given the Federal expenditure programs and the tax rates of that year. For the reasons explained earlier, the same budget program may yield a high surplus at full employment and a low surplus or a deficit at low levels of economic activity. The actual budget position in fiscal year 1960, a surplus of $2.2 billion or 0.4 percent of potential GNP, is shown at point A; this accompanied a level of GNP 5 percent below potential. Had full employment been achieved that year, however, the same basic budget program would have yielded a surplus of about $10 billion, or nearly 2 percent of gross national product (point F in the chart). The line labeled "1962 program" similarly shows the relationship between economic activity and the surplus or deficit, for the budget program of 1962; the expected deficit is shown at point B, and the full employment surplus at point G.

It is the height of the line in Chart 6 which reflects the basic budget program; the actual surplus or deficit depends both on the height of the program line and the level of economic activity. In other words, discretionary fiscal policy, by changing the level of Government expendi-

Chart 6

Effect of Level of Economic Activity on Federal Surplus or Deficit

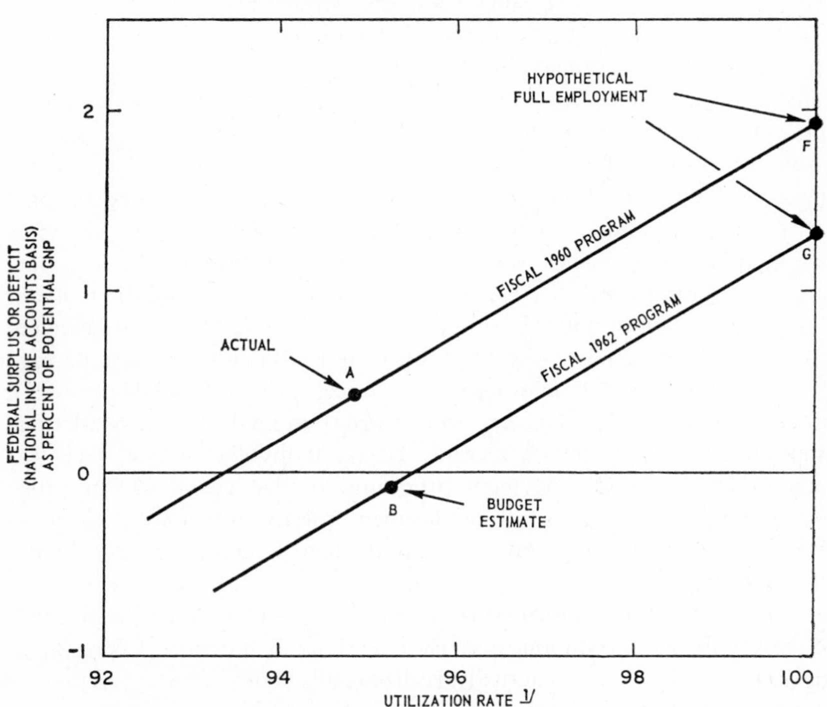

1 Actual GNP is percent of potential GNP.
Source: Council of Economic Advisers.

tures or tax rates shifts the whole program line up or down. The automatic stabilizing effects of a given budget program are reflected in the chart by movements along a given line, accompanying changes in economic activity. One convenient method of comparing alternative budget programs, which separates automatic from discretionary changes in surplus and deficits, is to calculate the surplus or deficit of each alternative program at a fixed level of economic activity. As a convention, this calculation is made on the assumption of full employment. In Chart 6, the points F and G mark the full employment surplus in the budget programs of fiscal years 1960 and 1962, respectively. The statement, "the fiscal

1960 budget had a larger full employment surplus, as a fraction of potential GNP, than the 1962 budget" is a convenient shorthand summary of the fact that the 1962 budget line was below the 1960 line, yielding smaller surpluses or larger deficits at any comparable level of activity.

The full employment surplus rises through time if tax rates and expenditure programs remain unchanged. Because potential GNP grows, the volume of tax revenues yielded by a fully employed economy rises, when tax rates remain unchanged. Full employment revenues under existing tax laws are growing by about $6 billion a year. With unchanged discretionary expenditures, a budget line drawn on Chart 6 would shift upward each year by about 1 percent of potential GNP.

The full employment surplus is a measure of the restrictive or expansionary impact of a budget program on over-all demand. Generally speaking, one budget program is more expansionary than another if it has a smaller full employment surplus. One budget program might have the smaller full employment surplus because it embodies greater Federal purchases of goods and services, in relation to potential GNP. By the same token, it leaves a smaller share of full employment output for private purchase. This means that full employment is easier to maintain under the budget program with the smaller surplus, because less private demand is required. It also means that inflation is more difficult to avoid, because there are fewer goods and services to meet private demand should it prove strong. Alternatively, one budget program might have a smaller full employment surplus than a second because it involves either lower tax rates or larger transfer payment programs. In that event, private after-tax incomes are larger at full employment for the first budget program than for the second. As a result, private demand would be stronger under the first program.

If the full employment surplus is too large, relative to the strength of private demand, economic activity falls short of potential. Correspondingly, the budget surplus actually realized falls short of the full employment surplus; indeed, a deficit may occur. If the full employment surplus is too small, total demand exceeds the capacity of economy and causes inflation.

But whether a given full employment surplus is too large or too small depends on other government policies, as well as on economic circumstances affecting the general strength of private demand. If the full employment surplus is too large, more expansionary monetary and credit policies may strengthen private demand sufficiently to permit full employment to be realized. Changes in tax structure, stimulating demand while leaving the yield of the tax system unchanged, might have the same effect. Similarly, restrictive changes in other government policies can offset the expansionary influence of a low full employment surplus.

49. THE FEDERAL BUDGET FOR 1963*

U.S. Bureau of the Budget

EXCERPTS FROM THE PRESIDENT'S BUDGET MESSAGE

The President transmitted the 1963 Budget to the Congress on January 18, 1962. Excerpts from his budget message follow:

I present with this message my budget recommendations for the fiscal year 1963, beginning next July 1.

This is the first complete budget of this administration. It has been prepared with two main objectives in mind:

First, to carry forward efficiently the activities—ranging from defense to postal services, from oceanographic research to space exploration—which by national consensus have been assigned to the Federal Government to execute;

Second, to achieve a financial plan—a relationship between receipts and expenditures—which will contribute to economic growth, high employment, and price stability in our national economy.

Budget expenditures for fiscal 1963 will total $92.5 billion under my recommendations—an increase of $3.4 billion over the amount estimated for the present fiscal year. More than three-quarters of the increase is accounted for by national security and space activities, and the bulk of the remainder by fixed interest charges.

Because of the increasing requirements for national security, I have applied strict standards of urgency in reviewing proposed expenditures in this budget. Many desirable new projects and activities are being deferred. I am, moreover, recommending legislation which will reduce certain budgetary outlays, such as the postal deficit and the cost of farm price and production adjustments.

It would not, of course, be sensible to defer expenditures which are of great significance to the growth and strength of the Nation. This budget therefore includes a number of increases in existing programs and some new proposals of high priority—such as improvements in education and scientific research, retraining the unemployed and providing young people with greater employment opportunities, and aid to urban mass transportation.

* U.S. Bureau of the Budget, *The Budget in Brief, Fiscal 1963* (Washington, D.C.: U.S. Government Printing Office, 1962), pp. 4–17.

Budget Expenditures as a Percent of Gross National Product

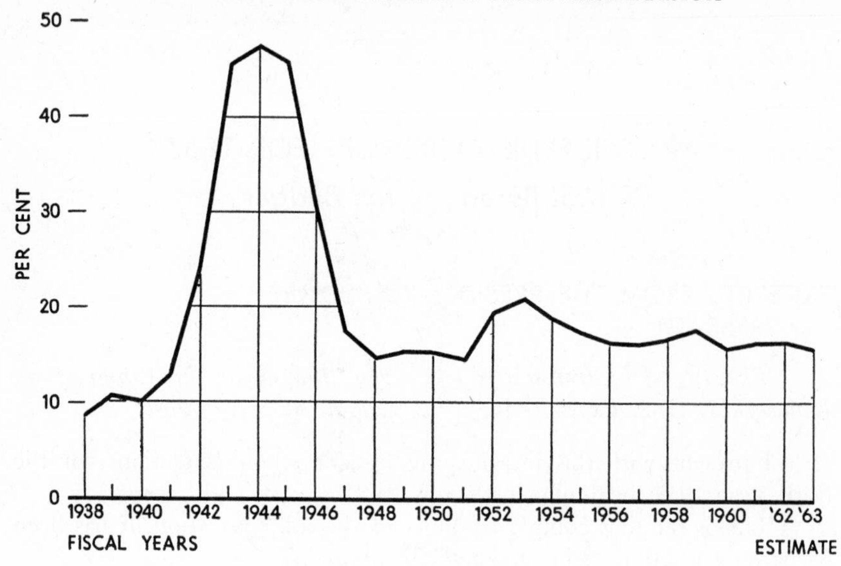

Public Debt as a Percent of Gross National Product

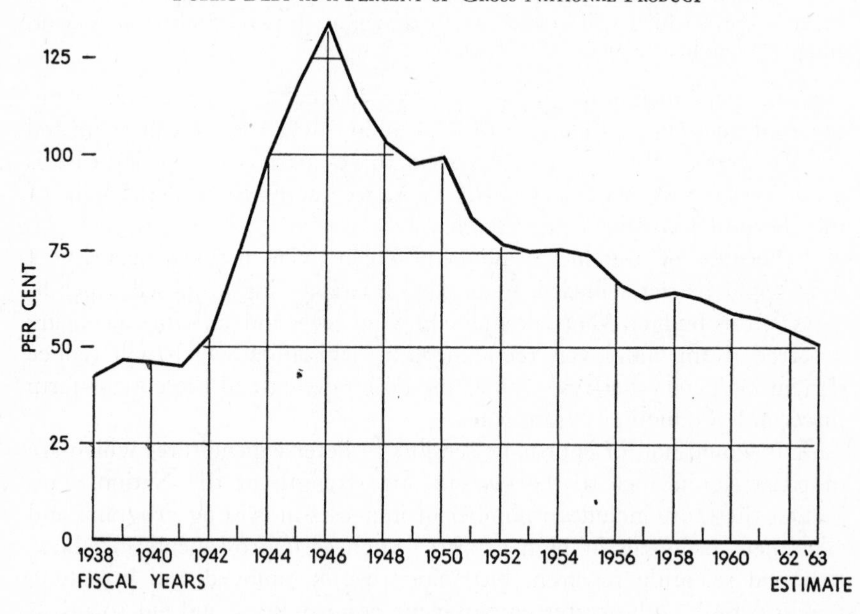

Budget receipts in fiscal year 1963 are estimated to total $93 billion, an increase of $10.9 billion over the recession-affected level of the present fiscal year. These receipts estimates are based on the expectation that the brisk recovery from last year's recession will continue through the coming year and beyond, carrying the gross national product during calendar 1962 to a record $570 billion.

SUMMARY OF FEDERAL FINANCES

(Fiscal Years, In Billions of Dollars)

Description	1959 Actual	1960 Actual	1961 Actual	1962 Estimate	1963 Estimate
Administrative budget:					
Budget receipts	67.9	77.8	77.7	82.1	93.0
Budget expenditures	80.3	76.5	81.5	89.1	92.5
Budget surplus (+) or deficit (−)	−12.4	+1.2	−3.9	−7.0	+0.5
Consolidated cash statement:					
Receipts from the public	81.7	95.1	97.2	102.6	116.6
Payments to the public	94.8	94.3	99.5	111.1	114.8
Excess of receipts (+) or payments (−)	−13.1	+0.8	−2.3	−8.5	+1.8
National-income accounts—Federal sector:					
Receipts	85.4	94.1	94.8	105.6	116.3
Expenditures	90.2	91.9	97.0	106.1	111.9
Surplus (+) or deficit (−)	−4.8	+2.2	−2.2	−0.5	+4.4
New obligational authority (administrative budget)	81.4	79.6	86.7	95.7	99.3
Public debt, end of year	284.7	286.3	289.0	295.4	294.9

The administrative budget for 1963 thus shows a surplus of about $500 million. Federal accounts on the basis of the consolidated cash statement—combining the administrative budget with other Federal activities, mainly the social security, highway, and other trust funds—show an estimated excess of receipts from the public of $1.8 billion over payments to the public. And in the terms in which our national-income accounts are calculated—using accrued rather than cash receipts and expenditures, and including only transactions directly affecting production and income—the Federal surplus is estimated at $4.4 billion.

By all three measures in current use, therefore, the Federal Government is expected to operate in 1963 with some surplus. This is the policy which seems appropriate at the present time. The economy is moving strongly forward, with employment and incomes rising. The prospects are favorable for further rises in the coming year in private expenditures, both consumption and investment. To plan a deficit under such circumstances would increase the risk of inflationary pressures, damaging alike to our domestic economy and to our international balance of payments. On the other hand, we are still far short of full capacity use of plant and manpower. To plan a larger surplus would risk choking off economic recovery and contributing to a premature downturn.

Budget Totals

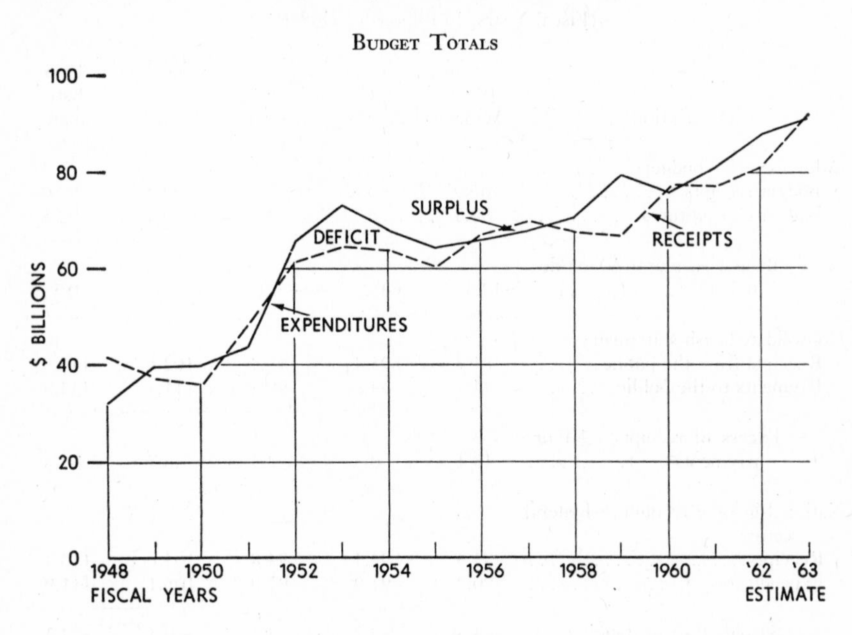

Under present economic circumstances, therefore, a moderate surplus of the magnitude projected above is the best national policy, considering all of our needs and objectives.

BUDGET EXPENDITURES

The total of budget expenditures is determined in large measure by the necessary but costly programs designed to achieve our national security and international objectives in the current world situation. Expenditures for national defense, international, and space programs account for more than three-fifths of total 1963 budget outlays, and for more than three-fourths of the estimated increase in expenditures in 1963 as compared to 1962. Indeed, apart from the expected increase in interest payments, expenditures for the so-called "domestic civil" functions of government have been held virtually stable between 1962 and 1963.

Within this total there are important shifts in direction and emphasis. Expenditures for agricultural programs, for the postal deficit, and

BUDGET EXPENDITURES
(Fiscal Years, In Billions of Dollars)

Function	1961 Actual	1962 Estimate	1963 Estimate
National defense	47.5	51.2	52.7
International affairs and finance	2.5	2.9	3.0
Space research and technology	.7	1.3	2.4
Subtotal	50.7	55.4	58.1
Interest	9.0	9.0	9.4
Domestic civil functions:			
Agriculture and agricultural resources	5.2	6.3	5.8
Natural resources	2.0	2.1	2.3
Commerce and transportation	2.6	2.9	2.5
Housing and community development	.3	.5	.8
Health, labor, and welfare	4.2	4.7	5.1
Education	.9	1.1	1.5
Veterans benefits and services	5.4	5.6	5.3
General government	1.7	1.9	2.0
Subtotal, domestic civil functions	22.4	25.3	25.4
Civilian pay reform	...	...	.2
Allowance for contingencies	...	.1	.2
Deduct interfund transactions	.7	.7	.7
Total budget expenditures	81.5	89.1	92.5

for temporary extended unemployment compensation are expected to drop. The fact that funds for these purposes can be reduced permits us to make increases in other important areas—notably education, health, housing, and natural resource development—without raising significantly total expenditures for domestic civil functions.

National Defense

This budget carries forward the policies instituted within the past 12 months to strengthen our military forces and to increase the flexibility with which they can be controlled and applied. The key elements in our defense program include: a strategic offensive force which would survive and respond overwhelmingly after a massive nuclear attack; a command and control system which would survive and direct the response; an improved anti-bomber defense system; a civil defense program which would help to protect an important proportion of our population from the perils of nuclear fallout; combat-ready limited war forces and the air and sealift needed to move them quickly to wherever they might have to be deployed; and special forces to help our Allies cope with the threat of Communist-sponsored insurrection and subversion.

Increases in expenditures for the Nation's defense are largely responsible for the rise in the budget of this administration compared to that of its predecessor. For fiscal years 1962 and 1963, expenditures for the military functions of the Department of Defense are estimated at about $9 billion higher than would have been required to carry forward the program as it stood a year ago.

For the coming year, the budget provides for:

Further increases in the capabilities of our strategic forces, including additional Minuteman missiles and Polaris submarines.

Additional measures to increase the effectiveness of our antibomber defense system, and further research and development at a maximum rate on antimissile defense possibilities.

An increase in the number of regular Army divisions from 14 to 16.

A substantial increase in the number of regular tactical fighter units of the Air Force and in the procurement of new fighter and reconnaissance aircraft.

Revision of the programs for organization and training of the reserve components so they will be better adapted and better prepared to serve in any emergency.

For civil defense, a new cost-sharing program with State and local governments and private organizations to provide shelters in selected community buildings such as schools and hospitals.

International Affairs and Finance

The new Agency for International Development has been providing needed leadership in coordinating the various elements of our foreign aid programs throughout the world. A consistent effort is being made to relate military and economic assistance to the overall capabilities and needs of recipient countries to achieve economic growth and sustain adequate military strength. To make our assistance more effective, increasing emphasis is being placed on self-help measures and necessary reforms in these countries.

In August 1961 the United States formally joined with its neighbors to the south in the establishment of the Alliance for Progress, an historic cooperative effort to speed the economic and social development of the American Republics. For their part, the Latin American countries agreed to undertake a strenuous program of social and economic reform and development through this decade. As this program of reform and development proceeds, the United States is pledged to help. To this end, I am proposing a special long-term authorization for $3 billion of aid to the Alliance for Progress within the next 4 years. In addition, substantial continued development loans are expected from the Export-Import Bank and from U.S. funds being administered by the Inter-American Development Bank. These, together with the continued flow of agricultural commodities under the Food for Peace Program, will mean support for the Alliance for Progress in 1963 substantially exceeding $1 billion.

Space Research and Technology

Last year I proposed and the Congress agreed that this Nation should embark on a greater effort to explore and make use of the space environment. This greater effort will result in increased expenditures in 1962 and 1963, combined, of about $1.1 billion above what they would have been under the policies of the preceding administration. With this increase in funds there has been a major stepup in the programs of the National Aeronautics and Space Administration in such fields as communications and meteorology and in the most dramatic effort of all—mastery of space symbolized by an attempt to send a man to the moon and back safely to earth.

Our space program has far broader significance, however, than the achievement of manned space flight. The research effort connected with

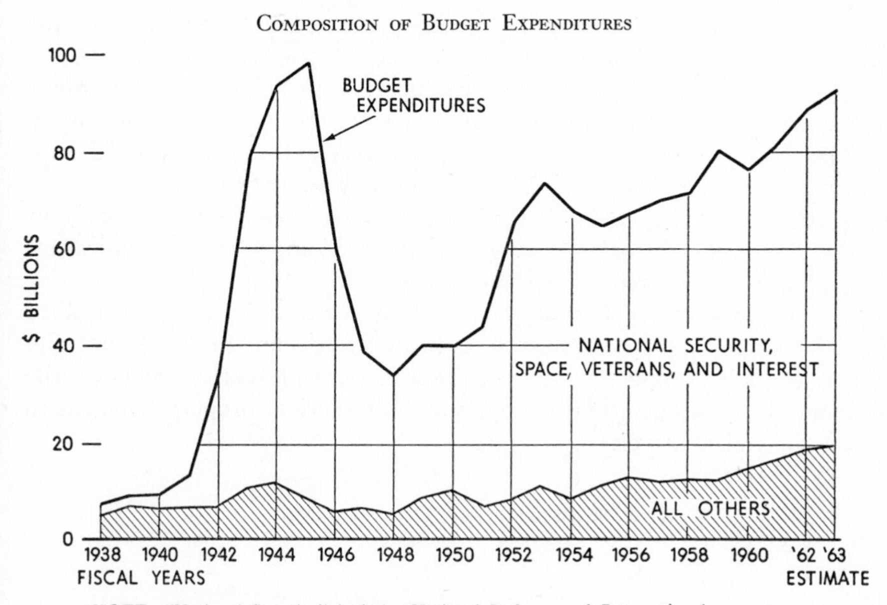

NOTE: "National Security" includes National Defense and International.

the space program—and particularly the tremendous technological advances necessary to permit space flight—will have great impact in increasing the rate of technical progress throughout the economy.

Domestic Civil Functions

Despite the necessary heavy emphasis we are giving to defense, international, and space activities, the budget reflects many important proposals to strengthen our national economy and society. Some of the more important proposals in domestic civil programs are mentioned below.

Agriculture and Agricultural Resources. In the development of farm programs we are striving to make effective use of American agricultural abundance, to adjust farm production to bring it in line with domestic and export requirements, and to maintain and increase income for those who are engaged in farming. The steps taken thus far, including the temporary wheat and feed grain legislation enacted in the last session of the Congress, contributed significantly to the rise in farm income last year and to some reduction—the first in 9 years—in surplus stocks. However, new long-range legislation is needed to permit further adaptation of our farm programs to the rapidly increasing productive efficiency in agriculture and to avoid continuing high budgetary costs.

Natural Resources. Estimated expenditures in 1963 for the conservation and development of our natural resources are higher than in any previous year. The 1963 budget makes provision for the Corps of Engineers, the Bureau of Reclamation, and the Tennessee Valley Authority to start construction on 43 new water resources projects with an estimated total Federal cost of $600 million. The long-range programs for the national parks and forests are also being strengthened.

One of our most pressing problems is the provision of outdoor recreational facilities to meet the needs of our expanding population. The Federal Government, State and local agencies, and private groups must all share in the solution. The Secretary of the Interior, at my request, is preparing a plan for the Federal Government to meet its share of the responsibility for providing outdoor recreational opportunities, including those related to fish and wildlife.

Commerce and Transportation. Budget expenditures for commerce and transportation programs are estimated to decline in 1963, reflecting my legislative proposal to increase postal rates to a level that will cover the costs of postal operations, except for those services properly charged to the general taxpayer.

COMMERCE AND TRANSPORTATION

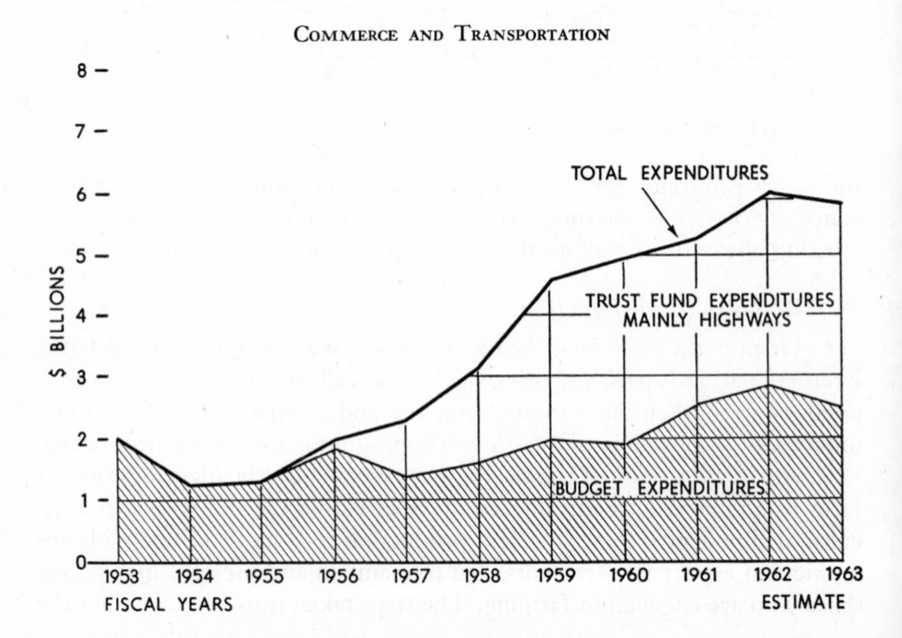

Outlays for the Federal-aid highway program are financed almost entirely through the highway trust fund and are not included in the budget total. Combined, Federal budget and trust fund expenditures for commerce and transportation programs in 1963 will amount to almost $6 billion.

Housing and Community Development. The long strides forward authorized by the Housing Act of 1961 are making it possible to accelerate progress in renewing our cities, in financing needed public facilities, in preserving open space, and in supplying housing accommodations, both public and private, within the means of low- and middle-income families and elderly people. The major new proposal I expect to make in this field will extend the authority for Federal aids to urban mass transportation.

Health, Labor, and Welfare. Budget expenditures for health, labor, and welfare programs are estimated at $5.1 billion and trust fund expenditures at $21.6 billion in 1963. The budget includes increased funds for health research and for a major strengthening of the programs of the Public Health Service, the Office of Vocational Rehabilitation, and the Food and Drug Administration. The budget and trust accounts also reflect the legislative recommendations which are pending in the Congress to provide increased aid for medical education and to enact health insurance for the aged through social security.

Many American families rely for help and for a new start in life upon the public assistance programs. Yet these programs frequently lack both the services and the means to discharge their purpose constructively. This budget includes substantial increases for public assistance. I am also

HEALTH, LABOR, AND WELFARE

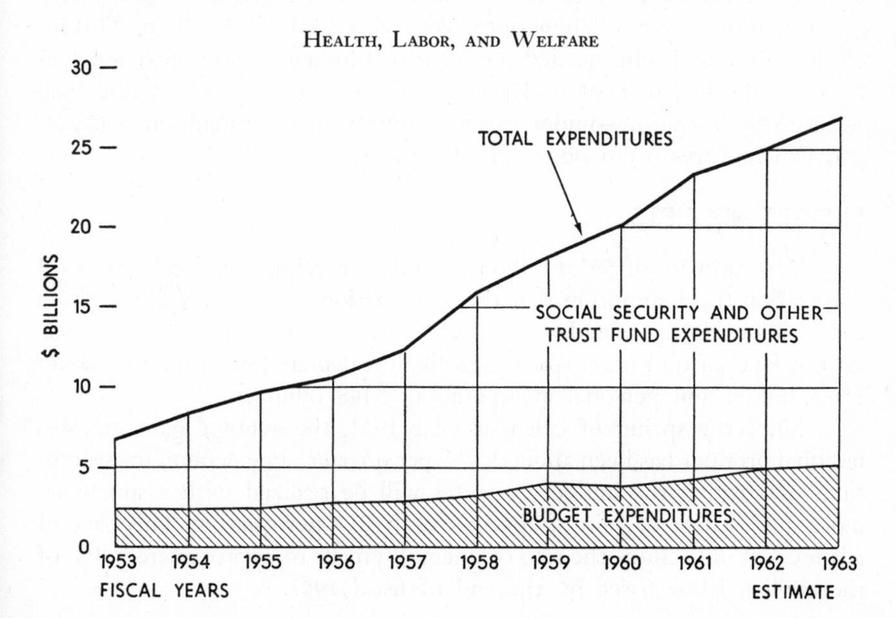

proposing a significant modernization and strengthening of the welfare programs to emphasize those services which can help restore families to self-sufficiency.

Education. A strong educational system providing ready access for all to high quality free public elementary and secondary schools is indispensable in our democratic society. Moreover, able students should not be denied a higher education because they cannot pay expenses or because their community or State cannot afford to provide good college facilities. This budget therefore includes funds for the legislative recommendations pending before the Congress to provide loans for the construction of college academic facilities and funds for college scholarships, and assistance to public elementary and secondary education through grants for the construction of classrooms and for teachers' salaries. The budget also includes funds for a new program of financial aid to improve the quality of education by such means as teacher training institutes.

Veterans Benefits and Services. Our first concern in veterans programs is that adequate benefits be provided for those disabled in the service of their country. The last increase in compensation rates for service-disabled veterans was enacted in 1957. To offset increases in the cost of living since that time, I again recommend that the Congress establish higher rates, particularly for the severely disabled.

NEW OBLIGATIONAL AUTHORITY

Before Federal funds can be spent, the Congress must enact authority for each agency to incur financial obligations. For 1963, my recommendations for new obligational authority total $99.3 billion. This includes substantial sums needed for forward funding of programs—such as those of the Department of Defense and the National Aeronautics and Space Administration—under which commitments are made in one year and expenditures often occur in later years.

BUDGET RECEIPTS

The estimate of $93.0 billion of budget receipts for fiscal year 1963 is based on the assumption that the gross national product will rise from $521 billion in the calendar year 1961 to $570 billion in calendar 1962. At this level of output, corporate profits in calendar 1962 would be about $56.5 billion and personal income about $448 billion.

Since the spring of calendar year 1961, the average gain in gross national product has been about 2½% per quarter. The economic assumptions underlying the budget estimates will be realized with a somewhat more modest rate of gain of approximately 2% per quarter. This pace of advance would reduce the rate of unemployment to approximately 4% of the civilian labor force by the end of fiscal 1963.

Budget Receipts

(Fiscal Years, In Billions of Dollars)

Source	1959 Actual	1960 Actual	1961 Actual	1962 Estimate	1963 Estimate
Individual income taxes	36.7	40.7	41.3	45.0	49.3
Corporation income taxes	17.3	21.5	21.0	21.3	26.6
Excise taxes	8.5	9.1	9.1	9.6	10.0
Estate and gift taxes	1.3	1.6	1.9	2.1	2.3
Customs	.9	1.1	1.0	1.2	1.3
Other receipts	3.5	4.4	4.1	3.5	4.2
Total	68.3	78.5	78.3	82.8	93.7
Deduct interfund transactions	.4	.7	.7	.7	.7
Total budget receipts	67.9	77.8	77.7	82.1	93.0

Tax Reform Proposals. Extensive and careful consideration has already been given to the tax reform proposals enumerated in my special tax message to the Congress last April. The House Committee on Ways and Means has made action on a similar set of recommendations its first order of business this year. I hope they will be enacted early in this session.

I particularly urge enactment of the tax credit for investment in depreciable equipment. The 8% credit as formulated by the Committee on Ways and Means, together with administrative revision of guidelines for depreciation now underway, will encourage modernization of productive equipment in private industry desirable alike to improve the Nation's potential for economic growth and the ability of our producers to compete with those abroad.

Any net reduction in fiscal 1963 revenues resulting from adoption of the investment credit is expected to be offset by additional revenues resulting from the enactment of measures to remove defects and inequities in the tax structure, including:

Corrective legislation with respect to the tax treatment of gains on real and personal property, which would prevent abuses that now occur.

A system of tax withholding on dividend and interest income, needed to overcome the serious loss of revenue and the unfairness resulting from the failure of some individuals to report these types of income on their tax returns.

Repeal of the exclusion from an individual's taxable income of the first $50 of dividends and the credit against tax of 4% of additional dividends.

Statutory provisions to cope with the problem of business deductions for entertainment and gifts and other expense account items.

Legislation to eliminate unwarranted tax preferences now received by several special types of institutions.

Revision of the tax treatment of foreign income to serve the overall objective of tax neutrality between domestic and foreign operations. This requires eliminating tax deferral privileges except in less-developed countries, and tightening up on other preferences given to foreign income under existing law.

Extension of Present Tax Rates. The budget outlook for 1963 requires that the present tax rates on corporation income and certain excises be extended for another year beyond their scheduled expiration date of June 30, 1962, to prevent a revenue loss of $2.8 billion in 1963.

Transportation Tax and User Charges. Under existing law, the 10% tax on transportation of persons is scheduled for reduction to 5% on July 1, 1962. This tax poses special problems for common carriers which must compete with private automobiles not subject to the tax. At the same time it is clearly appropriate that passengers and shippers who benefit from special Government programs should bear a fair share of the costs of these programs.

Accordingly, I recommend that the present 10% tax as it applies to passenger transportation other than by air be repealed effective July 1, 1962. I also recommend enactment of new systems of user charges for commercial and general aviation and for transportation on inland waterways.

C. Management of the National Debt

50. U.S. EXPERIENCE: AN EVALUATION*

Warren L. Smith

The Treasury's problems in managing the public debt have been the subject of much attention and concern recently. "Debt management," as we shall define the term, is different from both fiscal policy and monetary policy, although it is closely related to both. To a considerable extent, fiscal policy sets the framework within which debt management is conducted, while the kind of monetary policy being followed affects the Treasury's problems of debt management. At the same time, the debt management policies of the Treasury may interfere with the freedom of the Federal Reserve in conducting monetary policy, and the structure of the debt may significantly influence the way in which monetary controls function. Moreover, under our definition, the Federal Reserve has some

* Warren L. Smith, *Debt Management in the United States*, Study Paper No. 19, *Study of Employment, Growth and Price Levels* (Joint Economic Committee, 86th Cong., 2d sess.) (Washington, D.C.: U.S. Government Printing Office), 1960, pp. 1–7.

powers and responsibilities which come under the heading of debt management.

THE FEDERAL DEBT IN PERSPECTIVE

The Size of the Debt

There are several concepts of the public debt which are employed in discussions of debt management. On June 30, 1959, the "total gross debt" or "total Federal securities outstanding" amounted to $284.8 billion. The gross debt reached a level of $279 billion in February 1946 at the zenith of borrowing connected with the financing of World War II, then declined to $252.4 billion in June 1948 as a result of the immediate postwar budget surpluses and debt retirement. From mid-1948 to mid-1959 the gross debt grew by $32.4 billion.

However, the gross public debt does not represent the true debt of the Federal Government. At the end of the fiscal year 1959, $54.6 billion of Treasury securities was held by Government agencies and trust funds, i.e., within the Federal Government itself. A further $26 billion was held by the Federal Reserve System. Since purchases and sales of Government securities by the Federal Reserve are made for the purpose of controlling bank reserves and the money supply in the interest of maintaining financial and economic stability and since approximately 90 percent of the interest payments made to the Federal Reserve are returned to the Treasury at the end of each year, this portion of the debt is also essentially intragovernmental. The debt that is significant for most aspects of economic analysis is the publicly held debt—that is, debt held by households, business firms, commercial banks, and other financial institutions of the country. Changes in the amount and composition of the publicly held debt affect interest rates and the liquidity of spending units, and these effects may influence the level and composition of private expenditures. The publicly held debt amounted to $204.2 billion on June 30, 1959, and increased by only $9 billion between mid-1948 and mid-1959, compared with the $32.4 billion increase in the gross public debt.

Definition of Debt Management

We shall define debt management to include all actions of the Government, including both the Treasury and the Federal Reserve, which affect the composition of the publicly held debt. When defined in this way, debt management includes: (1) decisions by the Treasury concerning the types of debt to be issued to raise new money, (2) decisions by the Treasury concerning the types of debt to be issued in connection with the refunding of maturing securities, (3) decisions by the Federal Reserve concerning the types of debt to be purchased and sold in the conduct of open market operations.

It should be noted that under this definition of debt management, the amount of new securities to be sold by the Treasury to cover budget deficits or to be retired with the proceeds of budget surpluses is not a matter of debt management but of fiscal policy. Moreover, decisions by the Federal Reserve which change the publicly held money supply, including changes in reserve requirements and the amount (but not the composition) of open market purchases and sales, fall under the heading of monetary policy.

The Debt in Relation to Other Economic Magnitudes

Not only has the publicly held debt not grown greatly in absolute amount in the last decade, but it has actually declined substantially in relation to other relevant economic magnitudes. The publicly held debt was equal to 86.9 percent of GNP at the end of 1947; by 1958, due to the rise in GNP, the percentage had fallen to 44.2. Of course a substantial part of this decline in the percentage is the result of inflation, but the fact remains that the debt is much smaller relative to our productive capacity than formerly, and to the extent that this is a measure of our ability to carry the debt, it should sit much more lightly on our shoulders than it did a decade ago. Furthermore, between 1947 and 1958 total net public and private debt outstanding rose from $394.8 billion to $743.9 billion. As a result of this large increase, the publicly held Federal debt declined from 50.8 percent of the total in 1947 to 27.7 percent in 1958. Thus, the relative importance of the Federal debt in our debt structure has declined very substantially.

Interest on the Debt

Net interest paid by the Federal Government as shown in the national income accounts is the best measure of the interest cost to the Treasury, since it excludes the intragovernmental transfers involved in payments of interest to the trust funds. Net interest paid increased from $4.2 billion in 1947 to $5.5 billion in 1958 as a result of a steady upward trend in interest rates; however, due to rising incomes, net interest payments fell from 2.1 percent of national income in 1947 to 1.5 percent in 1958. Increases in interest payments have weak effects on the level of income, because the marginal propensity to spend out of interest receipts is relatively low and because such payments are subject to rather high marginal rates of taxation.

Nevertheless, interest costs on the public debt do represent a sizable sum and are a matter for concern. And since the administrative budget is frequently used as a tool of fiscal policy, for some purposes the interest included in this budget is the important thing. For fiscal 1960, interest payments in this budget are estimated at $9 billion, more than 11 percent of total budget expenditures, nearly three times the estimated expenditures of the Department of Health, Education, and Welfare, and nearly 40 percent larger than those of the Department of Agriculture.

With the present emphasis on balancing the budget without raising taxes, a rise in the interest burden tends to cut into other badly needed types of Federal expenditures. Thus, there is good reason for trying to avoid unnecessarily heavy interest costs on the public debt. That is, unless the increased interest payments serve some useful economic function, we should try to reduce them.

Volume of Debt Operations

In addition to exaggerating the size of the debt itself and of the interest payments on it, the statistics commonly used overstate the magnitude of current debt operations. For example, in the calendar year 1958, the total amount of certificates, notes, and bonds issued by the Treasury both for cash and in exchange for maturing securities amounted to $61.2 billion. However, out of this total, $22 billion represented securities issued to the Treasury trust accounts and Federal Reserve banks—almost entirely automatic (and fictitious) transactions involving no problems of debt management—so that the amount of securities issued to the public amounted to only $39.2 billion. Similar large differences are present in other years. Proper evaluation of the current problems of managing the debt requires that the transactions within the Government be eliminated from the calculations.

Ownership of the Debt

Holdings of Treasury securities by various investor groups have undergone substantial changes in recent years. With respect to debt ownership, investors may be divided into three broad categories.

1. *Investors Whose Holdings Have Declined Steadily.* This category includes insurance companies and mutual savings banks. Holdings of mutual savings banks declined by $4.7 billion from 1948 to 1959, while holdings of insurance companies declined by $10.8 billion during the same period. As a result of the prosperous conditions and heavy savings of the war period, these institutions grew rapidly during the war, and due to the limited private demand for funds, as well as pressures to assist the Treasury in war financing, most of the inflow of funds was invested in Government securities. In response to the heavy demands for funds which have characterized the postwar period, both of these types of institutions have steadily liquidated Government securities in order to shift their funds into more lucrative private investments—chiefly mortgages in the case of mutual savings banks and corporate bonds and mortgages in the case of life insurance companies. Liquidation of governments by these institutions has not shown any particularly strong tendency to speed up during periods of tight credit. The rate of liquidation appears to have slowed down somewhat as total portfolios have become smaller.

2. *Investors Whose Holdings Have Increased Steadily.* Several classes of investors have steadily added to their holdings of Government

securities in recent years. These include State and local governments, savings and loan associations, and foreign accounts and international agencies.

3. *Investors Whose Holdings Have Fluctuated Substantially.* Investments in Government securities by commercial banks and by nonfinancial corporations have exhibited substantial fluctuations from year to year with no discernible trend during the last decade. Fluctuations in the holdings of these two groups have shown a systematic pattern related to changes in monetary policy and credit conditions, which has made the task of conducting monetary policy more difficult for the Federal Reserve.

Composition of the Debt

In June 1959, out of a total publicly held debt of $204.2 billion, $5 billion represented convertible bonds and $54.2 billion represented all other nonmarketable and miscellaneous debt, chiefly savings bonds. The remaining $145 billion was marketable securities including Treasury bills, certificates of indebtedness, notes, and bonds. While there are problems connected with the savings bond program, our main concern is the management of the marketable portion of the debt. The percentage of the debt maturing in 1 year had risen from 24.6 in 1946 to 35.4 in 1959, while at the other end of the scale the percentage maturing beyond 10 years had fallen from 33.9 to 17.7. The maturity composition tends to shorten if nothing is done merely due to the passage of time, while debt operations in the form of cash borrowing, refunding operations, and debt retirement, introduce elements of irregularity into the behavior of the composition. Each time the Treasury refunds a maturing security by offering a new issue in exchange, the average maturity of the debt increases at least a little because securities having a maturity of zero are removed from the debt and replaced by other securities. Cash borrowings may increase or decrease the average maturity of the debt, depending on whether the securities being issued have a maturity longer or shorter than the existing average. Cash retirement of maturing securities lengthens the average maturity, because the securities removed from the debt have a maturity of zero. Consequently, the irregular pattern of debt operations makes the maturity structure and the average maturity behave in somewhat unpredictable fashion. Nevertheless, it is quite clear that the maturity of the debt, however measured, has declined substantially in recent years.

PRESENT DEBT MANAGEMENT TECHNIQUES

Bill Financing

The Treasury bill, which may have a maturity up to 1 year, has proved to be a very effective and useful debt instrument. Bills are sold at auction on a discount basis, and the bill auctions seem to interfere very little with the Federal Reserve's freedom of action. Until recently regular bill offerings were made only with maturity of 3 months. The Treasury has within the last year extended bill maturities first to 6 months and then to 1 year. At the present time, the Treasury has outstanding 13 issues of 3-month bills, 13 issues of 6-month bills, these 2 sets forming a pattern in which 1 issue matures and is replaced by a new bill offering each week. In addition, there are now four issues of 1-year bills maturing once each quarter in January, April, July, and October. The total amount of these regular bills was $31 billion at the end of July 1959, and this portion of the debt has been placed on a periodic rollover basis, which is efficient and economical and minimizes interference with Federal Reserve monetary policies. In addition to regular bill issues, the Treasury has recently been relying mainly on bills in its tax anticipation financing to meet seasonal gaps between receipts and expenditures.

Fixed Price Issues

The Treasury also borrows by issuing certificates of indebtedness, notes, and bonds, both to raise new cash to cover budgetary deficits and to refund maturing securities. Although refunding could be handled by selling new securities for cash and using the cash to retire the maturing securities, in practice refunding is almost always handled by means of exchange offerings. Certificates, notes, and bonds are sold on a fixed-price basis.

Several decisions must be made before a fixed-price issue can be offered to the public. These include the choice of a maturity, other provisions such as call or redemption options, and the selection of the coupon rate to be placed on the securities. In deciding upon the maturity and terms of a particular offering, the Treasury is guided by the advice from market experts—particularly the advisory committees of the American Bankers Association and the Investment Bankers Association—by potential investors, and by its own independent study of market conditions. The choice of the coupon rate is made by examining the yield curve at the time of the offering. However, it is necessary to set the interest rate on the new security somewhat above the yield on outstanding debt of the same maturity in order to induce the market to absorb a substantial offering.

Underwriting of Short-term Cash Offerings

The Treasury does not make use of formal underwriting in marketing its issues, such as is provided by investment banking syndicates in the case of corporate offerings. However, it is customary in the case of short-term cash offerings, such as certificates and shorter term notes, to permit commercial bank subscribers to pay for the issue by means of credits to Treasury tax and loan accounts, which means that banks are, in effect, able to obtain the securities by paying only a portion of the price equal to their reserve requirements until such time (commonly 2 to 3 weeks later) as the Treasury transfers the funds to its accounts at the Federal Reserve banks. The use of Treasury tax and loan account credits provides a kind of indirect underwriting.

The banks serve essentially as underwriters, reselling or distributing securities to other investors. The Treasury limits or discourages bank subscriptions on longer term issues apparently on the ground that such securities are unsuitable investments for banks. In restricting bank subscriptions to longer term issues, the Treasury is probably denying itself important support that could be of great help at times. The main underwriting device used by the Treasury to market long-term debt is to offer a rate sufficiently attractive to achieve the required sales.

Refunding Operations

Maturing securities are short-term liquid instruments and are likely to be in the possession of investors who are holding them for liquidity reasons. The securities being issued in exchange, on the other hand, if they are of intermediate or long maturity, are more likely to appeal to investors who want either permanent investments or prospective short-term speculative gains. The success of a refunding operation often depends, therefore, on the extent to which maturing securities have been shifted from their normal owners to investors desiring to obtain the new securities. This may require that the terms of the new security be sufficiently attractive to create a premium on the "rights" (i.e., the maturing issue) in order to induce the transactions in these "rights" that are needed to put them in the hands of investors who want the new issue.

Government security dealers buy and sell "rights," thus facilitating their distribution, and as soon as the subscription books open, the securities begin to trade on a "when issued" basis. During the subscription period dealers buy "rights" and sell "when issued" securities. These dealer operations, which contribute to the success of the exchange and the proper placement of the new offering, are the closest thing there is to systematic underwriting in connection with refunding operations.

RECENT DEBT MANAGEMENT PROBLEMS

Shortening of Debt Maturities

The shortening of debt maturities has been a matter of concern to Treasury officials, and debt management policy in the last few years has concentrated on trying to lengthen maturities. The orthodox theory of debt management calls for the issuance of long-term securities during periods of inflation in order to preempt funds from the capital market and reduce liquidity, and the issuance of short-term securities in recession periods in order to increase liquidity and leave the maximum amount of funds available for long-term investment. However, the Treasury has had little success in following the precepts of orthodox debt management theory and has been forced—or induced—to sell long-term securities in recessions. Thus, such debt lengthening as has occurred in the last few years has taken place largely in the recession or early recovery periods of 1953–55 and 1957–58.

The Competitive Position of Government Securities

In recent years, the Treasury has had considerable difficulty in selling long-term bonds. During the period of nearly 7 years since the present administration came into office with the intention of extending debt maturities, only $9.4 billion of bonds with a maturity of more than 10 years has been sold to the public altogether, both for cash and in exchange operations. Thus, the average is less than $1.5 billion per year. Nearly all the investor groups—including savings banks, life insurance companies, pension funds, etc.—who have traditionally shown an interest in Treasury bonds, have been reducing their holdings steadily or at most increasing them only very slowly. Certainly one important aspect of our debt management difficulties appears to be the declining popularity of Government securities, particularly of the longer term variety.

There are several possible explanations of the apparent deterioration of the competitive position of long-term Treasury securities. One is the greatly increased variability in the prices of Government securities as monetary policy has been employed more vigorously. This increased variability has lowered the liquidity, particularly of longer term Treasury securities, and reduced their attractiveness to many investors. Another reason is the increased attractiveness of corporate securities as investors' assessments of the risks associated with these securities have been reduced as a result of continued relatively prosperous business conditions. The increased importance of FHA-insured and VA-guaranteed mortgages has also cut into the market for longer term Government securities, since these mortgages are about as safe investments as Governments and yield the investor higher net returns. The fact that yields on Government securities have risen relative to those on private debt during the last decade, at the same time that the size of the publicly held Federal debt has been declining relative to the amount of private debt outstanding, appears to corroborate the view that Government securities have become less attractive to investors.

Other Problems

Interest rates have shown an increasing tendency to undergo rapid changes at turning points in business activity, as investors have become more aware of the implications of flexible monetary policy. This is rather troublesome to the Treasury, particularly at times when an improvement in business activity begins while the Treasury is still operating at a large deficit requiring heavy cash borrowing, as in mid-1958. In addition, speculation in Government securities has had a disorganizing effect on the Government securities market, especially in the case of the 2⅝-percent bonds of February 1965, which were issued in exchange for maturing securities in June 1958, at approximately the time that the outlook for business activity and monetary policy was changing from recession to recovery.

Part VIII: Questions for Analysis

1. Although government has grown both absolutely and relatively in the past four decades some people are convinced that further growth is vitally necessary.
   a) What does Barbara Ward Jackson think about this matter?
   b) What does Henry C. Wallich think about it?
   c) What do you think?
2. The Council of Economic Advisers describes the relationships of several budgetary concepts. Identify these concepts, and explain the relation of one to another.
3. Explain the meaning of the term "full employment surplus." How may government use this concept in planning its budget?
4. As submitted by President John F. Kennedy to Congress, does the federal budget for 1963 indicate a surplus or a deficit? By how much? If you cannot specify a single amount in answer to the last query, explain why you are unable to do so.
5. *a*) Who owns the national debt?
   b) What are the major techniques for managing the debt?
   c) What are the major problems in managing the debt?

IX ALTERNATIVE ECONOMIC SYSTEMS

The twentieth century is characterized by competing economic ideologies and systems. Economists have traditionally considered the market system as neutral with respect to the aims of economic life. John Maurice Clark points out that this is not strictly true, for the market system gives preference to marketable products.

Other economic systems, like communism, maintain that they are superior in achieving economic justice and social welfare. The divergence between the ideology and practice of communism is highlighted in several selections. Robert W. Campbell, of Indiana University, describes the procedures by which basic economic decisions are made in the planned Soviet economy. Calvin B. Hoover, of Duke University, describes the fascinating deviant economy of Yugoslavia, a unique market economy which combines collective ownership and the profit motive. Milovan Djilas, former Vice President of Yugoslavia and more recently a periodic inmate of his country's prisons, reveals how a new and exploiting class develops in the allegedly classless Communist society.

Among the vigorous critics of capitalism were the proponents of democratic or evolutionary socialism. The English and Swedish brands of democratic socialism, as reviewed by Paul T. Homan of the University of California and Calvin B. Hoover, have lost a good deal of their original zeal for nationalization of industry. Wilhelm Röpke, of the Graduate Institute of International Studies in Geneva, presents a dramatic description of the resurgence of the market economy in Western Europe since World War II. However, Röpke warns that the ultimate destiny of the market economy lies beyond supply and demand.

A. The Overview

51. THE AIMS OF ECONOMIC LIFE*

John Maurice Clark

Ask an economist what the goal or aim of the economic system is in a free society such as ours, and he will probably reply that the system, as a system, has no specific aims; the service it renders is to give its members a maximum of means and opportunity to pursue their several aims, whatever they may be. The system is conceived as neutral, ready to serve any and all kinds of wants; the responsibility of directing it to good wants, rather than bad, lies with those to whom the service is rendered. For the economist, people's wants are facts; those expressed in markets are economic facts; and his task as a scientist is to study facts, not to approve or disapprove them.

If that were all, this chapter might end here, having defined the attitude of economists toward the aims of economic life. But that is not all; the system is not as neutral as this definition suggests. No doubt its proper place is at the service of whatever ends the society may have. But the market naturally gives a preferred position to wants for marketable products. And it is taking generations of struggle to make slow progress in recognizing and making provision for other wants, some of which are far more important than an individualistic age has permitted itself to understand. To make goods cheaper and more plentiful, technical improvement has driven forward, from Adam Smith's pin factory to modern mass production; and only after we are committed to this irreversible movement do we arrive at the disturbing realization that something not fully understood has happened to conditions of work, to human relations on the job, and to the impact of work on the personality of the worker. Are we developing the kinds of personalities modern society needs, if it is to hold together and keep working, while maintaining freedom? If we fail in eternal vigilance in such matters, economic techniques could become our masters, precisely through our failure to realize that they are anything but docile servants.

Up to a point, economists realize that the market is not neutral, and they express this realization in their policies, if not in their theories. But

* Reprinted from *Economic Institutions and Human Welfare*, by John Maurice Clark, by permission of Alfred A. Knopf, Inc., New York, 1957, pp. 39–43, 70–72.

as to the more far-reaching human and social imponderables, even those who realize their importance are hardly equipped to deal with them. Economics is a quantitative discipline, and it does not know how to handle such qualitative material. Its most unqualified criteria of economic progress are more goods to consume and, on the side of conditions of production itself, a shorter work week and more leisure.

If you catch an economist in an expansive mood, he may define the goal as "the good things of life for the many, as widely distributed as practicable, in an ever-increasing flow." This adds several elements, and raises more questions than it settles. How wide a distribution is "practicable"? And who is to be the judge of what things are good? If the many are free to choose, they are free to choose wrong as well as right—that is what freedom means. We recognize this by practicing a limited censorship in the interest of health, safety, and, to a dwindling extent, morals. But outside these limits, economists traditionally think that the things people want for themselves and their families are likely to be less harmful than the goals that self-appointed mentors or rulers set for them. This question of the wisdom of wants economists prevailingly regard as somebody else's business, and they have satisfied themselves that quantitative economic gains are good as far as they go.

Our system stresses the self-interested (or family-interested) side of human nature as a prime mover in the business of producing and distributing goods and services, and undertakes to harness it to the economic requirements of the community by the most nearly voluntary methods, involving the least interference with its natural expression. Traditionally, the harness has been viewed as a rather simple matter of legal rights of person and property, plus competition as a game in which, to serve oneself, one must serve others. Ethical motives were thought of mainly as entering into the spending of incomes; they were good but not necessary to the working of the system, and pretensions to moral motivations in business were actually suspect.

In fact, the traditional harness depends on a general underlying sense of right, which is necessary to respect for property rights and faithfulness to contracts. This moral sense is also built into the legal machinery for interpreting and enforcing these rights. And as group power is less precisely limited by competitive checks, the sense of right becomes an increasingly active feature of economic life, and social responsibility in the use of group power has become an absolute necessity if the industrial system is to go on working on a basis containing enough freedom to be fairly characterized as voluntary. The tradition of utilizing self-interest has made us slow to realize this necessity, and thus the tradition is a source of weakness as well as of strength.

Furthermore, whatever responsibility for social ends there may be in our system needs to become explicit and conscious. It is not enough that the system be serviceable; serviceability must appear to flow naturally from its inherent character. Otherwise it concedes a dangerous propaganda advantage to rival systems. Our system must be animated by awareness of its obligation to be directed to serviceable ends, not merely tricked by an "invisible hand" into pursuing such ends in spite of the fact that the main preoccupation of its members is with self-interested motives.

In addition to self-interest, human nature has another and sharply contrasting side: the impulse to identify oneself with something bigger than oneself or one's family, to merge oneself in it, and to find there support, an inner sense of security and of sharing in a larger realization than an unattached individual could attain, supplying a sense of meaning that smaller objectives fail to convey. This self-identifying, self-merging, or self-dedicating impulse appears in many guises—in fraternal orders, in trade unions, in political parties, in any service that has a strong *esprit de corps*, and most profoundly in religions and in totalitarian systems. The last two have this in common, despite being poles apart in their objects of loyalty; and this is presumably the most deeply rooted reason for the attraction the Soviet system has had for many Western Christians, who set a high value on self-dedication and are repelled by the degree to which our economic system neglects this side of man's nature. While Soviet strength rests also on fear and ruthless coercion, it is a dangerous error to suppose that they are its sole source.

This system now threatens our own, in what amounts to an anti-religious holy war; and the requirements of defense against this threat will probably be the greatest single force determining the character of the changes our system will experience in the foreseeable future. Liberals are already warning us that we might win the contest and lose the thing we are fighting for. So we need not only to arm for defense, but to rediscover and redefine the qualities of our system that make it worth defending, the weaknesses of which it needs to be pruned, and the points at which the pruning may or may not involve risks to the essentials. Every generation needs such a rediscovery. Ours faces the need in the heat and confusion of conflict. It will make its decisions, with or without a clear eye to the values they affect and the valuations they imply.

. . . . . .

What we may fail to realize is that this challenge to a voluntaristic and self-governing society is a challenge to its members: the society will fail to meet its collective challenge if the members fail to develop the techniques and the ethics of voluntary working together. And this may impose a more exacting task on the individual than the individualistic tasks of which he has been partly freed, largely because it cannot be laid on him with the same automatic and compelling necessity. If he does his part, he does it voluntarily, as a moral act.

We can no longer rely on reaching economically correct results automatically, as an unintended by-product of what individuals do in pursuit of their private interests. We still need all we can get of such automatic adjustments; but there are growingly strategic areas in which the power of organized groups is such that, if sound terms of settlement are to be reached, people must consciously intend to reach them. This calls for some understanding of what economically correct adjustments are and a will to promote them rather than to pursue self-interest irresponsibly. This element of practical ethics has become an indispensable economic "factor of production."

Disagreements are inevitable, but underlying them there must be a basic general agreement on the conditions necessary to the health of the system, and a willingness to support them and to check the pursuit of private interest short of inflicting serious damage on these basic essentials, without robbing this motive of its dynamic force. This calls for a high quality of imagination in visualizing where the danger lines come, and for loyalty to the system in the face of specific dissatisfactions. And a system of free personal competition with widely differentiated rewards is a natural breeder, not only of ambition and opportunity, but of dissatisfaction.

Adequate opportunity and a fair contest may justify unequal results in the eye of the detached observer. But not every boy can become President, and the unsuccessful individual is not a detached observer. His inferior fortune may be in some respects all the harder to bear when it is not a predetermined status, sanctioned by accepted authority, but an evidence of inferior achievement in an open contest. He may be disinclined to concede the adequacy of the opportunity or the fairness of the contest, and he can always cite imperfections. Despite these inevitable defects, the system must somehow earn loyalty, and its constituent groups and individuals must accord it. Their loyalty must be tough-fibered enough to tolerate the amount of inequality that is an inescapable incident of a healthy economy dependent on individual incentives.

Without this tough-fibered loyalty, it will be all the more difficult to hammer out the necessary working compromise between the values of stability and the need for change. New and emergent needs must be met, without too much upsetting of the expectations on which people plan their lives. Some such disturbance is unavoidable; and a recognition of this fact is perhaps the first requirement for surmounting the resulting difficulties, some of which amount to injustice.

What remains to be seen is whether this can go on as a humanizing process rather than one of regimentation or disruption; and whether it can go far enough and fast enough to save Western society. Can we restore the saving positive value which medieval society had, by learning to act as members of one body under the strains of a dynamic, and not a static, society, maintaining the freedom and the vigor of individual incentive which are essential to progress? In short, can we do all this in ways that preserve an all-pervading basis of voluntary action, rather than replacing this with totalitarian discipline? It is a formidable assignment with destiny. Its moral requirements may well appear more exacting than those of any previous society.

B. Communism: Theory and Practice

52. THE SOVIET SYSTEM*

Robert W. Campbell

. . . There is a long tradition of argument in this country asserting that a planned economy will be wasteful and inefficient because planners cannot utilize resources "rationally." Before evaluating this argument, it will be helpful to explain briefly what is meant by rationality in an economic system. The task of achieving rationality in an economic system can be thought of as having two main aspects, namely, the problem of coordination and the problem of efficiency.

Coordination involves the achievement of internal consistency among the actions of producers and consumers. The output of coal must be great enough to supply the needs of all those who require coal for producing their output, such as steel or electric power, or there will not be enough steel and electric power. On the other hand to produce more coal than is needed would be a waste of resources. As another example, the relative volume of automobiles and clothing produced must be consistent with people's preferences, or there will be an excess of one and a shortage of the other. However, the achievement of internal consistency, the balancing of supply and demand, is not enough. It is also necessary that everything be produced in the most efficient way. For instance, satisfying the demand for fuel by producing enough coal is not by itself sensible if the fuel needs of the economy could be met at a lower cost, or with a smaller input of resources, by producing fuel oil and natural gas instead of coal. Throughout the economy the objective is to have producers follow courses of action which use the smallest possible input of resources to meet a required output. For an economic system to be rational, it must meet both these objectives more or less adequately.

In our economy the achievement of the two components of economic rationality depends on the operation of markets, utilization of the mechanisms of supply and demand, the price system, and profit maximization. Through the operation of supply and demand, the prices of things which are badly wanted or are in short supply move upward; the

* This selection from Robert W. Campbell's *Soviet Economic Power*, 1960, pp. 83–113, is reprinted by permission of and arrangement with Houghton Mifflin Company, the authorized publishers.

prices of those which are available in excess or which people no longer want so much are pushed downward. This is true for everything that is bought and sold, including the inputs used in producing goods, such as labor, materials, and capital, as well as the finished goods that are sold to ultimate consumers. Producers, whose aim is to make as much profit as they can, adjust their plans in accordance with these price movements. If the price of a given commodity increases, that encourages the production and discourages the consumption of that commodity—and conversely, lower prices encourage use and discourage production. This mechanism works flexibly in our economy to eliminate shortages and oversupplies, and to direct resources into the production of what is wanted most.

The price system also aids in achieving the second element of rationality, namely, efficiency. One way to increase profits is to cut costs, and in trying to do this, businessmen are guided by prices. In deciding whether to use one material or another, in choosing the best location for a plant, in selecting one production process over another, or in calculating to what extent they should substitute more machinery for labor, they consider the prices they will have to pay for inputs to see what the comparative costs of alternatives will be. The prices on the inputs bought by producers in running their businesses, just as the prices on other goods, can be thought of as a measure of how valuable these goods are in the overall estimation of society, taking into account how scarce they are, how much it costs to produce them, and how productive they are. In trying to cut costs and maximize profits, businessmen are at the same time minimizing the cost to society of producing their output. The mechanisms of supply and demand and profit maximization do not work perfectly, but they are constantly pushing our economy in the direction of greater rationality.

In the Soviet economy the tasks of coordination and deciding how to do things to get the biggest output from the smallest input are handled by the planners. How much of each good will be produced and how it will be distributed, what resources will be allotted to each producer, where and by what methods goods will be produced, are laid down beforehand in the national economic plan. It is often argued that when the flexible, automatic, instruments of the market economy are replaced by a set of human planners, confusion and waste will take over. The argument runs more or less as follows: The interrelationships between producers and consumers, between inputs and outputs, among innumerable other economic variables, are too intricate to be comprehended by human planners or encompassed within any plan. To the extent that the planners actually try to foresee and build all these details into their plans, the plans will be unwieldy, unworkable, and full of errors. The planners will be too far from the scene of action to see clearly what ought to be done in each case. How could people sitting in desks in Moscow possibly plan for the origin and destination of every nut and bolt in a factory in Novosibirsk, for instance, or how could they know whether some field on a collective farm somewhere in Kazakhstan should be planted to wheat or cotton next year? In a system where detailed orders come down from the top, there will be confusion, waste, imbalances of supply and demand, and orders to do things that do not make sense economically. Plans can be drawn up, all right, but they will be unrealistic in the sense that they contain contradictions, that they are not based on actual possibilities, and that they overlook important contingencies. The economy will not actually break down; people will be employed, goods will be produced, and the economy will be functioning, but in the process there will be a great deal of waste motion, and resources will not be used as productively as they might be.

Given this tradition of belief in the wasteful blundering to be expected from planning, it is not surprising that many people find it hard to accept the picture of Soviet economic performance shown in the statistics. The resolution of the apparent conflict turns on the fact that Soviet planning does not work so badly as the argument outlined above contends. It suffers from many faults and inefficiencies, but is nevertheless a tolerably effective substitute for the market economy, particularly when it is realized that the market economy does not work with the perfection usually ascribed to it in the textbooks. The purpose of this chapter is to make the conclusions about performance more nearly credible by providing a realistic picture of Soviet planning. We want to explain how the Soviet planners manage to formulate a set of plans that constitute a workable and relatively efficient blueprint for economic activity. Let us consider in turn the two problems of coordination and efficiency. . . .

COORDINATION

It is difficult to appreciate the complexity of the problem of coordination involved in a modern industrial economy. The intricacy of the interrelationships between different economic magnitudes staggers the imagination. The basic insight on which the science of economics is based is that almost all economic magnitudes depend on all other economic magnitudes. The number of automobiles that can be sold, for instance, depends on the price of automobiles relative to other goods and on the incomes of people. Each of these in turn depends upon other factors which are in their turn the result of other interrelationships and so on *ad infinitum.*

Input-Output Relationships

A good way to gain an appreciation of the kind of interrelationships that make practical planning so difficult is to look at the picture of an

TABLE 5.1

INPUT-OUTPUT TABLE FOR A HYPOTHETICAL ECONOMY

Unit of Measurement	Producing Sector \ Consuming Sector	Electric Power	Coal	Petroleum	Iron and Steel	Machinery	Chemicals
BKWH	Electric power	21.3	9.3	7.2	11.2	37.1	10.3
MT	Coal	83.1	10.0	4.0	55.1	16.3	4.8
Mbbls	Petroleum	22.3	7.1	13.9	1.4	9.2	8.4
$B	Iron and steel	0.02	0.40	0.62	23.9	13.94	0.15
$B	Machinery	0.20	0.60	0.30	1.70	50.8	0.20
$B	Chemicals	—	0.50	0.80	0.60	1.0	11.0
$B	Lumber and wood products	0.1	5.0	0.8	0.50	3.4	0.4
$B	Construction materials	0.4	0.2	0.1	0.7	0.2	1.1
$B	Textiles and apparel	—	—	—	—	1.2	2.1
$B	Food processing	—	—	—	—	0.02	1.34
$B	Agriculture	—	—	—	—	—	6.4
10BTM	Transport	0.02	34.24	15.53	14.34	1.71	2.29
$B	Other	0.9	1.0	1.8	1.2	4.1	3.2
TMY	Labor	320	1,402	143	696	5,941	670

BKWH = billion kilowatt-hours
MT = million tons
$B = billion dollars
TMY = thousand man-years
10BTM = ten billion ton-miles
Mbbls = million barrels

economy provided by an "input-output table." An input-output table is a sort of shorthand statistical description of an economy, organized in a special way. A highly schematic and oversimplified example is shown in Table 5.1. This table will merit some unhurried study. Some experimentation with it will help greatly in understanding the mutual independence among different parts of an economic system. Looking across any of the rows of this table, one can see the distribution of the output of any given industry among its various users. For instance, the first row shows that of the total output of 167.6 billion kilowatt-hours of electric power produced during the year in this hypothetical economy 21.3

Lumber and Wood Products	Construction Materials	Textiles and Apparel	Food Processing	Agriculture	Transport	Other	Households	Government	Investment	Total Output
6.2	6.7	5.5	6.0	3.5	8.4	9.2	15.4	5.6	4.7	167.6
6.7	13.0	7.5	10.3	4.0	60.3	10.9	62.1	2.3	—	356.4
1.6	1.0	2.1	7.2	94.9	82.0	6.2	45.2	46.9	7.8	357.2
0.01	0.04	0.02	1.70	0.20	1.39	0.80	0.51	0.30	5.2	49.20
0.30	0.20	0.20	0.40	5.6	6.4	0.3	10.8	50.0	57.2	185.2
1.1	2.0	2.1	1.8	4.0	1.9	1.0	5.3	1.6	1.9	43.6
11.0	0.8	—	1.9	2.4	1.7	1.8	8.5	3.3	19.1	60.7
1.0	5.7	0.1	1.4	0.5	0.1	—	2.6	1.5	17.7	33.3
0.3	0.05	100.1	0.41	3.8	0.05	1.2	68.6	2.3	—	180.1
0.02	0.03	5.77	55.31	4.18	0.24	0.2	113.7	3.5	—	184.31
0.9	0.3	23.9	52.5	—	—	0.9	60.0	1.0	—	145.9
19.67	10.21	1.02	5.66	8.07	0.16	1.50	10.02	7.16	2.00	133.60
1.7	1.7	1.3	2.1	1.2	2.3	1.3	6.1	2.3	0.4	32.6
2,931	1,149	3,256	2,085	38,697	5,319	1,662	2,491	14,832	5,830	87,424

billion kilowatt-hours was used by the electric power industry for its own needs, 9.3 billion kilowatt-hours went to the coal industry, 7.2 billion kilowatt-hours to the petroleum industry, various amounts went to other branches of industry, to agriculture and transport, and finally there was some left over for meeting the needs of households and other "final" consumers. Similarly in each of the other rows the disposition of the total output of some branch of the economy is shown. The bottom row of the table, below the heavy line, shows the distribution of the labor force of the economy among the various sectors. During the year a total of 87,424 thousand man-years were worked, and of this total, 320 thousand were for the electric power industry, 1,402 thousand were in the coal industry, 143 thousand in the petroleum industry, 696 thousand in the iron and steel industry, and so on across the row.

Looked at in another way, this table shows other important relationships as well. Glancing down any column, one can see the amounts of various goods and services that each industry bought and used in the process of producing its own output in the course of the year. For instance, in order to produce its 167.6 billion kilowatt-hours of electric power, the electric power industry had to consume 83.1 million tons of coal, 22.3 million barrels of petroleum fuel, and a certain amount of transportation, labor, and other inputs. For each industry the column shows the inputs from all other industries which were requried by the given industry for the production of the volume of output it produced. Thus, all the numbers to the left of the last four columns and above the "labor" row characterize the mutual interdependence of the demand for the output of any industry with the demand for the output of all other industries. How much coal will be needed depends on the levels of output of all those industries that require coal for their operation.

These interrelationships are more or less stable, at least for relatively short periods of a few years. This is because they are based on certain technological facts. In the case of the electric power industry, for instance, the consumption of 83.1 million tons of coal and 22.3 million barrels of fuel oil to produce 167.6 billion kilowatt-hours of electricity is a reflection of the fact that with the presently available technology, and given the efficiency of the equipment now in use, there is required on the average a certain number of BTU, or calories, to produce one KWH of electric power. . . . Similarly the input of iron and steel products required to produce the 185.2 billion dollars worth of machinery reflects the existing state of technology in the machinery industry, the kind of things that the machinery industry produces, and so on. Some of these interrelationships are more stable than others, and all can change over time as technology changes, and with other factors. By and large, such shifts proceed fairly slowly, and the relationships shown in the operation of the economy in a given year can be expected to hold fairly well for the near future.

This table will illustrate very neatly the task of the Soviet planners. A little experimentation shows that the amount of any commodity which the planners should produce depends on how much of everything else is going to be produced. In the table as we have shown it everything just matches. Each industry has been able to sell all the output it produced, and there is enough left over to meet household, investment, and government demands. But as the planners look forward to the task of drawing up the plan for the next year, obviously there will have to be some changes in output. Let us suppose, for example, that the planners want to increase the output of electric power used by households by 8 billion kilowatt-hours, which is an increase equal to about 5 per cent of the total output of 167.6 billion kilowatt-hours in the year to which the table refers. What will the impact of this single change be on the work of all the sectors of the economy? Clearly there will be some impact on all the different sectors, not just on the electric power industry alone. In order to produce this extra amount of power, the electric power industry will have to consume more coal, more labor, more transportation, and so on. If it took a certain number of tons of coal to produce the 167.6 billion kilowatt-hours in the previous year, it will take about 5 per cent more to increase output by 5 per cent, and so on down the line. The electric power industry will require larger inputs from all the industries which supply it, and this of course means that the output of every other industry will have to increase. But this is far from the end of the story. If each of the industries which supplies inputs to the electric power industry must increase its output, each will in turn require larger inputs from other industries. Thus there must be another round of adjustments, which will have to be followed by another, and so on in endless repercussion. Moreover, these are the kinds of interrelationships where there are wheels within wheels. For instance, the electric power industry will have to have more coal, but since considerable amounts of electric power are used in coal mining, the coal industry will have to be supplied with more electric power in order to meet the increased demand. So the electric power industry in turn will have to consume still more coal.

This example takes for granted that there is no bottleneck in the capacity of each of these sectors of the economy to produce the output required, if it gets enough current inputs. We have assumed that once the planners figure out just how much each industry should produce, and insure that there will be available to each industry all the required amounts of power, fuel, and materials, that each industry will be able to produce its assigned output. In fact, however, this may not always be true, since the production capacity of the industry, that is, the number of plants it has and the amount of equipment it has for turning out its product, might be inadequate to handle the assigned production program. In such a case it would be necessary to construct new capacity. In the case of the electric power industry, for instance, it might turn out that the assigned output of electric power could not be produced without construction of new power stations. When this happens there will be an induced need for more investment, and the amounts of goods available for investment, namely, the amounts shown in the next-to-last column of the input-output table, will have to be increased over whatever initial levels were previously planned. To build this electric power station will require some output from the machinery industry, from the iron and steel industry, from the construction materials industry, etc. This in turn will generate a new chain reaction of demands on all sectors of the economy. Whatever scheme the planners finally arrive at, it must not require more labor than is available or more capacity than is at hand or can be added.

Or consider the problem posed for the planners by the regime's decisions concerning the military program. Suppose that the government decides that it must provide a bigger defense program than in the previous year in the form of guided missiles, fissionable material, and an electronic defense network. Carrying out this policy would require more output from the corresponding industries, such as machinery and electrical equipment, and would probably also require construction and labor. Now try to trace the impact of this decision on all the sectors of the economy. The increased output of missiles from the machinery industry will require more output from the metal industry, which in turn will create new demands on the output of all the industries that supply inputs to the metals industry. Again from this one decision there will be almost endless ramifications reaching out into all areas of the economy. In the planned economy these interactions do not work themselves out automatically as the mysterious laws of price and of supply and demand go to work, but must be foreseen and taken care of ahead of time by the planners so that the required output will be included in someone's plan—and will be produced and available when required.

Finally the table also implies some other kinds of equilibria which the planners must consider. All those man-years shown along the bottom row imply wage-earners employed by enterprises, who will receive in the aggregate a certain amount of money income. But these laborers are the breadwinners of the households whose consumption is shown in the households column of the table. Obviously these two amounts have to be matched with each other. Suppose that in the previous year these magnitudes were nicely coordinated, so that employees were paid the right amount and were taxed the right amount and that the goods sold to households were priced in such a way that the total payments to the workers just enabled them to buy the amount that was made available for them to buy. Suppose that in the next year, an increase in total output of the economy is planned, which will require additions to the labor force. Or there may be some changes in the average wage level. As a result of such changes the total money incomes of households will be increased by a certain amount, and the planners will have to make some adjustments on the other side to balance this off. They could tax away the increased money incomes, they might plan to produce the same volume of consumer goods as in the previous year but sell them at higher prices, or perhaps they might increase the output of consumer goods appropriately, leaving the prices and the tax rates unchanged. If the latter is done, there will of course have to be a new round of adjustments in all the planned figures, since the production of more consumer goods will require the employment of more labor in those industries, additional inputs from other industries, and so on through the entire cycle all over again.

All the foregoing is just by way of describing the problem of coordination, rather than describing how the Russians actually go about solving it. It is obvious that the input-output table shown in Table 5.1

represents a highly oversimplified picture of the interrelationships involved in the economy. In a real economy there are not just thirteen branches but several hundred; moreover the final claimants on output comprise not just households, investment, and government—there are also exports, increases in inventory, military uses, and others. But even this simplified table illustrates clearly our main point, namely, that it is impossible to plan the activity of any one sector of the economy in isolation from the rest. The decisions of people in charge of planning any one aspect of the economy have an impact on the decisions of people planning the activities of all other sectors of the economy, and there must be some mechanism for coordination.

Actually the input-output approach makes it possible to express this problem of coordination as a mathematical problem, which although extremely complicated can be solved easily enough on high-speed electronic computers. But the input-output approach was developed, paradoxically, in the United States, rather than in the Soviet Union, where it would seem to be so much more useful. And only recently have the Russians begun to be interested in input-output analysis as an aid in planning. More will be said below about their interest in it, but for the moment we are more concerned with trying to understand how they have managed up to now to handle all these interrelationships in their planning.

The Soviet Mechanisms for Coordination

The mechanics of the Soviet planning process have not been studied very carefully in this country, and the details remain obscure. This is mostly because the Russian economists themselves have not done an adequate job of explaining how the system works. Our understanding must be pieced together from scattered indications, and many questions remain unanswered. The process defies easy description, but the following points will be helpful as guidelines in understanding its general operation.

1. Only the most aggregative kind of coordination is carried on at the center. The whole plan is not drawn up in Moscow, but rather the entire hierarchical pyramid of Soviet economic organizations participates in the process. At each level people operate with different degrees of detail, subject to varying degrees of constraint. The whole plan is finally produced by a process of negotiation and reconciliation between the different levels.

The process starts at the top with the formulation of very general goals by the Council of Ministers for such economic magnitudes as the increase in industrial and agricultural output, the level of new investment, the allocation for military expenditures, the volume of sales to households, and so forth. These recommendations are then sent to the State Planning Commission (usually called the Gosplan), which is the agency assigned primary responsibility for working out the national economic plan. Given these aggregate targets, the Gosplan goes through a process of trial-and-error balancing to see what is implied for every sector of the economy. The process of trial and error and successive approximation is manageable at this stage because the Gosplan is working with highly aggregated, and therefore a limited number of, economic magnitudes. In juggling such highly aggregated magnitudes the Gosplan can resort to rough projections of historical trends; detailed calculations need not be made at this stage. Suppose, for instance, that the instructions from the Council of Ministers call for a 10 per cent increase in industrial output. What are the implications for the industrial labor force? Naturally the economists of the Gosplan do not try to figure out what the increase in labor force in each industrial enterprise will be in order to increase total industrial output by 10 per cent. Rather they project rough indexes of historical experience. If output per worker has tended to rise in past years at something like 5 per cent, they will assume that output in the year they are planning for can be increased by 5 per cent with no increase in the industrial labor force at all. The remainder will have to be made up for by an increase in the labor force. Likewise, the central planners may postulate that this increase in output will require a certain amount of new investment, again on the basis of very aggregative relationships that have held in the past. At this stage, therefore, planning is partly the making of intelligent projections.

A plan in this form, however, would obviously not be an effective instrument for running an economy. To constitute a really operational plan it must be far more specific. The next stage is to pass these aggregative "limits and directives" for output, labor force, materials, investment, etc., down the administrative hierarchy, allocating each of them among subunits, and increasing the amount of detail along the way.

2. In the process the central planners concentrate their efforts on key commodities and key sectors. For instance, a long list of crucial commodities, totaling usually between one and two thousand, is subject to central rationing and allocation. The central planning organs keep even the fairly detailed planning of these commodities under their control. Reconciliation of supply and demand for these materials is effected through what are called "material balances," which are somewhat analogous to the input-output table described earlier. On one side of the ledger are listed all sources of supply, such as all the main producers, exports, stockpiles, etc.; on the other, the requirements of all the potential consumers of the item in question are shown. The disposition of other, less critical materials is settled by planning organs within ministries, with little inference from above, and others are planned at still lower levels.

In like manner the Gosplan is apt to give more attention to the planning of some sectors than others. This organ will specify much more detail in its plans for certain branches of industry, such as electric power or machinery, than for others, such as the textile and apparel industries. Many organizations producing consumer goods, such as local industry and producers' cooperatives, are treated only peripherally in the plans drawn up at the center, and are left mostly to their own devices in getting the investment funds, labor, and materials required. As another illustration, in investment planning, the central planners will consider in detail, and require central approval of, important projects, or those that involve expenditures above certain set limits, but will leave the planning and authorization of smaller ones to lower-level officials and planners, subject only to their staying within the totals assigned from above.

3. The third principle is that the planning process involves constant interaction between various levels of the administrative structure. The people at the top assign limits and directives to the next lower level of administrative organs; these further disaggregate and allocate these directives and limits among their constituent units, and so on down the line to the point where each enterprise receives a set of limits and directives for output, labor force, investment, materials, supply, and other indicators. At this point, the enterprise is to work out a detailed plan that will be consistent with these overall indicators. But in the process it may find that it cannot meet the output goal with its existing capacity, or that it needs more of some input than has been allocated to it. (Or as the Russians like to picture it, the limits and directives may not fully exhaust the capabilities of the enterprise and so the people in the enterprise may suggest how the plan might be made "harder." But this is more a hortatory myth than an accurate description.)

At this stage there will be arguments and conflicts back and forth between the enterprise and the superior level of administration. Suppose, for instance, that there is a conflict involving the allocation of a certain metal to a machinery plant. The plant management may insist that to produce the assigned output program it needs more of the metal than has been assigned. The superior organ (in most cases this will be the *glavk*, the Russian term for "chief administration," which is a division of a ministry or economic council) may counter that if the product is redesigned, or if waste and spoilage are cut, the assigned quota will be adequate. If the plant officials can convince their superiors that these are not practical possibilities, then the *glavk* may be able to give the plant a bigger allotment of the material by reducing the amount assigned to some other plant within its jurisdiction. If not, it may be necessary to get a larger allocation for the *glavk* as a whole, and ultimately, the planners at the center may have to alter the materials balance for this metal by reducing allocations to other industries, or by setting a higher goal for the production of the metal. Such a result will obviously call for the sort of chain reaction described earlier in connection with the input-output table. When such conflicts have been finally worked out, the final version of the aggregative plan is drawn up and ratified at the center, and the limits and directives are again passed down the hierarchy, and confirmed at each level, until each plant receives the final limits and directives from which it is to prepare its final plan. It does so, and when the plan is approved, it constitutes the basis for the work of the enterprise for the coming year.

4. One of the essential ingredients in this process is that some flexibility be built into the plan. It is a common practice, for instance, for the superior organs to overstate demands in distributing the limits and directives. That is, the *glavk* may assign to enterprises in the aggregate 10 per cent more output than its plan actually calls for. Then if some plant does not fulfill its plan, the *glavk* as a whole may still meet its goal. Likewise in the case of wage funds or materials allocations, the *glavk* may keep back some of the total allocated to it in order to meet emergencies that arise in the actual course of plan fulfillment. This flexibility makes it possible to handle unforeseen contingencies and to correct for some errors that are made in drawing up the plan. Also it is fairly common for plans to be changed in the course of the year, and such changes may even be made occasionally in the more aggregative indicators of the central plan. One might argue that these "cushions" constitute a tacit admission that the planning will be inaccurate, but, on the other hand, such flexibility enables the system to work in actual practice.

Somewhat akin to this concept of flexibility is the system of priorities implicit in the planning. For instance, the Gosplan might plan for a certain output of building materials and a labor force of so many people to carry out the construction program. If the plans for labor force, productivity, and materials supply work out, the successful completion of all the projects listed, from giant dams to factories to schools and housing, should be realized. But if it appears in the process of plan fulfillment that not all this program can actually be accomplished, the low-priority construction projects (housing has been a traditional example) are dropped, and the approximation, or error, involved in the original plan is corrected *ex post* by sacrificing the low-priority objectives.

5. The task of planning coordination in the Soviet economy is less complicated than it would be in the United States economy because of the relatively low level of consumption and the nature of the goals the planners have set for the economy. Consumption levels are still so low in the Soviet economy that the planners need be little concerned with getting just the right proportions between the output of different kinds of consumer goods. It is perfectly clear that what is needed is increases in output of the basic necessities of life, and even if the planned goals depart from the exact optimal proportions between different kinds of commodities, the goods produced will still be taken off the market easily enough, and will satisfy real needs of the population. The other com-

ponents of demand, the investment goods, and the military items which are so important in the pattern of Soviet production, are much more stable in composition than the consumer demands of an economy such as ours—and are therefore more susceptible to forecasting. Hence the required amounts of such goods can be programmed relatively easily. Incidentally, these features of the Soviet economy are shared by any underdeveloped country embarking on a program of industrialization. As a result, the difficulties of coordination which might make economic planning inappropriate for an economy with high levels of consumption such as ours are less important for the Russians or, by extension, for those underdeveloped countries that might be tempted to choose the Soviet planning approach to industrialization.

6. Finally, it should be emphasized that the planning process does not work perfectly. Often various limits and directives assigned to an enterprise contain inconsistencies; part of a plan may be changed without correcting the other parts that will be affected; and plans will fail to specify what is to be done with output, or where a plant is to get the materials it needs. Despite such mistakes, however, the planning process does what should probably be considered an acceptable job of coordinating supplies and demands.

Soviet Experiments with the Input-Output Approach

As indicated earlier, the Russians have recently become interested in the input-output approach as a technique that might enable them to deal with this problem of coordination more effectively. For many years the Russians blandly ignored developments in economic thought which took place in capitalist countries, except to issue an occasional ritual polemic to the effect that some bit of bourgeois theorizing was a hopeless attempt to shore up capitalism against its impending collapse. In the past few years, however, Soviet economists, like other technicians, have been encouraged to study the achievements of the capitalist countries in search of ideas that might be of use to them. One of the ideas that appealed to them was input-output, and they are now experimenting with applying it to their problem of balancing supplies and demands. The Russians apparently have very serious intentions in this area, as indicated by the high quality of the researchers assigned to these experiments, and by the amount of computer time that is available for them. If the Soviet planners can master all the informational and computational problems involved in input-output, they should be able to cope much more effectively with their job of coordination. Use of the computer will enable Soviet planners to take explicit account of many interrelationships that they now treat only in a vague way, to extend their efforts at coordination over longer periods of time, and to achieve generally better and more accurate long-range planning.

OPTIMIZATION AND EFFICIENCY

The second half of the problem of rational planning involves choices among different ways of doing things or, expressed in other terms, the allocation of available resources in such a way as to obtain the largest possible output from them. Subsumed in this general problem are thousands of different kinds of choices or decisions which must be made throughout the economy. Planners must choose the best place to locate a given plant, decide on the proper distribution of available capital among different investment projects, consider whether it is best to make certain components in one's own factory or to subcontract them to some specialized producer, select the optimum size for plants, determine which of several production processes is the most advantageous economically. These examples constitute only an illustrative list—the number of such decisions and choices is far greater in variety than the few items listed. The overall optimum in the sense of the largest possible output from the entire economy can be achieved only if each of these individually small decisions is made correctly.

Obviously not all these decisions can be made in Moscow. Only the largest ones, those involving the general lines of policy and aggregative allocations can be settled at the level of the central planning organs. Many of the decisions must be made by people in the enterprise in the actual process of working out the plan, in some planning bureau in the *glavk* or ministry, or at other subordinate levels.

The problem posed for consideration here is whether the Russians manage to make these decisions in an economically rational way. How close does the Soviet approach come to being a tolerable substitute for the profit-maximizing calculations of private firms in the market economy? There are two aspects of the problem of rational decision-making in the Soviet economy: (1) whether the Russians understand the issues involved in a given problem, and (2) whether the institutional setting and the available information will enable the planner to make the correct decision. The Russians have in Marxism an economic theory which is in some respects erroneous, and in others seriously incomplete. So their commitment to this body of doctrine may interfere with their understanding of some of the issues involved in "economizing." And even if their theoretical analysis of an economic problem is adequate, the planners may still be unable to make correct decisions because they do not have accurate information, or because they are subjected to pressures which lead them to make economically wrong decisions.

A full survey of the rationality of decision-making in the Soviet economy is too great a task to be dealt with conclusively here. Moreover, it is an aspect of Soviet planning that has not yet been fully explored by economists outside the Soviet Union. However, a brief examination of their treatment of some major areas of decision-making will illustrate some of the obstacles which their economic system has put in the way of rational decision-making.

Capital Allocation

One of the most controversial planning problems in the Soviet Union has been capital allocation. This is one of the relatively few cases where Marxist doctrine does deal explicitly with a practical problem confronting Soviet planners, and it is a case where Marxist theory and the demands of economic rationality are most openly in conflict. According to Marx's theory of value only labor creates value, and such returns as the interest which the capitalist gets on his investment or the landlord for the use of his land represent exploitation rather than compensation for some productive service which has been supplied by the capital or the land. Capital contributes nothing to production and it would therefore be absurd, once the power of the capitalists is overthrown, to require payment for the use of capital. In line with this general position, an interest charge for the use of capital is not made in the Soviet economic system. Enterprises are given their capital in the form of grants from the state and are not required to pay anything for the use of it.

This Marxist interpretation of capital and interest is erroneous; capital is productive in the sense that the addition of capital to a given process increases the output. Moreover, it is scarce, and some rule is required for allocating it to the most productive uses. In the capitalist economy the interest charge serves both as a payment for the productive services of capital and as a means for rationing it. Unless the prospective user of capital finds that it will increase his output or cut his costs enough to be worth the interest he must pay for it, he cannot obtain capital. So by means of the rate of interest capital is rationed out to those uses and in those amounts such that its overall productivity is greatest.

In the Soviet economy the basic circumstance that capital is both productive and scarce still holds. It is true that in the Soviet system there is no need for the state to pay interest to attract capital; interest is not necessary to persuade people to save. That problem is taken care of by a different mechanism. . . . Nevertheless, there cannot possibly be enough capital available to meet all the possible demands which Soviet planners might make for capital. Planners who are responsible for designing factories or machinery, choosing between automatic or non-automatic production lines, designing railroads, and so on, constantly find that if they could just use more capital in these projects the cost per unit of output in terms of current costs would decrease. Consider, for instance, the problem of a planner in the electric power industry who must decide whether to produce a given amount of electric power by building a steam station or a hydroelectric station. The hydroelectric station will require a much greater initial investment than a steam station of the same capacity, but once this investment is made the current costs per kilowatt-hour of electricity will be much lower forever after. In contrast to the steam station, there will be no cost for fuel, and there will be savings in other items, such as labor, as well. The possibility of cutting current inputs by increasing the capital investment, or as it is often called, the "capital intensity" of a project, occurs in many other situations as well. But if these planners were told that they should always increase the capital intensity of each of their projects up to the point where the cost per unit of output would be at the lowest possible point, their total requests for investment funds would far outstrip the amount available. This would not happen if interest were charged for the use of capital, since increases in the capital intensity of a project would add to current costs in the form of interest payments every year. This would set a rational limit to the amount of capital which the planner would find it attractive to use in the projected plant. But the Russians have been unable to use this simple approach because it is contradictory to the Marxist theory of value.

Nevertheless, a way had to be found to decide how far to carry the substitution of capital for current inputs in each case, and the Russian planners got around the obstacle of orthodoxy by using what is called the "payoff period" approach. In considering possible variants of a given investment project they ask how long it will take for the cost savings of the more intensive variant to recover the additional capital investment which it requires. For instance, suppose that in the example mentioned above, the hydroelectric power station requires 50 million rubles more investment than would a steam station of the same capacity, but that its annual operating costs will be 5 million rubles less than that of the steam station. The payoff period for the additional capital investment would thus be ten years. To guide engineers in making these choices the planners have often set up a general rule that additional investment in such cases can be justified only if the payoff period for the additional capital investment does not exceed a stipulated number of years.

A moment's reflection will show that the payoff period is essentially the rate of interest turned upside down. A recoupment period of five years, for instance, means that the return to the additional capital invested (in terms of the value of resources saved) amounts each year to 20 per cent of the investment. Or in other words, the productivity of the capital in this case is 20 per cent. If the authorities set a rule for plant designers that the payoff period must be no more than five years, they are in effect saying that capital should not be used unless the return to it is at least 20 per cent. Thus the planners manage to bring the condemned rate of interest in through the back door. In the early postwar years the anti-Marxist implication of this practice was realized and was officially condemned by the Marxist theoreticians. There followed a long controversy in which the necessity for some such device for capital allocation was made clear, and in the end it was decided to allow the payoff period approach to be used openly and universally. There are now even suggestions that the planners should pretend in their calculations that interest will be charged on the capital invested and some economists have even proposed that enterprises should actually pay a charge to the state in proportion to the amount of capital they are using. The Russians have not declared that Marx was wrong in his labor theory of value, but have simply chosen to ignore it when it conflicts with the demands of rationality in practical problems of planning.

It should not by any means be concluded that recent developments regarding capital allocation mean that the Russians actually achieve a rational allocation of capital. Having surmounted the difficulties in theoretical analysis, they have still not established the institutions for implementing the new understanding. No reasonable payoff period has yet been figured out, and in practice they charge different rates of interest to different users of capital. This is wrong, because it means that some planners are encouraged to use an extra thousand rubles of capital to save 50 rubles per year, whereas someone else might have a much more productive use for that 1,000 rubles of investment funds. But the point is that they are groping their way toward a more rational system of decision-making in this area.

Obsolescence and Replacement

Another illustration of the Soviet difficulties in achieving rational decisions is in the area of obsolescence. The problem which obsolescence poses for decision-makers is essentially the following. As an economy advances, more efficient ways of doing things are constantly being developed. This progress in technology is ordinarily embodied in specific capital goods, or, as they are often called, fixed assets. The improved possibilities in railroad haulage represented by diesel power are embodied in diesel locomotives, for instance, and the possibility of substituting better materials such as aluminum or plastics for traditional kinds of materials is embodied in the form of aluminum and chemical plants. So with the old technology—it is also embodied in the form of existing assets. As technological progress is made, existing assets representing the old technology begin to suffer a competitive disadvantage. The old buildings and machinery may still be in perfectly good working condition and they can still produce the output for which they were originally designed, but they suffer one big disadvantage in comparison with more modern replacements. This disadvantage consists essentially of the fact that using the old assets wastes inputs. Suppose, for example, that improved metalworking machines become available. Old metalworking machines still perform the same operations as the modern machines, but the amount of labor per unit of output will be much greater on the old ones. Keeping the old machines in operation therefore wastes labor.

Consider electric power generation, as another example. As improved boilers and turbines are designed, it is possible to build new generating plants which can produce electric power with a much smaller expenditure of fuel per kilowatt-hour than already existing plants can. Continued use of the existing plants thus involves a waste of fuel. Despite the great variety in the forms of obsolescence, it always involves some such waste of current inputs. In each concrete case there eventually comes a point when the total output of the economy will be increased by abandoning old assets—even though they are still capable of producing—and replacing them with more modern ones. The losses from scrapping obsolete assets and replacing them with new ones will be more than offset by the resources saved from more efficient production. The problem is to choose the correct point at which to abandon obsolete assets.

For a long time the Russians made the claim that a planned socialist economy enjoyed the advantage of having no obsolescence. In the late 1950's, however, this position was officially reversed. The leaders now admit that obsolescence does exist under socialism and Soviet planners are urged to consider very carefully the advisability of replacing obsolete equipment. This change in policy was all to the good, but Soviet practice in replacement decisions still leaves much to be desired. Incorrect decisions as to whether it is more economical to replace or to repair assets may result from confusion in their theoretical analysis. Furthermore, institutional restrictions often prevent the correct amount of replacement even in absence of theoretical errors. The enterprise director usually has funds which he can spend for repair of old assets in order to keep them in operation, but may find it impossible to get sufficient investment funds for a replacement. Or even if replacement funds are obtainable, physical rationing of equipment may make it impossible for him to get authorization to purchase replacement equipment. Most Western observers of the Soviet economy would probably agree that the Russians spend too much effort in repairing old, obsolete assets rather than replacing them with modern ones. It is pointed out by Soviet writers themselves that Soviet firms often spend more resources on repairing some old machine than it would cost to replace it with a completely new one.

On the other hand it is possible that the Soviet centralized system of economic decision-making has some advantages in dealing with a problem like this one. For instance, in many cases it is possible to rebuild and modernize obsolete machinery to make it reasonably similar to the latest replacement possibilities in terms of its productivity characteristics. And this can usually be done with less money than it would take to produce new machines. The Russians have decided at fairly high levels of decision-making that modernization of certain kinds of machines is in general economically advantageous and have established plans for modernizing a large share of the existing stock of metalworking machines, for example.

In carrying out a centrally determined plan for asset modernization undoubtedly many errors will be made. As the central plan is divided up among individual enterprises, there will be cases where a machine will be modernized, though it may not be economically rational for that particular machine, and other machines for which modernization would pay off handsomely will be bypassed. Nevertheless, the total result of this approach will be to get a lot of machinery modernized in a short period of time. In our own economy there will probably be no resources wasted on modernizing machines for which it is not rational, but because some firms are conservative, or lack funds, and because there is no central pressure, there may well be less than the optimum amount of modernization also.

Scale, Specialization, and Location of Plants

Planners must deal with an extremely complicated group of questions in deciding where to locate industrial plants, how large and how specialized to make them. The optimum size of plant in a given industry is determined by such considerations as the economies that come from large-scale production, transportation cost of shipping the product to the customers in a market area of a given size, flexibility in service to customers. In most kinds of industrial processes, up to a certain point, enlarging the plant brings reductions in costs because of the possibilities of better organization and other "economies of scale." There is, however, a point beyond which further expansion brings no economies in production costs, but does require that the plant must serve a larger and larger market area. The resulting increase in transport charges will affect delivered cost adversely. An indication of the best size for a plant for any given industry is obtained by balancing off all these different factors against one another. The capitalist attempts to evaluate all such factors in deciding the size and location of his plant, and in the long run the force of competition works to eliminate those producers whose calculations did not meet the demands of rationality.

It is often argued that the Soviet system, on the other hand, is prone to expensive errors in this area of decision-making. For example, policies of plant size and location in one important branch of the economy—the iron and steel industry—have been carefully analyzed in one study with the following conclusions. In the thirties, the designers of iron and steel units strove to make them as large and as specialized as possible in order to cut production costs to the minimum. In doing this, however, they more or less ignored a number of important factors which should have been taken into account in deciding the best size of plant from the overall national economic point of view. Rolling mills, for instance, were designed to be so big and so specialized that a single rolling mill could produce the entire output of a particular item for the whole country. This meant very low production costs for that output of course, but by the time the item was delivered to customers all over the Soviet Union the delivered cost was extremely high. The geographical location and the specialization of the rolling mill seriously restricted the responsiveness of the iron and steel industry to the needs of its customers. Because many customers were located at points far distant, it was difficult for them to communicate with or influence the rolling mill which was producing the goods they needed. That this could happen was partly the result of the institutional structure of the Soviet economy. The motivations of planners in Soviet industry are mostly concerned with costs and volume of output, and they follow policies in designing plants which will improve these indicators as much as possible. It made no difference to the designers of iron and steel mills that their decisions would involve extra work for the railroad system or that customers would be inconvenienced. That was the worry of the customers and of the railroads. Toward the end of the thirties the folly of this approach to planning became obvious. It was found that in a number of areas of the economy the emphasis on large-scale plants and neglect of transportation costs and customer service were wholly undesirable. There was an official condemnation and campaign against "gigantomania," i.e., a bias in favor of giant plants, and planners were instructed in the future to design smaller plants scattered throughout the Soviet Union.

Indeed it may well be that in this case, as often happens in the Soviet economy, the policy-makers at the top went too far in the other direction in their zeal to correct past errors. One of the most obvious results of the gigantomania was an excessive load on the transportation system. In order to correct this the Russian leaders announced a new policy in industrial location which was to emphasize regional self-sufficiency. Fairly large regions of the country were to be more or less self-sufficient with regard to production of many important items. In order to enforce this policy there was a reform in railroad freight rates which penalized shipments beyond a certain planned average distance for a particular commodity. Thus, for instance, it was planned that the average length of haul for coal should be about 700 kilometers, and when coal was shipped farther than this the rates began to rise very sharply. This was intended to discourage the shipment of coal from one region to another and thus to stimulate its production within each of the self-sufficient regions. But, in their efforts to make each of these regions self-sufficient the Russians failed to take full advantage of the possibilities of interregional specialization of labor.

The Soviet Price System

One obstacle to rational decision-making common to all these problems, and to many others as well, is the Soviet price system. Most economic decisions rest on a comparison of costs, and so are affected by the prices of the things that are being costed. When a planner is deciding between using coal or natural gas, whether to dieselize or electrify a section of railroad line, to locate a plant at one point or another, to buy a part or to make it, he has to choose one of several possibilities that will result in the lowest costs. And in making this calculation he must depend on prices. For instance, in deciding between dieselization and electrification, the estimate of the cost of electrification will be influenced by the prices that are set for the various inputs into the electrification project, such as copper and other materials involved in building the contact network, electric locomotives, and the price of electric power, which in turn depends on the price of coal. The costs for the dieselization project will likewise be influenced by the prices set on the corresponding inputs. But if these prices depart too much from real costs, there is a danger that the planners may choose an alternative that looks cheapest on paper, but is not really cheapest in terms of real national economic costs, that is, in terms of the real resources that go into it.

And indeed the Soviet price system seems to be a very imperfect measure of the real costs of resources. In the Soviet Union prices are set not by a process of supply and demand, but by administrative order. Most prices are set by fairly high-level organs of the government, others by price-setting organs in the ministries or the economic councils, and some are set by local authorities. Once set, they remain in effect for fairly extended periods of time, though they are overhauled from time to time. This kind of official, fixed price system is vitally important for purposes of planning and control. The process of drawing up cost plans, of planning investment, of estimating profits, and of making all other financial calculations is much easier when prices are known and stable. The point of departure for setting most prices is supposed to be the reported cost of production, but in practice, prices have usually departed considerably from the actual costs of production. The prices of some goods reflect large subsidies, while others have been set high enough to return very high rates of profit. Moreover, the prices customarily do not include any charges for rent or capital, and even calculations of cost of production have often been distorted by the errors of Soviet cost accounting. For instance, Soviet accountants have always considerably underestimated the real costs of depreciation and obsolescence in figuring costs. As a result of these peculiarities in their accounting and pricing system the price placed on a good has often been an inaccurate measure of what it really cost to produce it.

With such distortions in the price system, it is very difficult for planners to know whether their choice of the cheapest way of doing something is in reality correct. Soviet planners themselves have frequently expressed doubts about the validity of calculations based on existing prices, and in many cases have tried to make unofficial corrections of existing prices to render them more nearly accurate measures of real cost to the national economy. Even so, the Soviet price system often leads the planners to the wrong conclusion.

Price formation has seen great changes during the last few years however. Most of the postwar price reforms have aimed at eliminating subsidies and abnormal profits. And more recently, the Russians have become engaged in the most unfettered discussion of the theory of value and price formation in a socialist economy that has ever taken place in the history of the regime. There are radical proposals for changing the price system from its present basis, extending even to advocacy of the inclusion of interest and rent charges in prices. They have also been making a more careful study of their accounting, and have already set in motion plans for improving depreciation accounting. Their interest in the input-output technique is in part directed toward the possibility of using it for accurate computation of relative prices for most of the important goods in the economy in a simultaneous calculation. It is possible, therefore, that many of the errors in price formation which have confounded economic calculation in the past will be eliminated in the future, although this is still only a prospective development.

New Approaches in Maximizing

The Russians have been handicapped indirectly in other ways in their economic thinking by their commitment to Marxist economic theory. We are not referring here to the fact that some Marxist ideas are erroneous, as in the case of capital productivity and allocation. Rather the problem is that Marxism is a very incomplete sort of economic theory. Marx's ideas were developed in the third quarter of the nineteenth century, on the basis of economic theory as it existed at that time, and he simply has nothing to say on many of the issues that arise in the process of making correct economic decisions. Indeed, Marx was much more interested in other questions than he was in explaining how an economy should function to get the most out of its resources. Economics is a branch of science that has undergone extensive development in the capitalist countries since Marx's time, but Soviet economists have been cut off from these advances by their Marxist heritage. Much of this new economics involves more rigorous development of theories and concepts, often assisted by the use of mathematical approaches and models. Input-output, mentioned above, is one example, and another recent development is a device called "linear programming." Linear programming is a way of choosing the best solution from among what seem to be an endless list of possible ways of doing something. Planners or producers in business, or in the government, often come up against extremely complex problems, such as how to ship goods between a number of producing plants and a number of customers scattered over a wide area so that the total freight haulage will be a minimum, and so that the movement of empties between points will be a minimum. Or there may be a problem of distributing among different machines in a factory a number of operations, each of which might be performed on more than one machine, so that the output of a given number of machines will be a maximum. In a problem of this kind there is usually a large choice of ways of organizing the work, and a trial-and-error approach, or the selection of what *seems* to be a rational method, may give a result that is far from the best achievable solution. What linear programming does is to set up such problems in a mathematical form so that they can be solved for the maximum or minimum value of the variables one is interested in. This analytical tool was originated only a couple of decades ago, but already is used widely by business and government planners and decision-makers in the United States.

The interesting thing is that linear programming was actually invented independently in the Soviet Union somewhat earlier than it was in the United States, and its inventor, a mathematician named L. V. Kantorovich, showed how it could be used to find the best solutions to a number of practical problems of economic planning. However, Russian planners and economists never did anything with it. Kantorovich's work was ignored for nearly twenty years. The Soviet conception of economics involved a hostility to mathematical methods as bourgeois in origin and "formalistic." But here also the past few years have brought a revolution in the Russians' thought and practice, and they are now planning to make extensive use of linear programming in their planning. They are saved much embarrassment in doing this by being able to claim that the idea was invented by a Russian. But in any case, linear programming has become one of the favored fields in their economic research.

This turning to mathematical methods in general, and to linear programming in particular, holds great promise for better economic calculation in their planning. It is precisely when the perspective of a decision-maker takes in a very wide range of variables and interrelationships that linear programming is most likely to be useful, and, of course, this is the situation in which Soviet planners usually find themselves. So it is not unlikely that the use of these more precise methods of calculation will improve their economic decisions. But however extensively they use it, however many useful applications they find for it, the significant thing is that linear programming marks a turning point in their thought by focusing their attention on the problem of maximizing—of getting as much as possible out of limited resources. This is a concept they have only groped after in the past. The turn to linear programming is an important indication of the new interest they are now showing in the problem of rationality in economic planning.

THE RATIONALITY OF SOVIET PLANNING

Can we draw from this brief survey a balanced view as to the irrationality or rationality of Soviet planning? Do the Russians achieve tolerably correct coordination and decision-making in their planning? It should be admitted that on this issue, more than on any other, it would be difficult for specialists on the Soviet economy to reach a consensus. Certainly it is an ambiguous picture; it is possible to find many illustrations of their failure to achieve coordination, to understand the issues involved in certain economic problems, and to implement such understanding as they have. On the other hand, it is important to keep in mind some important reservations. After all, no economic system is perfectly rational—all suffer from errors in coordination, decision-making, and resource allocation. The errors we see in the Soviet case impress us with particular force because they are shortcomings to which our economic system is not particularly prone. The Soviet system is especially poor in the area of short-run flexibility and smooth operation, of rationality in the small. But it may work well enough in bigger issues, where really large amounts of resources are involved. The problem of modernization of assets discussed above is a case in point. Moreover, we should have some appreciation of the particular influences which their stage of economic development exerts on problems of economic rationality. In the process of industrialization the importance of short-run coordination and decisions that conform to short-run scarcity relationships was somewhat circumscribed. Any errors made in the short run were quickly corrected by growth in resources, by changes in scarcities, costs, and values. But as a result of industrialization the Soviet economy has undergone a significant metamorphosis. It has become a distinctly different kind of economy from what it was in the past—bigger, more complex, with more alternatives at every level of decision-making, more interrelationships and ramifications for every decision taken. Only now, in this new situation, do the crudities in techniques of coordination and the sterility of economic analysis characteristic of the past begin to involve waste of a really serious order of magnitude. Moreover, as changing circumstances make these problems more important, the attention of the leaders has shifted to finding ways of dealing with them, on both the theoretical and the institutional levels. To deal with the increased complexity of coordination, they are turning to input-output analysis and the electronic computer. As the problems of economic decision-making become more crucial, they are willing to allow more freedom in economic analysis and to reject old prejudices that interfered with rational decision-making. They are willing to reform pricing and to turn to the formerly scorned linear programming and other mathematical devices for aid in making economic decisions. And they are even willing to experiment with the institutional setting in order to shift the locus of some kinds of decision-making further down the administrative hierarchy, as a way of providing more flexibility and obtaining a more appropriate perspective on important considerations in any decision.

53. DEVIATIONISM: THE YUGOSLAV CASE*

Calvin B. Hoover

Before visiting Yugoslavia I was extremely doubtful whether the economic and political system of that country which had allegedly undergone fundamental change was in fact basically different from that of Soviet Russia. The recurring conflicts first between Stalin and Tito and more recently between Khrushchev and Tito had unquestionably been accompanied by the development of a Yugoslav economy no longer subsidiary to that of Soviet Russia. If, however, it had simply taken the form of a Yugoslav national soviet system, it would have had little interest for me, regardless of its significance in the international power struggle. After my stay in Yugoslavia I no longer doubted that the economic system had undergone changes, and that it now differs radically from that of Soviet Russia. These changes began with the setting up of workers' councils in 1948–49, following the break with Stalin. Further important changes were introduced in 1952–53, and others are still being made.

The break between Tito and Stalin was, indeed, an important factor in initiating changes in the Yugoslav economic system. It allowed Yugoslav Communists to personalize in the figure of Stalin those aspects of the Soviet system which had profoundly disturbed them, without repudiating Lenin and the October Revolution. Repudiation of the Soviet October Revolution was impossible for the Yugoslav Communist Party, since its own domination of the economic and political system was based upon similar revolutionary violence. The increasing bitterness of the current conflict between Tito and Khrushchev has gone far to remove the remaining inhibitions which Yugoslav Communists had felt about developing an economic system which deviated from Soviet

* Calvin B. Hoover, *The Economy, Liberty and the State* (New York: The Twentieth Century Fund, 1959), pp. 411–24.

Russia's. The virtual cancellation of Soviet loans to Yugoslavia while I was in Belgrade noticeably strengthened the decision to depart from the Soviet model.

Indeed, the Communist League of Yugoslavia (as the Communist Party now calls itself) has announced its determination to restore to the mass of the workers themselves the control of industrial plants and state farms which the state took over upon the successful seizure of power by Tito and his followers. The removal of the state from the control of industry and the substitution of worker control is visualized by Yugoslav Communists as that very process of the "withering away" of the temporarily necessary state after the dictatorship of the proletariat which was foreseen by Marx, Engels and Lenin. Whether this effort to have the mass of workers take over industry has any substantial chance of success is doubtful. It may even be that the readiness of Yugoslav Communist leaders to take this step is dependent upon the workers wanting to do no more than what the Communist leaders think they should. There can be no doubt, however, that the structural form of the economy has been basically altered by this effort to take industry out of the hands of the state and place it in the hands of the workers.

The conviction that state management of industry is not consistent with socialism was repeatedly stated to me by Yugoslav officials who were also Party members. As one official put it, "We came to the conclusion that the state is the enemy of socialism." Another said, "We had no doubt that a centrally planned and authoritatively directed economic system would work. We saw that it had worked in Russia. In a sense, it had worked with us. But we became convinced that it would only work at the greatest cost to personal freedom." The 1958 Program of the League of Communists expresses a similar view: "Our experience, as well as the experience of other socialist countries, has shown that the management of the economy and of the whole of social life by way of the state apparatus exclusively, leads perforce to greater centralization of power, to an ever closer merging of the state and party apparatus, to their further strengthening, whereby they tend to become independent and impose themselves as a force over and above society." This is in complete conflict with the position of the Communist Party of Soviet Russia, which does not admit the possibility of conflict of interest between the workers and the state controlled by the Communist Party.

With the purpose of removing the state from the management of the economy, the Yugoslav government proceeded to jettison the whole system of a state planned and directed economy. Expressed in its simplest and most extreme form, the intent has been to set up a competitive, free market economy but with collective ownership instead of private ownership of the means of production—a sort of capitalism without individual stockholders. The institutional structure and working rules by which this end has been pursued are fascinating to an economist. There are even some theoretical resemblances to the *soziale Marktwirtschaft* of the neo-liberals of present-day Germany and Austria.

In line with this objective, individual industrial plants in Yugoslavia are organized as "working collectives." These are controlled, in principle, by the workers themselves, through elected workers' councils, which in turn elect a smaller management committee that works with the manager. The manager is hired by a committee representing both the workers' council and the local commune in which the plant is located. In principle, each workers' collective produces and sells its goods for the best prices it can get in competition with the workers' collectives of plants producing similar products. Total wages earned by the working collective depend upon the cost of production, the volume of production and the selling price. Wage rates within the plant are determined by the workers' councils, within the limits set by the national trade union organizations.

No sooner had the working collectives been set up than it became apparent that it would not be either feasible or equitable to allow the workers in a particular plant or a state farm to profit by the more productive capital equipment one plant might have as compared with another, or the more fertile land one state farm might have as compared with another. Consequently, an interest charge is made on the capital value of a plant's assets which is paid to the state. Similarly, a rental charge is made for the use of agricultural land by state farms and the use of mines by state mining enterprises. The theory is that the working collective of a particular plant or state farm is only the operator of the particular enterprise. Society as a whole "owns" the assets.

But what is to prevent the workers' collective of a particular plant from profiting by a monopoly position? First of all, there are anti-monopoly regulations which are supposed to prevent cartels and agreements in restraint of trade. In fact, some working collectives have tried to arrive at illegal "gentlemen's agreements" to prevent "capitalistic cut-throat competition." In spite of the regulations attempting to enforce competition, various "working collectives" have found themselves in a quasi-monopolistic position in being able to raise their incomes more easily than others. As a result, a whole series of measures, in addition to the payment of interest on assets and rent on land and mines, has been introduced to prevent "undue profits" or to prevent such profits from being paid out as wages. Some of these measures are intended primarily to prevent the workers in one factory from getting wages "unduly" higher than those paid for similar work in other factories, or to prevent the workers in marketing enterprises from benefiting at the expense of those who are producers in the more limited meaning of the term. Such measures include the governmental fixing of prices on a limited list of basic industrial commodities, such as coal, steel, electric power and the most important food products. They include also the taxation of profits and the setting up of a whole series of reserve funds for the individual plant into which profits are paid instead of being disbursed as wages. There is also a regulation that prices of goods produced by any plant cannot be increased without obtaining a permit from the federal price office, that the commune may refuse to allow profits to be disbursed as wage bonuses if these are due to price increases rather than to increased productivity and, finally, that annual additions to wages out of profits may not exceed two months' wages.

Some of these measures are a quite logical part of a competitive economic system, such as the requirement that interest be paid to the state upon the assets of industrial plants, that rent be paid for land held by state farms and that rental payments be made by the richer mines. Others, however, reflect a shrewd unwillingness to follow blindly a policy of depending upon uncontrolled competitive processes to govern prices, wages and investment in a modern industrial economy. Almost all of the measures which limit "undue" payments of wages out of profits limit the incentive effect of allowing wages in each plant to depend upon the valuation which a free market would place upon the productivity of that plant. Almost all these measures also constitute a form of compulsory savings and investment.

There are other means also designed for this purpose, such as the 10 per cent payroll tax which is set aside for housing construction. In addition to the legally required withholding of profits from the wage fund of each working collective, the Communist leadership in the workers' councils continually tries to induce the workers' representatives to withhold as large an amount of profits as possible from the wages fund, even above the amounts legally required, in order that such withheld funds may be used for public purposes rather than for personal consumption by the workers.

Yugoslav government officials frankly claim that it is not possible at this time to have fully democratic control of the state and the economy in so poor a country. For economic growth and development, it is absolutely necessary to have much higher saving and investment than would be possible under full democracy. There can be no doubt that a high rate of saving and capital investment is taking place, accompanied by a high rate of economic growth. At the same time, there is some evidence that the profits withheld from wages are also going into the construction of unnecessarily elaborate administrative buildings in industry, on the state farms and at all levels of government.

With the development of the new type of partly autonomous, partly competitive industry the former system of centralized, authoritative planning was wiped out. No longer is there an elaborate central plan, with the various factories, mines, state farms and other economic enterprises assigned planned quotas to be fulfilled. No "plan orders" are issued. The state planning organization now only sets forth general objectives and lines of development. Monetary, fiscal and credit controls are primarily depended upon to implement this type of planning. However, a large measure of control over investment is provided by the state investment banking system, through which a large part of the funds withheld by the state are disbursed.

The dismantling of the huge bureaucracy by which the state previously operated the economy has been largely superseded by another large bureaucracy needed under the new system of "operation of the economy by the workers themselves." There is a system of dual legislative bodies, starting with the communes and going up through the republics to the federal government. At each level of government there is a council elected by all citizens which legislates on political matters and a Council of Producers elected by producers only which legislates on economic matters. These are connected by a People's Committee representing both councils. Each of the councils is served by numerous committees designed to insure maximum popular participation in the actual process of governing. This insures that a large number of citizens devote a vast number of man-hours to the performance of such duties. The system of self-government in industry through the workers' councils and the Management Committee has a similar purpose and a similar result.

The situation is very different from that in Poland, where there have been serious and even bitter conflicts between the workers' councils and the managers of plants. Communist leaders in Yugoslavia say that their real problem has been to develop continued and serious worker interest in the workers' councils. Indeed, it may well prove as difficult to induce active participation of the majority of the workers of a plant in its affairs as it is to induce individual stockholders of American corporations to attend stockholders' meetings or to induce the membership of American trade unions to participate actively in union affairs.

That the Communist League dominates the whole economic and political structure of the country is beyond question. Although only some 25 per cent of industrial workers are Communists, about 50 per cent of the membership of the workers' councils are League members. Almost 100 per cent of plant managers are members of the League. The process by which the Communist League decides who is to be appointed or "elected" to what office in the economy or in the government is a closely held secret in Yugoslavia, just as it always has been in Soviet Russia. There is no way of knowing whether anything like democratic processes operate within the League itself. Communist leaders, government officials and industrial managers, largely overlapping categories, were sometimes reluctant to admit the role of the Communist League in the "control of industry by the workers." Under persistent questioning, the very important role of the League was admitted. However, it was insisted that there was no direction from above and that in the workers' councils, for example, Communists voted simply as socially conscious individuals rather than as disciplined members of a Party cell. I frankly doubt that this is so.

The significance for the whole world of a Communist country in which the ruling class has come to recognize the state as at least the potential enemy of socialism cannot be overestimated. This significance is all the greater when a comprehensive economic system, fundamentally different from the Soviet system, has been set up with the purpose of removing the state from the operation of the economy. In my judgment the system functions with an impressive degree of success, measured both by the volume of production and by the success in preventing overt industrial conflict.

Paradoxically, what is not at all certain is whether the changed economic system really does what it was intended to do, that is, provide for the removal of state control and the implementation of industrial democracy through direct worker control of industrial plants. In the first place, as has been pointed out, industrial democracy may well be a utopian goal, impossible to make really effective. In the second place, control by the state may still exist through the Communist League's control of the economic and political apparatus. The Communist League in itself, like all other ruling Communist parties, constitutes a formidable state. One might say that the Communist League is now the state, which operates the economy through a new form of economic organization.

It may be that the whole system could not function without the monopoly of political power held by the Communist League or without at least the benevolent influence of the members of the Communist League exerted at all levels in the control and management of the economy. The explicit recognition by the Yugoslav Communist League of the dangers of permanent centralized management of the economy by the state, of the evils of bureaucracy and of the importance of personal liberty means, however, that an ideological foundation has been provided for those who would fight against these evils and dangers. Furthermore, the creation of actual machinery through which the protests of workers against managerial tyranny might be expressed appears to afford some protection against such tyranny developing.

I am limited in trying to make an appraisal of the new Yugoslav economic system by the fact that Yugoslavia is still a police state. True, these extraordinary police powers are primarily exercised against Yugoslav Stalinists and against those suspected of adherence to former Yugoslav governments. There is nothing in present-day Yugoslavia to correspond to the terror of Stalin's day in Soviet Russia or to the terror in present-day Hungary. One can carry on most interesting and fruitful discussions of the relations among the economy, liberty and the state with Yugoslav Communist leaders and governmental officials. Contrary to the situation in Soviet Russia, these leaders and officials are accessible to foreigners for such discussions. Indeed, Yugoslav officials were so friendly and helpful that I found it difficult to maintain an appropriately objective attitude.

Elections are not free in Yugoslavia. Neither is there freedom to publish critical comment on governmental policy or with respect to important Communist leaders. The press and all means of publication are closely controlled. One hears only the most limited and guarded criticism of the government among the populace, though, in fact, I had little opportunity to hear such criticism if anyone had felt like giving expression to it.

I could never forget that Yugoslavia is the country of the "New Class" about which Djilas wrote his book. Djilas is still in prison because of his criticism of the regime. His former high position and personal closeness to Tito did not protect him against the power of the state. Indeed, they seemed to aggravate the offenses with which he was charged. Dedier, who supported Djilas, is not in prison but is living in poverty, excluded from all employment.

The "cult of personality," the term used by Khrushchev to account for the "mistakes" of Stalin, still flourishes in Yugoslavia. A few days after I left Belgrade, Tito gave a public address in the mining town of Labin. In response, the crowd set up a rhythmic chant, in well-drilled unison, "Tito hero! We belong to Tito—Tito belongs to us!" Tito has a number of residences at his disposal. Besides his well-known retreat on Brioni Island, he lives in one palace in Belgrade and has another which he uses principally as a guest house for distinguished visitors. Driving through the residential area once occupied by the wealthy and by officials of former governments, I asked a resident of Belgrade who it was that now lived in these villas. He gave me a wry look and replied, "Whom do you suppose? The New Class, of course!" Yet it is not a fact that all such villas are occupied by the New Class. There are too many circumstantial accounts of eight or ten families, often formerly poor peasants from Montenegro or Macedonia, living, to the detriment of the plumbing system, in one villa formerly occupied by a single bourgeois family. When I had lunch with a Yugoslav couple high in the councils of the state and the Communist League, I found the villa in which they lived comfortable and furnished in unusually good taste but not lavishly. There was apparently one house servant and a chauffeur. Since both my host and his wife had heavy official duties, it would appear that this was close to the minimum standard of living necessary for the most effective performance of their functions. Yet in a country as poor as Yugoslavia this level of living was far above the average.

Thus, to an important degree, the higher level of living of the New Class reflects no more than the standard which any ruling class must maintain in order to function efficiently. Its superiority to their own inevitably shocks industrial workers and peasants who were told by the former revolutionists now comprising the New Class that a higher living standard was the special perquisite of the capitalist exploiters and that it would disappear with the overthrow of capitalism. A regime which takes power under the name of socialism is thus likely to find that it cannot permit free elections, at least until the potential voters have become accustomed to the higher level of living of the New Class. Without free elections, the danger always exists that the New Class will abstract for itself out of the national income a higher standard of living than is functionally necessary.

Yugoslav salaries, both of state officials and of plant managers, are, by all accounts, kept quite low. The salary of a plant or state farm manager is claimed to be no more than three or three and a half times the average wage of workers. Indeed, it is claimed that some skilled workers on piece rates occasionally receive higher wages than the plant manager. Communist leaders commonly maintained that the differential between the salaries of managers and the wages of workers is too low. However, the greater part of the compensation of the ruling class in Yugoslavia consists of "fringe benefits." These usually include a car with chauffeur and sometimes living quarters and servants, plus other "expense account" items.

Evidently stung both by the publication of Milovan Djilas' book and by labor unrest, the Executive Committee of the Yugoslav League of Communists in early 1958 denounced the widespread abuse of power and the privileges of office by bureaucrats of state and industry. The Committee cited as instances the purchase of expensive motor cars by factory directors and their use for personal pleasure, lavish spending for entertainment, the bestowing of the most desirable living quarters—allegedly to stimulate production—on personal favorites who had performed no real service, and other similar practices. In many factories and other economic enterprises the wishes of the elected representatives of the workers were disregarded. Workers who criticized such arbitrary actions were often transferred or even fired.

The construction of luxury apartments was banned and the use of official cars for personal purposes was brought under regulation. Thus the rulers of a totalitarian society may at times try to limit the power and privileges of the administrative ranks below them, just as the top management of corporations in a capitalistic society may try to limit the perquisites of corporation executives of lower rank.

My conclusion is that the "New Class" in Yugoslavia in setting up a new type of economic system is carrying out an experiment of profound importance to the whole world. This new economic system has already demonstrated its ability to carry on industrial production with substantial success. The "New Class" has declared through the 1958 Draft Programme of the League of Communists of Yugoslavia that "Legal order in Yugoslavia protects, and must protect, any citizen from the arbitrary action of any social factor or any state body." The League of Communists also considers ". . . proclamation of an absolute monopoly of the Communist Party to political power as a universal and 'perpetual' principle of dictatorship of the proletariat and of socialist development as an untenable dogma."

Whether the new Yugoslav economic system can be operated without intolerable interference with the liberties of individuals will depend in large degree upon whether the Communist League can and will carry out these expressed principles. The Communist League still expresses its devotion to the doctrine of the "withering away of the state'," and believes that the new economic system is a giant step in this direction. Personally, I do not believe that the new system can bring about the withering away of the state. That is impossible for any modern industrialized economy.

The results of the Yugoslav attempt, and to a lesser extent that of the present Polish government, to reduce the power of centralized autocratic bureaucracies over the economy are still inconclusive. If either should demonstrate that a state which came into existence by revolutionary violence, dedicated to the establishment of a collectivist economy, can operate such an economy without an intolerable degree of limitation of personal liberty while developing a form of government which is workably representative, it would be an immense service to mankind.

Until now there seemed little hope that a totalitarian economic and political system could ever evolve through internal processes into a system with the kind of personal liberty which exists in the quasi-capitalistic countries of the West. This hope may not be fulfilled, since trends in Yugoslavia and Poland may be reversed by events. Moreover, with the best of will on the part of the leaders of any form of economic and political system, it is not going to be easy to preserve personal liberties when, owing to the nature of modern industrial society, the power of the state must be great and widespread. Yet the recognition of the problem by the leaders of states which were previously totalitarian and the actual setting up of new forms of economic systems in an effort to solve the problem represent a most important step.

In a real sense the countries which have modern forms of modified capitalism face the same basic problem of how to reconcile the increased power of the state with liberty. The experience of France, for example, shows that the minimum authority needed to carry on the functions of the state may require limitations upon traditional forms of representative government. While the crisis which brought de Gaulle to power was not primarily economic, developments in France illustrate the kind of alternatives which might have to be faced in an economic crisis in other countries of the West. The 1957–58 economic recession in the United States, reflecting the need to control inflation while preventing economic depression, gives point to this observation. Yet it does not appear that any such powers of the state over the economy and over the individual as exist in totalitarian states would be required to deal with such a situation. The recollection that democratic and parliamentary institutions were adequate in most countries of the West to win through the far worse economic depression of the thirties offers substantial hope that these institutions can be adapted to solve the complex problems associated with the necessary growth of the power of the state over the economy. The high level of productivity which has been attained by the quasi-capitalistic economies of the West should mitigate the fierceness of the struggle for distributional shares among alternative recipient groups and thus facilitate the solution of these problems.

If the Yugoslav type of economic system, with production carried on by semi-competitive corporations, should some day come to be accompanied by a free political system, it would afford a striking comparison with the kind of economic and political system which would exist if the present trends in the countries of the West continue. There would still be differences in form between corporations of the Yugoslav type and the "privately owned" but managerially operated corporations which, for example, would still presumably operate under a Labor government in the United Kingdom. If the distribution of real income, including perquisites and fringe benefits, were essentially the same, the difference between the two systems would not be great. Indeed, there would not have to be much further evolutionary development of corporations in the United States or much further redistribution of income before the differences between the so-called capitalistic systems and the so-called socialist systems of the Yugoslav type would lose their sharpness.

Finally, the evolution of new institutional relations among the economy, liberty and the state depends upon the avoidance of armed conflict between states with varying economic systems. So long as the economic and political systems of the Soviet type of totalitarian state appeared immutable, war between the Soviet state and the free societies of the West seemed inevitable. Though as yet inconclusive, the evidence that free societies might develop out of collectivist states of revolutionary origin affords the best hope that the catastrophe which now menaces mankind can be averted.

54. THE NEW CLASS*

Milovan Djilas

Everything happened differently in the U.S.S.R. and other Communist countries from what the leaders—even such prominent ones as Lenin, Stalin, Trotsky, and Bukharin—anticipated. They expected that the state would rapidly wither away, that democracy would be strengthened. The reverse happened. They expected a rapid improvement in the standard

* Milovan Djilas, *The New Class* (New York: Frederick A. Praeger, 1957), excerpts from pp. 37–43, 47–54, 59, 60, 64, 68, 69.

of living—there has been scarcely any change in this respect and, in the subjugated East European countries, the standard has even declined. In every instance, the standard of living has failed to rise in proportion to the rate of industrialization, which was much more rapid. It was believed that the differences between cities and villages, between intellectual and physical labor, would slowly disappear; instead these differences have increased. Communist anticipations in other areas—including their expectations for developments in the non-Communist world—have also failed to materialize.

The greatest illusion was that industrialization and collectivization in the U.S.S.R., and destruction of capitalist ownership, would result in a classless society. In 1936, when the new Constitution was promulgated, Stalin announced that the "exploiting class" had ceased to exist. The capitalist and other classes of ancient origin had in fact been destroyed, but a new class, previously unknown to history, had been formed.

It is understandable that this class, like those before it, should believe that the establishment of its power would result in happiness and freedom for all men. The only difference between this and other classes was that it treated the delay in the realization of its illusions more crudely. It thus affirmed that its power was more complete than the power of any other class before in history, and its class illusions and prejudices were proportionally greater.

This new class, the bureaucracy, or more accurately the political bureaucracy, has all the characteristics of earlier ones as well as some new characteristics of its own. Its origin had its special characteristics also, even though in essence it was similar to the beginnings of other classes.

Other classes, too, obtained their strength and power by the revolutionary path, destroying the political, social, and other orders they met in their way. However, almost without exception, these classes attained power *after* new economic patterns had taken shape in the old society. The case was the reverse with new classes in the Communist systems. It did not come to power to *complete* a new economic order but to *establish* its own and, in so doing, to establish its power over society.

In earlier epochs the coming to power of some class, some part of a class, or of some party, was the final event resulting from its formation and its development. The reverse was true in the U.S.S.R. There the new class was definitely formed after it attained power. Its consciousness had to develop before its economic and physical powers, because the class had not taken root in the life of the nation. This class viewed its role in relation to the world from an idealistic point of view. Its practical possibilities were not diminished by this. In spite of its illusions, it represented an objective tendency toward industrialization. Its practical bent emanated from this tendency. The promise of an ideal world increased the faith in the ranks of the new class and sowed illusions among the masses. At the same time it inspired gigantic physical undertakings.

Because this new class had not been formed as a part of the economic and social life before it came to power, it could only be created in an organization of a special type, distinguished by a special discipline based on identical philosophic and ideological views of its members. A unity of belief and iron discipline was necessary to overcome its weaknesses.

The roots of the new class were implanted in a special party, of the Bolshevik type. Lenin was right in his view that his party was an exception in the history of human society, although he did not suspect that it would be the beginning of a new class.

To be more precise, the initiators of the new class are not found in the party of the Bolshevik type as a whole but in that stratum of professional revolutionaries who made up its core even before it attained power. It was not by accident that Lenin asserted after the failure of the 1905 revolution that only professional revolutionaries—men whose sole profession was revolutionary work—could build a new party of the Bolshevik type. It was still less accidental that even Stalin, the future creator of a new class, was the most outstanding example of such a professional revolutionary. The new ruling class has been gradually developing from this very narrow stratum of revolutionaries. These revolutionaries composed its core for a long period. Trotsky noted that in pre-revolutionary professional revolutionaries was the origin of the future Stalinist bureaucrat. What he did not detect was the beginning of a new class of owners and exploiters.

This is not to say that the new party and the new class are identical. The party, however, is the core of that class, and its base. It is very difficult, perhaps impossible, to define the limits of the new class and to identify its members. The new class may be said to be made up of those who have special privileges and economic preference because of the administrative monopoly they hold.

. . . . .

The social origin of the new class lies in the proletariat just as the aristocracy arose in a peasant society, and the bourgeoisie in a commercial and artisans' society. There are exceptions, depending on national conditions, but the proletariat in economically underdeveloped countries, being backward, constitutes the raw material from which the new class arises.

There are other reasons why the new class always acts as the champion of the working class. The new class is anti-capitalistic and, consequently, logically dependent upon the working strata. The new class is supported by the proletarian struggle and the traditional faith of the proletariat in a socialist, Communist society where there is no brutal exploitation. It is vitally important for the new class to assure a normal flow of production, hence it cannot ever lose its connection with the proletariat. Most important of all, the new class cannot achieve industrialization and consolidate its power without the help of the working class. On the other hand, the working class sees in expanded industry the salvation from its poverty and despair. Over a long period of time, the interests, ideas, faith, and hope of the new class, and of parts of the working class and of the poor peasants, coincide and unite. Such mergers have occurred in the past among other widely different classes. Did not the bourgeoisie represent the peasantry in the struggle against the feudal lords?

The movement of the new class toward power comes as a result of the efforts of the proletariat and the poor. These are the masses upon which the party or the new class must lean and with which its interests are most closely allied. This is true until the new class finally establishes its power and authority. Over and above this, the new class is interested in the proletariat and the poor only to the extent necessary for developing production and for maintaining in subjugation the most aggressive and rebellious social forces.

The monopoly which the new class establishes in the name of the working class over the whole of society is, primarily, a monopoly over the working class itself. This monopoly is first intellectual, over the so-called *avant-garde* proletariat, and then over the whole proletariat. This is the biggest deception the class must accomplish, but it shows that the power and interests of the new class lie primarily in industry. Without industry the new class cannot consolidate its position or authority.

Former sons of the working class are the most steadfast members of the new class. It has always been the fate of slaves to provide for their masters the most clever and gifted representatives. In this case a new exploiting and governing class is born from the exploited class.

· · · · ·

The development of modern Communism, and the emergence of the new class, is evident in the character and roles of those who inspired it.

The leaders and their methods, from Marx to Khrushchev, have been varied and changing. It never occured to Marx to prevent others from voicing their ideas. Lenin tolerated free discussion in his party and did not think that party forums, let alone the party head, should regulate the expression of "proper" or "improper" ideas. Stalin abolished every type of intra-party discussion, and made the expression of ideology solely the right of the central forum—or of himself. Other Communist movements were different. For instance, Marx's International Workers' Union (the so-called First International) was not Marxist in ideology, but a union of varied groups which adopted only the resolutions on which its members agreed. Lenin's party was an *avant-garde* group combining an internal revolutionary morality and ideological monolithic structure with democracy of a kind. Under Stalin the party became a mass of ideologically disinterested men, who got their ideas from above, but were wholehearted and unanimous in the defense of a system that assured them unquestionable privileges. Marx actually never created a party; Lenin destroyed all parties except his own, including the Socialist Party. Stalin relegated even the Bolshevik Party to second rank, transforming its core into the core of the new class, and transforming the party into a privileged impersonal and colorless group.

Marx created a system of the roles of classes, and of class war in society, even though he did not discover them, and he saw that mankind is mostly made up of members of discernible classes, although he was only restating Terence's Stoic philosophy: "*Humani nihil a me alienum puto*." Lenin viewed men as sharing ideas rather than as being members of discernible classes. Stalin saw in men only obedient subjects or enemies. Marx died a poor emigrant in London, but was valued by learned men and valued in the movement; Lenin died as the leader of one of the greatest revolutions, but died as a dictator about whom a cult had already begun to form; when Stalin died, he had already transformed himself into a god.

These changes in personalities are only the reflection of changes which had already taken place and were the very soul of the Communist movement.

Although he did not realize it, Lenin started the organization of the new class. He established the party along Bolshevik lines and developed the theories of its unique and leading role in the building of a new society. This is but one aspect of his many-sided and gigantic work; it is the aspect which came about from his actions rather than his wishes. It is also the aspect which led the new class to revere him.

The real and direct originator of the new class, however, was Stalin. He was a man of quick reflexes and a tendency to coarse humor, not very educated nor a good speaker. But he was a relentless dogmatician and a great administrator, a Georgian who knew better than anyone else whither the new powers of Greater Russia were taking her. He created the new class by the use of the most barbaric means, not even sparing the class itself. It was inevitable that the new class which placed him at the top would later submit to his unbridled and brutal nature. He was the true leader of that class as long as the class was building itself up, and attaining power.

The new class was born in the revolutionary struggle in the Communist Party, but was developed in the industrial revolution. Without the revolution, without industry, the class's position would not have been secure and its power would have been limited.

While the country was being industrialized, Stalin began to introduce considerable variations in wages, at the same time allowing the development toward various privileges to proceed. He thought that industrialization would come to nothing if the new class were not made materially interested in the process, by acquisition of some property for itself. Without industrialization the new class would find it difficult to hold its position, for it would have neither historical justification nor the material resources for its continued existence.

The increase in the membership of the party, or of the bureaucracy, was closely connected with this. In 1927, on the eve of industrialization, the Soviet Communist Party had 887,233 members. In 1934, at the end of the First Five-year Plan, the membership had increased to 1,874,488. This was a phenomenon obviously connected with industrialization: the prospects for the new class and privileges for its members were improving. What is more, the privileges and the class were expanding more rapidly than industrialization itself. It is difficult to cite any statistics on this point, but the conclusion is self-evident for anyone who bears in mind that the standard of living has not kept pace with industrial production, while the new class actually seized the lion's share of the economic and other progress earned by the sacrifices and efforts of the masses.

The establishment of the new class did not proceed smoothly. It encountered bitter opposition from existing classes and from those revolutionaries who could not reconcile reality with the ideals of their struggle. In the U.S.S.R. the opposition of revolutionaries was most evident in the Trotsky-Stalin conflict. The conflict between Trotsky and Stalin, or between oppositionists in the party and Stalin, as well as the conflict between the regime and the peasantry, became more intense as industrialization advanced and the power and authority of the new class increased.

Trotsky, an excellent speaker, brilliant stylist, and skilled polemicist, a man cultured and of excellent intelligence, was deficient in only one quality: a sense of reality. He wanted to be a revolutionary in a period when life imposed the commonplace. He wished to revive a revolutionary party which was being transformed into something completely different, into a new class unconcerned with great ideals and interested only in the everyday pleasures of life. He expected action from a mass already tired by war, hunger, and death, at a time when the new class already strongly held the reins and had begun to experience the sweetness of privilege. Trotsky's fireworks lit up the distant heavens; but he could not rekindle fires in weary men. He sharply noted the sorry aspect of the new phenomena but he did not grasp their meaning. In addition, he had never been a Bolshevik. This was his vice and his virtue. Attacking the party bureaucracy in the name of the revolution, he attacked the cult of the party and, although he was not conscious of it, the new class.

Stalin looked neither far ahead nor far behind. He had seated himself at the head of the new power which was being born—the new class, the political bureaucracy, and bureaucratism—and became its leader and organizer. He did not preach—he made decisions. He too promised a shining future, but one which bureaucracy could visualize as being real because its life was improving from day to day and its position was being strengthened. He spoke without ardor and color, but the new class was better able to understand this kind of realistic language.

. . . . .

After Lenin and Stalin came what had to come; namely, mediocrity in the form of collective leadership. And also there came the apparently sincere, kind-hearted, non-intellectual "man of the people"—Nikita Khrushchev. The new class no longer needs the revolutionaries or dogmatists it once required; it is satisfied with simple personalities, such as Khrushchev, Malenkov, Bulganin, and Shepilov, whose every word reflects the average man. The new class itself is tired of dogmatic purges and training sessions. It would like to live quietly. It must protect itself even from its own authorized leader now that it has been adequately strengthened. Stalin remained the same as he was when the class was weak, when cruel measures were necessary against even those in its own ranks who threatened to deviate. Today this is all unnecessary. Without relinquishing anything it created under Stalin's leadership, the new class appears to be renouncing his authority for the past few years. But it is not really renouncing that authority—only Stalin's methods which, according to Khrushchev, hurt "good Communists."

Lenin's revolutionary epoch was replaced by Stalin's epoch, in which authority and ownership, and industrialization, were strengthened so that the much desired peaceful and good life of the new class could begin. Lenin's *revolutionary* Communism was replaced by Stalin's *dogmatic* Communism, which in turn was replaced by *non-dogmatic* Communism, a so-called collective leadership or a group of oligarchs.

These are the three phases of development of the new class in the U.S.S.R. or of Russian Communism (or of every other type of Communism in one manner or another).

. . . . .

No class is established by its own action, even though its ascent is organized and accompanied by a conscious struggle. This holds true for the new class in Communism.

The new class, because it had a weak relationship to the economy and social structure, and of necessity had its origin in a single party, was forced to establish the highest possible organizational structure. Finally it was forced to a deliberate and conscious withdrawal from its earlier tenets. Consequently the new class is more highly organized and more highly class-conscious than any class in recorded history.

This proposition is true only if it is taken relatively; consciousness and organizational structure being taken in relation to the outside world and to other classes, powers, and social forces. No other class in history has been as cohesive and single-minded in defending itself and in controlling that which it holds—collective and monopolistic ownership and totalitarian authority.

On the other hand, the new class is also the most deluded and least conscious of itself. Every private capitalist or feudal lord was conscious of the fact that he belonged to a special discernible social category. He usually believed that this category was destined to make the human race happy, and that without this category chaos and general ruin would ensue. A Communist member of the new class also believes that, without his party, society would regress and founder. But he is not conscious of the fact that he belongs to a new ownership class, for he does not consider himself an owner and does not take into account the special privileges he enjoys. He thinks that he belongs to a group with prescribed ideas, aims, attitudes, and roles. That is all he sees. He cannot see that at the same time he belongs to a special social category: the *ownership* class.

Collective ownership, which acts to reduce the class, at the same time makes it unconscious of its class substance, and each one of the collective owners is deluded in that he thinks he uniquely belongs to a movement which would abolish classes in society.

A comparison of other characteristics of the new class with those of other ownership classes reveals many similarities and many differences. The new class is voracious and insatiable, just as the bourgeoisie was. But it does not have the virtues of frugality and economy that the bourgeoisie had. The new class is as exclusive as the aristocracy but without aristocracy's refinement and proud chivalry.

The new class also has advantages over other classes. Because it is more compact it is better prepared for greater sacrifices and heroic exploits. The individual is completely and totally subordinated to the whole; at least, the prevailing ideal calls for such subordination even when he is out seeking to better himself. The new class is strong enough to carry out material and other ventures that no other class was ever able to do. Since it possesses the nation's goods, the new class is in a position to devote itself religiously to the aims it has set and to direct all the forces of the people to the furtherance of these aims.

The new ownership is not the same as the political government, but is created and aided by that government. The use, enjoyment, and distribution of property is the privilege of the party and the party's top men.

. . . . .

All changes initiated by the Communist chiefs are dictated first of all by the interests and aspirations of the new class, which, like every social group, lives and reacts, defends itself and advances, with the aim of increasing its power. This does not mean, however, that such changes may not be important for the rest of the people as well. Although the innovations introduced by the new class have not yet materially altered the Communist system, they must not be underestimated.

. . . . .

In defending its authority, the ruling class must execute reforms every time it becomes obvious to the people that the class is treating national property as its own. Such reforms are not proclaimed as being what they really are, but rather as part of the "further development of socialism" and "socialist democracy." The groundwork for reforms is laid when the discrepancy mentioned above becomes public. From the historical point of view the new class is forced to fortify its authority and ownership constantly, even though it is running away from the truth. It must constantly demonstrate how it is successfully creating a society of happy people, all of whom enjoy equal rights and have been freed of every type of exploitation. The new class cannot avoid falling continuously into profound internal contradictions; for in spite of its historical origin it is not able to make its ownership lawful, and it cannot renounce ownership without undermining itself. Consequently, it is forced to try to justify its increasing authority, invoking abstract and unreal purposes.

This is a class whose power over men is the most complete known to history. For this reason it is a class with very limited views, views which are false and unsafe. Closely ingrown, and in complete authority, the new class must unrealistically evaluate its own role and that of the people around it.

Having achieved industrialization, the new class can now do nothing more than strengthen its brute force and pillage the people. It ceases to create. Its spiritual heritage is overtaken by darkness.

While the new class accomplished one of its greatest successes in the revolution, its method of control is one of the most shameful pages in human history. Men will marvel at the grandiose ventures it accomplished, and will be ashamed of the means it used to accomplish them.

When the new class leaves the historical scene—and this must happen—there will be less sorrow over its passing than there was for any other class before it. Smothering everything except what suited its ego, it has condemned itself to failure and shameful ruin.

C. Other Alternatives

55. DEMOCRATIC SOCIALISM: THE CASE OF ENGLAND*

Paul T. Homan

After the electoral defeat of the British Labour Party in 1951, the socialist intellectuals of the party began a process of what they called "rethinking Socialism." The problem was sharply stated by Kingsley Mar-

* Paul T. Homan, "Socialist Thought in Great Britain," *American Economic Review,* Vol. XLVII, No. 3 (June, 1957), pp. 350–62. Used by permission.

tin: "If there is something like an intellectual crisis in the Labour Party now, and if the Party had no positive policy for the 1951 election, that was largely because the leaders of both the Parliamentary Party and the trade union movement did not know where they were going after they had once established the principles of the Welfare State. . . ." (p. 1) The reassessment during recent years has been partly by individuals, partly organized on a group basis, especially by the group which calls itself Socialist Union and issues the monthly journal *Socialist Commentary*. One outcome has been a spate of pamphlets and, during the past year, two outstanding books by C. A. R. Crosland and John Strachey. The purpose of the present article is to review a select list of these documents and to set down a few reflections based on them.

The occasion for this reassessment arose out of the very success of the Labour Party program during the party's period in office. It had nationalized all the industries it had set out to nationalize (coal, electricity, gas, the transport industries, steel and The Bank of England); it had reenforced the position of the trade unions and tied their activities into national political objectives; it had initiated a large housing program; it had established a system of social welfare service as comprehensive and costly as the British economy could reasonably support; it had initiated a full employment policy based on financial controls; and through tax measures it had scaled sharply downward the personal income derived from property and high salaries. The Welfare State, as it came to be called, was a monumental accomplishment for a five-year tenure of power. It put into effect what Kingsley Martin called "a new list of Rights of Man," and he predicted that "No constitutional government in the future will dare directly withdraw these rights." This prediction is borne out by the ensuing behavior of the Conservative government, which with only slight modifications carried forward the social program.

The new question is whether the Welfare State and reformist measures, built on a private enterprise base, are all that is wanted; or whether socialism in the traditional sense is to be sought through progressive enlargement of the nationalized area. The intellectuals of the British left are deeply divided on the correct answer to this question. But there is little evidence that the Labour Party intends to move towards socialization of the means of production.

On the other hand, thinkers of the left are proposing rather far-reaching innovations in the way of social and economic change, and are still calling themselves socialists. In reviewing the recent writing within this field, I am left with three strong impressions: first, that the persistence of ideological stereotypes of capitalism and socialism muddies the discussion of ends and means—assuming that the ends in view are something definable in terms of public policies and potentially attainable in the calculable future; second, that the older socialists are frustrated in the attempt to formulate programs which give any considerable scope to their traditional socialist principles; and third, that action programs are tending to take a reformist turn which can be called socialist in principle only if the term takes on a much diluted and extended meaning.

The really impressive item in the programmatic literature is Crosland's *The Future of Socialism.* Mr. Crosland, a former member of the economics faculty at Oxford and former member of Parliament, engages in economic analysis marked by a high degree of competency. His critical thought is uncluttered by traditional socialist clichés, and his thought on policy by old political commitments. His purpose is at bottom to crystallize a working program for a party of the left comprising three qualities: expediency in the sense of promoting economic progress, morality in the sense of promoting social justice, and practicability in the sense of winning elections. In carrying out the task, he avoids three common defects of much socialist thinking; emotionally overwrought criticism of capitalism, the Utopian fallacy, and Marxist dogma. He takes a fresh new look at contemporary problems and possible solutions.

Crosland arranges his exposition under five headings: the transformation of capitalism, the aims of socialism, the promotion of welfare, the search for equality, and economic growth and efficiency. The broad pattern of his thinking may be stated somewhat as follows: the British reforms of the past two decades have been so far-reaching that the appellation "capitalism" is hardly applicable in the sense in which it was applicable for the preceding century. The resulting subordination of private industry to social purposes and social control has brought into effect much of what the older socialists sought: the end of primary poverty, full employment, stability of livelihood, and greater equality of both personal and real income distribution through the social services. On the economic front, further rise in the standard of living depends upon increasing productivity. There is no prima-facie case that this will be promoted by much extension of nationalization. As a basic industry, laggard in development and monopolistically controlled, steel should be renationalized; but there are few other good candidates for this treatment. In general, the proper role of the state can be defined by operating pragmatically without too much regard to older socialist doctrine. In the context of rising income, greater economic equality can be achieved by a variety of means —through higher wages, extension of social services, taxation, dividend limitation, death duties, capture of capital gains and so on. Where capital investment and technical innovation lag, government can intervene to force the pace, as it can also to minimize the effects of private monopoly.

Looking over this statement of directions for economic policy, an American Fair Dealer might find them on the whole both familiar and acceptable. This effect is, however, somewhat illusory, since Crosland is more of a "statist" than one would normally find in American policy-making circles. He finds more probable occasions for state intervention and a higher degree of necessary state control than would appear in any programmatic statement in the United States.

In any case, these precepts of economic action, while essential, do not provide the central focus to Crosland's agenda. To him, "socialism is about equality," but the greatest barrier to the kind of equality which should exist in a just world is social inequality. The peculiar British class basis of educational opportunity greatly restricts the field of "careers open to talent," poisons all social relations and exacerbates social resentments. The breaking down of class barriers therefore appears to Crosland as the first priority of social policy, and this cannot be directly accomplished by economic reforms, but only by a thorough-going revision of the educational system. Within the context of this reform, the approach to practicable degrees of economic equality, consistent with efficiency and growth, would be so much the easier.

From the economist's viewpoint, no doubt the most interesting point in Crosland's analysis is his treatment of the reasons for adjuring extensive nationalization. On this point he is detailed, pointed and persuasive. Part of the reason is the unsatisfactory performance of the industries already nationalized. The bill of particulars is extensive, including the administrative difficulties of monolithic monopolies, the failure to attract the best administrative talent, and so on. As an economist, Crosland lays special emphasis on their failure to contribute to the essential process of capital accumulation, comparing them unfavorably with private industry on this point. Their price policy has been a cost-covering one only.

This leads to a broader conjecture whether the democratic pressures on nationalized industries will not normally be toward low prices and high wages at the expense of business saving. From this, he presses on to analysis of reasonable expectations concerning progressiveness, flexibility, foreign trade, labor relations, wage levels, managerial structure, and so on. He finds no reason to suppose that nationalization, as a general rule, will either improve economic performance or contribute materially to a scheme of social relations conforming to the ideals of socialism. Given the powers of the state backed by a proper attitude toward their use, he finds the specific matter of ownership highly irrelevant. In developing this theme he provides a cogent refutation of Marxist thinking, as well as a deadly account of the Russian outcome.

Since social ownership of the means of production is usually considered the benchmark of socialism, one begins to wonder how Crosland, repudiating this approach, can call his book, *The Future of Socialism*. A better title would have been *In Place of Socialism*. One might attribute his title to the time-honored practice of retaining "good words" with emotive power while their meanings turn sharp corners—like "democracy" in the contemporary dictatorships. But there is no chicanery in Crosland. The semantic point does not bother him, since he is writing to persuade people who call themselves socialists, and who entertain certain ideals which they have heretofore thought could best be attained through particular institutional forms. To him the heart of the matter is in the ideals and not in the means. The economic role of government is large, its responsibility for promoting stability and growth is overriding, and its concern for just relations fundamental. These conditions place no taboo upon using private enterprise to the extent of its useful economic function consistent with pursuit of those ideals. The lines of policy already firmly embedded in British practice are described by Crosland as follows: ". . . it constitutes a major victory for the Left . . . that the majority of Conservatives today would probably concede the right, indeed the duty, of the state to hold itself responsible for (1) the level of employment, (2) the protection of the foreign balance by methods other than deflation, (3) the level of investment and the rate of growth, (4) the maintenance of a welfare minimum, and (5) the conditions under which monopolies should be allowed to operate" (p. 499).

The benchmarks of a Labour Party economic program are stated in the following terms: "The main objectives of planning . . . are then a steadily rising level of investment, and a sufficient volume of savings and risk-capital to match it; a volume of home demand which does not preempt goods away from export; a situation in the labour market which does not give rise to a wage-price spiral; and an increase in the proportion of the national income devoted to social expenditure—all these to be achieved against a background of growing social equality" (p. 502).

The little book issued by Socialist Union, *Twentieth Century Socialism*, represents a point of view substantially similar to that of Crosland. It contains little economic analysis and is concerned mainly with three objectives: first, to persuade people of the continuing necessity for active campaigning for the ideals of socialism; second, to restate those ideals; third, to indicate certain basic approaches to their attainment. The emphasis throughout is upon harnessing the economic apparatus to the attainment of human values. ". . . how to bring economic power under social control . . . has always been at the root of socialist thought . . . what socialists have sought is a system, an organization of the economy, based on principles which would ensure that economic power was made to serve social ends" (pp. 119–20).

The principles of institutional organization are stated in undogmatic terms, ". . . socialist planning aims at achieving economic security, fair shares and an expanding economy" (p. 134). The principles to be followed are three: the balance of power, strategic participation, and social accountability. The balance of power principle is based upon presumptions not greatly different from those of J. K. Galbraith's "countervailing power." Business, labor and consumer interests will organize to exercise power, and government will intervene to establish an appropriate balance between these conflicting private interests.

The principle of strategic participation requires the government to take possession of economic power, not by wholesale nationalization but by intervention at strategic points. Fiscal control through the budget is the most important instrument of planning, especially in pursuit of stability and full employment. Equality can be promoted by taxation and by acquiring equity shares and a portion of other accumulations of property. Direct investment may be required in some key industries, either by full nationalization or by operation of individual publicly owned competitive firms. The principle of public accountability is to be enforced by a variety of measures and sanctions for the protection of consumers and for elevating the status of workers in their productive environment. As will be seen from this catalogue, the thinking of Socialist Union runs along strongly reformist and interventionist lines, but stops far short of "socialism" in any of its traditional meanings.

Special interest attaches to the thinking of Mr. Gaitskell, the present head of the Labour Party. Gaitskell is an economist, an intellectual and a politician. These different roles necessarily create a certain ambivalence in his approach to problems of policy. At the same time, the combination of roles places his discussion of issues on a higher plane than would normally be expected of a political leader. As an economist he has a perfectly clear understanding of what economic reforms can be accomplished under a private enterprise system and the limitations to Utopian hopes under socialism. As an intellectual, the issues are very clearly sorted out in his mind. As a political philosopher, he has a deep respect for individual freedom and devotion to democratic processes. As a political leader, he has to hold the reins over an unruly team of persons with diverse interests and aspirations, and to promulgate lines of policy designed to win elections. As a socialist, he is the least dogmatic of men, willing to proceed pragmatically toward such goals of economic stability, justice and equality as are reasonably to be hoped for in the calculable future under democratic processes.

A British political leader in Gaitskell's position has to make his peace with the hard core of trade-union influences in the Labour Party. While many leaders and members of unions are no doubt socialists in principle, the basic unionist urge is toward some benefit in the here and now, not in some future socialist state. Consequently, any political leader, whatever his principles, is heavily committed to reformist policies consistent with the existing private enterprise basis of industrial life. This leaves a good deal of open territory for argument and maneuver, according to whether one thinks of reform as the goal or as a way station to some future socialist state. The difference of goals in view creates deep cleavages in the Labour Party, making it difficult to construct a platform on which to base its next electoral appeal. In this context, Gaitskell appears to lean to the reformist rather than the "subversive" side, placing him "at the right of the left."

The broad outlines of his philosophical position are best stated in his pamphlet on *Recent Developments in British Socialist Thinking*. The acid test of British socialists is, however, their attitude toward further socialization of the means of production. Gaitskell faces this problem in *Socialism and Nationalization* and I shall limit my attention to that pamphlet. He states socialist ideals as follows: "In short, the society we wish to create is one in which there are no social classes, equal opportunity in the sense described above ['for the pursuit of happiness, however people decide they can best achieve this'], a high degree of economic equality, full employment, rapidly rising productivity, democracy in industry and a general spirit of co-operation between its members." He approaches the subject of nationalization pragmatically, as a possible *means*, to be judged on its merits, toward the attainment of these *ends*. The traditional linking of public ownership with the ideals of socialism was based on its supposed necessity because: (1) the existence of unearned income is wrong; (2) capitalism inevitably engenders unemployment, economic insecurity and waste; (3) private possession of capital inevitably confers undue power; (4) economic competition is fundamentally unethical and unchristian, and prevents a real spirit of cooperation. Gaitskell proceeds to reexamine this traditional linkage.

On the first point he finds that, when compensation is paid to prior owners of nationalized industries, the redistributive effect is much diluted and that other methods are available which have a very considerable equalizing effect. On the second point, if full-employment policies are capable of successful application to a capitalist economy, the advantage of public ownership on this point disappears. He withholds judgment as to the probable degree of such success. On the third point, he finds that the earlier irresponsible power of capitalist enterprise has been much limited by trade-union and state action. While, as experience shows, nationalization in some degrees breaks up or diffuses power, it creates a new problem. As he says, "I doubt if there is any escape from the dilemma that the more independent the boards [of nationalized industries] are allowed to be, the more they will exercise power without responsibility, and the less independent they become, the greater the risk of over-centralisation and lack of enterprise" (p. 14). On the fourth point, the ethics of competition, he is noncommittal. Across the board, the general impression created is that Gaitskell regards the whole question of industrial organization to be open to reexamination, free of older socialist dogma.

Upon reviewing experience with the nationalized industries, he finds real accomplishments and is not "disillustioned." At the same time, serious problems have shown up. These very largely stem from large-scale management. The deadening effect of monopolistic centralism imposed upon these industries may yield to administrative improvement. But Gaitskell clearly has no conviction that the structure should be imposed upon others. A case-by-case, one-at-a-time approach is suggested without prior assumption that the circumstances will be found favorable to nationalization. He ends by drawing a distinction between nationalization and public ownership. He inclines to the idea that the state should gradually acquire equity shares in privately owned enterprises. "The state may become the owner of industrial, commercial or agricultural property without necessarily exercising detailed control even over an individual firm—much less a whole industry" (p. 35). Such assets—acquired from death duties, budget surpluses, and conceivably a capital levy—could be held by public investment trusts. To the extent of such investments, what is now private property income would become public income, and capital gains would accrue to the public, serving the objective of greater equality. "How far they [the investment trusts] would exercise control over the companies in which they held shares is not a matter on which it would be wise to be dogmatic now" (p. 35). Other possible forms of mixed ownership and control are envisaged as possibilities, especially where risks are too great for private enterprise alone or it is laggard in undertaking essential lines of production. The whole approach represents a thoroughly "statist" or interventionist viewpoint. But it parts company with traditional stereotypes of what a socialist economy would be like.

We now come to Mr. Crossman—journalist, member of Parliament, and long an influential force in party councils, especially on international political affairs. His pamphlet, *Socialism and the New Despotism*, is more narrowly focused than any of the writings referred to above. He is concerned specifically with the concentration of economic power. What he has to say illustrates the truly difficult situation of those ageing socialist politicians who try at once to be faithful to their socialist principles and to engage in program-making for the Labour Party.

Crossman has adopted as applicable to Great Britain J. K. Galbraith's stereotype for American industry under the name of "oligopoly"—a convenient and rather more realistic successor to "monopoly capitalism." He rejects Galbraith's favorable judgment of performance under American conditions—finding private power too concentrated, distributive injustice too pronounced and competitive safeguards too weak. Therefore the industrial oligopolies must be socialized. The case having been made, Crossman then goes programmatic—with astonishing results. He places three fields on the action agenda: municipal housing and nationalized transport and insurance—in other words, fields to which the discussion of industrial oligopoly is totally irrelevant. His excuse for this delimitation is that "Neither the workers in industry nor the voters are well acquainted with the serious Socialist case for public ownership." It is "prudent, therefore, to select industries where even the non-Socialist can be convinced that it is desirable" (p. 13).

Nationalization alone still would not quiet Crossman's anxieties about power. He distrusts concentrated economic power wherever found—on the boards of nationalized industries, in the state bureaucracy, in the trade unions. The Coal Board, for example, has powers greater than those of private industrial groups, and they are little linked to the broad objectives of a socialist program, while "the state bureaucracy itself is one of those concentrations of power which threaten our freedom" (p. 12). To Crossman, "the defence of personal freedom and personal responsibility in a managerial society" are equally important with economic aims.

His constructive thinking runs in two main directions. One is toward introducing a strong element of worker control into the structure—a shadowy remnant of the guild socialism so popular in the 1920's and now almost extinct in Great Britain. He has, however, no real notion of how this could be done. He also has no faith that nationalization would give rise to higher wages than those available from private industry. The reward to workers from the reorganization of control would presumably be a sense of participation.

His other, and principal, proposal is for constitutional reform designed to "enlarge freedom and stimulate an active democracy." On the economic side, this would entail a standing Parliamentary committee responsible for each nationalized industry; but his thought reaches further into fundamental reform of party structure and Parliamentary procedure. He regards such reform "at least as important as the extension of public ownership and redistribution of wealth." "Indeed, unless the two march in step, we shall merely create a new Leviathan" (p. 24).

Without further elaboration, it is difficult to assess this political thinking. But the economic proposal of direct supervisory control over nationalized industries by Parliamentary committees raises an issue of the most fundamental importance. Heretofore, nationalization has proceeded on the principle, so vigorously propounded by Herbert Morrison, that industrial management must be thoroughly insulated from direct political contacts. This was based on the presumption that making the course of industrial operations an immediate and perpetual occasion for political oversight, and therefore controversy, would be the surest blockade to efficient industrial management. This leads into the deeper question, whether comprehensive socialization is amenable to democratic controls, or whether it implies an essentially totalitarian structure of control. Crossman does not pose this question, but it crops up in the thought of Gaitskell, Crosland and others, and is, I judge, one of the reasons for their coolness toward an ambitious program of nationalization.

As against the moderation and reservations of people like Crosland and Gaitskell, Professor G. D. H. Cole, in his *World Socialism Restated*, continues his persistent advocacy of socialism in its traditional meaning. "I want to make an end of the entire system of capitalism" (p. 7). There is no need to repeat the general argument, since it is familiar. Even the old clichés crop up baldly. "American capitalism can sustain high production and employment only by giving an appreciable part of its products away . . ." (p. 17). Cole is the unreserved enemy of those moderate tendencies which I have reviewed above. ". . . The Labour Party has, I think, to choose between adopting a much more drastic Socialist policy and failing to act effectively even as a reformist party . . ." (p. 23). His attitude toward international socialism is equally unbending. The British socialists should support socialist tendencies and "anticolonial" movements, wherever found and whatever their political corollaries. This places him in total opposition, for example, to the American alliance. He is ambivalent toward the totalitarian tendencies of contemporary socialist states. He praises democracy, rejects the communist philosophy and deplores "the ruthlessness, the cruelty, and the centralized authoritarianism which are basic characteristics of Communist practice" (p. 14). At the same time, he enters excuses for the use of whatever methods are necessary to break down exploitive political and economic institutions (*e.g.*, pp. 10–12).

Having adopted this intransigent posture, Cole is quite unwilling to make his peace with those practical, everyday methods by which other well-intentioned people hope to effect some marginal improvement in the human state. He appears to have given up hope that the Labour Party will be an effective instrument of progress toward true socialism in the calculabe future. The elect, it appears, should isolate themselves into international enclaves of the true devotees—a sort of monastic order of the faithful awaiting the apocalyptic day.

To conclude this survey, we turn to Mr. Strachey's *Contemporary Capitalism.* It needs to be set apart from the documents reviewed above, since it is an entirely different sort of book. In the 1930's Strachey was convinced that the advent of communism was both inevitable and desirable—views defended in *The Nature of Capitalist Crises* and *The Coming Struggle for Power.* (I recall thinking, when first reading *The Coming Struggle for Power*, how convenient it was to possess a machine by which one could get clear answers to troublesome questions simply by turning the handle.) By 1940, he had discarded these views, due perhaps primarily to the influence of Keynes. From 1945 to 1950 he was a responsible member of the Labour government. Afterwards, he strongly defended the accomplishments of that government as a long step toward achieving socialist goals. He placed great faith in control over the central financial mechanism of the economy.

Strachey has now taken time out for reflective thought; his book is a restatement of his philosophical position and a reinterpretation of the process of social change. The title is somewhat misleading, since the book contains very little on the institutional characteristics of contemporary economic organization—in fact, hardly more than a stereotype of oligopoly. What he does, essentially, is to set up two abstract creatures, capitalism and democracy, put them in the prize ring, and let them fight it out, while he cheers in the corner of democracy. Capitalism is a sort of brutal monstrosity—the apotheosis of every inhumane, antisocial pursuit of private self-interest. Democracy is the champion of all generous-hearted efforts to attain general well-being and communal interest. The complete victory of democracy would usher in socialism.

In a series of early chapters, Strachey reviews Ricardian, neoclassical and Marxist theory, with special reference to the labor theory of value and the theory of absolute and relative immiseration. Economists will not find much to interest them, since Strachey is a biased and at times not very accurate reporter. The later marginalist and equilibrium theorists are disposed of summarily, as having dropped the really important question of the social distribution of income among classes or groups. He is especially interested in the development of social accounting as a method through which to reopen the old question of social distribution on a factual basis. Pending that basis, he commends Marx for asking the right questions and for devising a useful *method* of analysis, while he deplores the later translation of Marx into a rigid *system* of dogma and recognizes the failure in the field of prophetic vision.

Out of all this Strachey assembles a very personal, and highly debatable view of the validity of Marx's analysis, especially with respect to the prospects of the laboring classes. He takes the position that Marx's theory of progressive exploitation was a correct interpretation of a *tendency* inherent in capitalism as such. This tendency was, however, in practice offset by influences of a noneconomic character.

> Marx cut his way through to the essential tendency of capitalism, which, however you express the point, is to channel the whole of its ever growing *surplus* towards the owners of the means of production to spend or invest, and thus to deprive the mass of the wage earning population of any part of it . . . unless we keep this conclusion in view, there is no hope of our understanding the world in which we live (p. 86).

If this says what it appears to say, Strachey accepts as the central tendency of capitalism Marx's view that "the level of wages would be determined by what it took to produce the worker" (p. 88). "*In the political and social conditions with which Marx was alone familiar*, the tendency of wages to a subsistence level was over-riding" (p. 95; italics Strachey's).

Strachey at once points out that this is not what happened historically. His answer to the apparent paradox is that noneconomic forces lying outside capitalism "over-rode" the tendencies inherent in capitalism. This is the clue to his whole pattern of thought. His "capitalism" is an abstract model without sociological content; or else, if it has any such content, it is limited to what Marx thought he saw in his own immediate environment. Moreover, the model is so constructed that labor is always in such excess supply that employers will never be under the competitive inducement to bid up the rate of wages as productivity increases. Starting with a model of this sort, we must by definition attribute any improvement in the general standard of living to external forces.

For Strachey these moving forces are trade unions and political democracy. To them alone the *whole* of the improvement in real wages is attributed. "What has really happened is . . . that the wage earners, by political and trade unionist efforts, sustained over a century, have *forced up* their standards of life in the teeth of the economic tendencies of the system" (p. 109). He does not bother even to mention, much less to rebut, the idea that competitive bidding for scarce resources may have something to do with their rate of remuneration.

This doctrine encounters fairly rough going when one faces the circumstances of the United States. But Strachey is intrepidly dealing in universals, so he bravely faces the challenge. He says (p. 109 n):

> The apparent exception is America in the second half of the nineteenth century. There the wage earner's standard of life undoubtedly rose while trade unionism remained weak. But is not this accounted for, first, by the existence of free land? By taking up free land an American wage earner could at any time escape right out of the capitalist system, as it were, back into the world of "small commodity production." And, second, the *political* pressure exercised by the American wage earners, and more especially by the American farmers, during the whole period was far from negligible.

This is a nice, neat account of the foundations of economic well-being in the United States; and it would be a pity to deface it with critical commentary. He returns to the same subject at a later point (pp. 153–54) at greater length but to the same purpose.

Strachey proceeds to an analysis of contemporary democracy which he ultimately defines as "the diffusion of power throughout the community" (p. 179). This definition carries over from the political to the economic field, and ends up in the Utopian state of "perfect cooperation in perfect liberty" (p. 179). Since capitalism is by definition "strongly inequalitarian" and "potentially anti-democratic," clearly the end of the democratic process is socialism. Given this outcome an economic question arises, whether the process of accumulation necessary to economic improvement will be adequately cared for. Strachey enters an optimistic prophecy. The death knell of capitalism, he finds, is the fact that it is not self-regulating. The accumulative process makes it fundamentally unstable, so that the state is necessarily called in as a counterweight. Without this, it grows increasingly unstable. "What the democratic mechanism is forcing governments, more or less unconsciously, to attempt is, in a word, the socialisation of investment" (p. 211).

Strachey concedes the argument of Keynes that a sufficiently close and intelligent control of the central monetary mechanism can minimize the instability of the system. "But what Keynes never came to realize was that this growing loss of equilibrium was itself the result of that mutation of the system, which the growth in size, and the decrease in number, of its units, with the consequent atrophy of competition, had produced" (p. 219). So we are back at the concentration of economic power, the point from which Strachey set out. Even if relative stability is achieved, the consequences under private control will still be intolerable—in distributive terms and in terms of the democratic status and dignity of the working members of the system. The final verdict on Keynes, is "What he actually accomplished was something which he did not intend . . . to help the democratic, and, on this side of the Atlantic, the democratic socialist, forces to find a way of continuously modifying the system" (p. 253).

Strachey ends his book on a highly dramatic note.

> The general tendencies of last stage capitalism and democracy conflict because it is the purpose of the former to concentrate, and of the latter to diffuse power. . . . Their co-existence constitutes a state of antagonistic balance. . . . In the end the power of contemporary democracy must encroach upon capitalism until its last stage also has been completed; or, alternatively, capitalism must encroach upon democracy until this young, vulnerable and experimental method of government has been destroyed (p. 255).

The two great antagonists are locked in a struggle to the death. Having set up this posture of embattled giants, Strachey falls back into a series of interesting, intelligent and realistic observations upon political processes in Great Britain and the United States and upon the political and economic prospects of countries outside the limited realm of the Western democracies. But, in the end, the slow, shifting, indeterminate processes of institutional change are forced back into the dialectical mould. The framework of class war (a phrase Strachey does not use) is still there, a Marxist residue in his thinking; though he presents it more as a latter-day version of the legend of St. George and the dragon.

Strachey's analysis—for all his intelligence, thoughtfulness and worldly experience—will not give anyone a much deeper insight into the multiple intertwined influences which are shaping our destinies. Try as he will, he is not a creative thinker. His own private mythology makes a dramatic story, but it is not a very good guide to the intricate processes of social change or to possible lines of approach to "a better world." On the programmatic front, his expectations appear to be modest: "decade by decade" the party of the left must "show a certain minimum of social change" (p. 272).

"The road to socialism" used to imply a destination. The road itself was subversion. As Professor Gray says in *The Socialist Tradition*, socialists of all breeds could be described generically as people who "seek a better world, not by way of reform, but by way of subversion (using the word in its liberal and neutral sense)—or, if it be preferred, by a fundamental change in the nature and structure of society." There were different views of the process of subversion. In Great Britain the democratic process of gradualism has been the preferred method, although Laski used to toy with the idea of violence as the necessary way of removing the beleaguered forces of capitalism from their final strongholds. In any case, there was a destination. In the minds of many British socialists, the idea of such a destination appears to be dissolving. So I interpret, for example, the thinking of Crosland and Gaitskell.

The reasons, I think, are not hard to find. First of all, it has been demonstrated by experience how far social objectives can be achieved without expropriating private owners and without displacing the strong private motives which have beneficial economic effects. Second, the close view of what is involved in operating nationalized industries makes socialist politicians chary of undertaking much more of the same, and makes them skeptical of this route toward the attainment of their ideals. Finally, socialist thinking is under the shadow of Labour Party politics. Elections are won by votes; and voters have to be moved by appeal to some felt interest or incentive. There appear to be no British majorities to be won by promising an active program of subversion.

At least in the short run then, the only feasible programs in pursuit of economic well-being, and of economic justice too, appear to be reformist in character, to be carried out through an improved version of the present system and through other policies consistent with its continued existence. The more successful these improvements and policies, the less, one would think, anyone will want to practice subversion. What, then, is "the road to socialism"? Only, as far as one can see, through some unpredictable train of social disaster. But the Marxist imperatives on this point are no longer acceptable. As a thoughtful British socialist said: "The basis of present British Labour policy is not Marxian or Webbian, but Keynesian. And so it will remain unless the West has another slump, in which case it may again become what you call subversive."

One is tempted to conclude that the paths of economic destiny of Great Britain and the United States are not so very different—being basically the building of a welfare state on a predominantly capitalistic economic foundation. This might indeed turn out to be the case. But even if it did, the parallelism would probably not be very close. The history of the two countries has been very different, their sociological structure is different, and there is a striking difference of popular attitudes rooted in these two facts. Moreover, within the economic structure the United States retains a much more vigorous constituent of competition. Since the social rationale of private enterprise is heavily dependent on the reality of competition, it is not surprising that the British have a diminished confidence in the effects of private enterprise. But one cannot even speculate upon how nearly parallel the two courses may run without considering possible lines of social and economic change in the United States, a field into which I cannot now enter. In any case, it may, I think, be inferred from the body of current thinking reviewed above that socialism as a goal is waning in Great Britain, and that the British left is in process of reorienting its whole line of policy toward new combinations of public and private endeavor—not to be blue-printed in advance, but arrived at pragmatically as circumstances and popular attitudes warrant. This approach has, indeed, long been influential in the trade union segment of the Labour Party. It is now sweeping the field among the younger intellectual leaders. The day of the prophetic Utopian vision, equally with the day of the Marxist imperative, appears to be over.

56. DEMOCRATIC SOCIALISM: THE CASE OF SWEDEN*

Calvin B. Hoover

The development of the economic system in Sweden away from old-style capitalism has taken place during recent decades under a government in which an avowedly socialistic party has played the dominant role. As Hugo Hegeland points out, it was originally the belief of the Social Democratic Party that the goals of income equalization, full employment, social reforms and a rising standard of living could be attained only by the transformation of the private, capitalistic society into a socialistic one in which collaboration would be substituted for competition. In fact, the transformation of the Swedish economic system has taken place with relatively little nationalization of industry. Nationalization has not, however, been formally abandoned as party doctrine, and there have been some instances of it since World War II, as in the case of the Lapland iron ore corporation in 1956. There seems little prospect, however, that the Social Democratic Party will press actively for extensive further nationalization of industry. It has come to realize, first, that further nationalization has little appeal to the electorate as a political issue, second, that there are decided limitations upon the extent to which further nationalization would aid in attaining the goals desired, and, third, that the desired goals have been and are being achieved in large degree by other means.

The evidence indicates that in spite of increasing industrialization the share of large industrial enterprises in the total employment of labor has not been increasing during the last couple of decades. The importance of cartels in the economy has also apparently been declining. Recent legislation limiting the powers of cartels has been only a minor factor in this development. In larger part, it is due to full employment and a strong market demand for the products of industry, which have diminished the motivation for the formation and maintenance of cartels. Cooperative associations employ less than 1 per cent of the total labor force and control only about 14 per cent of retail trade.

* Calvin B. Hoover, *The Economy, Liberty and the State* (New York: The Twentieth Century Fund, 1959), pp. 315–20.

Yet group interests are probably more thoroughly organized in Sweden than in almost any other democratic country. Over 90 per cent of the workers in industry are organized in trade unions. These unions in turn are linked together in the Swedish Federation of Trade Unions (L.O.). Salaried workers are also organized in unions on a national basis. Employers forming 43 federations are linked in the Swedish Employers' Confederation (S.A.F.). The Swedish Federation of Trade Unions has followed a policy tending towards wage equalization through negotiating wage agreements giving greater percentage increases to unskilled than to skilled labor. Agreements with respect to the general level of wages and hours of labor in relation to the cost of living are worked out between the two organizations. For example, a comprehensive agreement covering the two years 1957 and 1958 was signed in February 1957. As Hegeland points out, the government has intervened in wage disputes only in tense situations in the early stages of wage negotiations and has then left it to the labor unions and employer associations to act "with a sense of social responsibility." This sense of social responsibility has been interpreted to mean limiting wage increases to those consistent with a stable price level. While this particular aspect of the *condominium* of government, labor unions and employer associations in the management of the economy has served well in maintaining industrial peace, it has not been so successful in maintaining a stable price level. Nor has it been wholly successful in protecting the interests of the less well organized elements of the population. However, the elaborate system of social insurance provides a welfare "floor" below which almost no one may fall. Since wage agreements provide only the minimum which may be paid for the various jobs, in a period of over-full employment wages have risen above these minima. It has been estimated that during the past decade from one-half to two-thirds of the increase in wages has been a direct result of collective bargaining.

Even though agriculture is overwhelmingly characterized by small-scale individual proprietors, agricultural prices are so regulated by the government that farmers receive the same income as "other comparable groups" in society, and farm laborers receive substantially the same wages as comparably employed industrial workers.

In spite of the abandonment of any dynamic policy for the nationalization of industry, the role of the state has continued to expand. Total taxes as a percentage of national income increased from 18 per cent in 1939 to 36 per cent in 1956. The current budget, as distinguished from the capital budget, of the national government now constitutes about one-fourth of the national income compared with one-tenth in 1938–39. Social expenditures such as old-age pensions, child contributions and rent contributions have grown from 23 per cent to 33 per cent of the governmental budget during the same period.

During a period when the proportion devoted to investment in total production increased from 25 per cent of gross national product in 1938–39 to 30 per cent in 1955, while the percentage of total production devoted to consumption shrank in proportion, public domestic capital formation doubled from 6.5 to 13 per cent of gross national product. Public investment amounted to 42 per cent of total gross investment in 1956. The total percentage of the gross national product attributable to the public sector increased from 14 per cent in 1938–39 to 25 per cent in 1956.

Perhaps the greatest instrument of governmental control over the economy has been the monetary and credit system. Comprehensive control over investment has developed primarily in an effort to prevent inflation. Governmental agencies have the power to set interest rates. New loans on the capital market have to be authorized by the central bank. As a consequence the traditional market mechanism no longer functions in the capital market. As a result of the difficulty of obtaining new funds for investment from outside sources, industrial corporations now depend very largely upon internally generated funds "plowed back" into the business. It is extremely difficult to obtain capital funds for new enterprises.

As Hegeland states:

> In its attempt to stabilize the economy, the Government has not only controlled the money supply but also the use of the country's "real resources." On the basis of the annual forecast by the national budget delegation concerning the expected changes in total current resources for the following year, the Government decides upon the distribution between an increase in total investment and in consumption. And it does not only determine the amount of total investment for the following year; it also determines its distribution between private and public investment, as well as its detailed allocation within each section of the economy and between factories, housing, highways, railroads, power dams, etc. Investment activity has been almost completely regulated during the whole period. In this way the Government has steadily increased the public sector of investment, as it considers public investments more profitable and necessary to society than private ones.

In spite of the extended role of the government in the control of the Swedish economy and in spite of the transformation from an individual-enterprise system to an organizational economy, a large role is left for the individual entrepreneur in small-scale industry, in trade and in agriculture, and for the managements of corporations in larger-scale industry, banking and commerce. The majority of operational decisions are still made by private and corporate managements.

During the period under review a substantial diminution in income inequality occurred. The percentage of total national income which would have to be transferred in order to attain complete equalization of income decreased from 41 per cent in 1935 to 34 per cent in 1948. The share of disposable income of the four lowest decile groups increased from 10 per cent to 14 per cent while the share of the tenth decile group, the highest, decreased from 37 per cent to 27 per cent. The share of employees in the national income increased from 70 per cent in 1930 to 77 per cent in 1954, while the share of employers declined from 21 per cent to 16.5 per cent. This change is largely accounted for by an increase in the number of employees in proportion to the number of employers. There has been a substantial diminution in the proportion of dividends in national income during the period. Individuals' income from capital fell from 7 per cent to less than 3 per cent. There has been a similar tendency towards the equalization of wealth. Tax policy has apparently played a relatively minor role in this tendency towards the equalization of income and wealth. The elimination of unemployment, the increase in productivity, the movement of labor from industries of low productivity to industries of higher productivity, the inflationary movement of prices acting upon a very progressive tax structure, compensation for increases in the cost of living extended to the lower-paid workers, and trade union policies favoring wage equalization, have all tended towards equalization.

During the period 1946–51, economic growth as reflected in the gross national product increased at an average rate of 4.5 per cent a year. With full employment and the necessity for restricting both consumption and investment through tightening money and credit, the rate of increase had fallen to 2 per cent by 1957.

Regardless of whether or not the economic and social policies of the Social Democratic Party have been the cause of full employment, a rising standard of living and a greater equalization of wealth and income in Sweden, it is easy to understand why that party no longer presses strongly for further nationalization of industry. Experience with a managed economy without extensive nationalization has demonstrated rather clearly that little if anything would be gained by nationalization and much might be lost. It has been demonstrated, for example, that restraining inflation while maintaining full employment is the major and extremely difficult problem of a managed economy. It has become clear that the attainment of a higher rate of capital investment and the further expansion of production are limited by the necessity for credit controls to prevent inflation. None of these problems would be ameliorated by the nationalization of the economy, but would instead be intensified. Similarly, it has been demonstrated, in Sweden as elsewhere, that a considerable degree of equalization of income and wealth can take place without nationalization. It has also become quite clear that a substantial degree of inequality would have to be retained even under nationalization.

57. THE RESURGENCE OF THE MARKET ECONOMY IN WESTERN EUROPE: AN INTERPRETATION*

Wilhelm Röpke

. . . The first question is this: To what extent and with what degree of lasting success has that economic order which is appropriate to a free society, namely, the market economy, been able to hold its own against the collectivist economic order, which is incompatible with free society in the long run?

At first sight it may seem as if the adherent of the market economy had good reason to feel both satisfied and hopeful when he considers the conflict between these two principles of economic order during the last fifteen years. He may feel all the more entitled to do so if he recalls the straits in which the cause of the market economy found itself when the Second World War and its outcome seemed to clinch the triumph of collectivism throughout the world. Founded upon the corresponding collectivist ideologies, controlled and planned economies, with their paraphernalia of forms, fixed prices, rationing, injunctions and permits, police checks, and penalties, seemed to be holding the field all along the line. When the Second World War was drawing to its close, few had the courage to give the market economy a good character, let alone a future. This small band was headed by a handful of men who had asked themselves long ago what were the fundamental difficulties on which the collectivist economy, with its central administration and compulsion, was bound to come to grief, and what incomparable advantages the market economy had on its side. Long before the market economy was again taken for granted and had become the source of prosperity, as they expected, these men in various countries had set to work to popularize the idea of economic order as a system of regulatory principles and incentives in the economy and to explain that in the last resort the choice lies between only two systems: the collectivist system, resting on planning and commands—as Walter Eucken says, the "economy of central administration" —and the opposite system of the market economy.

In our forgetful era it may be useful to recall how poor the prospects for the market economy appeared at that time and how hopeless the efforts of its advocates. What was the situation at the end of the Second World War? Throughout a whole century one of the principal reasons for the advance of socialism had been the myth of its historical necessity,

* Wilhelm Röpke, *A Humane Economy* (Chicago: Henry Regnery Company, 1960), pp. 20–35.

with which Marx, above all, had equipped the movement. This myth was well adapted to the mental inertia of the man in the street, and its propaganda value was bound to increase when the day of fulfillment actually seemed to be at hand. It is hard to withstand the appeal of an idea which is not only the winner-designate in the timetable of history, known only to the initiates, but which actually seems to have won through already. This is exactly what the situation was then.

Nearly everywhere in the world the purposes of planning, nationalization, and full employment had given rise to a mixture of expansionist monetary policy and official controls that paralyzed the price mechanism. The Leftist course of economic policy, with its varieties in different countries, owed its ascendancy in part to Keynes's oft-misunderstood ideas and in part to the heritage of war and war economy. The triumph was also furthered by the fiction that the Allied victory over the Fascist countries was tantamount to the victory of an anti-Fascist (that is, predominantly socialist and progressive) front over the bloc of powers mistaken for ultraconservatives, reactionaries, and monopoly capitalists. The blindness with which collectivist totalitarian Russia was accepted as a member of this anti-Fascist front was matched by stubborn refusal to accept any proof that German National Socialism had, at least in a formal sense, paralleled Soviet Russia as a textbook example of socialism in full bloom and had, on the spiritual side, more than one ancestor in common with "democratic" socialism. Those who, like F. A. Hayek and the author of this book, were so deplorably tactless as to explode this myth know from experience what it means to challenge a popular misconception.

Only in the light of all this can we appreciate the full significance of the fact that gradually a number of European countries began to form a center of opposition and had the temerity to disregard the timetable of history. In 1945, Switzerland stood alone as a kind of museum piece of liberalism which could be dismissed with an indulgent smile. The first jolt came when, in 1946, Belgium followed in the tracks of Switzerland and set her economy on an even keel by stopping inflation and reintroducing a free-market system. She was soon so successful that her balance-of-payments equilibrium disqualified her from direct Marshall Plan aid, which was tailored to the needs of socialist countries. At the same time, Sweden, which had started out from a situation comparable to Switzerland's, effectively demonstrated that determined Leftist policies, inspired by socialist theoreticians, enable even a rich country, and one spared by war, to soften the hardest currency almost overnight. But, the obtuse might have argued, did not Belgium possess the riches of the Congo, which would explain the miracle without destroying the socialist and inflationary creed? The answer was not long in coming. By adopting the now famous policy of Luigi Einaudi, then Governor of the Bank of Italy and later President of the Republic, who put a professor's knowledge of economics into practice, Italy, in 1947, rallied to the nucleus of liberal and anti-inflationary countries and managed to extricate herself from the morass of inflation and economic controls. It was a striking success and most probably saved Italy from the victory of Communism; however, its demonstration value was somewhat overshadowed by the host of problems peculiar to Italy.

The really decisive victory in the critical European economic situation was won by Germany in the summer of 1948. Again it was a professor who switched from theory to practice. Ludwig Erhard and his group, stepping into a situation of so-called repressed inflation which was really nothing less than the stark and complete bankruptcy of inflationary collectivism, countered with a resolute return to the market economy and monetary discipline. What is more, Erhard was unsporting enough to succeed beyond all expectations. This was the beginning of an impressive chapter in economic history when in the span of a few years we witnessed a nation's precipitous fall and its rebirth and the almost total collapse and subsequent swift recovery of its economy. The world was treated to a unique and instructive example of the paralysis and anarchy which can afflict an economy when utterly mistaken economic policies destroy the foundations of economic order and of how quickly and thoroughly it can recover from its fall and start on a steep, upward climb if only economic policy recognizes its error and reverses its course.

Germany lay prostrate, ravaged by war, impoverished by ten years of repressed inflation, mutilated, demoralized by defeat in an unjustified war and by the exposure of a hateful tyranny, and teeming with refugees: a country without hope which the passengers of international express trains traversed hastily, embarrassed by the children scrounging for leftovers of food on the embankments. And of all countries, it was precisely this one which had the courage to swim against the tide of collectivist and inflationary policies in Europe and set up its own—and contrary—program of free markets and monetary discipline, much to the dismay of the young economists of the Occupation Powers, who had been reared on the doctrines of Marx and Keynes and their disciples. Not only was the success overwhelming, but it also happened to coincide with the patent failure of socialism in Great Britain (which had replaced the hopelessly discredited Soviet Union as the promised land of the socialists). It began to look as if the country that had lost the war were better off than the winners.

This was an outrage because it meant the end of the socialist myth. What made it still harder to swallow was that defeated Germany should be the one to set this example of prosperity through freedom, for there were few who grasped that this was a not unworthy manner of making good some of the evil that this same country had brought upon the world by means of its previous, opposite example of inflationary collectivism, which had marked the beginning of National Socialism and had been lapped up all too eagerly by others. But the success of the new economic course was proscribed by every single chapter of the fashionable Leftist economic doctrine. This success simply could not be tolerated, and thus false theories combined with wishful thinking to produce those repeated prophecies of doom which accompanied German economic policy from one triumph to the next. When the false prophets, along with all their various disproved predictions, finally fell into ridicule, they took refuge in the tactics of either remaining as silent as possible on the success of the German market economy or of obscuring it with all kinds of statistical juggling and gross misrepresentation of facts. They also liked to dwell upon such problems as still required solution, exaggerating their importance and unjustly blaming the market economy for them. The annual reports of the United Nations Economic Commission for Europe in Geneva are a treasure-trove in this respect.

The dire warnings began with the assertion that truncated West Germany was not economically viable. This theme was repeated in a minor key in all sorts of variations until the symphony of disaster had to be broken off abruptly when it became obvious that Germany had become one of the world's leading industrial and trading nations, the major economic power on the Continent, and the possessor of one of the hardest and most sought-after currencies. Other arguments were then brought up. Some said that it was all a flash in the pan, others that currency reform and Marshall Plan aid were the good fairies rather than the market economy. Germany was a black sheep of sinister economic reaction and crippling deflation, the worst problem child of Europe besides Belgium and Italy, or so the annual reports of the European Economic Commission would have one believe. Still others said that even if Germany were quite obviously prospering, it had nothing to do with the market economy; it was only because the Germans were such a hard-working, frugal, and thrifty people. There is really no point now in continuing this list of embarrassed evasions and absurdities because they have long been answered by the facts. The lesson which Germany (and later Austria, in equally difficult conditions, and most recently France) taught the world with its example of market economy and monetary discipline gradually emerged from the sphere of demagogic disparagement and ideological party strife and became one of the most important reasons why the market economy has put collectivism on the defensive everywhere this side of the Iron Curtain—and, indeed, outside Europe, too, as the impressive example of Peru has shown.

If we look back today upon the economic development of the major countries of the West since the Second World War, the story is one of grave economic debility at first and subsequent recovery. True, the recovery is far from being complete, nor can we be certain that it will be lasting, but all the same, it has produced impressive improvements. The disease was caused by the economic experiments of dabblers and an unholy alliance of inflation and collectivism. The recovery, to the extent that it has taken place, is, we repeat, attributable to a very simple prescription: the re-establishment of a workable and stable currency system and the liberation of the economy from the fetters of planning, which had hampered or entirely paralyzed the regulatory and incentive effects of free prices and free competition. In some countries, especially Germany, the recovery was as unparalleled as the preceding sickness, and it is this recovery which opened the way to the spectacular revival of international economic relations, especially within Europe.

Under the impact of these experiences, the dispute over the principles of economic policy in a free society has now become much less acute. Nationalization and planning, the catch phrases of the immediate postwar period, have lost their appeal, and even in the socialist camp the response is now weak. Such enthusiastic reception as they still find—together with nationalism, which is closely connected with them—seems to be concentrated in the so-called underdeveloped countries, with their Nehrus and Sukarnos and Nassers and U Nus, or whatever their names may be. But even in these areas a cooling off may be expected in the near future. This is certainly a gratifying change in the climate of economic-policy discussions. However, a good many of the things which the open or—still more—the secret enemies of the market economy now demand under new labels come perilously close to those which are so discredited by their old name that one prefers not to mention them.

Nevertheless, it would be a mistake to overestimate the victory of the market economy or to think that its fruits are secure. First of all, we must not forget that the victory is anything but complete. We may perhaps neglect, in this context, the fact that the domination of total collectivism over approximately one-third of mankind remains unbroken, notwithstanding some minor concessions to personal independence and decentralization. But a good many countries of the free world, too, are still permeated by considerable remnants of collectivist policies, the elimination of which meets with stubborn resistance, even under non-socialist governments like the British. Some countries, especially in Scandinavia, are still so strongly influenced by the principles, institutions, and ideologies of the socialist welfare state that their efforts to combat the ensuing inflationary pressure do not hold out much promise of success. This is one of the reasons why the re-establishment of complete currency convertibility on the basis of balanced international economic relations remains an unsolved problem in spite of some progress and occasional determined efforts. It follows that the real basis of international economic integration also remains incomplete, that is, a universal currency system with free and stable foreign-exchange markets. This, in turn, creates a fertile field for all kinds of attempts at international economic controls. Certain aspects of European economic integration show quite clearly how this situation reacts on the separate national economies and weakens the market economy.

Furthermore, we would be greatly deluding ourselves if we regarded the market economy as secure, even in countries like Germany. First of all, we have to remove any misconception about what really happened. The German economic reform was not simply a once-and-for-all act of liberation, a removal of obstacles that blocked the way to an automatic and natural process of recovery and growth. It was not like that at all. The history of German economic policy since 1948 has proved that economic freedom is like any other freedom: it must, as Goethe says, be conquered anew each day. The act of liberation was a necessary but not a sufficient condition for recovery and growth. The German example shows the market economy must be won and secured over and over again and not just against new dangers and temptations or in the face of new tasks. Since 1948, the German market economy has had to grapple continuously, both with old and persistent problems and with new and changing ones. It was now this and now that, now foreign trade and now the capital market, the budget, social tensions, agriculture, or transport. Residues of collectivism, such as rent control, were scattered about the market economy like unexploded mines, and they proved to be exceedingly difficult to dispose of through normal democratic procedures and under the cross fire of vote-catching demagogy.

On all of these and other fronts, German economic policy has continued to fight, with varying fortunes. Some grave and almost irreparable mistakes were made. Some brilliant successes were scored, especially in the revival and expansion of foreign trade and the rehabilitation of the currency. In between the positive and negative poles there is a whole gamut of more or less satisfactory average results, half or three-quarter successes and—as in the case of agriculture and public finance—hitherto unavailing attempts to solve intractable chronic problems. The most serious feature was, and to some extent still is, capital shortage; in spite of all the progress achieved and in spite of an enormous rate of investment, this remained for a long time a dead weight on the German market economy, and its effects were aggravated until quite recently by the failure to create a really free and well-functioning capital market. There can be no doubt that in this field the German market economy suffered one of its most conspicuous defeats, and even though the setback was due to the disregard rather than to the application of the market economy's own principles, the fact remains that there was a serious threat from this quarter. The situation is much the same in Austria. Indeed, it is no exaggeration to say that nowadays the central and most pressing problem everywhere is how to insure the continuing economic growth of the countries of the free world by means of adequate capital supply resting on true saving and not on inflation and taxation or too much on business profits (self-financing).

Let us leave the instructive example of Germany and return to the general prospects of the market economy in its contest with collectivism.

It can, I think, by no means be taken for granted that the nature, conditions, and operation of the market economy are generally understood —in spite of all the lessons of experience and the best efforts of economists. Otherwise, how could people again seriously moot the idea of containing inflationary price rises with a new set of price ceilings and controls, as if the memory of decades of repressed inflation had simply been blotted out? Thus it is that the field still remains open, incredibly enough, to planned-economy sallies in various guises and in various places.

People are still in the habit of taking refuge in official regulations whenever a new problem turns up. In Europe, this takes the particularly absurd form of expecting any problem found intractable on the national scale to be solved on an international scale by a supra-national authority. Behind the façade of the market economy, people are still, consciously or unconsciously, promoting a development which leads to bureaucratic rigidity and the omnipotence of the state. They still tend, in the name of economic and social security, to heap new tasks on the government and thereby new burdens on the taxpayer.

Again and again we see ourselves cheated of the hope of reducing to tolerable limits the crushing weight of taxation, which in the long run is incompatible with a free or even moderately sound economy and society. It is not unusual today for the government's budget to absorb as much as 30 or 40 per cent of the national income through various kinds of compulsory contributions. This reinforces inflationary pressure and has a disintegrating and ultimately paralyzing effect on the market economy. In the presence of such excessive fiscal burdens, the market mechanism no longer works in the manner which theory assumes and economic order requires. The whole process of the economy is distorted by those households and firms whose financial decisions are made with an eye toward the tax collector rather than toward the market, and incentive is weakened at all levels and in all spheres. The tax system, which today is highly intricate and impenetrable but is at the same time of decisive importance for individuals and firms alike, has become, in the hands of government, a no less insidious than effective tool with which to sway and distort the market economy's processes and the natural selection of firms according to their true market performance. Saving is depressed below the level necessary to finance growth investment without inflationary credit expansion, and at the same time, the rate of interest loses its essential efficacy because, as a cost factor, it takes second place after tax payments. Thus the capital market is upset, and omnious encouragement is given to inflationary tendencies. Old-style public finance is turned into a kind of fiscal socialism which more and more socializes the use of income. It is, unfortunately, becoming quite plain that the combination of the overexpansion of public expenditure and the reorientation of its purposes in socialist directions constitutes a source of continuous inflationary pressure and is incompatible with the market system in the long run.

Still another circumstance accentuates this development. Not satisfied with their already enormous holdings of publicly operated enterprises, most governments, spurred on by the vested interests of the civil service, are still trying to acquire more and more such holdings and thus create veritable strongholds of public power and monopoly. This is happening even in Germany, the model of the market economy, to say nothing of Italy or France. At the same time, there remains a sense of social grievance, a hostile and economically irrational distrust of everything that goes by the name of capital or entrepreneur, together with a stubborn misconception of the latter's task and the conditions in which he can fulfill his functions, which are essential to the market economy. Free economy stands or falls with the free entrepreneur and merchant, just as such an economy is inconceivable without free prices and markets. There is no way of defending the free economy against the still powerful forces of collectivism except by having the courage to stand by these central figures of a free economy and protect them from the wave of distrust and resentment to which—more in the Old World than in the New—they are exposed.

We can do this more confidently and effectively if more entrepreneurs embrace free competition, which makes them the servants of the market and causes their private success to depend upon their services to the community. Otherwise they stab us in the back. But the task of safeguarding free competition and preventing concentration of economic power is exceedingly difficult and at best cannot be solved without compromises and concessions. At the same time, of course, there is the related task of making sure that competition does not degenerate in any way but remains a fair fight, so that the only road to business success is through the narrow gate of better performance in the service of the consumer and not through the many back doors of unfair and subversive competition, which are only too well known to the business world. In fact, these twin tasks have so far not been solved even tolerably satisfactorily in any country. At best they are being seriously tackled, as in the United States and Germany; at the worst no notice is taken of them at all.

Nevertheless, the progress made in safeguarding free competition among producers and protecting it from economic domination is sufficient to hope for eventual full success. But another monopoly position is gaining ground with uncanny speed and has, for very profound reasons, developed into the strongest and most dangerous bastion of social and economic power, and that is the monopoly of labor unions. This monopoly position remains unassailed, if indeed it is not further waxing in strength and danger. The concentration of supply on the labor markets in centralized trade-unions works with the whole arsenal of monopoly power and does not shrink from naked extortion. This monopoly is the most damaging of all because of its all-pervading effects, the most fatal of which is the inflationary pressure of our times. And yet the nature and significance of this labor monopoly are recognized by only a few, and even for them silence is the counsel of wisdom, unless they are free and independent or have the courage to face the consequences of openly stating unpopular truths. But since there is only a handful of people in the modern world with enough freedom and independence to save themselves from the suicidal effects of such courage, it is easy to imagine the prospects of solving a problem which cannot even be raised.

Behind all of these perils we always encounter one predominant problem which we must face whenever we stop to think about the fate awaiting the industrial nations that are built upon the principle of economic freedom, a fate which these nations approach with alarming complacency or even with pride in something they call progress. This all-pervading problem is the process of growing concentration in the widest sense and in all spheres: concentration of the power of government and administration; concentration of economic and social power beside and under the state; concentration of decision and responsibility, which thereby become more and more anonymous, unchallengeable, and inscrutable; and concentration of people in organizations, towns and industrial centers, and firms and factories. If we want to name a common denominator for the social disease of our times, then it is concentration, and collectivism and totalitarianism are merely the extreme and lethal stages of the disease.

We all know what consequences progressive concentration entails for the health, happiness, freedom, and order of society. First of all it destroys the middle class properly so called, that is, an independent class possessed of small or moderate property and income, a sense of responsibility, and those civic virtues without which a free and well-ordered society cannot, in the long run, survive. The obverse of the same medal is the steady increase in the number of those who are not independent, the wage and salary earners, whose economic focus is not property but money income. The workers and employees are progressively merging into a uniform type of *dependent labor*, the teeming millions which populate the factories and offices of giant concerns. It may be that in many cases the large firm has a superiority of technical and organizational methods, although this superiority is often exaggerated and frequently rests merely on the artificial, though perhaps not deliberate, support of the government's economic and fiscal policy. But if this means denying man and the society determined by human values their due, then our accounts go seriously wrong, and this miscalculation may become the source of grave perils to free society and free economy.

However, the most immediate and tangible threat is the state itself. I want to repeat this because it cannot be stressed too much. The state and the concentration of its power, exemplified in the predominance of the budget, have become a cancerous growth gnawing at the freedom and order of society and economy. Surely, no one has any illusions about what it means when the modern state increasingly—and most eagerly before elections, when the voter's favor is at stake—assumes the task of handing out security, welfare, and assistance to all and sundry, favoring now this and now that group, and when people of all classes and at all levels, not excluding entrepreneurs, get into the habit of looking on the state as a kind of human Providence. Is it not precisely this function which increases the power of the state beyond all bounds, even this side of the Iron Curtain? Is Frédéric Bastiat's century-old malicious definition of the state as *une grande fiction à travers laquelle tout le monde s'efforce de vivre aux dépens de tout le monde* not now becoming an uncomfortably close fit?

The bloated colossus of the state, with its crushing taxation and boundless expenditure, is also chiefly to blame for the smoldering inflation that is a chronic evil of our times. Its destructive action will continue as long as the state does not radically curtail its program and as long as we do not drastically revise some of the most cherished popular ideas of present-day economic and social policy, such as full employment at any cost, the welfare state, the use of trade-union power for inflationary wage increases, and so on. But what hope of this can there be in a "dependent labor" society and a mass democracy afflicted by concentration?

It is evident that the actually existing forms of market economy, even in Germany, Switzerland, and the United States, are a far cry from the assumptions of theory. What we have is a hodgepodge system in which the basic substance of the market economy is not always easily discernible, a cacophony in which the dominant note of economic freedom is not always clearly audible. The fact that the market economy still functions in spite of a hitherto unimagined degree of intervention is no proof that such distortions and handicaps are harmless, let alone useful. On the contrary, it it proves anything, it is the astonishing resilience of the market economy, which is obviously hard to kill.

On the other hand, there can be no doubt that there exists a critical point beyond which the symptoms of strain on such a market economy become alarming. This is a problem which has so far never been treated with the attention it deserves. One thing is certain: an excess of government intervention deflecting the market economy from the paths prescribed by competition and price mechanism, an accumulation of prohibitions and commands, the blunting of incentives, official price-fixing, and restrictions on primary economic freedom must lead to mistakes, bottlenecks, less-than-optimal performances, and imbalances of all kinds. At first these may be overcome comparatively easily, but with the proliferation of intervention, they end up in general chaos. The worst is that the disturbances caused by intervention are often taken as proof of the inadequacy of the market economy and so become a pretext for more and stronger intervention. It needs more understanding than can be generally expected to appreciate that intervention is at fault. Rent control, which, as every well-informed person knows, outdoes everything else in injustice and economic irrationality and not only tends to perpetuate the housing shortage but places an additional burden on the capital market, is a glaring and most depressing example, even in the model countries of the market economy.

This survey of the perils which today surround the market economy has shown that it is not nearly in such good condition as its outward success might suggest. We are concerned about the market economy. It is not that we think it is wrong; on the contrary, the reasons for defending it are as compelling as ever. It is precisely because we know how infinitely important it is to maintain, protect, and develop it in the face of the collectivist menace that we fear for the market economy in a world where social and political conditions are, on the whole, against it and threaten to become worse unless we remain vigilant and active. Market economy, price mechanism, and competition are fine, but they are not enough. They may be associated with a sound or an unsound structure of society. But whether society is sound or unsound will eventually decide not only society's own measure of happiness, well-being, and freedom but also the fate of the free market economy. Market economy is one thing in a society where atomization, mass, proletarianization, and concentration rule; it is quite another in a society approaching anything like the "natural order" which I have described in some detail in my earlier book *Mass und Mitte*. In such a society, wealth would be widely dispersed; people's lives would have solid foundations; genuine communities, from the family upward, would form a background of moral support for the individual; there would be counterweights to competition and the mechanical operation of prices; people would have roots and would not be adrift in life without anchor; there would be a broad belt of an independent middle class, a healthy balance between town and country, industry and agriculture.

The decision on the ultimate destiny of the market economy, with its admirable mechanism of supply and demand, lies, in other words, beyond supply and demand.

Part IX: Questions for Analysis

1. Is the American economic system neutral as regards the aims of economic life? Refer to the item by John Maurice Clark in preparing your answer.
2. Capitalism is associated with the free market. Soviet communism is associated with central economic planning by the State.

   a) According to Robert W. Campbell, what are the major planning techniques used in the Soviet Union?
   b) How well does such planning work?
3. The Yugoslav economy is an important and interesting deviant from Soviet Communism. Why?
4. According to Milovan Djilas, does communism bring a classless society? Explain.
5. *a*) For a number of years the British Labor Party has been debating the issue of further socialization (nationalization) of the ownership of industry. What major points are made by Paul T. Homan in his report on the controversy?
   b) Sweden is often thought of as an outstanding example of democratic socialism. According to Calvin B. Hoover, is further nationalization of industry a leading issue in that country? Why?
6. According to Wilhelm Röpke, how has the free market system fared in Western Europe since the end of World War II? Do you agree with his evaluation? Why?

INDEX OF AUTHORS

This book has been set on the Linotype in 10 point Janson, leaded 2 points. Part titles are in 18 point Spartan Heavy caps, section titles in 18 point Spartan Heavy caps and lower case, and article titles in 18 point Spartan Medium caps. The size of the type page is 27 by 47 picas.